COBOL and Visual Basic on .NET:
on .NET:
A Guide for the
Reformed Mainframe
Programmer

CHRIS RICHARDSON

APress Media, LLC

COBOL and Visual Basic on .NET: A Guide for the Reformed Mainframe Programmer
Copyright © 2003 by Chris Richardson
Originally published by Apress in 2003

ISBN 978-1-59059-048-5   ISBN 978-1-4302-0772-6 (eBook)
DOI 10.1007/978-1-4302-0772-6

Trademarked names may appear in this book. Rather than use a trademark symbol with every occurrence of a trademarked name, we use the names only in an editorial fashion and to the benefit of the trademark owner, with no intention of infringement of the trademark.

Technical Reviewer: Hung Tran

Editorial Directors: Dan Appleman, Gary Cornell, Simon Hayes, Martin Streicher, Karen Watterson, John Zukowski

Assistant Publisher: Grace Wong

Project Manager: Sofia Marchant

Developmental Editor: Valerie Perry

Copy Editor: Nicole LeClerc

Compositor: Argosy Publishing

Artist: Faith Bradford

Indexer: Kevin Broccoli

Cover Designer: Kurt Krames

Production Manager: Kari Brooks

Manufacturing Manager: Tom Debolski

The information in this book is distributed on an "as is" basis, without warranty. Although every precaution has been taken in the preparation of this work, neither the author(s) nor Apress shall have any liability to any person or entity with respect to any loss or damage caused or alleged to be caused directly or indirectly by the information contained in this work.

In loving memory of my parents,
Mable Lois and Carroll Wayne Richardson.

Contents at a Glance

Contents

Foreword

As RODNEY DANGERFIELD says, "I don't get no respect," so too COBOL doesn't "get no respect." The COBOL language has been underappreciated, disrespected, criticized, and bashed for much of its existence. It is generally perceived as an inefficient, verbose application development tool, irrelevant to modern software development methodologies. Nothing could be further from the truth. The very existence of Christopher Richardson's book, *COBOL and Visual Basic on .NET: A Guide for the Reformed Mainframe Programmer,* is a testament to COBOL's continued relevance.

COBOL Bashing

The timing of Mr. Richardson's book couldn't be better. The fourth official publication of the COBOL standard (COBOL o2002[1]) is pending as of this writing. It follows COBOL 68, COBOL 74, and COBOL 85. If you consider the Intrinsic Functions Addendum published in o1989, the new COBOL o2002 actually marks the fifth official release of standard COBOL.

The disrespect for the COBOL programming language, which is encouraged in many universities, is not new. The earliest gesture of "COBOL bashing" lies in the Computer Museum in Boston. It is a COBOL tombstone. Soon after the Conference on Data Systems Languages (CODASYL) committee was formed in o1959, a COBOL tombstone was given as a (gag) gift from some of the CODASYL COBOL committee members to the chairperson of CODASYL. It was meant to express their lack of confidence that this new "common business language" (CBL, later COBOL) would be used in the IT industry for very long. As it turned out, the COBOL language, defined by the CODASYL "short-range" committee and first published in o1960, has been an important part of the IT industry for 43 years—and still counting. Perhaps it is natural to presume that anything in the IT industry dating back to the o1950s/o1960s must be obsolete and irrelevant in the twenty-first century. The mistake in this logic is that the COBOL language (features and syntax) has evolved dramatically over its lifetime. I like to paraphrase an old

---

1. The use of five digits years (e.g., o2002) throughout this foreword is done so as not to be shortsighted in the year 9999 prior to the turn of the eleventh millennium. Sure, you might say, "Isn't it a bit early to be worrying about the Y10K problem?" But as we now know in retrospect, this is the same kind of thinking over the past three to four decades that led us to the Y2K crisis. Well, maybe I'm being a bit too cautious. If most enterprise applications are developed in COBOL for the next 8,000 years, I suppose the Y10K crisis, as the Y2K crisis, will turn out to be a "noncrisis." (Wink!)

General Motors commercial: "COBOL o2002 is not your father's/mother's COBOL."

Although the COBOL tombstone may have been the earliest example of COBOL bashing, it certainly wasn't the last. The annals of the IT industry are filled with other instances of public disrespect for COBOL. Dutch computer professor Edsgar Djikstra wrote in 1982, "The teaching of COBOL should be made a criminal offense!" For years, I have been speaking at universities around the world. Generally, COBOL has been on the defensive in these academic environments. Few people in my audiences (teachers included) were/are aware of what the modern COBOL language can do. COBOL has no real technical problems—it has "public relations" problems.

In the early o1980s, COBOL bashing took a turn for the worse. Serious efforts were underway to "kill" COBOL. In preparation for the publication of ISO/ANSI COBOL 85, there were serious legal and lobbying attempts (led by Travelers Insurance and joined by other respectable corporations) to block any new COBOL standardization effort. Some wanted to freeze the COBOL language as described in the ANSI COBOL 74 standard. Others wanted to roll back the COBOL standard to its "official" COBOL 68 version. The argument offered by these groups was that it involved a great corporate cost to update their enterprise applications in order for older COBOL programs to compile cleanly in newer COBOL compilers. No one told them that they didn't need to recompile any programs unless the business application required updating.

This frustration is still felt by many IT departments today. It's similar to the frustration experienced by many home computer users who object to frequent hardware changes, operating system upgrades, application updates, and the incompatibility issues surrounding all of this "progress." This is a legitimate dilemma. The ISO/ANSI COBOL committees became very sensitive to any change (addition, modification, deletion) to the COBOL standard that might affect programs written earlier. Still to this day, the (INCITS/ANSI) X3J4 COBOL committee, which is responsible for the technical evolution of COBOL, maintains a special list of new and changed features incorporated in COBOL o2002 that could possibly produce incompatible results with older COBOL programs. Special voting rules were put into effect before "potentially incompatible" features can be added to the COBOL language. COBOL features designated as "obsolete" are required to remain in the new COBOL standard for at least one more iteration before they're permanently removed from the official COBOL standard. This is done to give the COBOL community ample time (a decade or more) to update the affected programs and remove the obsolete features. COBOL is nonproprietary. The "official" COBOL standard is not owned by any one software manufacturer. It's developed by a cross-section of IT professionals, both COBOL compiler/tools manufacturers and COBOL users. This requirement of balancing the COBOL committee representation was built into the membership rules of the COBOL development committees so there would be a broad range of views regarding how COBOL could best serve the business application development community. It isn't accidental, therefore, that COBOL earned its reputation over the years as a solid, dependable application development language that protects its constituency—application developers—from whimsical changes. It is one of COBOL's many strengths.

Few things that were around in the IT industry in o1960 are still around today, except perhaps in museums and in basements. Yet the COBOL language, albeit highly evolved from its origins, remains relevant. The corporate assets represented by the billions (trillions?) of lines of COBOL code still running on commercial computers aren't about to be abandoned. Nor should they be. New tools that help integrate legacy (read: COBOL) systems with PC applications, Web services, new data formats, and protocols have been available since distributive systems emerged years ago. As today's application environment has evolved, .NET for instance, so has COBOL's capability to link to it, merge with it, and interact with it. Stretching the lifespan of an enterprise's legacy systems increases the value and productivity of its IT development staff and of the assets they produce.

Why Has COBOL Endured?

Given the rarity of anything in the IT industry surviving for over 40 years, it is appropriate to ask why has COBOL endured for so long. An underlying mission of COBOL language development during its entire lifespan has been to keep COBOL's syntax and new features relevant to modern application development methodologies and to do so with utmost respect for the large number of COBOL applications still running on computers around the world. The ISO COBOL o2002 language is an evolutionary product. Today's COBOL is the result of much determined work by the various COBOL committees that have contributed to its evolution, among them ISO, INCITS, ANSI, CODASYL, ECMA, and the national COBOL committees represented by individual countries (Netherlands, Canada, France, Japan, United Kingdom, Germany, United States, et al).

Change Is Natural

One thing is certain in the commercial IT world (and in life in general): Change is natural. Business computer systems are digital models of an enterprise and all of its operations. As an enterprise evolves so must its computer business systems (models) evolve. When designing any business application, we must anticipate changes, both corrective and perfective, in those applications. We must identify those parts of the system that will most likely need maintenance in the course of the system's lifetime.

When speaking to new systems designers, I often use an analogy of design techniques employed by the design engineers who build automobiles. It is absurd to think of a new line of cars being built without anticipating one of the basic maintenance chores required of all fuel-driven automobiles: refueling. Imagine for a moment that the car designers (system designers) placed the fuel cap underneath the car, hidden by the transmission. Would we tolerate dismantling our cars' transmissions each time we needed to refuel our cars? Of course not. This refueling (maintenance) chore was made easier by isolating those parts of the car that we need to reach to do this maintenance.

This is very similar to the design criteria that computer system designers must use. Thankfully, the original COBOL language designers knew this. When the COBOL language was first created, the CODASYL committee envisioned that the IT industry was fast changing and that most business systems would likely need to be modified during their lifetime. New hardware and new software development techniques were likely to follow. COBOL applications needed a way to adapt to ever-changing environments without causing chaos inside the enterprise systems development community. The solution was to make COBOL as adaptable as possible and to incorporate, inside the source program itself, whatever environmental documentation was required. This of course resulted in the Environment Division, one of four original Divisions still in the COBOL language. By isolating "all" the environmental dependencies of a COBOL application in one place, it was much easier to transport a COBOL application from one computer brand to another, from one operating system to another, from one database to another.

Today we take this concept for granted. Why should Microsoft Word behave differently on a Macintosh than on a Windows machine? In the late o1950s, however, this was a new concept just gaining popularity. Admiral Grace Hopper's contribution to the "birth" of COBOL is well documented. She was a member of the original CODASYL executive committee. A far greater contribution perhaps was her pioneering effort to develop and promote the concept of third-generation programming languages such as COBOL, Fortran, Algol, and so on. This allowed programmers to use a common, high-level set of instructions (higher than assembler languages). This high-level code was then translated (compiled) into the machine language of the particular hardware on which it would eventually execute. Further, to the point of adaptability, COBOL incorporated the CALL statement early in its development, as well as a COPY library source code facility. Later, the INVOKE statement was added as part of the object-oriented COBOL module.

These and other features in COBOL acknowledged the changing nature of computer business systems and anticipated the need for adaptability in COBOL language syntax. Rather than incorporate new COBOL syntax and data formats (borrowed from other programming languages) to map into every known programming language and database, COBOL simply chose to create flexible methods to interact with applications written in other languages and to pass data between modules effectively. You might say that the COBOL integrated development environment (IDE) is one of the earliest "open source" environments.

Another reason for COBOL's endurance lies in the large number of auxiliary tools available in a COBOL IDE: full-featured application development suites, code generators, software libraries, debuggers, conversion tools, compiler "add-ins," and so on. The sheer momentum over 43 years from so many programmers producing so many COBOL applications resulted in cottage industries of supplemental software to aid in the task of COBOL application development. No other programming language has such a robust IDE.

The Y2K "Noncrisis"

I have saved for last the most important reason perhaps for COBOL's continuing excellence: the superior maintainability of COBOL applications.

Much of the criticism of the COBOL language within the application development community is aimed at its "wordiness." It is true that COBOL is verbose. COBOL applications often require more lines of source code to be written than are necessary in applications written in other languages. This was by design. When the original members of the CODASYL COBOL committee set out to define the syntax for this Common Business Oriented Language (COBOL), they intentionally included many clauses, phrases, "noise words," and so on not to make the job of the development programmer harder, but rather to make the job of the maintenance programmer easier and the results more accurate. COBOL instructions such as "ADD this-weeks-salary TO previous-year-to-date-salary GIVING new-year-to-date-salary" are indeed more verbose than, say, "LET z = x + y." But no one can argue that the meaning/intent of the business logic coded in the former example is much clearer than in the latter example. This is by design. In application development, *clarity, not cleverness, is a virtue.*

COBOL contains syntax for coding its own shortcuts and clever programming techniques if a programmer is so inclined. The COBOL statement COMPUTE z = x + y is perfectly valid, but it is antithetical to good COBOL programming practices and is discouraged for all the reasons mentioned previously. Is this really important? You need only reflect on the Y2K "noncrisis" at the turn of the new millennium to determine how important this is. Many people blamed COBOL for the Y2K crisis, pointing to the huge number of legacy (read again: COBOL) programs still running on computers in o1999 as we prepared for potential disasters when switching over to o2000. This argument is fallacious. As any good application developer knows, the problems created by storing dates using the last two digits of the year (e.g., 85) instead of four digits (e.g., 1985) resulted from shortsighted system design, not from a poor choice of the programming language used. All applications (business applications and others), whether written in COBOL, Fortran, C/C++, or Visual Basic, had to be checked and modified to deal with the change from o1999 to o2000.

It's my firm belief that the Y2K crisis, anticipated by so many, turned out to be a Y2K "noncrisis" specifically because most of those legacy systems were in fact developed with COBOL. Because the COBOL source code is written with so much more clarity than source code written in other languages, the huge task of reviewing all of that legacy source code and making changes when/where necessary was made much easier because of COBOL than nearly everyone had expected. True, the Y2K crisis was a tremendous problem for the IT industry. But the efforts involved to fix the problem were made much easier, not harder, because of COBOL, not in spite of COBOL. In a way, COBOL turned out to be "too good." The clarity associated with COBOL source code made those earlier COBOL applications much more maintainable than anyone had predicted. After all, why discard an application that's performing most of its business functions properly simply because that application needs updating, when modifying the original source code is easier, less expensive, and adds years of productive life to business systems? As a result, the lifespan of legacy systems was stretched much further than people (systems designers) had expected. Is this bad? No, I think not; it's shortsighted perhaps, but it's not bad.

What we learned from the Y2K crisis was that COBOL provides "health insurance" to corporate assets. That is, it's the best way for an enterprise to protect its investment in its IT assets. The same can't be said for applications written in other languages. In many cases, applications written in lower level languages (assembler) or other third-generation languages (C, Pascal, and so on) were simply not worth deciphering to fix Y2K (and other) problems. Instead, many were discarded and replaced by newly written programs (hopefully in COBOL, but probably not).

COBOL and Visual Basic on .NET: A Guide for the Reformed Mainframe Programmer

Mr. Richardson tells the reader in this book, "The world has changed. The .NET Framework and VS .NET is part of that change . . . and so are you." We in the application development community must deal with ever-changing technologies. We're constantly faced with new challenges to keep our programming skills current.

These challenges confront us whether we're integrating legacy systems with modern (integrated Web) technologies or whether we're developing brand-new applications on PCs and/or mainframes incorporating Web services. Can we continue to keep our legacy systems running our enterprises in the midst of these emerging technologies? Or must we abandon those systems and start from scratch to take advantage of these new technologies? Can we "have our cake and eat it too"?

Yes, we can develop modern applications using COBOL, taking advantage of its superior maintainability while incorporating Web-based services into these systems as described in this book. COBOL is alive and well in the twenty-first century and its future is bright. A professor friend of mine from Purdue University, when discussing COBOL's future, likes to tell his students, "You better wear your sunglasses." There's much life still left in our legacy systems due to the myriad of integration tools available to us. And thanks to *COBOL and Visual Basic on .NET: A Guide for the Reformed Mainframe Programmer*, we can understand this new technology from the mainframe programmer's perspective and learn to apply it in our real lives.

Jerome Garfunkel
Woodstock, New York
February, o2003

About the Author

Chris Richardson has over 20 years experience in the information technology field. Over half of his career has been on the mainframe platform developing using COBOL, CICS, and DB2. Chris says that his mainframe background has served as a sound foundation for his Windows, Web, and .NET programming transition—a transition that has included becoming proficient in Visual Basic. Chris likes to point out that he has had the pleasure of being a senior programmer analyst, a lead developer, a systems architect, and a senior software engineer. With a smile, he explains that under each job title, the primary assigned and assumed duty has remained constant: to develop and optimize business solutions using technology as needed. Currently, he is a programming supervisor at a Fortune 500 company, offering his services to a team of Windows, Web, and .NET developers. He proudly reminds people of his mainframe background and jokingly refers to himself as a "reformed mainframe programmer."

Chris divides his leisure time between entrepreneurial endeavors (such as his recent start-up, California-based eClectic Software Solutions, http://eclecticsoftwaresolutions.com) and studying for his next Microsoft certification exam.

About the
Technical Reviewer

Hung Tran is a senior software engineer specializing in the design and development of financial service applications. He has an extensive technical background developing COM objects, client-server business applications, and Web applications. His multiprogramming language skill set includes C++, Java, Visual Basic, JavaScript, HTML, XML, and REXX, just to name a few. Upon the arrival of Visual Studio .NET Beta 1, Hung was participating in the .NET Early Adopter Program. Since then, Visual Studio .NET has become his main software development tool.

Living in Southern California with his wife and two children, Hung spends most of his spare time as a columnist, writing computer technical articles for *Phu Nu Gia Dinh Nguoi Viet,* an Orange County weekly magazine proudly serving the Vietnamese community; running his cofounded nonprofit organization, HopeToday.org; and playing computer games with his son.

About the Foreword Writer

Jerome Garfunkel is an international consultant and specialist in learning systems design. In the international commercial information technology (IT) community, he is recognized as one of the leading authorities in the field of programming languages and international computer standards. He has served as a senior technical advisor to the U.S. Department of Commerce. In addition, he sat on several American and international IT industry committees and has represented the United States in both the international and domestic IT standardization community in the ANSI Standards Planning and Requirements Committee, the ANSI Programming Language Study Group, the International Committee on Programming Language Guidelines, the American COBOL Committee, the International COBOL Committee, the CODASYL COBOL Committee, and the Object-Oriented COBOL Committee.

Jerome Garfunkel is a lecturer, an author, a consultant, an educator, an actor, a calligrapher, and a passionate motorcycle rider. As an educator and technologist, he lectures about leading-edge technologies such as the integration of legacy systems with Web-based services. Mr. Garfunkel was awarded the degree of Doctorate, Honoris Causa in Technology from De Montfort University in Leicester, England, for his lifetime contributions to the software engineering community. His collection of technical papers, memoranda, and notes is housed in the Charles Babbage Institute in Minnesota, for historical research. Included is the large body of his writings appearing in books, IT journals, magazines, and newspapers around the world.

Acknowledgments

FIRST AND FOREMOST, I would like to express my gratitude and thanks to my family for their patience, support, and encouragement. Throughout this 1-year+ journey, my loving wife, Lilia, my handsome son, Everette, and my charming daughter, Krystalynn, provided a sense of purpose that helped me focus and stay reminded of the importance of achieving my goals.

Next, I really owe an enormous thank you to my *other* family, the entire Apress team. To those at Apress working behind the scenes, thank you. To those at Apress that I've communicated with at one time or another (namely, Dan Appleman, Gary Cornell, Simon Hayes, Grace Wong, Valerie Perry, Sofia Marchant, Kari Brooks, and Nicole LeClerc), thank you! Working with each of you has been an extreme pleasure. Truly, I can't thank you all enough. My entire belief and understanding of teamwork, and the value of editing and project management has been reinforced and refreshed. You all are awesome!

To my technical reviewer, Hung Tran, thank you! Your comments and suggestions have certainly helped improve the accuracy of this book's technical content. Beyond that, the fact that you were there responding to my queries via instant messenger during those predawn hours was helpful in many ways.

To Dr. Basim Kadhim, Suad Lovic, and Doug Brown, all of Fujitsu Software, this entire effort would not have been possible without your assistance. Thank you for promptly answering and addressing each of my questions and comments as I installed and used your NetCOBOL for .NET product.

To Jerome Benjamin Garfunkel, thank you for agreeing to write the foreword for this book. It is truly my honor to have someone with your wealth of relevant experience and insight generously contribute to the success of this book. Again, thank you!

Finally, thank you to the community of COBOL mainframe developers for supporting a book such as this one. I was taught that it is a noble gesture to give back to the community, to remember where you came from, to honor your roots. Well, through this book, I can only hope that I have served you well.

Introduction

THERE I WAS, AT MICROSOFT'S Professional Developers Conference (PDC) 2001, surrounded by thousands of fellow developers. We were all looking forward to the various events that would take place during that week. Microsoft, with Bill Gates himself in attendance, was soon to launch Windows XP, their newest Windows version. Although this was going to be great, it was really just icing on the cake. What we really came to the PDC for was to hear about .NET (and, of course, to go home with the latest versions of various software titles). I was captivated during the general sessions as several Microsoft knowledge holders spoke rather eloquently about how the development world was changing and how we as developers were in the driver's seat. This all sounded extremely comforting. One Microsoft speaker after another presented and demonstrated some of the newest features of the .NET Framework. Each feature mentioned received loud applause and unanimous cheers. This was a pep rally to end all pep rallies. It really felt good. Until...

One particular Microsoft speaker (who will remain nameless) proudly announced the .NET Framework feature the .NET common language runtime (CLR), which allows developers to potentially develop Windows and Web programs in *practically any* language.[2] He mentioned Visual Basic .NET and the crowd cheered. He mentioned the new language C# and again the crowd cheered. Then it happened. The speaker mentioned (with emphasis) that you would *even* be able to code in COBOL! Yes, the standing-room-only crowd reacted. However, there were no cheers, no applause, and no ovations. Rather, the crowd booed, heckled, and laughed—loudly and continuously. Ouch! I slouched in my seat and pretended to join in.

> **NOTE**   Giving Microsoft the benefit of the doubt, I believe the assumptions may have been that any developer attending the PDC event naturally was devoted to developing in the .NET environment. They may have deduced that such developers could not possibly mind such ridicule and humiliation. Perhaps they only erred on the latter. For the record: No ill feelings harbored. All is forgiven.

---

2.   There is the requirement that a .NET version compiler be created to enable additional languages to be used in the .NET platform. Microsoft provides compilers for Visual Basic .NET and C#.

Having coded in this great language called COBOL for many years (both batch and CICS online applications), I concluded that most of the people joining the laugh-in had never actually carried the honorable title of COBOL/CICS/DB2 mainframe programmer. Simply put, they were either jealous or in denial.

Finally, Something for Us

There at the PDC 2001 event, I swore that I would do something for the group of developers interested in .NET that had a foundation similar to mine: mainframe COBOL programming. I wanted to create something that would speak positively to this group of developers. This group of mainframe programmers (those who are seeking *reformation*[3]) is now facing retraining challenges exacerbated by a void of mainframe-oriented guidance. This is a problem unique to mainframe programmers regardless of which new Common Business Oriented Language (COBOL) they choose to use on the .NET platform: Visual Basic .NET (VB .NET) or NetCOBOL for .NET (courtesy of Fujitsu Software).

This book is my attempt to address this need for mainframe-oriented guidance to tackling .NET. To the 90,000 COBOL programmers[4] that exist in North America and the uncounted many abroad, hold on to this book. As you strive to join the ranks of .NET developers, you will be hard-pressed to find other books (or Web sites, for that matter) that attempt to provide this type of mainframe-oriented .NET guidance.

My Reasons for Going to the PDC Event

Why was I there at the conference? Was it worth it? Additionally, what is the connection between that event and the topic of this book? Naturally, I had my reasons for going to this mainframe-hostile event:[5]

- Learning about the .NET Framework

- Leveraging previous versions and PC technologies

- Confronting the possibility of starting over

---

3. Please pardon my attempt at humor—my own chance to poke a little fun at those like myself who either have gone or will go through a career "technology transition." Yes, I too am a *reformed* mainframe programmer and proud of that fact.

4. According to published estimates of the analyst firm Gartner, there are approximately 90,000 COBOL programmers in North America.

5. OK, maybe using the phrase "mainframe-hostile" to describe the Microsoft PDC event may be an unfair exaggeration. I suggest that you take this lightly and view it as my weak attempt at humor (perhaps returning the favor at most).

Learning About the .NET Framework

I went to the PDC 2001 event to learn about the .NET Framework and all .NET-related technologies. Microsoft's technical team has included many features in the new .NET technology offering. As a result, many of my colleagues are referring to the new .NET Framework as a "revolution" (as opposed to an "evolution"). With the technological revolutions that I have subjected myself to in the past, this was right up my alley. Some people tend to object to the varying amount of marketing that you get at some of the Microsoft-sponsored events. Me, I welcome it. I want to be convinced and persuaded by the professionals.

As it turns out, the PDC 2001 event had a minimal amount of marketing material and a satisfying number of technical demonstrations and explanations. I recommend attending these types of events. Some of them are even free or nominally priced. Especially keep your eyes open for an annual Microsoft-sponsored event called Developer Days. Besides picking up information and free software, you can view this event as a good opportunity to network with fellow developers. Frankly, I had never attended an equivalent type of event while I was on the other side of the fence (in the mainframe world).

TIP There's an annual conference event that focuses on COBOL programming. If you haven't already heard about it, it's called the COBOL Expo. Be sure to check it out at http://cobolexpo.com/homepage.html.

Leveraging Previous Versions and PC Technologies

I wanted to hear from the horse's mouth (Microsoft, in this case) why the effort that I had invested into learning previous versions of Visual Basic and other PC technologies had to now be leveraged (or just forgotten, in some cases) in order to learn to develop on the new .NET Framework. I wanted to hear about the many other features (e.g., ASP.NET, ADO.NET, and XML Web services) and find out how I was to use these new technologies when developing tomorrow's applications. At the same time, I wanted to understand and have a healthy perspective on the fact that most of my bleeding-edge PC knowledge (gained over the last 4 years) is now slated to become *legacy* technology.

Allow me to remind you of the momentous transition that I had recently completed from the legacy mainframe technologies to the newer PC technologies. The explanations that were given, the cleanup that Microsoft has done to the "old" Visual Basic version 6.0 language, and the improvements made available by moving away from COM all combine to better enable developers to program complex business-solutions. Everything that I heard left me feeling very comfortable to join the .NET crowd and retrain. In other words, it was time for me to make a new investment, intellectually speaking.

Confronting the Possibility of Starting Over

I wanted to see the look on the faces of thousands of former experts and gurus while they struggled with the concept of "starting over." This last point deserves emphasis. The changes in the new .NET Framework and related .NET technologies are so encompassing that many have viewed them as a leveling of the playing field. Because practically everything is new, it is unreasonable for many to claim "expert" status—at least for now. That is right! If there were ever a great time for a mainframe programmer to consider crossing over, now is that time. This is a chance to get in on the ground floor:[6] .NET version 1.0.

NOTE The absence of .NET experts and gurus is being addressed quickly. I am witnessing the rapid consumption of various Microsoft-sponsored events, countless .NET-related Web sites and, of course, some very well-written books (perhaps such as the one you are currently reading). Many developers have started to code already!

Yes, there were times that I felt inferior mentioning that I started with Visual Basic version 5.0 (many "old-timers" started with Visual Basic version 1.0). Now, I (and many others) will stand shoulder-to-shoulder and start with .NET version 1.0, VB .NET version 1.0, and C# version 1.0. This is a great opportunity! To all of my former mainframe peers, please give this one some serious thought.

What This Book Covers

Simply put, this book is about .NET. It is a guide to approaching the .NET world written from the perspective of a former mainframe programmer and written for other mainframe programmers (soon to become *reformed*[7]). Beyond that, this book is about the new .NET Framework and related .NET technologies

---

6. I apologize for the multilevel direct-marketing sales-pitch tone.

7. Again, my attempt at a little humor. Please note that the *reformation* in question is a light reference to the career "technology transition" that this book focuses on. Having gone through this "transition" myself, it is much easier to treat the topic lightly. Bear with me. By the end of this book, you (too) will be proud of your reformation (err . . . transition).

(e.g., VS .NET, VB .NET, NetCOBOL for .NET, and ADO.NET). Concepts and considerations for future .NET developers are included as well.

What is unique about this book? I wrote it to serve as a bridge from the mainframe world to the new .NET universe. This book is filled cover-to-cover with mainframe-to-.NET comparisons, analogies, and translations (from the old way to the new way). When applicable, in-depth conceptual discussions are offered. These discussions serve to smooth the edges during the inevitable paradigm shifts that await mainframe programmers headed down the .NET path. I intentionally included a healthy amount of mainframe terminology to create a comfortable learning environment for former mainframe developers. The book assumes the role of a .NET "introductory" text. In other words, this is an entry-level .NET text for advanced mainframe programmers. It will adequately prepare you for further, more detailed learning.

What This Book Does Not Cover

This book is *not* about bashing any technology or company (even when it is deserved). For relational database discussions, I have only included IBM's DB2 database. Most of the SQL-related discussions are easily transferable to other mainframe DBMSs. The mainframe database system referred to as IMS is not discussed (I was never a big fan of this hierarchical type of data structure). The relational approach won me over long ago. In mainframe circles, I would be considered a DB2 bigot.

When I cover mainframe programming languages, I do not discuss the assembler programming language or any language other than COBOL, for that matter. You will also notice that I have omitted any discussion about available products/compilers that enable visual mainframe-type COBOL development to be done on the PC. With these types of PC-based products, a developer compiles the source code and uploads the binary load module from the PC to the mainframe. Although there are some great products out there, I do not discuss them in this book.

Supplemental References

I wrote this book to serve as your one-stop guide through the maze from the mainframe world to the Windows and Web world of .NET. To prevent this book from being over 1,000 pages in length, I chose to include more topics and at the same time cover less depth per topic. As a supplement, I include Web and text references for your continued learning and retraining effort. You will find these supplemental references located at the end of each chapter in the "To Learn More" section. This section is divided into the subsections "Books," "Magazines," and "Web Sites." Depending on your particular needs, some topics will deserve a more in-depth, step-by-step drill down. Additionally, for some topics, a list-oriented reference source will be helpful. These book, magazine, and Web references will go a long way toward the goal of filling those gaps. Please take advantage of them.

Technical Requirements

The following list presents the technical requirements for working through the examples and code listings in this book:

- Windows XP Professional operating system. I used Windows XP Professional during the sample application development and when capturing the screen shots. Although you can use Windows 2000 (Professional or Server) for .NET development, I recommend using Windows XP Professional (or newer) for your .NET development.

- Microsoft .NET Framework v.1.0 or v.1.1.

- Microsoft Visual Studio .NET v.1.0 or v.1.1.

- Fujitsu NetCOBOL for .NET v.1.1.

- Enterprise Services/COM+ v.1.5. This version of COM+ is bundled with Windows XP and is expected to be bundled with Windows .NET Server. If you use Windows 2000, and therefore COM+ v.1.0, you will notice some feature differences. This is one of several good reasons for doing your .NET development on Windows XP or newer operating systems.

- Internet Information Services (IIS) v.5 or greater. This is bundled with Windows 2000 and Windows XP Professional and greater. You will need to install IIS manually from your Windows installation source. It is not typically installed by default.

- Microsoft Message Queuing (MSMQ). This is bundled with Windows 2000 and Windows XP Professional and greater. You will need to install MSMQ manually from your Windows installation source. It is not typically installed by default.

- SQL Server 2000 (with a current Service Pack). The sample applications in this book that involve database access use Microsoft's database product, SQL Server 2000. With minimal changes, you can use other relational data-bases (e.g., Oracle).

- Internet Explorer v.6 or greater. This browser is installed and upgraded as part of your full .NET installation. You may choose to use other browsers. I used Internet Explorer exclusively throughout this book.

- Crystal Decisions's Crystal Reports v.8.5 or greater. A fully functional version of this software product is bundled with your full .NET installation. You will be required to complete a free online registration the first time you use it.

About the Source Code

You can download the code samples that I use throughout the chapters and appendixes from the Downloads section of the Apress Web site (http://www.apress.com). The source code is contained in two folders: Folder VS2002 and Folder VS2003.

Folder VS2002 has Visual Basic .NET and COBOL .NET code samples grouped by chapters that were developed using Microsoft's Visual Studio .NET version 1.0 and Fujitsu's NetCOBOL for .NET version 1.1, respectively.

Folder VS2003 has the same Visual Basic .NET samples as in folder VS2002, except that the samples were converted to run under Microsoft's Visual Studio .NET version 1.1 (also known as Microsoft's Visual Studio 2003).

You will notice that Folder VS2003 does not contain any COBOL .NET code samples. At the time of this writing, Fujitsu's current version (1.1) of NetCOBOL for .NET is fully compatible and integrates with Microsoft's Visual Studio .NET version 1.0, but not Microsoft's Visual Studio .NET version 1.1. Be sure to check the NetCOBOL Web site (http://www.netcobol.com) for the latest news of a compatible NetCOBOL for .NET release from Fujitsu.

Who This Book Is For

This book was written primarily for intermediate to advanced mainframe programmers who are seeking guidance toward converting/reforming[8] to the "other side." Additionally, those seeking to remain on the mainframe and extend their technological reach across platforms will also find this book very valuable.

Although most (if not all) of the discussion in this book speaks as though your decision to leave the mainframe is imminent, I do realize that there are still production applications to be maintained. After all, you *do* want to leverage your assets, and you will not complete a successful transition overnight.

My quandary is that I have seen what it is like on the other side and the grass *is* greener. Once you are bitten by .NET, it will be difficult to approach your legacy

---

8. Converting, reforming, transitioning—it's all the same. You get the point.

mainframe development with the same zeal and enthusiasm as before. My guess is that once you immerse yourself into .NET, you will find it more and more difficult to mentally switch back and forth from one platform to the other. Eventually, you *will* choose one platform over the other, and this book that you are holding in your hands will serve as your guide to make this choice a lot less confusing.

The ideal reader is someone who is already proficient in any of the following:

- Batch COBOL programming language

- Interactive online CICS screen development

- Batch or online COBOL database programming using DB2

The only other requirement is that you are genuinely interested in learning about the .NET Framework and .NET development tools. You should be prepared to commit and prioritize to allow for dedicated study and practice time.

NOTE   Reforming from the mainframe COBOL-oriented world is a significant accomplishment. A successful transition over to the .NET world requires that you embrace this new technology wholeheartedly. You will need to work hard, and the reward will reflect the amount of effort that you invest into this endeavor. Buying this book is one big step in the right direction.[9]

I've been there. I even straddled the fence (between the mainframe and the "PC") for a while. Eventually, I crossed over and proceeded to pursue the PC technologies with a relentless hunger and passion. When I first crossed over, I compared the new PC wilderness I entered to the "wild, wild West." I ended up wasting a lot of time and money trying to figure out *what* to learn first. I just needed some direction and a productive perspective. This book will be your time-saving guide. With guidance, your programming background will provide the foundation that will really make the big difference. I will go as far as saying that my mainframe foundation has better prepared me for this latest transition opportunity: the .NET transition. As a former mainframe programmer, that is your advantage as well.

Allow me to remind you (as I reminisce) that we mainframe programmers were groomed in an environment that has matured and continues to advance to this day—an environment that recognized the value of time-tested methodologies, standards, and disciplines. We took for granted that the old-timers were

---

9.   I know, I know, a shameless plug.

always there to serve as our mentors and that we could always pick up an IBM tome/manual for the "last word" on resolving a best practice debate. We looked at security mostly as something that kept us from accidentally editing production files, not something that protected us from faceless viruses.

The world has changed. The .NET Framework and VS .NET is part of that change . . . and so are you.

Chris Richardson
Richardson@eClecticSoftwareSolutions.com

Part One
The Mainframe Paradigm Shift

"Teach someone how to program with .NET and they will deliver .NET programs. Teach someone how to analyze, design, develop, troubleshoot, and architect with .NET and they will deliver enterprise business solutions using .NET technologies."

—Chris Richardson

Your Future with COBOL

Retrain or Plan to Retire
from Computer Programming

In this chapter

- Learning about the activities surrounding the pending new COBOL standard for the mainframe and how it will create retraining opportunities for tomorrow's mainframe COBOL programmers

- Contrasting the future for COBOL against the future for the average COBOL programmer

- Propelling yourself into reformation as you abandon the mainframe

LONG BEFORE .NET became the household techie buzzword that it currently is (in fact, before Microsoft itself existed), a former mentor of mine suggested a career survival strategy to me. The "strategy" was simple. It first examined one's commitment to being a "technical professional." It then made clear how "change" was inherent in the very nature of technology. To help cement his points, my mentor offered an analogy that I remember to this day:

> *"Keeping up with technology is like being on board a speeding train. The day that you decide to take a break from learning, you are essentially getting off of the train—and yes, the train will leave without you."*

I am entering into this discussion with the assumption that you, the reader, are interested in continued employment, competitive compensation, the opportunity to obtain marketable skills, and the chance to work on interesting and new development projects. The fact that you are reading this book is a strong indication that you are either still "on board the train" or looking for assistance to jump back on board (this includes those that may have been unknowingly *kicked off* the train). Either way, welcome.

In this chapter, I present a sampling of recent activities surrounding the COBOL language standardization effort. I choose to do this not only because I remain fond of the language, but also because I want to make a point: The world óf COBOL mainframe development is undergoing a significant change. I discuss this point in the context of the resulting retraining choices. That's where things become interesting. I discuss these choices and perhaps your choice—to abandon the mainframe and begin your reformation.

Reformations, Transitions, and Having Fun

Throughout this chapter (and this book) I have chosen to use the term "reform"—along with several conjugated forms of the term—to refer to the "technology transition" that you are embarking on. Although a *reformation* sounds more dramatic and intriguing than a "technology transition," I realize that the term may seem offensive to some. So, please note that I have gone through this same *transition* myself. Yet, I am and will continue to be proud of my mainframe background. The fact that you have brought me along as you embark on that same transitional journey is an honor for me. Please pardon my attempt at making that journey fun, interesting, and enjoyable—hence the humorous use of the term "reform" simply to refer to the exciting retraining effort that awaits you.

Now, let's get started.

Why Software Vendors Care About Mainframe COBOL

Consider this quote from none other than Bill Gates:

> *"As a result of the changes in how businesses and consumers use the Web, the industry is converging on a new computing model that enables a standard way of building applications and processes to connect and exchange information over the Web."*[1]

In other words, the way we build business programs needs to change with the times. On that point, the other major software vendors appear to agree with Microsoft. Where they seem to differ is in their strategy in accomplishing this goal. The way I see it, they each have unique challenges. The traditional mainframe product vendors are more likely to have established relationships with customers that are already using COBOL. I imagine that these loyal customers are asking vendors such as IBM questions like "Will I be able to build tomorrow's Web-enabled applications using your COBOL development tools?" and "What are you going to do to help me leverage my existing COBOL investments?"

---

1. Bill Gates, January 14, 2002 (http://www.microsoft.com/net/defined/net_today.asp).

On the other hand, Microsoft's challenge appears to be a bit different. Their challenge is helping two sets of customers with different needs. One set of Microsoft's customers has already left the mainframe and started developing Windows and Web applications both with and without COBOL. Those customers, now using nonmainframe tools, need to get closer to what they left behind: their legacy data, legacy business logic, and legacy talent pool. The other set of customers are actually future, potential customers—those contemplating a mainframe departure.

I suggest that neither Microsoft nor the other software vendors can ignore the fact that a windfall awaits the software/hardware vendor(s) that successfully taps the legacy-application market share. The legacy-developer talent pool is an attractive grassroots approach for entry into enterprises looking to take advantage of existing IT investments. That's right. You, I, and the billions of lines of legacy code that we helped write are now considered to be a commodity, and a very hot commodity at that.

NOTE   According to published estimates from the analyst firm Gartner, there are approximately 90,000 COBOL programmers in the United States and roughly 180–200 billion lines of COBOL worldwide.

CROSS-REFERENCE   For further general information about the new appreciation for COBOL, read the *Computerworld* article titled "Remember Cobol? If You Don't, Get Reacquainted" (http://www.computerworld.com/softwaretopics/software/appdev/ story/0,10801,60683,00.html) and the Micro Focus press release titled "Micro Focus Announces Support For New COBOL 2002 Standard" (http://www.microfocus.com/press/news/20011127.asp).

Many scenarios can unfold, all of which are aimed at getting at this gold mine. Companies will, in some cases, rewrite or convert their legacy applications under the guise of leveraging their existing investment. On the other hand, some companies will choose to replace their mainframe legacy applications with desktop and Web solutions written for and processed on nonmainframe platforms in search of ways to reduce their total cost of ownership (TCO). This latter approach sometimes includes techniques referred to as wrapping and screen scraping. *Wrapping* is the common process of including legacy modules within a component written in newer technology. Usually hiding the older module, the newer component is then integrated with other *new* components. *Screen scraping* is the common process of programmatically accessing, navigating to, and "reading" from online "screen" applications. Although they are slightly different, these two techniques can be found on either the mainframe or nonmainframe platforms.

It is a fact that the COBOL language is radically evolving—it has to. Here, I am attempting to answer the question of "Why?" You may disagree with my theory of corporations scrambling for market share and striving to please existing customers. Perhaps I could have taken a more plausible route. Suppose that the COBOL vendors are doing what is necessary to actually secure the continued existence of COBOL development and therefore their own corporate existence. In their individual and joint efforts to save the language, they may have actually sounded COBOL's own death knell.

NOTE   Please take a moment and read the previous paragraph again. Ponder that thought for a moment. Please read on.

Regardless of the motivation held by the various COBOL vendors, the fact remains that something *is* happening. COBOL, as we know it, is not just sitting still. Let's now explore the vendors' efforts to bring COBOL forward into the twenty-first century.

Creating a New Standard for Mainframe COBOL

Yes, that is right, the words "new" and "COBOL" in the same heading.

As you know, the current COBOL standard is the ISO/ANSI 85 standard (which replaced the ANSI 74 standard). During recent years, there have been only two amendments to the COBOL 85 standard (basically, intrinsic functions in 1989 and several corrections in 1993).

Now, ladies and gentlemen (drum roll, please), allow me to introduce the ANSI X3J4 committee. This group is working to create the next COBOL standard. Both the Draft International Standard (DIS) review and the Published International Standard (IS) are scheduled for 2002.

CROSS-REFERENCE   For the status of the standardization process, see `http://www.ncits.org/tc_home/j4.htm`.

Those of you who have followed this subject closely might respond, "Yeah right, I knew about the X3J4 (commonly abbreviated as J4) standardization process. They have been *working* on this for the past ten years. It is hardly new." Well, it looks like the committee's diligent efforts were not in vain. Although the standardization process is not actually complete, the expected hurdles have been cleared and it really looks like it is going to happen—*this time*.

With good reason, some view the expectation that 2002 will finally be *the* year as the J4 committee essentially "crying wolf." Citing several false alarms—missed targets in 1996, 1997, and 1998—some have adopted a wait-and-see attitude. In fact, maybe you have seen the news about a new COBOL 2002 existing. Because this effort of the J4 could have a very significant impact on your career, it's important that you learn a little about this committee.

CROSS-REFERENCE   A published article at CobolReport.com (`http://cobolreport.com/columnists/jerome/`) by the respected COBOL authority Jerome Garfunkel presents convincing insight into why the road to a newer COBOL standard has been fraught with challenge and conflict.

About the J4

The J4, also known as the COBOL Technical Committee of the InterNational Committee for Information Technology Standards (INCITS), is closely associated with the American National Standards Institute (ANSI) standardization body. They do, however, coordinate their efforts with the International Organization for Standardization (ISO) for international adoption of standards. The J4 has mostly corporate members and a few noncorporate members. I will limit this discussion to the corporate membership.

According to their October 23, 2001, Annual Report (`http://www.ncits.org/archive/2001/it010899/it010899.htm#members`), the J4 has eleven voting members and five advisory members. Among the voting members, the following six names should be familiar: Unisys Corporation; Micro Focus, Inc.; IBM Corporation; EDS; Fujitsu Software Corporation; and Compaq. Among the list of advisory members are the following companies: Acucorp; Boeing Company; Computer Associates; and Charles Schwab & Co., Inc. This is an impressive list! Well, I was impressed with this who's who of the J4. Suffice it to say, you have been properly introduced.

CROSS-REFERENCE   For the one or two of you genuinely interested in getting a "real" understanding of the INCITS, ANSI (J4), and ISO (WG4) organizations and how they are interrelated, see http://www.x3.org/incits/, http://www.ansi.org/, http://std.dkuug.dk/jtc1/sc22/wg4/, and http://www.iso.ch/iso/en/ISOOnline.frontpage.

Now, imagine this: You are one of the 11 voting members of this special committee that had been working to create a new programming standard. Then, you return to your corporate world. You submit your expense form for reimbursement for your latest expenditures (i.e., committee dues, travel, lodging, and so on). Because your superiors are creating next year's budget, they are eager for a debriefing and guidance.

They approach you and ask, "Since you know what the new 'standard' is *going* to be, how can we position ourselves technologically so that we are *ready*?" Then, with your job and entire reputation on the line, you start to explain how "Language interoperability, object orientation and XML will play a big part in the future of any enterprise-level programming language. However—" Your boss then interrupts you midsentence, pats you on the back, smiles, and says, "You are a true visionary." Under your breath, unheard by anyone, you continue your thought: "However, these very things are the areas that we continue to argue about. The full inclusion of these technologies is in doubt. And, I'm starting to question the motives of some of my fellow J4 members."

Does it take that much imagination to see this scenario as probable? Perhaps I do have a vivid imagination.

So, what are these J4 members doing in the "real world," outside of weighing in with their J4 membership votes? How are *they* preparing for a future that continues to include COBOL? The following corporate-specific sections are provided as a glimpse into how each company has apparently interpreted the information possibly delivered by someone similar to our "imaginary" J4 committee representative.

NOTE In all fairness, I must point out that many COBOL software vendors have added object-oriented extensions to the current COBOL standard (some "in anticipation of" and others "without regard to" the forthcoming COBOL standard). In addition to the J4-affiliated vendors discussed here, the following vendors have also extended their COBOL compilers with object-oriented features: Liant; Netron, Inc.; TechBridge Technology; Hitachi; and LegacyJ.

The Unisys Corporation J4 Committee Member

I visited the Unisys corporate Web site with one question on my mind: What are they doing today with COBOL? My search results first introduced me to some very interesting information that Unisys provides about e-business. Next, I started seeing the term "ClearPath" attached to several of their products. It became apparent to me that the ClearPath product line is very important to Unisys. There were two midrange servers prefixed with the ClearPath moniker (i.e., ClearPath IX6600 and ClearPathIX6800). I read on. They discussed the ClearPath platform and how well it serviced Web applications, database access, and application development. And then, finally, I found it: COBOL. I first noticed a reference to something called "Java Object Cobol." Interesting.

Pushing on, I followed one last link to a section titled "Object Oriented COBOL Compiler." So there, on the Unisys Web site, I found the answer to my question. Unisys has a "new" object-oriented COBOL compiler. They describe this compiler as being part of the overall ClearPath IX strategy of object-orientation and componentization. Additionally, according to Unisys, this object-oriented COBOL compiler is part of the continuing Unisys mission to enhance the programming environment of ClearPath systems by providing a workstation-based programming development environment for ClearPath IX systems. Unisys listed a few features and benefits of their COBOL compiler (e.g., "Object oriented features from the emerging COBOL 200x standard" and it "Brings the advantages of object oriented technology to the COBOL programmer").

CROSS-REFERENCE For additional information on Unisys's COBOL compiler, visit `http://www.unisys.com/products/clearpath_servers/index.htm`.

The Micro Focus, Inc. J4 Committee Member

First off, a small disclaimer: According to the J4's recent annual report, the chairman of the J4 committee is a gentleman by the name of Don Schricker. Judging from his published e-mail address, he appears to be a Micro Focus employee. Who cares, right? Consider it just a little trivia to lighten up things. While researching this particular corporation, looking for current[2] COBOL events, my search ended almost abruptly when I found information about the Micro Focus Object COBOL Developer Suite product.

After reading about this product, I realized that I needed to continue searching. Yes, they have an existing COBOL product with object-oriented extensions. However, I preferred to find something more current, something that might indicate an acknowledgement of the new standard. Then it happened—jackpot! A press release dated November 27, 2001, with the title "Micro Focus Announces Support For New COBOL 2002 Standard" and the subtitle "New standardized language to be implemented in all Micro Focus COBOL platform products."

The press release is interesting. It provides some insight into the company's products and general direction. Additionally, a positive point is shared about "standards" in general. The part of the press release that really caught my eye was the section that started out with the following phrase: "COBOL 2002 adds significant new features to the COBOL language including: . . ." I would rather not list all the features here. However, I will list one of them: "Object Orientation."

CROSS-REFERENCE   For additional information, see the previously mentioned Micro Focus press release (http://www.microfocus.com/press/news/20011127.asp?bhcp=1) and visit the COBOLPortal Web site (http://www.cobolportal.com/developer/).

---

2. Recent to the time of this writing (October 28, 2002), Micro Focus released a press release titled "Micro Focus COBOL Now Extended to the Microsoft .NET Framework." The implications of this press release are huge. Up to this point, there has been one COBOL vendor, Fujitsu Software, offering a COBOL compiler that integrates into VS .NET. If Micro Focus delivers what they mention in their press release, you will be faced with a choice of .NET COBOL compilers. Certainly, I will monitor this news as it unfolds. I invite you to do the same. The following links may be of interest to you: http://www.microfocus.com./press/releases/20021028.asp and http://www.informationweek.com/story/IWK20021028S0007.

The IBM Corporation J4 Committee Member

Like Micro Focus, IBM has an existing COBOL product (VisualAge for COBOL) that contains object-oriented features. So, my search continued for something "new." Interestingly, with IBM, I was also able to find a recent press release. On November 27, 2001, IBM announced the availability of IBM Enterprise COBOL for z/OS and OS/390 V3R1. Is it just me, or does the date of November 27, 2001, sound familiar?

In IBM's announcement, the stated goal of Enterprise COBOL V3R1 is "to enable developers to leverage 30 years' worth of applications in new endeavors." So, let's explore a little to discover how IBM intends to accomplish this rather ambitious goal. As you might have guessed, the term "object-oriented" is liberally sprinkled throughout the news announcement. However, what might be a little surprising is the equally liberal usage of the following two phrases: "Java interoperability" and "XML support."

Additionally, the announcement mentions the goal of leveraging existing development being done on IBM's Web application platform WebSphere. Apparently, developing on IBM's WebSphere platform implies a commitment to learn about Java 2 Enterprise Edition (J2EE). About midway through the press release, a particular statement from the announcement left me with my mouth wide open: "Object Oriented COBOL syntax is retargeted for Java-based OO programming. Further, the primary purpose of the OO syntax is not stand-alone OO COBOL programming, rather the syntax is intended to facilitate interoperation of COBOL and Java." Interesting! Otherwise, IBM's software announcement continues (in depth) to provide prospective customers with valuable information.

 CROSS-REFERENCE   For additional information on the IBM press release mentioned in this section, visit http://www-3.ibm.com/software/ad/cobol/zos/ and click the "IBM Enterprise COBOL for z/OS and OS/390 V3R1 (201-343)" link under the "News" heading.

The Electronic Data Systems (EDS) J4 Committee Member

Let's continue the investigation. Well, given my simplistic approach to investigating (going to corporate Web sites and searching for the word "COBOL"), perhaps I should say, "Let's continue the search." This particular J4 committee member provided an extremely in-depth essay about Extensible Markup Language (XML). (I discuss this technology in Chapter 4.)

I really liked EDS's suggestion of using XML as a central focus to fill the "legacy-to-Web information gap." Toward that end, EDS announces in an essay/article on its site a new tool named XML-inline. This tool (used in conjunction with EDS's COGEN 2000 tool) will Web-enable COBOL applications. As a result, legacy applications written in COBOL can now be extended to actually output XML-tagged data. This will offer efficiencies not realized today when legacy applications send their print streams to an external application for XML type parsing. This well-written article goes even deeper and discusses XML schemas and standards. It then generously provides an XML primer—a big bravo for EDS! By the way, the new COBOL standard appears to lack "full" XML support,[3] and EDS saves the day with its proprietary XML integration tools—how convenient!

CROSS-REFERENCE   For additional information on EDS's new XML tools, visit http://www.eds.com/news/home_page_xml.shtml.

What About Sun Microsystems and Microsoft?

Some may wonder why Sun Microsystems' name does not appear on the J4 committee list. You have to take a closer look. Please revisit the previous "corporate" update for IBM, and take note of the emphasis on Java and J2EE technologies. As you know, the Java standard and the J2EE platform standard are controlled by Sun Microsystems. Albeit indirect, herein lies the involvement of the Sun Microsystems via IBM's COBOL implementation approach.

Likewise, were you surprised that Microsoft's name was not included on the list of J4's who's who? People generally expect Microsoft to have their hands into every part of technology. As with Sun Microsystems, you have to take a closer look and consider indirect partnerships as involvement. This will make more sense when you read about the next corporate J4 member, Fujitsu Software Corporation.

---

3. I am concerned about the omission of XML support and Web enablement from the actual standard. For now, these are vendor-specific extensions. Perhaps 10 years ago no one predicted their importance. Likely, a committee will address this in a post-2002 COBOL standard.

The Fujitsu Software Corporation J4 Committee Member

Like several other J4 members, Fujitsu Software Corporation has several existing COBOL products with object-oriented extensions already implemented. One of these products is Fujitsu's PowerCOBOL. So, are they taking any "new" action? Yes. This corporate member has approached the new COBOL challenge in an interesting way (taking no thunder away from the other J4 committee members' announcements).

Fujitsu Software worked with Microsoft to become the first[4] COBOL vendor to formally announce support for Microsoft .NET and ASP.NET, including XML Web services. The development team over at Fujitsu Software has taken the new COBOL 2002 standard (or at least a large subset of the standard) and made the appropriate extensions needed for .NET. They have labeled this creation "Net-COBOL for .NET." Now, that is impressive to say the least. Those already familiar with Fujitsu's COBOL development tools will declare that this move toward Microsoft .NET integration is not necessarily a surprise. This is because Fujitsu Software has a reputation for providing tools for the COBOL community that assist in development integration with traditionally nonmainframe technologies (Windows GUI, MTS/COM+ compatibility, object orientation, and so on). In the next chapter, I discuss how the language interoperability and neutrality feature of .NET has kept the door open for this COBOL vendor (and other future vendors of other language compilers) to easily integrate into the .NET development environment.

CROSS-REFERENCE For additional information about Fujitsu Software's NetCOBOL for .NET, visit http://www.netcobol.com/products/windows/netcobol.html.

The Acucorp J4 Advisory Committee Member

Some of you may have used Acucorp's software products. They have several products designed to extend the life of legacy COBOL applications. They do this by

---

4. As pointed out in an earlier footnote, Micro Focus recently announced their planned entry into the "COBOL for .NET" arena. It appears that you will soon have two competing COBOL vendors (Fujitsu Software and Micro Focus) both offering a COBOL compiler extended for Microsoft's .NET platform.

successfully implementing Web-enabling, graphical front-end, and Windows platform technologies that integrate into their cross-platform version of the ANSI COBOL 85 compiler.

Additionally, it is known that Acucorp has joined the list of vendors with object-oriented COBOL extensions in their products. I was not surprised to see their name included on the J4 committee advisory member list. My guess is that they are in the process of revamping their product offering per the COBOL 2002 standard specifications, using firsthand information obtained from participation in the J4. Sounds like a wise business strategy for Acucorp.

For those of you who have not had the pleasure of using Acucorp's COBOL development tools and COBOL enabling technologies, they also offer a rather COBOL-friendly service. If a client wishes, Acucorp will (for a fee) take over the complete maintenance of the corporation's legacy COBOL applications. I assume that this typically results in the corporate client giving their existing legacy mainframe-programming staff generous amounts of time off to better address their retraining efforts.

CROSS-REFERENCE   For additional information on Acucorp, visit
`http://www.acucorp.com/News/Press/Presskit/about.html`.

What About Compaq?

I failed to include a detailed "corporate update" for Compaq. I could find no new announcements about the new COBOL on their Web site—just the same clear message that Compaq has strong support for the existing COBOL 85 standard. My guess is that they are sitting on the sidelines, waiting for the dust to settle and taking a more conservative approach than the other trailblazing vendors. A move that may prove to be a wise one. For additional information, see `http://www.openvms.compaq.com:8000/73final/cobol/cobum.htm`.

Committee Member Summary

Now you know what the J4 committee members have been up to. I have given you a glimpse into the future of the COBOL language: COBOL 2002. Perhaps you have come to some conclusion about the mainframe programmer's training requirements going forward. At the same time, you may have even concluded that you are ready to abandon the mainframe due to the inevitable training that awaits tomorrow's mainframe programmers. Some might even say, "If I need to retrain anyway, why not learn a new language and a new environment?" Others may have noticed a more subtle point: COBOL, something that has been very stable, virtually unchanged for decades, is about to burst from its cocoon. Following this metaphor, it may be fair to ask: Is the J4 giving birth to a butterfly that *will* actually fly?

Should I stop here? Have I made my point well enough? Is there any doubt in your mind that the J4 members are committed to creating a "new" COBOL language, one that will require retraining in various technologies? All right, you asked for it. Let's drill down further.

Mainframe COBOL: How Will It Look?

As you have figured out by now, *if* you plan to continue to code in COBOL on the mainframe (and *if* you are lucky[5]), retraining *will* be part of your future. Now, here is a case of irony for those ready for the .NET reformation and ready to abandon the mainframe. To be successful with Microsoft's .NET platform, you will have learning opportunities as well. In fact, the retraining requirements are practically the same. Whether you stay on the mainframe or not, the programming platforms of the future will require you to embrace the following technologies during your retraining effort:

- Object orientation

- Language interoperability

- Web enablement

- XML

- Web service support

---

5. I promise I will explain the thought behind this snide remark later in the chapter.

Obviously, in both retraining scenarios (staying on the mainframe or switching to .NET), this is an overly watered-down summary—to make a point. The J4 committee members recognized what they needed to do to retrofit yesterday's (legacy) applications to survive and compete in today's Web-enabled world—a world where businesses and processes will need to collaborate and interoperate. I call this the "the party did not come to them, so they came to the party" syndrome. This seems like a reasonable conclusion, given some further observation. Consider, for example, the Visual Basic language evolved for 10 years and then came .NET, a revolution for future application development. Now, consider the evolution of COBOL. It too has been in the making for 10 years.

"COBOL Has Been Around for Forty Years–I Repeat, FORTY Years"

Correct.[6] Nevertheless, the *new* COBOL standard that includes object-oriented syntax has been in the making for how long? Ten years. When the industry really implements COBOL 2002 (that together with all of the specific vendor implementations), you will have a new COBOL language. Go ahead, review the new COBOL 2002 standard in the context of each COBOL vendor's implementation. Although object orientation seems to get most of the attention, the details of the COBOL 2002 standard include many additional changes. I suggest that this "evolution" for COBOL is almost as "revolutionary" as .NET is for Visual Basic.

The business technology world has changed significantly over the last decade. The fact that the J4 committee (as committee members and as individual corporations outside of the committee) has positioned COBOL to enter the object-oriented, XML, and XML Web service–dominated world is certainly a good thing for the mainframe programmer community. Incidentally, I look at this as a confirmation that Microsoft has headed in the right direction with .NET. Everyone is coming to the party! All of the corporate J4 committee members, other software vendors, and Microsoft recognized this changing business world and the changes needed to provide developers with the tools to program for this changed world. Now comes your part: to use the tools. Confused about choosing your retraining path? I do not blame you. Now you understand why I wrote this book.

---

6. If COBOL's 40-year ticker is allowed to continue (what with all of the changes that the language is undergoing, including the Visual GUI COBOL development that has already begun), then one would have to also consider that Visual Basic's life actually started before the *Visual* was added to the *Basic*. In other words, both languages (COBOL and Visual Basic) are 40 years old. I am not taking sides—just trying to be fair.

Choose Your Vendor and You Choose Your Retraining Path

Aren't you glad that the apparent chaos in COBOL land will be someone else's problem? After all, you are abandoning the mainframe, right? So, what choices will *they* (those poor COBOL mainframe programmers that you leave behind) have? Let's review:

- Unisys and their ClearPath platform for developing object-oriented COBOL.

- Micro Focus presented as platform neutral. Still, there are proprietary development tools to learn.

- IBM's COBOL is captured in two acronyms: J2EE and Java (courtesy of Sun Microsystems).

- EDS, another apparently platform-neutral interpretation that offers proprietary development tools.

- Acucorp's COBOL offers Web enabling, graphical front-end, and Windows platform technologies.

- Fujitsu Software Corporation provides a bridge into .NET through their Microsoft partnership.

Depending on which COBOL vendor, and thus, which COBOL 2002 *implementation* they would be working with, those COBOL mainframe programmers will have a variety of retraining challenges. They will need to learn the vendor-specific language extensions, development tools, and proprietary development platforms. Think about it.

NOTE   I have heard some suggest that learning Microsoft .NET is a commitment to Microsoft. To that, I respond that in the future, learning any vendor's COBOL 2002 will be a "commitment" to that particular vendor. So there!

Should each vendor have the liberty to interpret the COBOL standard with a unique implementation? Of course! Alas, this is the "value" of having an "open" standard. Appropriately, vendors should have something that sets them apart from each other. It is good for business and good for future technological innovations. However, what is good for business and technology creates extra challenges for us, the developers. Training and learning does not occur overnight. Additionally, just saying that you are coding in one particular language is not enough. The choice of one vendor over another inherently brings additional opportunities for learning (e.g., the development tools, the platform, vendor-specific language extensions, and so on) that could be more significant than learning the specific language syntax itself.

Before you throw your hands up and declare that in the workplace, vendor selection is out of the individual developer's hands, take note: When you see the lines drawn between technologies and vendors, you may begin to see the role that developers play in their individual places of employment.

Choose a Software Vendor—Even for Desktop Tools

Perhaps you have ambitions to take your programming skills in the desktop-to-Web direction. You have heard there is a large market out there for "office collaboration and workflow" applications—a hot opportunity for entrepreneurs ready to cater to both enterprises and small businesses. Well, with IBM, you might be going down the path with Lotus Framework products (i.e., Lotus Notes, Corel WordPerfect, Domino.Doc, Domino Workflow, and so on).

On the other hand, with Microsoft and .NET, typically you would go down the path with Microsoft Office XP (i.e., Word 2002, Excel 2002, Outlook, and so on). You, the developer, understand that it is usually easier to develop integrated solutions when working within the boundaries of a particular vendor's product line. This is not an accident or coincidence. This concept applies to the mainframe just as it does to the desktop—the software vendors depend on it. Try to see the larger picture when choosing your career direction.

Be Concerned About Your Future with COBOL on the Mainframe

Upward compatibility was maintained from COBOL 2002 back to COBOL 85. This is not true for Visual Basic .NET back to Visual Basic 6.0. In order to really revolutionize the language, Microsoft took a bolder step toward a complete overhaul of Visual Basic. On the other hand, the J4 took a more customer-friendly approach, but the COBOL language will likely suffer as a result. In other words, the J4 held the upward compatibility restriction as a higher priority, and thus tied their own hands. Frankly speaking, I am deeply concerned about the future of COBOL programming, at least as it exists on the mainframe. But what about you? What are your concerns?

I realize that some of you have read this entire section of the book in total disbelief and shock. You may have had kind thoughts such as "This author has got to be joking. I have not heard anything about these revolutionary COBOL 2002 changes. My employer has not mentioned anything to me about retraining. I know that I will be able to do maintenance development to my legacy application until the day that I retire. My job and my career are secure. Besides, my company allows me to use PC-based visual COBOL development tools. We are modern. We recently upgraded to a 'latest versioned' COBOL compiler . . . uh, I am not sure if it was based on COBOL 85 or COBOL 2002. But either way, we have even used COBOL to develop a GUI front-end that rivals CICS to access our mainframe data. Worst case, a new standard will come out that will be upwardly compatible. In that case, it will be business as usual—good old structured programming with a few syntax enhancements."

Do these comments sound familiar? Have you had similar thoughts? When is the last time you discussed any of those topics with your employer?

 CAUTION Earlier I promised that I would give you an explanation of a snide remark I made. So, let's review. Here's the remark: "As you have figured out by now, *if* you plan to continue to code in COBOL on the mainframe (and *if* you are lucky), retraining *will* be part of your future." What's my point? My point is that some of you have been literally *kicked off* the train without even knowing it. Drawing on the words of that mentor of mine . . . well, you know how it ends: "Yes, the train will leave without you."

Taking Action: Do Your Homework

I suggest that you follow each of the Web links that I have provided. Then, ask your current employer some of these questions:

- Where are our COBOL 2002 migration plans?

- When will the object-orientation retraining schedule be published?

- When is the next major new development project starting up in *our* department?

You may discover that your employer has chosen to leave their COBOL legacy applications and their legacy developers as is—in maintenance mode[7]—avoiding the new COBOL 2002 standard, the object-oriented syntax, the XML support, and the XML Web services. From a business' point of view, this may be the most economically wise thing to do. This is great for your employer's bottom line, but it is *not* so great for your future marketability. I wish that I could say that this would only matter if (and when) you decide to seek employment elsewhere. From what I am hearing from several of my former mainframe coworkers, the latest trend is that companies are laying off entire groups of mainframe staff members—in some cases choosing to replace them with alternative platform software solutions.

CROSS-REFERENCE   Granted, not all of the layoffs I mentioned affect mainframe programmers. Nevertheless, if you have a chance, visit http://www.msnbc.com/news and type in **The Layoff List** in the SEARCH MSNBC box. Those are staggering numbers—just a little something for perspective. Keeping your skills inventory current helps reduce the impact of a surprise layoff.

Now, maybe your employer is much fairer than the "worst-case scenario" employer that I am describing. Just keep your eyes open. Communicate with your employer—the guardian of your career—and find out if they have already started to create tomorrow's nonmainframe "mission-critical" applications over in the Internet development department using a group of highly paid contractors. Find out if there are rumors that those guys over in the Internet development department are using a development approach called rapid application development (RAD). Rumor has it that when developers start using Microsoft .NET, RAD is going to get even faster. Do not worry. CIOs never listen to rumors.

CAUTION   You guessed it. This is not a rumor—this is real! In fact, .NET will extend the RAD capability beyond the GUI type of development to include "server" development. Naturally, I expand on this in later chapters.

---

7. Your employer always has the option of bringing in a company such as Acucorp to "help" them with the maintenance of their legacy applications. Try to be objective and answer the following question: If you owned the company, what would *you* do with your legacy COBOL applications?

OK, have I shaken you up a little? Right now, it's a risk I need to take. We can patch up our author-reader relationship in later chapters. So, let's continue forward for a little more motivational preaching. I promise I'll lighten up later.

Taking Action: Exercise Your Freedom to Choose

Remember that it is ultimately *your* career. Be the guardian of your own career. Let the choice of what technology you want to learn be influenced by (but not controlled by) what technology your current place of employment happens to be using. If it comes down to it, it is always each developer's option to *choose* his or her place of employment.

Regarding the notion of abandoning the mainframe and/or exercising your freedom to choose a different place of employment: For the record, I am very sensitive to the financial concerns of the business world at large. A mass exodus of all mainframe programmers from their current mainframe responsibilities would not be healthy for the average organization, and thus it would not be healthy in the end for the average employee. My challenge to you is this: Look for ways to serve yourself and at the same time address the needs of your employer. Look for creative ways to accomplish your goals while being sensitive to the needs of the organization as a whole. Think seriously about taking your responsibilities with you, even while leaving one platform for another. Seek opportunities to leverage your employer's current investment in business rule logic. A solution from which you and your employer both benefit will be better for all. Go for the win-win situation.

This unearths a subtle point. An important difference between developing on the mainframe (even for those using PC-based COBOL development tools) and developing real Windows applications on a PC is that for a small investment you can have major processing power (including your very own database) right in the comfort of your home. For some, *this* is where you may need to begin your retraining. Your (current) employer's choice and your choice (at least in the beginning) can be independent. Remember, when doing nonmainframe development, you can design, develop, debug, and deploy (even distribute for sale) real Windows and Web applications, all on your own personal computer, your own personal server, or your own home-based local area network (LAN). Having your *own* computer is empowering!

Assess Your Access to a Computer

Years ago when I was helping out my company's help desk, one of our mainframe business users called in with the following complaint: "Can you help me? I think *my* computer is broken." After helping the user and ending the phone call, I shared this user's plea with my coworkers. I can still remember the good laugh that we had. Why was this so funny? This was still in the days of the "centralized processing model." Remember, in those days there was only one computer—in the computer room, on top of a raised floor. Certainly, the user was mistaken. There was no computer on the user's desk, just a monolithic monochrome cathode ray tube (CRT). Those were the days.

Today, it has become common for companies to equip their users and their mainframe programmers with personal computer workstations with 3270-emulation software. There is no shame in people now referring to the CRTs of the past as "dumb" terminals. Naturally, the word "dumb" has nothing to do with how they looked or functioned.

As far as political correctness goes, if a "PC" workstation takes on the limited functionality our CRTs did, a more pleasant reference such as "thin client" is used. The term "thin client" serves both as a software and hardware term. At any rate, if you are among the many to have a "thick client" personal computer as your workstation running the Windows operating system, you are indeed fortunate.

Taking Action: Equip Yourself for Your Retraining Effort

You will need to equip yourself at home. Seriously, consider making a small investment at your local electronics store. What are the recommended hardware requirements? Allow me to first point out that your computer hardware needs as a new Windows programming professional are much different than the needs of a person who only uses his or her computer for home finances, e-mail, and games.

Some of you may already own an older computer at home. There is a remote possibility that doing an upgrade on your older computer may be a cost-justified solution. Granted, money does not grow on trees. However, this is your future—your career—that we are talking about. You *will* need these tools. Besides, the hours that you are going to invest into retraining cannot and should not be done all on your employer's resources. Cut the umbilical cord and prepare to reap many financial gains from your own investment.

The computer that you want to use as your *training hub* should be a beefy workhorse.

CROSS-REFERENCE   For a list of the minimum hardware and software requirements, visit http://msdn.microsoft.com/vstudio/productinfo/ sysreq.asp.

In other words, plan to spend about $1,500. A PC with a Celeron chip will be much cheaper than one with a Pentium chip. Either way, aim for a chip with a minimum of 600 MHz processing power. With the money that you save from buying this alternative Celeron chip, plan to purchase a random access memory (RAM) upgrade. You will want to upgrade your RAM to at least 512MB of memory. The current Windows operating system is Windows XP (Home Edition or Professional). The average new PC will already have Windows XP Home Edition installed. However, be prepared to pay a little extra for the upgrade to Windows XP Professional. The Home Edition of Windows XP does *not* provide Internet Information Services (IIS) and .NET requires IIS installation. Therefore, the Professional edition is required.[8]

.NET and Platform Independence

There is talk about the Microsoft .NET Framework eventually being available on other platforms. Otherwise, throughout this book, I take a Microsoft-centric view toward technology. Considering their dominant market share of Windows desktop applications and development tools, this is certainly a comfortable approach.

Windows 2000 has a server version. Additionally, Microsoft is expected to release a new server-versioned operating system (likely to be called Windows .NET) in the near future. If you choose to go down that route, be prepared to add more learning topics to your already full list. I suggest that you avoid the server-versioned operating systems for now. When you are ready to set up your own LAN at home, you will then prefer the actual server-versioned configuration.

For Windows and Web .NET development, the Professional-versioned Windows operating systems will be perfect. As you install all of your new software

---

8. The .NET Framework and all .NET technologies can be installed on a computer running the Windows 2000 Professional or Server operating system. If you get your hands on an older computer, these choices will likely be the ones that you will be working with (which will be fine).

tools, you will appreciate having the 40GB hard disks that are now a standard feature. A CD-ROM/DVD player, modem, and Internet connection are all required features. If you are serious about your retraining, this equipping step is not optional.

Perceptions and Opinions

Picking this book up, some of you might have anticipated reading dire predictions for COBOL as a language and, worse yet, degrading commentary about the mainframe developer community. Rather, you found just the opposite. Still, my perception may interest you. I believe that mainframe-based development does have a future—a future that may not include you. Having said that, you *should* be concerned about what is happening.

NOTE   Certainly, you have heard enough jokes comparing the mainframe and mainframe programmers to dinosaurs. This "humor" always hints at extinction. I am now saying something similar, not toward the mainframe, not toward the mainframe programmers, but toward the style and technology used for mainframe programming.

During the time that I continued to proudly call the mainframe my home, people constantly predicted that the PC was going to make the mainframe obsolete. Yes, everyone is entitled to his or her perceptions, opinions, and beliefs. Nevertheless, back in those days, I was always defending the mainframe platform (and myself). Even the mainstream press joined the cause, often drawing analogies between the extinction of dinosaurs and the extinction of the mainframe and mainframe programmers.

I remember telling people that "The world is big enough for the two platforms to coexist." Years have passed, and Y2K has come and gone. The mainframe is still here.[9] Therefore, it looks like I was right after all. However, what is happening now (the latest assault) is much more worrisome. The mainframe platform *itself,* with these new COBOL 2002 standard changes and the various vendor implementations of the standard, could potentially make today's mainframe programmers (those that fail to retrain) obsolete. Notice that I used the phrase "today's

---

9. Some companies are using their mainframes more or less like a data repository—a high-end data server—which is not necessarily a bad thing.

mainframe programmers," not "the mainframe (hardware) itself." Talk about being stuck in the back!

Acknowledging Industry Perceptions

I want to inject a few other industry perceptions at this point. They are not necessarily relevant or even within the current context. Nevertheless, to exclude them while discussing the transitional life of the reformed mainframe programmer would make this text seem less realistic. Other theories and perceptions are out there; some of them are even controversial.

Here is one perception that you may consider controversial. There is a perception that seasoned mainframe programmers typically are able to teach the typical Web developer a thing or two in general about disciplined quality assurance, production support practices, and application life-cycle methodologies.

Following this train of thought, interest in the mainframe programmer talent pool would then have little to do with actual technological expertise (COBOL or otherwise). Therefore, a perceived technological inferiority is more or less tolerated in order to leverage the "harder to come by" assets. Are you ready for another perception? Remember, these are not facts, just opinions that some people have. You might be surprised to see what people and how many people subscribe to these theories.

Try this one on for size. When hiring for Internet/Web development positions, some people believe a fresh-out-of-college intern makes a better hiring candidate than a seasoned COBOL mainframe programmer. They may add a supportive belief that the "newbie" college graduate will not require any "untraining" of old habits. The things that some people believe really amaze me. Nevertheless, though the perceptions may not be real, they do exist. Moreover, like opinions, everyone has one.

Undoubtedly, you have your own perceptions and opinions as well. Which, by the way, brings me to my next discussion topic: *Your* perception/opinion of your very own "technology transition" (see, I told you "reformation" sounds more exciting).

Your Reformation Has Begun

This is the point in this chapter and book where I will address you as if you had already decided to begin your reformation.

TIP   If you are undecided, please reread this chapter again. Remember, taking on new skills does not mean that you are being asked to forget all that you already know. Your legacy skills will ultimately set you apart from your peers. This is a good thing. You can offer valuable assistance in the harvest of legacy data while using nonmainframe technology.

From this point forward, you have my full support. However, you will need to be sure about *your* reformation. Do not expect to find much moral support for your new technological choices from your mainframe peers (I wish I could say that the opposite would be the case). Maybe you will be lucky enough to not experience the name-calling and cold shoulder treatment. Maybe your former coworkers will not refer to you as *the traitor.* I have seen this happen. This phenomenon has always reminded me of the scene viewed from the top of a pot of boiling lobsters. You know this scenario: An emerging comrade is pulled back down into the boiling water by the other lobsters so that they all die together. Now *that* is love.

Not to worry, the Microsoft .NET family of developers is waiting for you, ready to welcome you over to the other side with open arms. However, before you run toward these extended arms, you will want to prepare yourself. The remainder of this book will help you take full advantage of this warm reception. Be forewarned, though, first impressions do count. When your new peers see how serious you are about embracing "their" world, you *will* be welcomed as one of "them." So, as you emerge, prepare to grit your teeth as you occasionally hear snide remarks and jokes poking fun at the so-called stereotypical reformed mainframe programmer. Your skin will grow thick. One day soon, you will laugh again.

Spread the Word: Be an Evangelist!

Now, am I encouraging every mainframe programmer to quit his or her job? No, of course not. Am I running around sounding the alarm,[10] screaming that the sky is falling? Well, not really, but I would encourage you to view this as good reason to buy several more copies of this book as gifts for your fellow mainframe

---

10. Granted, I am an alarmist, which I know. Nevertheless, who would not have minded having an alarmist aboard the *Titanic,* alerting others about the shortage of flotation devices?

brothers and sisters, your closest mainframe buddies.[11] This would include those (soon-to-be) former coworkers who ridiculed you, the ones who were "trying to pull you back into the boiling water." Seriously, they will thank you.

....

Summary

This chapter's goals were as follows:

- To discuss the activities surrounding the pending new COBOL standard for the mainframe and how that will create retraining opportunities for tomorrow's mainframe COBOL programmers

- To contrast the future for COBOL against the future for the average COBOL programmer

- To propel you into your reformation as you abandon the mainframe

To accomplish these goals, I discussed the current events of COBOL and some possible scenarios that today's mainframe programmer stands to experience. I presented the choices of retraining: to *really* stay current on the mainframe or to continue to code on the mainframe with yesterday's COBOL 85 standard. It was my intention to use this chapter as an opportunity to shake loose any doubt that you might have had about abandoning the mainframe. This is a big step (and an exciting one).

I included the discussion about the J4 and COBOL 2002 to provide you with the appropriate information to enable an informed position from which you could have *your own* opinion about the current and future state of COBOL programming. To do otherwise, I think, would be a disservice to the average experienced mainframe programmer. You have invested 5, 10, maybe 20 years of your life learning to be an expert developer on the mainframe. I would not expect you to entertain the idea of abandoning the mainframe on a whim.

In the next chapter, I introduce you to the world of .NET. I have titled that chapter "What Is .NET?" And yes, it will take a full chapter to answer that question.

---

11. To obtain another copy, visit the Apress Web site (http://www.apress.com/), Amazon.com (http://www.amazon.com/), or your local bookstore.

To Learn More

The following are some suggested supplemental references to further your retraining efforts.

Books

Software Development on a Leash, by David C. Birmingham and Valerie Haynes Perry (Apress, 2002):

    http://www.apress.com/catalog/book/1893115917/.

Magazines

.NET Magazine:

    http://www.fawcette.com/dotnetmag/

Visual Studio Magazine:

    http://www.fawcette.com/vsm/

XML & Web Services Magazine:

    http://www.fawcette.com/xmlmag/

Web Sites

American National Standards Institute (ANSI):

    http://www.ansi.org/

Cobol Portal:

    http://www.cobolportal.com/developer/

Cobol Standards (and the J4 committee):

    http://www.cobolstandards.com/

InterNational Committee for Information Technology Standards (INCITS):

    http://www.x3.org/incits/

International Organization for Standardization (ISO):

    http://www.iso.ch/iso/en/ISOOnline.frontpage

Microsoft Developer Network (MSDN):

    http://msdn.microsoft.com/

Rapid Application Development for the Server:

    http://msdn.microsoft.com/vstudio/technical/articles/radserver.asp

Windows XP Home Page:

    http://www.microsoft.com/windowsxp/default.asp

CHAPTER 2

What Is .NET?

Defining and Connecting the Dots

In this chapter

- Covering the essentials of .NET programming

- Exploring the various ways to access data using .NET

- Reviewing the use of .NET to interface with the user

- Introducing advanced .NET technologies

- Understanding the roles of marketing and planning for .NET

THIS CHAPTER MARKS a significant milestone. You are now one quarter of the way into Part One of this book. Why is that a *significant* milestone? It just happens that Part One ("The Mainframe Paradigm Shift") focuses on preparing you for your .NET retraining effort. Therefore, you have progressed a quarter of the way toward your retraining preparation. So, congratulations! Now, what will you need to do to complete your preparation? Well, that is where this chapter comes in.

This chapter will provide you with a full definition of .NET. While revolving around the question of "What is .NET?", I will discuss several answers to that question. The .NET definitions will include everything from the basic programming aspects of .NET and the new .NET development tools to new .NET concerns centered on XML and Web services. To finish the chapter off, you will stretch your view of .NET to even include portions of the .NET platform that deal with enterprise servers, your career, and marketing concerns.

As you have deduced, this chapter will fulfill yet another quarter of your retraining preparation. The two chapters that follow this one (Chapters 3 and 4) will complete the remaining half of your retraining preparation. The four chapters in Part One of this book will have fully presented to you the mainframe paradigm shift.

NOTE This chapter is designed to introduce you to the scope of. NET, and it does not contain any code samples. Part Two of this book provides you with hands-on programming examples. There, you will find an ample supply of programming code samples.

Putting the .NET Question into Perspective

Instead of asking "What is .NET?" suppose for a moment that circumstances were reversed. Someone (aware of your impressive mainframe background) asked you, "What is mainframe programming?" In an attempt to give a full answer, would you start by telling the person about the collection of programming languages available from which to choose? Perhaps you would go into detail discussing the choices of user interface technologies. As you know, your answer would be terribly incomplete if you did not explain the various data access technologies, the Job Entry Subsystem (JES), and the development environment. Obviously, there is more—a lot more. Therein lies my point with this analogy: The world of .NET is also huge.

So, how do you get your arms around something this huge, this encompassing? Well, have you ever heard the saying "You eat an elephant one bite at a time"? To answer the question "What is .NET?" let's take that same approach. While staying at a rather high level, I've divided the topic of .NET (the "elephant") into the following "bites":

- Programming Essentials with a .NET Language

- Accessing Data the .NET Way

- Interfacing with the User Using .NET

- Understanding Advanced .NET Technologies

- Marketing and Planning for .NET

In the following sections, where appropriate, I've included Cross-Reference notes to later chapters in the book. In these cases, you'll find that specific chapters cover the .NET topics in much more depth. For now, in this chapter, I present a big-picture view while defining .NET. So, let's get started.

Programming Essentials with a .NET Language

In this section, I discuss .NET programming languages, the .NET development environment, and the core underlying .NET technologies. Of course, this discussion will begin our efforts to answer the question of "What is .NET?" Some people might expect that coverage of programming essentials alone would be sufficient to help define .NET. As you will see, it is easy to understand why some have that expectation.

 CROSS-REFERENCE   The topics in this section are further discussed in Part Two of this book.

This section explains how .NET qualifies as all of the following entities:

- Programming language choice

- Programming language support

- Development environment

- Collection of class libraries

- Virtual machine and runtime

- Object-oriented technology

.NET Is a Programming Language Choice

That's right, you have a chance to choose your .NET programming language. You make this language choice by selecting your specific .NET compiler. You can actually refer to a given language compiler as a .NET type of language compiler. However, to be technically correct, you would use other phrases such as "the language compiler supports the .NET Framework" and "the language is *managed*." Later, in this same "Programming Essentials with a .NET Language" section, I discuss the .NET Framework and what it means to be managed.

According to Microsoft, there are about 20 .NET language compilers. This count includes those compilers provided by Microsoft and other compilers developed by other software vendors (partners). A few of the .NET programming language compilers provided by Microsoft are as follows:

- Visual Basic .NET

- Visual C# (pronounced "C sharp") .NET

- Visual J# (pronounced "J sharp") .NET

- Visual C++ .NET

Among the list of partners, one in particular stands out (in my eyes[1]). Let the history books record that Fujitsu Software is the first vendor (and the only vendor for now) to come forth with a .NET compiler for COBOL. As mentioned in Chapter 1, this particular compiler version product is called NetCOBOL for .NET. For all reformed COBOL developers, this decision by Fujitsu Software to jump onboard (teaming up with Microsoft) will stand to be a critically valuable one. Therefore, when you do .NET development, you actually have choices related to the language syntax and language compiler with which you develop.

An Opportunity to Choose

Recall that the mainframe offered several popular programming language choices for business programming: COBOL, assembler, Easytrieve, and Dyl280, to name a few.[2]

Each of these mainframe languages had specific advantages over the others. Some of those advantages related to design and compile-level characteristics. In the case of Easytrieve and Dyl280, compilation (or rather, the lack thereof) was even an issue.

Fortunately, in the world of .NET, a language that is said to be a .NET language is able to stand shoulder to shoulder with any other .NET language. In other words, as far as functionality and performance is concerned, one .NET language does not have a clear advantage over another.

---

1. No offense intended to those who share a passion for other languages such as Fortran, Pascal, and so forth. If it is any consolation, even those languages (Fortran, Pascal, and others) have .NET compilers built (or being built) to .NET-enable them.

2. Using the words "Easytrieve" and "Dyl280" in the same sentence with the words "programming" and "language" may be a questionable approach. Later, in Chapter 4, you will see that the Web/Windows world has continued the tradition (as the mainframe world did) of loosely using the word "language" to describe various technologies.

Because the .NET development environment is designed such that languages are "neutralized," performance is not a criterion; in theory, all the languages will perform well. That being said, you may tend to make your .NET language choice based on personal preference. However, you should take many other things into consideration. Suffice it to say that whether your preference is Visual Basic, COBOL, C++, or even Java, there is a comparable .NET language compiler waiting for you.

CROSS-REFERENCE   Chapter 5 covers .NET language choices in further detail.

.NET Is Complete Programming Language Support

The previous section emphasized the availability of .NET as a language choice. Now, once you *do* select a .NET language (or languages), you will notice that your chosen .NET language has all of the normal language elements (i.e., conditional logic, loops, case statements, comparative operators, and so on) that you would expect of *any* programming language.[3] In that way, programming on the .NET platform becomes comparable with the legacy mainframe COBOL programming that you have (presumably) done for some time.

During your legacy mainframe development experience, you have likely used COBOL (and other languages) to implement your business rules using these normal language elements. Well, in .NET you will look to these familiar elements and concepts (or language features) to implement your business logic and presentation routines. Granted, the syntax will vary from one .NET language to the next. Nevertheless, you will find that these basic programming elements are there still.

CROSS-REFERENCE   Chapter 6 is devoted to the "nuts and bolts" of .NET programming.

---

3. This is at least true for each of the .NET languages that I discuss. Chapter 6 covers this topic in more depth.

.NET Is a Development Environment

In the mainframe world, you were accustomed to having an actual environment in which to develop your software. One mainframe tool comes to mind: Interactive System Programming Facility (ISPF). Some of you may have had the misfortune of working in mainframe environments where other products were in use—competing products that looked like and worked like ISPF (sort of). At any rate, you had a development environment. In this mainframe environment, you had an editor. Additionally, you had the ability to construct and compile in ISPF.

Whether you were doing batch programming or online programming, you typically did (almost) everything within this same environment. There were some exceptions—times when you left ISPF for certain tasks. Nevertheless, for the most part you leveraged the submenus on ISPF for your development needs. In that sense, you can say that ISPF (and products like it) represented an "integrated development environment."

Well, you guessed it, there is an *integrated development environment* (IDE) in the world of .NET. Microsoft has a product called Visual Studio .NET (VS .NET). In short, it is an awesome tool. In this IDE, you design, edit, compile, and test your programs. As in the case of the mainframe, there are times when you will work outside of VS .NET. Over time, vendors will attempt to create competing development environments. Only time will tell which one will rise to become the preferred IDE. For now, Microsoft's VS .NET is easily your .NET IDE of choice.

CROSS-REFERENCE   You will explore the VS .NET tool in great depth in Chapter 5.

.NET Is a Collection of Class Libraries

Imagine that you're developing a COBOL program on the mainframe. Perhaps you have a group of mainframe partitioned datasets (PDS) that make up an extensive library of copybooks, utilities, subprograms, and software routines. Let's say that this reusable software library has been proven bulletproof, so much so that you've come to rely on this library and you often reuse selected PDS members.

Now, add on top of all of this that you chose to leverage the inherent COBOL Report Writer module and internal COBOL SORT features. Obviously, your intention would be to maximize any plumbing that the COBOL compiler provided (that you may have a need for) and maximize any reuse opportunity that the reusable software library offered.

Well, with this mainframe analogy I have just about described the functionality of Microsoft's .NET Framework. However, to really be fair, I would have to take this imaginary reusable library and multiply it by a factor of 4,000. The .NET Framework contains several thousand reusable software *pieces*. Regardless of the .NET language that you happen to use, the full .NET Framework is available to you. The more that you leverage (reuse) the .NET Framework, the better off your .NET development experience and resulting .NET application will be.

CROSS-REFERENCE   Although selected portions of the .NET Framework will appear in almost every chapter in this book, you will focus directly on the .NET Framework in Chapter 7.

.NET Is a Virtual Machine and Runtime

Suppose for a moment that I asked you to define the mainframe's Job Entry Subsystem (also known as JES, JES2, or JES3). You might explain JES in this way: You submit your batch programs in the form of Jobs to the operating system. The operating system in turn hands your Jobs to JES for execution. JES then manages the priority execution of your Jobs. Following execution, JES handles the purging of your Jobs from the operating system. So, what does this have to do with defining .NET and answering the question "What is .NET?"

Well, sitting on the bottom of the entire .NET world is a foundation, an engine referred to as the *common language runtime* (CLR). The CLR manages the fine details of what your program is doing, in much the same way that JES manages your Jobs. As JES purges your Jobs from the operating system, the CLR might purge your software objects from memory. You could say that the CLR is a micromanager of sorts. As JES is a major piece of system-level software, the CLR is an equally major piece of system-level software.

CROSS-REFERENCE   Chapter 8 discusses the CLR in detail.

.NET Is an Object-Oriented Technology

The emphasis on the .NET Framework earlier in this chapter should also be applied to this topic of object orientation. Putting the two together will lead you to the creation of more maintainable and reusable components.

Good Design Practices Are Still Needed

For the reformed mainframe programmer, moving *toward* the object-oriented software development model means moving *away* from the following software development models:[4]

- Structured
- Procedural
- Top-down
- Spaghetti

Of course, well-seasoned developers (like us) have only developed applications using the structured development models. So, spaghetti code is a thing of the past, right?

Wrong. Although .NET is many things, it is not a panacea. As it turns out, even object orientation will not prevent developers from writing spaghetti code. However, fully leveraging all that .NET has to offer *will* encourage good program design. So, as you start writing great .NET applications using the new object-oriented development methodology, remember that design/code reviews and quality assurance processes continue to offer value.

In the world of .NET, you will be working with objects: Everything is an object. In your object-oriented program, you will create, reference, modify, and pass objects. After you understand the world of object orientation, you will prepare yourself to create maintainable, robust, and scalable applications. You will strive to create efficient code, and you will even learn not to create memory management problems in your application.

That's right, the concerns of memory management still exist. The concerns of managing memory will feel painfully familiar to the advanced mainframe Customer Information Control System (CICS) programmer who has worked with the GETMAIN and FREEMAIN storage commands. In addition, the phenomenon

---

4. This, of course, may not apply to those (few, relatively speaking) of you who have already begun object-oriented COBOL development on the mainframe.

referred to as "memory leak" is familiar to some advanced CICS mainframe programmers (like yourself). The good news is that .NET has implemented a solution to help developers in the area of memory management.

You will be introduced to this .NET-implemented feature, the garbage collector (GC), in Chapter 8. The GC will do some of what the mainframe FREEMAIN command did and more. As I mentioned earlier, in .NET everything is an object. The GC is just one aspect of what .NET offers to assist you in managing objects. Learn object orientation, and then prepare to work with .NET objects extensively.

CROSS-REFERENCE   I discuss the topic of object orientation in Chapter 4 in detail. In Chapter 9, I discuss object orientation in even more detail as it applies directly to the coding samples.

Sure, there are objects and the .NET Framework, but what about data? You were just about to ask that question, right? Eventually, you *are* going come across the need to read and/or write data. As I discuss in the next section, the .NET platform has great support for accessing data.

Accessing Data the .NET Way

I must admit that this is probably one of my least favorite topics because it clearly flags the departure from using Job Control Language (JCL). That's right, after all of these years of using JCL on the mainframe for most of your data needs, along comes .NET. So, for the reformed mainframe programmer, .NET is a fond farewell to JCL.

CROSS-REFERENCE   Part Three of this book further explores the topics presented in this section.

This section discusses using .NET to get data in the following ways:

• Without the help of JCL

• From a relational data source

• Described with XML

Getting Data Without the Help of JCL

As you know, on the mainframe JCL is used for many things, not just data access. JCL has been there for us through the years, providing a way to allocate the resources needed by our programs. Nevertheless, in the average mainframe JCL structure (Job), the data definition (DD) statements account for well over half of the JCL statements used. So, I repeat, it is time to say good-bye to JCL. Yes, as part of the package of your *reformation* away from the mainframe and into the .NET world, JCL is no longer a tool available in your arsenal. Period.

Now, here is the good news: .NET provides several ways to access data (and allocate other resources). Each of the available ways has a specific strength. As you learn about these approaches, you will discover that you will have a preference for one approach or another, depending on your needs. On the mainframe, you used one approach for regular sequential (Queued Sequential Access Method, or QSAM) files and a different approach for Virtual Storage Access Method (VSAM) files. By the way, for you, QSAM and VSAM files have joined JCL on the fond farewell list.

OK, before I upset a few people: Yes, I should have said QSAM and VSAM, *as we have known them.* First, the text files that you will work with on the Windows platform will remind you of mainframe QSAM files. Second, some vendors have created very useful tools that run on the Win32 platform to create indexed files. These indexed files behave similarly to mainframe VSAM files. For example, Fujitsu Software has a Win32 product called COBOL File Utility that will create an index for your Win32 text file. Granted, with this Win32 index file, you do not have all the power of a traditional mainframe VSAM file, but the Win32 file *is* indexed.

 CROSS-REFERENCE   Chapter 10 introduces a new perspective on data and covers several .NET tools for basic data access.

Obtaining Data from a Relational Data Source

Although a relational data source isn't your *only* choice for data access, it certainly is one of your choices. As it turns out, using relational databases in Windows and Web applications (and on .NET) is extremely popular. In Chapter 11, I discuss not only the actual coding concerns, but also the use of the SQL Server basic administrative tools.

On a similar note, Microsoft's SQL Server isn't your *only* choice of relational data source system. There are other good products on the market (e.g., Oracle,

Microsoft Access, and so forth). Nevertheless, in this book, you will use Microsoft's SQL Server (currently SQL Server 2000) for your database-related samples.

For those of you who have worked with IBM's DB2 RDBMS on the mainframe, you will feel right at home with Microsoft's SQL Server 2000. Well, sort of. The Structured Query Language, or SQL (now Transact-SQL, or T-SQL), is virtually the same as the SQL used to access DB2. You will realize the learning curve when you start looking around for some of the mainframe tools such as DB2 Interactive (DB2I), SQL Processor Using File Input (SPUFI), and Query Management Facility (QMF).

Working with SQL Server 2000, you will have a new set of tools to learn, namely Query Analyzer and Enterprise Manager. You can be certain that eventually you will need to write a database application. Therefore, time spent mastering these tools is time spent wisely.

CROSS-REFERENCE   I further explore the topic of T-SQL in Chapter 3. Then, to smooth out the learning curve for relational data sources, I discuss SQL Server 2000, along with a new set of related tools, in Chapter 11.

Getting Data Described with XML

As mentioned in Chapter 1 during the discussion of the J4 committee members' activities, practically every software vendor is using XML in one way or another. Well, so is Microsoft. But to what extent? Let's just say that XML is to .NET as blood is to the human body. Therefore, it is appropriate to use this topic to help answer the question "What is .NET?"

With XML, you will be accessing data. Specifically, you will find yourself describing, reading, and writing data with XML. You will be amazed at the various ways in which XML is used and can be used throughout the .NET platform. Generally, you can look at XML (especially XML Schemas) as a way to describe your data, much as you would use a mainframe COBOL copybook. Additionally, when you are writing (and reading) data in your .NET application, .NET makes it very convenient to write your data in the format of XML. You will even find that all of your .NET configuration concerns will be addressed using XML. XML truly runs through .NET inside and out. As you dig deeper into .NET (and XML), you will become more comfortable working with XML. You will quickly grow to view it as just another tool/standard to help you with your data concerns.

CROSS-REFERENCE   I expand on the topic of XML in Chapter 4. In Chapter 12, I further discuss XML in the context of describing and handling data.

Whether data is structured with the help of XML or a relational database, or accessed with ADO.NET (or any of .NET's innovative approaches), someone will want to see that data. In fact, a user will typically want to interact with your application and any data that is exposed. I discuss this aspect of .NET in the next section. As you continue through the chapter, perhaps you can appreciate (even more) that defining .NET *is* a significant undertaking.

Interfacing with the User Using .NET

In your previous career life, prior to your move toward *reformation,* you created user interfaces. Perhaps you used the Customer Information Control System (CICS) or the Interactive System Programming Facility (ISPF) to design and build useful screens. These screens provided the "face" in the word "interface." Welcome to the .NET world. You now have a new set of .NET tools for creating your graphical user interfaces (GUIs). Also, with .NET you will be creating nongraphical "program interfaces."

The User Is Still Always Right!

Regardless of the platform (mainframe or Windows/Web), all of the same "interface" design considerations apply. You will still want to clearly identify your target user group (those users who will interface with your application). Your interface should provide targeted users with the most pleasurable (hassle-free) experience. Although the term "user-friendly" may sound old-fashioned, to the user community this word is as fresh as ever. In some cases, you may find that the Windows/Web users are more demanding (remember, they do have a PC on their desk). In other cases, you may find just the opposite (with users being willing to do more on their own). The point being, you should learn the new .NET tools for developing application interfaces and remember to allow some time to understand the needs and expectations of your application's target audience.

Going forward with the "What is .NET?" question, this section discusses .NET in the following contexts:

- Windows, Web, and XML Web services development

- Use of a Toolbox during development

- State and event management

- Report creation and information delivery

- Deployment improvement

CROSS-REFERENCE   Part Four of this book further discusses the topics in this section.

.NET Is Windows, Web, and XML Web Services Development

This section explores a few additional .NET definitions that I have come across. These are my favorite so-called .NET definitions. Why? Because early on I recall using each of them myself.

.NET Is Windows Development

Windows programming on the .NET platform is an exciting sandbox to play in. Though the Windows Form may not get as much attention as its cousin the Web Form, Windows programming is more alive than ever.

Although you were able to develop Windows applications with previous versions of Visual Basic and Visual Studio, your development experience just got (much) better. For example, your .NET desktop applications can now leverage the full power of the .NET Framework. On top of that, you can now easily deploy Windows and desktop applications over the Internet directly to the remotely located user. Make sure to spend some time in the area of creating great applications for the desktop.

Portable Devices Have Windows

You may find yourself developing applications for portable devices—not just portable computers, but also personal digital assistants (PDAs), mobile phones, and wristwatches. In other words, .NET, when combined with the .NET Compact Framework and Smart Device Extensions for Visual Studio .NET, is a development platform for portable devices.

Windows development with .NET is a broad and exciting area to be in. Some developers will even include Microsoft Office objects (Word, Excel, and so forth) in their application solutions. In addition, collaborative workflow–type applications are gaining popularity. Although these solutions were possible prior to the existence of .NET, the enhancements that .NET brings to the table will make these types of implementations that much more attractive. Use .NET to build Windows applications—it is all possible.

.NET Is Web Development

In the previous section, I mentioned that Web Forms tend to get a lot of attention. As the Internet is very popular, the technologies used to create Web sites should follow that popularity. Becoming proficient in this area will have you learning about ASP.NET and HTML, along with many other technologies. If you have built mainframe CICS applications, ASP.NET and HTML will reintroduce you to many familiar concepts. You will find that the learning curve is not that steep, especially with the help of the great book in your hands.[5] Considering the popularity of Web sites and Web site development, it is easy to see why this particular answer for the question "What is .NET?" is a common one.

 CROSS-REFERENCE   Chapter 4 delves deeper into the topic of HTML.

---

5. Pardon me. Thanks.

.NET Is XML Web Services Development

What is .NET? Here is one very popular answer: XML Web services. Notice the three words: "XML," "Web," and "services." When combined (as in "XML Web services"), they equate to what is becoming *the* answer. Certainly, XML Web services are something to get excited about. However, for our purposes here, if .NET *is* XML Web services, then what *are* XML Web services?

Again, let's refer back to mainframe CICS application development. In the past, you may have created a special CICS transaction that didn't have an actual screen associated with it. This special CICS transaction was usually referred to as a *started task*. You would use a CICS START command to execute the started task, possibly passing data to the started task using the FROM option.

If you are familiar with this type of advanced mainframe CICS programming, you are already acquainted with the general idea of XML Web services. Obviously, there is more to the CICS started task technology. Likewise, XML Web services are very powerful and require further explanation.

CROSS-REFERENCE   Chapter 13 drills down further into Windows, Web, and XML Web services development.

.NET Is Using a Rich Toolbox During Development

As you dive deeply into VS .NET, you will explore the Toolbox. You will find that depending on the type of application that you are creating, the contents of the Toolbox will vary. For example, a Windows application may have certain types of controls (Toolbox contents) that are not applicable to a Web application and vice versa. The Toolbox can contain visual controls as well as other types of controls and components, such as data controls.

The Toolbox is designed to be exactly what its name implies: a container to hold tools that help you build applications. In Chapter 1, I mentioned rapid application development (RAD). Certainly, the Toolbox plays a large role in the RAD approach, especially when a developer fully leverages the contents offered in the Toolbox. The concept of having a Toolbox may be a bit strange at first for the reformed mainframe programmer. The good news is, you will quickly get used to using the Toolbox. To help get you started, I will present an analogy.

Imagine that you are developing a mainframe CICS application. At some point, you typically will create a screen for the user to interact with. This step requires that you create a BMS mapset and all of the corresponding map information. Now, suppose you have a PDS library available to you with several "pieces" of BMS mapsets that you could drag and drop to help you create your CICS screen. You can see how this type of reuse could lead to increased productivity and consistency (which also promotes maintainability).

Confused? Don't worry, you'll understand and master this feature later.

 CROSS-REFERENCE   Chapter 14 explores the Toolbox and its contents in more detail.

.NET Is Enhanced State and Event Management

Let's go back to your mainframe CICS development to understand state and event management. Recall the CICS DFHCOMMAREA and the CICS RETURN command. Together, these two CICS technologies provided a way to pass data from one execution of a transaction/program to the subsequent re-execution of the same transaction/program. In mainframe terms, these CICS technologies supported the idea of a transaction/program being *pseudo-conversational*. Well, the idea of saving this data while conducting a "conversation" with the user is a very general hint at what state management involves.

On .NET, you could define *state management* as a methodical approach by which you first identify an established conversation (being held between your application and your users). Once you identify the conversation, you will need to keep track of (manage) selected data specific to the established conversation (interaction) for any given user. Fortunately, .NET has some really cool features to make state management rather simple. You will learn more about them in Chapter 15.

Let's return to the mainframe CICS application analogy for a moment. To help explain what events are, I'll use one term: events. That's right. Well, in all fairness, when you do mainframe CICS development, you sometimes would use the phrase "event and response." You would use the Attention Identifier (AID) keys to determine what events had taken place.

On the mainframe, do you recall that there was an event/response chart you used when designing CICS programs to help manage the expected events and responses? Good—most programmers would have used this event/response chart right after the traditional flowchart was completed. This chart and the accompanying focus given to events and responses when designing a CICS program have prepared you for the type of event management awaiting you on the .NET platform. Even though the phrase "event management" is rarely used on the .NET platform, events are events, whether on the mainframe or off the mainframe. What's more, you'll need to manage your use of .NET's events. It's the same idea and concept, yet a very different implementation, as you'll see.

CROSS-REFERENCE   Chapter 15 further discusses state and event management.

.NET Is Report Creation and Information Delivery

I mentioned the mainframe COBOL Report Writer module earlier in this chapter. Recall how useful the COBOL Report Writer module was (when properly used). As mentioned before, the .NET Framework also has reusable classes to give you a big head start in creating reports.

For those of you who equate the phrase "report generation" with something that you get to do only when you are being punished, fear not. .NET has come to your rescue. Report generation has returned to reclaim its rightful distinction of being a glamorous endeavor.

With the .NET Framework objects and the built-in Crystal Reports objects, your interest in creating reports will be recharged as you create charts, spreadsheets, PDF documents, and other types of reports. You will see why the topic of report generation is now starting to blend in with the phrase "information delivery." Once again, you can hold your head high and proudly say that you are implementing a report generation (er, rather, an *information delivery*) application. If it sounds like I am getting excited about .NET, I am—and so will you.

CROSS-REFERENCE   Chapter 16 covers report generation and information delivery.

.NET Is Improved Deployment for .NET

You may have read about .NET's new XCOPY deployment feature. Next to .NET's improved packaging feature, the XCOPY feature is certainly highly regarded by many Web/Windows developers. Coming from the mainframe world, your reaction to this feature will certainly be different from the average pre-.NET Windows/Web developer's reaction. You see, the deployment that takes place on the mainframe already looks like XCOPY deployment. That is, as long as you are talking about offline batch program deployment. If you switch over to the mainframe CICS online type of program deployment, then, as you know, things get rather complicated.

So, when you see your new Windows/Web developer peers getting excited about .NET's improved deployment approach, try to get excited with them. You can feel fortunate that you are getting involved with the Windows/Web development world at a time when something like .NET exists. Hopefully, you will not have to maintain any legacy Web/Windows application. Then maybe you will never have to find out just *why* .NET deployment advances really *are* a big deal. If you had to live through what was called "DLL Hell," you too would gladly include this topic when answering the question "What is .NET?"

 CROSS-REFERENCE   Chapter 17 further explores .NET deployment.

Considering each subsection covered in this larger section, you may be surprised to find out that the next section deals with *advanced* .NET technologies. Yes, many of the previously discussed .NET explanations may have appeared advanced. Nevertheless, these previous sections were excluded from the advanced section. This is not to say that the topics covered up to this point are not important or even technologically superior—they are. This simply points out how enormous the .NET platform really is (and why it takes an entire chapter just to answer the question "What is .NET?"). In other words, .NET is not a toy. It is a real enterprise-caliber tool. So, please continue on to the next section to discover which topics are actually considered advanced.

Understanding Advanced .NET Technologies

The entire world of .NET *is* understandable. You may have to work hard, study hard, and practice hard. Nevertheless, it is doable. This section takes a quick look at the following advanced topics:

- Secure and configurable applications

- COM+ application creation

- Distributed and concurrent processing

- Interoperability

 CROSS-REFERENCE   Part Five of this book further discusses the topics presented in this section.

.NET Is Secure and Configurable Applications

Security is probably one of the most discussed topics in some circles. And yes, Microsoft has addressed this concern. So, when some people answer the question "What is .NET?" the security features will come to mind first. Portions of the .NET Framework you will learn about explore this topic completely. Additionally, the Global XML Web Services Architecture (GXA) WS-Security standard also increases the level of security available to .NET applications. You will want to learn about both.

Include Security As Part of Your Web Application Design

The area of security for a reformed mainframe programmer will seem strange. Not because the mainframe programmer does not appreciate the need and importance of the topic, but rather because the average mainframe programmer typically did not *need* to worry about security.

Even when you developed large mainframe CICS online applications, there was an entire team of security experts that secured the environment—mainly from internal employees. In the Web development world, your application is potentially exposed to the outside world. So now security is more of an application-level and enterprise-level problem, and thus your problem to share. You will need to take this paradigm shift very seriously.

Others will quickly refer to the enhanced, configurable features. .NET provides a host of configuration files. These configuration files are available at the user level, application level (both Windows application and Web application), machine level, and system level. .NET has certainly taken the idea of being configurable to a new level (pun intended).

For those programmers who have historically avoided hard-coding *anything* in their program code, these configuration files will be welcome. During your mainframe development, perhaps you created QSAM files and PDS members that contained configuration information and parameter values. Now you have this set of configuration files to take advantage of. Again, this is a similar idea and a similar concept—it's just the implementation that's different.

CROSS-REFERENCE   Chapter 18 discusses configuration and security in depth.

.NET Is COM+ Application Creation

In the next chapter, I define COM+. For now, I will just mention that COM+ on the Windows platform is similar to CICS itself. In other words, in the same way that individual transactions and application programs are installed on top of the system-level program CICS, you can have application-level programs installed on top of the system-level program COM+.

There are many services that COM+ offers to an application. If you want to leverage those services, you create a COM+ application and install your program into the COM+ application. I will provide step-by-step instructions on how to accomplish this.

CROSS-REFERENCE   I have extended this introduction to COM+ in Chapter 3. Later, in Chapter 19, I discuss COM+ further.

.NET Is Distributed and Concurrent Processing

If there were such a thing as a *really* advanced section in this book, this particular section would be it. That is the reason I chose to discuss these two topics in more detail near the end of the book. Allow me to point out that both distributed processing and concurrent processing are rather important topics. There is a possibility that one of your future applications will need to take advantage of either of these advanced features. That is certainly reason enough to not ignore these advanced topics. After all, this book is designed to be your one-stop guide to .NET.

CROSS-REFERENCE   Chapter 20 explores distributed and concurrent processing.

Distributed Processing

On the mainframe, have you ever used CICS's Distributed Program Link (DPL) feature? Don't feel bad if you haven't. Even on the mainframe, this is considered to be an advanced topic. Nevertheless, .NET has a feature called .NET Remoting that is similar to the DPL feature.

On the mainframe, if you had a CICS program on one CICS region that you wanted to be able to "connect" to from a different CICS region, you would use the DPL feature. On .NET, if you have a program on one machine that you want be able to communicate with a program on a different machine, you would use .NET Remoting.

You might wonder, "If this .NET Remoting feature is similar to the mainframe CICS DPL feature, will this feature be equally obscure?" To that, I would have to respond, "It depends." It depends on the particular needs of your users and the types of applications you plan on developing. Even more, it will depend on the physical configuration of your production (hardware) environment and your organization's security/firewall policies. You will explore these variables and others in Chapter 20. At that point, you will gain an understanding of when it is appropriate to include .NET Remoting as part of your application design.

Concurrent Processing

The topic of concurrent processing leads to the area of (.NET) threading. When I discuss concurrent processing further in Chapter 20, I compare it with the CICS features multitasking and multithreading.

.NET threading (or multithreading) is certainly a sensitive topic. There are those who will quickly swear to its usefulness. At the same time, there are those who have been "burned" so badly from previous attempts to use it that they will not even enter into an open discussion of the topic. And then there are those who are simply excited that the current version of Visual Basic (VB .NET) finally supports true multithreading.

Regardless of which camp you belong to, you will still want to know how to use threading—properly, that is—in the event that you can justify using it. Generally speaking, an application that has significant processing overhead may (I repeat, *may*) be a candidate. If the timely completion of key portions of this same application becomes critical (e.g., an online application that interacts with a user), this would further support the notion of the application being a candidate for explicit threading management. Furthermore, if you have designed your application such that multiple threads can safely be dealt with explicitly, you just might (I repeat, *might*) have yourself a candidate for .NET's threading.

Obviously, discussing *when* and *when not* to include explicit threading in your program design is important. Simply learning *how* to programmatically manage threads is equally important. In Chapter 20, when I further discuss this topic, I trust that you will be adequately informed, debriefed, and enlightened.

Yes, distributed processing and concurrent processing are rather advanced topics and should be treated as such. As you learn more about them, you will be armed with enough knowledge to use caution when traveling down the path of "alternative" processing models. Nevertheless, you *will* want to know that these features exist, just in case you ever need them.

.NET Is Interoperability

You can use multiple languages on .NET. However, what about the topic of interoperability? What about .NET's capability to allow modules of multiple languages to interact and coexist in the same application? With .NET, software modules written in one language (e.g., VB .NET) can easily interoperate with software modules written in a different language (e.g., C#). .NET is ready for these types of situations.

In fact, interoperability is a key characteristic of .NET that seems to get a fair amount of attention. I believe this can be attributed to the fact that when you need interoperability, you *really* need interoperability. Inclusion of interoperability as part of your application design usually means that there was not a more viable choice.

.NET Supports Component Object Model (COM) Interoperability

If you need to leverage existing Windows/Web legacy modules (i.e., COM modules), .NET's COM Interoperability (Interop) feature supports this need. For example, say that you have older COM objects that were written before .NET existed. If you need it to, your new .NET application can use COM Interop to directly integrate with the older, non-.NET module. Conversely, you can take new .NET (managed) objects and use them in your older COM (unmanaged) environment. Remember COM Interop just in case you inherit any legacy applications while you are becoming a .NET expert.

In your previous mainframe experience, you may have worked with applications written in COBOL that used subprograms written in assembler. You may have had Dyl280 programs that depended on subprograms written in COBOL or assembler. In other words, you are already familiar with the concept of language interoperability. What will be new for you here is how easy interoperability is with .NET. For example, with virtually no extra effort, you can interactively debug an application, stepping line by line, with execution transferring from a module written in one language to a module written in a different language. Now, that is a great feature.

Having multiple languages to choose among is great. It's also great that .NET fully supports multiple language integration and coexistence. While I'm on that topic, isn't it great that .NET fully supports each and every technological feature discussed so far? You've got to admit, there *is* a lot to .NET. So "What *is* .NET?"

Discussion from each of the previous sections has contributed to answering *that* question. Continuing on to the following section, you will take a slight turn away from this development/programming–centric focus. Although you will still ask the same question ("What is .NET?"), you will cast your view slightly outward toward the industry and the enterprise. You will find that these additional sides of .NET are in fact relevant and of importance to you.

 CROSS-REFERENCE   You can find a good example of language interoperability in Chapter 19.

Marketing and Planning for .NET

How are you doing so far? By now, I believe you are getting the point that .NET is quite huge. Remember, *you are eating this elephant one bite at a time* and you have just a few more bites.

In this section, I cover .NET in the following contexts:

- Multiple editions of VS .NET

- Group of Enterprise Servers

- Career choice

.NET Is Multiple Editions of VS .NET

That's right. Multiple editions of VS .NET are available. The good news is that regardless of the edition you happen to get, you will still have the core portions of .NET (VS .NET, the .NET Framework, and the CLR). What will differ are the tools, plug-ins, and features to which you avail yourself. The following list shows the available VS .NET editions (in the order of smallest feature set to largest):

- Professional

- Academic

- Enterprise Developer

- Enterprise Architect

For your initial training purposes, any edition should suffice—even the one with the fewest features. Obviously, as a developer, I could care less how Microsoft's marketing department decided to package the product. My concern is just to know what products are available and to clearly communicate that to you. Then, you can approach the subject with a bit of clarity.

If you happen to come across the following .NET software versions:

- VS .NET Beta 1

- VS .NET Beta 2

- VS .NET Release Candidate

- .NET Framework SDK

I recommend that you avoid installing them—at least they should not be your first choice. At best, use them for training purposes only. When it comes to deploying production code, you will want to have the retail version 1.0—any of the editions mentioned previously. Each of the prerelease versions in the preceding list had its time (the key word being "had"). Now that version 1.0 is out, make every effort to get it. In the worst-case scenario, visit Microsoft's Web site and download the free 60-day trial version.

CROSS-REFERENCE   Currently, a 60-day trial version (Visual Studio .NET Professional Edition) is available at `http://msdn.microsoft.com/ vstudio/productinfo/trial.asp`.

Additionally, as version 1.0 of the .NET product moves through its maturity phases (as with any product), service packs are certain to be made available. Periodically visit Microsoft's Windows Update Web site (`http://windowsupdatemicrosoft.com/`) for any available product updates (at a minimum, make it a habit to apply the updates that are marked as critical).

The .NET Compact Framework

As I discussed earlier in this chapter in the section ".NET Is Windows Development," you may choose to develop applications that target devices other than personal computers (i.e., mobile phones, PDAs, and so forth). For these devices, Microsoft has provided an edition of the .NET Framework called the .NET Compact Framework. The Compact Framework is a subset of the larger, fuller framework that you will use for Web and Windows development.

If you are interested in developing for portable devices, install the .NET Compact Framework (alongside the full .NET Framework) together with the edition of the VS .NET product you happen to have. Then, using the same VS .NET product, you have the option of developing applications for the Web, desktop, and/or portable devices.

Microsoft uses the term "smart devices" to generically refer to all types of devices other than traditional computers. Hence, the .NET Compact Framework software product is accompanied by the Smart Device Extensions for Visual Studio .NET software product.

.NET Is a Group of Enterprise Servers

As I mentioned earlier in this chapter in the section ".NET is Multiple Editions of VS .NET," I generally care less (as a developer) about the apparent decisions of Microsoft's marketing department. I am not here to cast judgment on them and the decisions probably influenced by them. In other words, if they want to slap the .NET label onto all of their software products, more power to them. So, rather than spending too much time on Microsoft's reasoning, just accept it as fact: Microsoft decided to name a collection of their software packages ".NET software."

What does all of this have to do with defining .NET? Well, to return to the original purpose here of defining .NET, consider the following list of Microsoft .NET Enterprise Servers:

- Microsoft Application Center 2000

- Microsoft BizTalk Server 2002

- Microsoft Commerce Server 2002

- Microsoft Content Management Server 2001

- Microsoft Exchange Server 2000

- Microsoft Host Integration Server 2000

- Microsoft Internet Security and Acceleration Server 2000

- Microsoft Operations Manager 2000

- Microsoft Mobile Information Server 2002

- Microsoft SharePoint Portal Server 2001

- Microsoft SQL Server 2000

- Windows 2000 Server

What *is* .NET? Well, to some, the answer would include some or all of these so-called .NET Enterprise Servers. For that reason, it is important for developers to know what the .NET distinction means (or will mean) when used in reference to one of Microsoft's software products.

In my opinion, the general marketing direction seems to support the following: In the short term, some of the server software packages will carry the .NET distinction for marketing purposes only. In the long term, each of the server software packages (eventually) will have native XML support, will run on top of the .NET CLR, will have its object model exposed via the .NET Framework, will be Web-enabled and Web service–enabled, and will then truly be a .NET server.

CROSS-REFERENCE   The Flash animation file at the following URL demonstrates the interoperation that is possible among the .NET Enterprise Servers: http://www.microsoft.com/servers/evaluation/interop.asp.

Extended Learning Objective

You will want to familiarize yourself with (at least a few to start, and eventually the majority of) the .NET Enterprise Servers. In order for you to reach (or retain) the level of a senior developer, consider it an expectation. Start by learning each server by name. Later, build a working knowledge of each server (particularly the ones in use at your place of employment).

Do you think this is going overboard? Let me remind you that on the mainframe, a senior developer was familiar with most (if not all) of the system-level software packages that were installed, especially the ones that affected production application development and processing. These software packages commonly came from software vendors such as IBM, Candle, and Computer Associates (among others). Software products such as CICS, DB2, OMEGAMON, and CA-7/11 all fall into this system-level software category.

.NET Is a Career Choice

Perhaps you are wondering, "If .NET *is* so many things, how will I be able to become a .NET developer? How will I be able to learn so many things *and* be so many things—all at once?" Well, my reader friend, with very few exceptions, most of the sections that you have read *can* represent areas broad enough for a specialization.

The idea of specialization is not foreign to the mainframe development community. I recall working with a gentleman (years ago) who was respected for his in-depth programming ability. Yet, he always programmed using Dyl280. That I knew of, he did not touch COBOL or assembler—only Dyl280. I repeat, he was respected and carried quite a bit of responsibility with his Dyl280 specialty. Granted, he probably *knew* of other technologies, but he was a master of the Dyl280 product.

So, in the mainframe environment, you had some who were known as great offline batch programmers or great CICS programmers. I am sure that you have worked with developers that spent their entire day creating powerful REXX and ISPF applications. You may have specialized in something yourself. Yes, occasionally you came across that exceptional person, the one who was a "Master of All Technology." Or, more often, you came across someone who just *thought* he or she was a "Master of All Technology."

Is there anything wrong with trying to eat the entire elephant? No, be my guest. Just do it *one bite at a time.* Perhaps you can start by specializing, and then either move on to other parts of the .NET landscape as time allows or find a good fit and stay put. What makes a good fit? Well, everyone is motivated by different things. Some will look at what skill sets demand the highest salary. Others will look at other factors for motivation. To each his own.

For our immediate concern, .NET is a career choice (after all, that is the bottom line). Microsoft has a great career roadmap on their MSDN site that I strongly recommend you examine. Whether you take the "learn everything" approach or the "specialization" approach, this roadmap will help you on your chosen path: `http://www.microsoft.com/traincert/training/roadmap/chart_tabloid.pdf`.

.NET Is a New Microsoft Certification

Twenty years ago, I worked with a team of mainframe CICS experts that happened to consist of independent contractors. On one occasion, I received a business card from one of the contractors and noticed his professional certification noted as "CDP" and "CCP." I remember asking the expert about his certification (CDP stands for *Certified Data Processor* and CCP stands for *Certified Computer Programmer*).

His reply was as follows:

> *"Chris, this certification means nothing if you cannot do the job. First, learn to do your job. Later, if you want a good challenge to keep you skills sharp, go for the certification. Otherwise, the certification would help you if you needed to market yourself for a promotion or in the case of being a contractor—for your next work assignment."*

Therefore, I spent the next 20 years learning how to do my job.

In keeping with the "What is .NET?" theme, .NET is a new distinction for Microsoft certification along with a new set of qualifying examinations. For application developers, there is the new Microsoft Certified Application Developer (MCAD) credential. For solution developers, there is the updated Microsoft Certified Solution Developer (MCSD) credential. Microsoft offers other types of certifications as well, including the one that I have obtained (so far): the Microsoft Certified Professional (MCP) credential.

Summary

This chapter's goals were as follows:

- To cover the essentials of .NET programming

- To explore the various ways of accessing data using .NET

- To review the use of .NET to interface with the user

- To introduce advanced .NET technologies

- To understand the roles of marketing and planning for .NET

So, what *is* .NET? Throughout this chapter, I have provided several answers to this question. I am certain that now you can appreciate the various ways that this question can be answered. Try it. Ask several people *the* question. Depending on whom you ask, you will get different answers. The great thing is that each answer is likely to be correct. .NET really is a lot of things, including this one thing: Practically the future of Microsoft Windows and Web (also portable/mobile) targeted development depends on it.

The Microsoft executives have gone on record as stating that Microsoft's .NET commitment amounts to a "betting of the farm" for Microsoft. In other words, .NET is not *just* the next big thing, it *is* the next big thing (especially for Microsoft, and thus for a developer community several hundred thousand strong).

In the next chapter, you will look at your retraining effort from a slightly different angle. You will explore (and remove) some of the common training obstacles that recently reformed mainframe programmers are likely to come across. My intention is to make sure that you have the proper foundation before you remove the brakes and dive even deeper into .NET.

To Learn More

The following are some suggested supplemental references to further your retraining effort.

Magazines

.NET Magazine:
    http://www.fawcette.com/dotnetmag/
Visual Studio Magazine:
    http://www.fawcette.com/vsm/
XML & Web Services Magazine:
    http://www.fawcette.com/xmlmag/

Web Sites

The .NET Compact Framework—Overview:
    http://msdn.microsoft.com/vstudio/device/compactfx.asp
.NET Enterprise Servers Overview:
    http://www.microsoft.com/servers/evaluation/overview/
.NET Training Roadmap:
    http://www.microsoft.com/traincert/training/roadmap/chart_tabloid.pdf
Microsoft .NET Basics: What Is .NET?:
    http://www.microsoft.com/net/defined/
Microsoft .NET Language Partners:
    http://msdn.microsoft.com/vstudio/partners/language/default.asp
Microsoft Certifications:
    http://www.microsoft.com/traincert/mcp/default.asp
Microsoft Developer Network (MSDN):
    http://msdn.microsoft.com/
Microsoft Windows Updates:
    http://windowsupdate.microsoft.com/
Visual Studio .NET Professional 60-Day Trial Edition:
    http://msdn.microsoft.com/vstudio/productinfo/trial.asp

CHAPTER 3

.NET Retraining Prerequisites, Part 1

Tools You Will Need for Web and Windows Programming

In this chapter

- Revisiting our mainframe past to establish the perspective of a (re)training effort

- Discussing tools and technologies of the Windows platform as prerequisites for .NET retraining

NOW YOU KNOW WHAT .NET is, at least from a high level. Additionally, you understand that a successful .NET retraining effort will include learning a new language syntax and learning much more about object orientation, language interoperability, Web enablement, and XML and Web services support. As you might have guessed, there is a lot more to learn. However, before I get into the details of the new Microsoft .NET platform and the .NET development tools offering, I should discuss a few topics to provide you with a better learning foundation.

Be patient. I can understand your eagerness to jump in and start developing new Windows, Web, and XML Web services applications—there's plenty of time for that later. My concern is that you have the proper foundation from which to attack the remaining chapters in this book efficiently. I'm certain that time spent here will increase your chances for a more productive and less frustrating learning experience.

Generally, this chapter focuses on two common areas where mainframe programmers—rather, *reformed* mainframe programmers—run into difficulty. The first is losing the perspective of a full training effort, and the second is not being prepared with prerequisites.

Now, let's continue to build your learning foundation.

Presenting a Historical View to Understand Our Future

In our former technology world, the mainframe, we were kings and queens. Yet, we often stumble with confused looks on our faces when making this journey to "the other side," to PCs and Windows programming. Based on our expectations, this should be a simple transition, right? We only set out to change programming languages and use a smaller, more personal piece of hardware. Yet, it seems that our new peers in the "PC world" are not only programming in a different language, but also talking and thinking in a different language. Actually, I hope that you are reading this book before subjecting yourself to what might sound like a nightmarish learning curve (the remainder of this chapter aims to flatten that learning curve out).

Consider this phenomenon: There has long been a push to reinstate the teaching of COBOL[1] in the college curriculum. Isn't it interesting that you hardly hear mention of the teaching of other technologies that a typical COBOL programmer equally depends on? I will illustrate the importance of these other technologies by recounting the details of a real-life story that occurred years ago at one of my former mainframe corporate homes.

NOTE   Bear with me while I go into significant depth. I am certain that you will later appreciate the relationship between this historical look backward and your .NET future. Remember, understanding (and remembering) our history helps us understand and plan for our future.

Years ago at company XYZ,[2] we hired a college graduate who had taken several COBOL computer-programming courses. For simplicity, I will refer to him as "Bob." Bob's job description called for a junior-level computer programmer. This looked like a good fit after a few adjustments. Our adjustments had more to do with our approach to training than anything else. Naturally, there was no need to "train" our new graduate how to code a program in the COBOL language.

---

1.   If that ever were to happen, I cannot help but wonder which "flavor" of COBOL they would teach. Would their approved textbook include any of the COBOL vendor-specific extensions?

2.   The company's name is not relevant. Nevertheless, in my 20-plus years of information technology experience, I have called the following corporations home at one time or another: HRT IND (aka Hartfield/Zodys); Tenet (aka National Medical Enterprises); Merisel (aka Softsel); Home Savings; The County of San Bernardino; FiServe (aka DataLine); Princess Cruises; Arco Products; Flying Tigers; Wyle Electronics; Pacific Life; Northrop; Experian (aka TRW); and Cendant (aka Coldwell Banker).

Bob took great pride in being able to quickly recite the COBOL syntax rules and COBOL statements in alphabetical order. We (the mainframe veterans) were impressed. Yeah, right! We constantly made joking comments about how this "newbie," "our rookie," was still wet behind the ears. Looking back, perhaps it was cruel. Admittedly, this new employee of ours would have put us to shame if we had to divulge our SAT scores. Nevertheless, we saw it as naive that someone would take a couple of COBOL classes and expect to be able to actually program afterward. To prove our theory, we gave Bob the simple task of creating restart/rerun documentation for a given production job stream. After seeing our new junior programmer struggle for a while, I am proud to say that we eventually created a training program[3] based on the following eight phases:

1. Roles and responsibilities

2. Production support

3. Systems support

4. Editing/browsing/program development environment

5. Third-party development aids

6. File access methods and utility programs

7. Relational database programming

8. Online interactive transactional programming

Phase 1: Roles and Responsibilities

We first laid out an entire map to communicate the roles and responsibilities of the various people and positions that existed in the organization. This went beyond the normal idea of an organizational chart. The focus was more on the tools, technologies, and responsibilities that existed in the organization. This map made clear how each technology's usage related to, interacted with, and depended on the others. In other words, we felt it was important to present the "big picture"— the interrelationships that existed in our organization from a technical point of

---

3. Incidentally, our training program included the practice of having a mentor.

view. Not only did this enable Bob to operate efficiently, but it also helped give him an accurate perspective of and appreciation for his own role.

Phase 2: Production Support

The next training step really seemed to confuse Bob at first. We had him spend a few days in the shoes of the computer operator and then in those of the production control analyst. We felt that it would be important for him to meet and "live the life" of those who would be ultimately responsible for scheduling, executing, monitoring, and possibly helping troubleshoot his programs. This worked out great. By the time we rescued Bob, he understood the difference between the Multiple Virtual System (MVS) operating system and the Job Entry Subsystem (JES2). He even understood what system initiators were and how to use basic MVS and JES2 commands. Had we retrieved him later, the support staff would have introduced Bob to his first system initial program load (IPL). As Bob was saying good-bye to his new pals, he turned and jokingly said, "Watch out for those SB37 and S122 system completion codes." We exchanged a stare and smiled.

Phase 3: Systems Support

We wanted to strike while the iron was hot. Therefore, we rushed Bob over to chat with the systems programming staff. There, he met staff members who proudly explained their roles and responsibilities. Bob seemed impressed as he quickly noticed the difference between a "systems" programmer and an "application" programmer. I remember him taking notes, writing down terms such as "database administrator," "network support," "Customer Information Control System (CICS) support," "direct access storage device (DASD) management," and "security administrator."

At this point, we decided that Bob had wandered around the building enough. We asked the security administrator for Bob's user login and off we went to Bob's new desk.

Phase 4: Editing/Browsing/Program Development Environment

Our first area of actual technical training was in the efficient use of the Time Sharing Option (TSO) and the Interactive System Programming Facility (ISPF). I admit, we assumed that any student who had learned COBOL in a formal class setting already would have been introduced to these tools. Much to our surprise, that was not the case. The college that Bob had attended opted to use a lesser-known editing/browsing tool. Bob seemed convinced that this was "transferable" knowledge. As it turned out, it was to be a significant training effort. For example, we started by explaining how he would want to use each of the ISPF options.

The next thing we knew, we had several subtopics that would each need an individual focus for explanation. Among the subtopics were source code management, SuperC Compare Utility, dataset file allocation, and TSO commands. We went through all of these with Bob. Just when we thought we were done, Bob stumbled across another ISPF option that we had not explained. It, too, brought to the surface a couple more subtopics: System Display and Search Facility (SDSF) and Job Control Language (JCL).

As Bob sat there looking dazed, I vaguely recall him mumbling something that sounded like "They lied. They had promised us that the college's editing tool was going to be transferable knowledge." This was the first time I had actually witnessed the deflation of an ego in real time. It was not a pretty sight. In fact, we were afraid that Bob might decide to not return to work the next day. We gave Bob a few days to absorb all of his new knowledge. Then we continued.

Phase 5: Third-Party Development Aids

We then decided to introduce Bob to the remaining set of tools accessed from ISPF. As you know, this would include tools such as the software packages that handled Job scheduling, tape management, Abend recovery, dump reading, and Abend-AID. Additionally, we introduced Bob to the DASD maintenance, interactive, and report archival and retrieval tools that are also accessed from ISPF.

Phase 6: File Access Methods and Utility Programs

It turns out that Bob's COBOL training had included introductions to the Virtual Storage Access Method (VSAM), partitioned datasets (PDS), and the Queued Sequential Access Method (QSAM). The problem was that he had received only *brief* introductions. Bob understood what a VSAM file was. However, he had no idea about VSAM-related topics such as alternate indexes and the IDCAMS utility program. We quickly discovered that other essential utility programs such as IEB-GENER, DFSORT, Dyl280, and even IEFBR14 were all foreign to Bob the graduate. Poor Bob.

Weeks passed, and as you might have guessed, Bob survived. He reviewed, he studied, and he became a well-rounded COBOL batch programmer.

Phase 7: Relational Database Programming

About 9 months into Bob's employment, we provided opportunities for him to learn more advanced levels of programming. We introduced him to database programming using Database 2 (DB2). He studied Structured Query Language (SQL) syntax on weekends. We grilled him daily at work on the various forms of normalization and other relational database concerns. Bob quickly became acquainted with going to the various ISPF options to access the database utility software packages. He said that his favorite was DB2 Interactive (DB2I) and SQL Processor Using File Input (SPUFI). Later, he expressed a strong preference for Query Management Facility (QMF). He bragged about how fast he was able to accomplish some of his ad hoc reporting tasks using his library of saved queries.

Phase 8: Online Interactive Transactional Programming

The day came when Bob celebrated his 1-year anniversary. We were all very proud of him and his accomplishments. As we celebrated with him, we emphasized that he had graduated from his first year of training with honors. As an anniversary gift, we told him that his entire second year of training would be limited to just one new training topic. Bob seemed relieved as he jumped up and down for joy. Then it occurred to him. Slowly, he looked us in the eyes and asked, "Did you say the *entire* year? Will it take *that* long?" We replied, "Yes, Bob, welcome to the programming world of CICS."

For the next 12 months, Bob was immersed in new concepts such as multitasking and multithreading. He studied to exhaustion the various CICS support tables: program control table (PCT), processing program table (PPT), terminal control table (TCT), and file control table (FCT). Later, we explained to Bob how he would need to build basic mapping support (BMS) mapsets to represent each of his screens. He then went on to conquer various CICS service transactions: command-level interpreter transaction (CECI), master terminal transaction (CEMT), and execution diagnostics facility (CEDF/CEDX). We emphasized to Bob the power of these transactions and how he would use them to test, troubleshoot, and control other CICS transactions. As you can imagine, he finished the remaining year perfecting the usage of CICS commands in his COBOL programs and learning how to properly use CICS's communication area, Execute Interface Block (EIB), and temporary storage queues.

That concludes our walk down memory lane. Bob, have a nice life.

Staying Onboard the Speeding Technology Train

Keeping up with technology is the main requirement for not having *the train leave without you*. However, you need to have a healthy perspective when doing so.

There is one critical point I would like to make here:

> If *all* you do is take one programming course (in any language), do not expect to hit the ground running. To write enterprise-ready programs, you have to jump in for the long haul.

Failure to thoroughly understand this point, I feel, is the root of many failed *reformation* attempts. Often, we veteran mainframe programmers venture into the "new" world—the nonmainframe world. We take one programming course (Visual Basic, for example). Upon completion of the course, we figure, "OK, I am ready to program." Then we, like Bob, are faced with a large dose of reality.

There is an entire infrastructure for any programming language on any platform. Naturally, learning the syntax of a particular programming language is important. However, you cannot stop there.

Take a Reality Check

To be a successful mainframe programmer, you are typically required to learn COBOL programming and many supportive technologies and tools. To illustrate this point in the previous section, I felt it was necessary to take a trip down memory lane in great detail. After being in the business for 10 to 20 years, it is likely that you have forgotten what it took to get where you are. After some time, you may take for granted just how many things you actually needed to learn to become proficient.

 NOTE The list of eight training phases in the previous section is by no means a "complete" training program for every company. Nevertheless, it is close enough for illustrative (and contrastive) purposes. Additionally, some organizations may prefer to alter the sequencing of the training phases.

Now, if you are really "getting" my point, the following thought may have occurred to you by now: In the mainframe world, it would have taken at least 20 textbooks and manuals to properly train my friend Bob across all eight training phases listed in the preceding section. Understanding this point, you can now appreciate the comprehensive approach taken in this one textbook that you have in your hands. In effect, this book will serve as your complete guide to continued learning as you transition from being a mainframe programmer to being (what I like to call) an enterprise developer.

To complete your learning objectives, you will want to drill down in further detail (truer for some topics than others). To aid you in the later phases of your training, I include many supplementary references (Internet links and text referrals) for your use in the "To Learn More" section at the end of each chapter. Please take advantage of these references. As you absorb the contents of this book, you should find yourself enabled to continue your training endeavor with more precision and confidence.

OK, you've been prepped, refreshed, warned, and perhaps even preached to. Still, you have continued forward with determination. Look, you're already well into the third chapter of this book. I suppose you've already decided that you're going to see this through. You're going to complete *this* journey. Good! Your next step, then, is to dive into the following section, which will introduce you to the first group (of two[4]) of .NET retraining prerequisites.

Building Blocks for Your .NET Training

I will start this section by showing you a brief snapshot of the technologies you will need to learn:

- Windows utilities (System Registry, Event Viewer, Task Scheduler, Windows Task Manager)

- Internet Explorer

- Microsoft Management Console (MMC)

- Open Database Connectivity (ODBC) configuration

- Microsoft Office (Outlook, Word, Excel, Access, and PowerPoint), Notepad, and Visio

- Microsoft Visual SourceSafe

---

4. You can find the second of the two groups of .NET retraining prerequisites in Chapter 4.

- Network protocols (TCP/IP, HTTP, FTP, and SMTP) and the URL

- T-SQL

- Active Directory

- Adobe Acrobat Portable Document Format (PDF)

- Internet Information Services (IIS)

- Enterprise Services (COM+) and Microsoft Message Queuing (MSMQ)

- Microsoft Developer Network (MSDN)

I need to let you in on a little secret. The preceding topics are actually just the *prerequisites*. In other words, you must have an understanding of these topics before you dive into .NET. As is the case with becoming a mainframe programmer, there is more to learning .NET than just learning a programming language. There is the .NET infrastructure and the supportive technologies. They are the tools and technologies surrounding .NET and the Windows platform.

CROSS-REFERENCE   In Chapter 4, I discuss four additional prerequisite topics: object orientation, Extensible Markup Language (XML), Hypertext Markup Language (HTML), and client-side scripting languages.

Allow me to remind you of my friend Bob (the COBOL graduate), whom you met earlier in this chapter in the section "Presenting a Historical View to Understand Our Future." Would not you have considered it "important" for Bob to be "familiar" with technologies/concepts such as JES2, IPL, and MVS? Would not you have considered it "critical" for someone in Bob's situation to have a working knowledge of TSO, JCL, and VSAM?

Now perhaps you are getting the point. Or maybe you're asking, "Why include network-related topics such as TCP/IP and HTTP in the .NET list for a programmer—an application programmer, no less?" I ask you, have you ever met a "real" mainframe programmer who wasn't at least "familiar" with network-related topics such as Virtual Telecommunication Access Method (VTAM), System Network Architecture (SNA), and System Application Architecture (SAA)? I could go on with analogy after analogy (in fact, as the chapters progress, I do).

Finally, do you question the applicability of the Active Directory topic being included on a .NET programming training list? You guessed it, there is a mainframe equivalent. You and the rest of the veteran mainframe programmer group are certainly familiar with one of the following security packages: IBM's Resource Access Control Facility (RACF) or Computer Associates' Access Control Facility (ACF2, now known as CA-ACF2).

Assumed Working Knowledge and Familiarity

As programmers, we have learned to never assume anything. However, we often forget this rule when it comes to our expectations of others' knowledge. I have argued the following point once or twice: How can you quickly criticize someone for not having "common sense"? Just because something is *common* to you does not mean that it makes *sense*, or even *good* sense. What is common to one person simply may not be common to another.[5] I think a wise person is someone who is aware of what *should* be common based on another person's background and experience.

To illustrate this point, consider the following abstract dialogue between three fictitious people: Victim John, Consoling Jane, and Confused Joe.[6]

Victim John: "Again, the coach accused me of being a hot dog. He just doesn't understand what being behind the eight ball is like. With him as the coach, I think we ended up with a lemon. Can you believe that he even asked me to put my John Hancock on the reprimand document? He's a real thorn in my side."

Consoling Jane: "So, that's why you are feeling blue. I think your coach is still wet behind the ears. In fact, when he said that he had ten years of experience, I think I saw his nose grow. So what. You were the coach before he was. That should be water under the bridge at this point. He really is over the hill, you know. By the way, I'm campaigning to have him kicked to the curb. It isn't final yet. Let's knock on wood for now."

Confused Joe: "Can the two of you please translate for me, in English? I have no idea, no clue, what the two of you are saying. I don't know where the bridge and hill are that you're speaking about. Who is John Hancock? I'm not sure what playing pool has to do with kicking the curb and hitting someone with wood. I don't see either of you turning blue. However, I would like to see your coach's nose grow. On top of that, all this talk about hot dogs and lemons is making me hungry."

---

5. Some scholars may wish to further debate this by making distinctions among acquired knowledge, wisdom, and common sense.

6. Yes, I am guilty of trying to create an interesting presentation of technical material. Since you have made it all the way to Chapter 3, it looks like I am doing OK so far.

Now, I ask, does it take common sense for Joe to understand what John and Jane are talking about? I think not. It takes prior experience with or exposure to *their* terminology. Then the terminology becomes "common" to Joe. In some cases, it may come down to cultural differences existing. I used this abstract example to introduce you to the next topic. As a reformed mainframe programmer, you are "switching" cultures now. You are the new kid on the block. All of your new peers will be speaking in a new language (and programming in a new language as well).

The following sections focus on these new technologies and concepts, which were presented in the earlier list. They may not be "common" to you at this time, but you should become familiar with them all the same.

Before you get into your .NET-specific training (the majority of this book), you will want this little bit of Windows platform "common sense." I know that some of you are more Windows programming–literate than some of your fellow former mainframe programmers. You may want to just use this section as a refresher. Otherwise, be patient. Understand that for some, using a PC has been akin to using another "dumb" terminal, a cathode ray tube (CRT). Turn the power on. Navigate to the 3270-emulation icon. Click. We have all been there at one time or another.

System Registry

To begin with, there is a very important database structure called the *System Registry*. The registry is a place where sensitive hardware, user, and software information can be stored and retrieved (manually or programmatically). The mainframe has several examples of this type of functionality. It is just that mainframe programmers traditionally used different names to describe those functionalities. In mainframe CICS terms, think of the roles that the PCT, TCT, and FCT played when providing a "registry" of sorts for CICS transactions.

When you ran batch COBOL programs, you typically needed a STEPLIB or JOBLIB JCL statement to "tell" JES2 where your compiled program was located. This type of "program location" feature is just one of the registry's main purposes in life. At least it used to be. After years of this program-location feature being in the middle of controversial application bugs (known as *DLL Hell*), .NET offers a less problematic approach.

 CROSS-REFERENCE Chapter 17 discusses the new .NET way of "locating" programs.

Here's one more mainframe analogy for registry types of functions: the System Master Catalog. Remember, after you cataloged a dataset, the system "knew" the location of your dataset. You no longer needed to specify volume-label information. The Windows System Registry is an old concept with a new name.

Going Forward, Registry Usage Will Amount to Two Typical Scenarios

In the first typical scenario, legacy dynamic link library (DLL) COM objects continue to exist.[7] These COM objects will typically be "registered." This registration enables their discovery when you are developing other portions of your application that will want to reference these COM objects. You will revisit this idea of "referencing" objects later. By the way, this reminds me of the continued existence of COBOL 74 programs long after COBOL 85 became the new standard.

In the second typical scenario for future registry interaction, some developers will design applications that (during runtime) will access the "registry" for configuration information. This might remind you of the way that mainframe programmers typically use CONTROL libraries—static PDS members with configuration information. The good news is that .NET design approaches are moving away from developers needing to design registry-dependent applications this way. There is a new .NET file called the .config file. Developers will gradually move toward taking more advantage of this new feature. Naturally, a later chapter (Chapter 18) discusses this .config file along with the other types of new .NET files.

To browse and edit the System Registry, you use the Regedit system program, as shown in Figure 3-1. This program is located in your Windows directory. You can run Regedit by clicking the Start button, selecting Run, and then typing **regedit** into the Run dialog box. Alternatively, you can double-click regedit.exe in the Windows directory in Windows Explorer. Figure 3-2 shows the resulting Registry Editor window.

---

7. That's right, the Windows and Web programming worlds have legacy applications. Remember, .NET is a revolutionary change for the Windows programming platform.

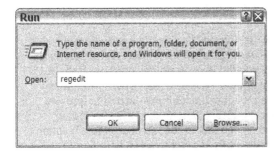

Figure 3-1. Typing regedit into the Run window

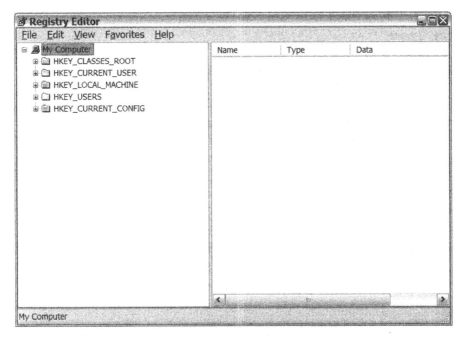

Figure 3-2. The Registry Editor window ready for viewing and careful editing

CAUTION   When you access the System Registry, use extreme caution. You could cause irreparable damage to your computer by inadvertently changing a registry entry. Using the Regedit utility could result in the need to reinstall your entire operating system. Make sure your emergency recovery disk and system/data backups are current before you mess around with your registry. Please refer to the "A Crash Course: Editing the Windows Registry" Web link in the "To Learn More" section ("Web Sites" subsection) later in this chapter to assist your continued learning on this sensitive topic.

Event Viewer

On the mainframe, if you had a question about the failure/Abend of a JES2 Job, a CICS online region, system software, or even an IPL, where would you have looked for logged error messages? One common repository storing this type of system-wide logging was the system log, which you could view through SDSF (you typically accessed SDSF via an ISPF option). As you know, there were exceptions to the practice of relying on the system log for error messages. Forward-thinking application developers knew to include error-trapping logic in their programs that would write to an application-level output file, sometimes resorting to COBOL DISPLAY statements.

Going forward, you will use the Windows Event Viewer when troubleshooting applications on the Windows platform. .NET introduces a few new types of helpful trace features that complement the functionality of the Windows Event Viewer.

 CROSS-REFERENCE   You will learn more about the new .NET debugging features in Chapter 18.

You access Event Viewer by clicking the Start button and choosing Programs ➤ Administrative Tools ➤ Event Viewer. As on the mainframe, multiple levels of messages (i.e., Application, System, and Security) are available. The Event Viewer tool (see Figure 3-3) makes it easy to view any of these message levels. Incidentally, you will be using a different language syntax (instead of the COBOL DISPLAY statement) to programmatically write application-level messages to the Event Viewer repository.

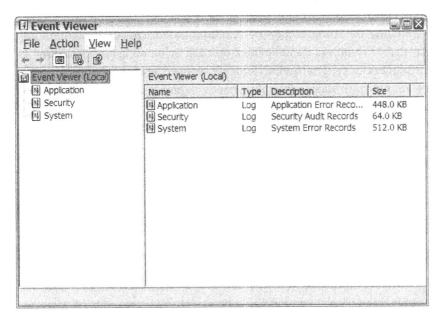

Figure 3-3. The Event Viewer window showing the three types of log choices

NOTE The instructions assume you are using Windows 2000 Server or Windows XP Professional. If you are using Windows 2000 Professional, for example, your menu selections may be different. For instance, instead of choosing Programs ➤ Administrative Tools ➤ Event Viewer, you may need to choose Settings ➤ Control Panel ➤ Administrative Tools ➤ Event Viewer.

Task Scheduler

Say that you have written a mainframe COBOL batch program. You need this batch COBOL program to execute on a periodic schedule. What do you do? You request to have your program (and its corresponding JCL Job) loaded into your available scheduling package. One common mainframe scheduling product is Computer Associates' CA-7. Allow me to emphasize that this is an extreme comparison: CA-7 to the Windows Task Scheduler. CA-7 is a full-featured software package sold by Computer Associates (a third-party software vendor). The Windows Task Scheduler feature is a Windows-bundled "freebie"—a basic Windows utility.

Although the features common to CA-7 (i.e., enhanced distributed-client terminal, forecasting, reporting, and event- and time-based scheduling features) are missing from the Windows Task Scheduler, for basic scheduling purposes (executing a program at a predetermined time or interval), the Task Scheduler is sufficient. For more advanced scheduling needs, a third-party software package would be appropriate.

You access the Scheduled Tasks menu option by clicking the Start button and choosing Programs ➤ Accessories ➤System Tools ➤ Scheduled Tasks (see Figure 3-4).

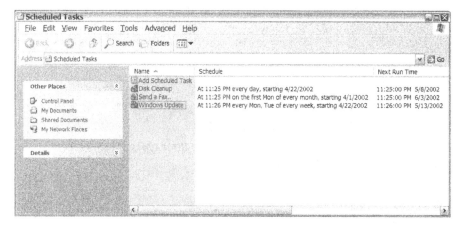

Figure 3-4. The Scheduled Tasks window showing several example tasks scheduled

Windows Task Manager

Sticking with the mainframe analogy approach, let's compare Windows Task Manager to a mainframe product that you know and love: SDSF. This is the second opportunity I have to use SDSF as a mainframe analogy. The first was earlier in this chapter under the section "Event Viewer." During your own mainframe development experience, you have likely used SDSF to view the status of application batch Jobs, CICS regions, and TSO user sessions.

For the sake of having something to compare SDSF with, Windows Task Manager is the closest thing you will commonly find in Windows to fill similar needs. Remember, there are third-party products out there. Windows Task Manager, on the other hand, is another Windows-bundled freebie, and a good one at that. Veteran Windows platform developers will swear by this Windows utility (and so should you). With it, you can view the status of any long-running application program,[8] any Windows processes (also referred to as *services*), and the

---

8. This applies to out-of-process programs only. This issue is further explained later in this chapter in the section "Enterprise Services (COM+)."

status of "local domain" users. Additionally, Windows Task Manager provides a fully customizable Performance view (memory, CPU, and so forth) for your local workstation (or server).

For those of you who had a glimpse of the operations side of the mainframe world, this performance-viewing feature may remind you of a legacy mainframe product by the name of OMEGAMON (courtesy of a company named Candle). Granted, the Windows Task Manager Performance tab appears to offer just barely 1 percent of what a full-featured product such as OMEGAMON offers. This is to be expected when you compare a Windows-bundled freebie utility to a product that certainly is not free. Taking nothing from either product, both (on their respective platforms) are respected tools for good reason.

You access the Windows Task Manager utility by simultaneously pressing the Ctrl, Alt, and Delete keyboard keys (see Figure 3-5).

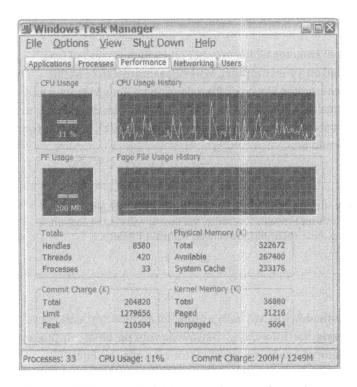

Figure 3-5. Windows Task Manager showing the Performance tab selected

Internet Explorer

Some of you might respond, "OK, Chris, this one topic *does* happen to be 'common' sense. We all know that Internet Explorer is the name of Microsoft's browser product. Additionally, we all know that a browser is software we use to view Web pages."

Right? Great. Therefore, I will not waste any time covering those two points. However, a few other points deserve mentioning. The first one is the most trivial: Do not confuse Internet Explorer with Windows Explorer (also known as NT Explorer if you happen to be using Windows NT). Windows Explorer is the Windows utility (click the Start button and choose Programs ➤ Accessories ➤ Windows Explorer) that provides a tree view of your local and network environment. Now that I have that one out of the way, let's move on to the remaining points.

CROSS-REFERENCE　In Chapter 4 in the section "Client-Side Scripting Languages," I discuss the topic of browsers from a different angle. The version and brand of browser that your intended customers use will influence your client-side scripting approach.

Please make a point of *knowing* which browser and which version of that browser you have installed on your computer. Why does this matter? For the average person, it does not matter. However, for a developer—for a Windows and Web developer—it is critical. For bleeding-edge Microsoft .NET development, you will want to go for the most current version of Internet Explorer (IE), which at the time of this writing is version 6.

NOTE　During your installation of Visual Studio .NET (VS .NET), the Internet Explorer browser (currently version 6) will also be installed. The underlying .NET technologies rely on Internet Explorer being installed.

It is inevitable that someday you will have a question about a particular error that you are troubleshooting. You may end up narrowing your problem symptoms down to a particular version of a software product (for example, the latest version of the Microsoft XML parser), and it will all boil down to knowing what IE version you have. That is right, occasionally other "dependent" software is installed when you install a browser (this is true with many browsers, not just Microsoft IE). If you take the time to read the README.TXT file that accompanies most major browser installations, you will discover these dependent software bundles in advance. There are, of course, other scenarios. For example, you may need a security patch to shield your computer from the latest viruses. The security bulletin may mention that the patch is only needed for certain versions of certain browsers. Again, you will want to know.

NOTE To the average legacy mainframe programmer, these sorts of things have traditionally been somebody else's responsibility—somebody else's problem. Remember, this was the advantage of the centralized computing model: one "big" computer, many "thin" clients. Rarely did yesterday's mainframe programmer have to deal with software installation (certainly not basic software) development tools. Welcome to the distributed computing model.

The final point. Microsoft is not the only company that makes browsers for the Windows platform. There are other browsers out there: Netscape, Opera, and so on. It is easy to find people who have a strong preference for one browser over another.

CROSS-REFERENCE The list of available browsers is constantly growing: http://ipw.internet.com/clients_servers/web_browsers/.

Personally, I have only one browser installed: Microsoft IE. Why only one? Simplicity. As you embrace your new responsibilities as the custodian of your own computer, you will grow to appreciate installing fewer things on your computer rather than installing everything that comes your way.

Carelessly installing every third-party utility (or worse, games and screen savers) on your computer will eventually bite you. I really didn't understand this until I had a memorable chat with a friend. I asked him, "Why on earth are you buying a second computer for home use? Isn't one enough?" He then explained that he was a "serious Windows and Web developer." He noticed that I still didn't get it. He then asked me the following question: "Chris, in the mainframe world, was the production environment treated as something sacred?" Of course, my answer was an emphatic yes. Then it hit me. For me, my own developer box is my own production environment[9]—my sacred environment to protect from "software pollution." So, unless you have the luxury of owning more than one computer . . . well, you get the point.

---

9. Additionally, remember that in the mainframe world, we *always* backed up production data—*always*. Yes, your development box is not "production" per se, but remember, you are ultimately responsible for your computer, your box, and the program source code developed on it. This emphasis applies more to a stand-alone computer—at home, for example. At work, this risk can be mitigated slightly. I explain this in more depth later in this chapter in the section "Microsoft Visual SourceSafe."

A Word of Caution About Installations

Just because somebody creates a software program and says "Install this" does not mean that it is the right thing to do. And just because that program is downloadable over the Internet or is delivered through e-mail does not mean that installing it is in your best interest. Something that looks harmless can cause irreparable damage to your system. Worse yet, even if everything "seems" OK on your computer, other third-party software (especially freeware) could be the one thing that is causing that weird program bug—the one that has kept you up late at night trying to figure out.

The fewer programs that you install, the fewer programs you will have on your process-of-elimination list. I do not want to sound paranoid, but be cautious of what you install—even other browsers. As you learn more about the Windows System Registry and COM DLLs, you will grow to appreciate this warning. Though this issue stretches beyond the discussion of browsers, it seemed like a good time to mention this concern.

By the way, there is a caveat to all of this. When you develop Web applications, multibrowser testing is important. If you are developing an intranet application and everyone is using IE, no problem. However, if the application is going to be accessed from the outside (i.e., it is a regular Internet application), you will not have any control over what browser is used. You can make recommendations, but you cannot control this. Therefore, depending on your target user, you may want to include a multibrowser testing scenario among your other test scripts.

CROSS-REFERENCE   When you develop ASP.NET applications, you have the opportunity to manually override the level (or type) of browser support through code and configuration settings. I further discuss this topic in Chapter 18.

Microsoft Management Console

I have referred to the mainframe tool ISPF throughout this chapter. This is appropriate given its usefulness. Think about it for a moment. Where would you typically go (on the IBM mainframe environment) to access standard tools, utilities, and third-party vendor utilities? Of course, you would use ISPF. Well, that is a good way to think of Microsoft Management Console (MMC).

By itself, MMC is just an empty container. However, you can add software utilities (snap-ins) to turn MMC into a common place to refer to when you need to access various software utilities. Tools used to administer advanced services such COM+ and IIS are typically (already) snapped into an MMC. It's common for multiple MMCs to exist on a system. MMCs have a Console mode that you can use to control a user's ability to modify specific MMCs. Additionally, Microsoft provides development kits to interested software developers to enable them to build custom snap-ins.

You access the MMC by clicking the Start button and choosing Programs ➤ Administrative Tools ➤ Computer Management. The listed Console.msc choice is an MMC that is provided for easy modification (see Figure 3-6). Alternatively, you can access MMC by right-clicking the My Computer icon on your desktop (on Windows XP, the My Computer icon is typically located on the Start menu) and then choosing Manage.

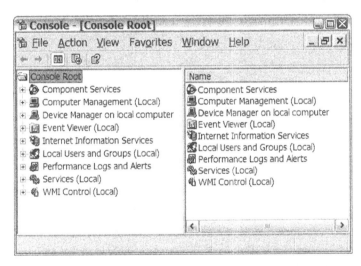

Figure 3-6. The Microsoft Management Console window showing default snap-ins

Open Database Connectivity Configuration

Although it is true that leaving the mainframe means saying good-bye to JCL, you will still need a way to "allocate" data sources. One way is using the Open Database Connectivity (ODBC) configuration tool. This tool allows you to create various types of data source names that you can then use in applications to access data. Specifically, ODBC is a standard protocol that facilitates the connectivity between applications and a variety of external database servers or files. The ODBC drivers (behind the scenes) permit access to SQL Server and several other relational database management systems (RDBMSs), and other data sources (including text files and Microsoft Excel spreadsheets).

You will soon discover (in Chapter 11 in the section titled "Accessing Data") that there are other, more preferable ways to create data source connectivity for your applications. Still, I wanted to introduce the ODBC tool, if for no other reason than you may run across legacy applications that use this approach.

You access the ODBC Data Source administrative tool by clicking the Start button and choosing Programs ➤ Administrative Tools ➤ Data Sources (ODBC). See Figure 3-7.

Figure 3-7. The ODBC Data Source Administrator window

Microsoft Office and Notepad

If you have not already done so, you will want to become proficient in the following Microsoft software packages:[10]

- Outlook (collaboration software)

- Word (word processing program)

---

10. Some of you will have to request that your employer install the "full" version of Microsoft Office (Professional version) on your computer. Visio is sold separately from all Microsoft Office versions. Notepad is a Windows freebie.

- Excel (spreadsheet program)

- Access (database program)

- PowerPoint (presentation software)

- Notepad (text editor)

- Visio (drawing design software[11])

You may choose to learn a competing vendor's product. If you have enough time to learn all of the competitors' products *and* Microsoft's tools, more power to you. However, if your time is limited, I would suggest starting with the Microsoft Office suite. Considering the market share that Microsoft has with these tools, you will be in good company.

The Importance of Learning the Microsoft Software Packages

Take the mainframe environment, for example. Try to imagine a mainframe programmer not knowing how to efficiently use TSO. Furthermore, think about some of the other common mainframe tools. How many times have you needed to do a quick-and-dirty extract or report program on the mainframe? Some of those times you reached for your trustworthy Dyl280 or Easytrieve software. What about those times that you got really creative with the SORT utility control cards to do OMITS and INCLUDES? How many times have you coded IEBGENERS and IDCAMS control cards while being pleased that you were avoiding the creation of actual programs? How many times has your advanced knowledge of the File-AID software tool practically saved your life? Are you beginning to get the idea of why learning some of the popular Windows tools is a good idea? The more tools that you have in your arsenal, the better off you will be.

For those who question the inclusion of PowerPoint and Visio in the context of "tell me what I need to know in order to learn .NET programming," allow me to remind you that being a senior programmer often creates opportunities beyond just banging out code. Your senior-level responsibilities will require you to design applications and to describe and document processes. In some cases, you will need to train junior staff members one day and give a presentation to senior

---

11. In the next chapter, when I discuss object orientation, I introduce a popular notation called the Unified Modeling Language (UML). One of the many features of the Visio software package is its capability to create UML drawings.

management the next day. Visio and PowerPoint are essential tools to have access to in each of these instances.

Are you still unconvinced? OK, did you ever create a flowchart in your mainframe days? Well, flowcharts *still* have value, even today. Visio is a great tool for creating charts (and performing many other design and drawing tasks). Have you ever given a presentation to a group of people using a whiteboard or an overhead projector? Now you get the point. Yes, you can use PowerPoint for a more effective presentation.

By the way, as an attractive bonus, the object model for each of these Microsoft software packages is exposed and accessible. This means that you can integrate all of the power and functionality from these existing tools into your own applications. When you learn more about "setting references" to existing objects, you'll be shocked at the things that you can programmatically do with the various Microsoft Office objects. In fact, many people have built entire careers and profitable businesses around exploiting these object models. There's just one catch: You have to learn how to use the object models efficiently first.

You access the Microsoft Office packages, Notepad, and Visio from your Programs list (click the Start button and choose Programs). Figure 3-8 shows Notepad.

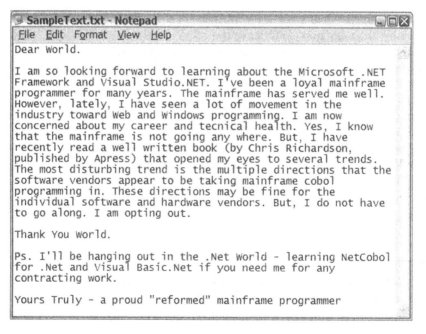

Figure 3-8. The Notepad editor showing some sample text

Microsoft Visual SourceSafe

What thoughts occur to you when you think of the mainframe software products ChangeMan or CA-Librarian? That's right, source code management. Fortunately, when you install either of the Enterprise versions of .NET, Microsoft Visual SourceSafe is included. Unless your organization has decided to go with a competing vendor's product, the Microsoft Visual SourceSafe software package will be your choice for source code management.

You access the Microsoft Visual SourceSafe software package from your Programs list (click the Start button and choose Programs).[12]

Network Protocols and the URL

In my days of mainframe programming, most of my peers passed through the ranks of computer operations. Time spent in computer operations provided in-depth exposure to system technologies and telecommunications protocols such as VTAM, SNA, and SAA. Interestingly, the Windows and Web programmers of today typically know nothing about the role of a computer operator.

At the same time, though, every Windows and Web programmer is (unknowingly) both a (personal) computer operator and a computer programmer. That is right, when I see the Windows and Web programmers of today "rebooting" their personal computers, I cannot help but recall the mission-critical mainframe IPL of yesteryear. You see, the responsibilities of Windows and Web programmers and their resulting knowledge extend beyond just programming to include intimate system and network knowledge. Hence, it is appropriate to present to you these "commonsense" network topics:

- Transmission Control Protocol/Internet Protocol (TCP/IP)

- Hypertext Transfer Protocol (HTTP)

- File Transfer Protocol (FTP)

- Simple Mail Transfer Protocol (SMTP)

- Uniform Resource Locator (URL)

---

12. The Visual SourceSafe product requires separate installation. You need to perform the installation before you can complete the suggested "access" steps mentioned in this section. The Visual SourceSafe product is bundled with the Enterprise Architect and Enterprise Developer VS .NET editions.

TCP/IP

TCP/IP is the basic network protocol for intranets, extranets, and the Internet. This low-level, stateless protocol takes care of the assimilation and routing of messages (packets) from one point to another point.

HTTP

Essentially sitting on top of TCP/IP are the higher-level protocols HTTP, FTP, and SMTP. HTTP is a set of rules facilitating the transfer of files (including text, graphics, and multimedia files) between a browser (client) and a Web server.

FTP

FTP is also a set of rules that facilitates the transfer of files. However, FTP is typically used for transferring program files and documents (not Web page requests).

SMTP

SMTP is also a set of rules that facilitates the transfer of files that happen to be e-mails.

URL

A URL is the address of a resource (a file) that can be accessed via TCP/IP. The type of resource (higher-level protocol) that the URL is referring to is actually indicated in the URL (prefix) itself. For example, in an address such as `http://msdn.microsoft.com`, "http" is shown to be the needed protocol to service this request. The remaining portion of the URL refers to the domain name, which translates to an actual Internet Protocol (IP) address (which in turn points to a specific computer). Optionally, you can include hierarchical folder structures to further categorize and access files on a specific Web server or FTP server.

T-SQL

My guess is that you have already learned SQL from your exposure to a mainframe-based RDBMS (e.g., DB2). If you have not been so fortunate, now is the time to do something about it. Perhaps you did not have DB2 available to you. This would be a good excuse to get your hands on Microsoft Access (better yet, install SQL Server 2000). That is right: You can practice and learn T-SQL on Microsoft Access. T-SQL is Microsoft's implementation of SQL (ANSI SQL) with Microsoft's extensions.

Adobe Acrobat Portable Document Format

On the mainframe, as you know, are various file formats (e.g., VSAM, QSAM, and PDS files). Each of these mainframe files has its own unique format and unique utility used to read and edit the contents. For example, to read VSAM files, you need a special version of File-AID or perhaps the IDCAMS utility.

Now, you may have wondered what types of files the Windows environment has. As it turns out, the Windows environment also has special formats for files and those files require certain software for reading (and editing). Externally, the Windows file format is indicated by the file extension. For instance, if the name of a file is README.TXT, the TXT extension indicates that the Notepad software can be used for reading and editing. If the file name is myspreadsheet.XLS, the XLS extension indicates that the Microsoft Excel software will be used. So, what if the file name is myreport.PDF? What does PDF mean?

Portable Document Format (PDF) is a file format that has become extremely popular. Business applications and special reporting software commonly use PDF as a format to create deliverable output reports. A user that receives a PDF file is required to have a software package called Adobe Acrobat Reader for reading the PDF file.

CROSS-REFERENCE   Adobe Acrobat Reader is available as a free download from the Adobe Web site (http://www.adobe.com/products/acrobat/readstep.html).

Once created, PDF files are read-only. This is useful when you want to preserve the printed appearance of an output report. You even have the option of creating secured PDF documents. A user ID and password are required to read secured PDF documents.

CROSS-REFERENCE   Learning to create reports in PDF format and other formats (DOC, XLS, TXT, and so on) will be one of your objectives as a Windows and Web programmer. Chapter 16 discusses the options that you have for creating PDF-formatted files and other types of reports with .NET (using the .NET Framework objects or Crystal Reports objects that are integrated into VS .NET).

Internet Information Services

I remember the first time someone tried to explain to me what Internet Information Services (IIS) was. This person, with the best of intentions, could not understand why I had a blank look on my face. Eventually, I asked him to define the term "server." Then, I realized where our communication gap was. As it turned out, the term "server" meant several things. Before our discussion, I thought a server was simply a piece of hardware—but this is not always the case.

It seems that you *can* have a piece of hardware that is a server. That piece of hardware can run a version of server software (e.g., the Windows 2000 Server operating system). You can have a system-level server software package such as IIS that sits on top of the actual Windows operating system (much like a CICS region sits on top of a mainframe operating system). Furthermore, IIS itself is really made up of other software servers (such as FTP server and HTTP server). The biggest job of IIS is to service HTTP and FTP requests. When IIS services HTTP requests, Active Server Pages (ASP, now ASP.NET) and static HTML files are processed. Are we all clear now? IIS is a Microsoft software package—a very powerful software package.

CROSS-REFERENCE   The Microsoft Windows features list shows IIS and other software as being included with Windows. Visit http:// www.microsoft.com/catalog/display.asp?site=656&subid=22&pg=2 for more information.

Using the MMC snap-in for IIS shown in Figure 3-9, you can set up, configure, and manage Web sites and virtual directories.

CROSS-REFERENCE   Chapter 17 discusses some of the common IIS configuration steps.

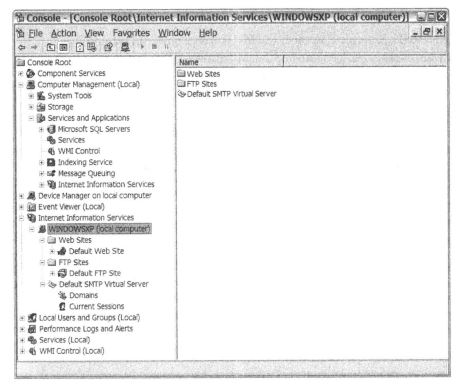

Figure 3-9. You can administer IIS through MMC.

Enterprise Services and Microsoft Message Queuing

Eventually (maybe sooner than later) you will develop multiuser, industrial-strength applications. Some of your applications will grow to support dozens, then hundreds, and later thousands and tens of thousands of users. Such applications will have a Service Level Agreement (SLA) detailing expected performance levels and acceptable levels of reliability. You will adjust your application designs to support such growth. Fortunately, at your disposal is system-level software designed to help support the increasing demands of your Windows and Web application software. Two very good examples of such (Microsoft-provided) software are Enterprise Services (COM+) and Microsoft Message Queuing (MSMQ).

COM+

Similar to IIS, Enterprise Services (COM+) is a very powerful system-level software package. As its name implies, Microsoft's COM+ is composed of several component services (resource management tasks, thread allocation, security, thread pooling, object pooling, transaction support, and object activation, just to name a few).

Take a look backward at the mainframe and think about the types of "services" that CICS itself provides for an application program. On the mainframe, your CICS application runs "inside" of CICS in much the same way that a component runs "inside" of a COM+ application. On the Windows platform, when you develop the components of your application, you can design your components to take advantage of these COM+ services (rather than create all of the needed plumbing yourself).

A properly designed component can be "installed" into COM+ as a COM+ application. The COM+ application can then service desktop or Web applications that depend on the programmatic processing provided by your component. .NET components can be designed to take advantage of COM+ services. Microsoft's COM+ software package is shipped with Windows 2000 and Windows XP.

CROSS-REFERENCE The Microsoft Windows features list shows COM+, MSMQ, and other software as being included with Windows. Visit http://www.microsoft.com/catalog/display.asp?site=656&subid=22&pg=2 for more information.

MSMQ

Microsoft Message Queuing (MSMQ) is Microsoft's answer to the need for an independent message-queuing software package. Why do I bring it up in a discussion about COM+? Because one additional service that COM+ includes is the Queued Components service (based on MSMQ).

Incidentally, you may have had the pleasure of working with message queuing software on the mainframe—perhaps IBM's MQSeries. Similar to MSMQ, MQSeries (as you recall) was a system-level software package that some IBM mainframe environments used to facilitate the passing of information between a mainframe CICS application and an application on an alternative platform.

Generally, message queuing products are called upon when there is a need for asynchronous communication or a guarantee of message delivery. The passing of messages asynchronously (application to application) may be needed between disparate platforms or on common platforms. Through the Queued Components service, the COM+ software package is able to leverage features of MSMQ. Conversely, MSMQ is able to leverage one other feature of COM+: transactional support. You see, MSMQ and COM+, whether together or apart, complement each other. I suggest you keep both of them on your radar.

Using the MMC snap-in for COM+ (the Component Services administrative tool) allows you to configure and manage COM+ applications. You can access all COM+ services, including the Queued Components service, from the MMC snap-in, as shown in Figure 3-10.

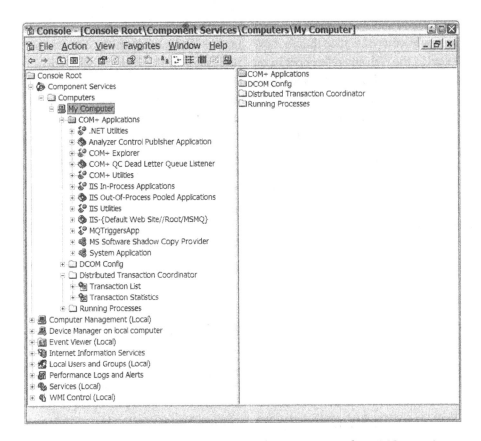

Figure 3-10. You can administer COM+ applications using the MMC snap-in.

CROSS-REFERENCE Chapter 19 covers some of the common Enterprise Services (COM+) application configuration steps.

Microsoft Developer Network

In my mainframe programmer days, we programmers had this thing called "the bible." Actually, we generally referred to the thick, printed reference manuals this way. These reference manuals were always reliable, always available. Nowadays, as a reformed mainframe programmer developing Windows and Web applications on the Microsoft platform, I have become reliant on the Microsoft Developer Network (MSDN, online and on CD and DVD).[13]

By the way, the online version of MSDN (`http://msdn.microsoft.com`) would naturally be the most current. I suggest that you bookmark this site. I cannot emphasize enough how often you should visit this site. In fact, I would go as far as to say that you should consider making the MSDN site your browser's home page. Incidentally, you will notice that in most chapters in this book, the MSDN site is included in the Web site references in the "To Learn More" section. Having said all of that, I suppose I should explain why.

Microsoft has done a great job of publishing tons of reference information on the MSDN site. There you will find programmer guides, columns and features, tutorials, and so forth. With all of the "new" discussions on .NET, a regular MSDN visitor will typically be the first to know when best practices are published. As an added bonus, you can search the MSDN Knowledge Base archives using keywords and error message numbers for those hard-to-figure-out problems.

From this point forward, I will refer to these so-called commonsense topics as if they *are* common.

Summary

This chapter's goals were as follows:

- To revisit our mainframe past to establish the perspective of a training effort

- To discuss tools and technologies of the Windows platform as prerequisites for .NET retraining

I have presented to you the areas that are typical stumbling points for the newly reformed mainframe programmer. First, I discussed the difference between learning a programming language and learning to *use* that language on a given platform. Second, I reviewed the technologies that should be on your "common sense" list—in other words, your prerequisites. My intention was to smooth out

---

13. Besides visiting MSDN, my need for additional supplemental reading is satisfied by investing in good technical books, such as the one that you are holding your hands. (Hey, if you don't ring your own bell every now and then, the bell may not be rung at all.)

the inevitable learning curve (and perhaps keep the discussion interesting at the same time).

The bottom line is, your prerequisites foundation is about half poured. In the next chapter, I will pour the remaining half. There, I will introduce you to an additional prerequisite section that I refer to as "Foundational Concepts for Web and Windows Programming."

Starting with Chapter 5 and continuing to the end of the book, you will remove the brakes and dive into .NET. In these subsequent chapters, I will spend more time explaining actual .NET topics. After all, I wrote this book to guide you through the .NET maze. I just cannot go forward (with a clear conscience) unless you first get all of your "foundational" learning out of the way. Thanks for your patience.

To Learn More

The following are some suggested supplemental references to further your retraining effort.

Books

Advanced Transact-SQL for SQL Server 2000, by Itzik Ben-Gan and Dr. Tom Moreau (Apress, 2000):
http://www.apress.com/catalog/book/1893115828/.

Magazines

.NET Magazine:
http://www.fawcette.com/dotnetmag/
Visual Studio Magazine:
http://www.fawcette.com/vsm/
XML & Web Services Magazine:
http://www.fawcette.com/xmlmag/

Web Sites

A Crash Course: Editing the Windows Registry:
http://msdn.microsoft.com/library/en-us/dnexnt01/html/ewn0201.asp
Adobe Acrobat Reader (available as a free download):
http://www.adobe.com/products/acrobat/readstep.html

COM+:

http://www.microsoft.com/com/tech/complus.asp

IIS 6.0: New Features Improve Your Web Server's Performance, Reliability, and Scalability:

http://msdn.microsoft.com/library/default.asp?url=/msdnmag/issues/02/03/
IIS6/toc.asp?frame=true

Internet Information Services Features:

http://www.microsoft.com/windows2000/server/evaluation/features/web.asp

Microsoft Developer Network:

http://msdn.microsoft.com/

Microsoft Message Queuing Services (MSMQ) FAQ:

http://www.microsoft.com/ntserver/support/faqs/MSMQfaq.asp

Microsoft Office (Outlook, Word, Excel, Access, PowerPoint) Home Page:

http://www.microsoft.com/office/default.asp

Transact-SQL Overview:

http://msdn.microsoft.com/library/en-us/tsqlref/
ts_tsqlcon_6lyk.asp?frame=true

Using COM+ Services in .NET:

http://msdn.microsoft.com/library/en-us/dndotnet/html/
comservnet.asp?frame=true

Using Visio:

http://www.microsoft.com/office/visio/using/default.asp

Visual Studio .NET Feature Comparison:

http://msdn.microsoft.com/vstudio/howtobuy/choosing.asp

CHAPTER 4

.NET Retraining Prerequisites, Part 2

Foundational Concepts and Technologies for Web/Windows Programming

In this chapter

- Learning about object-oriented programming (OOP)

- Understanding Hypertext Markup Language (HTML)

- Exploring client-side scripting languages

- Examining XML

THIS CHAPTER COVERS yet more prerequisites. I know, I know. You bought this book to learn .NET and all of the .NET technologies. My intention is to fully guide you toward and through that exact goal. However, I still have my conscience to deal with—plus, I like to sleep at night. As one reformed mainframe programmer to another, I *really* want you to be successful with your .NET retraining effort. On that note, I know that these two prerequisite chapters (the previous chapter and this one) will better prepare you for the entire .NET retraining (the remaining chapters in this book) that awaits you. Therefore, if you were able to extract any value at all from the previous chapter, you are certainly going to love this one.

I actually debated about classifying the four topics this chapter covers as *prerequisites* for a .NET retraining. What was the debate about? Well, on one hand, the four technologies (OOP, HTML, client-side scripting, and XML) are completely independent of .NET, predate .NET, and can be completely exploited without touching .NET. Yet, on the other hand, to properly leverage the .NET Framework and .NET technologies, you need to have a comfortable understanding about each of the four listed topics. After all, these technologies are critical for Web and Windows programming, and programming with .NET *is* Web and Windows programming.[1] Honestly, in the long term, your .NET journey will fail miserably[2] if you do not embrace (at some level) each of these technologies.

Object-Oriented Programming

The first time that someone tried to explain object-oriented concepts to me was several years ago in a Visual Basic class. I remember sitting there with a blank look on my face as the instructor used analogy after analogy to help the class grasp this *new* concept. The instructor's presentation went something like this:

> *"Class, let's explore some of the* basic *object-oriented concepts. The first one is the idea of a* class *and an* object. *Now, I want you to imagine that you are an architect who has designed a blueprint to build a house. With that blueprint, you can create an unlimited number of houses—each house would be identical to the next. According to your blueprint, each house would have the same number of windows, doors, and so on. Therefore, by following this analogy, the blueprint would mimic the general idea of a* class. *Each house that you created, using the same blueprint, would mimic the general idea of an* object. *In other words, an object is like a copy (an instance) that was based on a model or template (a class)."*

 TIP   Although it is possible to create a .NET program without good object-oriented design practices, this one characteristic will separate efficiently designed, scalable, and maintainable .NET applications from all the rest.

The Visual Basic instructor then went through several other analogies before we finally "got it." Probably the most amusing (attempted) analogy was one in which the instructor asked a student to stand up in front of the class. The

---

1. Actually, the list of platforms that can benefit from .NET (including these four *foundational* technologies) programming extends beyond the Web and the Windows platform. Let's just say that when you hear the word "platform," you should also think "device." Then allow for a broad definition of the word "device"—beyond just the Web browser and Windows desktop. Additionally, the possibility exists that someday you may be able to do .NET programming on operating systems other than Windows.

2. OK, maybe I am exaggerating a little. However, your .NET career growth *will* be limited, and you can only remain at the junior or intermediate level for so long before your peers start leapfrogging over and around you.

instructor then started to point out the characteristics (properties) of the student. As the student blushed, the instructor proceeded to ask the student to do all sorts of weird things (e.g., jump up and down, wave his arms, and so forth), which were supposed to demonstrate the idea of object-oriented methods. This analogy had taken a wrong turn somewhere. The instructor then switched course and went on to two other analogies. In one of these analogies, he described cookie cutters (as an object-oriented class) that created (instantiated) copies of cookies (objects).

The last analogy that I remember the instructor trying was that of an automobile factory assembly line. With this assembly-line analogy, the instructor described how each automobile (object) rolling off (being instantiated) the assembly line *matched* the master specification (class). The features (properties) of the automobile would match from one automobile to the next. The instructor explained that a person could make different types of requests (methods) of the automobile (e.g., opening a door, closing a door, pushing the horn, turning the key in the ignition, and so forth). I have to hand it to the instructor for not giving up.

NOTE   Generally, object orientation is object orientation. However, there can be a difference in the *degree* of the *orientation* (i.e., how strict the adherence is). For example, the .NET Framework *thoroughly* implements object-orientation practices. However, older versions of Visual Basic only partially implemented object-orientation practices.

In keeping with tradition (and in honor of all of those instructors out there struggling to teach the programmers of tomorrow), I will offer up my own analogy to help explain object orientation: the mainframe Job Control Language (JCL).

A Mainframe JCL Analogy

I will begin by stating that all mainframe programmers (unknowingly) have been using object orientation practices since the beginning of time (back when keypunch machines and UNIVAC computers were among us). One of the key areas of object orientation concerns the idea of flexible component reuse. Think for a moment about the Job Control Language Procedures[3] (JCL PROC) that every mainframe programmer has used through the years.

---

3.   For you JCL purists, I am referring to cataloged JCL PROCs, not instream JCL PROCs.

NOTE How ironic that JCL, which helped with your introduction *to* mainframe programming, will now help with your departure *from* mainframe programming.

Recall that one of the great things about a JCL PROC was the advantage of *flexible component reuse.* You could create one JCL PROC—a general one. Then, through the magic of symbolic substitution and JCL override (some creative JCL wizards even incorporated JCL INCLUDE members within their PROC), you would customize the JCL with "temporary" changes. Each individual executing Job then would create its own virtual/in-memory copy of the JCL PROC. Each customized step would execute for the specific needs of the particular executing Job. The executing steps essentially defined the behavior of the PROC and thus the behavior of the executing Job. Additionally, the executing Job would have ultimate control over which PROC steps executed (using JCL COND parameters).

One of the other great things about the JCL PROC was its capability to free programmers from having to worry about some of the unpleasant details involved in implementing a particular series of JCL PROC steps. The user of the PROC would need only minimal information (i.e., the name of the PROC and any necessary input symbolic parameters) to use the PROC. In this approach, mainframe programmers would use the JCL PROC as an extendable, customizable package of JCL statements.

As it turns out, the knowledge that you have from your mainframe past (even with JCL) will greatly assist your understanding of the object-oriented way of doing things in programming code. This JCL analogy may sound like a very abstract stretch (by the way, abstraction is part of OOP). For now, I touch briefly on each OOP topic in the sections that follow. The full applicability of object orientation will be further exploited throughout the remaining chapters of this book.

Extending the JCL Analogy to Introduce Key OOP Terminology

Well, now I (just like my Visual Basic instructor) have used an analogy to help explain the concept of object orientation. I can only hope that the use of JCL (a familiar technology) assisted in that high-level review. Now, let's drill down a bit into some of the specific portions of the OOP methodology. The following list[4] and the respective sections that follow present the basic OOP terminology that you will come across when you are developing on the .NET platform:

- Class

- Property

- Method

- Class library

- Base class

- Instantiation of objects

- Object construction

- Object finalization

- Inheritance

- Encapsulation

- Abstraction

- Polymorphism

- Overriding and overloading

- Shadowing

- Unified Modeling Language (UML)

---

4. This list is not meant to represent a complete list of OOP terms; rather, it is provided as a list of common OOP terminology. I will delay the discussion of persistence and state management until a later chapter (Chapter 16). Although both concepts apply to this OOP discussion, I would rather save them for the user interface section of this book. At that time, I will rely on your familiarity of common mainframe CICS technologies (COMMAREA, EIB, TS queues, and pseudo-conversational CICS design) to assist you in that discussion.

Class

In my analogy, the general PROC served as a template. From this template, virtual copies are produced and customized. When you design applications to solve real-life problems, using the object-oriented approach is significantly different from designing the structure of a PROC (or a structured program, for that matter). A PROC (my analogy of a class) generally is designed around functionality.

However, in general object-oriented approaches, functionality would be the responsibility of the methods. Think of object orientation in terms of nouns, verbs, and adjectives. A *class* typically represents the noun. In subsequent chapters, you will learn that the .NET Framework offers various types of classes/objects (value types, structure types, reference types, and so forth) that are each unique for different programmatic uses.

Property

Using the noun-verb-adjective approach again, a *property* represents the adjective of a class. Using the JCL analogy, the names of the PROC and JCL steps, and the names of the parameters available for symbolic substitution and overriding, would all mimic properties of a class.

Method

Using the noun-verb-adjective approach one last time, a *method* represents the verb of a class. In the mainframe JCL analogy, the JCL executable steps mimic the ability to invoke a class's methods. In subsequent chapters in this book, you will be further introduced to the various types of methods and the different ways to invoke them.

Class Library

Generic PROCs are stored in a PROCLIB library. In OOP, this library is referred to as a *class library*. In fact, the entire .NET Framework is one *big* class library filled with classes and objects that you will use. In addition, you will create your own classes (that inherit from classes in the .NET Framework).

Base Class

In OOP, the class library takes on a hierarchical structure/relationship. As an example, imagine if there was a main JCL PROC (at the top of the PROCLIB library) and all PROCs below it inherited basic characteristics from the PROC above, creating a parent/child relationship. In this analogy, the main JCL PROC (the one at the top of the PROCLIB) would represent the parent. The parent is analogous to the base class.

Instantiation of Objects

When a mainframe Job is submitted to the JES2 queue, a virtual/in-memory copy of the generic PROC is created. When you create your .NET applications, you will code programming statements that will cause the creation, or *instantiation*, of objects. Subsequent chapters will further introduce this topic with code examples.

Object Construction

At the point of instantiation, the construction of the object takes place. Let's say that you have a JCL step named "NEW" that executed automatically—as soon as the Job is submitted to the JES2 queue. This NEW step would be called your *constructor*. Any initializing or housekeeping that you want to do could be performed in this constructor step.

Object Finalization

Objects have a limited lifetime. Using the JCL analogy, when a JCL Job's execution is terminated and the in-memory copy (object) of the customized PROC "disappears," all resources[5] that the JCL statements had allocated are then released. Right before the in-memory copy of the PROC ceases to exist, if it was possible to execute one last JCL Job step (named Finalize or Dispose—see the following Note regarding a Destructor method) you would then be going down the path of object finalization.

---

5. When you think about "resources," remember that you will soon turn all of your focus toward a program and away from JCL. Start thinking about your legacy COBOL programs and the data that exists in your working storage and linkage section as some of the "resources" that you will be concerned about.

By the way, additional concepts branch off this topic, for example, deterministic versus nondeterministic finalization and the garbage collector. Chapter 8 expands on these additional topics using a different mainframe analogy: CICS's GETMAIN and FREEMAIN commands for resources management.

NOTE   At the time of this writing, it appears that the J4 Committee is in serious disagreement about *how* to implement all of the object-oriented features into the upcoming COBOL standard. In this case, what is in question is how (or whether) to include in the COBOL 2002 standard a Destructor/Finalizer method. The discussion surrounding the Finalizer method boils down to how the COBOL 2002 language will clean up after itself to free resources: clean up by default, when the program ends, clean up on demand via the call of the Finalizer method, or perhaps clean up periodically via a "garbage collector" when needed.

Now it looks like the J4 Committee has agreed to disagree on the question of standard inclusion for the Finalizer method. The J4 plans to create a technical report separate from the upcoming COBOL 2002 standard that will address the fate of the Finalizer method. That is too bad. My guess is that this will make it rather easy for the skeptics (and the OOP purists) to criticize the *partial* implementation of object orientation in the COBOL 2002 standard.[6]

CROSS-REFERENCE   For more information regarding the J4 Committee's discussion on the Finalizer method and their technical report, please see http://www.ncits.org/tc_home/j4htm/m230/01-0079.doc, http://www.ncits.org/tc_home/j4htm/m230/01-0081.doc, and http://www.microfocus.com/whitepapers/developmentcobolstandard.asp.

Inheritance

On the mainframe, some of the more advanced JCL users used the JCL INCLUDE statement. With this statement, a JCL PROC can *inherit* an INCLUDE group, which is usually a group of JCL statements saved in a partition data group member. In

---

6. Just look at how the OOP purists criticized Visual Basic (earlier versions) as not being truly object oriented. Up until recently, Visual Basic lacked inheritance as part of its object-oriented implementation. Now, the OOP purists are satisfied with VB .NET, considering that now it is *completely* object oriented.

.NET, the Framework (class library) offers thousands of classes that can be inherited. Additionally, other classes can inherit classes that you create yourself.

This is the portion of object orientation that fully exploits the idea of flexible code/component reuse. As you might have guessed, *this* mainframe "analogy" for inheritance is rather scaled-down compared to the real power of object-oriented inheritance. When I discuss the .NET Framework further in later chapters, I dig deeper into the topic of inheritance.

Encapsulation

Say you've created a JCL PROC that has many steps, and each step has many DD statements. Your main reason for creating it as a cataloged JCL PROC is to save others the trouble of reinventing the wheel (or rather, re-creating the same PROC). In effect, you have created an extendable, customizable package of JCL statements, as described earlier in this chapter. Regardless of whether the user chooses to override (customize) any of the statements, the user may be able to just refer to the PROC by name in the Job, execute it, and that's it.

The idea surrounding *encapsulation* is that of the black box, which furthers the idea of plug and play (with class/objects). You will appreciate this black box approach as you benefit repeatedly from the powerful classes offered in the .NET Framework (without always needing to look too far under the hood of each class/object). By the way, the information that you use to identify a class and its exposed characteristics makes up the *interface* of the class.

Abstraction

The concept of *abstraction* works hand in hand with encapsulation. As you go through the process of deciding which properties and methods to expose and which to "hide" in your class, you are assisted along the way by your ability to abstract the "important" characteristics. Given a business problem, an application designer will reduce a seemingly complicated problem down to its most essential characteristics (e.g., nouns, verbs, and adjectives). The result will be an object model of the problem. All of this will occur before any actual program coding is done.

This high-level design approach may remind some of you of the mainframe programming flowcharts that you have created at one time or another. In this case, however, you would create the object model before you would create a flowchart. After you create the object model, it is time to define how the objects relate to each other. This latter design step (defining how objects relate to each other) might be closer to the idea of flowcharting.

Polymorphism

Polymorphism refers to the ability to have a class or any of its members (properties and methods) behave differently depending on how it's inherited (or on how it's implemented). The approach of customizing generic JCL PROCs with JCL override and symbolic substitution leans heavily toward the idea of polymorphism.

Using the mainframe JCL analogy, a given JCL step might behave differently depending on how a particular Job has implemented the override statements. A very common approach that I am sure you have encountered is to have one JCL PROC that has a symbolic substitution parameter that is used to indicate whether the PROC is being used for production or for testing. By overriding the JCL, the behavior of each JCL step will differ greatly, accessing either testing/development resources or production resources.

Overriding and Overloading

Much like the mainframe JCL overriding that I have discussed, when one class inherits from another, you can choose to *override* the properties and methods of the "parent" class to modify the characteristic or behavior that takes place in the "child" class.

However, *overloading* is different from *overriding*. Overloading is more similar to the idea of having one Job step and a series of JCL override statements that override the same step conditionally. As you dig into the practice of inheritance, you will come across .NET Framework classes that have methods that are *overloaded*. Depending on how you use the class, the method execution will differ. This is good example of polymorphism (discussed previously).

Shadowing

Shadowing is similar to overriding, but it's much more powerful. Let's stretch the JCL analogy a bit. Imagine a type of JCL statement that allowed you to cause all of the PROC Steps and PROC DD statements to be "hidden" from the system. Let's say that this same imaginary JCL statement caused only the JCL override statements found in the JCL Job to be recognized. Well, this is heading in the direction of describing the power of shadowing—when you're looking for an extended way to override properties and methods that exist in the inherited *parent* class.

Unified Modeling Language

Recall what I said earlier about the flowcharting that you have done before. Typically, before you created a mainframe COBOL program, as standard practice you would create a flowchart (OK, maybe you just intended to create one). The flowchart did what you would expect from its name: It charted out the flow of the program. Well, I mentioned earlier that the practice of designing an object model is similar to the idea of flowcharting, except that it includes much more than just "the flow." An object model shows everything there is to possibly know about an object. This would include what class the object was derived from, any attributes (properties) and methods, how the object will relate to other objects, and much, much more. Fear not, a language and a tool exist to assist you through your object model design efforts.

Through a collaborative effort, a notation language called Unified Modeling Language (UML) is available to help you with documentation of object models that you create using object-oriented design and analysis methodologies.

CROSS-REFERENCE   UML is now an accepted specification of the Object Management Group (OMG). For more information, please visit http://www.omg.org/uml/.

In the previous chapter, I mentioned that Microsoft has a diagramming product called Visio. Using Visio, you can create UML object model drawings (see Figure 4-1) to document your object models.

But you can do more with this program than just create drawings. Using Visio, you can build a program code skeleton like the one shown in Figure 4-2 from your UML object model drawing.[7] That's right—using this software tool, you can design your entire object model using UML notation, and then with a few mouse clicks you can have all of your program class files created for you. You then simply need to edit your program class files to add in the business rules and program logic. By the way, Visio 2002 Professional[8] supports all nine of the diagram types defined by the UML 1.2 specification.

---

7. Of course, you can also do this with other, non-Microsoft software packages. Also, you could do this manually, without the aid of a software tool.

8. Visio Professional 2002 is included with Visual Studio .NET Enterprise Architect edition. The code generation and reverse engineering features are applicable to the version of Visio that is bundled with Visual Studio .NET Enterprise Architect edition, but not the Visio 2002 stand-alone version.

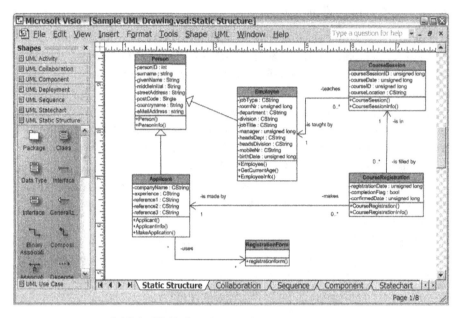

Figure 4-1. A sample Visio UML drawing

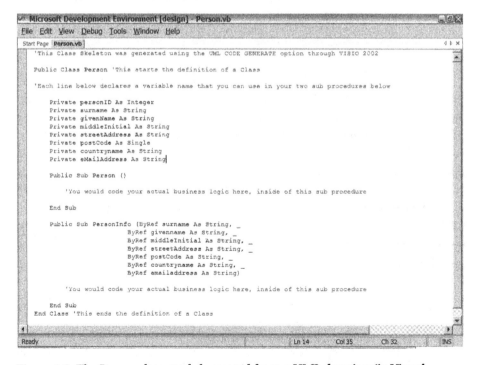

Figure 4-2. The Person class module created from a UML drawing (in Visual Basic .NET)

But Wait, There's More to Microsoft Visio 2002

The features list for the Microsoft Visio 2002 product is extensive. As much as I would like to discuss each feature here, doing so would extend far beyond the scope of this discussion. That said, there are two additional features that I would like to point out:

- *You can create many types of drawings other than UML-based object models.* To help get you started, Visio ships with various types of sample drawings. In fact, I used one of the sample drawings to give me a head start in creating the drawing in Figure 4-1. Notice the Visual Basic .NET (VB .NET) class (skeleton) that was automatically generated using Visio.

- *You can take an existing .NET application with the classes, properties, methods, and program logic created already and then have Visio create the UML-based object model drawing for you.* This process is called *reverse engineering.* Some of you may have had experiences (many years ago) on the mainframe with computer-assisted software engineering (CASE) tools. Some of those experiences may have not been pleasant. Keep in mind that this is a different platform now and the technology has improved.

Once you create your Visio diagram, leveraging the full support for UML, you will want to save the diagram. When you proceed to do that, you will be presented with the Save As dialog box. Near the bottom of this dialog box is the Save As Type drop-down list. There, you have many choices to pick from—everything from the default Visio format (.vsd) to common graphic formats (i.e., Graphics Interchange Format [.gif], Adobe Illustrator File [.ai], and so forth). You can even choose to save your Visio UML diagram in the Hypertext Markup Language (.htm or .html) format. This may be helpful to remember while you read the next section.

Hypertext Markup Language

On the mainframe, you built COBOL CICS screens and you loved what basic mapping support (BMS) mapsets could do for you. Maybe you coded your BMS mapsets manually or maybe you were fortunate enough to have a screen-painting tool that built the mapsets for you. Either way, the concept of designing a screen and assigning attributes to field positions (i.e., length, color, and so on) is something very familiar to you. Well, CICS/BMS, scoot over and make room for Hypertext Markup Language (HTML).

HTML is one of the main languages that you will be working with (directly and indirectly) when you develop the graphical user interface (GUI) portions of Web pages. When you develop Web pages, not only will you have an opportunity to set "field" attributes (font sizes, text color, and so on), but you will also build entire user interface features. In some cases, you will take full advantage of a screen-painting tool (Visual Studio .NET or other software) that will create the HTML code for you. In other cases, you will need to manually modify the HTML code. HTML (currently version 4.01) is used to present documents and information in all types of browsers. Thanks to the World Wide Web Consortium (W3C), HTML is an accepted standard. HTML is multivendor-, multibrowser-, and multiplatform-friendly.

Please familiarize yourself with the following basic HTML terminology:

- *Publishing:* When HTML files (and ASP.NET files) are deployed to a Web server and made available to the public, *publishing* has taken place.

- *Content:* HTML is not just about showing different types of fonts on Web pages. Most often, a company or organization is presenting valuable information, documents, and graphics on their Web pages. The HTML formatting tags and the text information, documents, and graphics are referred to collectively as *content.*

- *Authoring:* Someone needs to create the content for the Web site, a process that is referred to as *authoring.* Authoring is the task of the Web author.

- *Rendering:* When a client browser makes an HTTP request for an HTML page, the Web server[9] "delivers" the file to the browser. The HTML file and all of the HTML tags contained within the file are then "interpreted" by the browser[10] and the results are shown to the client. In this context, "rendering" and "HTML browser interpretation" are synonymous.

---

9. This basic explanation deals just with "static" HTML pages. In a later chapter (Chapter 14), I discuss Active Server Pages (ASP.NET). With ASP.NET, pages take on a more dynamic nature. The Web server processes the ASP.NET page before sending the resulting HTML page to the client browser.

10. If there was a client-side script (VBScript, JavaScript, or JScript), the interpretation of the script would also occur at this point. In the next section in this chapter, I discuss client-side scripting.

- *Tags/elements/attributes:* These terms refer to the predefined syntax used to build an HTML file. Each represents the code and values you use to control things such as font size and color, background pattern, buttons, input fields, and structure.

- *Cascading Style Sheets (CSS):* Rather than repeatedly apply the same detailed format information in separate HTML tags and/or separate HTML files, you can create a style sheet. The style sheet contains groups of format styles. Depending on the type of style sheet (local, global, or linked), your multiple HTML tags and files can then inherit the formatting rules specified by your style sheet and the appropriate format style group. The cascading effect follows a simple rule of precedence (first local, then global, and finally linked). Style sheets provide a way to separate the presentation of content from the content itself. Although you can also use CSS with XML, there is yet another type of style sheet syntax, Extensible Stylesheet Language Transformations (XSLT), which is available for XML programmers. CSS and XSLT serve similar purposes. However, they are not the same thing. Later in this chapter, I discuss XML and XSLT in more detail.

CROSS-REFERENCE   The W3C has more information available regarding the CSS Recommendations at http://www.w3.org/Style/.

- *Tables:* Adding tables to a page is a common technique to assist with the organization/structure of content on a page.

- *Frames:* You have choices about how to build your Web pages. For example, you may choose to divide your page into various frames. This is useful when you want to make only a portion of your screen scrollable.

Using your browser, navigate to any Web site or HTML page of your choice (see Figure 4-3 for an example). Then select View ➤ Source from your browser window to view the HTML (shown in Figure 4-4) that is behind the page of the Web site. Viewing the HTML code of Web pages can help you discover new HTML coding techniques.

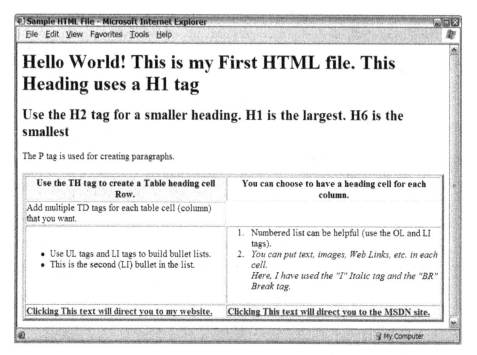

Figure 4-3. Sample HTML rendered in the Internet Explorer browser window

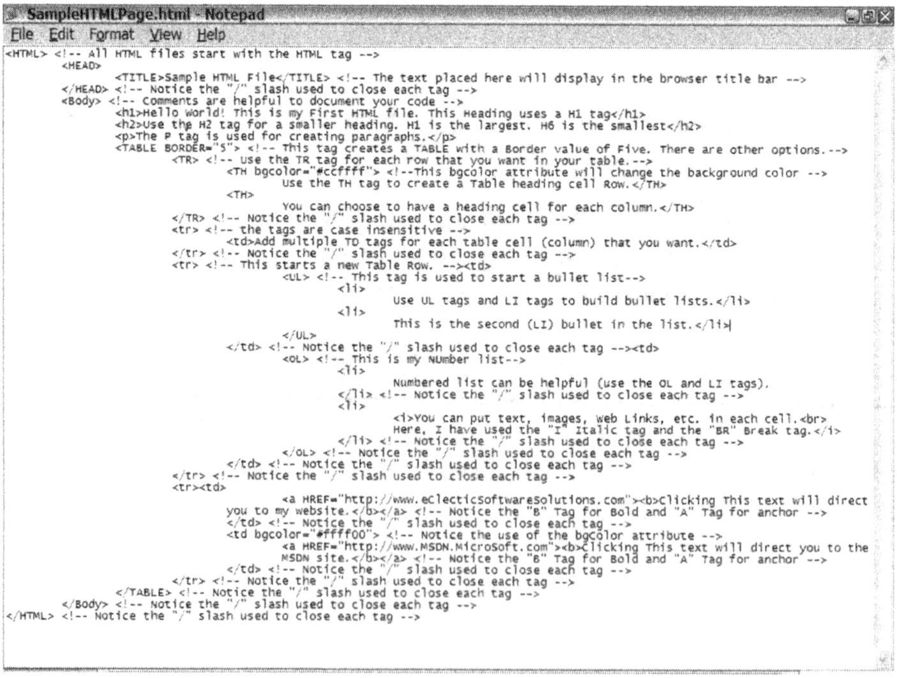

Figure 4-4. Sample HTML as text data in the Notepad editor

Though the HTML in Figure 4-4 is displayed using Notepad, you could create your own HTML files in Notepad. However, you would be missing out on a lot of great editing enhancements that are available to you. Among many other things, Visual Studio .NET (VS .NET) includes a great editor.[11] This will mean much more to you when you are creating your ASP.NET Web applications and occasionally (with confidence) tweaking the HTML code.

CROSS-REFERENCE   You can find more information on the W3C's HTML Recommendation at http://www.w3.org/MarkUp/.

The Future of HTML: XHTML

The W3C is now working on the "extension" of HTML: XHTML. They have improved HTML by making it follow some of guidelines that XML follows. Due to sheer volume of the lines of HTML code in existence (responsible for the entire world's Web pages), the move toward XHTML is likely to be slow, not to mention difficult with regard to the cost of justifying a rewrite. Either way, you can adopt XHTML-type habits when you code your HTML files today, which will result in better HTML coding.

Visit the W3C Web site for more information about the XHTML Recommendation: http://www.w3.org/TR/xhtml1.

Eventually, after you become an HTML expert, you will want to add logic to your Web pages. Perhaps you will want to add simple input validation to your Web pages. When you reach that point, you will want to explore the topic of client-side scripting. For your convenience, the next section serves to point you in the right direction.

---

11. Generally, if a person prefers a tool designed *just* for Web page design/publishing (minus all of the great power that programming brings), that person might choose one of the following products to author Web content: WYSIWYG, Dreamweaver 4.0, GoLive 5.0, FrontPage 2002, or Microsoft Publisher.

Client-Side Scripting Languages

Many years ago, in my junior-programmer mainframe days (when COBOL, CICS, and VSAM were still relatively new to me), I created a mainframe application that used three technologies: Command List (CLIST), REXX, and ISPF Dialogs/PDF. The application was my version of a homegrown paperless change-control system. I designed, coded, and deployed the application on schedule. The entire company started using it. Generally, it was a big success. That is, until the user load exceeded my wildest expectations. The success of the application ended up being its doom. That was my first lesson about scalability.

TIP *Scalability* (in general) is the ability of an application to maintain a given level of performance as physical changes are introduced to the application in an attempt to service an increased user load. The phrases "scale upward" and "scale outward" are commonly used in discussions about scalability. In a given situation, "scale upward" can refer to increasing the size of your computer processor or adding more memory. In that same situation, "scale outward" might refer to adding additional processors.

At any rate, as the system started to show serious signs of stress, a more senior programmer came to consult with me. His advice sounded something like this:

"This Command List (CLIST) language is much too slow because it is being interpreted each time a user makes a request. Did you know that you could have compiled your REXX Command List code? There is a time and place for scripts and command list. When you have the choice, a compiled binary module should be your first choice. Nevertheless, you should recode this application with a real language like COBOL or assembler. I still cannot believe that you coded this application with flat files. How are you handling concurrent updates? Have you not heard of VSAM? Besides that, you could have preprocessed your ISPF panels."

NOTE A code review would have been a good idea before I coded and deployed the application.

As that scolding senior programmer had told me, there's a time and place for scripts and command list. Well, the time is today and the place (at least one of the places) is in many of the Web pages that you'll create. That's right. We *still* have languages that are being interpreted at runtime.

JavaScript, JScript, and VBScript

If you have a Web page that you wish to add dynamic features to, you will need to use an interpretive language—a script language. Your basic choices[12] are JavaScript, JScript, and VBScript. If your users are all using Microsoft's Internet Explorer (IE) browser, then VBScript or JScript will be good a choice. Otherwise, plan on brushing up on your JavaScript. The popularity of JavaScript can be attributed to the fact that virtually all browsers fully support it (including IE). By the way, you should be concerned with not only the *type* of browser your users have, but also the *version* of that browser.

 TIP I discussed already how the browser "renders" the HTML and prepares it for display (as a Web page). There is a lot to be said for what the Web browser actually does for us. The browser has a scripting engine that takes care of the script code. Now it may be easier to appreciate the emphasis (in the previous chapter) about "knowing" your browser type and version.

When the browser detects an HTML script tag such as the one in the following example, the browser interprets and executes the code:

```
<HTML>
<script language="JavaScript">
. . .
<!-- client-side script code goes here  -->
. . .
</script>
</HTML>
```

In this script code, you can code logic that manipulates or processes the "other" HTML elements and style sheets.

---

12. If you are targeting IE version 5.0 or later, you can set the LANGUAGE attribute of the HTML script element to XML (or to one of the other choices previously mentioned).

Client-Side Field-Level Validation

Client-side scripts are useful when you perform field-level validation.[13] In other words, why make an expensive trip across the network only to find out that the user has not filled in all of the required fields? For example, when a user enters a date into the Date field in your Web page, your script checks that the information entered is in a valid date format. Then, after the client-side script code has served as your gatekeeper, your application makes the call to the Web server and processes the server-side code. Finally, the server-side code executes the database update logic.

CROSS-REFERENCE   Chapter 14 covers client-side validation in more detail and provides sample code.

NOTE   One of the major advances of ASP.NET is that when you write server-side code you can now use a full-powered language (such as VB .NET) instead of being limited to VBScript. The scripting languages VBScript and JavaScript are subsets of Visual Basic and Java, respectively. Additionally, with ASP.NET, the server-side code is compiled code now. Gone are the days of coding your ASP files with VBScript interpretive code for server-side execution. Scripts have their time and place, and server-side execution is no longer the place.

Client-Side Scripts, HTML, and Cascading Style Sheets

When you use client-side scripts to *manipulate* HTML and CSS, you are creating dynamic Hypertext Markup Language (DHTML). You can leverage the client-side Document Object Model (DOM) to manipulate HTML tags and CSS. DHTML, as its name implies, is a way to make your HTML and CSS displays more dynamic. The W3C (to the rescue again) has worked toward a DOM Specification. The standard will increase the compatibility of your DHTML on multiple browser types (IE, Netscape, and so forth).

---

13. Validation code is just scratching the surface of script code usefulness. However, keep in mind that if a security-conscious user disables script support on his or her browser, your Web application may not perform as you expect it to.

The Windows Script Host

The client-side script that I just discussed dealt with "running" the script code on the client side, in the browser. Well, there is another use for script code: You can use script code with the Windows Script Host (WSH)[14] on your regular desktop.

The WSH approach to scripts actually reminds me quite a bit of my mainframe CLIST days and even of my Windows DOS batch (BAT) file days. In each of these cases (CLIST and Windows DOS batch), you create a text file, save it, and execute it. That's it—no compiling. So, with WSH, right on your desktop you can use the Notepad editor (or any other editor), type in some VBScript code (or even JScript), and save the file. Then double-click and run the file. Optionally, you can execute the file from your Command Prompt window (click the Start button and select Run).

Of what use are these "stand-alone" script files? Well, other than making it easy for people to create script viruses (remember the I Love You.txt.vbs virus?), they can help you create very friendly and safe routines to automate user and administrative tasks—just like mainframe programmers do with CLIST.

If you want to experiment a little, open Notepad and then type in the following four lines of VBScript code:

```
Dim obj
Set obj = WScript.CreateObject("InternetExplorer.Application")
obj.Navigate "http://www.EclecticSoftwareSolutions.com"
obj.Visible = true
```

Next, save the file with a .vbs extension (e.g., SampleWSH.vbs). Then double-click the saved .vbs file. This little VBScript logic will open an instance of IE (using the Windows Script Host object model) and navigate to my Web site. Of course, this will only work if you have the IE browser installed and you have an Internet connection. Don't worry if you don't understand the actual syntax of the preceding VBScript code. I provided this sample just to demonstrate the power of a very small WSH script file.

---

14. Yes, this topic has little to do (directly) with .NET programming. However, I do believe that removing any potential misunderstanding can be helpful to your .NET retraining effort. With all of the concern that you will have about scripting (in the browser when doing client-side logic), I felt it important that you know the difference between the common uses of the term "scripting." Besides, scripting with the WSH is a powerful and useful technique to add to your arsenal—for the proper time and place.

CAUTION I don't advise sending any file attachments in your e-mails that have the .vbs file extension. Your network e-mail system will likely detect the script file and send you a nasty warning. It's not that script files are bad, it's just that some people use them in bad ways sometimes. So, create them, have fun with them, but just don't try to send them through your e-mail system.

How Many Prerequisite Languages Are There?

You have gone from UML to HTML to XHTML, and you'll move on to XML in the next section. For those of you in shock from the seemingly large number of "extra" languages (and tools) that are included in this prerequisites chapter, allow me to point out that we, too, have many languages on the mainframe. You may be keeping count of the additional languages you need to learn to be a well-rounded .NET Windows/Web developer. Before you get discouraged, remember your own mainframe past: How many *extra* languages (and tools) are normally required to be a well-rounded mainframe programmer? When you start counting, remember to start your mainframe tally with JCL being number one. Then keep counting: Dyl280, Easytrieve, CLIST, REXX, CICS, BMS macros, TSO commands, ISPF Dialogs, SDSF, advanced control card syntax for various utilities such as DFSORT, IDCAMS, batch File-AID, and so on.

My guess is that you may question the fact that I have referred to some of these mainframe technologies as "languages." Good. That is my point. Just because some of these Web/Windows platform technologies include the word "language" in their acronyms does not mean that they are full-fledged languages per se—rather, they may simply require a certain syntax.

Now that you've learned about HTML and client-side scripting, I may have left you with the impression that those two technologies combined are the only tools that you need to do *all* of your Web page development. Well, for basic Web pages, there was a time when this was true. However, the trend has been to incorporate more modern, more flexible technologies into your Web page development arsenal. Among the technologies topping the list is the one I discuss in the following section: Extensible Markup Language (XML). Striving to make the best of your .NET development experience, you will want to learn this additional technology.

Extensible Markup Language

In some of your past mainframe assignments, you may have had the pleasure of exploring the Electronic Data Interchange (EDI) format.[15] You may have had an assignment where you needed to exchange data with a business partner. After struggling with delimited and positional files, perhaps you and your business partner both agreed that EDI would be "the" format. You found an EDI specification that matched your needs. While your systems department was setting up your expensive EDI server, you began to learn the cryptic EDI document specifications. Finally, after much effort and preparation, you formatted your data accordingly, and the data exchange was then established.

Yes, legacy applications (particularly business-to-business applications) survived with EDI. However, XML has taken the idea of data packaging and data description many steps forward.

 NOTE Those of you (lucky ones) who never touched EDI have probably worked with COBOL copybooks, the COBOL Data Division file descriptions (FDs) and record descriptions, and COBOL PICTURE clauses and VALUE clauses. Well, what you can do with these COBOL legacy technologies you can do with XML. However, the opposite is far from true—let's just say that XML is almost in a league of its own.

You have used these COBOL legacy technologies as a way to design, package, and deliver data (even if just within your COBOL program), right? The COBOL syntax (or the EDI specification) has helped document the electronic transport of data. Likewise, XML helps you accomplish similar objectives within a program, but more important, it helps you do so outside your programs and outside your company.

You can understand the significance of XML if you first realize that Microsoft has integrated their entire .NET product offering with XML. It is virtually impossible to find a portion of .NET that does not use XML—it is everywhere, inside and out. So, what *is* XML? XML is a complete set of rules for designing, representing, and delivering text-based, delimited, self-documenting, structured data. Now, that was a mouthful, which reminds me of another point: XML is referred to as being "verbose by design" (as a compliment).

---

15. You may know the EDI standard by a different name: The American National Standards Institute (ANSI) and The Accredited Standards Committee version is "X12"; the European version is Guidelines on Trade Data Interchange (GTDI); and The International Organization for Standardization (ISO) and United Nation's version is called Electronic Data Interchange for Administration, Commerce, and Transport (EDIFACT).

CROSS-REFERENCE The W3C has several Recommendations as well as Proposed Recommendations in progress for the various XML related technologies. You can find more information about these Recommendations and the various kinds of W3C technical reports available for XML at http://www.w3.org/TR/#About.

Looking at the sample XML file in Figure 4-5, you will notice that XML looks similar to HTML when you view it in the Notepad editor.

```
SamplegradesXMLpage.xml - Notepad
File  Edit  Format  View  Help
<?xml version="1.0"?>
<grades>

        <student id="Jim">
                <test_scores>125</test_scores>
                <homework_scores>228</homework_scores>
                <quiz_scores>56</quiz_scores>
        </student>

        <student id="John">
                <test_scores>150</test_scores>
                <homework_scores>200</homework_scores>
                <quiz_scores>98</quiz_scores>
        </student>

        <student id="Jane">
                <test_scores>180</test_scores>
                <homework_scores>160</homework_scores>
                <quiz_scores>110</quiz_scores>
        </student>

                <student id="Sally">
                <test_scores>110</test_scores>
                <homework_scores>250</homework_scores>
                <quiz_scores>89</quiz_scores>
        </student>

</grades>
```

Figure 4-5. Sample XML viewed in the Notepad editor

Figure 4-6 presents the same XML file in the IE browser after it's been double-clicked. Notice that the same file is displayed in two separate browser windows to demonstrate the ability to collapse and expand each XML element.

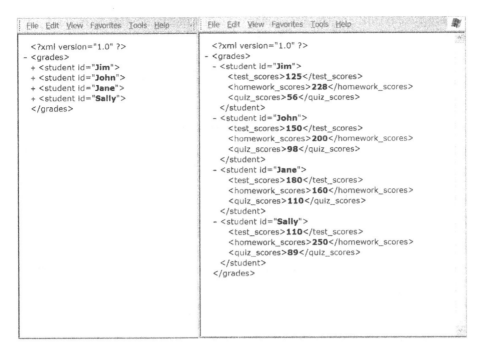

Figure 4-6. Sample XML file (parsed) viewed in the IE browser

You can type XML statements into a regular text file using Notepad.[16] Then, save the file with an .xml extension. That's it. When you double-click it, the XML parser that lives in IE parses it and creates the collapsible XML tree structure display shown in Figure 4-6. Although XML looks like HTML, XML differs from HTML in a couple of ways:

- With XML, you have the flexibility to create your own names for your tags. For example, a valid XML tag could look like this: <createYourOwnName> <createYourOwnName/>. With HTML, however, you must use the standard, predefined tags.

- With XML, you are packaging and documenting data, whereas with HTML you are formatting a screen display.

One additional difference between XML and HTML is that XML must be *well-formed*. This is one of the main reasons that the W3C has created XHTML, or

---

16. Later you will use VS .NET for most of your programming and editing. However, you will still find Notepad useful for some quick and dirty editing, especially in emergency situations when you need an editor and no other editor is installed on the server that you happen to be working on.

well-formed HTML. To give you an idea of what it means for XML to be *well-formed*, consider the following list of rules:

- The XML document must begin with the XML declaration
  (`<?xml version="1.0"?>`).

- Any elements must not overlap, but they may nest.

- Elements must have both a start and end tag if there is data in the element.

- Empty elements must end with a /> if only a single tag is used.

- Quote marks must be used on attribute values.

I present this list of rules just to give you a sense of what well-formed means. There are more rules that you will want to learn about. Also, the rules for well-formed HTML are slightly different. As you continue your retraining exploration, be sure to keep these points in mind, and for more information, please visit `http://www.w3.org/TR/REC-xml#sec-well-formed`.

NOTE In the previous chapter and this one, I reiterated the importance of "knowing" your browser. I pointed out that you really want to know the type and version of browser that sits on your desktop. Well, even with XML, your browser choice will have an impact. Your browser (type and version) choice influences what version (if any) of an XML parser and XSL processor you may already have, not to mention that it impacts the HTML, DHTML, and scripting-related technologies discussed earlier. By the way, you can install an XML parser separately, without having any specific browser to go along with it.

XML Learning Kick Start

To give your XML learning experience a little kick start, I have included the following sampling of the basic XML terminology:

- *XML:* XML, or Extensible Markup Language, is a markup language that allows you to create your own tags to document the data contained within the tags. Both humans and machines can then read the entire XML document. Additionally, XML files are text based, which makes it easy to transmit them over HTTP and through security firewalls. (For more information, visit `http://www.w3.org/XML/`.)

- *XML declaration:* `<?xml version="1.0"?>` is the one tag that you must have as the first line in your XML document. Beyond that, there are many other terms and syntax rules to dig into. Be on the lookout for terms such as "elements," "attributes," "data islands," "entity," "template," and "nodes." Please take advantage of the references that I have provided for your continued learning at the end of the chapter.

- *XML Schema and XML Schema Definition (XSD):* XML Schema is to XML as COBOL copybooks are to mainframe VSAM files and QSAM files. You can create your own customized schemas. In addition, there are "approved" schemas for most major industries (similar to the proprietary EDI specifications). XSD, simply put, is the W3C language standard that you use to define XML Schemas (which have their own W3C Recommendation). The XML Schema defines the structure and semantics of the well-formed XML documents that you will be creating. XML Schemas and XSD replace the older approach of document type definition (DTD) and XML-Data Reduced (XDR).

CROSS-REFERENCE   You can find more information about the W3C's XML Schema Recommendation at `http://www.w3.org/XML/Schema`.

Although I referred to the topics just listed as "basic XML terminology," allow me to point out that I am using the word "basic" rather loosely. Be prepared to devote some time to these "basic"-level XML topics during your retraining effort. Later, you may need to extend your XML knowledge with other, more advanced topics. When that time comes, the following section should be useful.

Advanced Topics to Take Your XML Skills to the Next Level

The XML technologies are so vast that a person could easily specialize in this area and remain there. For your immediate purposes (to learn .NET for Windows and Web programming), I suggest learning the basics of XML and XML Schemas. Then revisit the remaining XML topics later. Considering the overwhelming presence that XML has in the industry, you will not want to exclude these additional XML-related technologies from your future training.

The upcoming sections discuss these advanced topics:

- XSL, XSLT, XPath, and XQuery

- DOM, SAX, and SOM

- MSXML

XSL, XSLT, XPath, and XQuery

Generally speaking, Extensible Stylesheet Language (XSL) is a W3C technology that you use to transform XML into HTML. XSL is really much more than that, though. To begin with, XSL is three interrelated technologies combined into one: XSL Transformations (XSLT), XSL Formatting Objects, and XML Path Language (XPath). Together, these XSL technologies offer a very flexible and powerful way to format, calculate, arrange, add to, delete from, and otherwise transform XML data into HTML[17] for display. The style sheet processor and formatter used with XSL are built right into your Web browser.

CROSS-REFERENCE   For more information about XSL and XSLT, visit http://www.w3.org/Style/XSL/ and http://www.w3.org/Style/XSL/WhatIsXSL.html, respectively.

Specifically, XSL is an XML-based language that you use to express style sheets. Your XML document and your XSL style sheet are processed together by the XSL style sheet processor to create the desired display result. This process involves the transformation and formatting of the XML document. The XSL Formatting Objects and formatting properties assist in the actual formatting semantics. To manipulate your XML beyond the Formatting Objects' capabilities, you can use

---

17. XSLT can transform XML into text-based formats other than HTML.

the XPath language. You use XPath to navigate the hierarchical node structure of your XML document to perform conditional testing, expressions, functions, and logic for varying desired results.

CROSS-REFERENCE   For more information about XPath, go to
http://www.w3.org/TR/xpath.

On the other hand, you might use XML Query (XQuery) instead of XPath. XQuery makes it possible to query XML documents much as you would an actual relational database. It has its own syntax that some claim is easier than XPath. I liken it to the comparison between programming against a mainframe IMS database and programming against a mainframe DB2 database. With IMS, you had a hierarchical approach to querying for data. However, with DB2 you had a more direct, dynamic approach due to the relational database structure. Given this comparison, my bet is on the direct, dynamic approach.

CROSS-REFERENCE   For more information about XQuery, go to
http://www.w3.org/XML/Query.

It has been said that a picture is worth a thousand words. I have provided a few figures to help further explain the XML technologies. First, as shown in Figure 4-7, an XML document is displayed as-is using the Notepad editor. Following that figure, you will notice in Figure 4-8 that I have prepared the XSLT that will be used to transform the XML. It is shown here using the Notepad editor. Lastly, in Figure 4-9, the transformed HTML is shown in the Web browser. I trust that Figures 4-7 through 4-9 will help introduce the XSL technologies.

```
SamplegradesXMLpagewithXSLT.xml - Notepad
File Edit Format View Help
<?xml version="1.0"?>
<?xml-stylesheet type="text/xsl" href="sampleXSLT.xsl"?>
<grades>

        <student id="Jim">
                <test_scores>125</test_scores>
                <homework_scores>228</homework_scores>
                <quiz_scores>56</quiz_scores>
        </student>

        <student id="John">
                <test_scores>150</test_scores>
                <homework_scores>200</homework_scores>
                <quiz_scores>98</quiz_scores>
        </student>

        <student id="Jane">
                <test_scores>180</test_scores>
                <homework_scores>160</homework_scores>
                <quiz_scores>110</quiz_scores>
        </student>

                <student id="Sally">
                <test_scores>110</test_scores>
                <homework_scores>250</homework_scores>
                <quiz_scores>89</quiz_scores>
        </student>

</grades>
```

Figure 4-7. An XML document viewed in Notepad

```
SampleXSLT.xsl - Notepad
File Edit Format View Help
<?xml version='1.0'?>
<xsl:stylesheet version="1.0"
      xmlns:xsl="http://www.w3.org/1999/XSL/Transform">
<xsl:output method="html"/>
<xsl:template match="/">
<html>
    <head><title>Grades Results By Student</title>
    </head><body>
        <table border="1">
            <tr>
                <th>student</th>
                <th>test_scores</th>
                <th>homework_scores</th>
                <th>quiz_scores</th>
            </tr>
            <xsl:for-each select="grades/student">
                <!-- order the result by test_scores -->
                <xsl:sort select="test_scores"
                          data-type="number"
                          order="descending"/>
                <tr><td>
                        <em><xsl:value-of select="@id"/></em>
                    </td>
                    <td><xsl:if test="test_scores &gt; 150">
                            <xsl:attribute name="style">
                                <xsl:text>color:red</xsl:text>
                            </xsl:attribute>
                        </xsl:if>
                        <xsl:value-of select="test_scores"/>
                    </td><td><xsl:value-of select="homework_scores"/>
                    </td><td>
                        <xsl:value-of select="quiz_scores"/>
                    </td>
                </tr>
            </xsl:for-each>
        </table>
    </body>
</html>
</xsl:template>
</xsl:stylesheet>
```

Figure 4-8. XSLT used for transformation viewed in Notepad

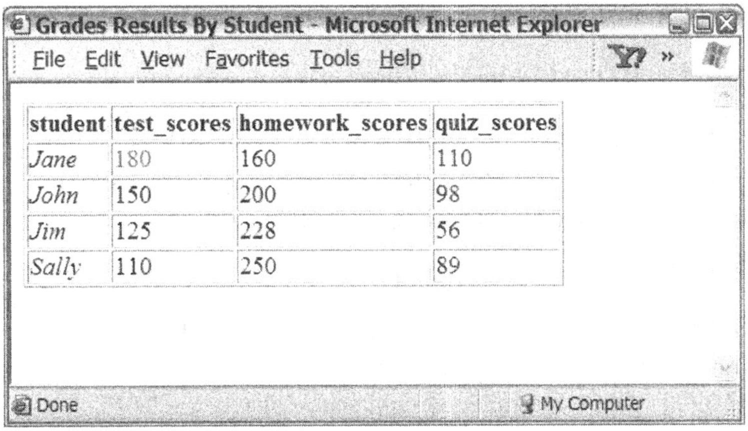

student	test_scores	homework_scores	quiz_scores
Jane	180	160	110
John	150	200	98
Jim	125	228	56
Sally	110	250	89

Figure 4-9. HTML in IE after being rendered

To further appreciate what XSL has to offer, imagine that you have created a very informative Web site with your best HTML skills[18] (using lots of the HTML <p></p> tags for your data). Now, let's say that you want to create two versions of your HTML (static) Web site. Each Web site will display mostly the same content, but the content will be formatted very differently on each site. The format will be so different, in fact, that even the use of CSS is not a practical choice. Therefore, you go into development mode.

First, you edit the old HTML file to copy and paste your content (data). Next, you create the second page and paste in your content. You deploy both HTML pages to their respective Web sites. Great—mission accomplished. Congratulations, you have just created a maintenance problem. When the time comes to update your "static" data, you will now need to maintain *both* versions.

Let's say that you later learn about XML and the XSL technologies. You open one of your HTML files and copy the data (again), except this time you paste your data into a new XML document, making the appropriate changes to meet the well-formed XML requirement. Next, you create separate XSLT for each Web site as per each Web site's formatting requirement. Then, you copy the respective XSLT to each Web site. Each distinct XSLT will read the same XML data and output uniquely formatted HTML for a customized Web site display. Now, when it is time to maintain the data, you edit your *one* XML document and affect the multiple Web site implementations. Later, you can read the same XML document for other Web sites (or other devices), all the while not disturbing the original two Web sites. This is just one example of the value that XSL can bring to XML. The list of benefits is not short.

18. Even when you are creating powerful, dynamic Web pages with ASP.NET, there is still much value in what the XSL technologies offer.

DOM, SAX, and SOM

Recall that the DOM is also used for HTML. When you want to dynamically access and/or update the structure, content, and style of XML (or HTML) documents, the DOM is available for you to exploit. Because the DOM is a W3C Specification, it is appropriate for multibrowser use. A similar technology is Simple API for XML (SAX). SAX is also multibrowser-friendly. However, SAX is not a W3C Specification (yet).

Both SAX and DOM have specific advantages and disadvantages. Depending on your application and design, you may want to choose one or the other. By the way, when you are done reading up on SAX and the DOM, remember to look up Schema Object Model (SOM), a complementary technology for the DOM.

 CROSS-REFERENCE   For more information about SAX, the DOM, and SOM, go to http://msdn.microsoft.com/library/en-us/xmlsdk/htm/ sax_concepts_8kaa.asp, http://msdn.microsoft.com/library/en-us/ xmlsdk/htm/sax_concepts_0v1p.asp, and http://msdn.microsoft.com/ library/en-us/xmlsdk/htm/som_devguide_overview_73g7.asp, respectively.

MSXML

MSXML is the name of Microsoft's XML parser. This is the parser that I mentioned earlier that does all of the XML magic for you in the browser. The actual translation of the acronym MSXML used to be *Microsoft XML Parser.* Now, the translation is *Microsoft XML Core Services.* My guess is that they changed the name to more accurately reflect the impressive power and functionality of MSXML.

At the time of this writing, MSXML 4.0 is the latest version of the parser and is available for download from the MSDN site. At some future date, it is likely that MSXML will be included with a version of the IE browser. Today, the default MSXML parser that comes with IE is an older version (version 2.0). However, it is simple to upgrade to one of the newer MSXML parsers (version 2.6 or 3.0) if you have IE 5.5 or later.

CROSS-REFERENCE   For more information about MSXML, go to
http://msdn.microsoft.com/library/en-us/dnmsxml/html/
dnmsxmlnewinjuly.asp.

Getting Comfortable with XML

You should become comfortable with XML because I discuss it further in the following chapters:

Chapter 11 covers accessing data with the new .NET technology ADO.NET. Guess what? When you use ADO.NET to return data from a Web service, it is it XML format. How convenient!

Chapter 12 explores the topics of relational data and accessing it using T-SQL, and introduces the subject of Microsoft SQLXML 3.0 technology. With SQLXML, you are able to query your database and receive data in XML format. Being comfortable with XML will certainly help you leverage the new opportunities that SQLXML offers.

Chapter 13 covers Web services and explores three technologies that Web services depend on: Simple Object Access Protocol (SOAP), Web Services Description Language (WSDL), and Universal Description, Discovery, and Integration (UDDI). Here's the catch: If you haven't established a good comfort level with XML, you'll feel very uncomfortable during the discussion about Web services and its supportive technologies.

Chapter 18 presents examples where you'll need to configure some aspect of your .NET environment—for example, manually editing a file in your .NET development environment. You can bet that you will be editing an XML file.

XML Is Everywhere in .NET

As noted in the preceding section, the use of XML is apparent in several portions of the .NET platform. It was this fact that convinced me to include XML in this .NET prerequisite chapter. My most recent example of needing to know XML came as

I was installing the beta version of Fujitsu's NetCOBOL for .NET[19] to integrate it into the VS .NET environment. Fujitsu's installation instructions included the following step:

> *". . .you must incorporate the configuration changes found in the file Examples\Web\web.config into your machine's global configuration file."*

The ...\web.config file contained XML code similar to the following:

```
<?xml version="1.0" encoding="UTF-8" ?>
<configuration>
    <system.web>
        <compilation debug="false" explicit="true" defaultLanguage="vb">
            <compilers>
                <compiler language="COBOL;cob" extension=".cob"
                type="Fujitsu.COBOL.COBOLCodeProvider,
                Fujitsu.COBOL.CodeDom,version=99.9.9.9,
                 Culture=neutral,PublicKeyToken=999999999999999" />
            </compilers>
        </compilation>
    </system.web>
</configuration>
```

Next, I opened up my machine's global configuration file (...\CONFIG\machine.config) to discover that there were a total of 793 lines of XML code. Interesting. So, where should I make the change mentioned in the Fujitsu NetCOBOL for .NET installation document? Well, if you understand XML, the answer is obvious. Do you get my point? Yes, you will need to learn XML.

Because I felt comfortable editing XML, I proceeded to update my machine's global configuration file. For my first step, I made a complete backup copy of my machine.config file (just to be safe). I then opened the file (I used VS .NET, but I could have used Notepad) to begin the navigation down into the 793 lines of XML. The goal now was to look for the node names mentioned in Fujitsu's XML sample. For example, first I looked for <configuration>, which was on the second line. Then I looked for <system.web>, which was on line 113. Finally, I looked for <compilers>, which was on line 157. Bingo! To finish the process off, I copied and pasted the <compiler .... /> XML line below the other similar lines that were there already.

---

19. I promise I will spend almost a whole chapter (Chapter 6) talking about Fujitsu's NetCOBOL for .NET product. After all, it is one of the .NET language choices.

My guess is that this vendor's assumption that the reader is comfortable editing an XML file is a reasonable approach to take. After all, other platforms (such as the mainframe) assume that certain technologies are known. Take JCL, for example. Recall how JCL tended to be rather ubiquitous. It was common for mainframe programmers to use JCL for everything, so it was assumed that every mainframe programmer knew JCL. Yes, JCL was used for "packaging and describing" your program execution and request for resources. XML, on the other hand, is used to package and describe your data. Nevertheless, XML is every bit as omnipresent on the .NET platform as JCL was on the mainframe.

Summary

This chapter's goals were as follows:

- To discuss object-oriented programming

- To understand HTML

- To explore client-side scripting languages

- To examine XML

In this chapter, you were introduced to a number of prerequisite topics. I like to refer to this set of topics as "foundational concepts and technologies for Web/ Windows programming." You started with object-oriented concepts. Then, you moved on to HTML. You saw some actual HTML code in a very basic example. I included a discussion about client-side scripting and explained the time and place for its usage. Lastly, you reviewed XML and several XML-related technologies.

You covered a lot of ground in this chapter. Honestly, I think this will be one of those chapters that some of you will choose to revisit and reread a few times. Certainly be sure to take advantage of the supplemental links and references provided in the "To Learn More" section at the end of this chapter (and every chapter).

In the next chapter, you will move into .NET drill-down mode. You will explore the choices for program editors (Notepad and Visual Studio .NET, among others). To support that discussion, you will review the actual .NET programming language choices. Early in the chapter, I state my recommendations. Lastly, you will review several illustrative code samples.

To Learn More

The following are some suggested supplemental references to further your retraining effort.

Books

Doing Web Development: Client-Side Techniques, by Deborah Kurata (Apress, 2001):
> http://www.apress.com/catalog/book/1893115879/.

Managing Enterprise Systems with the Windows Script Host, by Stein Borge (Apress, 2001):
> http://www.apress.com/catalog/book/1893115674/.

XML Programming Using the Microsoft XML Parser, by Soo Mee Foo and Wei Meng Lee (Apress, 2002):
> http://www.apress.com/catalog/book/1893115429/.

Magazines

.NET Magazine:
> http://www.fawcette.com/dotnetmag/

Visual Studio Magazine:
> http://www.fawcette.com/vsm/

XML & Web Services Magazine:
> http://www.fawcette.com/xmlmag/

Web Sites

A User's Guide to Style Sheets:
> http://msdn.microsoft.com/library/en-us/dnie40/html/css.asp

HTML Elements:
> http://msdn.microsoft.com/workshop/author/html/reference/elements.asp

MSDN:
> http://msdn.microsoft.com

XML Developer's Guide:
> http://msdn.microsoft.com/library/en-us/xmlsdk/htm/
> xml_devgd_overview_91b9.asp

XML Query Language Demo:
> http://xqueryservices.com

XSLT Tutorials:

```
http://www.xslt.com/resources_tutorials.htm
```

Using Visio:

```
http://www.microsoft.com/office/visio/using/default.asp
```

Windows Script (VBScript, JScript, and WSH):

```
http://msdn.microsoft.com/scripting
```

Part Two
.NET Programming Essentials

"Visual Studio .NET offers great interactive debugging features. I have grown to expect that of a modern tool. Now, I'm spoiled. Now, developing software without modern tools reminds me of trying to mount pictures on a wall without the help of a stud finder."

—*Chris Richardson*

Inside the .NET Integrated Development Environment

Bringing Visual Studio .NET to Life

In this chapter

- Introducing Visual Studio .NET

- Reviewing the .NET project types and project templates

- Choosing among the .NET language alternatives

- Developing your first .NET programs

IN THE PREVIOUS TWO chapters, I emphasized that learning to program on the .NET platform will require you to learn much more than just a new programming language or a new development tool. In those chapters, I covered several prerequisite topics. Now you have a foundation that you are ready to build upon. You will find that this chapter is rather different from the previous chapters.

Beginning with this chapter and continuing in each subsequent chapter, I not only discuss .NET, I also illustrate *how* to use .NET tools and .NET technologies. That's right. It's time to roll up your sleeves. I start by showing you the many features contained in Visual Studio .NET (VS .NET), your new integrated development environment (IDE). I explain the project template feature and the various project types. From there, you'll move on to choose among the .NET languages. Last, but certainly not least, you'll develop your first .NET programs.

Incidentally, I now assume that you have acquired an edition of VS .NET and installed it (review the section ".NET Is Multiple Editions of VS .NET" in Chapter 2 for information about the available VS .NET editions). When you perform the installation using the VS .NET installation disks, pay particular attention to the choices available for Language Selection and Documentation Location Selection.

The Language Selection options control which Microsoft-provided language compilers and project types are installed. The Documentation Location Selection options offer you a choice of location for the documentation that accompanies the installation disks: either your CD/DVD drive or your hard disk. The examples and screen shots in this book are based on the Enterprise Architect edition of VS .NET, version 1.0.

Integrated Development Environments

In Chapter 2, I referred to the mainframe tool Interactive System Programming Facility (ISPF) as an IDE. I mentioned that on the .NET platform, your IDE of choice *is* VS .NET. Well, it is now time to take a closer look at both IDEs.

The IDE of Yesterday: ISPF

For perspective, let's revisit the mainframe. There, you might have not normally used the phrase "integrated development environment" when referring to ISPF. Nevertheless, the phrase does fit. By the way, as a reformed mainframe programmer, you can now add ISPF to your fond-farewell list.

That is right. It is time to say goodbye to your old friend ISPF. OK, call me an old, sentimental you-know-what. Just think about it: no more JCL, no more VSAM, and now no more ISPF. Of course, the real point here is just to realize how critical these tools and technologies have been in your day-to-day mainframe development. Why is this point important? Because the requirements that *were* addressed with these legacy tools and technologies *still* need to be addressed. The basic requirements include the following:

- Creating program code

- Viewing and editing program code

- Compiling program code

- Testing and debugging program code

As ISPF did, your new IDE, VS .NET, will now easily take care of all of these basic needs. I discuss each of these needs in the next section, "The IDE of Today and Tomorrow: VS .NET."

What About the Modern Mainframe Tools?

There *are* products available now that are hosted on the Windows platform to enable developers to create applications targeted for the mainframe. These modern tools, being more graphical than their predecessors, even offer drag-and-drop features. It is not my intention to ignore those mainframe programmers who use these types of development tools and products that are hosted off the mainframe, on the Windows platform. Likewise, it is not my intention to pretend that these products do not exist. Yes, several companies, including Micro Focus, Fujitsu, and IBM, have made great advances with graphical Windows-based mainframe development products.

However, many of our mainframe brothers and sisters have not been fortunate enough to transition over to these modern development tools. Many are still stuck in the twentieth century. If you are currently using any of these types of Windows-based development tools, consider yourself lucky. Your .NET learning curve will not be as steep as it will be for others. Even so, from what I have seen so far, even these modern graphical mainframe tools pale in comparison to Microsoft's Visual Studio .NET (VS .NET) IDE. After you have spent some time with VS .NET, please share your opinions regarding this comparison with me via e-mail at Richardson@eClecticSoftwareSolutions.com.

At this point, perhaps you are asking the following question: "If I am saying good-bye to ISPF, what about *all* of the other tasks that ISPF performed for me?" You are right; I have only mentioned the so-called basic tasks. Nevertheless, there is a VS .NET feature available for the other, "nonbasic" ISPF tasks. As Figure 5-1 shows, the typical ISPF Primary Option Menu offers several menu options.

```
  Menu   Utilities  Compilers  Options  Status  Help

                       ISPF Primary Option Menu
   Option ===>

   0  Settings      Terminal and user parameters        User ID . :
   1  View          Display source data or listings     Time. . . :
   2  Edit          Create or change source data        Terminal. :
   3  Utilities     Perform utility functions           Screen. . :
   4  Foreground    Interactive language processing     Language. :
   5  Batch         Submit job for language processing  Appl ID . :
   6  Command       Enter TSO or Workstation commands   TSO logon :
   7  Dialog Test   Perform dialog testing              TSO prefix:
   8  SDSF          Spool Display and Search Facility    System ID :
```

Figure 5-1. The basic choices on the ISPF Primary Option Menu

Table 5-1 shows the chapter and section in which the comparable VS .NET feature is discussed in this book.

Table 5-1. ISPF Options and Comparable VS .NET Features

ISPF OPTION	ISPF DESCRIPTION	CHAPTER AND SECTION WHERE COMPARABLE VS .NET FEATURE IS DISCUSSED
0	Settings: configure ISPF	Chapter 5, "My Profile"
1	View: browse text	Chapter 5, "The IDE of Today and Tomorrow: VS .NET"
2	Edit: create and update	Chapter 5, "The IDE of Today and Tomorrow: VS .NET"
3	Utilities	Chapter 11, "Client-Side Tools"
4	Foreground: compile	Chapter 5, "The IDE of Today and Tomorrow: VS .NET"
5	Batch: execute	Chapter 5, "The IDE of Today and Tomorrow: VS .NET"
6	Command support	Chapter 5, "Executing Programs and Commands at a Command Prompt"
7	Dialog Test: program	Chapter 5, "VS .NET Customization Through Automation"
8	SDSF (Spool Display and Search Facility)	Chapter 3, "The Event Viewer"
(Other)	Third-party utility applications	Chapter 5, "NetCOBOL for .NET"

At a high level, this section has just about addressed the entire mainframe ISPF feature set. I have discussed ISPF as an IDE for perspective. Perhaps I have given you the impression that there is a one-to-one correspondence between the ISPF and VS .NET feature sets. As you will see in the next section, that is not the case. Yes, you *can* find an equivalent feature in VS .NET for each ISPF feature. However, with that, you will just be scratching the surface of what VS .NET has to offer.

NOTE Any features you find in ISPF that are not represented (in some form) in VS .NET are likely to be features not directly related to program development. For example, third-party Job scheduling software is commonly accessed from an ISPF menu option. For the Windows and Web development platform, this sort of production support software is located outside of VS .NET.

Are you ready to explore your new IDE, VS .NET? OK, let's do it.

The IDE of Today and Tomorrow: VS .NET

In the previous section, I discussed the many features of ISPF. Naturally, I will do the same for VS .NET in this section. It may seem that comparing (rather than contrasting) one IDE with the other is almost unfair. After all, the basic structure of ISPF has gone unchanged for as long as I can remember. VS .NET, along with the platform it was created for, is much newer and more oriented around graphics (hence the "visual" in "Visual Studio .NET") than ISPF. Nevertheless, the mainframe platform typically uses one IDE: ISPF. The .NET platform, on the other hand, uses VS .NET.

Chapter 2 discussed VS .NET as being one of the answers to the "What is .NET?" question. VS .NET is *the* feature-packed IDE that you use to develop .NET applications. Now, let's drill down to find out how to take advantage of the features offered in this tool.

Launching VS .NET

You have installed VS .NET and you are ready to put it to use. After the installation is complete, you launch VS .NET by clicking the Start button and selecting the Programs menu, as shown in Figure 5-2. Depending on the edition of VS .NET that you installed and the options you chose during installation, your Programs menu may differ slightly from the one shown in Figure 5-2.

Figure 5-2. Launching VS .NET from the Programs menu

VS .NET Start Page

By default, the VS .NET Start Page is set to Show At Startup. Because VS .NET is configurable, you can turn this option off if you don't want to have the Start Page show at startup. However, I do *not* recommend doing so. At least wait until you have had a chance to discover the usefulness of this screen. Then decide.

 TIP If you happen to close the Start Page (or maybe you accidentally turned off the Show At Startup option) and you would like to bring it back for display, choose Help ➤ Show Start Page. In my opinion, having the Show Start Page option under the Help menu is not intuitive. I think a more appropriate location for this option is under the View menu (under the Other Windows submenu) or under the File menu. However, I believe the location of the Show Start Page option is Microsoft's way of clearly indicating that the Start Page is intended as a page to provide help as opposed to just a page from which to start tasks.

When you launch VS .NET for the first time, the default setting is to show the My Profile view of the Start Page, as shown in Figure 5-3.

On subsequent launches of VS .NET, the Get Started screen view will be selected. For now, leave the default settings as they are on the My Profile view. I further discuss the My Profile view in the section "My Profile."

Now, I want to point out that there are a total of nine options on the Start Page. You navigate from one to the other with your mouse, selecting any choice you wish. As shown in Figure 5-3, the available Start Page options are as follows:

- Get Started

- What's New

- Online Community

- Headlines

- Search Online

- Downloads

- XML Web Services

- Web Hosting

- My Profile

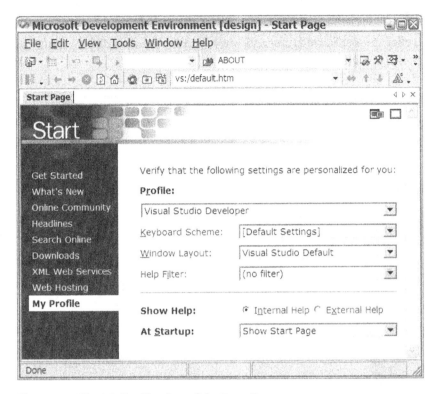

Figure 5-3. The My Profile view of the Start Page

NOTE Except for Get Started and My Profile, the Start Page screen views require an Internet connection in order to function. The What's New screen view will function offline (somewhat). However, in order to get updated with current information, even the What's New screen view requires an Internet connection. Integrating with the Internet for value-added features appears to be a trend in Microsoft products and products from other vendors. (Considering the liberal use of Web site references in this book, even I have opted to integrate with the Internet—for value-added features, of course.)

As the Primary Option Menu is to ISPF, so is the Start Page to VS .NET. Now, let's learn about each[1] of these "menu" (Start Page) options. The first one I discuss is the Get Started option, which appears at the top of the Start Page.

---

1. I defer discussion of the XML Web Services screen view and Web Hosting screen view Start Page options until later chapters. I discuss the XML Web Services screen view in Chapter 13, and I discuss the Web Hosting screen view in Chapter 17.

Get Started

After you click the Get Started screen view tab, you should see a display similar to what is shown in Figure 5-4.

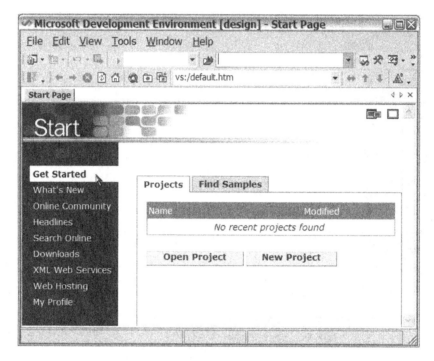

Figure 5-4. The Get Started view of the Start Page

The following are the basic requirements that you have when approaching program code in an IDE:

- Creating

- Viewing

- Editing

- Compiling

- Testing

- Debugging

On the Get Started screen view, notice there are two tabs: a Projects tab and a Find Samples tab. The Projects tab is where you accomplish each of the basic requirements in the preceding list. The Projects tab has three features:

- Recent projects found list

- Open Project button

- New Project button

NOTE   The term "project" is *almost* synonymous with the traditional mainframe term "program," with significant exceptions. Soon you will need to learn additional terms such as "solution," "assembly," "execut-able" (EXE), and "dynamic link library" (DLL). I explain these terms (and others) in Chapter 6.

Because you have not created any projects yet, the first two options (the recent projects found list and the Open Project button) are of little use at this point. To create a new project, click the New Project button. The dialog box shown in Figure 5-5 will appear.

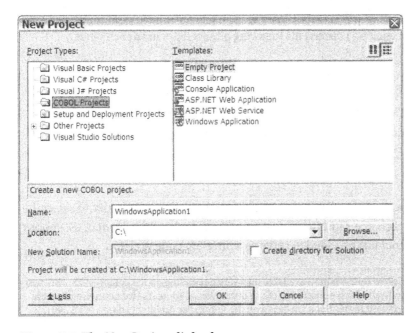

Figure 5-5. The New Project dialog box

Notice the Project Types options shown on the left side of the dialog box. This list includes programming languages, among other things. Additionally, notice the Templates choices shown on the right side of the dialog box.

Two factors influence what project type and language choices you have. First, when you install VS .NET, you have the chance to choose among the Microsoft-provided languages: Visual Basic .NET (VB .NET), Visual C# .NET (C#), and Visual C++ .NET (C++ .NET). Second, you can obtain (for a reasonable price) .NET language compilers provided by other software vendors.

In my case, I selected VB .NET and C# when I installed VS .NET. Separately, I obtained a copy of Fujitsu's NetCOBOL for .NET product and installed it after I completed installing VS .NET. Presumably, you have not installed Fujitsu's NetCOBOL for .NET product yet. Please refer to the documentation that accompanies Fujitsu's product for any needed installation assistance. I further discuss the topic of .NET language choices later in this chapter, in the section "Choosing Your .NET Language."

Choosing a VS .NET Project Type Extends Beyond Language Choice

You might have noticed that VS .NET shows several other types of projects in the New Project dialog box (in the Other Projects folder and the Setup and Deployment Projects folder).[2] The discussion in this chapter focuses on the language-specific project types. The other project types have various purposes. Among the choices, I discuss the following project types in later chapters:

- I discuss the Application Center Test Project in Chapter 13.

- I discuss Database Projects in Chapter 11.

- I discuss Enterprise Template Projects in Chapter 13.

- I discuss Setup and Deployment Projects in Chapter 17.

With regard to the Templates choices, if you love to type, then always select the Empty Project choice. Otherwise, if you are like the other 99 percent of us, choose one of the templates provided to serve as a program code skeleton.

---

2. The project types that you have available may vary depending on the edition of VS .NET you have installed and which options you chose during installation. As I mentioned earlier, the examples I present in this book are based on the Enterprise Architect edition of VS .NET, version 1.0.

In the mainframe environment, you created code skeletons, right? Perhaps you had a partitioned dataset (PDS) member into which you typed the minimal COBOL structure. For example, maybe you had a member that contained the appropriate Identification Division, Environment Division, Data Division, and Procedure Division statements. You may have even added the appropriate COBOL Section statements (i.e., the Input-Output, File, and Working-Storage Sections). Then, whenever you need a new program, the first step would be to copy the code skeleton to get a head start.

Honestly, when was the last time you created a mainframe COBOL program from *scratch*? Exactly. That is what the templates are for: to increase productivity. However, for those who insist on starting from scratch, the Empty Project template shown in Figure 5-6 is available just for you.

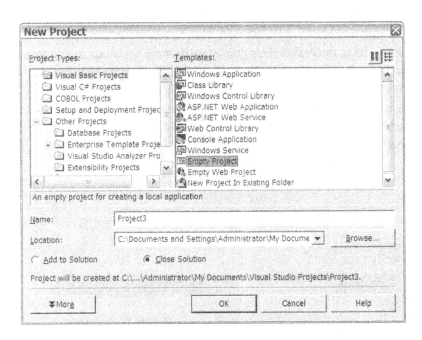

Figure 5-6. The Empty Project template

The available template choices vary depending on your project type choice. With regard to this chapter's discussion, that choice would relate to language. In other words, VB .NET offers a different set of project template choices than does NetCOBOL for .NET. However, I do expect that this list of template choices will continue to grow (particularly for NetCOBOL).

What's New

On the VS .NET Start Page, the second choice from the top is the What's New tab. When you click this tab, a screen view displays that is divided into three tabbed sections: a Technology tab (for software updates and highlights), a Training and Events tab, and a Tips and Walkthroughs tab.

It appears to me that the What's New tab will be one of those tabs that everyone should visit, but few will. Why do I say that? It is the second tab from the top. In other words, most will dive into the first tab (the Get Started screen view discussed in the previous section) and never come up for air. Therefore, I am spending time *now* on these *other* VS .NET Start Page options. I believe these supportive Start Page screen view options are worthwhile and offer great value.

I gave some thought to offering some sort of analogy, some sort of comparison of this What's New page to anything like it on the mainframe. Well, I suppose that a contrast can be just as useful as a comparison. That fact is, these "Internet-connected," interactive, integrated tools greatly surpass the tools that mainframe programmers have relied on for years. Honestly, the closest that we have come is the proliferation of mainframe help Web sites. Although there are a few good sites out there, not one of them (that I know of) is integrated into the mainframe development environment. *That* is the big difference. So, take some time and visit the What's New page (see Figure 5-7). You will be glad that you did.

Figure 5-7. You can access the What's New screen view from the Start Page.

Online Community

The Online Community tab offers several ways to extend your reach when you are away from your desktop, away from your desk, and even away from your home and work location. After you click the Online Community tab on the Start Page, you will see the options displayed in Figure 5-8, which can potentially open the entire .NET development world up for you.

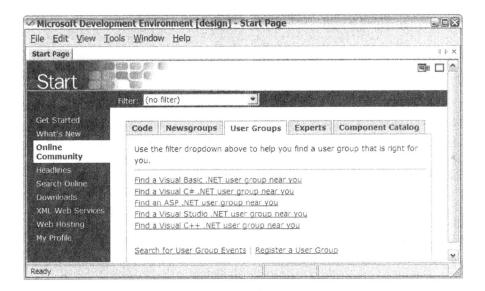

Figure 5-8. The Online Community screen view

The first tab is labeled Code (for code sharing) and includes several Web links. Each of these links will lead you to part of an online community where people are sharing code for free. Eventually, as you progress in your own knowledge, you too can contribute. The same holds true for other tabs on this same page, except the other tabs approach sharing from a different direction.

The second and third tabs are labeled Newsgroups and User Groups, respectively, and again they promote sharing knowledge, enthusiasm, and even motivation.

The fourth tab, Experts, is the one that I really love. In this community, people volunteer to help others, which is similar in effect to what happens on the other tabs I just discussed, except that self-proclaimed experts are answering the questions. If this is not enough, there is even a Technical Chat option available on this Expert tab.

Although these features are also available elsewhere (see the "Web Sites" subsection of the "To Learn More" section at the end of this chapter), the real value here (as with the What's New tab) is that this wonderful feature is integrated right into the development environment—right into VS .NET. As Figure 5-8 shows, the community has various points of entry.

I admit that it took me a while to get into the electronic "community" idea. This sort of faceless sharing—even anonymous sharing—was new to me. I believe it is new to the average mainframe programmer. Certainly, if this is the wave of the future, perhaps there is hope for humankind yet.

The Electronic Mentor

In this book's Introduction, I discussed how things have changed over time. In that discussion, I referred to the "mainframe old-timers who were always there for us as mentors." Well, coming from the mainframe environment, you will be hard-pressed to find the types of mentor programs that you may remember from "the old days." However, the same value that you realized from these partnering/sharing/grooming relationships you can now realize from other types of relationships: electronic relationships.

Consider the following points for this new approach to mentoring:

- It is no longer practical to *be* an old-timer due to the rapid evolution of technology.

- Online communities facilitate rapidly built relationships at the appropriate Internet era rate.

- The new, distributed electronic communities are integrated right into your new IDE: VS .NET.

Headlines

The Headlines screen view has four tabs. Each tab has "headline" news. The first tab, News, has content that is very familiar to me. It appears that most of the content on the News tab uses as its source the MSDN Web site. You see, for some time now I have had the MSDN site as my browser's home page. Naturally, I appreciate having the MSDN content show up in real time as one of the options of the VS .NET IDE.

The second and third tabs, .NET Platform and XML Web Services, respectively, should prove useful in your .NET retraining effort. The fourth tab, Development Life Cycle, provides good reading. However, this might be the one area where the average mainframe programmer has the upper hand (as discussed in Chapter 1 in the "Acknowledging Industry Perceptions" section). Nevertheless, consider yourself introduced to yet another VS .NET IDE feature.

Search Online

This is a great feature. As shown in Figure 5-9, it appears to be just a simple search tool. To appreciate its usefulness, you have to take into consideration the manner in which many developers perform their MSDN searches. For example, it's likely that you perform MSDN searches by opening up a browser window, navigating to the MSDN site, and then entering your search into the "Search for" box.

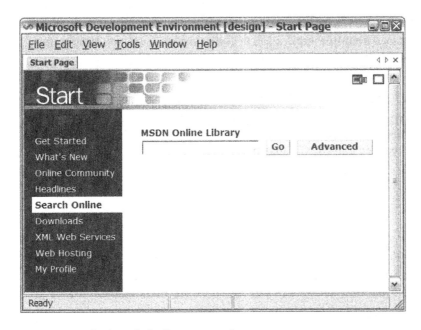

Figure 5-9. The Search Online screen view

Alternatively, you can use the search feature built right into VS .NET. Obviously, using this search feature will save you a few steps, as you don't need to navigate to the MSDN site outside of VS .NET. Beyond the step savings, another great thing about this feature is that the search results are returned in a "tabbed" window that is integrated with the VS .NET environment. This allows you to easily switch back and forth between your application and the MSDN search results. There will be times when you will prefer to open a separate browser window. No problem—at least you know that you have a choice.

Yes, the value of this feature drops considerably when an Internet connection is not available. Nevertheless, the term "integrated" is starting to take on a much larger meaning. Are you starting to look at the mainframe IDE (ISPF) in a slightly different light now? Perhaps it may not be so hard after all to part company with some of the mainframe tools that you hold near and dear.

Downloads

Downloads, free downloads. The Downloads screen view has two tab options: Free Downloads and Subscriber Downloads. You may be surprised to learn that the Free Downloads section actually has *good stuff* available to download. Some very well-written sample applications are available for download from that section. Integrated into the VS .NET IDE is the capability to download working examples. In some cases, you will find an answer to some confusing problem. In other cases, for sake of productivity (in other words, so you do not have to reinvent the wheel), you can download a sample application or code snippet. Then, you simply copy, paste, and modify it to meet your particular needs.

NOTE   The common thread running through each of these Start Page discussions is as follows: Each Start Page tab represents a great feature integrated into VS .NET that increases productivity.

My Profile

Recall that with mainframe ISPF (menu option 0), you were allowed to perform a small amount of configuration. As Figure 5-10 shows, you typically configured the programmable function (PF) keys to suit your personal preferences.

Editor Basics Yesterday and Today

As Figure 5-10 shows, the common setup for ISPF PF keys 5 and 6 was RFIND (repeat Find) and RCHANGE (repeat Change). Which reminds me that it was possible to perform a FIND and/or a REPLACE. Well, guess what? VS .NET also offers a Find and Replace feature. If you refer once again to Figure 5-10, you are reminded that ISPF PF keys 2 and 9 supported the ability to SPLIT the ISPF screen into two separate screens. Yes, you guessed it. VS .NET also offers a feature that allows you to split your screen (rather, window) in two.

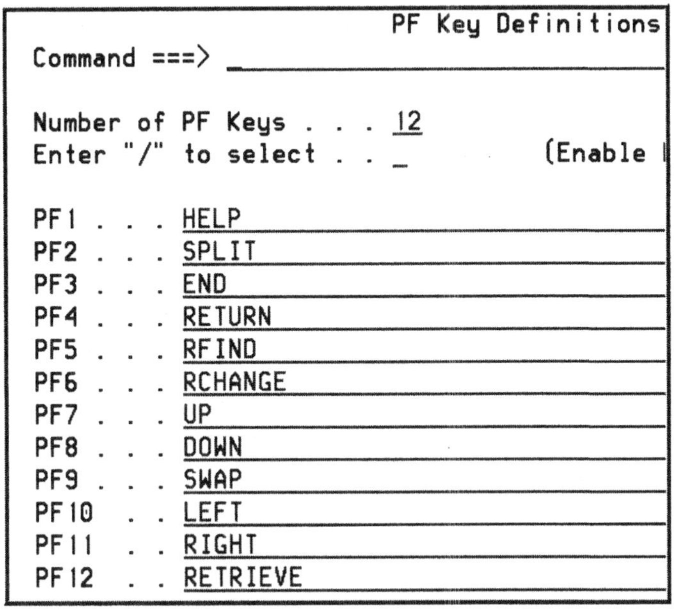

```
                         PF Key Definitions
  Command ===>  _____

  Number of PF Keys . . . 12
  Enter "/" to select . . _            (Enable

  PF 1 . . . HELP_____
  PF2 . . . SPLIT_____
  PF3 . . . END_____
  PF4 . . . RETURN_____
  PF5 . . . RFIND_____
  PF6 . . . RCHANGE_____
  PF7 . . . UP_____
  PF8 . . . DOWN_____
  PF9 . . . SWAP_____
  PF10  . . LEFT_____
  PF11  . . RIGHT_____
  PF12  . . RETRIEVE_____
```

Figure 5-10. Mainframe ISPF PF key definitions

With the VS .NET IDE, you are able to configure your IDE. The VS .NET config-uration options extend far beyond (yet include) the ability to set the keyboard function keys to your personal preference.

Navigate to the My Profile screen view from the Start Page. Notice that the My Profile screen view offers options for you to configure your IDE. Take some time to click each drop-down window and view the available choices. You can always return to the My Profile view later to configure the IDE. Optionally, you can perform advanced-level configuration by selecting Tools ➤ Options. As shown in Figure 5-11, the options to change the font and color styles for the text editor (under the Environment category) are among many other options for configuration.

All of the options shown on the My Profile view are also included on the Options dialog box. Again, for the purposes of this discussion, let's leave the con-figuration options at their default settings. Remember, you can always come back and change them later.

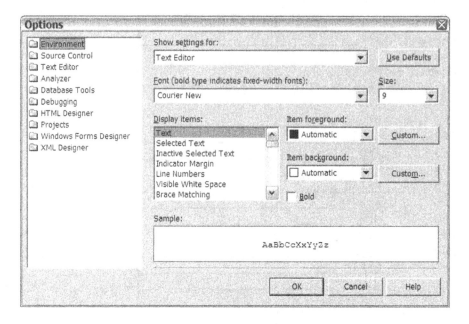

Figure 5-11. The Options dialog box contains advanced configuration options.

Getting Help

Here are a few suggestions for what to do when you want more details on a specific topic:

- Use the Help search feature from within the VS .NET environment.

- Use the Dynamic Help feature from within the VS .NET environment.

- Use the Microsoft VS .NET documentation, which is available outside the VS .NET environment.

- Press F1 while you edit/view programming code and the item in question is selected.

- Take advantage of the various tools available from the VS .NET Start Page.

- Visit the MSDN Web site (http://msdn.microsoft.com/) and search the Knowledge Base.

- Consider adding to your personal library (see the "Books" subsection of the "To Learn More" section at the end of each chapter for recommendations).

- Consider joining an online discussion group and submitting questions (see the "Web Sites" subsection of the "To Learn More" section at the end of each chapter for recommended groups).

More VS .NET

With everything that this chapter has covered so far, you might expect that the topic of VS .NET would have been exhausted already. Perhaps your expectations were set too low. Honestly, VS .NET does so much, has so much to offer, and can be used for so many tasks, you would almost expect it to be able to make coffee and help solve world hunger.

In this section, I discuss two more topics related to VS .NET: customization through integration and automation. For your convenience, I will defer some remaining VS .NET discussions until I cover the actual topics that focus on various *applications* of .NET technologies. Table 5-2 details each forthcoming VS .NET discussion topic and the related chapter that provides a context for specific VS .NET features.

Table 5-2. VS .NET Discussion Topics and Related Chapters

DISCUSSION TOPIC	CHAPTER
Learning about the Solution Explorer, the Task List, and the Properties window	Chapter 6
Using the Class View window, the Object Browser, and IntelliSense	Chapter 7
Leveraging the Server Explorer	Chapter 11
Exploring the Toolbox	Chapter 14

VS .NET Customization Through Integration

Most mainframe installations of ISPF include some *value-added products,* some third-party products that have been added to one of the main menu options. These value-added extensions usually range from various production support and/or disaster recovery software to DASD management and/or security software.

With VS .NET, you also have independent software vendors (ISVs) integrating their extensions into VS .NET. To make this possible, Microsoft offers a program called the Visual Studio .NET Integration Program (VSIP). Microsoft provides support to partners who want to create products that integrate into VS .NET. These products would program against the VS .NET automation object model that Microsoft provides.

Two examples of this type of collaboration that I discuss in this book are as follows:

- Fujitsu Software Corporation's NetCOBOL for .NET product (discussed in the section "COBOL for .NET" later in this chapter)

- Crystal Decisions' Crystal Reports for Visual Studio .NET product (discussed in Chapter 16)

There are many other good products available. In fact, the number of ISVs ready to "plug" their proprietary products into VS .NET is rapidly increasing. This is, by the way, a good thing. The more ISVs that create products for VS .NET, the more certain the long-term success of the .NET platform becomes.

VS .NET Customization Through Automation

You may recall the experience I shared with you earlier that dealt with the creation of an application based on script languages and customized ISPF Dialogs/PDF technologies (see the section "Client-Side Scripting Languages" in Chapter 4). Well, as that experience illustrated, it is certainly possible (and common) to create customized ISPF screens. Typically, mainframe ISPF Dialogs/PDF screen development is aimed at adding value and even improving productivity.

Likewise, you may choose to modify VS .NET with programmatic automations. That is right: You do not need to get into the formal VSIP to be able to programmatically customize VS .NET. The VSIP would be appropriate if you wanted to market your customizations. However, if you are doing something on a smaller or private scale, Microsoft has an answer for your needs: *customization*.

Earlier in this chapter in the section "My Profile," I discussed VS .NET features that allow you to configure your personal preferences in VS .NET. The opportunities available using *customization* go far beyond the options reviewed earlier for *configuration*. Microsoft has made customization of VS .NET possible by exposing the entire Visual Studio .NET automation object model.

What Is an Object Model?

Having an object model is equivalent to building custom ISPF Dialogs/PDF screens and having someone provide information that explains every single detail needed to accomplish your task, at one time. (See the section "Abstraction" in Chapter 4 for details.) For example, imagine if someone created a diagram that laid out all of the ISPF Dialogs/PDF Display, Variable, and Table Services. Additionally, suppose that all of the names of the ISPF development libraries were included in the diagram (for example, ISPSLIB, ISPTLIB, ISPMLIB, and so on). Picture this type of graphical aid presented in a hierarchal (flowchart-style) structure and you now have a rough idea of what an object model looks like.

On the mainframe, you typically used CLIST and/or REXX to implement the logic portions of the ISPF Dialog/PDF modules. With VS .NET, you could use VB .NET or NetCOBOL.

VS .NET provides three options for those looking to program against the Visual Studio .NET automation object model:

- Add-ins

- Wizards

- Macros

Depending on your particular need, one of the preceding three approaches may be more appropriate than the others. Of the three approaches, the macros option may be the easiest way to get started. It offers a Record feature that will build your programming code for you. You can then view the code[3] that it creates for you and modify it as needed.

TIP The program logic associated with macros automation is displayed and edited in the Macros IDE, which is an IDE within the VS .NET IDE. You can access the macro Record feature from the Macros IDE. From within VS .NET, you have two ways to launch the Macros IDE: either select Tools ➤ Macros ➤ Macros IDE or press Alt-F11.

The opportunities available through programmatically manipulating ISPF panels have always interested me. If you share that sort of interest, consider looking further into this topic with VS .NET. Naturally, adding value and gaining productivity would be the motivating factors to undertake this challenge.

---

3. There is one caveat: The code that VS .NET creates for you using the macro Record feature is in VB .NET.

CROSS-REFERENCE   From within the MSDN site
(http://msdn.microsoft.com/), navigate to /library/en-us/vsintro7/
html/vxoriManipulatingDevelopmentEnvironment.asp. This area provides lots of useful information related to VS .NET customization
and automation.

Working Outside of VS .NET

Now it is time to learn about those few times when you might perform a development task outside of the VS .NET environment. With everything you have read,
you may ask, why would anyone ever work outside of VS .NET? After all, it is such a
great IDE.

Well, let's not forget that even on the mainframe, you occasionally found the
need to do some things outside of ISPF. You know, I'm referring to those times that
you chose ISPF Menu Option 6 to access the Command window. Perhaps there
was a mainframe CLIST or TSO command that you needed to execute. In some
cases, you may have exited ISPF completely to work from the TSO READY prompt.

In this section, I review the following examples of common situations in which
temporarily working outside of VS .NET is justified:

- Editing in Notepad

- Executing programs and commands at a command prompt

- Using utilities provided by ISVs

Editing in Notepad

In the section "Microsoft Office and Notepad" in Chapter 3, I emphasized the
importance of learning the tools available on the Windows platform. Notepad is
one of those types of tools. Now I will give you one specific example of needing to
use this tool.

Say that you have developed a great application and deployed it to your production servers. Time passes and one day your application crashes. For the sake of
this example, say that you are away from your desk (and thus away from your great
VS .NET development environment) when the crash happens. You happen to be in

an area where a group of people is fulfilling an operations/production support role and the group is asking you to fix your application. Using the great logging and tracing information output from your application, the group members have narrowed the problem down to one line of code. This troubleshooting information has been logged in a well-publicized report.

Just as you are about to mention that you need to get back to your desk (and back to VS .NET), the president of the company walks in and he's holding the well-publicized report in his hand. The president then asks why the online application is taking so long to fix, given that only one line of code needs to be corrected.

Continuing with this imaginary example, you, thinking quickly, ask one of the production support staff members if you can access the server where your application is running. You see the file that needs to be changed. Knowing that development tools such as VS .NET are not installed on the production server, you launch the Notepad editor. Looking at the file in question, you notice that the file is text based (i.e., HTML with VBScript) and does not require compilation after editing, so you make the one-line correction and save the file. Then, as you are signaling to the production support staff that all has been resolved (using the traditional two-thumbs-up sign), you notice that the president of the company is nodding his head in definite approval.

OK, how is that? I hope that you are convinced that there are some occasions when a very crude, feature-stripped editor such as Notepad (which happens to be available on all Windows servers, even production servers) can be useful.

 CAUTION   It is generally not advisable to edit production files directly while on a production server. It is generally against all modern security standards for an application developer to have access to production servers. It is generally bad practice to immediately deploy program code without taking the code through an extensive quality assurance and change control process.

Executing Programs and Commands at a Command Prompt

A few situations you will encounter will require you to execute programs and commands using VS .NET's command prompt. As Figure 5-12 shows, you access VS .NET's command prompt by clicking the Start button and selecting Programs ➤ Microsoft Visual Studio .NET ➤ Visual Studio .NET Tools ➤ Visual Studio .NET Command Prompt.

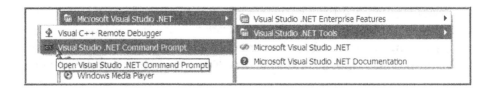

Figure 5-12. Displaying the Visual Studio .NET Command Prompt menu option

For those instances when you need to access the command prompt, you will need to familiarize yourself with a couple of basic DOS commands: CD for changing the directory/path and DIR/P for displaying a list of files in a particular directory. OK, before you drop this book to the floor, let me explain.

If you were teaching someone who was transitioning to the mainframe about ISPF, eventually you would have to mention something about CLIST, right? And what does CLIST contain? TSO commands. So, in this context, look at DOS commands on Windows as being equivalent to TSO commands on the mainframe. In the cases where you occasionally do things outside of VS .NET, I will be sure to provide adequate detail to walk you through some of these tricky areas when appropriate.

The VS .NET command prompt has many uses. However, in Table 5-3 I mention only a few uses that pertain to VS .NET development in addition to the chapters of this book where I discuss them in context.

Table 5-3. Command Prompt Uses and Related Chapters

COMMAND PROMPT USE	CHAPTER
Executing stand-alone programs (EXE files)	Chapter 6
Creating and using strong-named assemblies	Chapter 18
Adding a Serviced Component to COM+	Chapter 19

The Windows Command Prompt

There is *another* command prompt. The other one is referred to as the Windows command prompt, which you launch by clicking the Start button, selecting Run, typing **cmd**, and clicking OK. At the Windows command prompt, you use DOS commands to interact with the operating system. Compare the VS .NET command prompt with the mainframe ISPF Menu Option 6 command. Then, compare the

Windows command prompt with the mainframe command prompt that you access when you totally leave ISPF to go to native TSO.

TIP   When you get a chance, look into using the Windows command prompt to execute the program named DEVENV.EXE. When you execute this program, you will launch VS .NET. Now, imagine that you combined the execution of this program with some other program logic. Wow! The list of automation opportunities you can get yourself into is endless.

The Command Window

This other "command prompt" is actually referred to as the Command window. Additionally, this other command prompt is accessed from *within* the VS .NET IDE. I mention it here just to avoid confusion with the other two command prompts I just discussed.

Let me first briefly mention that the VS .NET IDE has multiple windows (all of which you will learn about in this book). One of those windows is the Command window, which you launch from within the VS .NET IDE by selecting View ➤ Other Windows ➤ Command Window. This VS .NET Command window has two modes: Command and Immediate. In Command mode, you can enter VS .NET IDE commands (as opposed to DOS commands).

TIP   During development debugging, the VS .NET Command window (in either Command mode or Immediate mode) will prove to be very useful. I provide examples of its use in Appendix A.

Using Utilities Provided by ISVs

There are many great products on the market. (It so happens that Microsoft doesn't make all of them.) Many ISVs have leveraged the VSIP and developed products that are integrated right into VS .NET. I mentioned some of these products earlier this chapter in the section "VS .NET Customization Through Integration." Still, some great ISV products are not integrated into VS .NET (for various reasons). By the way, even some of Microsoft's own products are not integrated into VS .NET (yet).

The point being, there will be times when you work outside of VS .NET during the application development life cycle. In some cases, you will access software products via a command prompt (see the section "Executing Programs and Commands at a Command Prompt" earlier in this chapter). In other cases, you will access ISV products by clicking the Start button and selecting Programs.

Some of you will even choose to regularly edit certain file types outside of the VS .NET IDE. There is a product that you can install on your PC that looks and works similar to ISPF. The one that I am aware of is made by Command Technology Corporation (http://www.commandtechnology.com/). The product, SPF/SourceEdit (SPF/SE), is 32-bit application that you can run on all current versions of Windows.

Additionally, companies such as Micro Focus and Fujitsu have great Windows-based IDEs (workbenches) that are all worthy of mention. The challenge you will face with regard to some of the ISV products is choosing *when* to install them and *when not* to install them. With that challenge, I will only advise you to keep integration and simplification in mind. Personally, I try to minimize the number of vendors whose products I use. Microsoft being one vendor, I start to count conservatively from there.

CROSS-REFERENCE   See the sidebar titled "A Word of Caution About Installations" in Chapter 3 to review the recommended considerations before installing software.

Besides that, advising you on each product is beyond the scope of this book. Also, considering that I am not familiar with each and every product on the market (and who is?), it would likely be unethical for me to attempt to persuade you away from one product or the other.

TIP   Keep integration and simplification in mind when you install new products.

It is possible that you will not need to worry *that* much about the available product choices. Some of these product choices will be made for you if you happen to work for a company of considerable size. For better or worse, the person signing the checks (or approving your department's expense budget) ultimately calls the shots. If you have a chance to influence product choices, consider yourself lucky (hence, the value of at least being familiar with the available choices).

Speaking of choices, choices will be made (by you or someone in your organization) regarding the available .NET programming languages. The following section introduces you to the .NET languages *chosen* for discussion in this particular book.

Choosing Your .NET Language

Earlier in this chapter in the "Get Started" section, I discussed the New Project button. After you click that button, the New Project dialog box appears, allowing you to choose project types. I have emphasized (more than once, I think) that the choices you make during your VS .NET installation influence the project types that appear in this dialog box. The upper portion of the New Project dialog box shows an example of the project types (see Figure 5-13) that are language specific. (Your display may differ.)

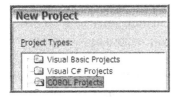

Figure 5-13. The upper portion of the New Project dialog box

When I installed VS .NET, I chose to include VB .NET and C# (pronounced "C sharp"). Later, I acquired NetCOBOL for .NET from Fujitsu and installed it. In this section, I discuss these languages.

CROSS-REFERENCE In addition to the .NET languages provided by Microsoft, ISVs such as Fujitsu are providing .NET languages. At this time, 15 ISVs are developing .NET languages. Visit the Microsoft .NET Language Partners Web site (http://msdn.microsoft.com/vstudio/ partners/language/default.asp) for more information.

VB .NET

The first language I learned after venturing into my own reformation was Visual Basic. As I mentioned in the book's Introduction, my involvement with Visual Basic started with version 5.0. As we (I and the rest of the Visual Basic community) pull ourselves away from Visual Basic 6.0 and gravitate toward VB .NET, I still remember my initial reaction to Visual Basic several years ago: "Wow, so they have created another Common Business Oriented Language!"

Because I had an extensive background in COBOL, learning Visual Basic seemed easy to me (it was all of the prerequisites covered in Chapters 3 and 4 that took more time). After all, Visual Basic was rather English-like and verbose (something that I liked about COBOL). Another deciding factor for me was Visual Basic's market share in the business application world. Coming from the mainframe, I was always comfortable with my marketability (even before Y2K). Naturally, I wanted to maintain or enhance my marketability. Having Visual Basic in my skill set has certainly fulfilled (and continues to fulfill) that requirement. Now, with .NET, I have the opportunity to learn another new language: VB .NET.[4]

Although not everyone will choose to use VB .NET as his or her main .NET programming language, I definitely consider it a wise move to include VB .NET as part of *your* retraining effort. Having said that, I can now disclose that (everywhere possible) the code samples in this book will be presented in both languages: VB .NET and NetCOBOL for .NET. Not that you need to be convinced, but as you comb through the generous amount of tutorial information that is available on MSDN, you will notice that the sample code is written in either C# or VB .NET. Learning VB .NET (and/or C#) will make these tutorial and sample code offerings that much more valuable to you.

 CROSS-REFERENCE By the way, language interoperability and COM Interoperability (COM Interop) are features of .NET that I further discuss in Chapter 19.

As many will tell you, and as you'll soon develop an understanding for, learning to program .NET involves many things. It's much more than just learning

---

4. Generally, the industry refers to VB .NET as a new language rather than just a new version of Visual Basic. Perhaps this is due to a little influence from the Microsoft marketing department, yet the changes *are* significant enough to justify the new language label.

the syntax rules of one language or another. I'll strive to keep emphasizing that your language choice is a lesser issue. I demonstrate this idea later in the section "Developing Your First .NET Program."

COBOL for .NET

As you know, COBOL has come a long way. And now, COBOL has headed into the future with an entry onto the .NET landscape made possible through the partnering of Fujitsu and Microsoft via the Visual Studio .NET Integration Program (VSIP, which I discussed earlier in section "VS .NET Customization Through Integration"). Fujitsu has named this COBOL edition NetCOBOL for .NET. Going forward, I refer to Fujitsu's NetCOBOL for .NET product unofficially as "COBOL .NET".

CROSS-REFERENCE   You can download a free trial version of Fujitsu's NetCOBOL for .NET from Fujitsu Software's Web site (http://www.netcobol.com/products/windows/netcobol.html).

Given the affection that we mainframe programmers have for the COBOL language,[5] COBOL .NET just has to be the coolest thing since the invention of sliced bread. Just think, you can leverage the full power of the .NET Framework using COBOL. Granted, using COBOL .NET still requires that you learn how to use the other portions of .NET. Also, it is still advisable to clear the retraining prerequisites discussed in Chapters 3 and 4. Nevertheless, we have arrived.

As of this book's writing, Fujitsu has included support for several project templates. Therefore, with COBOL .NET, you can create .NET Windows applications. That's not all: Fujitsu has also included support for ASP.NET in their COBOL product. In other words, you can also create Web applications. Now, is that great or what? Obviously, I'm excited about this and you should be too.

---

5. You have got to admit, COBOL is a great language—there is a reason why it has survived for so long. So please pardon my inclusive reference. I believe that I am speaking correctly on behalf of the average reformed mainframe programmer.

What an Opportunity!

I am sure there are those who will say, "But I can already create Windows applications with COBOL." On top of that, some of you may already be using one of various flavors of object-oriented COBOL. My response is this: Try .NET, try VS .NET, and then tell me if you think this whole thing is worth getting excited about. I am betting (and hoping) that the mainframe community realizes what a great opportunity .NET is. I am hoping that we can lay down our gauntlets and join forces with the Web and Windows developers and not waste time criticizing the implementation that Fujitsu (and Microsoft) have made available. Seize the opportunity!

By the way, there are also business reasons to justify being excited about COBOL .NET. COBOL's availability on .NET means that the dream for companies to leverage several investments can now be made a reality. The investments in people as well as the investments in business rule logic can now be leveraged. Not only can the developers get excited, but the managers and executives can get excited as well. As I mentioned in the previous section, I attempt to present all code samples in this book using both COBOL .NET and VB .NET. You will be amazed at the opportunities that you will create for yourself (and your employer) by becoming "bilingual."

What About C#?

Appendix B is a brief primer covering the basics of two additional languages provided by Microsoft: C# (pronounced "C sharp") and J# (pronounced "J sharp"). Otherwise, as mentioned in Chapter 2, many other language choices are available to you—about 20 of them, to be exact. Discussing all of those choices is beyond the scope of this retraining effort.

Regardless of which .NET language (or languages) you end up spending more time with, ultimately you will want to actually develop applications. After all, that is what you do, right? Taking a bilingual approach, the following section provides you with an opportunity to develop simple .NET applications.

Developing Your First .NET Programs

In this section, you will create a .NET program. You will use the Console Application project template type. The application will display text onto the console window. First you will use COBOL .NET and then you will use VB .NET.

COBOL .NET Example

Start your COBOL .NET example as follows:

1. Launch VS .NET.

2. From the Get Started screen view (see Figure 5-14), click New Project to display the dialog box.

Figure 5-14. Select New Project from the Get Started screen.

3. Select COBOL Projects from the Project Types window (as shown in Figure 5-15). Select Console Application from the Templates window. Change the name of the application to **MyFirstCobolExample**, and then click OK.

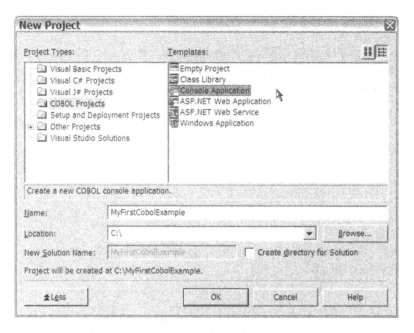

Figure 5-15. The New Project dialog box after making selections and changing the default project name

---

TIP   If you want to see the traditional COBOL line numbers, select Tools ➤ Options ➤ Text Editor ➤ COBOL ➤ Reference Format.

---

4. You should now see an empty program template. All of the lines of code provided should look very familiar to you. Make small adjustments to lines 20 and 80 in the template as shown here:

```
000010 IDENTIFICATION DIVISION.
000020 PROGRAM-ID. MAIN.
000030 ENVIRONMENT DIVISION.
000040 DATA DIVISION.
000050 WORKING-STORAGE SECTION.
000060 PROCEDURE DIVISION.
000070
000080 END PROGRAM MAIN.
```

5. Using the DISPLAY statement and a variable definition that you are familiar with, enter the following basic pieces of code into the console, starting at line 60:

```
000010 IDENTIFICATION DIVISION.
000020 PROGRAM-ID. MAIN.
000030 ENVIRONMENT DIVISION.
000040 DATA DIVISION.
000050 WORKING-STORAGE SECTION.
000060 01 NULL-X PIC X(1).
000070 PROCEDURE DIVISION.
000080     DISPLAY "Hello, .NET World.".
000090     DISPLAY "I Cannot believe how simple this is!".
000100     DISPLAY "Enter X and Press Enter to Exit.".
000110     ACCEPT NULL-X.
000120 END PROGRAM MAIN.
```

6. Before you are able to build (compile) the program, you need to change the project properties. To perform this function, begin by opening the Solution Explorer window.

NOTE The Solution Explorer window may already be open. If it isn't, you can open it by selecting View ➤ Solution Explorer or by pressing Ctrl-Alt-L.

7. In the Solution Explorer window, locate the project file, as shown in Figure 5-16.

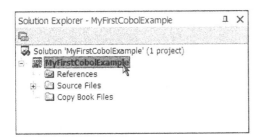

Figure 5-16. Find the project file in the Solution Explorer window.

8. Right-click the MyFirstCobolExample project.

9. Select Properties from the shortcut menu to display the Property Pages window.

10. Locate the entry name (about three lines from the top) and change it from Program1 to **MAIN**. Click OK.

11. It is now time to build (compile) the solution. Select Build ➤ Build Solution. The Output window should appear at the bottom of the screen, indicating that the build was successful.

12. Run the application by selecting Debug ➤ Start.

Congratulations! Your completed code should resemble Figure 5-17.

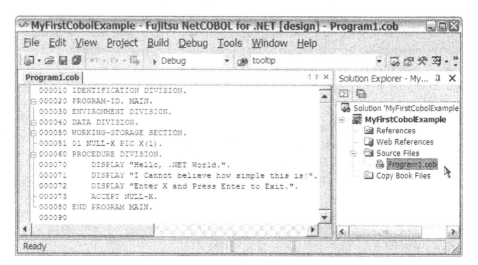

Figure 5-17. The completed code example looks like this.

I provided this sample application to warm you up a little. Naturally, I had to stick with tradition and create a "Hello, World" program to get things started (even if I did change it slightly). Obviously, there is much more to learn about COBOL on the .NET platform, .NET's common language runtime (CLR), XML access, the .NET Framework, and much more. You have gotten off to a good start. I am sure that you will enjoy the learning experiences that await you in each and every remaining chapter.

VB .NET Example

You should be all warmed up now. You have seen some COBOL code (or rather COBOL .NET code). In this section, you will move on to create another console application using VB .NET.

1. Click the New Project button on the Get Started screen, as shown in Figure 5-18.

Figure 5-18. Notice that the previous COBOL .NET example is shown in the recent projects found list.

2. In the New Project dialog box, select Visual Basic Projects from the Project Types window and Console Application from the Templates window. This time you will change the name of the project to **MyFirstVBExample** (see Figure 5-19). After you have done so, click OK.

3. As in the previous section's example, you should now be viewing an empty template. The template contains a very basic skeleton into which you will build your application. The following lines represent your "skeleton code" in the VB .NET console application template:

```
Module Module1
    Sub Main()
    End Sub
End Module
```

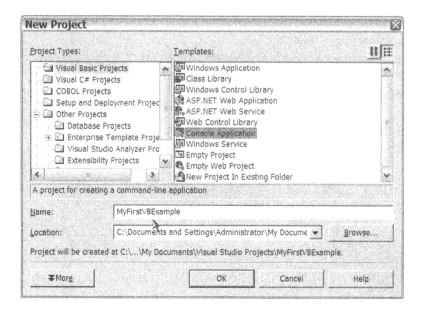

Figure 5-19. The New Project dialog box with VB .NET selections

4. Enter some VB .NET code to display in the console window. In keeping with tradition, use the following lines of code to complete the "Hello, World" application:

```
Module Module1
    Sub Main()
        Console.WriteLine("Hello, .NET World.")
        Console.WriteLine("I Cannot believe how simple this is!")
        Console.WriteLine("Press Enter to Exit.")
        Console.ReadLine()
    End Sub
End Module
```

5. Build (compile) the solution by selecting Build ➤ Build Solution. As before (with the COBOL .NET example), the Output window should appear at the bottom of the screen, indicating that the build was successful. Start the VB .NET application by selecting Debug ➤ Start. (Optionally, you can press F5 to start the application.)

Again, congratulations! You are now an official VB .NET programmer. Your completed console application should resemble the one shown in Figure 5-20.

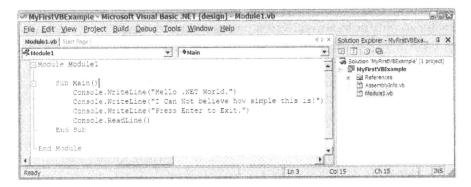

Figure 5-20. The completed VB .NET console application looks like this.

Now that you have completed your obligatory "Hello, World" applications, suffice it to say that you are officially welcomed into the .NET world. You are now prepared for the deep dive into .NET.

Summary

This chapter's goals were as follows:

- To introduce Visual Studio .NET

- To review the .NET project types and project templates

- To choose among the .NET language choices

- To develop your first .NET programs

In this chapter, you reviewed several features of VS .NET. You started with launching the application and then you learned about the application's feature set. You reviewed the project types and project templates, and you explored several specific choices. You then moved on to read about the choice I made in this book of limiting the code chapter code samples to VB .NET and COBOL .NET (two very good language choices). Finally, you created two console "Hello, World" applications.

I trust that the sample "Hello, World" applications whetted your appetite for more .NET code using both COBOL .NET and VB .NET. There is a lot more to come. You have come far, yet you are just getting started. In subsequent chapters, you will learn more about the .NET platform, additional VS .NET features, how to build Web and Windows applications, and more. You will find that each chapter will bring you one (big) step closer to being proficient and comfortable developing .NET applications.

In the next chapter, you will examine yet more program code. In that chapter, you will start with the basics and review common programming tasks at a granular level. From there, you will drill down further to look at Microsoft intermediate language (MSIL). The next chapter concludes with a review of some debugging and testing options. Sound interesting? Good. See you in the next chapter.

To Learn More

The following are some suggested supplemental references to further your retraining effort.

Books

Visual Basic .NET or C#? Which to Choose?, by Dan Appleman (Desaware, 2002):
http://desaware.com/Ebook2L2.htm.

Magazines

.NET Magazine:
http://www.fawcette.com/dotnetmag/
Visual Studio Magazine:
http://www.fawcette.com/vsm/
XML & Web Services Magazine:
http://www.fawcette.com/xmlmag/

Web Sites

Automation Samples for Visual Studio .NET:
http://msdn.microsoft.com/vstudio/downloads/automation.asp
Microsoft .NET Language Partners:
http://msdn.microsoft.com/vstudio/partners/language/default.asp
Microsoft Community (discussion groups, e-newsletters, and so forth):
http://communities2.microsoft.com/
MSDN:
http://msdn.microsoft.com/
NetCOBOL for .NET:
http://www.netcobol.com/products/windows/netcobol.html
Visual Studio .NET home page:
http://msdn.microsoft.com/vstudio/default.asp

CHAPTER 6

The Nuts and Bolts of .NET Programming

Some Things Just Never Change

In this chapter

- Taking a new look at old programming syntax

- Examining Microsoft intermediate language (MSIL)

AT THIS POINT, YOU have dabbled with the prerequisites discussed in Part One of this book. You have installed your Visual Studio .NET (VS .NET) software. You have explored several of the basic features offered in the VS .NET IDE. To top it off, you have written an extremely simple .NET program. Yet you want more.

That is where this chapter begins. Get prepared to cover several programming elements. You will examine the programming syntax that you would expect any language or platform to support. To keep it interesting for you, this chapter presents code examples in both the COBOL .NET[1] and Visual Basic .NET (VB .NET) syntax (being bilingual is your chosen direction, after all). However, there is no need to stop there.

You will then take a look under the hood at the Microsoft intermediate language (MSIL or IL) code. Those days of peeking at assembler language will seem just like yesterday as you are reminded of the relationship assembler has with COBOL (and that MSIL has with any .NET language).

Taking a New Look at Old Programming Syntax

You are eager to implement complex business rules in your programs, right? As you know, simple programming statements hold even complex programming

---

1. In this chapter and throughout this book, I use "COBOL .NET" as a casual, unofficial reference to Fujitsu's NetCOBOL for .NET product.

logic together. This is true regardless of the programming language and regardless of the platform. Therefore, this chapter will address the following questions:

- How do you go about implementing the various programming elements in .NET?

- To what extent can you leverage your current COBOL programming skills?

- Does .NET change some of the basics of COBOL syntax?

Certainly, you've implemented conditional and looping logic many times before. Practically every program you've written has contained variable declarations—some of them even containing constants. But now you're dealing with .NET and it's time to see what's changed and what's stayed the same when it comes to the common programming syntax. I use the following areas to organize this discussion:

- Defining data items

- Coding logic statements

- Noting observations

- Using the VS .NET Solution Explorer

Perspective Check

Trying to see the technical world through the eyes of another is an interesting challenge. Trying to develop a guide (such as this book) that is useful for a cross-section of the mainframe community is no less of a challenge. This is *one* book, yet the mainframe community certainly is made up of more than just *one* type of mainframe programmer. Yes, we are a diverse group. So, I have to request a couple of things from you (if you don't mind).

To begin with, please keep in mind the objective of this book: to assist *all* (or as many as possible) of our mainframe brothers and sisters who are looking at .NET as a vehicle for a "technology transition" (remember, the *reformation*). Next, keep in mind that some of us have never programmed outside of the 3270-Rumba-mainframe-JCL-VSAM-type environment.

Please be conscious of the fact that not everyone reading this book has experience creating mainframe applications on the Win32 platform, compiled using a Windows-based tool and uploaded to run on the host. Some among us have not developed COBOL applications using a Win32 tool and then executed modules on the Windows platform. Finally, not all of us "mainframers" have had the pleasure of coding in object-oriented COBOL.

I am reminding myself of these facts as well. Although my goal is to provide value in *each* chapter for *every* reader, I realize that some chapters will be of more interest to you than others will. You may prefer to simply skim this section (or others). However, skipping entire sections may yield unpredictable results. Therefore, I do not recommend taking that approach.

Defining Data Items

On the mainframe, when you coded COBOL logic, you declared variables, structures, literals, and constants in your program. You were able to do this in your COBOL program's File Section, Working-Storage Section, or Linkage Section. You used the COBOL PICTURE clause to identify the type of data that you planned to store in the field.

For perspective, let's continue. To complete your mainframe COBOL field definition scenario, you simply used one of three characters (in your PICTURE clause) to identify the type of data: either "A," "X," or "9" for alphabetic, alphanumeric, or numeric, respectively. When you planned to perform calculations with your numeric data or had a subscript (index) in the Working-Storage Section, you were advised to add the USAGE clause. Once you had the USAGE clause in your code, you would typically choose between COMP and COMP-3 (COMP was the abbreviation for COMPUTATIONAL) depending on your need.

To complete your mainframe COBOL field definitions, you chose whether or not to add implicit or explicit decimals or other printable characters in your PICTURE clause. Then, after explicitly specifying the exact length of your field, you decided whether or not to add a VALUE clause. The VALUE clause was useful for assigning an initial value to your new field.

Well, guess what? With one caveat, practically *all* of your prior mainframe knowledge (when it comes to basic COBOL syntax) is transferable to the .NET platform.

The caveat? You will only use this familiar syntax and terminology (i.e., File Section, Working-Storage Section, and so forth) when you use COBOL .NET[2] as your .NET language of choice. Given that you are assuming a bilingual programming retraining approach (COBOL .NET and VB .NET), you already have a head start.

---

2. Just a kind reminder: "COBOL .NET" is my own unofficial reference to Fujitsu's NetCOBOL for .NET product.

So now you'll examine some code snippets to see how this looks in practice (both past and current). The legacy mainframe COBOL code snippet in Listing 6-1 should look familiar.

Listing 6-1. Legacy Mainframe COBOL Code

```
Data Division.
File Section.
. . .
Working-Storage Section.
77  My-First-Number      Pic S9(4) USAGE IS COMP.
77  My-Second-Number     Pic S9(9) USAGE IS COMP-3.
77  My-Third-Number      Pic 9(3)V99.
. . .
Linkage Section.
. . .
Procedure Division.
. . .
```

Listing 6-1 shows an example of defining variables. Although you will not perform a strict one-to-one type conversion (from legacy COBOL to COBOL .NET), the code snippet in Listing 6-1 will help define the context for further discussion.

TIP From within the VS .NET IDE, while you have an existing project open, the Solution Explorer window is available to provide full access to all files that exist in your .NET solution. Learning to navigate in this window will increase your productivity during development. Be sure to familiarize yourself with the various pop-up context windows (right-click and so forth) that are accessible from within the Solution Explorer window.

COBOL .NET Example

To convert the legacy COBOL example definitions in Listing 6-1 to COBOL .NET definitions (declarations), you have a choice to make. You need to decide whether to use .NET data types directly (as object references) or to use the COBOL .NET equivalent data types that are intrinsically supported. First, you'll take a look at the code, and then I'll discuss this topic further.

Using a Console Application as my Visual Studio .NET (VS .NET) COBOL template type, I have created a COBOL project and named it DefineDataTypesSampleCobol. The COBOL .NET code sample (copied from the Program1.cob module) is presented in Listing 6-2.

Listing 6-2. COBOL .NET Program Showing Fields Being Declared

```
000010 IDENTIFICATION DIVISION.
000020 PROGRAM-ID. MAIN.
000030 ENVIRONMENT DIVISION.
000040 CONFIGURATION SECTION.
000050 REPOSITORY.
000060* .NET Framework Classes
000070    CLASS SYS-INT16 AS "System.Int16"
000080    CLASS SYS-INT32 AS "System.Int32"
000090    CLASS SYS-DOUBLE AS "System.Double".
000100*
000110 DATA DIVISION.
000120 WORKING-STORAGE SECTION.
000130* Declare Data Items with COBOL.NET Data Types
000140    77  My-First-Number-Intrinsic  PIC S9(4) USAGE IS COMP-5.
000150    77  My-First-Number-Int8Demo   PIC S9(5) USAGE IS COMP-5.
000160    77  My-Second-Number-Intrinsic PIC S9(9) USAGE IS COMP-5.
000170    77  My-Third-Number-Intrinsic USAGE IS COMP-2.
000180* Declare Data Items using .NET Data Types
000190    77  My-First-Number-ObjectRef  OBJECT REFERENCE SYS-INT16.
000200    77  My-Second-Number-ObjectRef OBJECT REFERENCE SYS-INT32.
000210    77  My-Third-Number-ObjectRef  OBJECT REFERENCE SYS-DOUBLE.
000220
000230    01 NULL-X PIC X(1).
000240 LINKAGE SECTION.
000250*
000260 PROCEDURE DIVISION.
000270* Move numeric literal to Data Item
000280     MOVE 32767 TO My-First-Number-Int8Demo.
000290     MOVE 32767 TO My-First-Number-Intrinsic.
000300
000310     Display "Pic5 " My-First-Number-Int8Demo
000320     Display "Pic4 " My-First-Number-Intrinsic
000330
000340     DISPLAY "Enter X and Press Enter to Exit.".
000350     ACCEPT NULL-X.
000360*
000370 END PROGRAM  MAIN.
```

NOTE   On lines 20 and 370, the PROGRAM-ID has been changed to
MAIN. You will need to modify the ENTRY NAME on the PROPERTY
PAGES for this project to reflect the value of "MAIN." I generally follow
this approach in the remaining samples in this chapter.

As you can see, the code is not performing any logic yet, hence the empty Procedure Division. You will fill in the Procedure Division in a later section (in the
section titled "Logic Statements"). Notice that there is a correlation between the
fields suffixed with "Intrinsic" and those suffixed with "ObjectRef". The first set
of fields (lines 140 through 170) consists of COBOL .NET data types that have an
equivalent mapping to the corresponding .NET data type.

CROSS-REFERENCE   I expand on the topic of variable declaration and
include examples of other data types (i.e., Strings and Booleans) in the
section "Logic Statements" later in this chapter. There are other intrinsically supported data types. Please refer to the COBOL .NET
documentation for a complete list.

You may have noticed that I haven't yet discussed a few things in the COBOL
.NET code in Listing 6-2. For example, lines 70 through 90 present an example of
using three classes from the .NET Framework. I discuss this type of .NET
Framework usage and much more in Chapter 7.

Additionally, notice the use of the REPOSITORY paragraph on line 50. The
REPOSITORY paragraph represents an area where you will store information
about classes, interfaces, functions, and properties. In the previous COBOL .NET
sample code, you are using the REPOSITORY as a place to connect your "internal"
variables (those defined with the "ObjectRef" suffix) to the class name of the referenced .NET Framework class. Again, when I discuss the .NET Framework in
Chapter 7, you will see much more usage of the REPOSITORY paragraph.

The OBJECT REFERENCE clause may look new to most of you. However, if you
refer back to your advanced legacy mainframe COBOL experience, you may recall
coding statements that included a USAGE IS POINTER clause. You would have
used this clause following the PICTURE clause for a data item definition. Subsequently, you were likely to use the ADDRESS OF special register along with a SET
statement. Sound familiar? Good, then you have an idea of what the OBJECT
REFERENCE is accomplishing in the COBOL .NET example in Listing 6-2 (lines

190 through 210). Nevertheless, I further discuss this topic of referencing objects in Chapter 9.

Choosing Between COBOL .NET Data Types and .NET Data Types

Typically, you would not include a complete set of definitions using both approaches as I have in the COBOL .NET code example in Listing 6-2. I did this just for demonstration purposes. These declarations demonstrate a choice that is available when you code your COBOL .NET declarations. So, what difference does it make when you choose one way or the other to define your variables?

There is one opinion that says to give preference to the COBOL .NET data types over the .NET data types. A few reasons that may support this opinion are as follows:

- If you use .NET data types that are value types,[3] the entire object, not just the pointer, is allocated in your Working-Storage area.

- If you use .NET data types, you will need to write extra lines of programming code.

- Fujitsu must have had a good reason for going to the trouble of making sure that many of the COBOL .NET data types map directly to the .NET data types. The opposite was more likely—they probably wanted to map all of the .NET data types back to COBOL .NET data types.

There is another opinion that says to go ahead and create the object references and use the .NET Framework classes directly. Some reasons that may support this opinion are as follows:

- The .NET Framework classes have valuable built-in methods and properties.

- The more you use the .NET Framework classes, the quicker you will learn how to leverage .NET technology in general.

- The average VB .NET programmer will be able to understand and maintain your COBOL .NET code.

Then, I have my opinion, which is plan to use both data types. When possible, use the .NET Framework classes (including the .NET data types). Otherwise,

---

3. I explain the concept of value types further in Chapters 8 and 9.

use the COBOL .NET data types, *but be careful*. Please keep in mind the following considerations:

> *First consideration:* For those who would avoid the .NET data types just because of the way that the Working-Storage memory allocation is handled for value types, I kindly remind them of the last time that COBOL programmers made design sacrifices to save a negligible amount of memory (remember Y2K?). Times have changed, and memory is cheaper and more available.

> *Second consideration:* The built-in properties and methods available to users of .NET data types offer significant value. Yes, there is the *ToString* method that can convert the typical .NET data type to a *String*. I say, go for any chance to use .NET Framework classes and any built-in methods and/or properties. To me, this type of "reusability" is one important step toward an OOP mindset.

> *Third consideration:* Use the .NET Framework members as much as possible. The more you use them, the more familiar you will become with them. This will lead to a definite increase in programming productivity. How? You will begin to use many *other* built-in methods and properties and thus write less *duplicate* code. In Chapter 7, you will explore many of these .NET Framework members.

> *Fourth consideration:* Plan to use both approaches, but *do* be careful. When you need to manipulate indexes and perform mathematical problems, the COBOL .NET data types are likely your best choices. When you need to pass data items between .NET programs, typically you will choose the .NET data types.[4] Nevertheless, choose your data types carefully. For example, you could end up inadvertently truncating your data. In some cases, the compiler will produce code for you that I feel is not intuitive. I believe this will be a source of hidden program bugs for those who approach this topic without caution.

Let's dig deeper into the fourth consideration. Take, for example, the following COBOL .NET code snippet:

```
...PIC S9(4) USAGE IS COMP-5.
```

As explained in Fujitsu's COBOL .NET documentation, this type of data declaration is intended to map directly to the .NET type *System.Int16*, a 16-bit signed

---

4. In Chapter 20, I discuss data marshaling. At that time, I make a distinction between the concerns of marshaling data items (whether native .NET data types or not) and objects (whether managed .NET objects or not).

integer. (I prove later in the section "Examining Microsoft Intermediate Language" that this mapping actually does occur.)

This is a good thing. However, it is not so good when you attempt to move data into your COBOL .NET data type field. As it turns out, the maximum *useable* value for a field, using the definition shown previously, is 9999. You might say, "Chris, that is fine. It is, after all, a four-digit PICTURE clause."

The concern that I have is that it *does* map directly to a 16-bit signed integer .NET data type. This becomes more of a concern when you take into consideration that (according to .NET's documentation) the 2-byte System.Int16 data type should have a maximum value range of –32768 to 32767. Please take note that this value range is significantly more than maximum *useable* value 9999 (the word "useable" is a hint here). Well, if you move the value of 32767 to the "intrinsically" supported COBOL .NET data type, your high-order digit is truncated, resulting in a stored value of 2767. As shown in the following code snippet, the value of 32767 is being moved to the field in question (My-First-Number-Intrinsic):

```
...
000270* Move numeric literal to Data Item
000280     MOVE 32767 TO My-First-Number-Int8Demo.
000290     MOVE 32767 TO My-First-Number-Intrinsic.
000300
000310     Display "Pic5 " My-First-Number-Int8Demo
000320     Display "Pic4 " My-First-Number-Intrinsic
000330
000340     DISPLAY "Enter X and Press Enter to Exit.".
000350     ACCEPT NULL-X.
000360*
000370 END PROGRAM  MAIN.
```

How nice! I do not think so. Interestingly enough, the compiler generates the following warning message and compilation completes with a "Build Succeeded" message:

```
JMN3328I-W  WHEN NUMERIC LITERAL IS MOVED TO 'MY-FIRST-NUMBER-INTRINSIC'
            IN MOVE STATEMENT,OVERFLOW IS OCCURRED.
```

Doesn't this remind you of "condition code 4"s from the legacy mainframe COBOL compiles? Because compilation was usually allowed to complete with a "condition code 4," some developers habitually ignored those innocent warning messages. Later, after they got burned a few times, experienced developers learned that there is no such thing as an innocent warning message. I believe those lessons learned still apply here with COBOL .NET.

NOTE I find it somewhat interesting that attempting to move 99999 into the field also produces an OVERFLOW compile error. However, in this case, the severity of the message is high enough to prevent compilation from continuing. Following the attempted compilation, the VS .NET IDE Task window will display the recommended correction.

You may ask, "Why not just bump the PICTURE size from 9(4) to 9(5)?" Well, if you do that, you are no longer mapping directly to the .NET System.Int16 data type; rather, you are mapping to the unsigned *Int8* data type (also known as *System.BYTE*). I prove this in the section "Examining Microsoft Intermediate Language," where you will take a look at the MSIL that is being generated behind the scenes.

To that, perhaps you might respond, "So what, I'm mapping to the Int8 instead of System.Int16. At least the number value isn't truncated now." The thing that puzzled me is that if you're mapping to Int8, then you're essentially mapping to the .NET data type System.BYTE. As you may have guessed, System.BYTE has a value range of 0 to 255. Therefore, why is the value of 32767 *not* being truncated, given that it clearly exceeds 255?

As it turns out, by changing the PICTURE size from 9(4) to 9(5), you've requested that the compiler create a zero-based, *one-dimensional array*. Isn't it nice of the compiler to do this for you? (I'm being sarcastic, by the way.) Honestly, if I really wanted to create an array, I'd prefer to do so explicitly to make what's *really* going on more obvious.

 NOTE An *array* is similar to the tables (sometimes referred to as arrays) that you created during your legacy mainframe COBOL experiences. With tables, you used the OCCURS clause to define how many elements were contained in the table. Sometimes you would create single-level (or one-dimensional) tables. Other times, you would create double-level (or two-dimensional) tables. Then, using a subscript or an index, you would retrieve the individual elements of your table (or array). To access the first element, you would access the element item that had an index or subscript value of "1". So, you were working with a 1-based array.

Now, what do you think about using the COBOL .NET data types? I guess this is what Fujitsu meant by providing "intrinsic" support. One minute you are mapping to the System.Int16 data type (also known as the *Short* data type) and the next minute you are mapping to a one-dimensional array of type Int8.

NOTE The Help text provided with VS .NET does state that there is general memory overhead associated with arrays ("...*an array uses extra memory for the array itself and also for each dimension ... this overhead is currently 12 bytes plus 8 bytes for each dimension. ...*"). So, if you are avoiding object references in an attempt to save memory, you may be introducing more memory usage than the amount you are trying to save.

My suggestion is to choose your approach to creating your data types carefully. Choose your data types even more carefully. Plan to use both approaches: COBOL .NET intrinsic data types and *native* .NET data types. You will notice that in the sample code in this book, I restrict my usage of these COBOL .NET data types to manipulating indexes and some arithmetic functionality. To Fujitsu's credit, I am glad they built in the ability to declare data items using either approach. That way, you *do* have a choice.

To Be or Not to Be CLS Compliant

Why does Fujitsu care (and why should you care) whether the COBOL .NET language provides direct intrinsic support for the .NET data types? The question of being Common Language Specification (CLS) compliant is what it boils down to. When you take the bold step to .NET-enable your language compiler (as Fujitsu has), being CLS compliant is one measure of just how .NET-enabled the language compiler is. Although there are many requirements for such compliance, supporting (intrinsically) the main .NET data types is obviously one such requirement. (See the "Web Sites" subsection in the "To Learn More" section at the end of this chapter for a CLS-related link.)

Have I exhausted the "data type with COBOL .NET" topic? All right, this seems like a good breaking point. In the next section you'll look at some VB .NET code.

VB .NET Example

Using VB .NET, I demonstrate the declaration of three numeric fields as I did in the preceding legacy COBOL and COBOL .NET code examples. Again, using a Console Application as my VB .NET template type, I have created a VB .NET project and named it DefineDataTypesSampleVB. Listing 6-3 shows the VB .NET code sample (copied from the Module1.vb module).

Listing 6-3. VB .NET Code Showing Two Approaches for the Declaration of Three Data Items

```
Module Module1
    Sub Main()
        'Declare Data Items using VB .NET Data Types
        Dim MyFirstNumberVBNET As Short
        Dim MySecondNumberVBNET As Integer
        Dim MyThirdNumberVBNET As Double

        'Declare Data Items using Native .NET Data Types
        Dim MyFirstNumberNative As System.Int16
        Dim MySecondNumberNative As System.Int32
        Dim MyThirdNumberNative As System.Double

    End Sub
End Module
```

In the VB .NET code sample in Listing 6-3, you will notice that three data items have been *dimensioned* (declared) using the VB .NET data types. Then, a similar set of data items has been declared using the native .NET data types.

In the case of VB .NET, there truly is *not* a difference between the VB .NET data types and the native .NET data types. They (intuitively) map exactly as you would expect them to. Of course, I have verified this by taking a quick look at the MSIL. (Yes, I demonstrate this in the section "Examining Microsoft Intermediate Language.") With VB .NET, use either approach.

Just to be fair, I decided that even the VB .NET sample deserved the same scrutiny as that of the COBOL .NET sample. I wanted to move a "maximum" value numeric literal into the Int16 and Short data type data items. The code snippet in Listing 6-4 demonstrates this.

Listing 6-4. VB .NET Code Showing a Numeric Literal Being Moved into the Data Items

```
Module Module1
    Sub Main()
. . .
        'Place a numeric literal in Data Item
        MyFirstNumberVBNET = 32767
        MyFirstNumberNative = 32767
    End Sub
End Module
```

As expected, both fields accepted the maximum value of 32767 without any truncation.

> **TIP**   You have a choice between copying and pasting this source code or typing it in (line by line). If you copy and paste you can rest assured that the sample code will work (this approach avoids typos). On the other hand, you do want to start coding soon for real learning. Here, I just want to point out that both approaches offer value. (This applies to both the VB .NET samples and the COBOL .NET samples.)

Naturally, you can only do so much with just data item declarations. In fact, you can't really *do* anything. Therefore, let's look at the logic statements. I like to refer to logic statements as the "glue" that holds everything else together.

Logic Statements

Logic statements represent the real purpose of your application. After all, the reason that you are creating an application in the first place is to implement business rules, providing some type of valuable service to your business (whether directly or indirectly). Regardless of the platform, regardless of the language, this is true.[5] You have written logic statements in your legacy mainframe COBOL applications. This requirement will remain constant, even with .NET.

---

5.   Unless, of course, you are writing programs as a hobby sitting at home.

In your previous programming experiences, have you ever created an infinite loop? Granted, an infinite loop is not something to be proud of. Nonetheless, you are certainly familiar with the concept of conditional logic, even if the condition is never met. Of course, a program is not necessarily made up of looping logic alone.

In the samples that follow, you will take a look at logic used to perform (finite) loops. Additionally, you will review other types of logic statements (e.g., case-type statements and comparative operators). I even throw in a few intrinsic COBOL functions. In this section, you will briefly review some of the more common types of logic statements. The following types of logic statements are included in the sample code:

- Conditional logic

- Constants

- Intrinsic functions

In the following COBOL .NET code sample, most (if not all) of what you will see should be familiar to you. I have coded this particular sample program for these reasons:

- To demonstrate that you *can* use most of the COBOL syntax that you are already familiar with in .NET

- To provide a comfortable context from which to derive future code samples for the later chapters

Following the COBOL .NET code sample, I include a VB .NET code sample. With the VB .NET sample, my assumption is that this will be a good opportunity for you to learn some more of the VB .NET syntax basics.

COBOL .NET Example

Using a Console Application[6] as my VS .NET COBOL template type, I have created a COBOL project and named it LogicSampleCobol. Listing 6-5 presents the COBOL .NET code sample (copied from the Program1.cob module).

---

6. In Chapter 13, I introduce other template types (i.e., Windows, ASP.NET, and Web services). For now, I am limiting the samples to the use of the Console Application template. This is intended to encourage more focus on other targeted topics.

Listing 6-5. A COBOL .NET Sample Program Demonstrating the Use of Basic Syntax

```
000010 IDENTIFICATION DIVISION.
000020 PROGRAM-ID. MAIN.
000030 ENVIRONMENT DIVISION.
000040 CONFIGURATION SECTION.
000050 REPOSITORY.
000060*
000070*** .NET Framework Classes
000080*
000090      CLASS SYS-STRING AS "System.String"
000100      CLASS SYS-INTEGER AS "System.Int32"
000110      CLASS SYS-BOOLEAN AS "System.Boolean".
000120*
000130 DATA DIVISION.
000140 WORKING-STORAGE SECTION.
000150*
000160*** Declare Data Items using .NET Data Types
000170*
000180 01 MY-String OBJECT REFERENCE SYS-STRING.
000190 01 MY-Integer OBJECT REFERENCE SYS-INTEGER.
000200 01 MY-Boolean OBJECT REFERENCE SYS-BOOLEAN.
000210*
000220*** Declare Data Items with COBOL .NET Data Types
000230*
000240 01 My-Index PIC S9(9) COMP-5.
000250 01 My-SecondIndex PIC S9(9) COMP-5.
000260 01 My-Accum PIC S9(9) COMP-5.
000270 01 My-Flag PIC 1 USAGE BIT.
000280      88 My-Flag-True       Value B'1'.
000290      88 My-Flag-False      Value B'0'.
000300 01 NULL-X PIC X(1).
000310 01 SystemDate.
000320      05 YYYY PIC 9999.
000330      05 MM   PIC 99.
000340      05 DD   PIC 99.
000350 01 My-FixedLengthString PIC X(50).
000360*
000370*** Demonstrate creation of Table-Array
000380*
000390  01 MONTH-VALUES.
000400      05      PIC X(09) VALUE "January".
000410      05      PIC X(09) VALUE "February".
000420      05      PIC X(09) VALUE "March".
```

```
000430      05        PIC X(09) VALUE "April".
000440      05        PIC X(09) VALUE "May".
000450      05        PIC X(09) VALUE "June".
000460      05        PIC X(09) VALUE "July".
000470      05        PIC X(09) VALUE "August".
000480      05        PIC X(09) VALUE "September".
000490      05        PIC X(09) VALUE "October".
000500      05        PIC X(09) VALUE "November".
000510      05        PIC X(09) VALUE "December".
000520 01  MONTH-TABLE REDEFINES  MONTH-VALUES.
000530      05  MONTH-ITEMS OCCURS 12 TIMES.
000540          10 MONTH-ITEM      PIC X(9).
000550 PROCEDURE DIVISION.
000560*
000570*** Demonstrate Intrinsic Function accessing System Date
000580*
000590      MOVE FUNCTION CURRENT-DATE TO SystemDate
000600      DISPLAY "Today is " SystemDate
000610
000620*
000630*** Demonstrate Boolean fields, Constants, Conditional/Computational Logic
000640*
000650      PERFORM UNTIL My-Flag = B"1"
000660                 ADD 1 TO My-Index
000670        IF My-Index > 12
000680           SET MY-Boolean to B"1"
000690           SET My-Flag to MY-Boolean
000700        END-IF
000710      END-PERFORM
000720      IF My-Flag-True Then
000730         SET MY-String to "The 88 Level Boolean is now set to TRUE"
000740         SET My-FixedLengthString to MY-String
000750         DISPLAY My-FixedLengthString
000760      END-IF
000770*
000780*** Demonstrate usage of Conditional and Computational Logic
000790*
000800      PERFORM VARYING My-SecondIndex
000805         FROM 0 BY 1 UNTIL My-SecondIndex = My-Index
000810         COMPUTE My-Accum = My-SecondIndex + 1
000820      END-PERFORM
000830      SET MY-Integer to My-Accum
000840*
000850*** Demonstrate Intrinsic Functions, Conditional and Computational Logic
```

```
000860*
000870      MOVE 1 to My-Index
000880      INITIALIZE My-FixedLengthString
000890      PERFORM 12 TIMES
000900          EVALUATE MONTH-ITEM (My-Index)
000910              WHEN "December"
000920              WHEN "January"
000930              WHEN "February"
000940                  STRING
000950                      MONTH-ITEM (My-Index) DELIMITED BY " "
000960                      " " DELIMITED BY SIZE
000970                      "is" DELIMITED BY SIZE
000980                      " " DELIMITED BY SIZE
000990                      "Winter" DELIMITED BY SIZE
001000                      INTO My-FixedLengthString
001010                  END-STRING
001020                  DISPLAY My-FixedLengthString
001030                  INITIALIZE My-FixedLengthString
001040              WHEN "March"
001050              WHEN "April"
001060              WHEN "May"
001070                  STRING
001080                      MONTH-ITEM (My-Index) DELIMITED BY " "
001090                      " " DELIMITED BY SIZE
001100                      "is" DELIMITED BY SIZE
001110                      " " DELIMITED BY SIZE
001120                      "Spring" DELIMITED BY SIZE
001130                      INTO My-FixedLengthString
001140                  END-STRING
001150                  DISPLAY My-FixedLengthString
001160                  INITIALIZE My-FixedLengthString
001170              WHEN "June"
001180              WHEN "July"
001190              WHEN "August"
001200                  STRING
001210                      MONTH-ITEM (My-Index) DELIMITED BY " "
001220                      " " DELIMITED BY SIZE
001230                      "is" DELIMITED BY SIZE
001240                      " " DELIMITED BY SIZE
001250                      "Summer" DELIMITED BY SIZE
001260                      INTO My-FixedLengthString
001270                  END-STRING
001280                  DISPLAY My-FixedLengthString
001290                  INITIALIZE My-FixedLengthString
```

```
001300              WHEN "September"
001310              WHEN "October"
001320              WHEN "November"
001330                  STRING
001340                      MONTH-ITEM (My-Index) DELIMITED BY " "
001350                      " " DELIMITED BY SIZE
001360                      "is" DELIMITED BY SIZE
001370                      " " DELIMITED BY SIZE
001380                      "Autumn" DELIMITED BY SIZE
001390                      INTO My-FixedLengthString
001400                  END-STRING
001410                  DISPLAY My-FixedLengthString
001420                  INITIALIZE My-FixedLengthString
001430          END-EVALUATE
001440          ADD 1 to My-Index
001450      END-PERFORM
001460      DISPLAY "Enter X and Press Enter to Exit.".
001470      ACCEPT NULL-X.
001480*
001490 END PROGRAM MAIN.
```

If you were to run this program, you would produce a console window display as shown in Figure 6-1.

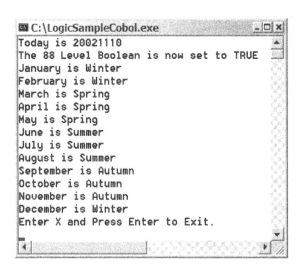

Figure 6-1. The console window display produced by the LogicSampleCobol program

Please take a moment and familiarize yourself with this program. Remember, you will *derive* future sample code snippets from this sample application.

TIP You have probably noticed that I included comments in the sample code. Even with .NET, good programming practices still apply. Rather than restate what has already been included in the preceding sample code (if you do not mind), I will simply refer you to the following sample code comment lines: 370, 570, 630, 780, and 850. That is it—a new look at some old programming practices.

NOTE The "current date" logic (lines 590 and 600) will retrieve and display your system date at runtime.

Before you move on to the VB .NET sample code, I would like to mention a great VS .NET feature at this time: the Clipboard Ring.

VS .NET Feature: The Clipboard Ring

During your coding experience, there will be times when rather than repeatedly type something you'll choose to copy and paste. Everyone does this. It's not because we're lazy; rather, we're cost conscious and seek to improve our productivity. Well, with the VS .NET IDE feature called the *Clipboard Ring*, your productivity just received another boost.

To use the Clipboard Ring (while viewing your .NET program in the VS .NET IDE), you will first need to display the Toolbox. To do this, choose View ➤ Toolbox. The icon and menu option associated with the Toolbox are shown in Figure 6-2.

Figure 6-2. The Toolbox menu option and icon

The next step is to select the program code lines that you want to copy (or cut). You can use the options displayed on the Standard toolbar for this. Notice that in Figure 6-3, I have selected three lines of code and subsequently copied them.

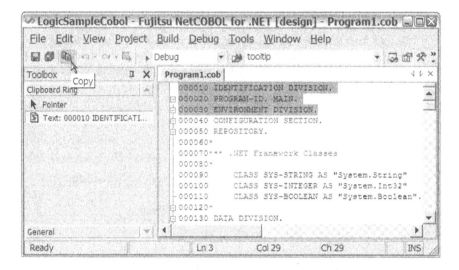

Figure 6-3. I have selected three lines of code and copied them. An item now shows in the Clipboard Ring.

You will notice that after "copying" the selected text, an item shows up in the Clipboard Ring (as shown in Figure 6-3). Items will continue to accumulate as you repeat the select and copy steps. You will realize the true value of the Clipboard Ring as you drag and drop these accumulated items one by one (in any order) from the Clipboard Ring to targeted areas in your program modules. Whether you are working with text-formatted files in your COBOL .NET projects or your VB .NET projects, you will notice that this great VS .NET IDE feature is available.

VB .NET Example

Staying with the Console Application template type, I have created a new project in VS .NET with VB .NET as the language choice. The new project is named LogicSampleVB. Listing 6-6 presents the VB .NET code sample (copied from the Module1.vb module[7]).

---

7. In your own, real-life projects, you will choose to name your modules appropriately. For simplicity's sake, I left the modules with their default names.

Listing 6-6. A VB .NET Sample Program Demonstrating the Use of Basic Syntax

```
Module Module1
    Sub Main()
        '*
        '*** Declare Data Items using .NET Data Types
        '*
        Dim MYString As System.String
        Dim MYInteger As System.Int32
        Dim MYBoolean As System.Boolean
        '*
        '*** Declare Data Items with Visual Basic.NET Data Types
        '*
        Dim MyIndex As Integer
        Dim MySecondIndex As Integer
        Dim MyAccum As Integer
        Dim MyFlag As Boolean
        Dim systemDate As Date
        Dim MyFixedLengthString As String
        '*
        '*** Demonstrate creation of String Array
        '*
        Dim MonthValues() As String = _
        {"January", "February", "March", _
        "April", "May", "June", _
        "July", "August", "September", _
        "October", "November", "December"}
        '*
        '*** Demonstrate Intrinsic Function accessing System Date
        '*
        systemDate = Now
        Console.WriteLine("Today is " & systemDate.ToShortDateString)
        '*
        '*** Demonstrate Booleans, Constants, and Conditional/Computational Logic
        '*
        Do Until MyFlag = True
            MyIndex += 1
            If MyIndex > 12 Then
                MYBoolean = True
                MyFlag = MYBoolean
            End If
        Loop
        If MyFlag Then
            MYString = "The Boolean is now set to TRUE"
```

```vb
            MyFixedLengthString = MYString
            Console.WriteLine(MyFixedLengthString)
        End If
        '*
        '*** Demonstrate usage Conditional and Computational Logic
        '*
        For MySecondIndex = 1 To MyIndex
            MyAccum = MySecondIndex + 1
        Next MySecondIndex
        MYInteger = MyAccum
        '*
        '*** Demonstrate Intrinsic Functions, Conditional/Computational Logic
        '*
        MyIndex = 1
        MyFixedLengthString = String.Empty
        Dim x As Int32
        For x = 0 To 11
            Select Case MonthValues(x)
                Case "December", "January", "February"
                    Console.WriteLine _
                    (MyFixedLengthString.Concat(MonthValues(x), _
                    " is ", "Winter"))
                Case "March", "April", "May"
                    Console.WriteLine _
                    (MyFixedLengthString.Concat(MonthValues(x), _
                    " is ", "Spring"))
                Case "June", "July", "August"
                    Console.WriteLine _
                    (MyFixedLengthString.Concat(MonthValues(x), _
                    " is ", "Summer"))
                Case "September", "October", "November"
                    Console.WriteLine _
                    (MyFixedLengthString.Concat(MonthValues(x), _
                    " is ", "Autumn"))
            End Select
        Next
        Console.WriteLine("Press Enter to Exit")
        Console.ReadLine()
    End Sub
End Module
```

NOTE   I hope that you have started experiencing the VS .NET IDE. Whether you have chosen to type the sample code or to copy and paste the code, it is *time to get your hands dirty.*

Now that you have had a chance to view the sample VB .NET code in Listing 6-6, what do you think? Which do you think is easier or more straight-forward: COBOL .NET or VB .NET? Can I ask that you hold that thought? I do not think it is fair to judge either language *yet.* How one language or the other implements the features of .NET will vary—that is a fact. Moreover, that is my point: You are just beginning to scratch the surface. Please wait until you have read a few more chapters in this book before you make this sort of judgment. At that time, you will be well prepared to weigh in on one side or the other. In the meantime, you have to admit that being bilingual is actually rather *cool.*

To wrap up this sample code section, let's run the VB .NET sample program. The program produces the console window display shown in Figure 6-4.

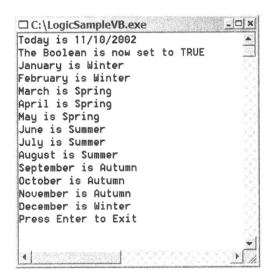

Figure 6-4. The console window display produced by the LogicSampleVB program

Noting Observations

In the preceding section, I suggested that you delay judgment of the two languages. However, that does not mean that you cannot make note of your observations and even formulate constructive criticism. In previous sections, you have worked with the basic programming syntax (both with COBOL .NET and VB

.NET). Undoubtedly, working with the previous sample applications has given you a glimpse into a few feature differences.

Throughout this book, I will point out any product features that may be available in one language (i.e., VB .NET), but not available in the other language (i.e., COBOL .NET). I suspect that this will typically position VB .NET to sit on the "available" side of the comparison. Consequently, you might consider creating your own "wish list." Then, you could use your wish list as a constructive communication vehicle to forward to Fujitsu Software Corporation.

What does this say about COBOL .NET's feature set? Well, if my opinion about COBOL .NET's feature set was based solely on pointing out the things that Fujitsu's product was missing (when compared to VB .NET), I would be left with a slightly negative opinion. But, that is just it. I am *not* basing my opinion on what COBOL .NET is *missing*. Rather, it is what COBOL .NET is *not missing* that makes it a .NET language worthy of consideration.

Applauding Fujitsu Software Corporation

Considering that Fujitsu's NetCOBOL for .NET product is in an early version (currently v1.1), Fujitsu has done an outstanding job. The product actually works! Not many companies can say that about their early product releases. (By the way, you can also include Microsoft in this distinguished category. Remember, this *is* also an early version—currently going from v1.0 to v1.1—of the entire .NET platform. I take my hat off to both companies.)

Additionally, it appears to me that we (the mainframe community) owe it to ourselves and to Fujitsu to embrace and support this product. I applaud Fujitsu for supporting the COBOL language. The *least* that we can do is support the COBOL .NET product. Allow me to point out that the long-term success of this product (any product, for that matter) is directly related to the support (adoption, use, and interest) received from its users.

Lastly, it should be noted that Fujitsu's software support group has been extremely responsive. I have been left with the impression that some (if not all) of the feature differences will be addressed in future releases of the NetCOBOL for .NET product. I suggest that we use Fujitsu's product, make notes of any improvement opportunities, and forward our *constructive* feedback directly to Fujitsu.[8] Together, we can help what is now a good product become an even better, more feature-rich product.

---

8.   You can e-mail Fujitsu Software's technical support directly. Optionally, feel free to forward an e-mail to me and I will forward it to Fujitsu. Include the description "COBOL .NET Wish List" in the e-mail subject header. My e-mail address is Richardson@eClecticSoftwareSolutions.com.

NetCOBOL for .NET Code Samples from Fujitsu

Included with your NetCOBOL for .NET product installation are a generous number of code samples. You can locate these code samples by browsing the specific hard disk location where the Fujitsu NetCOBOL for .NET product is installed on your machine and navigating to the Examples subfolder. The typical installed disk location is

```
<Hard drive>:\Program Files\Fujitsu NetCOBOL for .NET\Examples
```

I have browsed these samples and found them to be very useful. You should spend some time familiarizing yourself with them. The samples I have provided in this book will serve as a complement to the ones provided by Fujitsu. I have made an attempt to not duplicate the Fujitsu samples.

NOTE   Naturally, the samples provided by Fujitsu are in COBOL .NET only. That makes the *bilingual* approach (i.e., samples in both COBOL .NET and VB .NET) of this book slightly unique.

Rather, I preferred to add value by seeking out alternatives, variations, and extensions in my own "simple" code examples. When you combine both sets of samples together, you should have more than enough to get you off to a good start. Nevertheless, you will notice that my sample code and Fujitsu's provided samples both take a simplistic approach, avoiding a realistic business rule approach. Most agree that this approach allows for more focus on the actual technology.

Consider leveraging the VS .NET IDE toolset to help you explore these sample applications. In the next section I introduce to you the Solution Explorer window, a VS .NET IDE tool. This is one VS .NET IDE tool that you may find yourself using quite often.

Using the VS .NET Solution Explorer

In Chapter 5, I referred to the Solution Explorer window, which you can access by selecting View ➤ Solution Explorer or pressing Ctrl-Alt-L. You used this window to access the property pages of the project. Well, there are a few other treats awaiting your discovery with the Solution Explorer. As shown in Figure 6-5, not only can you view your editable program modules, but you can also use the Show All Files feature to view *all* the files stored in your local application path.

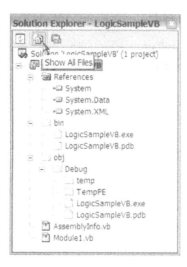

Figure 6-5. The Solution Explorer window with the Show All Files feature activated. The LogicSampleVB project is being viewed.

You will notice that the display style is that of a collapsible tree. You will also notice that the top item on the tree is the solution file (in this case, LogicSampleVB.sln). In this solution file, you can have one or more projects. The second item from the top of the tree is the project file (in this case, LogicSampleVB.vbproj). Basically, all of the files related to your project will be stored "under" the project in question. As shown in Figure 6-5, even the executable file (LogicSampleVB.exe) falls under the project. Please note the executable file (EXE) is stored in a subfolder named *bin*. If you were creating dynamic link library (DLL) files instead of executable files, you would see the DLL file in the bin sub-folder as well.

NOTE In some .NET languages, a .NET assembly can consist of one or more DLL files or EXE files. In VB .NET and COBOL .NET, an assembly is composed of just one EXE or one DLL. For our purposes, the term "assembly" can be used loosely as a synonym for executable or dynamic link library. The AssemblyInfo.vb file that appears in the Solution Explorer can be used to provide metadata for the assembly.

This brief introduction to the Solution Explorer should be sufficient for now. I reference the Solution Explorer in this book when it is useful to do so. In the meantime, go ahead and explore and discover. I encourage you to further explore the Solution Explorer feature of VS .NET.

Examining Microsoft Intermediate Language

In my previous mainframe COBOL programming days, there were occasions when a question arose about the behavior of the COBOL compiler. Inevitably, I would resort to compiling my COBOL program with the appropriate compile directive to include the actual assembler language output. I suppose you can call me a "curious geek"—the shoe certainly does fit.

.NET offers a similar opportunity to view MSIL with a handy utility called *ILDASM*. You execute this utility using the VS .NET command prompt (Chapter 2 covers this command prompt feature). With the ILDASM utility, you have the option of displaying your program's MSIL in the ILDASM GUI, or you can send the output to a text file.

For this discussion, refer back to the sample code project you created earlier in this chapter (DefineDataTypesSampleCobol). Recall there were a couple of things that I wanted to show you. For example:

- How do you know that the COBOL .NET data type 9(4) COMP-5 does in fact map to the .NET data type Sysetm.Int16?

- How do you know that the changed COBOL .NET PICTURE description 9(5) COMP-5 will cause a mapping to the .NET data type System.Int8 as a one-dimensional array?

Let's execute the ILDASM utility. As you can see in Figure 6-6, you execute the ILDASM utility from the Visual Studio .NET Command Prompt window. The path information used for your executable file (and output file, if you so choose) will differ.

NOTE   Figure 6-6 shows the executable file named DefineDataTypesSampleCOBOL.exe.

Figure 6-6. The Visual Studio .NET Command Prompt window. The command line has been prepared for execution of the ILDASM utility.

I have included a snippet of the COBOL sample program code in Listing 6-7 to assist in this ILDASM discussion.

Listing 6-7. A Portion of the Original Sample DefineDataTypesSampleCobol Code

```
. . .
000050 REPOSITORY.
000060* .NET Framework Classes
000070    CLASS SYS-INT16 AS "System.Int16"
000080    CLASS SYS-INT32 AS "System.Int32"
000090    CLASS SYS-DOUBLE AS "System.Double".
000100*
000110 DATA DIVISION.
000120 WORKING-STORAGE SECTION.
000130* Declare Data Items with COBOL.NET Data Types
000140    77  My-First-Number-Intrinsic  PIC S9(4) USAGE IS COMP-5.
000150    77  My-First-Number-Int8Demo   PIC S9(5) USAGE IS COMP-5.
000160    77  My-Second-Number-Intrinsic PIC S9(9) USAGE IS COMP-5.
000170    77  My-Third-Number-Intrinsic  USAGE IS COMP-2.
000180* Declare Data Items using .NET Data Types
000190    77  My-First-Number-ObjectRef  OBJECT REFERENCE SYS-INT16.
000200    77  My-Second-Number-ObjectRef OBJECT REFERENCE SYS-INT32.
000210    77  My-Third-Number-ObjectRef  OBJECT REFERENCE SYS-DOUBLE.
000220
000230    01 NULL-X PIC X(1).
000240 LINKAGE SECTION.
000250*
000260 PROCEDURE DIVISION.
000270* Move numeric literal to Data Item
000280     MOVE 32767 TO My-First-Number-Int8Demo.
000290     MOVE 32767 TO My-First-Number-Intrinsic.
000300* Commented out to shorten ILDASM output display.
000310*    Display "Pic5 " My-First-Number-Int8Demo
000320*    Display "Pic4 " My-First-Number-Intrinsic
000330*
000340*    DISPLAY "Enter X and Press Enter to Exit.".
000350*    ACCEPT NULL-X.
000360*
000370 END PROGRAM  MAIN.
```

I have added a field called My-First-Number-Int8Demo at line 150 with the PIC value of S9(5). Additionally, I have added logic statements at lines 280 through 350.

By default, the ILDASM GUI is used to view the MSIL, as shown in Figure 6-7.

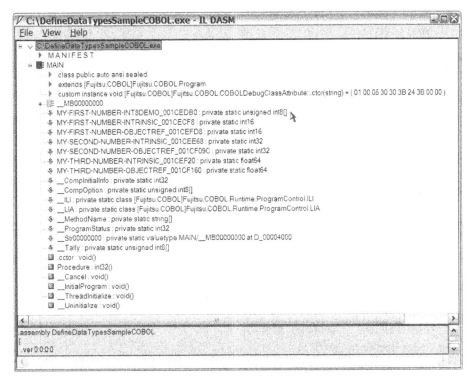

Figure 6-7. The ILDASM GUI window showing the mapped .NET data types

In the ILDASM display, notice the difference between My-First-Number-Intrinsic and My-First-Number-Int8Demo. If you are interested, you can doubleclick the Procedure tag (see Figure 6-8). Then, get ready for a lesson in learning to read intermediate language. Well, since you insisted, double-click the Procedure tag and look inside.

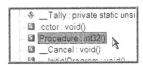

Figure 6-8. The ILDASM GUI window showing the mapped Procedure tag

After you double-click the Procedure tag, you will see the full MSIL file for this program. I will grab a snippet from the ILDASM display to discuss further. The MSIL code snippet in Listing 6-8 is actual MSIL. Please take a look the entire snippet and pay special attention to lines IL_0058 through IL_0070.

Listing 6-8. MSIL Code Snippet Taken from the ILDASM Utility Display

```
IL_0026:  stloc      __MainSubInfo
IL_002a:  ldc.i4.s   32
IL_002c:  ldsfld     int32 MAIN::__CompInitialInfo
IL_0031:  or
IL_0032:  stsfld     int32 MAIN::__CompInitialInfo
IL_0037:  ldsfld     int32 MAIN::__CompInitialInfo
IL_003c:  ldc.i4.4
IL_003d:  and
IL_003e:  brtrue.s   IL_004a
IL_0040:  call       void MAIN::__InitialProgram()
IL_0045:  call       void MAIN::__ThreadInitialize()
IL_004a:  ldsfld     int32 MAIN::__CompInitialInfo
IL_004f:  ldc.i4.4
IL_0050:  or
IL_0051:  stsfld     int32 MAIN::__CompInitialInfo
IL_0056:  br.s       IL_0058
IL_0058:  ldsfld     unsigned int8[] MAIN::'MY-FIRST-NUMBER-INT8DEMO_001CEDB0'
IL_005d:  ldc.i4.0
IL_005e:  ldelema    unsigned int8
IL_0063:  ldc.i4     0x7fff
IL_0068:  conv.i4
IL_0069:  stind.i4
IL_006a:  ldc.i4     0x7fff
IL_006f:  conv.i2
IL_0070:  stsfld     int16 MAIN::'MY-FIRST-NUMBER-INTRINSIC_001CECF8'
IL_0075:  leave.s    IL_009b
```

Let's take just a few lines of MSIL and figure out exactly what's going on. Remember, this MSIL represents two lines (two MOVE statements, both moving the value of 32767) of original COBOL .NET logic. Table 6-1 shows the MSIL code and a brief description what the MSIL accomplishes.

Table 6-1. MSIL Code and Descriptions

MSIL CODE		DESCRIPTION
IL_0058:	ldsfld	Load the static field (the Int8 array).
IL_005d:	ldc.i4.0	Load the numeric constant, which is zero for now.
IL_005e:	ldelema	Load the address of the array element.
IL_0063:	ldc.i4	Load the numeric constant, 0x7fff or 32767.
IL_0068:	conv.i4	Convert the length to Int32.
IL_0069:	stind.i4	Store a value of type natural int.
IL_006a:	ldc.i4	Load the numeric constant, 0x7fff or 32767.
IL_006f:	conv.i2	Convert the length to Int16.
IL_0070:	stsfld	Replace the value of a static field.

So, you can see that the COBOL .NET field that you kept with the original picture definition of S9(4) maps to an Int16 (as intended). Additionally, as the MSIL line IL_006f shows, after the value of 32767 is moved, the data type remains as Int16. On the other hand, the field that you changed to S9(5) appears to transition from an Int8 type array up to an Int32 type data item. Interesting? Fun? Remind you of assembler programming?

Now it is your turn. Perhaps you can execute the ILDASM utility against the Visual Basic sample code DefineDataTypesSampleVB. Check to see *why* I made the claim that the VB .NET data types and the native .NET data types are equivalent. This ILDASM utility will really help answer these types of questions and many more. Have fun with it.

TIP Run ILDASM with the /? option at the command line to discover the many options available when executing this utility.

Summary

This chapter's goals were as follows:

- To take a new look at old programming syntax

- To examine Microsoft intermediate language (MSIL)

You have covered enough of the basics in this chapter to get you off to a good start. You reviewed some familiar concepts using the new VS .NET IDE. First, you went through several data type declarations and then you moved on to some common logic statements. The focus was on using basic, familiar syntax to answer the question "Can you use legacy-style syntax in the new .NET environment?" You then examined sample applications using both COBOL .NET and VS .NET. To wrap up the discussion in this chapter, you explored the ILDASM utility and MSIL.

This chapter focused on doing things the old-fashioned way. In the next chapter, you will make a sharp turn toward focusing on doing (some) things the "new" .NET way. Your exploration of the .NET Framework will provide many opportunities for discovery. During that exploration, you will dive much deeper into code.

To Learn More

The following are some suggested supplemental references to further your retraining effort.

Magazines

.NET Magazine:
> http://www.fawcette.com/dotnetmag/

Visual Studio Magazine:
> http://www.fawcette.com/vsm/

XML & Web Services Magazine:
> http://www.fawcette.com/xmlmag/

Web Sites

.NET Framework Developer's Guide's "What is the Common Language
Specification?":

```
http://msdn.microsoft.com/library/en-us/cpguide/html/
cpconwhatiscommonlanguagespecification.asp
```

ILDasm Tutorial:

```
http://msdn.microsoft.com/library/en-us/cptutorials/html/
il_dasm_tutorial.asp
```

Microsoft Communities (discussion groups, e-Newsletters, and so forth):

```
http://communities2.microsoft.com
```

MSDN:

```
http://msdn.microsoft.com
```

CHAPTER 7

The .NET Framework

A Class Library Designed for Use and Reuse

In this chapter

- Discussing what the .NET Framework has to offer

- Exploring the (re)use of the .NET Framework

IN CHAPTER 2, I offered a mainframe analogy to begin my explanation of the .NET Framework. The analogy concerned a group of mainframe partitioned datasets (PDSs) being used as an extensive library of copybooks, utilities, subprograms, and software routines. As you recall, this previous discussion was one of several digestible bites of the much larger (.NET) elephant. As I attempted to answer the question "What is .NET?" in Chapter 2, I included the .NET Framework as one of several "correct" answers to that question. Well, in this chapter, I propose two new questions:

- What is the .NET Framework?

- How can you (re)use the .NET Framework?

After you obtain an understanding of the .NET Framework and how to use and reuse the .NET Framework, you will begin to see the *real* power behind developing on the .NET platform.

Dicing the .NET Framework

Are you ready to digest another bite of the .NET elephant? OK, it is time to examine the bits that make up this particular byte (bite). Imagine for moment that you are sharing the following feedback about this book with a coworker: "Chris Richardson *dices* the subject matter into digestible bits." Then you will appreciate the fact that I have created a convenient acronym[1] from this feedback that maps to the parts of the .NET Framework. Taking the five letters of the word "dices" to create the acronym DICES, you can say that the .NET Framework is

- **Delegates**

- **Interfaces**

- **Classes**

- **Enumerations**

- **Structures**

These five high-level groupings make up the types of objects in the .NET Framework. Collectively, these objects are available to you as a class library. The class library is broken down into namespaces. As you can see in Figure 7-1, the .NET Framework is a layer of abstraction that sits between your programming code and the common language runtime (CLR).[2]

Before I interject unneeded confusion, allow me to point out the following:

- The entire .NET Framework is loosely referred to as a class library, but it does contain more than classes.

- The classes in the .NET Framework can be base classes or classes *derived* from base classes.

Now that I have cleared all that up, let's discuss how you might go about learning more about the delegates, interfaces, classes, enumerations, and structures. You will start off with the topic of namespaces. Following the discussion of namespaces, you will drill down further to explore delegates, interfaces, classes, enumerations, and structures.

---

1. All right, I admit it is not that impressive, but it might help you remember the parts of the .NET Framework. I suppose I should leave the acronym creating to the Microsoft marketing gurus.
2. I discuss the common language runtime (CLR) in Chapter 8.

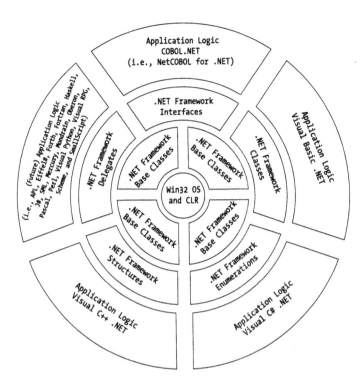

Figure 7-1. The .NET Framework abstraction layer

The .NET Namespaces

For a moment, let's revisit the mainframe analogy of the PDSs that represented an extensive library of reusable modules. On the mainframe, if you created PDSs such as this that you wanted other developers to be able to share, you would have made a few decisions along the way, for example:

- You would have decided which members (objects) should be organized into which PDSs.

- You would have decided on names for your PDSs.

- You would have decided on meaningful names for each *member* that would be stored in each PDS.

These are exactly the types of decisions that Microsoft apparently faced when they organized the thousands of delegates, interfaces, classes, enumerations, and structures. Their choice was to use namespaces. Fortunately, Microsoft did not stop there.

First, Microsoft organized the namespaces in a hierarchy according to function. Second, Microsoft provided useful tools to assist your research when you need detailed information about namespaces.

NOTE On occasion, you will create your own "custom" namespaces. These custom namespaces are useful as you create code targeted for reuse. Microsoft recommends that the namespaces organizations and individuals create be prefixed with a unique value. For example, the "high-level" qualifier could be the name of your company. This will help distinguish your custom namespaces from those provided by Microsoft (or third-party vendors). In Chapter 9, I demonstrate how to create custom namespaces.

The Functional Hierarchy of Namespaces

I recently had a .NET-related discussion with a friend of mine. Specifically, we discussed the .NET Framework. As the discussion went on, I found myself involved in a deeper, low-level explanation about individual namespaces. We then discussed how .NET's hierarchical namespace structure would help people locate the appropriate .NET objects and so forth. Continuing our discussion, we started to group the namespaces by function: those for client-side user interface versus those for Web development, those for I/O and data versus those for security and configuration, and so on.

As I noticed my friend's eyes glazing over and his face contorting, he asked, "How on earth will anyone ever remember the names of all of the namespaces?" I answered, "Why try to remember *all* of the names?" I suggested to my friend that he simply remember just *one* thing: Use the Microsoft Visual Studio .NET documentation (see Figure 7-2).

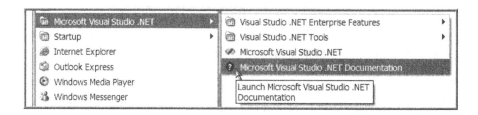

Figure 7-2. Preparing to launch the Microsoft Visual Studio .NET documentation

That may sound like a slick way to avoid helping someone. However, to be fair, I did include the following additional instructions (after all, this is my friend I am talking about):

1. Click the Start button and select Programs ➤ Microsoft Visual Studio .NET ➤ Microsoft Visual Studio .NET Documentation.

2. Locate the URL window on the Standard toolbar.

3. Type **ms-help://MS.VSCC/MS.MSDNVS/cpref/html/cpref_start.htm** into the URL window.

4. Press Enter.

The resulting display is a *complete* list of the .NET Framework namespaces. You will notice that in Figure 7-3, I have scrolled down to locate the System namespace. Note that the namespace names are displayed in a hierarchical fashion by function.

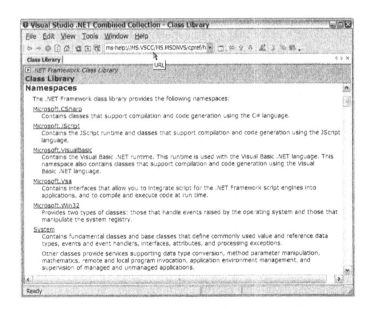

Figure 7-3. The .NET Class Library Help page from the Microsoft Visual Studio .NET Documentation feature

The approach that I chose when helping my friend follows the traditional saying, "Give a man a fish and he'll eat for a day. Teach a man to fish, and he'll eat for a lifetime." Please consider this book (especially sections like this one) as your guide to *learning how to fish*. On that note, let's continue fishing.

Browsing a Namespace

Recall that your ultimate objective is to drill down into the appropriate namespace. Your purpose for doing that is to locate, understand, and use the appropriate delegates, interfaces, classes, enumerations, and structures.

Using the Microsoft Visual Studio .NET documentation approach to locating the hierarchical display by function of a namespace, you could simply click the appropriate namespace name and locate the lower-level object. For example, say that you selected the *System.Text* namespace, as shown in Figure 7-4.

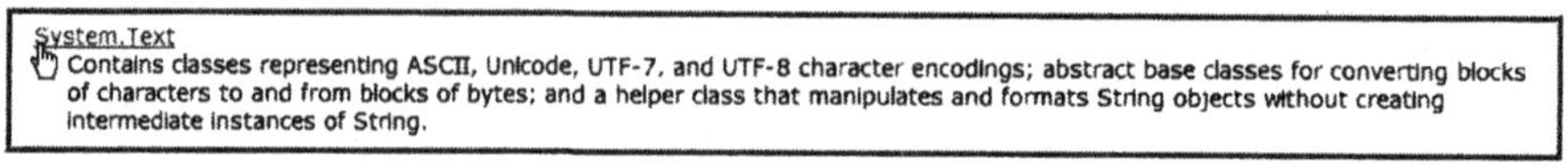

System.Text
Contains classes representing ASCII, Unicode, UTF-7, and UTF-8 character encodings; abstract base classes for converting blocks of characters to and from blocks of bytes; and a helper class that manipulates and formats String objects without creating intermediate instances of String.

Figure 7-4. A portion of the .NET Class Library Help page (via the Microsoft Visual Studio .NET documentation) showing the selection of the System.Text namespace

You will notice that the System.Text namespace contains eight classes. However, there are no delegates, interfaces, enumerations, or structures. Good observation. So, to be accurate, let's agree that a namespace will contain zero or more delegates, zero or more interfaces, zero or more classes, zero or more enumerations, and zero or more structures. Some namespaces will contain one or more of *each* type of object, whereas other namespaces (such as System.Text) will contain just one type of .NET object (in this case, classes).

Using the information that you have now, you could easily use the Help feature that is located within the Visual Studio .NET (VS .NET) IDE. For example, you could do a search (setting the appropriate search filter) using the value of System.Text. Better yet, now that you have the names of the eight classes that this namespace contains, you may have noted that there is a class named StringBuilder. You could do a search on the StringBuilder class to get detailed information about this particular .NET reusable object.

There are several scenarios involved with and corresponding approaches taken toward the goal of exploring and leveraging the .NET Framework. Up to this point, I have suggested an approach suitable for the scenario where uncertainty exists with regard to either the .NET namespace name or the name of a specific class/object. Suppose for a moment that you came from a different direction. Consider the following (other) scenarios:

- You already know the namespace name, but you have no idea of what assembly[3] implements the namespace.

---

3. In Chapter 6, I briefly mentioned the .NET assembly. In this context, the .NET Framework namespaces are implemented by the Microsoft-supplied assemblies (DLLs).

- You already know the class name, but you forgot the namespace name.

- You already know the assembly name, but you are not sure about the namespace name or the namespace members.

Though the preceding scenarios could direct you toward a variety of search methods, the fact that there is overlap between them is indicative of the nature of Windows and Web development. You have several ways to do practically everything. In some cases it will boil down to a matter of preference. Having said that, let's explore another way to get information about namespaces (and thus information about delegates, interfaces, classes, enumerations, and structures): the Object Browser feature. •

VS .NET Feature: The Object Browser

The very name of this particular VS .NET feature, Object Browser, practically explains its purpose in life. Yes, you use this tool to browse objects. Too simple, huh? OK, there is a little more to it. To begin with, the objects that you are interested in (for now) are just the .NET Framework objects contained within the Microsoft-supplied namespaces (which are delegates, interfaces, classes, enumerations, and structures). Yet, there is more.

I need to emphasize that assemblies implement namespaces (recall that generally speaking, an *assembly* is a compiled unit of code). Having said that, in order to display information about the namespaces using the Object Browser, you will need to have a "reference" to the appropriate assembly. The following assemblies are referred to as the .NET *default assemblies:*

- mscorlib.dll

- System.dll

- System.Data.dll

- System.Design.dll

- System.DirectoryServices.dll

- System.Drawing.dll

- System.Drawing.Design.dll

- System.Messaging.dll

- System.Runtime.Serialization.Formatters.Soap.dll

- System.ServiceProcess.dll

- System.Web.dll

- System.Web.Services.dll

- System.Windows.Forms.dll

- System.XML.dll

You will become familiar with these .NET default assemblies (and others) over time. Depending on the .NET language and the project template type you use, you may have to manually set a reference to the appropriate assembly.

Referencing the Appropriate Assembly

During your mainframe batch travels, you undoubtedly used STEPLIB and JOBLIB JCL DD statements. Your reason for doing this was to provide a "reference" to a program via a load library. The name of the load library was typically associated with a PDS that contained precompiled modules. Granted, there was additional programming needed to CALL the external program. Your understanding of this practice (common in legacy mainframe COBOL development) provides you with a conceptual understanding of the *reference* used in the context of referencing a .NET assembly.

Now let's look at the Object Browser. From an open VS .NET IDE window, access the Object Browser feature by selecting View ➤ Other Windows ➤ Object Browser. As you can see in Figure 7-5, the Object Browser feature is an available menu option. Notice that I have yet to open a project of any type.

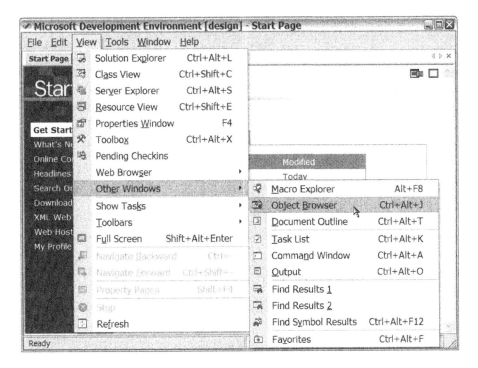

Figure 7-5. Selecting the Object Browser feature

The resulting display may be an empty Object Browser window. Now select the Customize toolbar option to begin the steps of adding an assembly reference to the Object Browser (see Figure 7-6).

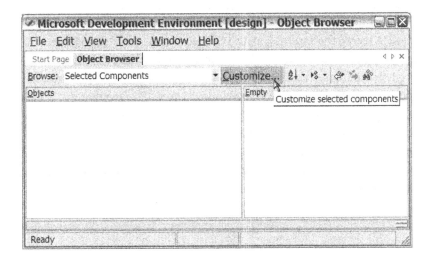

Figure 7-6. Clicking the Customize option in the Object Browser

In the Selected Components dialog box, click the Add button (see Figure 7-7).

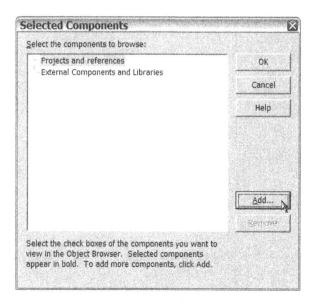

Figure 7-7. Clicking the Add button in the Selected Components dialog box

At this point, you should be viewing a window titled Component Selector, with the .NET tab selected.

Now recall the "other" scenarios mentioned in the previous section. Suppose that you had worked with the System.Text namespace before, but you could not remember the details of the *StringBuilder* class. In this scenario, also suppose that you know that the System.Text namespace is implemented in the mscorlib.dll assembly. You are now prepared to select mscorlib.dll from the list of assemblies. After you scroll to locate the assembly in the Component Selector dialog box, select the assembly, and click Select (as shown in Figure 7-8), you can click OK twice to complete the steps of adding an assembly reference to the Object Browser.

After you return to the Object Browser window, you will notice that the mscorlib assembly is included, along with a plus sign (+). Click the plus sign to expand the tree view and scroll past several namespaces to locate the System.Text namespace. Then proceed to expand the tree view and locate the StringBuilder class. After you click to select the StringBuilder class, you are finally able to see detailed information about the class, as shown in Figure 7-9.

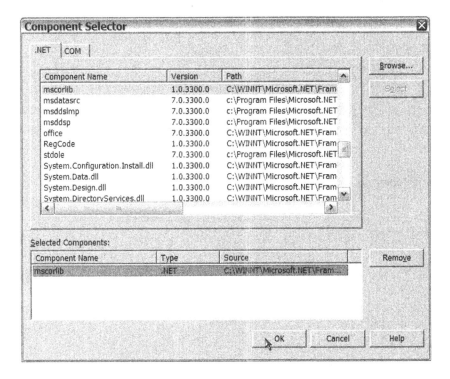

Figure 7-8. Selecting mscorlib.dll from the Component Selector dialog box

During your application development, this detailed class information would prove to be critical if you wanted to use the StringBuilder class.

That is one scenario in which you know the assembly. During your development, there will be times when the assemblies will already be referenced in the Object Browser. In those instances, knowing the name of the assembly will be less of a requirement (e.g., when you view the Object Browser from an open Visual Basic .NET project). Additionally, assembly references added to the Object Browser (such as the one that you have just added) will remain available until they are manually removed.

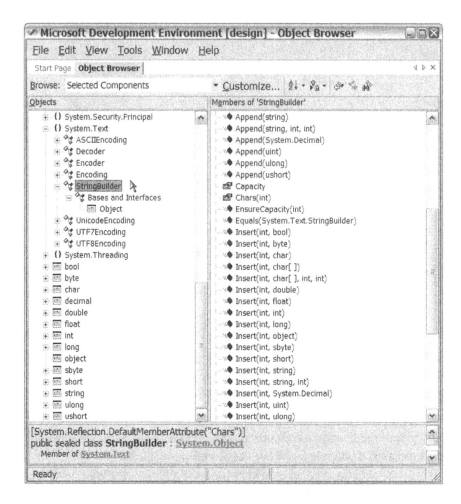

Figure 7-9. The Object Browser window displaying information about the StringBuilder class

So far in this section, you have covered namespaces, assemblies, and the Object Browser. You should now feel better prepared to drill down into the topic of the .NET Framework. Although I have used the example of a class to assist in the namespace discussion, I still have delegates, interfaces, enumerations, and structures to cover (remember the DICES acronym?). Do not worry. The remaining discussions should be much easier. In the upcoming discussions, you will be able to refer back to your new understanding of namespaces and assemblies. Additionally, you will use the Object Browser again for further illustration. These parts will feel like review for you.

Delegates

As you browse various namespaces, you will notice that some namespaces contain delegates; for example, the System namespace contains six delegates. Therefore, you need to establish a general understanding of what exactly a delegate is. Consider for a moment the lexical[4] meaning of *delegate*: "To commit or entrust (as task or power) to another."

Let's see how "To commit or entrust . . . to another" relates to the technical use of the term. In Chapter 6, in the COBOL .NET DefineDataTypesSampleCobol sample program, you briefly referred back to the legacy mainframe COBOL use of the USAGE IS POINTER clause. As you know, when you used that clause (occasionally with the ADDRESS OF register) you were pointing to (referencing) the actual memory storage location of one data item for the shared use of a second defined "data item." Again, you were working with data items. In this instance, you can easily see the issue of *trust* being important. If you have ever had a memory violation (especially with CICS applications), you had simply violated the *trust* that had been extended to you.

Now, in the current century, some of you have moved on to use the modern mainframe COBOL features of the USAGE IS PROCEDURE-POINTER clause or the USAGE IS FUNCTION-POINTER clause. Unlike the legacy USAGE IS POINTER clause, which pointed to data items only, these other clauses were available for pointing to procedures and/or functions. Naturally, the matter of trust has continued to be important. As before, violating that trust will produce undesirable results.

 NOTE Using these newer USAGE clauses will be more familiar to those COBOL programmers who have already started to move away from legacy procedural/structured COBOL programming and toward object-oriented programming (OOP).

On .NET, delegates are practically identical to the USAGE IS FUNCTION-POINTER implementation. In other words, a *delegate* is a special object (actually, a class) that you use to point to (store a reference for) a method. The matter of trust is dealt with by using a feature called a *signature*. By restricting the storage of method references to those whose signatures match, the chances of violating the trust are virtually eliminated (some trust, huh?).

---

4. According to *The American Heritage College Dictionary, Third Edition* (Houghton Mifflin, 1995).

CROSS-REFERENCE I discuss delegates further in Chapter 15. In that chapter, you will learn several ways to use delegates (e.g., events and asynchronous execution).

For now, having a general understanding of what delegates are is sufficient. You will want to keep in mind that the System namespace contains two classes that are inherited (recall the discussion on object orientation in Chapter 4) by other classes implemented in the form of a delegate: *System.Delegate* and *System.MulticastDelegate*. The System.MulticastDelegate class is *derived* from the System.Delegate class. All other delegates are *derived* from System.MulticastDelegate.

Reuse Through Object-Oriented Design

To get an idea of how the .NET Framework uses object-oriented design, consider the following observation. As noted in this section, all delegates derive directly from System.MulticastDelegate, which itself derives from System.Delegate. Now, here is the amazing part: The .NET Framework class library has approximately 147 delegates, all deriving from the System.MulticastDelegate delegate. Now that is what I call reuse!

Interfaces

When you browse the System namespace, you will notice that it contains 11 interfaces. (Perhaps you will also notice that the names of most of the interfaces are prefixed with an *I*.) So, what are interfaces, and why are they among the namespace constituents?

Simply put, an *interface* is a contract. This contract specifies a set of functionality that must be followed by any class that chooses to implement the interface. In your legacy mainframe COBOL applications (before object orientation), you had a very limited concept of an interface.

For example, say that you wanted to call a subprogram from within your main COBOL program. You would have added a CALL statement followed by the name of the subprogram. But that was not all. Depending on the requirements of the subprogram, you would have also added a USING statement to indicate the parameters being passed to and returned from the subprogram. In other words, the subprogram was enforcing a "contract."

At this point, perhaps you are reflecting on the occasions when you had to debug some program logic dealing with calling subprograms. On some of these occasions, you may have inadvertently violated this subprogram contract. Although you may have been careful to pass in the correct number of parameters, you failed to adhere exactly to the requirements expected by the subprogram. For example, you may have put the parameters in the wrong order or you may have defined data items of the wrong type (numeric versus alphabetic). Maybe you thought everything was right, only to discover that your receiving fields were truncating your values due to short data field lengths.

Reflecting on these memorable legacy mainframe events, you can say that the subprogram had an interface that needed to be adhered to. The enforcement of the contract between the subprogram and the calling program meant that the requirement of the subprogram's interface was met. Therefore, in legacy mainframe terms, this is an example of the limited use of an interface that served as a contract.

In the context of .NET, the .NET Framework, and a .NET namespace, an interface includes the general concept of the mainframe "subprogram using" scenario. However, thanks to object-oriented design features, the more complete understanding of an interface includes much more.

On .NET, an interface can describe methods (conceptually similar to the legacy subprogram), fields, properties, and events. Classes can then "implement" this description (interface) and thus the class will be required (by contract) to provide all of the functionality described in the interface.

CROSS-REFERENCE   I discuss interfaces further in Chapter 15. In that chapter, you will review several ways to use delegates (e.g., events and asynchronous execution).

Object-oriented design plays an important role in the .NET Framework and its parts. The existence of Microsoft-supplied interfaces (contained in various namespaces) provides developers the opportunity to reuse existing code. As shown in Figure 7-10, the System namespace contains 11 interfaces.

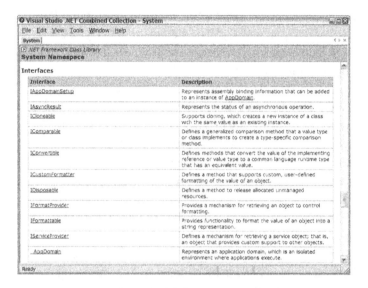

Figure 7-10. A portion of the .NET Class Library Help page (via the Microsoft Visual Studio .NET documentation) showing the interfaces available in the System namespace

Classes

If you were the type of proficient legacy mainframe COBOL developer who leveraged the COBOL intrinsic functions as often as possible, you will want to become extremely familiar with this particular namespace constituent. You can practically draw a one-to-one match from each of the legacy COBOL intrinsic functions to a particular .NET Framework class. But then, by far, the .NET Framework collection exceeds the quantity of the legacy COBOL offering.

Although you can create applications without explicitly creating classes, this will typically *not* be the case. The sample applications that you created in Chapter 6 were simple applications that did not justify the structure of a class. The sample code that you will create in this chapter presents an example of explicit class creation.

You will see object-oriented design being used in the creation of the .NET Framework classes. (Recall that a basic understanding of OOP was listed as a .NET prerequisite in Chapter 4.) As you browse the list of namespaces, notice that practically all of them contain classes. Practically all of the classes derive from another class (a base class).

That is, all but *one* of the classes derive from another class. One class in the System namespace is the *root,* the superclass of all classes in the entire .NET Framework. All classes are derived (either directly or indirectly) from the *System.Object* class (or the *Object* class, for short). As shown in Figure 7-11, System.Object sits at the very top of the .NET Framework type hierarchy.

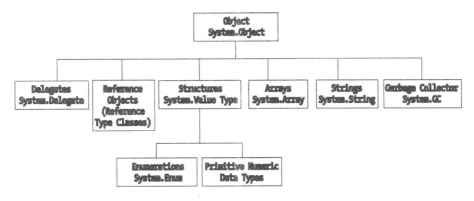

Figure 7-11. A portion of the System.Object superclass hierarchy

To quickly review, a *class* serves as a template (roughly speaking). The class can contain methods, properties, and events. To access the functionality of a class, you need an *instance*. The instance then is an object.

NOTE   This is an extremely abbreviated explanation. For example, there are value type objects and reference type objects, each with their own style of instantiation. Look for further discussion of this subject in Chapter 9.

To finish the namespace classes discussion, you will revisit the StringBuilder class from the System.Text namespace previously discussed in this chapter. You will use the StringBuilder class as an example to introduce the use of a class viewing tool: the .NET Framework Class Viewer.

.NET Framework Tool: Class Viewer

What would you do if you were coding a COBOL .NET program and wanted to use the StringBuilder class? Assume that you had used the StringBuilder class before, but you could not remember which namespace contains the class. At worst, you could not locate any code samples. Additionally, assume that you could not remember the name of the assembly that implements the namespace.

Armed with the question "What are the methods and properties of the StringBuilder class?" you would begin your search. For some, the first choice might be to conduct a search using either the VS .NET IDE Help/Search feature or the

Microsoft Visual Studio .NET documentation's Help/Search feature. Others may even take advantage of the online MSDN Search feature.

The good news is that each of these Help/Search choices would eventually lead you to your answer. The bad news is that some of these choices may not be the fastest method of accessing the information you're after. Depending on the filter you use, you'll get about 500 results returned from your search. With practice, you'll learn how to recognize the *right* result out of the 500 *potential* right results. Fortunately, you have an alternative.

Microsoft provides a .NET Framework tool called the *Class Viewer* (not to be confused with the Class View option available in the VS .NET IDE). Using this tool, you will receive multiple results from your search as well. The difference is that each result that you receive will directly relate to a class/namespace/assembly relationship.

You execute the Class Viewer tool from the VS .NET Command Prompt window. As shown in Figure 7-12, you type in **WinCV.exe** to access the Class Viewer user interface.

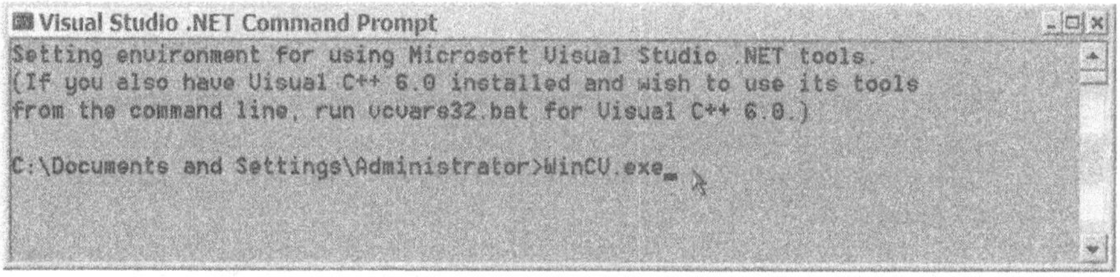

Figure 7-12. Enter WinCV.exe in the Visual Studio .NET Command Prompt window to execute the Class Viewer.

The Class Viewer user interface is rather intuitive. You simply type in the name of the class that you are interested in. In this case, you would enter **StringBuilder**. Notice that as you type, the window display on the right immediately updates to display the information you are looking for. Using the Option feature on the Class Viewer toolbar, you can easily copy the output. I have pasted portions of the output display here:

```
'c:\winnt\microsoft.net\framework\v1.0.3705\mscorlib.dll'
. . .
    // Constructors
    public StringBuilder();
    public StringBuilder(int capacity);
    public StringBuilder(int capacity, int maxCapacity);
    public StringBuilder(string value);
    public StringBuilder(string value, int capacity);
    public StringBuilder(string value, int startIndex, int length, int capacity);
```

```
// Properties
public int Capacity { get; set; }
public char Chars { get; set; }
public int Length { get; set; }
public int MaxCapacity { get; }

// Methods
public System.Text.StringBuilder Append(short value);
public System.Text.StringBuilder Append(char value);
public System.Text.StringBuilder Append(long value);
public System.Text.StringBuilder Append(int value);
public System.Text.StringBuilder Append(bool value);
public System.Text.StringBuilder Append(string value);
public System.Text.StringBuilder Append(byte value);
public System.Text.StringBuilder Append(SByte value);
```

. . .

```
public System.Text.StringBuilder Append(char[] value);
public System.Text.StringBuilder Append(object value);
public System.Text.StringBuilder Append(double value);
```

. . .

```
public System.Text.StringBuilder Append(Decimal value);
public System.Text.StringBuilder Append(char value, int repeatCount);
```

. . .

```
public int EnsureCapacity(int capacity);
public virtual bool Equals(object obj);
public bool Equals(System.Text.StringBuilder sb);
public virtual int GetHashCode();
public Type GetType();
public System.Text.StringBuilder Insert(int index, double value);
public System.Text.StringBuilder Insert(int index, int value);
public System.Text.StringBuilder Insert(int index, char[] value);
public System.Text.StringBuilder Insert(int index, float value);
public System.Text.StringBuilder Insert(int index, long value);
public System.Text.StringBuilder Insert(int index, UInt64 value);
public System.Text.StringBuilder Insert(int index, object value);
public System.Text.StringBuilder Insert(int index, UInt32 value);
public System.Text.StringBuilder Insert(int index, Decimal value);
public System.Text.StringBuilder Insert(int index, UInt16 value);
public System.Text.StringBuilder Insert(int index, SByte value);
public System.Text.StringBuilder Insert(int index, bool value);
public System.Text.StringBuilder Insert(int index, string value);
public System.Text.StringBuilder Insert(int index, byte value);
public System.Text.StringBuilder Insert(int index, char value);
```

```
    public System.Text.StringBuilder Insert(int index, short value);
. . .
    public System.Text.StringBuilder Remove(int startIndex, int length);
    public System.Text.StringBuilder Replace(char oldChar, char newChar);
. . .
    public System.Text.StringBuilder Replace(string oldValue, string newValue);
. . .
    public virtual string ToString();
    public string ToString(int startIndex, int length);
```

This Class Viewer tool is nice. The ability to easily copy the output is an added bonus. As I have copied and pasted portions of the output here, you can copy and paste portions of output directly into your program code. This has productivity written all over it. Can you tell that I am excited about this tool?

TIP So far, I have introduced you to two "Microsoft-provided" tools that actually fall under the category of ".NET Framework tools": the ILDASM.exe tool (introduced in Chapter 6 during the Microsoft Intermediate Language [MSIL] discussion) and the WinCV.exe tool (the Class Viewer discussed in this section). The .NET Framework has many other tools. To find information on the other tools the .NET Framework provides, please visit the Microsoft Visual Studio .NET Documentation Help page using the following URL: `ms-help://MS.VSCC/MS.MSDNVS/ cptools/html/cpconnetframeworktools.htm`.

That concludes this chapter's discussion of classes and the Class Viewer tool. In the following sections, you will explore the remaining types of objects you are likely to come across when you use the .NET Framework: enumerations and structures.

Enumerations

Believe or not, you have worked with a data structure similar to the .NET enumeration object before. How many times in your legacy mainframe COBOL past have you seen tables or group items defined that listed a collection of numeric values? Sometimes, "88" levels were used, other times not. You would then use the individual items as constants. In the legacy COBOL code snippet in Listing 7-1, the group of data items called My-Days-Of-Week is implementing this type of behavior.

Listing 7-1. Legacy COBOL Code Snippet Showing a Group Item Definition

```
Data Division.
    File Section.
    FD  My-File
        Record Contains . . .
    01  My-Record.
        05  My-fields.
            . . .
    Working-Storage Section.
    01  My-Days-Of-Week.
        05  Sunday              Pic 9(1) value = 0.
        05  Monday              Pic 9(1) value = 1.
        05  Tuesday             Pic 9(1) value = 2.
        05  Wednesday           Pic 9(1) value = 3.
        05  Thursday            Pic 9(1) value = 4.
        05  Friday              Pic 9(1) value = 5.
        05  Saturday            Pic 9(1) value = 6.
    01  My-Other-Fields         Pic x(20).
    . . .
    Procedure Division.
        . . .
```

In the .NET Framework, you will come across namespaces that provide enumerations (you can also create your own). All enumerations (about 477) are derived from the System.Enum class. When you examine the System namespace, you will notice that there are eight enumerations, one of which is the *DayOfWeek* enumeration. The functionality of the System.DayOfWeek enumeration is the same as that in the legacy COBOL code snippet in Listing 7-1.

For example, if you were to type in **DayOfWeek** in the .NET Framework Class Viewer, you would see the display shown in Listing 7-2.

Listing 7-2. The DayOfWeek Enumeration Declaration in C#

```
public enum DayOfWeek
{
    Friday = 0x00000005,
    Monday = 0x00000001,
    Saturday = 0x00000006,
    Sunday = 0x00000000,
    Thursday = 0x00000004,
    Tuesday = 0x00000002,
    Wednesday = 0x00000003,
} // end of System.DayOfWeek
```

By design, the Class Viewer output is in C#. Just for fun, let's quickly translate the enumeration declaration in Listing 7-2 to Visual Basic .NET (VB .NET). Listing 7-3 shows the result.

Listing 7-3. The DayOfWeek Enumeration Declaration in VB .NET

```
Public Enum DayOfWeek
    Friday = 0x00000005
    Monday = 0x00000001
    Saturday = 0x00000006
    Sunday = 0x00000000
    Thursday = 0x00000004
    Tuesday = 0x00000002
    Wednesday = 0x00000003
End Enum
```

NOTE In the cases of enumeration creations, you will notice that there is not a big difference between C# and VB .NET.

CROSS-REFERENCE Appendix B reviews the basics of the C# language.

The enumeration declarations in Listings 7-2 and 7-3 demonstrate what Microsoft has already done for you. For the predefined enumerations, you simply use the predefined enumerations. You use enumerations in a similar way to other numeric data types (e.g., Int16 and Int32). In the case of the DayOfWeek enumeration, you would declare data items with the type DayOfWeek.

Many of the common number constants that you would have coded (over and over again) in your legacy applications have already been coded for you. Familiarize yourself with what is available—many times you will avoid having to reinvent the wheel. Again, the .NET Framework, as a class library, offers many opportunities for reuse. In the cases where an enumeration does not already exist, you can create an enumeration that derives from the System.Enum base class.

NOTE   COBOL .NET does not allow the creation of enumerations. However, you can reference and use the existing enumerations provided by the .NET Framework.

Structures

The My-Days-Of-Week group item shown in Listing 7-1 provides the perfect starting point for a brief discussion about structures. If you can, try to imagine the previous group item declaration on steroids.

At first, it may appear that a *structure* (also referred to as a *value object*) is functionally similar to an enumeration. For example, you can use a structure to "declare" data items that behave as traditional fields (or properties). However, that is where the similarities end. A structure adds the following to its feature list:

- You are not limited to numeric data types.

- You can add methods with executable logic.

In Chapter 6 in the COBOL .NET code sample, you used a few structures. These were structures from the System namespace. In the sample code, you used the .NET data types System.Int16, System.Int32, and System.Double. Well, each of the numeric .NET data types (e.g., Int16, Int32, and Double) actually is a structure in the System namespace.

CROSS-REFERENCE   In Chapter 9, I further discuss value types. In that chapter, I contrast these types of objects with reference types. Additionally, I discuss appropriate considerations when using each type of object.

As with enumerations (discussed in the previous section), Microsoft has provided predefined structures in the .NET Framework class library. You will notice that there is a base class in the System namespace called *System.ValueType*.

Approximately 100 structures (or value objects) are derived from System.ValueType. As you now know, you can create your own enumerations deriving from the *System.Enum* base class. Likewise, you can create your own structures deriving from the System.ValueType class.

This concludes the chapter's discussion of delegates, interfaces, classes, enumerations, and structures (DICES). In the following section, you will explore some interesting ways to use (rather, to *reuse*) some of the .NET Framework objects.

(Re)using the .NET Framework

In the previous sections (under the "Dicing the .NET Framework" heading), I emphasized that the .NET Framework was designed to encourage reuse. The objects that make up the class library are all available for your exploitation. In this section, that is exactly what you will do.

In the sample code that follows, I demonstrate how to both use and reuse the .NET Framework objects. In my demonstration, I use Microsoft's predefined delegates, classes, and structures. Each code sample introduces the creation of a class.

CROSS-REFERENCE Chapter 9 covers classes in more detail.

COBOL .NET Example

As you will notice in Listing 7-4, I have created a console application and named the project FrameworkExampleCobol. For your convenience, the sample code from the .cob module is provided in Listing 7-4.

Listing 7-4. A COBOL .NET Sample Program Demonstrating the Use of the .NET Framework Objects

```
000010*
000020 CLASS-ID. MYFIRSTCLASS.
000030 ENVIRONMENT DIVISION.
000040 CONFIGURATION SECTION.
000050 REPOSITORY.
000060*
000070*    Reference a .NET Framework Class
000080*    These classes are from the
000081*    System.Text.RegularExpressions Namespace
000090*
```

```
000100      CLASS Regex AS "System.Text.RegularExpressions.Regex"
000110      CLASS Match AS "System.Text.RegularExpressions.Match"
000120*
000130*     Reference a .NET Framework Delegate
000140*     The Delegate is from the
000141*     System.Text.RegularExpressions Namespace
000150*
000160      DELEGATE MatchEvaluator AS
000170              "System.Text.RegularExpressions.MatchEvaluator"
000180*
000190*     Reference a .NET Framework Class
000200*     This Class is from the System Namespace
000210*
000220      CLASS SYS-STRING AS "System.String"
000230
000240 STATIC.
000250 PROCEDURE DIVISION.
000260 METHOD-ID. MAIN.
000270 DATA DIVISION.
000280 WORKING-STORAGE SECTION.
000290 01 OBJ OBJECT REFERENCE MYFIRSTCLASS.
000300 PROCEDURE DIVISION.
000310      INVOKE MYFIRSTCLASS "NEW" RETURNING OBJ.
000320 END METHOD MAIN.
000330 END STATIC.
000340
000350 OBJECT.
000360 DATA DIVISION.
000370 WORKING-STORAGE SECTION.
000380 PROCEDURE DIVISION.
000390*
000400 METHOD-ID. NEW.
000410 DATA DIVISION.
000420 WORKING-STORAGE SECTION.
000430 PROCEDURE DIVISION.
000440      INVOKE SELF "MYFIRSTMETHOD".
000450 END METHOD NEW.
000460*
000470 METHOD-ID. MYFIRSTMETHOD.
000480 DATA DIVISION.
000490 WORKING-STORAGE SECTION.
000500*
000510* Establish appropriate References to the .NET Framework objects
000520*
```

```
000530  01 MY-DELEGATE OBJECT REFERENCE MatchEvaluator.
000540  01 INPUT_STRING OBJECT REFERENCE SYS-STRING.
000550  01 OUTPUT_STRING OBJECT REFERENCE SYS-STRING.
000560  01 STRING_PATTERN OBJECT REFERENCE SYS-STRING.
000570  01 DISPLAY_LINE PIC X(100).
000580  01 NULL-X PIC X(1).
000590
000600 LINKAGE SECTION.
000610 PROCEDURE DIVISION.
000620*
000630*    Assigning the Delegate via the Class Constructor
000640*
000650     INVOKE MatchEvaluator "NEW"
000660          USING BY VALUE SELF "EvaluatorMethod"
000670          RETURNING MY-DELEGATE.
000680*
000690     SET INPUT_STRING TO "I think programming on the .NET platform is 0."
000700     SET STRING_PATTERN TO "\d"
000710*
000720*    Using a .NET Framework Class and doing an INLINE Invoke
000730*
000740     SET OUTPUT_STRING TO REGEX::"Replace"
000750         (INPUT_STRING, STRING_PATTERN, MY-DELEGATE)
000760     SET DISPLAY_LINE TO OUTPUT_STRING
000770
000780     DISPLAY DISPLAY_LINE
000790     DISPLAY "Enter X and Press Enter to Exit.".
000800     ACCEPT NULL-X.
000810
000820 END METHOD MYFIRSTMETHOD.
000830*
000840*    Using the Public Shared Function that is
000850*    fired each time the Regex.Replace method finds a match
000860*
000870 METHOD-ID. MatchEvaluatorMethod as "EvaluatorMethod".
000880 DATA DIVISION.
000890 WORKING-STORAGE SECTION.
000900 LINKAGE SECTION.
000910  01 MY-MATCH OBJECT REFERENCE Match.
000920  01 MyReturnString OBJECT REFERENCE SYS-STRING.
000930 PROCEDURE DIVISION USING BY VALUE MY-MATCH
000940                      RETURNING MyReturnString.
000950*
000960* Optionally, you could make the return value
```

```
000970* conditional depending on the MATCH value.
000980*
000990     SET MyReturnString TO "Easy"
001000 END METHOD MatchEvaluatorMethod.
001010
001020 END OBJECT.
001030 END CLASS MYFIRSTCLASS.
```

NOTE   The PROGRAM-ID has been changed to MAIN. You will need to modify the Entry Name on the property pages for this project to reflect the value of "MYFIRSTCLASS,MAIN".

In the COBOL .NET sample in Listing 7-4, the *System.Text.RegularExpressions* and System namespaces were used. Additionally, a Microsoft-provided delegate was used (the *MatchEvaluator*). Please take some time to review the code. The comments included in the sample code describe what the code is accomplishing. Listing 7-1, of course, represents just a sample of what is possible when you leverage the existing .NET Framework objects. Incidentally, the .NET Framework *Regex* class (the main class for regular expressions) used in this sample code *is* capable of much more.

Irregular Regular Expressions

When possible, consider looking into the topic of *regular expressions*. That is right, there is a toolset (namespace) within the .NET Framework called *RegularExpressions*. This toolset includes a very powerful, very flexible syntax that allows the creation of conditional matching and replacing logic that will really surprise you. What you might spend ten to fifteen lines of code doing in VB .NET, C#, or COBOL .NET, you could likely do with just one line of regular expressions. A word of caution: The syntax for regular expressions can appear to be quite cryptic until you spend some time deciphering it (see the "Books" subsection of the "To Learn More" section at the end of this chapter for a helpful resource). One good application for this type of flexible matching logic is in the area of *screen scraping* (scraping HTML Web pages). Validation logic is yet another area where regular expressions really shine. You can use this recommended addition to your retraining effort from any .NET language.

To wrap up the discussion of the COBOL .NET sample code in Listing 7-4, I thought it would be interesting to execute the Class Viewer .NET Framework tool to display your own class: MyFirstClass. Because you have compiled your project, the executable (similar to the legacy mainframe COBOL load modules) will be located in the bin subfolder. By the way, your bin subfolder will be located within the folder location that you chose to save your .NET project in. The code in Listing 7-5 is from the Class Viewer display of the MyFirstClass class. (The following option was used: **WINCV /r:FrameworkExampleCobol.exe**.)

Listing 7-5. The Class Viewer Showing MyFirstClass

```
public class MYFIRSTCLASS :
    object
    // Constructors
    public MYFIRSTCLASS();
    // Methods
    public virtual bool Equals(object obj);
    public virtual string
            EvaluatorMethod(System.Text.RegularExpressions.Match MY-MATCH);
    public virtual int GetHashCode();
    public Type GetType();
    public static void MAIN();
    public virtual void MYFIRSTMETHOD();
    public virtual string ToString();
    // end of MYFIRSTCLASS
```

In Listing 7-5, notice the "extra" methods that appear on your class. Recall that you did not "need" to create these yourself. As discussed earlier in the section "Classes," all classes—even the ones that you create—indirectly or directly inherit from System.Object. These "extra" methods being in your class is the result of this inheritance.

VB .NET Example

For the VB .NET sample code, I have created a console application and named the project FrameworkExampleVB. Listing 7-6 presents the sample code from the Module1.vb module.

Listing 7-6. A VB .NET Sample Program Demonstrating the Use of the .NET Framework Objects

```
' IMPORT a .NET Framework Namespace.
' By importing the Namespace, you can then refer
' to objects from the Namespace without typing the full
' name of the namespace - provides a shortcut.
Imports System.Text.RegularExpressions


Module Module1

        Sub Main()

                'Call the Sub Procedure
                MyFirstClass.MyfirstSubProcedure()


        End Sub


End Module

'Create our own Class
Class MyFirstClass
        Public Shared Sub MyfirstSubProcedure()

                'Declare variables by reusing the String Class
                'The SYSTEM Class is from the SYSTEM namespace
                'Including name of the namespace is optional
                'I could have just had "STRING" instead of "SYSTEM.STRING"

                Dim MyStringPattern As System.String = "\d"
                Dim MyfirstOutputString As System.String
                Dim MyfirstInputString As String _
                = "I think programming on the .NET platform is 0."

                'Using the .NET Framework class REGEX and its Replace method.
                'Our Declared String variable will "receive" the returned result
                'Notice that the AddressOf Operator is used
                'The AddressOf Operator is used to reference the Shared Function.

                MyfirstOutputString = _
                Regex.Replace(MyfirstInputString, MyStringPattern, _
                AddressOf Evaluator)
```

```
            Console.WriteLine(MyfirstOutputString)
            Console.WriteLine("Press Enter to Exit")
            Console.ReadLine()


    End Sub


    '  Using the Public Shared Function that is
    '  fired each time the Regex.Replace method finds a match

    Public Shared Function Evaluator(ByVal passedString As Match) As String

            'Optionally, you could make the return value
            'conditional depending on the MATCH value.
            Return "Easy"


    End Function


End Class
```

Please take a moment to read the comments included in Listing 7-6. Although this sample code is simple, it is a good example of how to leverage an existing .NET Framework delegate.

There are many other delegates (e.g., the popular *System.EventHandler* delegate). The sample code provided in this chapter provides examples of how to leverage these .NET Framework objects. Additionally, the interfaces, classes, enumerations, and structures are all available and waiting for you to exploit them.

 TIP   In Listing 7-6, there is a reason why it is optional to use the System namespace name when declaring the String data types. Even though the *Import* statement was not included in the code, the System namespace is actually *imported* by default. View the property pages to see the other namespaces that are *imported* by default. Compare this with the Import statement that was added for the System.Text. RegularExpressions namespace. From the property pages, you can add or remove namespaces for Import. Importing from the property pages will spread the "effect" across the entire project. Using the Import statement in code affects just the module that contains the Import statement.

The Visual Basic class MyFirstClass is available for you to examine in the Class Viewer. The code in Listing 7-7 shows the output from the Class Viewer tool when viewing FrameworkExampleVB.exe. The command line used to view this specific assembly is **WINCV /r: FrameworkExampleVB.exe**.

Listing 7-7. The Class Viewer Output Display

```
class FrameworkExampleVB.MyFirstClass :
    object
    // Constructors
    public MyFirstClass();
    // Methods
    public virtual bool Equals(object obj);
    public static string
            Evaluator(System.Text.RegularExpressions.Match passedString);
    public virtual int GetHashCode();
    public Type GetType();
    public static void MyfirstSubProcedure();
    public virtual string ToString();
    // end of FrameworkExampleVB.MyFirstClass
```

As with the COBOL .NET sample in Listing 7-4, notice that there are members in the MyFirstClass class that you did not explicitly code. Again, this provides you with a glimpse into the role of the .NET Framework's object-oriented design.

Referencing the .NET Framework Assemblies

In the previous VB .NET sample, FrameworkExampleVB, I mentioned that the Import statement was available for namespace typing shortcuts. This feature (in VB .NET) can be implemented explicitly in code or in the property pages.

Now that you understand all of that, I need to point out that the *importing* of .NET Framework namespaces should not be confused with the *referencing* of the assemblies (that contain the namespaces).

You may recall that I discussed the referencing of assemblies earlier in this chapter, when I needed to make the assemblies "visible" to the Object Browser. Well, this same "visibility" needs to exist for the application itself (remember the mainframe analogy of using STEPLIB and JOBLIB DD JCL statements to reference mainframe compiled load modules).

In COBOL .NET, you are accomplishing this "assembly reference" when you add the name(s) of the .NET Framework namespace(s) in the REPOSITORY paragraph.

In VB .NET, the "assembly reference" is accomplished by adding the name(s) of the .NET Framework namespace(s) in the Reference node in the Solution

Explorer window. Figure 7-13 shows the assembly references that are automatically added for the VB .NET Console Application template.

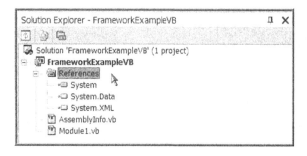

Figure 7-13. The VS .NET IDE Solution Explorer window with the Reference node expanded to show the referenced assemblies

I realize that it may be a little confusing that you would use the namespace names to reference particular assemblies. In this context, the two names (assembly and namespace) are practically synonymous without the "dll" suffix. This is made even more confusing when you realize that several namespaces could potentially be stored all in the same assembly. For example, both the System and System.Text.RegularExpressions namespaces are stored in the System.dll assembly. Aren't you glad that you had a chance (here) to clear that all up?

VS .NET Feature: IntelliSense

While you've edited various lines of code, you've certainly noticed the IntelliSense feature by now. Basically, IntelliSense is a productivity feature. As you start to type, the VS .NET IDE attempts to assist you by displaying a "type ahead" list (see Figure 7-14).

For example, say that you intend to type in **System.Text.RegularExpressions**. After you type in the period to signal the end of the second namespace level (i.e., **System.Text.**), you will notice that a list will appear. You can use your up and down arrow keys to navigate the list and select RegularExpressions from the list. Pressing Enter (or the Tab key) will enter the list item selection into your code as if you had typed it yourself.

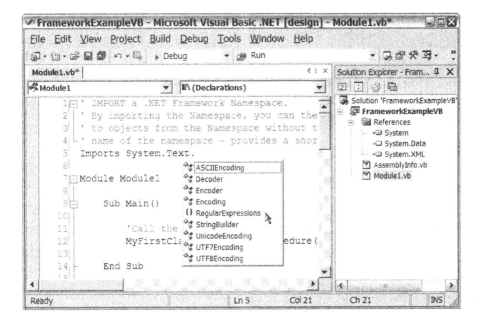

Figure 7-14. The VS .NET IntelliSense feature

Property Pages and the Project File

For each sample application I've presented in Chapter 6 and in this chapter, there have been occasions when I've referenced updating the project property pages. In those instances, I mentioned using the VS .NET IDE to perform these updates. Although I still recommend that you take advantage of the VS .NET IDE for these types of updates, you may find it interesting to know that you have a choice. You can also browse and/or update the project files directly.

In the case of each sample application (VB .NET and COBOL .NET), a project file is created and stored in the application folder. The project file for COBOL .NET (in this case) is named FrameworkExampleCobol.cobp. The VB .NET file, on the other hand, is named FrameworkExampleVB.vbproj.

If you use Notepad as your editor and open the FrameworkExampleCobol.cobp file (using a right-click, Open With approach), you will see the contents of the project file. Listing 7-8 presents a snippet of the file. Note the C# structure.

Listing 7-8. A Portion of the COBOL .NET Project File

```
"General"
{
"ProjectIdGuid" = "{864B8329-105D-4818-BCB6-41CA912020D7}"
"NestedProjectID" = "{930598EC-661E-4688-8812-014B15FBAC44}"
"EntryName" = "MYFIRSTCLASS,MAIN"
"OutputType" = "Exe"
"AssemblyName" = "FrameworkExampleCobol"
"Version" = ""
"Company" = ""
"Copyright" = ""
"ProductName" = ""
"Trademark" = ""
"Description" = ""
"Title" = ""
"DelaySign" = "False"
"KeyFile" = ""
"KeyName" = ""
}
"Configurations"
{
    "Debug|.NET"
    {
    "OutputPath" = "bin\\Debug\\"
    "GenerateListFile" = "False"
    "AdditionalOptions" = ""
    "ReferencePaths" = ""
    "CopyBookPaths" = ""
    }
    "Release|.NET"
    {
    "OutputPath" = "bin\\Release\\"
    "GenerateListFile" = "False"
    "AdditionalOptions" = ""
    "ReferencePaths" = ""
    "CopyBookPaths" = ""
    }
}
```

Optionally, you can browse and edit the VB .NET project file. Listing 7-9 shows the code as displayed in the Notepad editor. Note the XML structure.

Listing 7-9. The VB .NET Project File

```
<VisualStudioProject>
    <VisualBasic
        ProjectType = "Local"
        ProductVersion = "7.0.9466"
        SchemaVersion = "1.0"
        ProjectGuid = "{ABD5521A-28AA-4676-905E-0D8F0418D5CF}"
    >
        <Build>
            <Settings
                ApplicationIcon = ""
                AssemblyKeyContainerName = ""
                AssemblyName = "FrameworkExampleVB"
                AssemblyOriginatorKeyFile = ""
                AssemblyOriginatorKeyMode = "None"
                DefaultClientScript = "JScript"
                DefaultHTMLPageLayout = "Grid"
                DefaultTargetSchema = "IE50"
                DelaySign = "false"
                OutputType = "Exe"
                OptionCompare = "Binary"
                OptionExplicit = "On"
                OptionStrict = "Off"
                RootNamespace = "FrameworkExampleVB"
                StartupObject = "FrameworkExampleVB.Module1"
            >
                <Config
                    Name = "Debug"
                    BaseAddress = "285212672"
                    ConfigurationOverrideFile = ""
                    DefineConstants = ""
                    DefineDebug = "true"
                    DefineTrace = "true"
                    DebugSymbols = "true"
                    IncrementalBuild = "true"
                    Optimize = "false"
                    OutputPath = "bin\"
                    RegisterForComInterop = "false"
                    RemoveIntegerChecks = "false"
                    TreatWarningsAsErrors = "false"
                    WarningLevel = "1"
                />
```

```xml
            <Config
                Name = "Release"
                BaseAddress = "285212672"
                ConfigurationOverrideFile = ""
                DefineConstants = ""
                DefineDebug = "false"
                DefineTrace = "true"
                DebugSymbols = "false"
                IncrementalBuild = "false"
                Optimize = "true"
                OutputPath = "bin\"
                RegisterForComInterop = "false"
                RemoveIntegerChecks = "false"
                TreatWarningsAsErrors = "false"
                WarningLevel = "1"
            />
        </Settings>
        <References>
            <Reference
                Name = "System"
                AssemblyName = "System"
            />
            <Reference
                Name = "System.Data"
                AssemblyName = "System.Data"
            />
            <Reference
                Name = "System.XML"
                AssemblyName = "System.Xml"
            />
        </References>
        <Imports>
            <Import Namespace = "Microsoft.VisualBasic" />
            <Import Namespace = "System" />
            <Import Namespace = "System.Collections" />
            <Import Namespace = "System.Data" />
            <Import Namespace = "System.Diagnostics" />
        </Imports>
    </Build>
    <Files>
        <Include>
```

```
            <File
                RelPath = "AssemblyInfo.vb"
                SubType = "Code"
                BuildAction = "Compile"
            />
            <File
                RelPath = "Module1.vb"
                SubType = "Code"
                BuildAction = "Compile"
            />
        </Include>
    </Files>
  </VisualBasic>
</VisualStudioProject>
```

Although I am encouraging you to explore the files that are created in your local application folder, I ask that you do so with caution. Generally, you will be better off using the VS .NET IDE for your project properties editing. However, I believe that the more you understand what is going on behind the scenes, the more efficiently you will be able to leverage the .NET Framework.

 NOTE   At this time, I am only noting the observation that the structure of the project file contents is different: The COBOL. .NET project uses a C# structure, and VB .NET project uses an XML structure. However, it is fair to say that the XML structure is generally more common for .NET file content.

So, you have taken a good look at the contents of the project file. Perhaps you are debating whether to continue using the VS .NET IDE to update *your* project files. Well, before you make up your mind, here are a couple of alternative ways to access the property pages (*still* from within the VS .NET IDE). You may prefer either of these two methods over going to the Solution Explorer, right-clicking the project file, and selecting Properties.

- The first alternative is via the Standard toolbar. From your open VS .NET IDE, select the project file in the Solution Explorer window. Next, on the Standard toolbar, simply select Project ➤ Properties.

- The second alternative is via the Properties window. From your open VS .NET IDE, select the project file in the Solution Explorer window. Then, display the Properties window by pressing F4 (or on the Standard toolbar, select View ➤ Properties). The last step is to click the Property Pages icon, as shown in Figure 7-15.

Figure 7-15. Clicking the Property Pages icon in the Properties window

Summary

This chapter's goals were as follows:

- To discuss what the .NET Framework has to offer

- To explore the (re)use of the .NET Framework

This chapter covered quite a bit of ground. I discussed the .NET Framework in general. To fully explore this "Microsoft-provided class library," I discussed namespaces, assemblies, and the .NET Framework tools first. Then, I used an acronym (DICES) to introduce the types of objects available in the .NET Framework for your use and reuse. The sample code provided examples of .NET Framework usage. Naturally, I used several legacy mainframe analogies to assist your understanding: COBOL intrinsic functions, partitioned datasets, copybooks, subprograms, and the STEPLIB and JOBLIB JCL statements).

As you learned in this chapter, the .NET Framework is very powerful. In the next chapter you will turn your focus to .NET's common language runtime (CLR). As you will see, that portion of .NET is equally as critical to .NET as the other .NET features covered up to this point.

To Learn More

The following are some suggested supplemental references to further your retraining effort.

Books

Regular Expressions with .NET, by Dan Appleman (Desaware, 2002):
http://desaware.com/Ebook3L2.htm.

Magazines

.NET Magazine:
http://www.fawcette.com/dotnetmag/
Visual Studio Magazine:
http://www.fawcette.com/vsm/
XML & Web Services Magazine:
http://www.fawcette.com/xmlmag/

Web Sites

.NET Framework Class Library:
http://msdn.microsoft.com/library/en-us/cpref/html/cpref_start.asp
Dr. GUI .NET #1: Introduction to .NET Framework Types and Other Classes:
http://msdn.microsoft.com/library/en-us/dnguinet/html/
drguinet1_update.asp
Microsoft Community (discussion groups, e-newsletters, and so forth):
http://communities2.microsoft.com/
MSDN:
http://msdn.microsoft.com/

The .NET Common Language Runtime

What Is Done Under the Hood Does Matter

In this chapter

- Understanding .NET's common language runtime (CLR)

- Discussing the garbage collector (GC)

IF THERE WERE SUCH a thing as an "under-the-hood" type of chapter, this chapter would certainly fit the mold. The common language runtime (CLR) and its various features are well hidden. Even worse, the CLR's most important tasks are done automatically for the most part. Nevertheless, a full understanding of the CLR could easily separate those who simply *develop using .NET* from those who *use .NET to develop*.

In this chapter, I introduce the basic features of the CLR. I explore one of the CLR's features, the garbage collector (GC), in detail, particularly the role that the GC plays in memory management.

Understanding the Common Language Runtime

In Chapter 2, the terms "managed" and "unmanaged" were introduced. Also in that chapter, the CLR was (very) briefly introduced. Basically, I discussed how .NET-enabled program code was considered *managed* code and programming code executed outside of the .NET environment was considered *unmanaged* code. Consequently, the CLR is the "manager" of .NET-enabled code. The mainframe analogy offered in this earlier discussion suggested the "managing" that JES2 on the mainframe performs is similar to the managing performed by CLR on .NET. So, is there more? Yes, there is a lot more.

Having Fun with Acronyms

It is purely a coincidence that Microsoft chose the CLR acronym to describe a critical portion of .NET and that CLR happens to be the initials of my name: Christopher Lynn Richardson. If Microsoft had asked me to name this portion of .NET, they probably would have ended up with a name like "the engine of .NET." So, then we would have had an acronym like "TEN." Although that does spell .NET backwards, it would have left many developers in a state of confusion (except for those skilled in the art of [1]*gnidaeR drawkcaB)*. So, again, I tip my hat to Microsoft for their marketing genius.

I begin this discussion by looking at the name of the feature itself: common language runtime. Obviously, Microsoft chose that name to communicate that *all* .NET-enabled languages, once brought down to a "common" code form, will "run" on this virtual machine of sorts. In fact, that is the basic premise of Microsoft intermediate language (MSIL, or IL for short). Once each "high-level" language is taken through the appropriate compiler to create the intermediate language (a *common* denominator), the CLR then just runs the IL code without any discrimination. Understandably, some people refer to MSIL as CIL, which stands for *common intermediate language*. CIL is the generic specification that MSIL is based on.

There is one problem: This explanation is incomplete. To begin with, the CLR does not actually "run" the intermediate language. Does the mainframe "run" assembler code? No, the assembler code is "compiled" into machine code. The same concept applies here. The intermediate code is taken through a "compiler" that creates the machine code. The machine code is actually "run." (The compilation of IL to machine code occurs in the just-in-time [JIT] compiler.)

CROSS-REFERENCE I discuss the JIT compiler further in Chapter 17.

---

1. "Backward Reading." Recall that I warned you that I would make an attempt to present this information to you in an interesting yet useful way. This is in response to my peers who always thought that it was unusual that I was able to read IBM technical manuals as if they were novels—and not fall asleep.

Beyond that, there is still a problem with this brief and incomplete explanation. Yes, it is important to realize that the CLR's use of IL basically opened the door for Fujitsu Software and other ISVs to create .NET-enabled compilers. And yes, the use of IL even opened the door for Visual Basic .NET (VB .NET) to stand shoulder to shoulder with Visual C++ .NET (C++ .NET) and Visual C# .NET (C#). Still, the CLR *is* more—much more—than just the topic of IL.

For a moment, let's use the legacy mainframe JES2 system software as an analogy for the CLR. Just to review, I discussed in Chapter 2 the scenario of you submitting your batch programs in the form of Jobs, JES managing the priority execution of your Job, and JES being involved in the purging of your Job from the operating system. As you know, it is not *that* simple.

Up to this point, I have omitted many other COBOL mainframe (batch) development concerns. When it came to management of your "code," "process," and "resources," you had decisions to make. Typically, before you got to the point of being able to process your mainframe program, you (a veteran mainframe programmer) asked yourself most of the following questions:

- Which compiler directives should I use?

- What libraries should I include when I "link edit" my program?

- How much memory will my Working-Storage Section consume?

- Is my main program making static or dynamic calls to subprograms?

- Is my program going to be statically or dynamically called by a different program?

- Where is my compiled (binary) load module located?

- Did I remember to use a DISP=SHR on my JCL data definition statement when referring to my program load library?

- Am I going to execute my program in a JCL cataloged procedure?

- Do I need to override the default REGION allocation for memory (by Job or by Job Step)?

- When are any requested system resources going to be deallocated?

- Should I manually deallocate any system resources?

To those veteran mainframe programmers who happen to think in terms of CICS online application development, the additional following questions should be familiar:

- Does my CICS program design require me to use GETMAIN and FREEMAIN commands for explicit storage (memory) allocation and deallocation?

- Does my CICS program design require me to use ENQ and DEQ commands to explicitly reserve and release system resources?

- I want to use a temporary storage queue. Does it matter to my CICS application design if the queue is main storage or auxiliary storage?

- I want to use a transient data queue. Just how "transient" is the data that goes into the queue and what design considerations will I need to make to prepare for it?

Having gone through the exhaustive list of legacy mainframe development, perhaps you are saying, "Right, but what does this have to do with the CLR?"

Well, mainframe development—both batch and online—required that *you* actively participate in the various aspects of *managing* your application. Yes, the mainframe JES2 package, along with a host of other system software, was at your disposal. Basically, everything from JCL to the operating system played a part in this *management*. For instance, you have dealt with memory management, resource allocation, and code optimization. Can you now see where this analogy is leading? That is right. When you are developing on the .NET platform, the CLR will be there (in the background, mostly) assisting with these types of *management* concerns. And yes, you still have opportunities to actively participate.

Let's now move further into the CLR to review its feature set. Generally speaking, the CLR has the following features:

- Memory management through the garbage collector (GC)

- Code optimization through the just-in-time (JIT) compiler

- Process and application domain management

- Code access security

- Thread pool management

- .NET Remoting (distributed processing)

In this chapter, you will learn about the GC feature in detail. I delay discussion of the remaining features until later chapters, as shown in Table 8-1.

Table 8-1. CLR Feature Discussion

FEATURE	CHAPTER
The JIT compiler	Chapter 17
Code access security	Chapter 18
Process and application domain management	Chapter 20
Thread pool management and .NET Remoting	Chapter 20

The Garbage Collector

Considering all the accolades the Microsoft marketing gurus have received, you might think that they perhaps *blinked* while naming this particular CLR feature. Who would have thought that a name as unglamorous as the "garbage collector" would stick? Well, considering what the GC actually does, I cannot think of a more appropriate name myself. Believe me, I tried—for example, "memory space reclaimer" and "managed heap recycler." These entries just do not seem to have the same pizzazz as the "garbage collector." So, sticking with GC, let's examine the "garbage" that gets collected.

Memory Management

On the mainframe, when your COBOL batch Job ended, you knew that you were freeing resources. Additionally, when you did mainframe COBOL CICS development, you knew that the completion of your CICS task freed resources. Now, if I were to ask you to list the "resources" that were freed, you would likely begin with external input and output devices (including disk storage). Perhaps you might continue by mentioning the operating system's Job processing initiator as a freed resource.

Naturally, you would not stop there. You would include the resources associated with the variables defined in your program's Working-Storage Section and Linkage Section as freed resources. Lastly, you would mention the virtual copy of your COBOL program and JCL Job as freed resources. Now for a question: Have you ever given thought to the disposition of these "resources" after they were freed? As I recall, we referred to this as "concerns for the electronic heavens."

These freed resources represented *garbage:* resources that had been used and discarded. As unsettling as it is to admit, we mainframe programmers just did not care about (or need to care about) the disposition of our garbage as long as the resources were in fact freed. Little did we know, our resident system programmer kept a watchful eye on the available resources systemwide using system-level software to identify the freed resources (our garbage), reclaim unused memory, and compact freed space to minimize fragmentation.

Creating .NET Garbage

On the .NET platform, you will create lots of garbage.[2] That is to say, your well-written applications will contain many managed objects that eventually are freed. Once freed, the objects become garbage and candidates for collection.

In Chapter 7, you learned about the .NET Framework. As you recall, the Framework includes delegates, interfaces, classes, enumerations, and structures (which I referred to using the acronym DICES). With the exception of enumerations and structures, these .NET Framework objects are destined to become collected garbage. So, why are enumerations and structures treated differently?

Well, in Chapter 7, you learned that enumerations could only contain numeric data types (structures), right? You also learned that all enumerations are *derived* from the System.Enum class. So, where do you think the System.Enum class is *derived* from? That is right. System.Enum is *derived* from the System.ValueType class. As you know, *all* structures are derived from the same class: System.ValueType. There you have it: Enumerations and structures are excluded from garbage collection because they are both derived from the System.ValueType class and are considered ValueType objects.[3]

NOTE ValueType objects can participate in garbage collection if they are *boxed*. Boxing is further discussed in the section "The Boxing of ValueType Objects" later in this chapter.

Basically, that leaves you with delegates, interfaces, and classes (and any boxed ValueTypes) to be garbage collected. As the GC makes its rounds looking for garbage (objects that are no longer referenced and available for collection), one of several things can occur:

2. Pun intended.
3. I further discuss ValueType objects in Chapter 9.

- Dead objects can be collected (i.e., they are effectively removed from the managed heap).

- Dead objects that happen to have a *Finalizer* method can be flagged and moved to a different managed heap[4] (I discuss this further in the section "Garbage Collection Schedule" later in this chapter).

- Live objects can be promoted from one heap generation to the next heap generation (i.e., from frequently scanned generation 0 to less frequently scanned generation 1, and so forth).

Figure 8-1 illustrates boxed structures and other .NET Framework objects on the managed heap waiting to be collected by the GC.

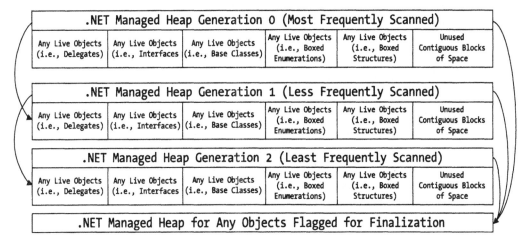

Figure 8-1. The .NET Framework objects on the managed heap

As you will notice in Figure 8-1, your installed system will typically support multiple heap generations. As garbage collections occur, any objects that survive will be promoted to the next heap generation. These objects are said to have *aged*. The following set of code samples is provided to demonstrate the CLR promoting an object from one heap generation to the next. The CLR does this for performance reasons.

NOTE The System namespace and GC class are introduced in each code sample to support this demonstration. Comments are included in each code sample to help explain the GC methods being used.

---

4. This "other heap" is sometimes referred to as the *finalization queue.*

COBOL .NET Example

As you will notice in Listing 8-1, I have created a console application and named the project HeapGenerationExampleCobol. For your convenience, the sample code from the .cob module is provided in Listing 8-1.

Listing 8-1. COBOL .NET Example of How the CLR Promotes Aged Objects

```
000010 IDENTIFICATION DIVISION.
000020* This is an example of how the CLR Promotes Objects
000030* from one HEAP Generation to the next - as an object ages
000040 PROGRAM-ID. MAIN.
000050 ENVIRONMENT DIVISION.
000060 CONFIGURATION SECTION.
000070 REPOSITORY.
000080* .NET Framework Classes
000090    CLASS SYS-OBJECT AS "System.Object"
000100    CLASS SYS-INTEGER AS "System.Int32"
000110    CLASS GC AS "System.GC".
000120*
000130 DATA DIVISION.
000140 WORKING-STORAGE SECTION.
000150    77 obj    OBJECT REFERENCE SYS-OBJECT.
000160    77 GC_OBJ OBJECT REFERENCE GC.
000170    77 My_Int OBJECT REFERENCE SYS-INTEGER.
000180    77 My_String PIC X(20).
000190
000200    01 NULL-X PIC X(1).
000210 LINKAGE SECTION.
000220
000230 PROCEDURE DIVISION.
000240
000250    DISPLAY "Begin Heap Generation COBOL.NET Example"
000260    DISPLAY " "
000270
000280* Instantiate Object from .NET Framework Classes
000290    INVOKE SYS-OBJECT "NEW" RETURNING obj
000300
000310* Execute GC "GetGeneration" Method Using Inline Invoke syntax
000320    SET My_Int to GC::"GetGeneration" (obj)
000330* Execute ToString Method Using Inline Invoke syntax
000340    SET My_String to My_Int::"ToString"
000350    Display "HEAP Generation of obj BEFORE FIRST collection: "
000360            My_String
```

```
000370
000380* Manually Induce Garbage Collection on all Generations
000390     INVOKE GC "Collect".
000400
000410* Execute GC "GetGeneration" Method Using Inline Invoke
000420     SET My_Int to GC::"GetGeneration" (obj)
000430* Execute ToString Method Using Inline Invoke syntax
000440     SET My_String to My_Int::"ToString"
000450     Display "HEAP Generation of obj AFTER FIRST collection: "
000460          My_String
000470
000480* Manually Induce Garbage Collection on all Generations
000490     INVOKE GC "Collect".
000500
000510* Execute GC "GetGeneration" Method Using Inline Invoke
000520     SET My_Int to GC::"GetGeneration" (obj)
000530* Execute ToString Method Using Inline Invoke syntax
000540     SET My_String to My_Int::"ToString"
000550     Display "HEAP Generation of obj AFTER SECOND collection: "
000560          My_String
000570
000580* Remove Object reference
000590* This will make it eligible for Garbage Collection
000600     SET obj to NULL
000610
000620* Manually Induce Garbage Collection on all Generations
000630     INVOKE GC "Collect"
000640
000650* Optionally, I could have induced a collection
000660* specifically on the generation # containing my obj.
000670* Using the syntax "GC.Collect USING BY VALUE var1"
000680* with var1 having the value of 1, to target generation 1
000690
000700     DISPLAY "Enter X and Press Enter to Exit.".
000710     ACCEPT NULL-X.
000720
000730 END PROGRAM  MAIN.
```

After you execute the HeapGenerationExampleCobol project, the output shown in Figure 8-2 will appear.

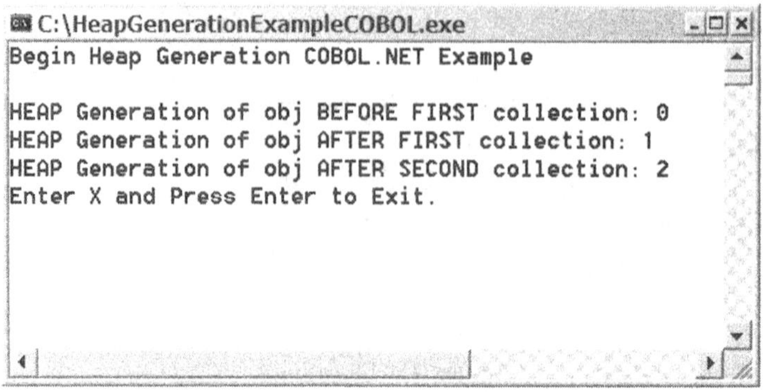

Figure 8-2. The console display of the HeapGenerationExampleCobol project

Feel free to view the associated IL (using ILDASM) for this assembly. The more that you do this, the better you will understand the effect your coding statements have on application processing. (Please see the related common intermediate language [CIL] reference in the "Books" subsection of the "To Learn More" section.)

Let's now take a look at this heap generation example implemented using VB .NET.

VB .NET Example

As you will notice in Listing 8-2, the VB .NET code sample also is created as a console application. The .vb code for HeapGenerationExampleVB is provided in Listing 8-2.

Listing 8-2. VB .NET Example of How the CLR Promotes Aged Objects

```
Module Module1

        'This is an example of how the CLR Promotes Objects
        'from one HEAP Generation to the next - as an object ages

        Sub Main()

                Console.WriteLine _
                ("Begin Heap Generation Visual Basic.NET Example")
                Console.WriteLine(String.Empty)

                'Instantiate Object from .NET Framework Classes
```

```
          Dim obj As New Object()

          'Execute GC "GetGeneration" Method and ToString Method
          Console.WriteLine _
          ("HEAP Generation of obj BEFORE FIRST collection: " _
          & GC.GetGeneration(obj).ToString)

          'Manually Induce Garbage Collection on all Generations
          GC.Collect()

          'Execute GC "GetGeneration" Method and ToString Method
          Console.WriteLine _
          ("HEAP Generation of obj AFTER FIRST collection: " _
          & GC.GetGeneration(obj).ToString)

          'Manually Induce Garbage Collection on all Generations
          GC.Collect()

          Console.WriteLine _
          ("HEAP Generation of obj AFTER SECOND collection: " _
          & GC.GetGeneration(obj).ToString)

          'Remove Object reference
          'This will make it eligible for Garbage Collection
          obj = Nothing

          'Manually Induce Garbage Collection on all Generations
          GC.Collect()

          'Optionally, I could have induced a collection
          'specifically on the generation # containing my obj.
          'Using the syntax GC.Collect(1) to target generation 1

          Console.WriteLine("Press Enter to Exit")
          Console.ReadLine()

    End Sub

End Module
```

For your convenience, I have executed the HeapGenerationExampleVB project. As you can see in Figure 8-3, the display shows that the CLR has promoted the object from heap generation 0 to heap generation 1 and then to heap generation 2.

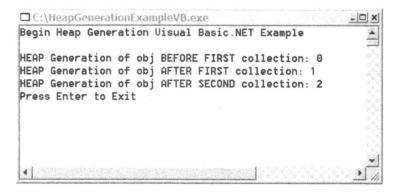

Figure 8-3. The console display of the HeapGenerationExampleVB project

The Boxing of ValueType Objects

As previously mentioned in the section "Creating .NET Garbage," structures and enumerations (in other words, ValueType objects) can participate in garbage collection through the CLR feature called *boxing*. Using the boxing feature, you can reference a structure or an enumeration (value type) as a reference type object. Usually, this conversion is done implicitly as the result of a coding assignment. Likewise, there is an *unboxing* feature, which is the boxing operation occurring in reverse. The COBOL .NET and VB .NET code snippets in this section illustrate the boxing feature in practice.

Listing 8-3 presents the COBOL .NET code snippet (using a Console Application template).

Listing 8-3. COBOL .NET Code Snippet from the BoxingExampleCOBOL Project

```
000010 IDENTIFICATION DIVISION.
000020* This is an example of IMPLICITLY BOXING a Structure
000030 PROGRAM-ID. MAIN.
000040 ENVIRONMENT DIVISION.
000050 CONFIGURATION SECTION.
000060 REPOSITORY.
000070* .NET Framework Classes
000080            CLASS SYS-OBJECT AS "System.Object".
000090*
000100 DATA DIVISION.
000110 WORKING-STORAGE SECTION.
000120
000130* Declare Data Items with COBOL.NET Data Types
```

```
000140* this Data Type maps to a Structure/Value Type.
000150* Initialize with the value of 9999 (Hex x'270F).
000160* The myFirstInt variable is allocated on the Stack
000170* does not get Garbage Collected
000180
000190   77  myFirstInt PIC S9(9) USAGE IS COMP-5 Value 9999.
000200* Declare Data Items using .NET Data Types
000210* that References an Object
000220* The myobject variable is allocated memory on the HEAP
000230* and will be Garbage Collected
000240
000250   77  myobject              OBJECT REFERENCE SYS-OBJECT.
000260
000270   01 NULL-X PIC X(1).
000280 LINKAGE SECTION.
000290*
000300 PROCEDURE DIVISION.
000310* Reference the Value of the Value Type
000320     SET myobject to myFirstInt.
000330
000340     DISPLAY "Use ILDASM to view the BOXing of the Structure"
000350     DISPLAY "Enter X and Press Enter to Exit.".
000360     ACCEPT NULL-X.
000370
000380 END PROGRAM  MAIN.
```

Listing 8-4 presents the VB .NET code snippet (which also uses a Console Application template).

Listing 8-4. VB .NET Code Snippet from the BoxingExampleVB Project

```
Module Module1

    Sub Main()
          'This is an example of IMPLICITLY BOXING a Structure

          'Declare a Structure/Value Type.
          'Initialize with the value of 9999 (Hex x'270F)
          'The myFirstInt variable is allocated on the Stack
          'and does not get Garbage Collected
          Dim myFirstInt As Integer = 9999

          'Declare a Reference Type Object
          'Reference the Value of the Value Type
```

```
                     'The myobject variable is allocated memory on the HEAP
                     'and will be Garbage Collected
                     Dim myobject As Object = myFirstInt

                     Console.WriteLine _
                     ("Use ILDASM to view the BOXing of the Structure")
                     Console.WriteLine _
                     ("Press Enter to Exit")
                     Console.ReadLine()
              End Sub
       End Module
```

Now, let's take a peek at the ILDASM display and look at the MSIL for evidence that this boxing feature is actually executed. You will notice that the box command appears in the MSIL for each language. Notice also that the hex value of x'270F' is used to initialize the value type variable.

Listing 8-5 presents the MSIL snippet for the COBOL .NET BoxingExampleCOBOL project.

Listing 8-5. MSIL Snippet for COBOL .NET Showing the Box Command Being Performed

```
. . .
<copied from the _InitialProgram Method Output>
  IL_0016:  ldc.i4     0x270f
  IL_001b:  stsfld     int32 MAIN::MYFIRSTINT_001CE9F8
  IL_0020:  ldnull
  IL_0021:  stsfld     object MAIN::MYOBJECT_001CEAB8
. . .
<copied from the Procedure Method Output>
  IL_006a:  stelem.ref
  IL_006b:  br.s       IL_006d
  IL_006d:  ldsfld     int32 MAIN::MYFIRSTINT_001CE9F8
  IL_0072:  box        int32
  IL_0077:  stsfld     object MAIN::MYOBJECT_001CEAB8
  IL_007c:  ldloc      _DisplayInfo
  IL_0080:  ldc.i4.0
  . . .
```

Listing 8-6 shows the MSIL snippet for the VB .NET BoxingExampleVB project.

Listing 8-6. MSIL Snippet for VB .NET Showing the Box Command Being Performed

```
<copied from the Main Method Output>
.method public static void  Main() cil managed
. . .
  .locals init ([0] int32 myFirstInt,
              [1] object myobject)
  IL_0000:  nop
  IL_0001:  ldc.i4      0x270f
  IL_0006:  stloc.0
  IL_0007:  ldloc.0
  IL_0008:  box         [mscorlib]System.Int32
  IL_000d:  stloc.1
. . .
  IL_002a:  nop
  IL_002b:  ret
} // end of method Module1::Main
```

I included this small amount of COBOL .NET and VB .NET code to demonstrate the activities that go on behind the scenes. Some of these activities result in different amounts of garbage being created by your application. Some of these things *will* matter to you.

You may come across information in the future (and even in the next chapter of this book) that will point out advantages of value type objects over reference type objects. But as you can see here, depending on how you use them, you could end up actually creating reference type objects that will get garbage collected.

In other words, there are times when you should use value type objects and other times when reference type objects are more suitable. Each object type has special program coding considerations. Each object type has its pros and cons. However, once a value type object is boxed, the playing field is somewhat leveled.

CROSS-REFERENCE　In Chapter 9, you will explore value type objects and reference type objects in detail.

TIP Just for clarification, the distinction made in Chapter 6 between COBOL .NET data types and .NET data types shouldn't be confused with the distinction made here between value types and reference types. For example, within the category of .NET data types, you have both value types and reference types. This was further explained in Chapter 7 in the section "Structures." Did I confuse you? Don't worry, in Chapter 9 I thoroughly discuss the topic of objects. Then, having come full circle, I'm sure your understanding will be complete.

Garbage Collection Schedule

In the section "Creating .NET Garbage" earlier in this chapter, I mentioned that the .NET GC "makes its rounds." Then, I turned around and used a GC.Collect method in the heap generation code samples to manually *induce* a garbage collection. Of course, this is an obvious contradiction.

At this point, you are ready to have the following questions answered:

- What is the garbage collection schedule?

- Can you control the garbage collection schedule?

- Should you control the garbage collection schedule?

The real answer to the first question is "Who knows?" Now, this does not sound like a polite way to answer a question, right? Given the technical nature of the topic, some will say that this answer is just barely acceptable. We reformed mainframe programmer types have been trained for years to never guess, to never assume anything. So, in our honor, here is a more appropriate answer. (Be sure to take a deep breath before you continue!)

The GC has an optimizing engine that determines how often to perform a collection. The GC is described as following a *heuristic approach*. Depending on the actual characteristic of managed heap allocation attempts and available space at the time, the GC follows an established algorithm.[5] For example, if an application attempts to allocate space, the first target managed heap generation is generation 0. The GC checks to see if there is enough space to complete the allocation (this also

---

5. Some believe that a particular phase of the moon or the velocity of the northern wind has some influence on the GC schedule as well. Well, if a groundhog's vision can influence seasonal weather patterns, anything is possible.

involves processing of objects and generation promotion of objects). If the needed space is not available on generation 0, the GC then follows the same algorithm on generation 1 and then again on generation 0 (remember that eligible objects are being removed, disposed, finalized, and/or promoted). The GC compacts the free space found on the managed heap. The GC, if needed, then goes through the same process with generation 2, then generation 1, and then generation 0. Again, it is processing objects, promoting objects, reclaiming and compacting space, and so forth.

All right, now exhale. That was certainly a mouthful. Can you do me a favor? The next time that someone asks *you* about the GC's schedule, try giving *them* this same answer. As you watch the person's jaw drop, calmly sum things up by saying something like "It's really intuitive and simple." Hey, why not have a little fun every now and then?

 NOTE Just a reminder: The GC is a feature of the CLR.

Let us now tackle the remaining two questions, which both speak to the topic of controlling the GC schedule.

Yes, for better or for worse, you *can* control the GC schedule. Why "for better or for worse"? Well, first understand that generally speaking, you should not even think about controlling, influencing, manipulating, or otherwise intervening with the GC's schedule.

My liberal use of the *GC.Collect* method in this chapter in various code samples is for demonstration purposes only. Some of the same coding statements available (e.g., GC.Collect) for increasing the frequency of collection could in some cases improve one application's performance but seriously degrade a different application's performance. This also holds true for the use of the *Dispose* and *Finalize* methods. You should use the Dispose and Finalize methods only after you have performed detailed analysis regarding the intended benefit and any potential negative impact of using them. Having said that, here are a few other legitimate scenarios for explicitly influencing the GC schedule:

- Your managed code makes use of unmanaged resources (e.g., file, window, or network connections).

- Your managed code makes use of unmanaged objects (e.g., legacy applications, COM objects, and so forth).

- Your managed code makes use of only managed objects and managed resources, yet your application fits a rare example of one that has the need to adopt a "deterministic" cleanup approach.

I strongly recommend that if your application falls into one of these three scenarios you refer to the "To Learn More" section at the end of this chapter. You will find a healthy number of useful references to support your continued learning.

CAUTION   A few of you might feel a little uncomfortable with the idea of my mentioning a piece of technology only to turn around and discourage its use. First, I wish to only discourage its *misuse*. Second, we highly skilled reformed mainframe programmers have done this sort of thing before. Haven't you cautioned others on the use of the FREEMAIN and GETMAIN commands when doing mainframe COBOL CICS development? As you know, the misuse of these "memory management" commands can have grave consequences. Suffice it to say that a warning is appropriate in this context as well.

Are you ready for one more stab at the GC topic? Good! I think you will like the next discussion.

Monitoring the GC

Perhaps you are starting to get a feel for this CLR feature, this powerful engine called the GC. Maybe, just maybe, you have a feel for the scheduling concerns that surround the GC. Through discussion and sample code you have even explored the heap generation promotion behavior of the CLR and GC. But still you are curious; you are thirsty for more. OK, here you go.

Included with the Windows and .NET platform are many tools that monitor performance. Given the impact that memory management (and mismanagement) can have on performance, familiarity with these monitoring tools is relevant. I will use this section to give you yet another view of the actual "behavior" of the GC.

Among the many Windows-based performance-monitoring tools are a few that are bundled with various Windows and .NET software editions:

- Windows Task Manager (discussed in Chapter 3)

- Application Center Test (ACT) (discussed in Chapter 13)

- Performance Monitor (Perfmon)

As noted, the Windows Task Manager and Application Center Test are discussed elsewhere in this book—in Chapter 3 and Chapter 13, respectively.

TIP To access the Windows Task Manager utility, press Ctrl-Alt-Delete. Depending on your version of the Windows operating system, you may have to click Task Manager after you press the keyboard combination. Optionally, you can access the Windows Task Manager utility by right-clicking an empty space on the taskbar and then clicking Task Manager.

At this time, I will introduce you to the Windows product called *Performance Monitor* (Perfmon). Functionally, you might (loosely) compare this product with some of the various OMEGAMON-type mainframe-monitoring products. As you will soon see, with Perfmon you can obtain a rather granular view of your application's performance (including the general performance of your system-level processes).

You can access the Perfmon tool in one of several ways:

- From your desktop, click the Start button and select Programs ➤ Administrative Tools ➤ Performance.

- From an open Windows Task Manager window on the toolbar, select File ➤ New Task (Run). Then enter **Perfmon** in the Open text box and click OK.

- From your desktop, click the Start button and select Run. Then enter **Perfmon** in the Open text box and click OK.

- Programmatically, you can access the Perfmon objects (or performance counter objects) via an instance of the .NET namespace *System.Diagnostics.PerformanceCounter*.

For this discussion, you will access Perfmon using the last two approaches. First, you will take a look at the "programmatic" approach with a set of sample applications. Following that discussion, I introduce the actual Perfmon tool.

NOTE You will notice a large block of COBOL .NET DISPLAY statements and VB .NET Console.WriteLine statements in the following set of sample applications (PerfmonCobol and PerfmonVB). As you execute the sample applications for the first discussion in the section "Creating a Performance Counter Component," simply disregard these code comments/instructions. I provided these code comments/ instructions as preparation for the discussion in the section "Using the Windows Performance Monitor Tool" later in this chapter. In this later section, you will again execute this same set of sample applications. At that time, you should pay attention to the code comments/ instructions.

Creating a Performance Counter Component

In the following set of code samples, you will separately create a COBOL .NET project and a VB .NET project. I created each using the Console Application template type. I chose to name the applications PerfmonCobol and PerfmonVB, respectively. In each project, you will focus on the *PerformanceCounter* class from the *System.Diagnostics* .NET namespace. The following five properties of the PerformanceCounter class are used:

- Input: `CategoryName = ".NET CLR Memory"`

- Input: `CounterName = "# Bytes in all Heaps"`

- Input: `MachineName = "."`

- Input: `InstanceName = "PerfmonVB"`

- Output: `RawValue`

I chose this particular performance object (the value specified in the *CategoryName* property) and this particular performance counter (the value specified in the CounterName property) for demonstration purposes only. In the section "Performance Counter Objects" later in this chapter, I list a few of the other performance objects that are directly related to the .NET CLR.

COBOL .NET Example

The COBOL .NET code in Listing 8-7 will programmatically create a performance counter component. Please examine the code and the included comments before you run the application. This application demonstrates the activity of the GC. By showing how the total allocated heap bytes fluctuate (without manually inducing a garbage collection), you can see that the GC is alive and actively clearing space from the managed heaps.

Listing 8-7. COBOL .NET PerfmonCobol Example

```
000010 IDENTIFICATION DIVISION.
000020* This is an example of how the CLR
000030* actively performs memory management.
000040 PROGRAM-ID. MAIN.
000050 ENVIRONMENT DIVISION.
000060 CONFIGURATION SECTION.
000070 REPOSITORY.
000080* .NET Framework Classes
000090     CLASS SYS-INT64 AS "System.Int64"
000100     CLASS PERFCOUNTER AS "System.Diagnostics.PerformanceCounter"
000110     PROPERTY PROP-CategoryName AS "CategoryName"
000120     PROPERTY PROP-CounterName AS "CounterName"
000130     PROPERTY PROP-MachineName AS "MachineName"
000140     PROPERTY PROP-InstanceName AS "InstanceName"
000150     PROPERTY PROP-RawValue AS "RawValue".
000160*
000170 DATA DIVISION.
000180 WORKING-STORAGE SECTION.
000190    77 PERFCOUNTER_Obj OBJECT REFERENCE PERFCOUNTER.
000200    77 myLong OBJECT REFERENCE SYS-INT64.
000210    77 My_String PIC X(20).
000220    77 myString1 PIC X(40) VALUE "This is an example of creating Garbage".
000230    77 i PIC S9(9) COMP-5.
000240* Set this variable to the number of times to process the loop
000250    77 maxInt PIC S9(9) COMP-5 VALUE 999.
000260
000270    01 NULL-X PIC X(1).
000280 LINKAGE SECTION.
000290
000300 PROCEDURE DIVISION.
000310
000320* Set Properties of PerformanceCounter Class
000330     INVOKE PERFCOUNTER "NEW" RETURNING PERFCOUNTER_Obj
```

```
000340        SET PROP-CategoryName OF PERFCOUNTER_Obj TO ".NET CLR Memory"
000350        SET PROP-CounterName OF PERFCOUNTER_Obj TO "# Bytes in all Heaps"
000360        SET PROP-MachineName OF PERFCOUNTER_Obj TO "."
000370        SET PROP-InstanceName OF PERFCOUNTER_Obj TO "PerfmonCobol"
000380
000390        SET myLong to PROP-RawValue OF PERFCOUNTER_Obj
000400        INITIALIZE My_String
000410        SET My_String to myLong::"ToString"
000420
000430        DISPLAY "Begin Performance Monitor COBOL Example"
000440        DISPLAY " "
000450        DISPLAY "1St Performance Monitor Reading: " My_String
000460        DISPLAY " "
000470        DISPLAY "Warning: This loop will run for a long time."
000480        DISPLAY "!! Depending on the Value of the maxInt variable !! "
000490        DISPLAY "I suggest that you let it run for a while"
000500        DISPLAY "at the same time, you can View the Perfmon Tool info."
000510        DISPLAY "You can either let the loop run and end normally or"
000520        DISPLAY "you can manually terminate the sample application"
000530        DISPLAY "by CLOSING the opened console window."
000540        DISPLAY " "
000550        DISPLAY "Please Prepare your Perfmon window as follows:"
000560        DISPLAY "Performance Object = .NET CLR Memory"
000570        DISPLAY "Counter = # Bytes in all Heaps"
000580        DISPLAY "Machine Name = Local computer"
000590        DISPLAY "Instance Name = PerfmonVB and/or PerfmonCobol"
000600        DISPLAY " "
000610        DISPLAY "Enter X and Press Enter to Resume Sample Application."
000620        ACCEPT NULL-X.
000630
000640        PERFORM VARYING i
000650              FROM 0 BY 1 UNTIL i >= maxInt
000660                  MOVE "This String had been modified." TO myString1
000670                  SET myLong to PROP-RawValue OF PERFCOUNTER_Obj
000680                  INITIALIZE My_String
000690                  SET My_String to myLong::"ToString"
000700                  Display "Allocated Heap: " My_String
000710        END-PERFORM
000720
000730        DISPLAY "The loop has completed. Enter X and Press Enter to Exit.".
000740        ACCEPT NULL-X.
000750
000760 END PROGRAM  MAIN.
```

If possible, please run the application. After it displays hundreds of output lines, the application will complete. Take a moment and scroll through the console window display. It should be obvious at which point the GC performed its collection (at each point where the displayed value decreased).

In the sample code, please notice the approach to "creating" the Performance-Counter object. In object-oriented terms, this is referred to as *object instantiation*.

VB .NET Example

In Listing 8-8, the performance counter component has been programmatically created. Please examine the code and the included comments. When you run this application, a stream of lines will be written to the console window. Notice how the RawValue amount fluctuates constantly. Well, this value is showing the total amount of allocated spaces across all of the managed heaps in each generation. Why does it fluctuate so? Because the GC is busily clearing space as the application continues to add space. This demonstrates that garbage collection will occur, even without any manual intervention.

Listing 8-8. VB .NET PerfmonVB Example

```
'This is an example of how the CLR
'actively performs memory management.

Module Module1
  Sub Main()
    Dim i As Int32

'* Set Properties of PerformanceCounter Class
      Dim myCounter As New System.Diagnostics.PerformanceCounter()
      With myCounter
              .CategoryName = ".NET CLR Memory"
              .CounterName = "# Bytes in all Heaps"
              .MachineName = "."
              .InstanceName = "PerfmonVB"
      End With
'Set this variable to the number of times to process the loop
      Dim maxInt As Int32 = 999
      Console.WriteLine("Begin Performance Monitor VB Example")
      Console.WriteLine(String.Empty)
      Console.WriteLine("1St Performance Monitor Reading: " & _
                    myCounter.RawValue.ToString())
      Console.WriteLine(" ")
      Console.WriteLine("Warning: This loop will run for a long time.")
```

```
        Console.WriteLine("!! Depending on the Value of the maxInt variable !! ")
        Console.WriteLine("I suggest that you let it run for a while")
        Console.WriteLine("at the same time, you can View the Perfmon Tool info.")
        Console.WriteLine("You can either let the loop run and end normally or")
        Console.WriteLine("you can manually terminate the sample application")
        Console.WriteLine("by CLOSING the opened console window.")
        Console.WriteLine(" ")
        Console.WriteLine("Please Prepare your Perfmon window as follows:")
        Console.WriteLine("Performance Object = .NET CLR Memory")
        Console.WriteLine("Counter = # Bytes in all Heaps")
        Console.WriteLine("Machine Name = Local computer")
        Console.WriteLine("Instance Name = PerfmonVB and/or PerfmonCobol")
        Console.WriteLine(" ")
        Console.WriteLine("Then Press Enter to Resume Sample Application.")
        Console.ReadLine()
        Dim myString1 As String = "This is an example of creating Garbage"
        For i = 0 To maxInt
                myString1 = "This String had been modified."
                Console.WriteLine("Allocated Heap: " & _
                myCounter.RawValue.ToString())
        Next
        Console.WriteLine("The loop has completed. Press Enter to Exit.")
        Console.ReadLine()
End Sub
End Module
```

Please run the VB .NET example application. If you scroll through the console window display, you will notice that the "TOTAL of BYTES in ALL HEAP" value increases and decreases. Each decrease signals that a garbage collection has occurred.

Please notice use of the *With* and *End With* language statements in the VB .NET sample code. The use of these statements is considered good coding practice when you need to access multiple properties on one object.

Performance Counter Objects

In the sample applications, you have used the System.Diagnostics. PerformanceCounter class. You set a few of its properties. One of those properties is CategoryName.

Now, what will you do when you want to use categories *other* than the one you used here (".NET CLR Memory")? Given that you have many performance categories to choose from (approximately 66), there has to be a way to find out what choices are available, right? Well, there is. You have a few options:

- You can view the MSDN Web references included at the end of this chapter in the "Web Sites" subsection of the "To Learn More" section.

- You can view the drop-down menus of the Perfmon GUI tool.

- You can write a small program to instantiate the appropriate .NET namespace class: *System.Diagnostics.PerformanceCounterCategory*. Then, execute the appropriate method (i.e., *GetCategories*) to receive an array that contains all of the available performance categories. The following sample code demonstrates this:

```
'This is an example of how to retrieve
'the Performance Categories
Module Module1
    Sub Main()
    Dim myCounterCategories As New _
    System.Diagnostics.PerformanceCounterCategory()
    Dim x As Array = myCounterCategories.GetCategories()
    For Each myCounterCategories In x
        Console.WriteLine(myCounterCategories.CategoryName)
    Next
    Console.WriteLine("Press Enter to Exit.")
    Console.ReadLine()
    End Sub
End Module
```

NOTE   The preceding code sample is one of a few exceptions where I provide just the VB .NET code. Converting the sample to COBOL .NET would be a good exercise for you to do.

After running the small sample application GetPerfCategoriesVB, I did a little copying and pasting to include *some* of the following performance categories, which are directly related to .NET:

- .NET CLR Data

- .NET CLR Exceptions

- .NET CLR Interop

- .NET CLR JIT

- .NET CLR Loading

- .NET CLR LocksAndThreads

- .NET CLR Memory

- .NET CLR Networking

- .NET CLR Remoting

- .NET CLR Security

- ASP.NET

- ASP.NET Applications

- ASP.NET Apps v1.0.3705.0

- ASP.NET v1.0.3705.0

There will be occasions when you'll want to use some of the other performance categories (ones that don't appear in the preceding list). Feel free to run the GetPerfCategoriesVB application for a complete list.

TIP For your continued learning, I invite you to experiment with the many other performance objects and counters. I have provided several references related to performance objects and counters in the "To Learn More" section at the end of this chapter.

Using the Windows Performance Monitor Tool

Before I get into the fun stuff, please recall that the focus here is the performance concerns of .NET managed code, particularly as it relates to the CLR. Specifically, this section of the book focuses on the GC and its various aspects of memory management. Why am I making this point?

Well, Perfmon has a large set of objects available (a partial list appears in the section "Performance Counter Objects"). About 15 percent (10 of 66) of those objects are directly tied to the .NET CLR. Several more are directly related to other .NET managed code concerns (e.g., ASP.NET, Web services, WMI, and so on). Although most of the remaining Perfmon objects are indirectly related to .NET and the CLR, you can appreciate the fact that Perfmon provides both a granular view and a comprehensive view.

Using the GUI (front-end) that Windows provides to expose these objects, you can select one or more objects, which are referred to as *performance objects*. Once you select your performance object, you can select one counter, several counters, or all counters listed for that particular performance object. You will typically make two additional choices: choosing an Instance and choosing a Computer. The Instance option provides you the opportunity to see all executing processes or to narrow your view to just one executing process. The Computer Selection option provides you the opportunity to target just your local workstation or other remote servers.

 NOTE   To prepare for the steps that follow, I have modified the two Perfmon sample programs. I have modified the variable maxInt from 999 to 99999. This will cause the loop to run for "a long time." Please locate your two compiled sample code executables (PerfmonCobol.exe and PerfmonVB.exe). These files should be located in the bin subfolder within the folder location of each actual sample application. When you have located the .exe files, double-click them to launch the sample applications. Each sample application was designed to "pause" (remember the block of Display/Console.WriteLine statements?). Leave each sample application paused with the console window open.

Figure 8-4 shows each sample application launched and paused. Please do this before you proceed to the following Perfmon setup steps.

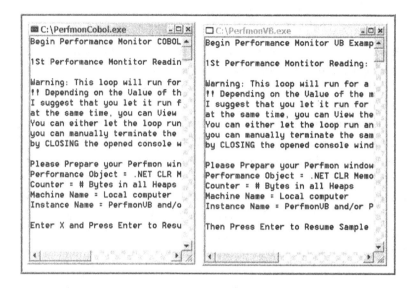

Figure 8-4. The two sample applications, PerfmonCobol and PerfmonVB, have been launched and paused.

The following series of figures illustrates the basic steps in starting and setting up Perfmon. Figure 8-5 shows the initial launch of Perfmon.

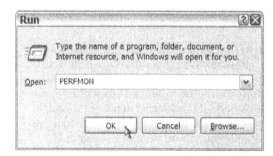

Figure 8-5. Launching Perfmon by clicking the Start button and selecting Run

Figure 8-6 shows how to access the Add counter button. Figure 8-7 shows how to select a .NET CLR-related performance object.

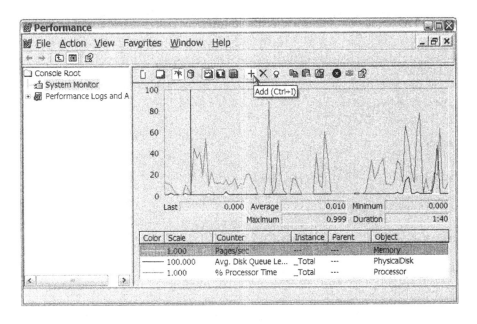

Figure 8-6. Accessing the Add counter button to add performance counters

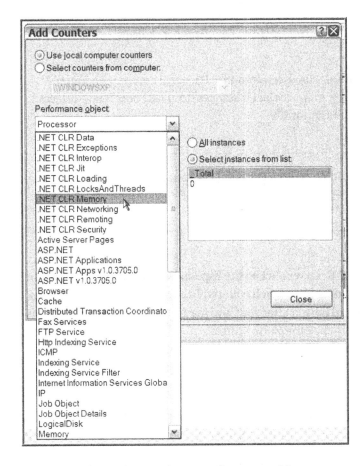

Figure 8-7. Preparing to select a performance object

Figure 8-8 shows how to select a specific counter.

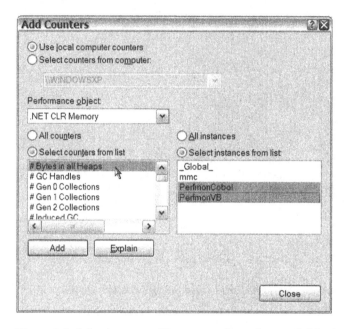

Figure 8-8. Selecting a specific counter from the available choices

As shown in Figure 8-9, I have selected the "Use local computer counters" radio button. Additionally, in the "Select instances from list" box, I have selected both PerfmonCobol and PerfmonVB.

NOTE If you do not see the PerfmonCobol and PerfmonVB applications as available choices, launch each sample application by clicking its respective .exe file.

As shown in Figure 8-9, I have clicked the Explain button. You use this button to get a better understanding about each counter. To complete the Perfmon setup, make sure to click the Add button after you have made *all* of the selections on this screen. Afterward, simply click the Close button.

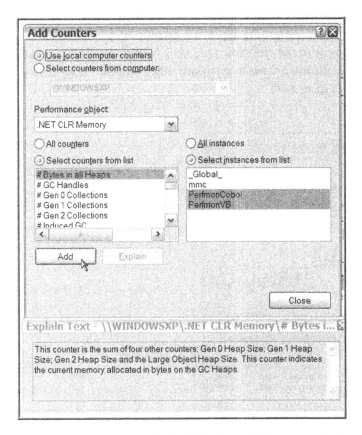

Figure 8-9. Preparing to click Add in the Add Counters window to complete the setup

NOTE Optionally, you can format your Perfmon display (e.g., change the scale, colors, and so on) by pressing Ctrl-Q. If you select View from the toolbar, you can customize your Perfmon window—for example, you can remove the console tree. Also, you can remove any instance displays (as I have done) that you may not have an immediate interest in. You do this by first selecting the instance in the box where the PerfmonCobol and PerfmonVB instances are displayed and pressing Delete.

After you start each Perfmon sample application (PerfmonVB and PerfmonCobol) and perform the appropriate setup on the Perfmon tool, you should see a display similar to the one shown in Figure 8-10. You will notice that I have moved the two console windows next to each other with the Performance window sitting on top of them both.

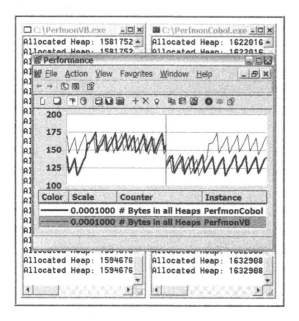

Figure 8-10. The Performance window, with the two Perfmon sample applications processing. Their console windows are behind the Performance window.

If you have the time, let each application process to completion. It is rather interesting to watch the graphs change (well, more interesting than watching paint dry). I actually found it interesting that the behavior of the GC varied slightly between the two sample applications. One minute, their graphs (reflecting their total bytes allocated across each heap generation) are going up and then down (as the GC performs its collections and heap compactions), almost in unison. Then, occasionally, the VB .NET application will "break out" ahead and grab more storage (having less collected). But then, COBOL .NET (not to be left behind) "catches up" each time.

NOTE If you let these sample applications run for a while, you will eventually need to adjust the default scale for the graph (from 0-100 to 0-500, for example). You do this by pressing Ctrl-Q to access the System Monitor Properties page. Next, click the Graph tab. You will see a Vertical Scale section near the bottom portion of the dialog box. To adjust the vertical scale, change the Minimum and Maximum values as needed.

You will notice that over time, the allocated heap count continues to inch upward as the GC collects less. My theory about this is that perhaps there is a gradual increase in the amount of aged objects that have been promoted to managed heap generation 2. Obviously, you are welcome to modify the Perfmon sample applications as needed to prove or disprove this theory. And as for me? That is fun enough—for now.

I believe that I've discussed the GC in sufficient depth. Although there's certainly more to discover, you're well equipped for that leg of the journey. The discovery process will be great.

Samples, Samples, and More Samples

You are sitting on top of a gold mine. Well, a gold mine's worth of free samples— right on your own hard disk. A large number of Microsoft samples are bundled with the Visual Studio .NET (VS .NET) product. It is likely that you installed them when you installed your edition of VS .NET. Although you will not find any COBOL .NET samples there, you *will* find lots of good VB .NET and C# samples. Remember, you also have a good "stash" of free COBOL .NET samples sitting on your hard disk courtesy of Fujitsu. The locations of these samples, both Microsoft provided and Fujitsu provided, are as follows:

- *Microsoft:* <Hard drive>:\Program Files\Microsoft Visual Studio .NET\FrameworkSDK\Samples

- *Fujitsu:* <Hard drive>:\Program Files\Fujitsu NetCOBOL for .NET\Examples

Summary

This chapter's goals were as follows:

- To understand .NET's common language runtime (CLR)

- To discuss the garbage collector (GC)

This chapter focused on the common language runtime (CLR). I began with a brief review of the role that Microsoft intermediate language (MSIL) plays in enabling languages to have a *common* platform on which to run. You were then introduced to the various portions of the CLR. Chapter references were provided to direct you to the chapters where "in-context" discussion will occur. You spent a healthy amount of time exploring the garbage collector (GC) feature of the CLR. I provided several sample applications to demonstrate the memory management characteristics of the GC.

In the next chapter, you will explore the creation and passing of objects. There, finally, you will come full circle with discussions about value type and reference type objects. You will learn about various programming concerns as well. Naturally, I will provide sample applications to help illustrate pertinent details.

To Learn More

The following are some suggested supplemental references to further your retraining effort.

Books

CIL Programming: Under the Hood of .NET, by Jason Bock (Apress, 2002):
    http://www.apress.com/book/bookDisplay.html?bID=88.
Windows 2000 and Mainframe Integration, by William H. Zack (Macmillan
    Technical Publishing, 1999):
    http://www.amazon.com/exec/obidos/ASIN/1578702003/.

Magazines

.NET Magazine:
    http://www.fawcette.com/dotnetmag/
Visual Studio Magazine:
    http://www.fawcette.com/vsm/
XML & Web Services Magazine:
    http://www.fawcette.com/xmlmag/

Web Sites

Automatic Memory Management (with the CLR):
    http://msdn.microsoft.com/library/en-us/cpguide/html/
    cpconautomaticmemorymanagement.asp
Cleaning Up Unmanaged Resources:
    http://msdn.microsoft.com/library/en-us/cpguide/html/
    cpconcleaningupunmanagedresources.asp
Common Language Runtime Overview:
    http://msdn.microsoft.com/library/en-us/cpguide/html/
    cpconcommonlanguageruntimeoverview.asp
Dr. GUI .NET #4: System.Object and Garbage Collection:
    http://msdn.microsoft.com/library/en-us/dnguinet/html/
    drguinet4_update.asp
Finalize Methods and Destructors:
    http://msdn.microsoft.com/library/en-us/cpguide/html/
    cpconfinalizemethodscdestructors.asp
Microsoft Community (discussion groups, e-newsletters, and so forth):
    http://communities2.microsoft.com/
MSDN:
    http://msdn.microsoft.com
Performance Considerations for Run-Time Technologies in the .NET Framework:
    http://msdn.microsoft.com/library/en-us/dndotnet/html/dotnetperftechs.asp
Performance Counters:
    http://msdn.microsoft.com/library/en-us/cpgenref/html/
    gngrfperformancecounters.asp

CHAPTER 9

Creating and Using Objects

Objects: Backward, Forward, Inside, and Out

In this chapter

- Discussing object creation

- Comparing the Object and ValueType classes

- Examining the behavior of objects

- Exploring object visibility and availability

ALMOST SINCE THE beginning of this book, you have read that *this* chapter was on the horizon. First, in Chapter 2, as I offered an answer to the question "What is .NET?" one of the answers offered was "object orientation," which included a reference to this chapter. Then again, in Chapter 4, as I discussed object orientation as one of the .NET retraining prerequisites, I included a reference to this chapter. In Chapter 6, when I introduced the topic of referencing objects, I included yet another reference to this chapter.

This trend continued as I made reference to this chapter repeatedly in Chapter 7 when I discussed namespaces and value type objects references. Finally, in Chapter 8, during the discussion of the garbage collector's impact on objects, I found it appropriate to include a reference to this chapter.

Suffice it to say that I discuss objects in this chapter. I discuss where objects come from and how they are created. Additionally, I contrast the basic two groups of objects by looking at their behavior and general usage considerations.

The Origin of "the Object"

Many years ago, I was happily programming COBOL batch and CICS applications on the mainframe (before my own reformation). At that time, I recall the topic of "object orientation" coming up in a friendly workplace debate. My coworkers and I had read how COBOL was going to become an object-oriented language. With much anticipation, we started to discuss the meaning of this "new" way of programming. Oh, how I remember the way we drilled down into defining the words "virtual," "physical," and "logical." All the while, we were trying to apply the "idea" of object orientation to our COBOL 85 procedural/structured code mainframe way of doing things.

As you know, with limited success, object-oriented COBOL eventually became a reality. Also, as discussed (at great length) in Chapter 1, the new COBOL standard has continued in that direction. You have to wonder, why in retrospect have "we"[1] struggled so with this subject?

Part of the problem (of course, we did not realize this at the time) was that we simply did not have the "right" context from which to discuss the topic. Hence, the object orientation analogy offered in Chapter 4. Recall that I suggested that Job Control Language (JCL) and its pieces could loosely be viewed as classes, objects, and so forth. Although I still stand behind that analogy, the fact remains that you need to understand more (much more) about objects. Specifically, you need to *really* understand the *.NET* objects.

The Elusive Object

If it's any consolation, even the nonmainframe programming community has struggled somewhat with the topic of object orientation. Although the Windows and Web programmers certainly have gotten a head start, even *they* are learning new things today. For example, the object orientation purist contends that the .NET platform avails a "first-time" opportunity to the Visual Basic programmer to perform "real" object-oriented program design.

Beyond that, others have suggested that if you limit your view of object orientation to the functionality of programming routines, you will miss the more complete object-oriented "business" view. This, of course, speaks to the practice of designing objects that represent entities, activities, patterns, and relationships found in business.

---

1. I am using the general reference of "we" to include the average legacy mainframe COBOL/CICS programmer.

That JCL analogy was provided to give you a place to start. Chapter 4's discussion presented a high-level view into object-oriented concepts. I would expect that Chapter 4's high-level discussion answered a few questions. At the same time, though, new questions undoubtedly arose. For example:

- Where do .NET objects come from?

- How exactly do you create .NET objects?

- What types of .NET objects are there?

- How do you handle .NET objects?

Let's now move toward answering these questions.

Where Do .NET Objects Come From?

I start this discussion with the System.Object class, the class from which all .NET objects derive. Listing 9-1 was generated from the .NET Framework's Class Viewer tool.[2] It shows the contents of the System.Object class. (The line numbers in Listing 9-1 were added manually.)

Listing 9-1. Output from the Class Viewer for System.Object

```
(1) // from module 'c:\winnt\microsoft.net\framework\v1.0.3705\mscorlib.dll'
(2)   public class object
(3) // Constructors
(4)   public Object();
(5) // Methods
(6)   public virtual bool Equals(object obj);
(7)   public static bool Equals(object objA, object objB);
(8)   public virtual int GetHashCode();
(9)   public Type GetType();
(10)  public static bool ReferenceEquals(object objA, object objB);
(11)  public virtual string ToString();
(12) // end of System.Object
```

Well, from the self-documenting System.Object class name alone, you already know that "Object" belongs to the System namespace. Additionally, from the Class

---

2. This tool was first introduced in Chapter 7. It is a command-level tool you use by executing WinCV.exe.

Viewer tool output, you can see in line 1 that this particular Namespace.Class is in mscorlib.dll.

Line 2 indicates that this particular class is *Public*. This means that the *scope* of this class is fully visible (I further explain the concept of scope in the section "Object Visibility and Availability" later in this chapter). The next set of code lines, 3 and 4, introduce the topic of constructors. Basically, the *constructor* is the method responsible for initializing an instance of the object. In the following section, I further discuss the topic of constructors. The remaining code lines, 6 through 11, are a list of methods.

TIP As you have noticed, the code output of the Class Viewer tool is in Visual C# .NET (or simply C#). Fear not, Microsoft has provided several very useful translation guides. You can easily translate the C# statements into Visual Basic .NET (VB .NET) statements. I have included the URL that links to this collection of Microsoft documents at the end of this chapter in the "Web Sites" subsection of the "To Learn More" section (please see the reference for "Language Equivalents"). I am sure that you will find this URL to be worthy of a bookmark.

Using the list of included methods, let's make a few more observations. Notice that lines 6 and 7 both define a method with the name *Equals* that will return a *Boolean* type (indicated by "bool"). However, you will notice that the characteristics of each are different (i.e., one of the methods has the attribute *Virtual* and the other has the attribute *Static*—for more information, see the section "Object Visibility and Availability").

Additionally, please note that the static Equals method (line 6) is defined as taking in one input parameter, whereas the other Equals method is defined as taking in two input parameters. These two methods, having the same name and appearing as they do with the other appropriate differences, are said to be *overloaded*. I discuss this concept further in the section "Availability via Object Orientation" later in this chapter.

Lastly, note the lines 9 and 11 in Listing 9-1. *GetType* and *ToString* are two very common methods that you'll see used in various code examples. Seeing them defined here, as methods of System.Object, you now know which base class actually defined these two useful methods. More interestingly, notice that the GetType method is defined to have a return type of *Type*. On the other hand, the ToString method is defined to have a return type of *String*. Why do I think this is interesting? Because it actually makes sense, that's why. This isn't always the case, so when it happens, why not acknowledge it?

A Minimalist View

One of my coworkers once stated, "Computer programming is just a matter of moving data from one place to another place." Although that is true, I would like to offer a similar statement, one that reflects a .NET minimalist perspective: ".NET computer programming is just a matter of creating objects and using objects."

There you have it. Within those few code snippet lines, you have *the* object that every (yes, I do mean *every*) .NET object is derived from. As you drill down a bit further, you will refer back to the code in Listing 9-1.

Bringing an Object to Life

When I discussed lines 3 and 4 in Listing 9-1, I mentioned the term "constructor." So, you already know that a constructor initializes an object. The other purpose that a constructor serves is to allocate memory on the heap (or stack) for the object in question. In COBOL .NET and VB .NET code, you will recognize a constructor as "a method of a *class* that happens to have the name of NEW." In other words, when you execute code to instantiate an object using the *NEW* clause, you are actually executing a method that has the name "NEW." This causes the following to occur:

- Memory is allocated on the heap or stack.

- The object gets initialized.

Let's say for example that a COBOL .NET class had the constructor method shown in Listing 9-2.

Listing 9-2. COBOL .NET Code Snippet Showing a Constructor

```
000020 CLASS-ID. AClass.
. . .
000400 METHOD-ID. NEW.
000410 DATA DIVISION.
000420 WORKING-STORAGE SECTION.
000430 PROCEDURE DIVISION.
000440* Do something
000450 END METHOD NEW.
. . .
```

Then, it would be reasonable to also use a COBOL .NET statement as shown in Listing 9-3 to create an instance of that class (in other words, to instantiate an object).

Listing 9-3. COBOL .NET Code Snippet Showing How to Instantiate an Object

```
. . .
PROCEDURE DIVISION.
000260 METHOD-ID. MAIN.
000270 DATA DIVISION.
000280 WORKING-STORAGE SECTION.
000290 01 OBJ OBJECT REFERENCE AClass.
000300 PROCEDURE DIVISION.
000310     INVOKE AClass "NEW" RETURNING OBJ.
000320 END METHOD MAIN.
000330 END STATIC.
. . .
```

Likewise, if you saw a VB .NET class that had the following constructor method:

```
Public Class AClass
    Sub New()
      ' Do Something
    End Sub
End Class
```

you might also use the following VB .NET statement to instantiate the object:

```
Sub ADifferentProcedure()
    Dim AnObject As New AClass()
End Sub
```

Are you confused now? Are you wondering what the previous code snippets have to do with the System.Object class? Well, since you know that the System.Object class contains a NEW method (a constructor) similar to the ones shown in the previous code snippets, you can visualize the type of method that gets called every time that you instantiate an object.

Let's try a little question and answer (Q&A):

Question 1: What happens if you create a class, but you do not explicitly code a constructor?

Answer 1: The constructor of the base class is implicitly executed.

Q2: Can you pass parameters into the constructor?

A2: Yes. In fact, if the constructor happens to be inside of a *value type* object, you *must* have at least one input parameter.

Q3: Can you have more than one constructor in a class?

A3: Yes, thanks to the concept of overloading in object orientation.

Q4: If you have multiple constructors (overloaded), which one is the default constructor?

A4: The default constructor is the NEW method that is defined as *parameterless*—in other words, lacking input parameters.

Q5: Why is it that the value type object's constructor cannot be "parameterless"?

A5: The default constructor (the one that is parameterless) is "reserved" for the value type object's initialization needs.

Q6: Why is it that some constructors have as their first coded statement an instruction similar to "Mybase.New()"?

A6: This is true (generally) if you define a class that derives from another class. Because constructors are not inherited, you must explicitly execute the constructor of the base class.

Q7: Is there more to learn about constructors?

A7: Yes, but not too much more. This is certainly enough for now.

Now, wasn't that fun? The preceding Q&A list (hopefully) addressed most of your questions about constructors. As you learn more throughout this chapter, some of these answers will become clearer. On that note, I need to clear up one additional point before I conclude this discussion of constructors.

The discussion here has focused strictly on *instance* constructors. You should be aware of the existence of the other constructor type: *Shared* constructors. Shared constructors are used to initialize *Shared* variables, in other words, variables that are declared with the Shared access attribute are Shared variables. Shared constructors provide a convenient way to initialize these types of variables. Access attributes are further discussed in the section "Object Access and Scope" later in this chapter.

NOTE COBOL .NET does not support the creation of Shared constructors. The constructors (methods with the name NEW) that you will use in COBOL .NET are instance constructors. However, you will find that VB .NET does provide support for both types of constructors: Shared and instance.

You will recognize a Shared constructor as a method with the name NEW *and* the access attribute Shared. For example, in VB .NET, the coding statement to define a Shared constructor looks like this: `Shared Sub New()`.

When you come across the need to use Shared variables and Shared constructors, please take advantage of the Microsoft Visual Studio .NET Documentation (`ms-help://MS.VSCC/MS.MSDNVS/vbls7/html/vblrfVBSpec7_2_2.htm`). Recall that you can access this Microsoft documentation package (locally, on your desktop) as follows: Click the Start button and select Programs ➤ Microsoft Visual Studio .NET ➤ Microsoft Visual Studio .NET Documentation.

OK, is that all clear now? Are you totally comfortable with the topics of constructors and object creation? Are you ready to move on to the next section? Great, let's do it.

TIP COBOL .NET coding introduces a few special considerations for constructors (i.e., the constructor name "new" must always be capitalized: NEW). Fujitsu has provided a "NetCOBOL for .NET Language Reference" document bundled with their NetCOBOL for .NET product. I suggest that you refer to this document, particularly its last chapter (Chapter 12). This useful document happens to be in PDF format. You can simply navigate to its installed location, which is typically the following: <hard disk>\Program Files\Fujitsu NetCOBOL for .NET\doc\.

Finally, Value versus Reference Objects

At this point, you have encountered the term "value" several times. I have covered value objects, value types, value this, and value that. Are you ready to look under the hood at these value "things"? All right, here we go.

As you know, all classes in .NET are derived from System.Object. This, of course, includes the System.ValueType class. If you view the System.ValueType class using the Class Viewer tool, you will see the output shown in Listing 9-4. (The line numbers in Listing 9-4 have been added manually.)

Listing 9-4. Class Viewer Output of the System.ValueType Class

```
(1) // from module 'c:\winnt\microsoft.net\framework\v1.0.3705\mscorlib.dll'
(2) public abstract class ValueType :
(3)     object
(4)     // Constructors
(5)     // Methods
(6)     public virtual bool Equals(object obj);
(7)     public virtual int GetHashCode();
(8)     public Type GetType();
(9)     public virtual string ToString();
(10) // end of System.ValueType
```

Let's take a closer look at each displayed line in Listing 9-4. Starting with line 1, you can see that the ValueType class is *physically* located in the same module (i.e., mscorlib.dll) as the System.Object base class. In line 2, the word "abstract" is used. This is where value type objects begin their departure from the System.Object class. The "abstract" term is C# (and C++) lingo for *MustInherit*. MustInherit is VB .NET lingo for a class that can't be instantiated directly but can be inherited.

You will notice that line 3 states the class that the ValueType class is derived from. Then, on line 4, you see that there are no constructors shown. Although there *is* actually a constructor, there is not a Public constructor. The System.ValueType constructor is defined as *Protected*. This is a more restrictive setting than Public. A Protected method (including the methods that have the name NEW, as in the constructor) can only be called from within the local class (or a derived class).

 NOTE The System.Object class is (ultimately) the base class for all objects. The System.ValueType class is (ultimately) the base class for all value type objects. Generally, the former are said to be reference type objects and are allocated on the heap, and the latter are said to be value type objects and are allocated on the stack. Loosely speaking, people will use the term "reference objects" or simply "objects" to refer to reference type objects. Value type objects are loosely referred to as "value types" or simply "types."

Lines 6 through 9 of Listing 9-4 should look familiar. Recall that these methods were also in System.Object. Therefore, this is a good example of inheritance in action. Because System.ValueType is derived from the base class System.Object, it is able to inherit those four methods. This type of inheritance is provided (or restricted) according to the definition (visibility and accessibility) of the method found in the base class. The derived class (in this case) is able to either use the inherited method as-is or use one of several object-oriented techniques to change the behavior of the exposed method.

Putting the System.ValueType Class into Perspective

The System.ValueType class uses the object-oriented technique of overriding for the inherited methods Equals, GetHashCode, and ToString. The GetType method is simply inherited. Through overriding, the ValueType class is able to implement logic that is more appropriate for a value type object.

For now, let me offer a few more value type facts to you (if you do not mind):

- Once declared, value type objects simply "exist" on the stack.

- Value types do not require declaration *and* instantiation—just declaration.

- It is not necessary to explicitly call the constructor on a value type.

- The default (parameterless) constructor that is implicitly called for value type objects simply initializes them.

- You can optionally create and call and constructors that have been added to a value type (i.e., overloaded constructors).

Just in case you were wondering, the variables that you have grown accustomed to creating in the Working-Storage Section of your COBOL .NET program are value types. These include the variables that look like the legacy COBOL data types (using PICTURE clauses and so on) you are familiar with. In Chapter 6, these data types were referred to as the COBOL .NET data types that provided intrinsic support for .NET data types.

NOTE In your legacy mainframe COBOL development, when you used pointers and address registers to refer to memory allocations, you were closely mimicking the type of behavior of .NET's reference type objects.

Well, that is about it as far as contrasting the two types of objects. Are you now wondering what this "value versus reference" issue looks like in real life? Good! Let's continue.

Objects: Use with Care

Let's say, just for example, that you are creating a collection of data items. You stumble across the .NET class *System.Collections.ArrayList* and decide to use it. In some cases, this is a great idea. But in other cases, this could prove to be disastrous. Sometimes it may be better to choose the basic *System.Array* class over the *ArrayList* class. But why?

NOTE These days, on the mainframe, the term "array" has become synonymous with the term "table." Both terms represent data items defined with the COBOL OCCURS clause. Legacy mainframe COBOL programmers will recall that we generally used arrays to store data to be used as output. A table, on the other hand, was typically used for lookup functionality. In hindsight, this was simply an exercise in semantics. After all, arrays and tables looked the same, acted the same, and were defined and stored the same. The Array and ArrayList classes discussed here, on .NET, are functionally similar to the arrays and tables used in mainframe COBOL development.

Well, the elements of the ArrayList class have the generic data type of Object (remember the System.Object class). The Array class, on the other hand, allows you to use specific types (i.e., Integer, Boolean, and so forth). Although you could even choose Object as the type for your Array class, ideally you should try to avoid this. The ArrayList, however, does not give you this choice. This becomes critical if the collection of data items that you want to store (in your Array or ArrayList class) happens to be a collection of value type data items (do you remember the discussion about boxing in Chapter 8?).

Naturally, this *does not* mean that you should always avoid the ArrayList class. It *does* mean that you should put some thought into the data types you choose, the classes you use, and how you use them.

Are you convinced that this topic is important? Good! Because you appreciate the significance of this topic, I have created two sets of sample applications that will illustrate object type choice and object type usage. I believe you will find the code in the following two sections rather interesting.

Object Type Sample Code

When you create your managed .NET applications, you might want to know how normal, everyday programming code can potentially affect performance. Eventually, most *good* developers get around to observing the performance of their applications. On the other hand, a *great* developer (like yourself) will have had this question of performance already in mind, simply as a habit. Thus, performance of the reference type object and the value type object is the focus in the sample applications that follow.

The first set of sample applications (StringBuilderExampleVB and StringBuilderExampleCobol) demonstrates the difference between using the new .NET StringBuilder class for string concatenation versus the more traditional string concatenation approaches.

COBOL .NET Example

The sample application in Listing 9-5 makes use of the *System.Environment* class. Observe the technique of using the *TickCount* property that is exposed by the System.Environment class. This technique may be useful to you for other coding scenarios. Now, let's explore the code sample.

Listing 9-5. The StringBuilderExampleCobol Project

```
000010 IDENTIFICATION DIVISION.
000020* This is an example of how traditional String
000030* Concatenation differs from using the
000040* .NET StringBuilder Class for Concatenation.
000050 PROGRAM-ID. MAIN.
000060 ENVIRONMENT DIVISION.
000070 CONFIGURATION SECTION.
000080 REPOSITORY.
000090* .NET Framework Classes
000100     CLASS SYS-ENVIRONMENT_Obj AS "System.Environment"
000110     CLASS SYS-STRINGBUILDER AS "System.Text.StringBuilder"
000120     PROPERTY PROP-TickCount AS "TickCount".
000130*
000140 DATA DIVISION.
000150 WORKING-STORAGE SECTION.
000160     77 sb OBJECT REFERENCE SYS-STRINGBUILDER.
000170     77 sb1 OBJECT REFERENCE SYS-STRINGBUILDER.
000180     77 i PIC S9(9) COMP-5.
000190     77 ibeg PIC S9(9) COMP-5.
000200     77 myStartTick PIC S9(9) COMP-5.
000210     77 myFinishTick PIC S9(9) COMP-5.
000220     77 myComputedTick PIC S9(9) COMP-5.
000230     77 myDisplayTick PIC Z(9).
000240     77 myString1 PIC X(430000).
000250     01 NULL-X PIC X(1).
```

```
000260 LINKAGE SECTION.
000270
000280 PROCEDURE DIVISION.
000290
000300     DISPLAY "Begin String Builder Example."
000310     DISPLAY " "
000320
000330* Start logic for String (FUNCTION) Compare
000340     SET myStartTick to PROP-TickCount of SYS-ENVIRONMENT_Obj.
000350     MOVE "I am creating .NET Garbage to be Collected" TO myString1
000360     MOVE 50 to ibeg
000370     PERFORM VARYING i
000380       FROM 0 BY 1 UNTIL i >= 9999
000390         STRING " * One Piece of Garbage to be collected * "
000400              DELIMITED BY SIZE
000410              INTO myString1
000420              WITH POINTER ibeg
000430         END-STRING
000440     END-PERFORM
000450     SET myFinishTick to PROP-TickCount of SYS-ENVIRONMENT_Obj.
000460
000470     DISPLAY "Milliseconds for traditional String concatenation: "
000480     COMPUTE myComputedTick = (myFinishTick - myStartTick)
000490     MOVE myComputedTick to myDisplayTick
000500     DISPLAY myDisplayTick
000510
000520* Start logic for StringBuilder Compare using Default size of 16
000530     SET myStartTick to PROP-TickCount of SYS-ENVIRONMENT_Obj.
000540     INVOKE SYS-STRINGBUILDER "NEW"
000550         RETURNING sb.
000560     INVOKE sb "Append"
000570         USING BY VALUE "I am creating .NET Garbage to be Collected : "
000580         RETURNING sb.
000590
000600     PERFORM VARYING i
000610         FROM 0 BY 1 UNTIL i >= 9999
000620           INVOKE sb "Append"
000630             USING BY VALUE " * One Piece of Garbage to be collected * "
000640             RETURNING sb
000650     END-PERFORM
000660     SET myFinishTick to PROP-TickCount of SYS-ENVIRONMENT_Obj.
000670
000680     DISPLAY "Milliseconds for StringBuilder - using default Size: "
000690     COMPUTE myComputedTick = (myFinishTick - myStartTick)
```

```
000700      MOVE myComputedTick to myDisplayTick
000710      DISPLAY myDisplayTick
000720
000730* Start logic for StringBuilder(500) Compare
000740      SET myStartTick to PROP-TickCount of SYS-ENVIRONMENT_Obj.
000750      INVOKE SYS-STRINGBUILDER "NEW"
000760          USING BY VALUE 500
000770          RETURNING sb1.
000780      INVOKE sb1 "Append"
000790          USING BY VALUE "I am creating .NET Garbage to be Collected : "
000800          RETURNING sb1.
000810
000820      PERFORM VARYING i
000830          FROM 0 BY 1 UNTIL i >= 9999
000840            INVOKE sb1 "Append"
000850                USING BY VALUE " * One Piece of Garbage to be collected * "
000860                RETURNING sb1
000870      END-PERFORM
000880      SET myFinishTick to PROP-TickCount of SYS-ENVIRONMENT_Obj.
000890
000900      DISPLAY "Milliseconds for StringBuilder - initialized Size : "
000910      COMPUTE myComputedTick = (myFinishTick - myStartTick)
000920      MOVE myComputedTick to myDisplayTick
000930      DISPLAY myDisplayTick
000940
000950      SET SB TO NULL
000960      SET SB1 TO NULL
000970
000980      DISPLAY "Enter X and Press Enter to Exit.".
000990      ACCEPT NULL-X.
001000
001010 END PROGRAM  MAIN.
```

Please take a moment to review the sample code in Listing 9-5. In this sample project, StringBuilderExampleCobol, you will notice that I used the traditional COBOL STRING function first. Then, for comparison, I included two instances of the new .NET System.Text.StringBuilder class. Notice the inclusion of constructors for the StringBuilder class. After you run the program, the console window will display the output lines shown in Listing 9-6.

Listing 9-6. Console Display Output of the StringBuilderExampleCobol Project

```
Begin String Builder Example.

Milliseconds for traditional String concatenation:
      40
Milliseconds for StringBuilder - using default Size:
      220
Milliseconds for StringBuilder - initialized Size :
      161
Enter X and Press Enter to Exit.
```

> **NOTE** The displayed "millisecond" results (shown in several demonstration code samples) should be used for relative comparisons. The actual values will likely vary each time you run them on your own computer. In fact, the relative comparison of the "millisecond" results from one computer as compared to those of a different computer could vary as well. Depending on the any number of variables (i.e., the type of processor, amount of memory, type of hard disk, and so on), results should and will vary. The resulting numbers displayed here are for demonstration purposes only.

Interesting! In this COBOL .NET example, the traditional string concatenation approach (using the native COBOL STRING function) is actually faster than the .NET Framework StringBuilder class. I have to admit that this was a bit surprising. Nevertheless, the numbers speak for themselves.

Of course, the curiosity factor alone would drive any developer to want to understand this, right? For now, I can only give you a hint: *MSIL*. This hint will be explained later in the section "Same Reference Object, Different Languages." Beyond that, it will really help if you first review the VB .NET example you will find in the next section. In that section, the string concatenation functionality has been reproduced using VB .NET.

VB .NET Example

For your bilingual learning pleasure, Listing 9-7 presents the StringBuilderExampleVB project. After you review the code, please take a moment to actually execute the program. The program will output a few lines to the console window.

Listing 9-7. The StringBuilderExampleVB Project

```
Module Module1
  Sub Main()
      Dim i As Int32
      Dim myStartTick As Int32
      Dim myFinishTick As Int32

      Console.WriteLine("Begin String Builder Example")
      Console.WriteLine(String.Empty)

      'Start logic for String Compare
      myStartTick = System.Environment.TickCount
      Dim myString1 As New String("I am creating .NET Garbage to be Collected")
      For i = 0 To 9999
          myString1 = myString1 & " * One Piece of Garbage to be collected * "
      Next

      myFinishTick = System.Environment.TickCount
      Console.WriteLine("Milliseconds for traditional String concatenation: ")
      Console.WriteLine(myFinishTick - myStartTick)

      'Start logic for StringBuilder Compare using Default size of 16
      myStartTick = System.Environment.TickCount
      Dim sb As New System.Text.StringBuilder()
      sb.Append("I am creating .NET Garbage to be Collected : ")
      For i = 0 To 9999
          sb.Append(" * One Piece of Garbage to be collected * ")
      Next

      myFinishTick = System.Environment.TickCount
      Console.WriteLine("Milliseconds for StringBuilder - using default Size: ")
      Console.WriteLine(myFinishTick - myStartTick)
      'Start logic for StringBuilder(500) Compare
      myStartTick = System.Environment.TickCount
      Dim sb1 As New System.Text.StringBuilder(500)
      sb1.Append("I am creating .NET Garbage to be Collected : ")
      For i = 0 To 9999
          sb1.Append(" * One Piece of Garbage to be collected * ")
      Next
```

```
        myFinishTick = System.Environment.TickCount
        Console.WriteLine("Milliseconds for StringBuilder - initialized Size ")
        Console.WriteLine(myFinishTick - myStartTick)

        myString1 = Nothing
        sb = Nothing
        sb1 = Nothing

        Console.WriteLine("Press Enter to Exit")
        Console.ReadLine()

    End Sub
End Module
```

The lines in Listing 9-8 are written to the console window when StringBuilderExampleVB is executed.

Listing 9-8. The Lines Written to the Console Display for the StringBuilderExampleVB Program

```
Begin String Builder Example

Milliseconds for traditional String concatenation:
89839
Milliseconds for StringBuilder - using default Size:
41
Milliseconds for StringBuilder - initialized Size
30
Press Enter to Exit
```

Wow! Now, *that* is a big difference in performance (as shown in Listing 9-8). When you use VB .NET, it is easy to see why people get so excited about the StringBuilder class.

 TIP The .NET Framework StringBuilder class has *other* very useful methods. Although the Append (and ToString) method seems to get all the attention, the StringBuilder class offers the following useful methods: AppendFormat, Insert, Remove, and Replace.

I'd like to point out a few more things about the VB .NET code sample. Let's begin by looking closely at the following code lines copied from Listing 9-7:

```
. . .
Dim i As Int32
Dim myStartTick As Int32
Dim myFinishTick As Int32
. . .
Dim sb As New System.Text.StringBuilder()
. . .
Dim sb1 As New System.Text.StringBuilder(500)
. . .
```

Notice that the three Int32 variables are being declared *without* the word "NEW" in the Dim statement. The Int32 Dim statements are declaring *value type* objects and relying on their default constructor. On the other hand, both StringBuilder declarations have the word "NEW" included in their Dim statements. The StringBuilder Dim statements are declaring reference type objects and explicitly "calling" the constructor.

As you have certainly noticed, the second StringBuilder in the preceding code (sb1) includes an input parameter of 500. This value of 500 will be input into the constructor. The other StringBuilder in the preceding code (sb) is using the default constructor (in other words, the parameterless constructor). Figure 9-1 shows the list of overloaded constructors for the StringBuilder class as shown in the VS .NET Object Browser.

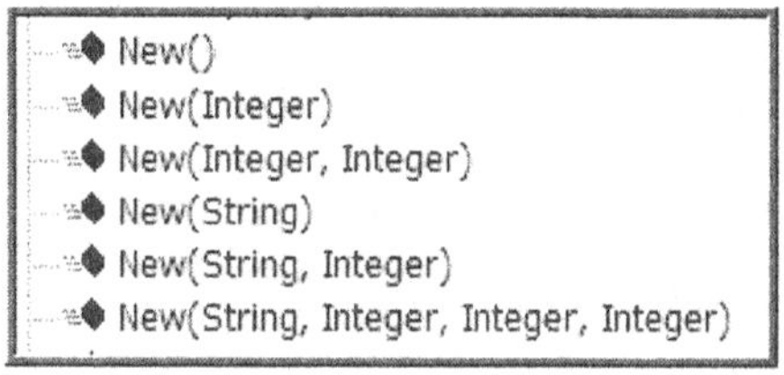

```
New()
New(Integer)
New(Integer, Integer)
New(String)
New(String, Integer)
New(String, Integer, Integer, Integer)
```

Figure 9-1. The overloaded constructors of the StringBuilder class

If you explore a bit, it will become apparent that the StringBuilder class (being a reference type object) has inherited from the System.Object class. Further exploration will show that Int32 is derived from the System.ValueType class. That just leaves one additional point to mention: the *String* class.

TIP The String class offers many valuable methods. It would be wise to spend some time familiarizing yourself with them. In some cases, you can replace several lines of programming code with the proper usage of an existing String method (e.g., *Format, Trim, TrimEnd, ToLower,* and *PadLeft,* among others). You might compare the String class's collection of methods to the functionality available with the legacy COBOL STRING function. However, you will find that the features of the .NET String class meet and then surpass those of the legacy COBOL STRING function.

The sample application demonstrated a performance concern when using the String class (a reference type object that inherits from System.Object). Although the String class is extremely useful, you really should think twice if you need to implement logic that results in repetitive modifications of the string (i.e., typical concatenation routines). It turns out that the String class is *immutable*—in other words, it cannot be changed.

Therefore, the system ends up creating a new String object each time you attempt to update an existing object. This is the reason for the large performance hit. The StringBuilder, on the other hand, allows "underlying" String objects to be updated (without needing to create new String objects).

Same Reference Object, Different Languages

You have learned up to this point that you can take any logic example and easily implement the functionality in either COBOL .NET or VB .NET. However, as you saw in the previous set of sample applications, the performance behavior can vary. The same reference object (in this case, the StringBuilder class) exhibits different behavior when one sample project is compared with the other.

NOTE In the previous sample applications, the fastest COBOL .NET string concatenation processing time (about 40 milliseconds) is nearly equivalent to the second-fastest processing time of the VB .NET application (about 41 milliseconds). Is this just a coincidence? I think not. My guess is that Fujitsu may have taken the same "optimal" approach in the NetCOBOL for .NET compiler (assuring that the COBOL STRING function was updating the String reference type object *in place*) as Microsoft did in the VB .NET compiler (providing the StringBuilder class for *in-place* updating of the String reference type object).

In the StringBuilderExampleCobol COBOL .NET example, the .NET StringBuilder class performed less efficiently than the intrinsic COBOL STRING function. On the other hand, in the StringBuilderExampleVB VB .NET example, the StringBuilder class performed more efficiently than the intrinsic Visual Basic String function. Here is why.

I mentioned earlier (when reviewing the StringBuilderExampleCobol results) that *MSIL* was a hint. As you know, MSIL is an abbreviation for Microsoft intermediate language. And it is in reviewing the resulting MSIL for both StringBuilderExampleCobol and StringBuilderExampleVB that the explanation lies.

Using the ILDASM tool (at the command-prompt level) to review the MSIL for each sample project executable, you will be able to locate MSIL code showing the use of the StringBuilder class. Please review the MSIL snippets from each sample project in Listings 9-9 and 9-10.

First, Listing 9-9 shows the MSIL for the COBOL .NET project. Notice the five original lines of code that directly relate to the StringBuilder class (these are the lines that are prefixed with a double slash [//]—for example, //000054 through //000058).

Listing 9-9. A Portion of the MSIL for the COBOL .NET Sample Application

```
//000054: 000540      INVOKE SYS-STRINGBUILDER "NEW"
      IL_0453:  newobj     instance void class
[mscorlib]System.Text.StringBuilder:::.ctor()
      IL_0458:  stloc      __Temp001F06D0
      IL_045c:  ldloc      __Temp001F06D0
      IL_0460:  stsfld     class
[mscorlib]System.Text.StringBuilder MAIN::SB_001CEB18
//000055: 000550      RETURNING sb.
//000056: 000560      INVOKE sb "Append"
      IL_0465:  ldsfld     class
[Fujitsu.COBOL]Fujitsu.COBOL.Runtime.ProgramControl.ILI MAIN
::__ILI
      IL_046a:  ldloca     __LocalTempCOBOLDATA0
      IL_046e:  initobj    valuetype [Fujitsu.COBOL]Fujitsu.COBOL.COBOLData
      IL_0474:  ldloca     __LocalTempCOBOLDATA0
      IL_0478:  ldsfld     unsigned int8[] MAIN::__LiteralArea
      IL_047d:  ldc.i4     0x10a
      IL_0482:  ldc.i4.s   45
      IL_0484:  call       instance void
[Fujitsu.COBOL]Fujitsu.COBOL.COBOLData
:::.ctor(unsigned int8[],int32,int32)
      IL_0489:  ldloc      __LocalTempCOBOLDATA0
```

```
    IL_048d:  ldc.i4.s    45
    IL_048f:  ldloca      __LocalTempCOBOLDATA0
    IL_0493:  initobj     valuetype [Fujitsu.COBOL]Fujitsu.COBOL.COBOLData
    IL_0499:  ldloca      __LocalTempCOBOLDATA0
    IL_049d:  ldloc       __Temp001F06EC
    IL_04a1:  ldc.i4.0
    IL_04a2:  ldc.i4.s    90
    IL_04a4:  call        instance void
[Fujitsu.COBOL]Fujitsu.COBOL.COBOLData
::.ctor(unsigned int8[],int32,int32)
    IL_04a9:  ldloc       __LocalTempCOBOLDATA0
    IL_04ad:  ldc.i4.s    90
    IL_04af:  ldloca      __Temp001F0698
    IL_04b3:  call        void
[Fujitsu.COBOL]Fujitsu.COBOL.Runtime.Intrinsics.Unicode
::JMP8UCS2(class
[Fujitsu.COBOL]Fujitsu.COBOL.Runtime.ProgramControl.ILI,
valuetype [Fujitsu.COBOL]Fujitsu.COBOL.COBOLData,int32,
valuetype [Fujitsu.COBOL]Fujitsu.COBOL.COBOLData,int32,int32&)
    IL_04b8:  ldloc       __Temp001F0698
    IL_04bc:  brfalse.s   IL_04d2
    IL_04be:  ldloc       __Temp001F06EC
    IL_04c2:  ldc.i4.0
    IL_04c3:  ldloc       __Temp001F0698
    IL_04c7:  call        string
[Fujitsu.COBOL]Fujitsu.COBOL.Runtime.OmeLib.Setc
::ConvCobolTOString(unsigned int8[],int32,int32)
    IL_04cc:  stloc       __Temp001F0708
    IL_04d0:  br.s        IL_04d7
    IL_04d2:  ldnull
    IL_04d3:  stloc       __Temp001F0708
    IL_04d7:  ldsfld      class
[mscorlib]System.Text.StringBuilder MAIN::SB_001CEB18
    IL_04dc:  ldloc       __Temp001F0708
    IL_04e0:  call        instance class
[mscorlib]System.Text.StringBuilder class
[mscorlib]System.Text.StringBuilder
::Append(string)
    IL_04e5:  stloc       __Temp001F0724
    IL_04e9:  ldloc       __Temp001F0724
    IL_04ed:  stsfld      class
[mscorlib]System.Text.StringBuilder MAIN::SB_001CEB18
//000057: 000570   USING BY VALUE "I am creating .NET Garbage to be Collected : "
//000058: 000580   RETURNING sb.
```

Listing 9-10 shows a snippet of MSIL for the VB .NET project. In this case, there are two lines of original code related to the StringBuilder class (again, these are the two lines prefixed with a double slash [//]—for example, //000025 and //000026).

Listing 9-10. A Portion of the MSIL for the VB .NET Sample Application

```
//000025:              Dim sb As New System.Text.StringBuilder()
  IL_0068: newobj     instance void [mscorlib]System.Text.StringBuilder::.ctor()
  IL_006d: stloc.s    sb
//000026:          sb.Append("I am creating .NET Garbage to be Collected : ")
  IL_006f: ldloc.s    sb
  IL_0071: ldstr      "I am creating .NET Garbage to be Collected : "
  IL_0076: callvirt   instance class [mscorlib]System.Text.StringBuilder
[mscorlib]System.Text.StringBuilder::Append(string)
  IL_007b: pop
```

Ignoring the difference in the number of original code lines, *please note the difference in the resulting MSIL lines.* It is, after all, the MSIL that counts.[3] Because both examples end up accessing the System.Text.StringBuilder class via mscorlib.dll (shown in the MSIL listings as [mscorlib]), it is fair to say that you *are* comparing "apples to apples." The conclusion (apparently) is that one of the "apples" has a significant amount of *MSIL* overhead added. This explains the inconsistent performance behavior of the StringBuilder class.

 TIP In the future, when you need to do repetitive string concatenation, I suggest that you use the intrinsic STRING function in your COBOL .NET programs. On the other hand, VB .NET programs should use the .NET StringBuilder class (a reference type object). This suggestion would stand until Fujitsu modifies their compiler to produce more streamlined MSIL code (for implementing the StringBuilder class).

This behavior observation certainly underscores my point. When you code in .NET, choose your objects wisely—both value type objects and reference type objects. Think about the variables involved in *your* application. Experiment with the .NET Framework classes to find the most efficient coding combinations. Have fun.

Now you'll drill down deeper into the usage of value types and reference types. The following set of sample applications will help set the stage for further discussion.

---

3. This is partially true. The Microsoft intermediate language is ultimately compiled into machine code by the .NET just-in-time (JIT) compiler.

More Sample Code

This next set of sample applications (ValueTypeSampleVB and ValueTypeSampleCobol) illustrate a difference between using value types and reference types. These samples focus on the "usage" factor—showing that *how* you use value type objects and reference type objects does in fact make a difference.

COBOL .NET Example

This sample application demonstrates the use of the structure value type object and the basic reference type class object. For each object type, you will see an Integer and a String used.

NOTE   The group data type is COBOL .NET's way of providing intrinsic support for the .NET structure value type object.

You will also notice that I have broken the ValueTypeSampleCobol COBOL .NET sample application code into three physical files:

- Program1.cob

- mybarInt.cob

- mybarStr.cob

I did this to demonstrate a common approach to organizing your own classes. Please review the following code from the three COBOL .NET ".cob" files. Listing 9-11 presents the ValueTypeSampleCobol Program1.cob file.

Listing 9-11. The ValueTypeSampleCobol Program1.cob File

```
000010* 'ValueTypeSampleCobol Console Application
000020 CLASS-ID. A-CLASS.
000030 ENVIRONMENT DIVISION.
000040 CONFIGURATION SECTION.
000050 REPOSITORY.
000060*
000070* ADD References for .NET Framework Classes
000080
```

```
000090      CLASS SYS-ENVIRONMENT_Obj AS "System.Environment"
000100      PROPERTY PROP-TickCount AS "TickCount"
000110
000120* ADD references for the Classes created in this Project
000130      CLASS mybarInt
000140      CLASS mybarStr.
000150
000160 STATIC.
000170 PROCEDURE DIVISION.
000180 METHOD-ID. MAIN.
000190 DATA DIVISION.
000200 WORKING-STORAGE SECTION.
000210 01 OBJ OBJECT REFERENCE A-CLASS.
000220 PROCEDURE DIVISION.
000230      INVOKE A-CLASS "NEW" RETURNING OBJ.
000240 END METHOD MAIN.
000250 END STATIC.
000260
000270 OBJECT.
000280 DATA DIVISION.
000290 WORKING-STORAGE SECTION.
000300 PROCEDURE DIVISION.
000310*
000320* The method below is known as the CONSTRUCTOR
000330 METHOD-ID. NEW.
000340 DATA DIVISION.
000350 WORKING-STORAGE SECTION.
000360 PROCEDURE DIVISION.
000370      INVOKE SELF "A-METHOD".
000380 END METHOD NEW.
000390*
000400 METHOD-ID. A-METHOD IS PUBLIC.
000410 DATA DIVISION.
000420 WORKING-STORAGE SECTION.
000430* Misc Fields
000440   77 myStartTick PIC S9(9) COMP-5.
000450   77 myFinishTick PIC S9(9) COMP-5.
000460   77 myComputedTick PIC S9(9) COMP-5.
000470   77 myDisplayTick PIC Z(9).
000480   77 i PIC S9(9) COMP-5.
000490   01 NULL-X PIC X(1).
000500
000510*  NOTE: A Group Data Type is COBOL.NET's intrinsic support
000520*  for .NET Structures
```

```
000530
000540* Create my own Structure that contains a Int32 (equivalent)
000550  01 WS-myfooInteger_Test1.
000560     05 WS-myInt PIC S9(9) USAGE COMP-5.
000570  01 WS-myfooInteger_Test2.
000580     05 WS-myInt PIC S9(9) USAGE COMP-5.
000590
000600* Create my own Structure that contains a String
000610  01 WS-myfooString_Test1.
000620     05 WS-myString PIC X(30).
000630  01 WS-myfooString_Test2.
000640     05 WS-myString PIC X(30).
000650
000660  01 mybarInt_Obj_Test1 OBJECT REFERENCE mybarInt.
000670  01 mybarInt_Obj_Test2 OBJECT REFERENCE mybarInt.
000680  01 mybarStr_Obj_Test1 OBJECT REFERENCE mybarStr.
000690  01 mybarStr_Obj_Test2 OBJECT REFERENCE mybarStr.
000700
000710 LINKAGE SECTION.
000720 PROCEDURE DIVISION.
000730*
000740     DISPLAY "Starting the ValueTypeSampleCobol Console Application."
000750     Display " "
000760     SET myStartTick to PROP-TickCount of SYS-ENVIRONMENT_Obj.
000770     PERFORM VARYING i
000780       FROM 0 BY 1 UNTIL i >= 999999
000790         MOVE 1 to WS-myfooInteger_Test1
000800         MOVE 2 to WS-myfooInteger_Test2
000810         MOVE WS-myfooInteger_Test1 to WS-myfooInteger_Test2
000820     END-PERFORM
000830     SET myFinishTick to PROP-TickCount of SYS-ENVIRONMENT_Obj.
000840
000850
000860     COMPUTE myComputedTick = (myFinishTick - myStartTick)
000870     MOVE myComputedTick to myDisplayTick
000880     DISPLAY "Total milliseconds: Integer Structures: " myDisplayTick
000890           Display " "
000900
000910     SET myStartTick to PROP-TickCount of SYS-ENVIRONMENT_Obj.
000920     PERFORM VARYING i
000930       FROM 0 BY 1 UNTIL i >= 999999
000940         MOVE "This is the String" to WS-myfooString_Test1
000950         MOVE "This is the Second String" to WS-myfooString_Test2
000960         MOVE WS-myfooString_Test1 to WS-myfooString_Test2
```

```
000970        END-PERFORM
000980        SET myFinishTick to PROP-TickCount of SYS-ENVIRONMENT_Obj.
000990
001000        COMPUTE myComputedTick = (myFinishTick - myStartTick)
001010        MOVE myComputedTick to myDisplayTick
001020        DISPLAY "Total milliseconds: String Structures: " myDisplayTick
001030        Display " "
001040
001050        SET myStartTick to PROP-TickCount of SYS-ENVIRONMENT_Obj.
001060        PERFORM VARYING i
001070          FROM 0 BY 1 UNTIL i >= 999999
001080            INVOKE mybarInt "NEW" USING BY VALUE 1
001090                    RETURNING mybarInt_Obj_Test1
001100            INVOKE mybarInt "NEW" USING BY VALUE 2
001110                    RETURNING mybarInt_Obj_Test2
001120          SET mybarInt_Obj_Test2 TO mybarInt_Obj_Test1
001130        END-PERFORM
001140        SET myFinishTick to PROP-TickCount of SYS-ENVIRONMENT_Obj.
001150
001160        COMPUTE myComputedTick = (myFinishTick - myStartTick)
001170        MOVE myComputedTick to myDisplayTick
001180        DISPLAY "Total milliseconds: Reference -Int Objects: " myDisplayTick
001190        Display " "
001200
001210        SET myStartTick to PROP-TickCount of SYS-ENVIRONMENT_Obj.
001220        PERFORM VARYING i
001230          FROM 0 BY 1 UNTIL i >= 999999
001240            INVOKE mybarStr "NEW" USING BY VALUE "This is the String"
001250                    RETURNING mybarStr_Obj_Test1
001260            INVOKE mybarStr "NEW" USING BY VALUE "This is the Second String"
001270                    RETURNING mybarStr_Obj_Test2
001280          SET mybarStr_Obj_Test2 TO mybarStr_Obj_Test1
001290        END-PERFORM
001300        SET myFinishTick to PROP-TickCount of SYS-ENVIRONMENT_Obj.
001310
001320        COMPUTE myComputedTick = (myFinishTick - myStartTick)
001330        MOVE myComputedTick to myDisplayTick
001340        DISPLAY "Total milliseconds: Reference - Str Objects: " myDisplayTick
001350        Display " "
001360
001370        Display "The Test is now complete.".
001380        DISPLAY "Enter X and Press Enter to Exit.".
001390        ACCEPT NULL-X.
001400
```

```
001410 END METHOD A-METHOD.
001420*
001430 END OBJECT.
001440 END CLASS A-CLASS.
```

The preceding Static class instantiates objects using the two classes shown in Listings 9-12 and 9-13.

Listing 9-12. The ValueTypeSampleCobol mybarInt.cob File

```
000010 IDENTIFICATION  DIVISION.
000020 CLASS-ID. mybarInt.
000030 ENVIRONMENT DIVISION.
000040 CONFIGURATION SECTION.
000050 REPOSITORY.
000060    CLASS SYS-INT32_Obj AS "System.Int32".
000070 OBJECT.
000080 PROCEDURE DIVISION.
000090 METHOD-ID. NEW.
000100 DATA DIVISION.
000110 WORKING-STORAGE SECTION.
000120 01 myInt1_Obj OBJECT REFERENCE SYS-INT32_Obj.
000130 LINKAGE SECTION.
000140 01 myInt1 PIC S9(9) USAGE COMP-5.
000150 PROCEDURE DIVISION USING BY VALUE myInt1.
000160    SET myInt1_Obj TO myInt1.
000170 END METHOD NEW.
000180 END OBJECT.
000190 END CLASS mybarInt.
```

Listing 9-13. The ValueTypeSampleCobol mybarStr.cob File

```
000010 IDENTIFICATION  DIVISION.
000020 CLASS-ID. mybarStr.
000030 ENVIRONMENT DIVISION.
000040 CONFIGURATION SECTION.
000050 REPOSITORY.
000060    CLASS SYS-STRING_Obj AS "System.String".
000070 OBJECT.
000080 PROCEDURE DIVISION.
000090 METHOD-ID. NEW.
000100 DATA DIVISION.
000110 WORKING-STORAGE SECTION.
000120 01 myStr_Obj OBJECT REFERENCE SYS-STRING_Obj.
```

```
000130 LINKAGE SECTION.
000140 01 myStr OBJECT REFERENCE SYS-STRING_Obj.
000150 PROCEDURE DIVISION USING BY VALUE myStr.
000160    SET myStr_Obj TO myStr.
000170 END METHOD NEW.
000180 END OBJECT.
000190 END CLASS mybarStr.
```

After you run the ValueTypeSampleCobol sample application, the lines in Listing 9-14 are written to the console display window.

Listing 9-14. Console Display Window Output from ValueTypeSampleCobol

```
Starting the ValueTypeSampleCobol Console Application.
Total milliseconds for Integer Structures:         40
Total milliseconds for String Structures:        4647
Total milliseconds for Reference -Int Objects:   7561
Total milliseconds for Reference - Str Objects: 21831
The Test is now complete.
Enter X and Press Enter to Exit.
```

The console display output is quite revealing. Please take a moment to notice the significant difference (in processing time) between the reference type String and value type Integer usage. A significant difference is also apparent when you compare the value type structure usage to the reference type object usage.

Would you have guessed that such a big performance difference would surface? It certainly is good to be aware of the "cost" of one coding design over another. Things that appear to be subtle choices (e.g., object types, data types, and so forth) can make a big difference in the performance of your application.

In the next section, you'll take a look at the same value/reference object type comparison, this time using VB .NET.

VB .NET Example

Please take a moment to review the sample application in Listing 9-15. You will see the definitions for two structures (myfooInteger and myfooString) and two classes (mybarInt and mybarStr). Near the end of the application, you will notice that there is one larger class (MyFirstClass) defined that actually uses the other defined structures and classes. As with the other applications, this ValueTypeSampleVB application is a console application. If you can, please execute the application to generate the console display output.

Listing 9-15. The ValueTypeSampleVB Application

```vb
'ValueTypeSampleVB Console Application


'Create my own Public Structure
Public Structure myfooInteger
        Public myInt As System.Int32


        'Define a Constructor Method
        Public Sub New(ByVal Input As Int32)
                Me.myInt = Input
        End Sub
End Structure


Public Structure myfooString
        Public myString As System.String


        'Define a Constructor Method
        Public Sub New(ByVal Input As String)
                Me.myString = Input
        End Sub
End Structure


'Create my own Class
Public Class mybarInt
        Public myInt1 As System.Int32


        'Define a Constructor Method
        Public Sub New(ByVal Input As Int32)
                Me.myInt1 = Input
        End Sub
End Class


'Create my own Class
Public Class mybarStr
        Public myStr As System.String


        'Define a Constructor Method
        Public Sub New(ByVal Input As String)
                Me.myStr = Input
        End Sub
End Class


Class MyFirstClass
```

```
Shared Sub Main()
    Console.WriteLine _
    ("Starting the ValueTypeSampleVB Console Application.")
    Dim tick1 As Integer = System.Environment.TickCount
    Dim i As Integer
    For i = 0 To 999999
        Dim test1 As myfooInteger = New myfooInteger(1)
        Dim test2 As myfooInteger = New myfooInteger(2)
        test2 = test1
    Next
    Dim tick2 As Integer = System.Environment.TickCount
    Console.WriteLine _
("Total milliseconds for Integer Structures: " & _
(tick2 - tick1))
    Console.WriteLine(" ")

    Dim tick1a As Integer = System.Environment.TickCount
    Dim ia As Integer
    For ia = 0 To 999999
        Dim test1 As myfooString = _
        New myfooString("This is the String")
        Dim test2 As myfooString = _
        New myfooString("This is the Second String")
        test2 = test1
    Next
    Dim tick2a As Integer = System.Environment.TickCount
    Console.WriteLine _
("Total milliseconds for String Structures: " & _
(tick2a - tick1a))
    Console.WriteLine(" ")

    Dim tick1d As Integer = System.Environment.TickCount
    Dim id As Integer
    For id = 0 To 999999
        Dim test1 As mybarInt = New mybarInt(1)
        Dim test2 As mybarInt = New mybarInt(2)
        test2 = test1
    Next
    Dim tick2d As Integer = System.Environment.TickCount
    Console.WriteLine _
("Total milliseconds for Reference - Integer Type Objects Loop: " & _
(tick2d - tick1d))
    Console.WriteLine(" ")
```

```
            Dim tick1e As Integer = System.Environment.TickCount
            Dim ie As Integer
            For ie = 0 To 999999
                    Dim test1 As mybarStr = _
                    New mybarStr("This is the String")
                    Dim test2 As mybarStr = _
                    New mybarStr("This is the Second String")
                    test2 = test1
            Next
            Dim tick2e As Integer = System.Environment.TickCount
            Console.WriteLine _
        ("Total milliseconds for Reference - String Type Objects Loop: " & _
        (tick2e - tick1e))
            Console.WriteLine(" ")

            Console.WriteLine("The Test is now complete. Press Enter to Exit")
            Console.ReadLine()
        End Sub
End Class
```

Please review the output shown in Listing 9-16 that is displayed in the console window when the ValueTypeSampleVB application is executed.

Listing 9-16. Console Output Display for ValueTypeSampleVB

```
Starting the ValueTypeSampleVB Console Application.
Total milliseconds for Integer Structures: 50
Total milliseconds for String Structures: 60
Total milliseconds for Reference - Integer Type Objects Loop: 320
Total milliseconds for Reference - String Type Objects Loop: 341
The Test is now complete. Press Enter to Exit
```

Now, aren't those displayed numbers revealing? Notice the pattern. The value type objects (the structures) that are defined to contain just an Integer will generally be faster to process than the other structures (in this case, those defined to contain a String). Additionally, the same pattern exists with the performance of the reference type objects. The Integer type reference object is generally faster than the String reference type object.

NOTE There are times when you will choose a particular data type because you absolutely need *that* particular data type. In those cases, these performance issues will have little meaning. However, when you actually have a choice, then of course you will want to choose the most efficient data type for your application.

For the structures, it boils down to this fact: When you define your value type data type to be part of a structure, it will actually have its value stored with the structure on the stack. These "true" value type structures will generally process faster. On the other hand, when the reference type object was defined as part of a structure, you were actually just storing the reference pointer there. Naturally, the pointer (just like any other reference type) is pointing to allocated space on the heap. This difference can help explain the relative variance in the processing times.[4]

TIP Always strive to allocate your value type *and* reference type objects using specific data types. In other words, good coding practices might result in rare usage of the System.Object data type and more common usage of System.Int32, System.String, and so on. Following this guideline, your code will typically run faster[5] and be more maintainable.

Continuing with the sample code output observation, you will notice that the reference type objects (created in the form of our own classes) produced similar processing variances (relatively speaking). Additionally, you will notice that the processing times *are* higher for the reference types than for the value type objects. Given the extra heap storage allocation concerns, this variance is to be expected. There are many times that you will appropriately choose to use reference type objects in spite of this apparent overhead. The fact remains that

---

4. As the byte size of your structure increases, the processing time comparison "gap" will tend to narrow.

5. This did not appear to be the fact with some of my COBOL .NET testing. With COBOL .NET, the System.Object usage actually yielded faster results than the more specific data types of Integer and String. Interesting, to say the least!

reference type objects have a lot to offer, but there is a price to pay. Investigate, experiment, and choose wisely.

In this section, I contrasted value type objects against reference type objects. Additionally, I reviewed general object usage concerns and potential performance issues. In the remaining section of the chapter, you'll explore yet another object usage concern: visibility and availability.

Object Visibility and Availability

In preparing to write this section, I reflected on my legacy mainframe COBOL days. I pondered the questions "When did *we* ever have to deal with visibility or availability of components?" and "When, on the mainframe, did we take into consideration the exposure and access of a component (or even the attributes of a component)?"

Mainframe Analogy: JCL and PROCs

One possible answer to these questions can be found in the legacy mainframe coding of JCL Jobs and procedures. Say that you are preparing to use a JCL Procedure (JCL PROC) in a particular Job. As you know, it is very common to use JCL overrides and symbolic variables in your Job to override portions of the PROC. Using either approach you can override EXEC statement parameters, OUTPUT JCL, and DD statements. However, there is a limit.

While all of the internal JCL portions of the PROC are visible (Public) to the external JCL job, the PGM parameter (alone) is the one portion of the EXEC statement that is not available for override (*NotOverridable*). On the other hand, all of the remaining JCL parameters are available for override (*Overridable*). Reflecting on this typical JCL scenario (as an analogy) will support further discussion on the visibility and availability of objects.

So, there is at least one possible answer to the question of whether the legacy mainframe coding arena dealt with visibility and availability of components. This JCL analogy speaks to that. I actually have another analogy that will help drive the point home. Let's (re)visit the practice of legacy mainframe COBOL programs calling subprograms.

Mainframe Analogy: COBOL Subprograms

Imagine, if you will, that you are creating a rather useful legacy mainframe COBOL routine. Wanting to move in the direction of code reuse, you design the routine to be used as a subprogram. Potentially, several other "main" programs will call[6] your subprogram. Typically, what design choices have you made (in your subprogram) to make all of this possible?

At some point in your subprogram design, it is likely that you made a decision to declare certain fields (variables) in your Linkage Section and other fields in your Working-Storage Section. As you know, this *is* the way that you make certain fields visible to any calling program while leaving others hidden. Those declared in the Linkage Section (exposed) would then be visible (Public) to the outside world. A calling program (calling the subprogram) would not "see" the (Private) fields defined in the Working-Storage Section.

NOTE When you work with legacy mainframe COBOL subprograms, the *calling* program has a choice of whether to include any of the following "Using By" clauses: BY CONTENT, BY REFERENCE, or BY VALUE (with BY REFERENCE being the default). Naturally, any senior-level legacy mainframe programmer is already familiar with this COBOL coding convention. This is a good thing. It makes it much easier for you to understand the concept of using the *ByVal* and *ByRef* coding options on the .NET platform. Just be aware that value type objects and reference type objects behave differently depending on whether you have passed them as ByVal or ByRef. Also note that ByVal is the default on the .NET platform.

Alternatively, you may have worked with the COBOL COPY statement (instead of the CALL statement). Still in the spirit of code reuse, you may have had components shared between programs in the form of copybooks.[7] Well, how about those times when you included the REPLACING clause on the COPY statement? You would have used the REPLACING clause to cause your COPY statement to "modify" all matching text inside of the target component—that is, all matched text that was "available" for update. Besides that, if the targeted component (to be copied) was nested, then all bets were off and the REPLACING clause simply could

---

6. To settle your curiosity, in the context of this analogy, it would not matter if you were designing the subprogram to be called/linked dynamically or statically.

7. I am loosely using the term "copybooks" to include legacy mainframe COBOL copybooks targeted for the Environment, Data, and Procedure Divisions of a consuming program.

not be used. Thus, depending on established criteria, the contents of the targeted component were either Overridable *or* NotOverridable.

Point made, right? Perspective established, correct? Good. OK, let's return to the twenty-first century and .NET. The following sections introduce you to the terminology used in COBOL .NET and VB .NET programming in the context of object visibility and availability.

Object Access and Scope

The terms "scope" and "access" are used interchangeably. Both terms speak to the determinable extent to which an object is visible or accessible. For defining scope attributes (or access attributes), COBOL .NET and VB .NET both use syntactical terms such as Private, Public, and Protected.

The Public access attribute provides for the highest degree of visibility and access. The Private access attribute is the most restrictive, providing the least amount of visibility.

In the case of COBOL .NET, these access attribute terms (Private, Public, and Protected) apply only to the class's methods. On the other hand, VB .NET allows these same access attributes to also be used at the class, structure, enumeration, property, and field levels. Additionally, VB .NET includes the *Friend* and *Shared* access attributes. Both COBOL .NET and VB .NET implement an additional "access attribute": *Static*.

 TIP   You will find that the Static access attribute is an opportunity for confusion. Understand that the access attribute of Static in COBOL .NET is equal to the access attribute SHARED in VB .NET. Usually when you see the term "static" used in the Class Viewer and other .NET tools, it will most likely be referring to the COBOL .NET definition of Static. On the other hand, when you see the term "static" used in the VB .NET context, the definition is completely different than COBOL .NET's. The way that VB .NET defines a Static access attribute specifically applies to VB .NET. For further details on this subject, please take advantage of the references provided at the end of this chapter in the "To Learn More" section.

Basically, a Static (or Shared in VB .NET) variable is instantiated once per class. The content is then visible to all instantiated objects (of that same class). In the COBOL .NET context, Static is used when defining a class. Optionally, you can include a Static Definition for data and methods within the class. In VB .NET, you can use the Shared (equivalent to Static in COBOL .NET) access attribute only at module, namespace, or file level—in other words, everywhere except inside of a procedure.

At a high level, almost in summary fashion, you have been introduced to object visibility. Is that a lot to digest? Understanding will come with practice and experimentation. Additionally, I believe that you will find the following Tip rather helpful.

 TIP You can consult the Fujitsu NetCOBOL for .NET Help text along with Microsoft's VB .NET Help text (both via Visual Studio .NET) for further details. Additionally, I have included URLs in the "To Learn More" section ("Web Sites" subsection) at the end of this chapter for your continued learning on the topic of access attributes. In fact, the URLs present a chart-style display that you can print out for frequent cross-referencing.

Availability via Object Orientation

In the two previous mainframe analogies (presented in the sections "Mainframe Analogy: JCL and PROCs" and "Mainframe Analogy: COBOL Subprograms"), the terms Overridable and NotOverridable were introduced. Guess what? I have a surprise for you! You were actually introduced to the term Overridable much earlier in this chapter. Recall the section "Where Do Objects Come From?" where I discussed System.Object? There was a section of code displayed from the Class Viewer tool similar to Listing 9-17.

Listing 9-17. A Portion of System.Object As Shown in the Class Viewer Tool Output

```
. . .
(5) // Methods
(6)   public virtual bool Equals(object obj);
. . .
(8)   public virtual int GetHashCode();
. . .
. . .
(11)  public virtual string ToString();
(12) // end of System.Object
```

Notice that lines 6, 8, and 11 include the word "virtual." What is the significance of this? Well, virtual is the C# (and C++) term for Overridable.

TIP   See the "Web Sites" subsection of the "To Learn More" section at the end of this chapter for a useful URL that should ease the translation of key terms from one .NET language to another.

All right, you know that a method can be Overridable. So what, right? Again, I will refer back to one of those .NET retraining prerequisite topics presented in Chapter 4. In this case, I'm talking about object orientation. So, you ask, what does object orientation have to do with object availability?

Using the System.Object class as an example, the three methods marked "virtual" are made available to other classes as Overridable. In order for this to become relevant to other classes, the System.Object (base) class would first have to be *inherited* by the "other" classes. When you are talking inheritance and base classes, you certainly are talking object orientation. What's more, whether a member is Overridable or not is just scratching the surface in terms of object availability.

As with object "scope" (discussed earlier in the section "Object Access and Scope"), there are various levels (or degrees) of object availability. Though I prefer not to repeat the entire object orientation content presented earlier in the book here, I do feel it is useful to emphasize the applicability of the topic in this context. To affect object availability, you will expose (or hide) members of a class (using any of the Override-related keywords). On other occasions, you may choose to "add" functionally new objects to a class (using the *Overloads* and/or *Shadows* keywords). Yes, your focus here is on "the object," yet you have proven that eventually you *will* go full circle.

Going Full Circle Around the Object

In order to program on .NET, you really need to understand what System.Object is. That will lead you to understanding the difference between the value type objects and reference type objects. In order to effectively use these objects, you need to understand how to influence their scope and availability. Once you have gone that far down the path, you are not only programming the .NET way, you are programming the object-oriented way.

Summary

This chapter's goals were as follows:

- To discuss object creation

- To compare the Object and ValueType classes

- To examine the behavior of objects

- To explore object visibility and availability

This is, by far, my favorite part of every chapter. As I lick my wounds and crack my knuckles, I get a chance to reflect. This chapter is no exception. You have come a long way.

I started this chapter by acknowledging the many references to this chapter that you found in previous chapters. I discussed the omnipresence of the System.Object class for greater appreciation of its usefulness. I then discussed the System.Object class and its derivative System.ValueType class. That set the stage for various discussions that examined the object types from various perspectives: coding, behavior, performance, and scope. I finished the chapter by revisiting the topic of object orientation and illustrating the relationship between object orientation and object availability.

The next chapter covers how to get data without the help of JCL.

To Learn More

The following are some suggested supplemental references to further your retraining effort.

Books

Software Development on a Leash, by David C. Birmingham and Valerie Haynes Perry (Apress, 2002):
http://www.apress.com/catalog/book/1893115917/.

Magazines

.NET Magazine:
> http://www.fawcette.com/dotnetmag/

Visual Studio Magazine:
> http://www.fawcette.com/vsm/

XML & Web Services Magazine:
> http://www.fawcette.com/xmlmag/

Web Sites

Dr. GUI .NET #5: Strings in the .NET Framework:
> http://msdn.microsoft.com/library/en-us/dnguinet/html/
> drguinet5_update.asp

Dr. GUI .NET #6: Arrays in the .NET Framework:
> http://msdn.microsoft.com/library/en-us/dnguinet/html/
> drguinet6_update.asp

Microsoft Community (discussion groups, e-newsletters, and so forth):
> http://communities2.microsoft.com/

MSDN:
> http://msdn.microsoft.com

Visual Basic Attributes for the Dim Statement (scope/visibility):
> http://msdn.microsoft.com/library/en-us/vblr7/html/vastmDim.asp

Visual Basic Attributes for the Sub Statement (availability):
> http://msdn.microsoft.com/library/en-us/vblr7/html/vastmSub.asp

Visual Studio Language Equivalents (translation between .NET languages):
> http://msdn.microsoft.com/library/en-us/vsintro7/html/
> vxgrfLanguageEquivalents.asp

Part Three
Reading, Writing, and Describing Data

*"I do not know everything. At least I am intelligent enough to know that.
I do not know everything about .NET. At least I know enough about
.NET to know that."*

—*Chris Richardson*

A New Perspective Toward Data

Leaving No Stone Unturned in the Search for Data

In this chapter

- Exploring basic data access with text files

- Learning to work with data repositories

- Working with metadata as data

THE LINGUISTS IN the crowd are certain to grind their teeth while they read this chapter. They would argue the following:

> *"The technical community leaves no room on their bookshelf for the honorable lexicon. It's enough that they abuse the use of acronyms as a way to shorten sentences. At their whim, they repurpose terms such as 'mouse,' 'window,' and 'scroll.' They include capital letters in the middle of terms just to identify syllables. Those technical folks can't even use the term* data *correctly. Don't they know that the term* data *was intended to be used as the plural form of the term* datum.*"*

Although I certainly will not argue with those who have mastered the English language (or Latin, for that matter), I would like to go on record as stating that as language evolves over time, so should those that profess to use it. So, on the note of evolution, the very meaning of the term "data" has in fact evolved. Yes, the various ways of storing and accessing data have changed. More important, there are many *newer* ways of identifying and classifying data. The .NET platform fully supports these changes.

The topics I cover in this chapter embrace that fact. I start the discussion with the most basic type of data access: the text file. Then, I move on to cover data repositories, a more complex view of data. I could easily stop there. But, I will not. Relentlessly, I will push forward. To finish off the chapter, I discuss a very different type of data: metadata.

A Basic View of Data: Files

Let's start by reflecting on the most basic types of data files that are available on the mainframe:

- Queued Sequential Access Method (QSAM)

- Partitioned Access Method (PAM, but more commonly known as partitioned dataset or PDS)

- Virtual Storage Access Method (VSAM)

NOTE On the mainframe, database-stored data is as common as QSAM, PDS, and VSAM data formats. I further discuss database-oriented data formats the section "An Extended View of Data: Data Repositories" later in this chapter.

Any discussion of mainframe data would not be complete without mention of the QSAM file (rather, the *flat file*). For a lot of us *reformed* mainframe types, this simply structured, easily accessed file served as our initial entry into programmatic data processing. (Well, that is, for those of us who have no idea what keypunch cards are.) Combine the QSAM file with JCL, and we were happily creating great applications that consisted of nothing more that a few IEBGENER utility programs being executed in succession, copying one QSAM file on top of another, and perhaps sorting and printing the data.

In those early days, just as you had gotten used to Logical Record Lengths (LRECLs) and Data Control Blocks (DCBs), it happened. Someone came along and pointed out that the PDS file that you had been using to store your JCL Jobs could also be used to store regular text. Then, you used these PDS members for all of your basic data storage needs (e.g., status reports, resumes, and so on). Perfecting your abilities to read and write programmatically, your QSAM and PDS files meant that now you were really a data processing professional.

Let's jump forward a few mainframe years, when you "graduated" to VSAM files. For many of you, this would have occurred around the same time that you were making your entry into mainframe CICS programming. With VSAM files, you were now (generally) able to choose between *sequential* or *random* access of your data. You were introduced to the IDCAMS utility (which was comparable to the IEBGENER utility). So, with QSAM, PDS, and VSAM files, you went along creating mission-critical solutions.

Users Putting the "I" in "I/O"

It's likely that you've written some type of application that accepted user input. It may have been an online mainframe CICS application that had the user entering values on the screen. Besides the fact that you had to add input validation logic, you were now getting input directly from the user. Similar to getting input from files, you had the opportunity to process this direct user input data as you saw fit. In Chapter 13, when I further discuss user interaction, you'll be introduced to the .NET ways of accepting user input (including input validation and other techniques).

As you make your transition to the Windows platform, you will be looking for suitable replacements for the common mainframe data file formats of QSAM, PDS, and VSAM. Naturally, you will want to explore data access in the absence of mainframe JCL. Equally (if not more) important, you are eager to find out what type of support .NET provides for Windows-based basic data access.

Moving from Flat Files to Text Files

Simply put, the Win32-based *text file* (or American Standard Code for Information Interchange [ASCII] file) is going to be your replacement for the mainframe type of *flat file* (or Extended Binary Coded Decimal Interchange Code [EBCDIC] file).

NOTE The Windows NT file system (NTFS) is the preferred underlying system-level application responsible for general file allocation concerns in the Windows 2000 environment. The older Win32 file systems, file allocation table (FAT) and FAT32, continue to be supported for backward compatibility.

On the Windows environment, text-type files are generally recognized as the files that are readable by humans. Suffix extensions are associated with each grouping of text-type files (.txt, .xml, and .htm, just to name a few). The groupings of text-type files that use .txt as the suffix extension are sometimes simply referred to as *text files* (even though this grouping is just one among other text-type files). For the remainder of this chapter, I use this particular grouping of text-type files (files ending with .txt), and I also loosely refer to them as "text files."

File-type suffix extensions typically have a default program associated with them for reading/editing. Therefore, each specific grouping of text-type files can be associated with a specific reading/editing program. The default program typically associated with text files (files with the .txt suffix, in this context) is the Windows utility Notepad.

TIP You can override the default program-to-file-type association in Windows. This is generally referred to as the Open With option on the Windows platform. Consult your Windows Help text for further details. (Search on the topic "File Type" or "File Name Extension.")

Outside of your own application development, you can use Notepad to easily create and edit text files (I discussed Notepad in Chapter 3 in the section "Microsoft Office and Notepad"). Understanding this, you are then faced with the choice of how to access text files (when capturing and modifying your own data): the traditional legacy way or the newer .NET way.

TIP On the Windows platform, when you want to create a text file, you simply create it. Gone is the need to worry about LRECLs, block sizes, and DCBs. Variable-length and fixed-length record formats . . . huh? What does that mean? The questions you might ask during the creation of a Win32 text file might involve file name and folder choice for saving. That is about it. Pretty simple. Oh—and no JCL.

Accessing Text Files in .NET the Old Way

Before you throw up your hands, bear with me for a moment. You might ask, "Why on earth even mention doing something the 'old way' on the .NET platform?" Well, I suppose it comes down to *dollars and cents*—or maybe *dollars and sense*: the *dollars* that it may cost to rewrite the application using the newer approach (in most cases, the better approach) and the *sense* that it typically makes to do so. My suggestion is that if you have time, quickly learn and master the "newer" way and use it. If you don't have time, simply use the "older" way and effortlessly port your existing legacy business logic to your new .NET application. Now, let's take a look at both the traditional approach (on .NET) and the modern approach (on .NET).

NOTE Large vendors (e.g., Microsoft and Fujitsu) include support for the traditional syntax mainly to ease the upgrade experience (both software-wise and training-wise). As they do, you should remain sensitive to the financial bottom line that exists in every organization. In some cases, your legacy application may have some life left in it. That is, according to the expected life span of your legacy application, management may have issues with expediting the trashing of a software investment.

COBOL .NET Code Snippet

The pseudo-code snippet in Listing 10-1 (showing a basic data access structure) should look familiar to you. Even though this code is being presented in the context of COBOL .NET sample code, notice that the approach is basically the same as that you would expect to see in the traditional mainframe COBOL code. Although the SELECT/ASSIGN statement may look a little strange, the remaining statements (OPEN, WRITE, CLOSE, and so forth) are the same COBOL statements that you have used in your legacy mainframe applications. It is great to know that you *can* continue to use this type of legacy COBOL syntax in your new COBOL .NET development.

Listing 10-1. A Pseudo-Code COBOL .NET Snippet Showing Traditional File Access Syntax

```
IDENTIFICATION DIVISION.
PROGRAM-ID. My-program.
. . .
 FILE-CONTROL.
     SELECT a-file
       ASSIGN TO "C:\SampleText.txt".
DATA DIVISION
 FILE SECTION.
 FD a-file
 01 your-record   PIC X(80).
PROCEDURE DIVISION.
```

```
    OPEN OUTPUT a-file.
[Open mode could have been I-O, INPUT, or EXTEND]
    WRITE your-record.
[You may have READ your a-file]
    CLOSE a-file.
  . . .
END PROGRAM My-program.
```

This continued traditional syntax support is, of course, a good thing when you are porting existing coded logic from the mainframe platform over to the Windows platform. There is one significant caveat to this convenience: If you are developing new code, you might consider leveraging the newer .NET way of accessing files. I believe this latter approach (using the .NET Framework) will further support your ultimate retraining goal.

VB .NET Code Snippet

Yes, Visual Basic .NET (VB .NET) also supports a traditional approach. Knowing this may be of more value to those with a legacy Visual Basic (that is, Visual Basic 6.0) background, but it may (one day) be of use to you as well. Who knows? You may end up being tasked with converting legacy Visual Basic 6.0 applications over to VB .NET. After all, you *are* acquiring .NET expertise. You will be surprised at the doors that you are opening for yourself.

The following VB .NET pseudo-code snippet demonstrates a typical way,[1] using traditional Visual Basic 6.0 syntax, to access text file data in a .NET application.

Listing 10-2. VB .NET Pseudo-Code Snippet Showing a Traditional Approach of Accessing a Text File

```
. . .
Dim myString As System.String
Dim myInt As System.Int32
. . .
'The code below Demonstrates how to Write to the Text file.
'Open File Number 1
Microsoft.VisualBasic.FileOpen(1, "MyFile.txt", OpenMode.Output)
'Write a String to File Number 1
Microsoft.VisualBasic.Write(1, "This is a Test")
```

---

1. Some Visual Basic 6.0 developers have used an alternative traditional approach to access data in Win32 text files. This other approach is commonly referred to as the FileSystemObject (FSO) approach. For our purposes here, please just make a note that this *other* traditional approach does exist.

```
'Write a Number to File Number 1
Microsoft.VisualBasic.Write(1, 99)
'Close File Number 1
Microsoft.VisualBasic.FileClose(1)
'The code below Demonstrates how to read from the Text file.
'Open File Number 1
Microsoft.VisualBasic.FileOpen(1, "MyFile.txt", OpenMode.Input)
'Read a String from File Number 1
Microsoft.VisualBasic.Input(1, myString)
'Read an Integer from File Number 1
Microsoft.VisualBasic.Input(1, myInt)
'Close File Number 1
Microsoft.VisualBasic.FileClose(1)
. . .
```

Whether you bilingual developers are coding in COBOL .NET or VB .NET, you are certainly ready now to see the newer .NET way of accessing Win32-based text file data.

Accessing Text Files in .NET the New Way

Microsoft has created a .NET Framework namespace specifically designed for data access. This namespace, *System.IO*, contains a healthy number of delegates (sorry, no interfaces), classes, enumerations, and structures. Although it is advisable to eventually familiarize yourself with each one of them, I will introduce only the following few here:[2]

- File (or *System.IO.File*)

- TextReader (or *System.IO.TextReader*)

- TextWriter (or *System.IO.TextWriter*)

 TIP   There are System.IO objects available that support path/directory logic as well as security/access logic. There are even special methods you can use when reading and writing binary data. As time (and your need) dictates, do explore the System.IO namespace.

---

2. You will actually use a few additional classes and enumerations simply through the course of using the three classes File, TextReader, and TextWriter.

Reviewing System.IO.File

Let's start by using the Class Viewer (WinCV.exe) tool to take a quick peek into the System.IO.File class.[3] It has a handful of members, as Listing 10-3 shows.

Listing 10-3. The Methods of the System.IO.File Class

```
// from module 'c:\winnt\microsoft.net\framework\v1.0.3705\mscorlib.dll'
public sealed class System.IO.File :
    object
. . .
    // Methods
public static System.IO.StreamWriter AppendText(string path);
public static void Copy(string sourceFileName, string destFileName);
public static void Copy(string sourceFileName, string destFileName, bool
                overwrite);
public static System.IO.FileStream Create(string path);
public static System.IO.FileStream Create(string path, int bufferSize);
public static System.IO.StreamWriter CreateText(string path);
public static void Delete(string path);
public virtual bool Equals(object obj);
public static bool Exists(string path);
public static System.IO.FileAttributes GetAttributes(string path);
public static DateTime GetCreationTime(string path);
public virtual int GetHashCode();
public static DateTime GetLastAccessTime(string path);
public static DateTime GetLastWriteTime(string path);
public Type GetType();
public static void Move(string sourceFileName, string destFileName);
public static System.IO.FileStream Open(string path, System.IO.FileMode mode);
public static System.IO.FileStream Open(string path, System.IO.FileMode mode,
                System.IO.FileAccess access);
public static System.IO.FileStream Open(string path, System.IO.FileMode mode,
                System.IO.FileAccess access, System.IO.FileShare share);
public static System.IO.FileStream OpenRead(string path);
public static System.IO.StreamReader OpenText(string path);
public static System.IO.FileStream OpenWrite(string path);
public static void SetAttributes(string path, System.IO.FileAttributes
                fileAttributes);
```

---

3. Yes, you can choose to abbreviate System.IO.File to just File (and then remember to use the IMPORTS statement when coding in VB .NET). However, I generally find it more useful to just go ahead and use the entire namespace. This approach (to me) seems more informative and self-documenting.

```
public static void SetCreationTime(string path, DateTime creationTime);
public static void SetLastAccessTime(string path, DateTime lastAccessTime);
public static void SetLastWriteTime(string path, DateTime lastWriteTime);
public virtual string ToString();
} // end of System.IO.File
```

Notice that each member of the System.IO.File class is a Public Static method (the Class Viewer tool uses Visual C# .NET or just C# syntax in its display). This, of course, is in reference to the access attributes being shown. Recall that if I were coding in VB .NET, I would have rephrased this as Public Shared method.

From the list of methods in Listing 10-3, take a closer look at the *Open* method. You can see that there are actually three methods shown for Open. This is an example of the object-oriented overloading approach. In other words, the Open method is overloaded. Looking at the overloaded Open methods (displayed using C# syntax)

```
. . .
public static System.IO.FileStream Open(string path, System.IO.FileMode mode);
public static System.IO.FileStream Open(string path, System.IO.FileMode mode,
              System.IO.FileAccess access);
public static System.IO.FileStream Open(string path, System.IO.FileMode mode,
              System.IO.FileAccess access, System.IO.FileShare share);
. . .
```

you can see that if you were to code *System.IO.File.Open*, the *type* of object that would be returned is a *System.IO.FileStream* object. As its name indicates, *FileStream* is a class housed in the System.IO namespace. By using the overloaded approach, the only thing that differs with each overloaded Open method is the input parameters. Depending on your use of input parameters, you will dictate which Open method you actually use. With the exception of the string/path input parameter, the *System.IO.FileMode, System.IO.FileAccess*, and *System.IO.FileShare* input parameters are enumerations from the System.IO namespace.

Reviewing System.IO.TextReader

This next class, *System.IO.TextReader*, contains just over a dozen methods. Please take a moment to review Listing 10-4, which contains the Class Viewer display that shows these few methods.

Listing 10-4. The Methods of the System.IO.TextReader Class

```
. . .
public abstract class System.IO.TextReader :
. . .
// Methods
public virtual void Close();
public virtual System.Runtime.Remoting.ObjRef CreateObjRef(Type
               requestedType);
public virtual bool Equals(object obj);
public virtual int GetHashCode();
public virtual object GetLifetimeService();
public Type GetType();
public virtual object InitializeLifetimeService();
public virtual int Peek();
public virtual int Read();
public virtual int Read(char[] buffer, int index, int count);
public virtual int ReadBlock(char[] buffer, int index, int count);
public virtual string ReadLine();
public virtual string ReadToEnd();
public static System.IO.TextReader Synchronized(System.IO.TextReader reader);
public virtual string ToString();
. . .
```

You will notice that the System.IO.TextReader class is defined as Public Abstract (near the top of the Class Viewer display). This is C# syntax for Public MustInherit. In other words, you can't use the System.IO.TextReader class directly—you must first inherit this class. Then, you simply take advantage of System.IO.TextReader via your derived class. For your convenience, the majority of the methods (as shown in Listing 10-4) are defined as Public Virtual (again, C# syntax). You can interpret this as Public Overridable. So, if you found the need to, you could actually override most of the System.IO.TextReader methods in your derived class.

You are in luck. Microsoft has actually provided two .NET "*derived* classes"— two classes that both inherit from System.IO.TextReader. These classes are *System.IO.StreamReader* and *System.IO.StringReader.* Of course, if you were so looking forward to exercising your object orientation skills, feel free to create your own *derived* classes (that inherit from System.IO.TextReader). Just remember, you also need to add all of the additional logic to override the appropriate methods. In other words, plan to use these two *derived* classes (System.IO.StreamReader and System.IO.StringReader) that Microsoft has provided as part of the .NET Framework each time that you want the functionality exposed by the System.IO.TextReader class.

> **NOTE** My emphasis here on the word "derived" is actually misleading. As you learned in Chapter 9 (in the section "Where Do .NET Objects Come From?"), *all* .NET Framework classes are either directly or indirectly derived from the System.Object class. So, these are two classes that just happen to derive from the System.IO.TextReader class.

Take a moment to review each of the System.IO.TextReader methods carefully. For example, take note of the following facts:

- The *Read* method is overloaded.

- There are several methods for reading (e.g., *ReadLine*, *ReadBlock*, and *ReadToEnd*).

- The *Peek* method returns an Integer.

- The ToString method returns a String.

The name of the System.IO.TextReader class is obviously self-documenting. Given that fact, it should not surprise you that there *is* a .NET Framework class for writing text that has the name System.IO.TextReader.

Reviewing System.IO.TextWriter

This particular data access–oriented class also happens to be an abstract class (that must be inherited and used via a derived class). Listing 10-5 shows a partial Class Viewer display of the *System.IO.TextWriter* class.

Listing 10-5. The System.IO.TextWriter Class

```
. . .
// Methods
public virtual void Close();
. . .
public virtual void Write(char[] buffer);
public virtual void Write(char[] buffer, int index, int count);
public virtual void Write(string format, object[] arg);
public virtual void Write(string format, object arg0);
public virtual void Write(string format, object arg0, object arg1);
public virtual void Write(string format, object arg0, object arg1, object arg2);
public virtual void Write(int value);
```

```
public virtual void Write(UInt32 value);
public virtual void Write(char value);
public virtual void Write(bool value);
public virtual void Write(long value);
public virtual void Write(Decimal value);
public virtual void Write(string value);
public virtual void Write(object value);
public virtual void Write(UInt64 value);
public virtual void Write(float value);
public virtual void Write(double value);
public virtual void WriteLine();
public virtual void WriteLine(char[] buffer);
public virtual void WriteLine(char[] buffer, int index, int count);
public virtual void WriteLine(string format, object[] arg);
public virtual void WriteLine(string format, object arg0);
public virtual void WriteLine(string format, object arg0, object arg1);

. . .

public virtual void WriteLine(Decimal value);
public virtual void WriteLine(string value);
public virtual void WriteLine(object value);
public virtual void WriteLine(double value);
public virtual void WriteLine(int value);
public virtual void WriteLine(bool value);
public virtual void WriteLine(char value);
public virtual void WriteLine(UInt32 value);
public virtual void WriteLine(float value);
public virtual void WriteLine(UInt64 value);
public virtual void WriteLine(long value);

. . .
```

Wow! Now, *that* is what I call truly exercising an object-oriented design. Take a look at the extent to which the two methods Write and WriteLine are overloaded. You can see that the System.IO.TextWriter class supports practically all data types. Using the appropriate derived class, you can write data to your heart's content. Among your choices of derived classes provided by Microsoft (as part of the .NET Framework) are

- System.IO.StreamWriter

- System.IO.StringWriter

- System.Web.HttpWriter

- System.Web.UI.HtmlTextWriter

Demonstrating How to Access Data in Text Files

Now that you have reviewed the System.IO.File, System.IO.TextReader, and
System.IO.TextWriter classes, it is time for a quick demonstration. The code
shown in the following two sample projects, SystemIOExampleVB and
SystemIOExampleCobol, should help you get off to a great start. Please review the
VB .NET and COBOL .NET code. When you execute the project, a few lines will
display on your console that show the data contents of your text file.

> **NOTE** When you execute the sample applications, a text file will be
> created. Until you explicitly delete the newly created text file (named
> myTextFile.txt), the file will continue to exist.

Listing 10-6 shows the data access logic in a VB .NET sample project.

*Listing 10-6. VB .NET Project SystemIOExampleVB Demonstrating the Use of the
System.IO Namespace*

```
Module Module1
    Sub Main()
        Call WriteMyData()
        Call ReadMyData()
    End Sub


    Sub WriteMyData()


        'Declare a StreamWriter Object
        'which inherits System.IO.TextWriter
        Dim myStreamWriter As System.IO.StreamWriter
        'Return Value of File.CreateText Method = StreamWriter
        myStreamWriter = _
        System.IO.File.CreateText("myTextFile.txt")
        Dim myInt As System.Int32
        For myInt = 0 To 3
            myStreamWriter.WriteLine("This is a Test")
        Next
        'Close the StreamWriter and file
        myStreamWriter.Close()
    End Sub


    Sub ReadMyData()
```

```
            'Declare a StreamReader Object
            'which inherits System.IO.TextReader
            Dim myStreamReader As System.IO.StreamReader
            'Return Value of File.OpenText Method = StreamReader
            myStreamReader = System.IO.File.OpenText("myTextFile.txt")
            'Read Until Reaching the End of the StreamReader
            Dim myReadString As System.String
            Do Until myStreamReader.Peek = -1
                myReadString = myStreamReader.ReadLine()
                Console.WriteLine(myReadString)
            Loop
            'Close the StreamReader and file
            myStreamReader.Close()
               Console.WriteLine("Press Enter to Exit.")
            Console.ReadLine()
        End Sub
End Module
```

Listing 10-7 shows similar data access logic implemented in a COBOL .NET sample project.

Listing 10-7. COBOL .NET Project SystemIOExampleCobol Demonstrating the Use of the System.IO Namespace

```
000010 IDENTIFICATION DIVISION.
000020 PROGRAM-ID. MAIN.
000030 ENVIRONMENT DIVISION.
000040 CONFIGURATION SECTION.
000050 REPOSITORY.
000060* .NET Framework Classes
000070*    Declare a StreamWriter & StreamReader Object
000080*    which will inherit from
000090*    System.IO.TextWriter & System.IO.TextReader
000100    CLASS Sys-StreamWriter AS "System.IO.StreamWriter"
000110    CLASS Sys-StreamReader AS "System.IO.StreamReader"
000120    CLASS Sys-Integer      AS "System.Int32"
000130    CLASS Sys-String       AS "System.String".
000140*
000150 DATA DIVISION.
000160 WORKING-STORAGE SECTION.
000170    77 mySys-StreamWriter OBJECT REFERENCE Sys-StreamWriter.
000180    77 mySys-StreamReader OBJECT REFERENCE Sys-StreamReader.
000190    77 mySys-String  OBJECT REFERENCE Sys-String.
000200    77 mySys-Integer OBJECT REFERENCE Sys-Integer.
```

```
000210   77 myDisplayString PIC x(30).
000220   77 myInt PIC S9(9) COMP-5.
000230   77 myOtherInt PIC S9(9) COMP-5.
000240   01 NULL-X PIC X(1).
000250 PROCEDURE DIVISION.
000260
000270      Perform 1000-WriteMyData.
000280      Perform 2000-ReadMyData.
000290      Stop Run.
000300   1000-WriteMyData.
000310
000320*     Explicitly Create StreamWriter Object with Constructor
000330      INVOKE Sys-StreamWriter "NEW"
000340      USING BY VALUE "myTextFile.txt"
000350      RETURNING  mySys-StreamWriter
000360
000370      PERFORM VARYING myInt
000380        FROM 0 BY 1 UNTIL myInt >= 4
000390          INVOKE mySys-StreamWriter "WriteLine"
000400            USING BY VALUE "This is a Test"
000410      END-PERFORM.
000420*     Close the StreamWriter and file
000430      INVOKE mySys-StreamWriter "Close".
000440   2000-ReadMyData.
000450
000460*     Explicitly Create StreamReader Object with Constructor
000470      INVOKE Sys-StreamReader "NEW"
000480      USING BY VALUE "myTextFile.txt"
000490      RETURNING  mySys-StreamReader
000500
000510      PERFORM UNTIL myOtherInt = -1
000520         SET mySys-String TO mySys-StreamReader::"ReadLine" ()
000530         SET myDisplayString TO mySys-String
000540         DISPLAY myDisplayString
000550*     Read Until Reaching the End of the StreamReader
000560         SET mySys-Integer TO mySys-StreamReader::"Peek" ()
000570         SET myOtherInt to mySys-Integer
000580      END-PERFORM
000590*     Close the StreamWriter and file
000600      INVOKE mySys-StreamReader "Close".
000610
000620      DISPLAY "Enter X and Press Enter to Exit.".
000630      ACCEPT NULL-X.
000640 END PROGRAM MAIN.
```

You will notice that both sample projects (SystemIOExampleCobol and SystemIOExampleVB) make use of the System.IO namespace. Although the syntax varies slightly between the two languages, the approach is similar for accessing data in text files. The next step could be to explore further the System.IO namespace. With practice, you will be better prepared to take advantage of these (and other) .NET Framework classes to support your basic needs to write data to and read data from text files.

I have discussed both traditional and state-of-the-art approaches to accessing data in text files. Now you will switch gears and move beyond the text file and flat file. As you well know, there are times when a flat file or text file will not meet all of your development needs.

What About the PDS and VSAM Data Formats?

Coming from a legacy mainframe COBOL environment, you will likely seek out something representative of the mainframe PDS and VSAM types of data formats. These "other" data formats certainly have had their time and place. So, on that note, their time was yesterday, and their place was on the mainframe.

All right, to be fair, there are comparable replacements. The Win32 directory/folder structure mimics the functionality of the PDS data format. You can read from, navigate the "tree" structure of, and write to the Win32 directory/folder data structure. As for VSAM, a product available from Fujitsu called the COBOL File Utility that ships with NetCOBOL for .NET allows you to create indexed text files. These indexed text files mimic the functionality of the mainframe VSAM files that you have used through the years.

Besides the file utility products (such as the one Fujitsu provides), many companies are following a growing trend where they will create or purchase an application programming interface (API) to access mainframe VSAM files. The modern acronym being used for these types of APIs is EAI, which stands for *Enterprise Application Integration*.

 TIP A reformed mainframe programmer can be a big asset to his or her organization when EAI and host integration projects are launched.

An Opportunity to Redefine Data

When I decided to transition over to the Windows/Web development world,[4] among other things, I remember having to actually *redefine* data. You, reading this, may assume that I am using the phrase "redefining data" to refer to the REDEFINES data definition clause used in COBOL programs. Actually, I am referring to the notion that an expanded definition of the term "data" does exist. In other words, there are many things (other than QSAM, PDS, and VSAM text-type structures) that can be categorized as data, especially when you are doing Windows/Web development.

Take image files, for example. As a Windows/Web developer, you may grow to recognize an image file as just another type of data file. You could become familiar with image formats such as bitmaps, Joint Photographic Experts Group (JPEG) files, and Tagged Image File Format (TIFF) files. In your Web development work, you will certainly work with the Graphics Interchange Format (GIF) image file format. If you are lucky, you may even end up working with GIF animation files.[5] They are part of an impressive list that consists of data files (while redefining the term "data") available for your application to consume. (I further discuss graphic data in the next section, "The .NET Framework Supports Graphic Data.")

> **NOTE** .NET objects themselves can even be considered to be data.
> .NET has a feature referred to as *object serialization*. With this feature,
> you can "turn" a previously instantiated object into XML structured
> data. The serialized object can then be *persisted* (saved) or transmitted.
> Later, the *deserialization* process brings the object back to life.
> Chapter 12 goes into this topic in more depth.

Once you redefine what data actually is (or rather, what *is* data), the list is endless. In addition to image files, there are data files for supporting audio and video needs. Speech, network streams, and even HTML would also fall into the (redefined) data category. The types of data formats that I have listed in this section ("A Basic View of Data: Files") are those that are more "file" oriented. In

---

4. The day I joined forces with the dark side.

5. For those interested in programming with graphic data, be sure to do a search on the Macromedia Flash technology. A reference is included at the end of this chapter to give you a head start.

other words, as exhaustive as this "redefined" data list appears, it just scratches the surface. For example, a look beyond the data "files" will reveal the following "other" types of data:

- Data repositories (see the section "An Extended View of Data: Data Repositories" later in this chapter)

- Metadata (see the section "A Meta View of Data: Metadata" later in this chapter)

The redefinition of data may sound like a stretch, I know. It was a stretch for me. Legacy mainframe development tools (for the most part) simply were not equipped to support these types of data. As you've probably guessed, the .NET platform is equipped to support *all* of your data needs.

The .NET Framework Supports Graphic Data

In the event that your application needs to work directly with graphic data, you will want to familiarize yourself with several .NET Framework namespaces:

- *System.Drawing* for basic graphics functionality

- *System.Drawing.Drawing2D* for advanced two-dimensional graphics

- *System.Drawing.Imaging* for advanced imaging functionality

- *System.Drawing.Text* for advanced typography functionality

- *System.Drawing.Design* for design-time user interface and drawing

- *System.Drawing.Printing* for print-related services

These .NET namespaces all have one thing in common (other than "System.Drawing" being part of their name): They each support a technology known as GDI+, which is the successor to Graphical Device Interface, or GDI. GDI+ is a broad and powerful graphics-based technology worthy of further research. For your convenience, I have provided a few GDI+ references at the end of this chapter in the "To Learn More" section.

Walk Before Running with GDI+

In the meantime, it is possible to accomplish your most basic (graphically oriented) tasks without an extensive investment into GDI+ expertise. Start with something simple (e.g., the *System.Drawing.Graphic* class) and build up from there. Better yet, how about the System.Drawing.Printing namespace? That could be a starting point.

You could combine your knowledge of the System.IO.StreamReader class (discussed earlier in the section "Reviewing System.IO.TextReader") with classes from the System.Drawing.Printing namespace. This will be helpful when you want to read a regular text file for the purpose of printing the contents of the file. You can even add Print Preview functionality into your application using features you will find in the System.Drawing.Printing *PreviewPageInfo* and *PreviewPrintController* classes.

> **NOTE** Depending on the type of business applications that you will be writing, your perspective toward "a basic view of data" could vary significantly. For example, rather than depending on Win32-based text files, you could find yourself working with many "other" types of data formats, including image files.

Have fun exploring these "graphic" data namespaces. As you encounter the need to incorporate graphic data into your applications, your use of them (as well as your comfort in using them) will increase. As you grow to look at image files as *just* another data file format, you will also grow to see these System.Drawing namespaces as *just* another set of namespaces. Seek to take advantage of the delegates, interfaces, classes, enumerations, and structures in the System.Drawing namespaces.

Having fun so far? Good. Perhaps this is a good time to refresh your hot or cold beverage and rest your eyes for a moment or two. You will want to be fully prepared for the rest of the discussion. You will consider yet another view of data: an extended view. The upcoming extended view will introduce the group of data formats commonly referred to as *data repositories*.

An Extended View of Data: Data Repositories

Those of you who have worked on an application that used a database as its data source have a good idea of what a *data repository* is. On the mainframe, a common data repository may have been a relational (e.g., DB2) or hierarchical (e.g., IMS) database that your application accessed. The description of a data repository would then begin with the same basic characteristics of a database: *a grouping of data that supports systematic access.*

Although the database is a great common choice, it's not the only data repository choice. There are other data repositories available to the Windows/Web developer.

NOTE On the Windows platform, it is common to have a database available to serve as your data source. In a Microsoft-centric environment, the database product would typically be SQL Server. The .NET platform offers the technology ADO.NET for database access. When you combine ADO.NET with the appropriate .NET Framework namespaces—*System.Data, System.Data.Common, System.Data.SqlClient,* and *System.Data.SqlTypes*—you are ready to take full advantage of your data repository of choice.

CROSS-REFERENCE I further discuss the System.Data namespace, the ADO.NET technology, and the SQL Server database in Chapter 11.

Introducing the Data Repositories

Some of the following product and technology names will be new to you. It is not my intent to provide a tutorial to each individual data repository. Rather, I want to make sure that you are simply aware of the choices that are available to you for data. As you enter into .NET development and begin to create Windows- and Web-based applications, being somewhat familiar with these products and technologies will be to your advantage. Please take a look at the following list of Windows-based data repositories:

- Active Directory (a Windows directory service)

- Microsoft's Web Storage System[6] (WSS) (a Web-accessible database)

- XML documents (further discussed in Chapter 12)

- Screen scraping (further discussed in Chapter 13)

- XML Web services (further discussed in Chapter 13)

Some will prefer that the preceding list be more inclusive. At the same time, some will argue against the inclusion of one entry or another. Nevertheless, the main point here is that products and technologies are available that support the organization and retrieval of information (data). These products and technologies more closely resemble a database than a text file. Yet, they are not normally referred to as databases; hence, I call them *data repositories*. Oh, I almost forgot one other very important point: The .NET platform fully supports your programmatic access to these data repositories through appropriate .NET Framework namespaces.

NOTE In Chapter 3 in the section "Microsoft Office and Notepad," I introduced the Microsoft Word and Excel products and mentioned that their object model is exposed for programmatic use. When you incorporate Microsoft documents into your programming logic, you are using these documents as data repositories.

Know this one fact, before I do harm and injustice to all: The technologies surrounding Active Directory and WSS are extensive enough to fill several thick textbooks. Having said that, let's briefly peek at the support that .NET provides for these data repositories.

---

6. Some refer to the Web Storage System (WSS) as the Exchange Server Information Store. Good luck with keeping up with the names of Microsoft's products and technologies!

Active Directory As a Data Repository

You have worked with directories before on the mainframe. You most likely used the term "catalogs" to refer to these directories. The catalog was used (indirectly) each time you wanted to create or retrieve a cataloged dataset. Recall that the mainframe environment basically had two types of catalogs: master catalogs and user catalogs. When retrieving a cataloged dataset, the system would first search the one master catalog and then any one of the user catalogs to look up the appropriate dataset pointer. The most recent "type" of cataloging system implemented on the mainframe was the Integrated Catalog Facility (ICF) catalog system.

The Windows 2000 environment offers a catalog/directory-type system as well: Active Directory. You can use Active Directory to "locate" data (similar to the mainframe catalog). Active Directory then goes on from there—practically without end—being able to store and retrieve all types of information (not just datasets). For example, an organization might use Active Directory to organize and store information for users, groups, computers, printers, and so on. As a Windows directory service, you would generally look to this product to store and retrieve static data (as an alternative to using a relational database, for example). Active Directory's data is stored in a treelike structure.

TIP   Active Directory uses the term "domain" to refer to both the physical domain controller and a logical relationship-type grouping of data. This supports the use of the Active Directory schema. The groups of related domains then become *domain trees* (in reference to Active Directory's hierarchical storage design). Groups of trees are then called a *forest*.

If you find that your Windows/Web application has a need to access this particular data repository, you will be able to leverage the .NET Framework through several managed objects (in this case, classes and enumerations).

NOTE   When you work with Active Directory, it is common to also use Active Directory Services Interfaces (ADSI). The .NET Framework provides classes that are able to use the features of ADSI. This provides for flexible Active Directory programmatic support. References are provided at the end of this chapter in the "To Learn More" section for your convenience.

If you take a look at the .NET Framework's *System.DirectoryServices* namespace, you will notice an extensive list of classes and enumerations. Of these, I suggest that you start with the two classes *DirectoryEntry* and *DirectorySearcher*. The methods and properties exposed by these two components will quickly enable you to add ADSI support to your application.

> **NOTE** A general understanding of Active Directory should be considered a prerequisite to any attempted use of the System.DirectoryServices namespace.

Simply put, you would use the .NET System.DirectoryServices.DirectoryEntry class to manipulate information in your Active Directory tree. When you want to query your Active Directory, the .NET System.DirectoryServices.Directory-Searcher class will be your choice. Through the use of these two classes, you will end up using additional classes (and the enumerations) from the System.DirectoryServices namespace.

The Web Storage System As a Data Repository

Nowadays, practically everyone has had the experience of sending e-mail, both in their personal and professional life. Similarly, it is becoming commonplace for organizations to expose calendar/scheduling, online forms, and voting/polling features to employees, all online. Additionally, we have all grown comfortable with sharing electronic versions of documents. A grouping of these features would fit nicely into our description of a data repository. Microsoft's Web Storage System (WSS) is exactly that. The WSS is a hierarchical database that supports the storage of unstructured and semistructured data.

Two major products take advantage of the WSS technology: Microsoft's Exchange Server 2000 (or Exchange) and Microsoft's SharePoint Portal Server 2001 (or SPS). The WSS is bundled with Exchange and SPS.[7] Exchange is a very powerful messaging system. It uses the WSS to store e-mails, calendars, contacts, and other related data. SPS, on the other hand, allows organizations to extend the WSS to include advanced document management, searching, and collaboration features.

---

7. In Chapter 2 (in the section ".NET Is a Group of Enterprise Servers"), Exchange Server and SharePoint Portal Server were included in the list of .NET Enterprise Servers.

TIP   Given the enormity of these three topics (Exchange, SPS, and the WSS), I strongly suggest that you take advantage of the related references provided in the "To Learn More" section at the end of this chapter.

Your typical configuration (as a Microsoft-centric shop) would have Microsoft Outlook client stored on each employee's desktop. Each person's local Outlook software would then have the appropriate options set to use the central Microsoft Exchange Server (for sending and receiving e-mails, scheduling, and so forth). Optionally, Outlook Express could be used through an Internet browser. SPS also has a browser-based user interface available. Exchange and SPS both expose fully customizable interfaces.

You're creating your .NET application and now you wish to consume data that's stored in the WSS. After all, what good is a data repository if you can't access the data? Fear not, .NET provides support for those who wish to access the WSS.

When you seek out .NET Framework support for various tasks, you will search for .NET namespaces. Take this case as an example. Say that you read about Microsoft Exchange Server and its e-mail storage functionality. Then, when you seek guidance, a well-intentioned Windows developer may point you in the direction of the Collaborative Data Objects (CDO) and CDO for Windows NT Server (CDONTS) technologies. So, your search begins.

Then, you come across the .NET Framework namespace *System.Web.Mail*. You are certain that you have hit the jackpot. After all, you see the word "Mail" in the namespace and you see a new form of the CDO acronym. Then you read further.

You discover that with this namespace, you can construct and send messages using the Collaboration Data Objects for Windows 2000 (CDOSYS) component. There is just one catch: CDOSYS and the System.Web.Mail namespace directly support Simple Mail Transfer Protocol (SMTP)[8] and Network News Transfer Protocol (NNTP). Furthermore, the component that fully exposes the Exchange object model is CDO for Exchange 2000 Server (CDOEX).[9] SPS uses a different component to expose its object model: Publishing and Knowledge Management Collaboration Data Objects (PKMCDO).

---

8.   I discussed these network protocols in Chapter 3 in the section "Network Protocols and the URL."

9.   CDOEX is a superset of CDOSYS.

TIP Microsoft offers a Software Development Kit (SDK) for both SharePoint Portal Server and Exchange Server. See the "To Learn More" section at the end of this chapter.

So, where is the .NET support for the WSS? Fortunately, the .NET platform offers a feature called COM Interop. To use this feature, you simply *register* and *reference* the appropriate COM DLL. Basically, you then are able to programmatically access (in your .NET managed code) the public methods and properties exposed by the COM DLL. The components mentioned previously (CDOEX and PKMCDO) have a COM DLL associated with them. The "To Learn More" section at the end of this chapter will help you in your further pursuit of information about the WSS.

CROSS-REFERENCE I discuss COM Interop further in Chapter 20.

I have discussed two types of data repositories in this section. The discussion supported an extended view toward the topic of data. In the next section, I discuss yet another type of data: *metadata*. I am sure that you will find this to be an interesting discussion. By the way, to illustrate the support that .NET provides for metadata, you will get into some sample code.

A Meta View of Data: Metadata

Metadata is one of those terms that usually receives a quick confirming nod when explained. At the same time, it is one of those terms that almost always requires an explanation. Basically, metadata is data about data, or even data about objects. In other words, information that might be used to identify or describe something is metadata.

Say that you are coding a mainframe COBOL batch program. When the program is complete, you might also create a JCL Job structure to use for program execution. Then, if I was to come along behind you and browse the PDS library where your JCL Job is saved and open the JCL Job, I would be able to "read" your JCL, right? What would I know at that point? Just from "reading" your JCL, I would be able find out several facts.

The very first JCL statement in every JCL Job describes (at a minimum) the Job name of the JCL Job. Typically, I would also be able to find out the input class and message class values, chargeback/accounting information, execution priority, and whether the "type of run" will be held or not. I could possibly obtain all of that information just from the first JCL statement: the Job statement. If I were to look further into the JCL Job at other JCL statements, I would be able to obtain even more pieces of descriptive information (e.g., which load libraries are referenced, the names of any cataloged procedures being used, and possibly the names of the programs being executed).

That's right. All of the descriptive information, the data about the JCL Job, is *metadata*. Now, imagine if you were to write a mainframe batch utility program to read the PDS member (the one that actually contains the JCL Job) as text data. Your utility program would be able to take the text line by line, and display/report on the so-called metadata. All right, how about another confirming nod? Thanks. Let's now see how metadata is accessed on the .NET platform.

.NET Supports Metadata with Reflection

Fortunately, there is no need to write your own program to do the low-level data mining needed for gathering metadata. .NET provides a namespace specifically designed to gather metadata. Naturally, the namespace, *System.Reflection*, contains delegates, interfaces, classes, enumerations, and structures. The mainframe JCL analogy had the JCL Job as the focal point for metadata excavation. With .NET, the assembly (.exe or .dll) becomes the target for exploration using the System.Reflection namespace.

Adding Metadata with Attributes

Attributes make up a special breed of metadata for your .NET applications. There are two groups of attributes: intrinsically available attributes and custom attributes that you create yourself. Take a look at your assembly manifest sometime (using the ILDASM tool or programmatically via reflection). You will see the metadata provided by attributes. You can use attributes to further document/ describe your application. Attributes also have other uses. For example, you can use them to help manage your production deployments through version control (I further discuss deployment in Chapter 17). That is not all. When you combine the use of attributes with metadata, you can easily choose to add compiler directives to your application. You see, the support for metadata is an important feature in .NET.

Each time you use the ILDASM tool, you get a taste of what "reflection" looks like. Recall that the first page displayed when the ILDASM tool is used simply describes the assembly. It is after drilling down that you get to the actual Microsoft intermediate language (MSIL). To demonstrate this, you will use the two sample code assemblies created earlier in this chapter in the section "Demonstrating How to Access Data in Text Files": SystemIOExampleCobol.exe and SystemIOExampleVB.exe. As shown in Figures 10-1 and 10-2, the first page displayed with the ILDASM tool basically describes each respective assembly.

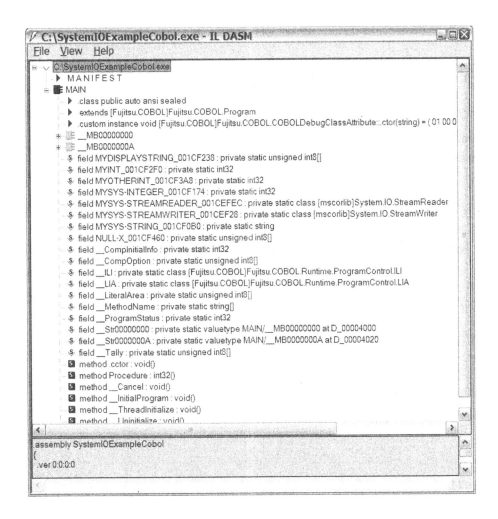

Figure 10-1. The ILDASM display of SystemIOExampleCobol.exe

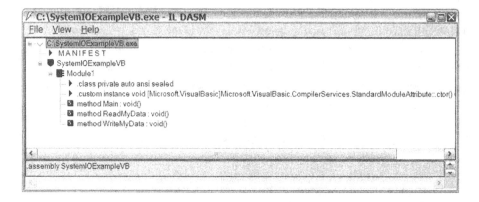

Figure 10-2. The ILDASM display of SystemIOExampleVB.exe

As you look at each assembly's ILDASM display, are you reminded of the main-frame analogy of looking inside a JCL Job? Good. Now you will take a look at some sample code to understand the programmatic access of metadata.

Using the System.Reflection Namespace

I have created two sample projects: MetaDataExampleVB and MetaDataExampleCobol. You will see that each project programmatically accesses the metadata for the System.Text.StringBuilder class that is contained in the Microsoft assembly mscorlib.dll.

To help prepare for the demonstration code, please review the ILDASM display shown in Figure 10-3. You will notice that even the Microsoft assembly mscorlib.dll is not immune to this type of metadata observation. The ILDASM tool uses *reflection* to display the types contained in the mscorlib.dll assembly. The StringBuilder class is one of the types.

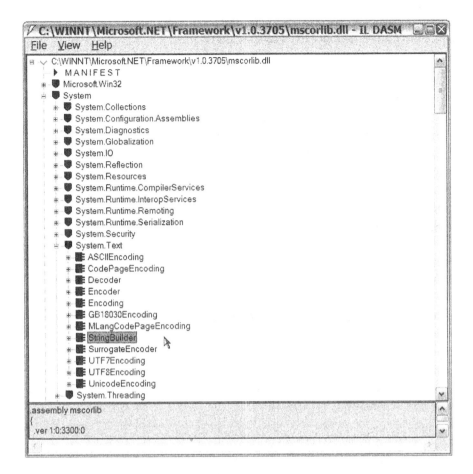

Figure 10-3. The ILDASM display of mscorlib.dll for the System.Text.StringBuilder class

VB .NET Metadata Example

The code in Listing 10-8 demonstrates the use of two *System.Reflection* classes: *System.Reflection.MemberInfo* and *System.Reflection.Assembly*. The code was copied from the MetaDataExampleVB.exe sample project.

Listing 10-8. MetaDataExampleVB.exe Project Demonstrating the Use of the
System.Reflection Namespace to Obtain Metadata

```
Module Module1
Sub Main()
     'Create Objects from System.Reflection Namespace
     Dim myMemberInfoArray() As System.Reflection.MemberInfo
     Dim myAssembly As System.Reflection.Assembly

     Dim MyTypes() As System.Type
     Dim MyType As System.Type
     Dim indexA As Integer
     Dim indexB As Integer

     'Create Object from StringBuilder Class
     Dim sb As New System.Text.StringBuilder()

     'Get the Type associated with the StringBuilder
     MyType = sb.GetType
     'Get the Assembly associated with the StringBuilder Type
     myAssembly = myAssembly.GetAssembly(MyType)
     'Get the Types found in the Assembly
     MyTypes = myAssembly.GetTypes()

     For indexA = 0 To UBound(MyTypes)
     'Select specific Type for further processing
        If MyTypes(indexA).Name = "StringBuilder" Then
        'Display appropriate Information
        Console.WriteLine(MyTypes(indexA).FullName)
        'Get members found in the selected Type
        myMemberInfoArray = MyTypes(indexA).GetMembers()
           For indexB = 0 To myMemberInfoArray.Length - 1
           'Display appropriate Information
                sb.Length = 0
                With sb
                 .Append("MemberType - ")
                 .Append(" ")
                 .Append(myMemberInfoArray(indexB).MemberType.ToString())
                 .Append(" ")
                 .Append("Name -")
                 .Append(" ")
                 .Append(myMemberInfoArray(indexB).ToString())
                 .Append(" ")
                 Console.WriteLine(.ToString())
```

```
            End With
          Next indexB
        'Exit Loop after StringBuilder Type is located
        Exit For
        End If
      Next
      Console.ReadLine()
  End Sub
End Module
```

COBOL .NET Metadata Example

With a little practice, using the reflection namespaces is not very difficult. The sample code in Listing 10-9 demonstrates exactly how to go about doing so. Please take a moment to read the code. I will assume that you are continuing to approach your .NET retraining with a bilingual flavor. With that understanding, I am sure you will find the comparisons between the two sample projects (MetaDataExampleVB.exe in Listing 10-8 and MetaDataExampleCobol.exe in Listing 10-9) rather interesting and informative.

Listing 10-9. MetaDataExampleCobol.exe Project Demonstrating the Use of the System.Reflection Namespace Objects

```
000010 IDENTIFICATION DIVISION.
000020* This is an example of how to use the
000030* System.Reflection Classes to obtain MetaData
000040 PROGRAM-ID. MAIN.
000050 ENVIRONMENT DIVISION.
000060 CONFIGURATION SECTION.
000070 REPOSITORY.
000080* .NET Framework Classes
000090     CLASS SYS-sb AS "System.Text.StringBuilder"
000100     CLASS SYS-MyString As "System.String"
000110     CLASS SYS-MyInt As "System.Int32"
000120     CLASS SYS-MyType As "System.Type"
000130     CLASS SYS-MyTypes As "System.Type[]"
000140     CLASS SYS-myMemberInfoItem As "System.Reflection.MemberInfo"
000150     ENUM ENUM-myMemberTypes As "System.Reflection.MemberTypes"
000160     CLASS SYS-myMemberInfoArray As "System.Reflection.MemberInfo[]"
000170     CLASS SYS-myAssembly As "System.Reflection.Assembly"
000180     PROPERTY PROP-Length as "Length"
000190     PROPERTY PROP-FullName as "FullName"
000200     PROPERTY PROP-Name as "Name"
```

```
000210      PROPERTY PROP-MemberType as "MemberType".
000230*
000240 DATA DIVISION.
000250 WORKING-STORAGE SECTION.
000260    77 sb OBJECT REFERENCE SYS-sb.
000270    77 MyString OBJECT REFERENCE SYS-MyString.
000280    77 MyInt OBJECT REFERENCE SYS-MyInt.
000290    77 MyType OBJECT REFERENCE SYS-MyType.
000300    77 MyTypes OBJECT REFERENCE SYS-MyTypes.
000310    77 MyTypeItem OBJECT REFERENCE SYS-MyType.
000320
000330* Reference Objects from System.Reflection Namespace
000340    77 myMemberInfoItem OBJECT REFERENCE SYS-myMemberInfoItem.
000350    77 myMemberInfoArray OBJECT REFERENCE SYS-myMemberInfoArray.
000360    77 myAssembly OBJECT REFERENCE SYS-myAssembly.
000370    77 myMemberTypes OBJECT REFERENCE ENUM-myMemberTypes.
000380
000390    77 indexA PIC S9(9) COMP-5.
000400    77 indexB PIC S9(9) COMP-5.
000410    77 ArrayBoundaryA PIC S9(9) COMP-5.
000420    77 ArrayBoundaryB PIC S9(9) COMP-5.
000430    77 MyDisplayString  PIC X(100).
000440    01 NULL-X PIC X(1).
000450 LINKAGE SECTION.
000460
000470 PROCEDURE DIVISION.
000480
000490* Create Object from StringBuilder Class
000500     SET sb to SYS-sb::"NEW" ()
000510* Get the Type associated with the StringBuilder
000520     SET MyType TO sb::"GetType" ()
000530* Get the Assembly associated with the StringBuilder Type
000540     SET myAssembly TO SYS-myAssembly::"GetAssembly" (MyType)
000550* Get the Types found in the Assembly
000560     SET MyTypes TO myAssembly::"GetTypes" ()
000570
000580     SET MyInt to MyTypes::"GetUpperBound" (0)
000590     SET ArrayBoundaryA to MyInt
000600     PERFORM VARYING indexA
000610       FROM 0 BY 1 UNTIL indexA >= ArrayBoundaryA
000620* Select specific Type for further processing
000630             INVOKE MyTypes "Get" USING BY VALUE indexA RETURNING MyTypeItem
000640* Display appropriate Information
000650             SET MyDisplayString to PROP-Name of MyTypeItem
```

```
000660            IF MyDisplayString = "StringBuilder" Then
000670                SET MyDisplayString to PROP-FullName of MyTypeItem
000680                Display MyDisplayString
000690* Get members found in the selected Type
000700            SET myMemberInfoArray to MyTypeItem::"GetMembers" ()
000710            SET MyInt to PROP-Length of myMemberInfoArray
000720            SET ArrayBoundaryB to MyInt
000730              PERFORM VARYING indexB
000740                FROM 0 BY 1 UNTIL indexB >= (ArrayBoundaryB - 1)
000750                INVOKE myMemberInfoArray "Get"
000760                 USING BY VALUE indexB RETURNING myMemberInfoItem
000770
000780                SET myMemberTypes to PROP-MemberType of myMemberInfoItem
000790                SET MyString to myMemberInfoItem::"ToString" ()
000800                SET PROP-Length of sb to 0
000810* Display appropriate Information
000820                INVOKE sb "Append" USING BY VALUE "MemberType - "
000830                        RETURNING sb
000840                INVOKE sb "Append" USING BY VALUE " "
000850                        RETURNING sb
000860                INVOKE sb "Append" USING BY VALUE myMemberTypes
000870                        RETURNING sb
000880                INVOKE sb "Append" USING BY VALUE " "
000890                        RETURNING sb
000900                INVOKE sb "Append" USING BY VALUE "Name -"
000910                        RETURNING sb
000920                INVOKE sb "Append" USING BY VALUE " "
000930                        RETURNING sb
000940                INVOKE sb "Append" USING BY VALUE MyString
000950                        RETURNING sb
000960                INVOKE sb "Append" USING BY VALUE " "
000970                        RETURNING sb
000980                SET MyDisplayString to sb::"ToString" ()
000990                DISPLAY MyDisplayString
001000              END-PERFORM
001010* Exit Perform after StringBuilder Type is located
001020              EXIT PERFORM
001030            End-IF
001040      END-PERFORM
001050      DISPLAY "Enter X and Press Enter to Exit.".
001060      ACCEPT NULL-X.
001070 END PROGRAM  MAIN.
```

Why Care About Metadata and Reflection?

Why speak about .NET's support for metadata? The answer to this question is different for each person. For myself, I see this as a great opportunity to easily document an assembly. Basically, the assembly ends up documenting itself. You can capture metadata and write the information to a text file (using System.IO.TextWriter). Then, you can archive the text file for application documentation.

For a better idea of the "documentation" that is automatically available, run either sample project (MetaDataExampleVB.exe or MetaDataExampleCobol.exe). Your console display will reveal some of the metadata that is available for this mscorlib.dll assembly, specifically for the StringBuilder type. I have included a small portion of that display in Listing 10-10.

Listing 10-10. A Portion of the Metadata Captured from the mscorlib.dll Assembly

```
System.Text.StringBuilder
MemberType -    Method  Name -   Int32 GetHashCode()
MemberType -    Method  Name -   Boolean Equals(System.Object)
MemberType -    Method  Name -   System.String ToString()
MemberType -    Method  Name -   Int32 get_Capacity()
MemberType -    Method  Name -   Void set_Capacity(Int32)
MemberType -    Method  Name -   Int32 get_MaxCapacity()
MemberType -    Method  Name -   Int32 EnsureCapacity(Int32)
. . .
MemberType -    Method  Name -   System.Type GetType()
MemberType -    Constructor    Name -   Void .ctor()
MemberType -    Constructor    Name -   Void .ctor(Int32)
MemberType -    Constructor    Name -   Void .ctor(System.String)
MemberType -    Constructor    Name -   Void .ctor(System.String, Int32)
. . .
MemberType -    Property       Name -   Int32 Capacity
MemberType -    Property       Name -   Int32 MaxCapacity
MemberType -    Property       Name -   Int32 Length
MemberType -    Property       Name -   Char Chars [Int32]
```

As you can see, with metadata and .NET's reflection technology, an application moves closer to being "self-documenting." I see that as being a great thing with great potential. Learn to leverage your metadata.

Summary

This chapter's goals were as follows:

- To explore basic data access with text files

- To learn about data repositories

- To work with metadata as data

This chapter was all about discussing data. I started the data discussion using *reflection* as a theme. Interestingly, I ended the chapter using the same theme. Of course, the first case was that of *reflecting* back to the mainframe types of data access to contrast them with the newer .NET approaches. The latter case for reflection was that of the Reflection namespace found in the .NET Framework for metadata support. In the middle of the chapter, I presented data repositories as a type of data.

In the next chapter, you will take a turn toward relational data. The support available in .NET for database programming is astonishing. Several .NET Framework namespaces await you. Additionally, you will learn about SQL Server data storage and retrieval, the GUI tools that you will use as a developer, and the ADO.NET technology.

To Learn More

The following are some suggested supplemental references to further your retraining effort.

Books

GDI+ Programming in C# and VB .NET, by Nick Symmonds (Apress, 2002):
    http://www.apress.com/book/bookDisplay.html?bID=107.
Object-Oriented Macromedia Flash MX, by William Drol (Apress, 2002):
    http://www.apress.com/book/bookDisplay.html?bID=84.

Magazines

.NET Magazine:
http://www.fawcette.com/dotnetmag/

Exchange & Outlook Magazine, DevX Newsletter (by Jim Minatel, Editor-in-Chief):
http://www.devx.com/free/newsletters/exo/exoed031601.asp

Visual Studio Magazine:
http://www.fawcette.com/vsm/

XML & Web Services Magazine:
http://www.fawcette.com/xmlmag/

Web Sites

Choosing Among File I/O Options in Visual Basic .NET:
http://msdn.microsoft.com/library/en-us/dv_vstechart/html/
vbtchUseFileStreamObject.asp

Collaboration Data Objects Roadmap:
http://msdn.microsoft.com/library/en-us/dncdsys/html/cdo_roadmap.asp

Drawing and Editing Images (using GDI+):
http://msdn.microsoft.com/library/en-us/cpguide/html/
cpcondrawingeditingimages.asp

Fujitsu NetCOBOL for .NET (the product I use when discussing COBOL .NET):
http://www.netcobol.com/products/windows/netcobol.html

Microsoft Communities (discussion groups, e-Newsletters, and so forth):
http://communities2.microsoft.com

Microsoft Exchange Server:
http://www.microsoft.com/exchange/default.asp

Microsoft Exchange Software Development Kit:
http://msdn.microsoft.com/library/en-us/wss/wss/
_exch2k_welcome_to_exchange.asp

Microsoft SharePoint Technologies:
http://www.microsoft.com/sharepoint/

MSDN:
http://msdn.microsoft.com

SharePoint Portal Server Software Development Kit:
http://www.microsoft.com/sharepoint/downloads/tools/SDK.asp

Types of Bitmaps (image file format):
http://msdn.microsoft.com/library/en-us/cpguide/html/
_gdiplus_types_of_bitmaps_about.asp

Web Storage System Schema Usage and Best Practice Guide:
http://msdn.microsoft.com/library/en-us/dnmes2k/html/wssschemause.asp

CHAPTER 11

Database Programming with .NET

A SQL Server and ADO.NET Primer

In this chapter

- Providing an overview of the SQL Server Enterprise Manager tool

- Discussing the use of the SQL Server Query Analyzer tool

- Exploring the ADO.NET technology

FOR THOSE OF YOU who have had the pleasurable experience of using a relational database as a data repository, this chapter will bring back exciting coding memories. For that majority, allow me to say that you will love this chapter. I am certain that you will find the few mainframe analogies to be useful. The information in this chapter will leave you feeling empowered and ready (again) to query every database that you can get your hands on.

For the few of you who have yet to experience relational database programming, welcome aboard! The ride will be fun and informative. I include enough information in this chapter to get you off to a solid start—a start sure to whet an insatiable appetite. The chapter's discussion does assume familiarity with basic SQL query syntax. The references at the end of the chapter in the "To Learn More" section will assist those in need of a review.

In this chapter, I begin the discussion with an overview of Microsoft's SQL Server 2000 product,[1] with a focus on the developer-friendly tools bundled with the product. Following the SQL Server 2000[2] discussion, you will explore the topic

---

1. Microsoft's SQL Server product has a Relational Database view and a Data Warehousing and Online Analytical Processing (OLAP) view. I limit this discussion to the relational database topics.

2. The functionality and features discussed in this chapter could apply equally to the previous version of Microsoft's SQL Server product (i.e., SQL Server 7.0). Nevertheless, as with most products, upgrading brings new possibilities. For example, SQL Server 2000 offers support for XML.

of ADO.NET. Combining these meaty topics into one chapter was a challenge. Nonetheless, as with all of the other "meaty" chapters in this book, the time you spend reading this chapter should prove to be time well spent.

> **NOTE**   To get the full value of this chapter's discussion, you'll want to have access to the Microsoft SQL Server 2000 database product. In particular, you'll want to have access to the SQL Server 2000 client-side tools. As with most of Microsoft's server products, you can easily obtain a free, fully functional 120-day trial version from the Microsoft Web site (http://www.microsoft.com). Optionally, an evaluation kit for SQL Server 2000 is available from the Microsoft Web site. The SQL Server Evaluation Kit includes the 120-day trial version product and lots of extras (demos and so forth). You'll need to pay a small shipping and handling charge to have the Evaluation Kit mailed to you. Visit the following Web address for more details: http://www.microsoft.com/sql/evaluation/trial/default.asp.

SQL Server 2000: A .NET Enterprise Server

It is likely that any experience you have had on the mainframe platform with relational databases was associated with IBM's DB2 database product. DB2 has long been the dominant player in that arena. In the Windows/Web arena, Microsoft has joined the ranks of database software vendors with their SQL Server 2000 product.

> **NOTE**   If by chance you are using a competing database product (e.g., Oracle's Oracle9i database or IBM's DB2 Universal Database), the majority of this chapter will still be of value to you and your .NET retraining. The ADO.NET and Application Blocks for .NET discussions apply to any vendor's (Microsoft, Oracle, IBM, and others) database product.

In Chapter 2, I referred to the Microsoft SQL Server 2000 (or just SQL Server) product when I listed the .NET Enterprise Servers. Then, as I discussed various views of data in Chapter 10, I mentioned Microsoft's database product again, this time as a data repository.[3] Now, this product will serve as a backdrop for this chapter's relational database programming discussion.

Getting Started

For simplicity, I'll assume that you downloaded the free, 120-day trial version of
SQL Server 2000 and installed it (client tools and database) locally on your own
workstation. A few very basic things are worthy of mention. You should choose to
include Books Online (you are prompted about this during installation). Additionally, you should choose to include the SQL Server Service Manager, Query
Analyzer, and Enterprise Manager (all installation choices).

NOTE If your company's software installation policy does not allow
you to install a SQL Server database to your local workstation, ask your
database administrator (DBA) for access to a remote development
server. Mention to the DBA that you are only interested in accessing the
SQL Server default sample databases for training purposes. This is typically not a problem. This type of configuration will require you to install
just the client tools to your local workstation. Additionally, your DBA
(or the documentation in SQL Server Books Online) can assist you in
the server registration required to "connect" to the remote development server (the server registration is needed only if you wish to
connect to a database other than one locally installed).

SQL Server Books Online

When you install the SQL Server product, select the option to install Books Online.
Once the installation is complete, you can access the online documentation by
clicking the Start button and selecting Programs ➤ Microsoft SQL Server ➤ Books
Online (see Figure 11-1). You will find this set of online documentation to be
extremely informative.

---

3. You'll find that some desktop and smaller applications use Microsoft Access (a member of
   the Microsoft Office family) and/or Microsoft Data Engine (MSDE) as a relational data
   source, although they aren't as powerful and feature rich as SQL Server. You may even find
   that for quick prototyping development, Microsoft Access or MSDE will suit your database
   needs.

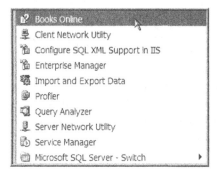

Figure 11-1. Accessing the SQL Server Books Online option

Starting the SQL Server Service

Along with the choice of whether or not to install the Service Manager comes the choice of whether or not to have the SQL Server service automatically started every time you reboot your computer. Some developers prefer to manually start the service each time they are ready to access the locally installed database. As shown in Figure 11-2, the Service Manager is easily accessed.

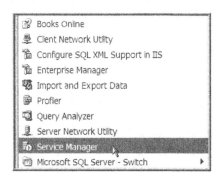

Figure 11-2. Accessing the SQL Server Service Manager

TIP You may notice the SQL Server Service Manager icon also appears in the area of the desktop taskbar referred to as the *notification area*. The notification area of the taskbar is where you typically see the time displayed (pre–Windows XP operating systems called this taskbar area the System Tray). By clicking (optionally, right-clicking) the SQL Server Service Manager icon, you can start, stop, and pause the SQL Server service. Accessing the SQL Server Service Manager icon here may be more convenient than using the Start button/Programs menu approach, as shown in Figure 11-2.

Optionally,[4] you could choose to access the SQL Server Service Manager from the Microsoft Management Console (MMC) snap-in interface: Computer Management. After you navigate to the Computer Management console and expand the tree view node for Microsoft SQL Server, you right-click the SQL Server Service icon (see Figure 11-3).

Still in Shock

Not long after I began my own "reformation"—my technology transition over to the "other side"—I was introduced to the SQL Server product. I recall the feeling of being in shock after realizing that I was able to download and install my very own copy of an industrial-strength database product. With this local copy, I was able to start and stop an entire database service, create and delete databases, and create tables and views. I find that having that type of freedom and power is simply amazing. Can you imagine walking into the mainframe data center and telling the systems programmer or database administrator that you would like to spin up your very own copy of a mainframe DB2 service?

---

4. Depending on your installation choices, you may also have the option of accessing the SQL Server Service Manager from your Windows desktop taskbar notification area (next to the clock).

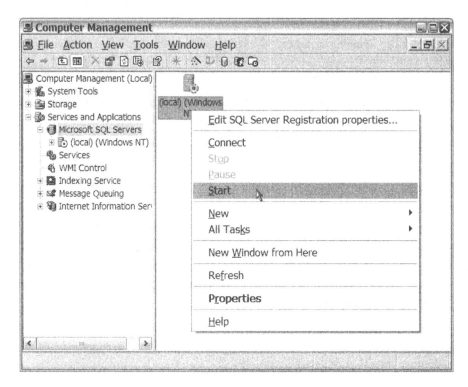

Figure 11-3. Starting the SQL Server Service Manager from the Computer Management console

Client-Side Tools

You could loosely divide the SQL Server product into two basic portions: the client-side tools and the server-side database software. To give you an idea of the general purpose of the client-side tools, you can compare them with the tools of IBM's mainframe DB2 database product. On the mainframe, you typically had the following tools to support your DB2 development:

- Database 2 Interactive (DB2I)

- Query Management Facility (QMF)

Traditionally, the QMF tool usage is sometimes reserved for special querying and reporting needs. On the other hand, the DB2I tool is used by practically all mainframe DB2 developers. As shown in Figure 11-4, the DB2I tool is supported as a mainframe ISPF option.

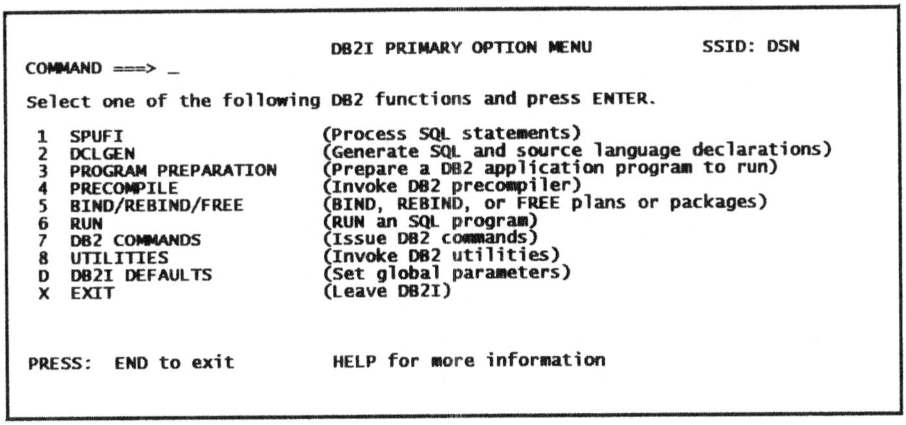

```
┌──────────────────────────────────────────────────────────────────────┐
│                        DB2I PRIMARY OPTION MENU           SSID: DSN    │
│   COMMAND ===> _                                                       │
│                                                                        │
│   Select one of the following DB2 functions and press ENTER.          │
│                                                                        │
│     1   SPUFI                   (Process SQL statements)               │
│     2   DCLGEN                  (Generate SQL and source language declarations)│
│     3   PROGRAM PREPARATION     (Prepare a DB2 application program to run)│
│     4   PRECOMPILE              (Invoke DB2 precompiler)                │
│     5   BIND/REBIND/FREE        (BIND, REBIND, or FREE plans or packages)│
│     6   RUN                     (RUN an SQL program)                    │
│     7   DB2 COMMANDS            (Issue DB2 commands)                    │
│     8   UTILITIES               (Invoke DB2 utilities)                  │
│     D   DB2I DEFAULTS           (Set global parameters)                │
│     X   EXIT                    (Leave DB2I)                            │
│                                                                        │
│                                                                        │
│   PRESS:  END to exit          HELP for more information               │
│                                                                        │
└──────────────────────────────────────────────────────────────────────┘
```

Figure 11-4. The main menu of IBM's DB2I tool

If you were to navigate to the SQL Server Programs list (by clicking the Start button and selecting Programs ➤ Microsoft SQL Server), you would notice about seven client-side utilities (not including Books Online and Service Manager). Of those seven SQL Server utility options, I discuss the following two in this chapter:

- Enterprise Manager

- Query Analyzer

Interestingly, you can almost draw a one-to-one comparison between the mainframe DB2 tools and the Win32 SQL Server tools. In other words, the mainframe DB2I tool is very similar to the SQL Server Enterprise Manager tool. Likewise, the mainframe QMF tool is similar to the SQL Server Query Analyzer tool. Generally, you used DB2I for administrative and development preparation tasks. Some of those types of tasks for SQL Server you will perform using the Enterprise Manager tool. You typically used the mainframe DB2's QMF tool for querying and ad hoc reporting capabilities. You guessed it: Now the Query Analyzer tool will serve your SQL Server querying and ad hoc needs.

Is It Fair to Compare?

In fairness, I should emphasize that these comparisons of *legacy mainframe* DB2 tools to *modern Win32* SQL Server tools are loosely tied. As you will see, you can find features absent or present on one platform's toolset or the other. This is understandable given that there are some platform-specific requirements supported as needed on both sides (the mainframe DB2 side and the Win32 SQL Server side).

On one hand, you may read my statements as positioning the Win32 platform tools as more user- and developer-friendly (given the more graphic presentation of the SQL Server's toolset) than the mainframe tools. On the other hand, I must tell you that in more modern times, IBM has created newer versions of the DB2 client-side tools. For example, there is a new version of QMF called QMF for Windows. Additionally, there exist newer DB2 SQL client tools such as Operations Navigator, Interactive SQL, and Query Manager.

Understand that I am contrasting the traditional/legacy mainframe environment with the newer .NET Windows/Web environment. This is appropriate given that many mainframe installations continue to develop under the older legacy configurations. The bottom line is that if you have used the mainframe database support tools before, you immediately have a head start toward learning the Win32 SQL Server support tools. The contrasting presentation in this chapter simply seeks to help you leverage that advantage.

Enterprise Manager

Basically, Enterprise Manager[5] is a graphical user interface (GUI) tool you use to manage your SQL Server objects (databases and tables are examples of such objects). To access SQL Server's Enterprise Manager, click the Start button and select Programs ➤ Microsoft SQL Server ➤ Enterprise Manager. As shown in Figure 11-5, Enterprise Manager includes a total of seven groups of options.

Each option grouping is presented as a folder in the left pane of the Enterprise Manager window. The option grouping that appears above the others (Databases) is used for database-specific tasks. The other six options (Data Transformation Services, Management, Replication, Security, Support Services, Meta Data Services) are available for non-database-specific needs.

To address your immediate concerns, you will narrow your focus to the options you can access via the Databases grouping. When time allows, please revisit the other Enterprise Manager options. The references provided at the end of this chapter in the "To Learn More" section, in addition to the Books Online documentation, will help with your continued learning.

---

5. Some of the functions you can access via Enterprise Manager's graphical interface are also available through the Computer Management console snap-in interface of Microsoft Management Console (MMC).

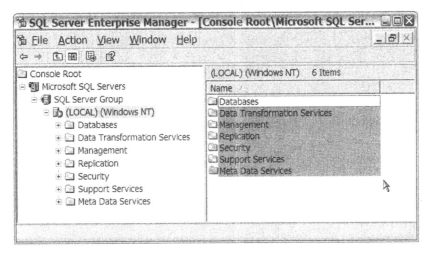

Figure 11-5. Enterprise Manager offers several administrative and non-database-specific features.

Exploring the Databases Feature

A typical SQL Server installation includes two sample databases: the Northwind database and the Pubs database. You will use each of these Microsoft-provided sample databases to help illustrate several points (see Figure 11-6).

Sample Databases

The Northwind sample database provided by Microsoft represents sales data for a fictitious company. The fictitious company, Northwind Traders, is an importer and exporter of specialty foods. The Pubs sample database contains the type of fictitious data typical of a book publishing company.

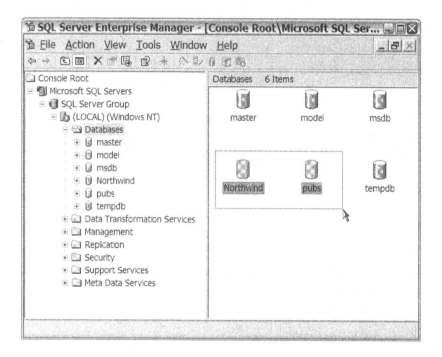

Figure 11-6. SQL Server's Enterprise Manager showing the default and sample databases

If you double-click the Tables icon (below the Northwind database folder), the list of User and System tables displays. Obviously, the User tables are for your querying needs (both input and output). The SQL Server service makes use of the System tables. On some occasions, you may find it useful to even query the System tables (typically, you would not update the System tables yourself). Figure 11-7 shows the User tables of the Northwind sample database.

> **NOTE** The default installation of the sample databases includes the two users guest and dbo (database owner). The tables will show dbo as the owner. It is not uncommon when you are doing a demonstration/ training setup that the login name of "sa" is used for dbo, using a blank password. You can leave the settings for Users and Roles as is for demonstration/training purposes. However, for actual development, you should change these security/access settings as per your particular organization's requirements.

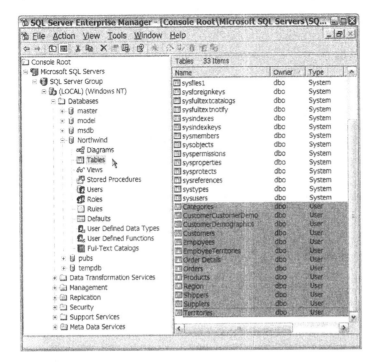

Figure 11-7. The User tables of the Northwind sample database

Let's use the Categories table (one of the User-type tables) of the Northwind database as an example to demonstrate how easy it is to perform a query. If you select the table by right-clicking it and then choosing Open Table ➤ Return all rows, you will dynamically build and execute a SELECT query. Figure 11-8 shows the menus you will see after you right-click the Categories table.

Your resulting display (in grid format) should list the eight existing rows of the Categories table. Optionally, you can click the Show/Hide SQL Pane icon. In Figure 11-9 you can see the selected rows of the Categories table with the SQL Pane shown.

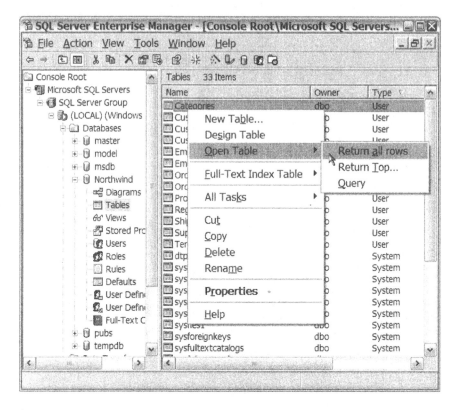

Figure 11-8. Performing a SELECT query on the Categories table

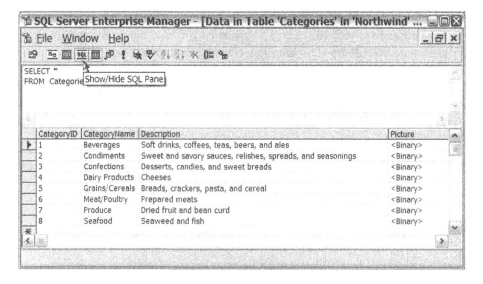

Figure 11-9. The selected rows of the Categories table

TIP You can toggle between this displayed grid-style window and the main Enterprise Manager window. On the menu bar, click Windows. You will then see a list of available windows to toggle to.

Having seen this SELECT query capability, you now know at least one area where the feature set of the Enterprise Manager tool is similar to that of the mainframe DB2I tool. Specifically, you typically used DB2I's SQL Processor Using File Input (SPUFI) option to perform similar query execution tasks.

NOTE The SQL Server client tools fully support all types of queries; you are not limited to SELECT queries. Additionally, you can use either Enterprise Manager or Query Analyzer to create SQL stored procedures.

Please continue to explore the other features of the Enterprise Manager tool. Keep in mind that your ultimate goal is to create Windows/Web applications that will use SQL Server tables. When you perform database programming, the tables (similar to those found in the Northwind and Pubs databases) will serve as your data source. Look to the various functions exposed in the Enterprise Manager tool to support your development activity.

TIP Through your retraining effort, you may end up wanting to restore the Northwind or Pubs sample database back to its original state. There is a SQL script available that will reinstall each sample database. Consult the SQL Server Help feature (or Books Online) for further details.

SQL Server's Query Analyzer

The Query Analyzer tool is designed to support your needs to query the SQL Server tables. Although there is some overlap[6] between the Enterprise Manager tool and the Query Analyzer tool, each tool has its strengths. As you could use the mainframe QMF tools to support your query needs on the mainframe with the DB2 database, you can use SQL Server's Query Analyzer in much the same way. The way you work with Query Analyzer may remind you of the Query-by-Example (QBE) feature of QMF.

NOTE As you know, the mainframe tool QMF served two primary purposes: to quickly run queries on DB2 databases and to easily create formatted reports using the query results. The SQL Server Query Analyzer tool is comparable to the query functionality in QMF. Although you can create basic, ad hoc reports with Query Analyzer, most Windows/Web developers seek out other tools to address their need for formatted reports.

You can launch the SQL Server Query Analyzer tool in two ways. From within the Enterprise Manager main window (as shown in Figure 11-10) on the menu bar, you can select Tools ➤ SQL Query Analyzer. Optionally, you can access the SQL Server Query Analyzer tool by clicking the Start button and selecting Programs ➤ Microsoft SQL Server ➤ Query Analyzer.

TIP There is one advantage to accessing the Query Analyzer tool from within Enterprise Manager. The Query Analyzer window will open, showing that you are already connected to a specific SQL Server (WINDOWSXP in my case, user SA). Also, whichever database you happened to have selected in Enterprise Manager will be selected in the newly opened Query Analyzer window.

---

6. The mainframe DB2 tools of DB2I and QMF also had a small amount of overlap. The SPUFI feature of DB2I and QMF supported query capabilities.

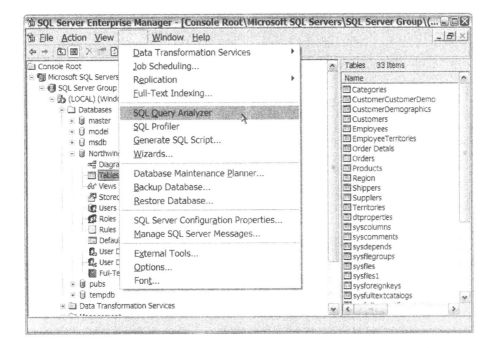

Figure 11-10. Launching Query Analyzer from within the Enterprise Manager window

Using Query Analyzer

Once you've launched the Query Analyzer tool (I chose the option of launching from within Enterprise Manager), you can navigate through the tree view shown in the Object Browser window by expanding and collapsing nodes. As shown in Figure 11-11, I have expanded the Northwind/User Tables node to locate the Categories table.

As you can see in Figure 11-11, if you right-click a given table, you will be presented with many options. Naturally, these options include building a SELECT query (to do so, after right-clicking, navigate using Script Object to New Window As ➤ Select). After you build your query in the new window, simply press F5 to execute the query. The results will be displayed in a grid at the bottom of your Query window.

You can choose to change the grid output display. You can easily change the grid style output to text or a file (see Figure 11-12) by clicking the Execute Mode icon.

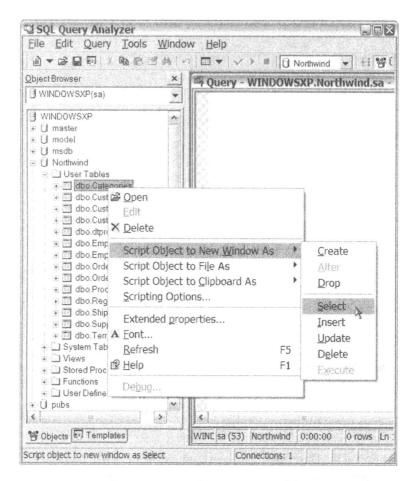

Figure 11-11. Preparing to query the Categories table using the Query Analyzer tool

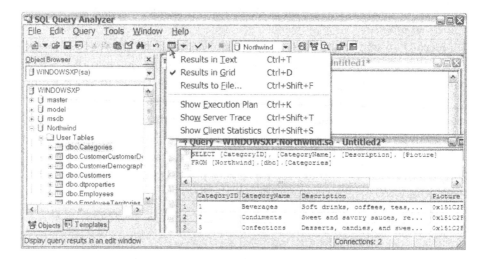

Figure 11-12. Preparing to click the Execute Mode icon to change the option from "Results in Grid" to either "Results in Text" or "Results to File"

For those of you who have used the mainframe DB2 EXPLAIN function and PLAN_TABLE when working to optimize[7] your queries, and perhaps the mainframe QMF tool to format your output, Query Analyzer offers a comparable feature. You can launch the Display Estimated Execution Plan feature via its toolbar icon or by pressing Ctrl-L. As shown in Figure 11-13, the Estimated Execution Plan is displayed (in the lower window) for the SELECT query (shown in the upper window).

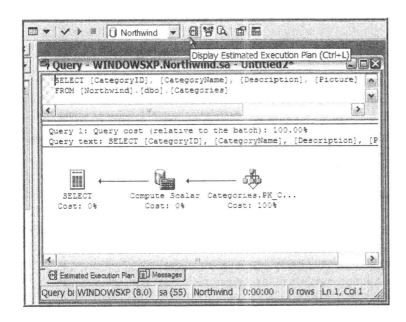

Figure 11-13: The Estimated Execution Plan for a given query. This feature will assist you in optimizing your query.

TIP The Object Browser window contains a Common Objects folder and a Templates tab. These two features offer significant development shortcuts. You will notice that the Common Objects folder will assist you in the use of built-in functions. The Templates tab gives you a "skeleton" of SQL code. In both cases, you can "drag" the object in question from the Object Browser window over to a target Query Analyzer window.

---

7. Some of you may have also used the DB2 SQL Performance Analyzer (SQL PA).

Saving Queries and Data

Using the mainframe QMF tool, you regularly executed the SAVE command to save objects. Any objects that you saved went to your QMF database. Among the SAVE commands that you were able to execute were the following:

- SAVE QUERY

- SAVE DATA

- SAVE PROC

With SQL Server's Query Analyzer tool, you can also save your queries and data. However, there are a few differences.

On QMF, you were limited to one SQL statement per saved query. In Query Analyzer, that limitation does not exist. You are able to include multiple SQL commands that will execute sequentially. Optionally, you can actually *highlight* a specific SQL command separately from the others. When you press F5, only the query that is highlighted will execute.

TIP   In Query Analyzer, after you have created your query, executed it, and optimized it, you may wish to save the query for later execution. To do this, simply navigate to the regular menu bar. Then, select File ➤ Save or Save As. (Optionally, you can press Ctrl-S.) Your query will be saved in a file with .sql as the file extension. You can choose to save your queries in an appropriate folder for yourself or for others to share.

As you know, on QMF you were able to save the results of your SELECT query using the SAVE DATA command. However, you needed the QMF FORM or QMF REPORT objects to actually SHOW the saved data. With Query Analyzer, you can save your SELECT query results (e.g., as a CSV file or comma-separated values) and easily use the saved file outside of Query Analyzer.

On QMF, the SAVE PROC feature was used to save QMF commands. You would use these QMF commands to process QMF objects in a batch mode (i.e., using the RUN command to execute multiple saved queries in succession). Query Analyzer does not have any intrinsic commands to support this type of a batch PROC. However, the support Query Analyzer provides for SQL stored procedures can easily surpass that of a QMF PROC.

TIP The next time that you are in the Visual Studio .NET (VS .NET) IDE preparing to create a new project (looking at the New Project dialog box), take a quick look at the Other Projects folder. One of the subfolders that you will see within the Other Projects folder is the Database Projects folder. Basically, this folder contains a template you can use to create a special type of project. If you use this project template, you will notice that an actual project will be created for you. However, the project will look more like a place to store multiple types of saved queries. In other words, it will remind you of the use of QMF when saving your queries. The Database Projects template VS .NET feature is certainly worthy of your time.

In an abbreviated fashion, that concludes this chapter's overview of SQL Server's Enterprise Manager and Query Analyzer tools. Using these two tools, you can build and test your SQL queries. You can also use these tools to help familiarize yourself with the sample databases Northwind and Pubs. Now I'll move on to discuss the .NET technology that you'll use in your programming code to access the SQL Server databases.

TIP From the VS .NET IDE window, you can access the Server Explorer. The VS .NET Server Explorer offers functionality similar to that of the SQL Server client tools. The fact that it is integrated directly into the VS .NET IDE may make it more convenient to use (on some occasions). When time allows, be sure to take a look at it. To access the Server Explorer from the VS .NET menu bar, select View ➤ Server Explorer. (Optionally, you can press Ctrl-Alt-S.)

Database Programming with .NET

You are now ready for relational database programming. At this point, you have established your access (user logon, password, and so forth) to a SQL Server 2000 installation. Your local workstation is equipped with the SQL Server client-side tools (Enterprise Manager, Query Analyzer, and so on). Perhaps you have even toured the Northwind and Pubs sample SQL Server databases. You are now ready to actually write some code. So, you may ask, "Where should I start?"

Let's assume for the moment that you have heard of ADO.NET. Maybe you have read somewhere that ADO.NET is "the" new database technology for .NET. So, your search begins.

It is likely that you might open VS .NET and do a search using the Help option on the menu bar. I tried this myself. I used "ADO.NET" as my "Look for:" value and "Fujitsu NetCOBOL for .NET" as my "Filtered by:" value. As shown in Figure 11-14, the search was unable to locate any Help items (as indicated by the "0 topics found" message at the bottom of the window).

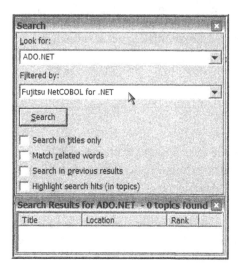

Figure 11-14. Searching VS .NET for ADO.NET information (filtered by "Fujitsu NetCOBOL for .NET")

Why Do I Use the VS .NET Help Option?

I have set out to *guide* you to (and through) the voluminous amounts of Help text that is available (in some cases, attempting to supplement what is available). Hence, I need to first confirm the availability of such Help text. Typically, after digesting the available material (if I am able to find any), I ask myself questions such as the following: Was this information clear or misleading? Is there anything that I can add, reword, or rephrase to improve the Help text that is already available? Will a mainframe analogy be helpful? Is this a good candidate to include in the "To Learn More" section at the end of the chapter? Naturally, the desired end result in following this approach is a useful guide to .NET for the mainframe programmer.

What, no topics found? How can that be? ADO.NET *is* after all a major .NET topic. After scribbling a note to myself (*Chris, remember to ask the helpful and responsive Fujitsu Software technical support contact about adding ADO.NET to their Help text...*), I decided to do yet another search. This time, I changed the "Look for:" value to "(SQL) or (DATABASE)". I kept the "Filter by:" value set to "Fujitsu NetCOBOL for .NET". As you can see in Figure 11-15, the search returned about 28 relevant Help text items.

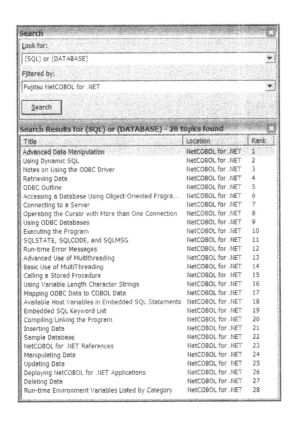

Figure 11-15. Searching VS .NET for "(SQL) or (DATABASE)"–related information (filtered by "Fujitsu NetCOBOL for .NET")

If you drill down into each of the 28 relevant Help text items, you will find full discussions on "how to use embedded SQL" in your COBOL .NET applications. You will also find supportive discussions (e.g., "how to connect to a server/database"). About 90 percent of this information will look familiar to you. In other words, these 28 relevant Help text items will be helpful to you if (and only if) you needed to continue coding your database logic using the mainframe DB2 legacy style.

TIP Giving Fujitsu Software the benefit of the doubt, I decided to search their NetCOBOL for .NET Web site (http://www.netcobol.com/) and eventually found a link to an extremely useful Web site. As it turns out, Fujitsu Software provides the following Web site, which contains a healthy number of ADO.NET QuickStart samples (and other types of samples): http://www.netcobolsamples.com/. Although I hope Fujitsu will add additional VS .NET Help topics (even for ADO.NET) in future releases of their NetCOBOL for .NET product, the NetCOBOL samples Web site will certainly suffice for the time being.

Legacy-Style Database Programming in .NET

Obviously, I am biased when faced with the choice of using a "legacy" coding style or a "contemporary" coding style. Looking at this from a developer's point of view, sometimes it is just more exciting to use newer technology. Nevertheless, you cannot ignore that there are other points of view.

There could, in some cases, be good arguments for using a legacy coding style. Even when the playing field is leveled, when productivity and performance are equal, a case could be made for choosing one style over the other. However, be forewarned. Some developers may find themselves having to deal with "perceptions" as much as "reality." Who knows? In the worst-case scenario, you may even need to deal with political issues.

Commendation vs. Condemnation

Fujitsu Software should not be criticized for providing backward compatibility in their .NET product. Rather, they should be commended. Some companies will see this as a way to gradually transition legacy applications over to the .NET platform—a less steep learning curve.

Fujitsu is not alone in taking this approach of building backward compatibility into their products. Microsoft has also designed .NET to support its own legacy style of database programming. In pre-.NET Win32/Web applications, you will find Active Data Objects (ADO) being used for database programming. The technology of ADO preceded ADO.NET and continues to be supported in .NET. Using .NET's COM Interoperability technology, you can continue (when needed) to use ADO in your .NET applications.

Given these possibilities and unknowns, it will be prudent to at least take a quick peek at what legacy-style database programming looks like in COBOL .NET. The pseudo-code in Listing 11-1 shows the basic language elements and the required syntax. Please take a moment to read the programming code and the comments included within the pseudo-code project, LegacyDatabaseAccessCobol. Notice the use of embedded SQL encased within EXEC statements—just like in the old days.

Listing 11-1. A COBOL .NET Pseudo-Code Project Demonstrating Legacy-Type Database Access

```
000010 IDENTIFICATION DIVISION.
000020 PROGRAM-ID. Program1 AS "Program1".
000030 ENVIRONMENT DIVISION.
000040 DATA DIVISION.
000050 WORKING-STORAGE SECTION.
000060
000070* Include the code below to represent the legacy
000080* style Host Structure or Host Variable.
000090* The Northwind/Categories Table is used as an example.
000100* In the past, you may have used the DCLGEN
000110* (or the Declaration Generator) in DB2I for this.
000120* A more traditional way of doing this would have
000130* been to have the "declared Host Structure" in a
000140* copybook. Then an INCLUDE statement would have been
000150* used. The same thing applies to the use of the
000160* SQL Communication Area. Legacy Styles might have
000170* normally used an INCLUDE statement. The SQLSTATE
000180* Variable below is used for this purpose.
000190     EXEC SQL BEGIN DECLARE SECTION END-EXEC.
000200 01 Table-LIST.
000210     05 CategoryID        PIC S9(4) COMP-5.
000220     05 CategoryName      PIC X(15).
000230     05 Description       PIC X(16).
000240     05 Picture-Image     PIC G(15) DISPLAY-1.
000250 01 SQLSTATE              PIC X(5).
000260     EXEC SQL END DECLARE SECTION END-EXEC.
000270
000280 PROCEDURE DIVISION.
000290
000300* Include the code below to Connect to your data source
000310* Your Server and database connection information may vary
000320     EXEC SQL
000330         CONNECT TO '(LOCAL)' AS 'DemoODBC' USER 'sa/'
```

```
000340    END-EXEC.
000350
000360* Include the code below to declare a Cursor for
000370* Query. As with Legacy Styled coding, you would
000380* do this whenever you were expecting more than
000390* one row returned in your result set.
000400* The Northwind/Categories Table is used as an example.
000410    EXEC SQL DECLARE CategoriesCUR CURSOR FOR
000420        SELECT * FROM Categories
000430    END-EXEC.
000440
000450* Naturally, you need to Open your Cursor before using it.
000460    EXEC SQL OPEN CategoriesCUR END-EXEC
000470
000480* The code statement below would be used to actually
000490* Read the "Next Record" in the database table
000500    EXEC SQL
000510      FETCH CategoriesCUR INTO :Table-LIST
000520    END-EXEC.
000530
000540* Good housekeeping: you close your cursor when done
000550    EXEC SQL CLOSE CategoriesCUR END-EXEC.
000560
000570* Include the code below to Query your Data Source
000580* You would use this when only expecting one row in your
000590* return set. Notice the legacy style usage of a
000600* colon being used for the Host Variables.
000610* The Northwind/Categories Table is used as an example.
000620    EXEC SQL
000630    SELECT CategoryID,CategoryName,Description
000640                    INTO      :CategoryID,
000650                              :CategoryName,
000660                              :Description
000670            FROM Categories
000680            WHERE CategoryID = 7
000690    END-EXEC.
000700
000710* Include the code below to Disconnect from your data source
000720    EXEC SQL DISCONNECT CURRENT END-EXEC.
000730 END PROGRAM Program1.
```

NOTE   The use of COMMIT and ROLLBACK commands as a way to simulate a logical unit of work (to ensure data integrity) continues to be supported in COBOL .NET. As you did in your legacy mainframe COBOL (database) applications, you can continue to use these two commands within the legacy-style EXEC delimiters.

I have referred to the COBOL .NET code in Listing 11-1 as being in *pseudo-code* form. In other words, although the code is syntactically correct and will compile, you will need to complete a few tasks before actually executing it. For example, you will need to add actual business logic to the Procedure Division. Additionally, the required environment setup needs to be completed as per Fujitsu's documentation.

NOTE   Most legacy mainframe developers are likely to welcome a departure from the concerns of BINDING and PACKAGING their mainframe COBOL database programs.

The Environment Setup: To Do or Not to Do?

The typical environment setup may be familiar to those of you who have done COBOL coding on the Win32 platform before (using earlier COBOL compilers from Fujitsu Software or Micro Focus). For the rest of you, this will represent a learning curve. Assume for a moment that you were thinking about staying with the legacy style of database programming (in .NET). You would then need to review the environment setup steps detailed in Fujitsu's documentation. The following four environment setup topics would be of concern to you:

- Using Fujitsu's runtime Environment Setup tool

- Creating a runtime initialization file

- Using Fujitsu's Open Database Connectivity (ODBC) Setup utility

- Creating an ODBC information file

NOTE With all of the other things that you will be learning, I cannot see any practical reason why you might want to go through the effort of setting up your environment to support legacy database–style programming. At most, just know that it *is* possible (just in case).

Now, assume that you have decided to "upgrade" your database programming coding style. In that case, there would be very little reason to complete the environment setup. However, there would still be value gained simply from viewing the COBOL .NET pseudo-code shown in Listing 11-1. Why? The legacy coding–style code, whether done on the mainframe or here in COBOL .NET, will serve as an opportunity for analogies during the discussions in the next section.

Although I encourage you to learn more about working with ODBC (see the section "Open Database Connectivity Configuration" in Chapter 3), I'll stop just short of really questioning why anyone wanting to learn *.NET* and wanting to create *.NET* applications would choose to avoid using a *.NET way* of database programming (i.e., the ADO.NET technology). After all, there are two very good reasons why you *should* use the newer .NET programming style when coding .NET applications:

- ADO.NET is designed to support a *disconnected* model for database programming. This is more appropriate for distributed Web applications.

- ADO.NET is integrated with XML (I discuss this further in Chapter 12). XML integration becomes critical when you are working with Web and Web service applications.

Convinced yet? Don't worry. You'll turn now to explore the *newer* .NET way of database programming using the ADO.NET technology. After you see how easy it is to use the ADO.NET Framework objects, your choice will be much clearer.

.NET-Style Database Programming in .NET

Generally speaking, the .NET style of database programming means using the ADO.NET technology (managed objects) to access your database source. As mentioned in the previous section, the ADO.NET technology is characterized by its support for the Disconnected Application Model and XML. To further understand this technology, you will explore the following two major components that make up ADO.NET (see Figure 11-16):

- .NET data providers

- .NET Dataset

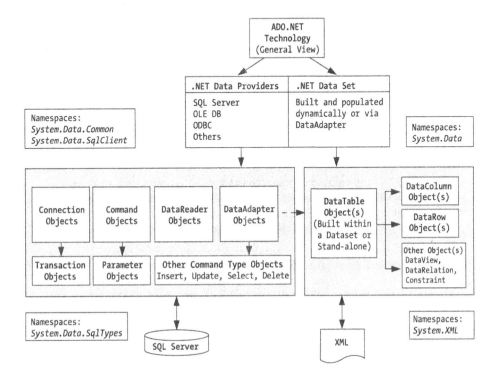

Figure 11-16. A general view of the ADO.NET technology

.NET Data Providers

In your legacy mainframe database development (when using DB2), you understood that DB2 provided *attachment facilities*. These attachment facilities provided the connections (referred to as *threads* on the mainframe) between your application and the actual DB2 database. Furthermore, you may have been familiar with some of the other mainframe DB2 components, including Database Services, Relational Data Systems, Data Manager, and Buffer Manager. Functionally, these DB2 components are similar to the .NET data providers.

Each time you coded the EXEC delimiters to execute SQL commands in your mainframe COBOL programs, you were using the services of the DB2 components. With ADO.NET, you will use classes from the .NET Framework to leverage the services offered by the .NET data providers. .NET ships with the following data providers:[8]

- SQL Server .NET Data Provider

- Oracle .NET Data Provider

- OLE DB .NET Data Provider

Each .NET data provider has a .NET namespace (containing classes and so forth) associated with it. If you were using the SQL Server .NET Data Provider, you would be interested in the *System.Data.SqlClient* namespace. If you were using the OLE DB .NET Data Provider, the *System.Data.OleDb* namespace would be most important to your ADO.NET development.

TIP   If you want to do a search in VS .NET to find information on ADO.NET, simply remove the "Fujitsu" filter from the earlier search. Practically any other "Filter by:" choice (even the choice that reads "No Filter") will allow the search to retrieve ADO.NET-related Help topics.

Depending on the type of database (or data source) you are targeting, you would choose to use one provider/namespace over another. The SQL Server .NET Data Provider is optimized for Microsoft's SQL Server database (version 7.0, version 2000, and later) and the Microsoft Data Engine (MSDE). The OLE DB .NET Data Provider would be appropriate for older SQL Server database versions (version 6.5 and earlier) and Microsoft's Access database product. Because you are using the SQL Server 2000 product, you will use the SQL Server .NET Data Provider and the System.Data.SqlClient namespace.

---

8.   As of .NET version 1.0, the Oracle .NET Data Provider is available as a free download from Microsoft's Web site. I expect that this .NET Data Provider will eventually be bundled and shipped with the other .NET Data Providers. Likewise, there's an Open Database Connectivity (ODBC) Data Provider available as a separate download from Microsoft's Web site. Optionally, you're free to write a .NET data provider for any data source.

NOTE If you find that you need to use another data provider
(e.g., the OLE DB .NET Data Provider) in your own development, you
will be able to apply all of the information I discuss here. Moving from
one namespace (e.g., System.Data.SqlClient) to another (e.g.,
System.Data.OleDb) is rather easy. After making an adjustment for a
small name "prefix" difference, you will find the namespaces to be
almost identical. Incidentally, you will notice that both data provider
namespaces (System.Data.SqlClient and System.Data.OleDb) contain
objects that derive from the *System.Data.Common* namespace.

The System.Data.SqlClient Namespace

Let's now drill down into the System.Data.SqlClient namespace. Of the sixteen or
so classes and the three delegates that this namespace contains, you should begin
by first gaining a solid understanding of the following four classes:

- *System.Data.SqlClient.SqlConnection*

- *System.Data.SqlClient.SqlCommand*

- *System.Data.SqlClient.SqlDataReader*

- *System.Data.SqlClient.SqlDataAdapter*

You will use the SqlConnection class to connect to the SQL Server database.
This class has properties and methods that you will use to accomplish this. One of
the properties, *ConnectionString*, is used to communicate details such as the
server name, user ID, and password. As you might have figured out by now, there is
an *Open* and a *Close* method exposed by the *SqlConnection* class.

TIP There is a *SqlTransaction* object that you can create using the
BeginTransaction method of the SqlConnection class. The use of the
ADO.NET SqlTransaction class will remind you of your use of the DB2/
SQL COMMIT and ROLLBACK commands in your legacy COBOL
programs.

Once you have a "Connection" object (providing a connection to your database), you will want to use the *SqlCommand* class. This class has properties and methods that facilitate the association between your *Command* object and your *Connection* object. You then set other properties and methods depending on whether or not you are executing a stored procedure, and depending on what type of results (in your result set) you are expecting to return. You are basically "executing" your command to achieve a desired result. Among the Command object's *Execute* methods are the following:[9]

- *ExecuteScalar:* Use this method to send commands to the Connection object to return a single value.

- *ExecuteNonQuery:* Use this method to execute commands that do not return rows.

- *ExecuteReader:* This method sends commands to the Connection object to return a *DataReader* object (which I discuss further in this section).

NOTE You can use the constructor of the SqlCommand class to create a Command object. Optionally, you can use the Connection object's *CreateCommand* method to create Command objects.

This leaves you with the SqlDataReader and SqlDataAdapter classes (*DataReader* and *DataAdapter* objects, respectively). Your choice of one of these classes really depends on your ultimate "data" need and application design. Generally speaking, you use DataReader objects when your data needs are met by a read-only, forward-only stream of data (output from your database). On the other hand, if your data needs extend beyond that, use of the SqlDataAdapter class may be more appropriate for your ADO.NET development.

---

9. There's another "Execute" method offered by the SQLCommand class named ExecuteXmlReader. I further discuss this method in Chapter 12.

NOTE The use of these ADO.NET "data provider" classes should remind you of your use of SQL/DB2 commands in your legacy mainframe DB2 applications. After all, during your years of legacy mainframe development, you understood the ideas of connecting to your database, executing SQL commands, and handling result sets.

Though this section presented a brief mention of the SqlDataAdapter class, you will have an opportunity to revisit this topic. In the next section, when you explore the "other" major component of ADO.NET, I further discuss the SqlDataAdapter class. (Hint: You use the SqlDataAdapter class as a bridge between your database and a Dataset object.)

TIP Soon after you are comfortable with the System.Data.SqlClient classes discussed in this section, be sure to look into the *System.Data.SqlClient.SqlError* class. You will find that the *SqlError* class provides similar functionality to that provided by the mainframe DB2 SQL Communications Area (SQLCA). As you recall, you used the SQLCA to collect any available "warning and error" information generated by the database engine. Typically, you included the SQLCA and appropriate conditional logic when you did database programming in your legacy mainframe COBOL applications. Good defensive programming design will direct your usage of the SqlError class.

.NET Dataset

I hinted in the previous section that the SqlDataAdapter plays a key role with the Dataset object. This is only the beginning—I'm just scratching the surface of the Dataset topic. Nevertheless, before you go below the surface (and dive into the .NET namespace objects), I want to assist you in moving toward a better perspective of why .NET Datasets are important and when you might want to use one.

I have included a discussion in the following section that should make it easier for you to understand the usefulness offered by the new .NET Dataset object. The discussion follows an imagined scenario that draws from your legacy mainframe experience.

Increasing Data Demands

If you will, please imagine the following scenario: You are on the mainframe. You have reviewed a requirements document detailing the legacy COBOL DB2 application that you will create.[10] You turn to your trusted ISPF/DB2I tool to perform a Declaration Generator (DCLGEN) task.

Once the DCLGEN is complete, you use the COBOL INCLUDE statement to introduce the DB2 host structure/host variables to the Working-Storage portion of your COBOL program. You then proceed to code a complex SQL statement that will perform a database SELECT query (perhaps JOINing a few tables in the process). You embed the SQL inside of the EXEC delimiters and successfully complete your application development.

Then it happens. You discover that your query is actually going to return multiple records. No problem. First, you confirm that this was omitted from the requirements documentation. Next, you modify your code to include the appropriate DB2/SQL statements to support *cursor-type*[11] processing (e.g., CURSOR DECLARE, FETCH, and OPEN/CLOSE).

 TIP   As it would have been wise to use DB2I/SPUFI in this case (to test your query outside of your actual application), SQL Server's toolset (discussed earlier in the section "Client-Side Tools") offers similar advantages.

When your business analyst discovers that you are modifying the program, the analyst requests an additional business requirement: Change the application from read-only to read and update. Your "completed" application now needs to be modified. You quickly add the FOR UPDATE clause to your SQL/DB2 query to enable your cursor for database updating. As you prepare your mainframe database program for production deployment, your business analyst comes back with "just one more" requirement.

---

10. Wouldn't it be great if you always had a complete requirements document on which to base your software development?

11. You'll come across the term "cursor" in the SQL Server context. Be aware that in legacy ADO technology, there was a server-side cursor and a client-side cursor. With ADO, a server-side cursor was used when "scrolling and updating" was desired. With ADO.NET, the trend has been to use the new .NET Dataset in cases where a legacy ADO server-side cursor would have been used.

NOTE As contrived as this scenario may appear, some developers (on the mainframe and Windows/Web environments) actually experience this on a daily basis. If you have not, consider yourself lucky.

You now find out that your program will need to be able to scroll (bidirectionally) through your result set. After silently swearing to yourself, you go ahead and add a SCROLL clause to your CURSOR declaration. With foresight, you even add an ARRAY in your program to create an in-memory table to hold the result set. Your business analyst then pays you another visit.

TIP In the case of ADO.NET's data provider classes, these two business requirements (bidirectional scrolling ability and updatable) would have been reasons to not use the SqlDataReader class. Recall that the SqlDataReader class is for read-only and forward-only data usage. The SqlDataAdapter class then becomes a more appropriate data provider class choice.

The business analyst informs you that there are a few more requirements. You are now told that your application will need to perform a second database query, dynamically join with the first query (the saved array), perform searches using the combination of both queried result sets, update the virtually joined data, apply the updates to the database, and then write out the virtually joined data in XML format to use as input for the new Web service[12] audit application.

As you sit there, stunned and amazed, your business analyst then informs you that the business users want the flexibility of being able to load your database application onto their laptops, pocket PCs, and tablet PCs to use while they are offline, in the field.

---

12. I further discuss Web services in Chapter 13.

Business Users Are Not the Enemy

Our job, our professional livelihood, is given purpose by satisfying the growing needs of business users. The .NET platform's ADO.NET technology better enables your software development to address the new needs of your business users.

The way that this imagined scenario ends is really up to you. Perhaps you can end it by imagining that you eventually convert your legacy mainframe database application to a .NET application that uses ADO.NET. Imagining a happy ending to this scenario, you then discover ADO.NET offers an object called the .NET Dataset. Further discovery reveals to you that the .NET Dataset supports flexible, relational-like, in-memory data needs, XML formatting, and disconnected/offline usage.

TIP You can use the SqlDataAdapter class to create the Dataset class. Understand that there is additional overhead incurred with the SqlDataAdapter class. The overhead is justified only when it helps you meet your data usage needs. If your data needs can be satisfied with the SqlDataReader class, you should use it instead of the SqlDataAdapter (and Dataset) class.

To conclude this imagined scenario, say that you completed your application development using ADO.NET's Dataset class, easily satisfying all of the business requirements that your business analyst threw your way—on schedule. On that note, let's return to reality and move on to learn about the details of the .NET Dataset.

The System.Data Namespace

As you certainly expected, there is a namespace provided to support the use of the .NET Dataset: *System.Data*. This namespace provides ADO.NET objects (delegates, interfaces, classes, and enumerations) for you to exploit. To better

understand the usefulness of the System.Data objects, you will want to know
the general structure of the .NET Dataset. (Please briefly revisit Figure 11-16 in the
earlier section ".NET-Style Database Programming in .NET").

NOTE   You can create a .NET Dataset in one of two ways: as a return
type of the SqlDataAdapter class or independently without a
SqlDataAdapter. Your choice typically will depend on what data source
you are targeting to "fill" your Dataset. If you intend on filling your
Dataset from a database query, then the SqlDataAdapter class is a good
choice to create your Dataset. On the other hand, if you are filling your
Dataset using any other data source (including data that is internal to
your program), you can directly create your Dataset totally independent of any database or data provider objects.

Generally speaking, the .NET Dataset (*System.Data.Dataset*) is made
up of one or more tables (*System.Data.DataTableCollection*). Each table
(*System.Data.DataTable*) is made up of a collection of columns
(*System.Data.DataColumnCollection*) and a collection of rows
(*System.Data.DataRowCollection*). The DataColumnCollection object is
made up of individual columns (*System.Data.DataColumn*), with each
column having a specific data type (*System.Data.DataType*). The
DataRowCollection object is made up of individual rows (*System.Data.DataRow*).

NOTE   You can create a System.Data.DataTable object either as part of
a Dataset or as a stand-alone DataTable.

Of course, you will want to become familiar with many other System.Data
objects. However, familiarizing yourself with the Dataset, DataTable, DataColumn,
DataType, and DataRow objects should get you off to a good start. Remember, you
will need the SqlDataAdapter object (discussed earlier in the section "The
System.Data.SqlClient Namespace") if you are filling the Dataset from a database
connection.

TIP Use the references in the "To Learn More" section at the end of this chapter to further your retraining effort. Additionally, the VS .NET Help text will prove to be very useful. Recall that the filter you use can greatly impact your ability to locate ADO.NET-related information.

I have discussed the ADO.NET data providers and the Dataset. Additionally, you have been introduced to the .NET namespaces associated with ADO.NET. In the next section, you will take a look at some sample programming code. There you will see the simplicity involved in putting ADO.NET to use.

TIP As you further your ADO.NET training, you will come across one other ADO.NET namespace: *System.Data.SqlTypes.* You will learn that this namespace mostly contains structures that offer a preferable way of mapping to native SQL Server data types.

Using ADO.NET

To demonstrate the use of the Data Provider and Dataset classes, I will use the SQL Server 2000 product as my data source. I will query the Microsoft-supplied sample Northwind database using a simple SQL SELECT command. I will create both the COBOL .NET and Visual Basic .NET (VB .NET) code using a VS .NET console template. First, I present the VB .NET sample code project (DataBaseAccessExampleVB), and then I present the COBOL .NET sample code project (DataBaseAccessExampleCobol). I suggest that you familiarize yourself with each sample code project (taking the bilingual approach). You should soon feel comfortable enough to enhance the sample code projects and further explore the relevant namespaces (e.g., consider writing the queried result set out to a text file).

TIP Microsoft has created a collection of components called *Application Blocks for .NET.* One of the Application Blocks available is the *Data Access Application Block.* This component set offers convenience by first packaging several ADO.NET classes and then exposing a collection of "shortcut" methods. When you take advantage of the Data Access Application Block, you can significantly reduce the number of coding lines required to use ADO.NET. I suggest that you first learn to use the ADO.NET class directly (as explained in this chapter). Later, you can easily switch to take advantage of the Data Access Application Block. You will find that the packaged routines will meet your needs *most* of the time. Use of the Data Access Application Block will require that you first download from Microsoft's Web site the Microsoft.ApplicationBlocks.Data.dll assembly. Afterward, you will be able to leverage the members of two managed classes: *SqlHelper* and *SqlHelperParameterCache.* For further details of this useful feature, see the reference provided in the "To Learn More" section (in the "Web Sites" subsection) at the end of this chapter. (For those using Oracle's database product, there is a corresponding Data Access Application Block assembly and managed "helper" class set available via Microsoft's MSDN Code Center Web site.)

ADO.NET with VB .NET Sample Code

You will notice in the sample code in Listing 11-2 (copied from the Module1.vb file of DataBaseAccessExampleVB) that I have avoided the use of the VB .NET IMPORT statement. Although this statement is a good coding shortcut, for illustrative and training purposes it seems more useful to see exactly what namespace each object is coming from. In your own code, you may wish to use the IMPORT statement to make your code less verbose. It is up to you and your coding style/preference.

NOTE The ADO.NET assembly (System.Data.Dll) is already referenced by default in the DataBaseAccessExampleVB VB .NET project.

Listing 11-2. Sample VB .NET Code Demonstrating the Use of ADO.NET

```vbnet
'Sample Code using ADO.NET Technology
Module Module1

    Sub main()

        Call UseSqlDataAdapter(OptionalPreTableBuild)
        Console.WriteLine(" ")

        Call UseSqlDataReader()
        Console.ReadLine()


    End Sub

    Public Function OptionalPreTableBuild() As DataSet
            'It is possible to obtain the "schema" or table structure
            'directly/automatically from the SQL Server Database
            'This section is added for training purposes.
            'The information found in this section would be critical
            'in the case of building a disconnected .NET dataset
            'that may have a non-SQL Server Data Source.

            ' Create new DataTable.
            Dim myDataTable As DataTable = _
            New System.Data.DataTable("myCategories")

            ' Declare DataColumn and DataRow variables.
            Dim myDataColumn As System.Data.DataColumn
            Dim myDataRow As System.Data.DataRow

            ' Create 1st myDataColumn.
            myDataColumn = New System.Data.DataColumn()
            myDataColumn.DataType = System.Type.GetType("System.Int32")
            myDataColumn.ColumnName = "CategoryID"
            myDataColumn.Unique = True
            myDataTable.Columns.Add(myDataColumn)

            ' Create 2nd myDataColumn.
            myDataColumn = New System.Data.DataColumn()
            myDataColumn.DataType = Type.GetType("System.String")
            myDataColumn.ColumnName = "CategoryName"
            myDataTable.Columns.Add(myDataColumn)
```

```vb
' Create 3rd myDataColumn.
myDataColumn = New System.Data.DataColumn()
myDataColumn.DataType = Type.GetType("System.String")
myDataColumn.ColumnName = "Description"
myDataTable.Columns.Add(myDataColumn)

' Create 4th myDataColumn.
myDataColumn = New System.Data.DataColumn()
myDataColumn.DataType = Type.GetType("System.Byte[]")
myDataColumn.ColumnName = "Picture"
myDataTable.Columns.Add(myDataColumn)

' Assign primary key column to CategoryID column
Dim PrimaryKeyColumns(0) As System.Data.DataColumn
PrimaryKeyColumns(0) = myDataTable.Columns("CategoryID")
myDataTable.PrimaryKey = PrimaryKeyColumns

' Reference the DataSet.
Dim myDataSet As New System.Data.DataSet()
' Associate the Table with the Dataset.
myDataSet.Tables.Add(myDataTable)
myDataTable = Nothing
Return myDataSet


End Function


Public Sub UseSqlDataAdapter(ByVal myDataset As DataSet)
    'Reference Data Provider Objects
    Dim mySqlConnection As New System.Data.SqlClient.SqlConnection()
    Dim mySqlDataAdapter As New System.Data.SqlClient.SqlDataAdapter()
    Dim mySqlCommand As New System.Data.SqlClient.SqlCommand()

    'Reference Dataset Objects
    Dim myDataRow As System.Data.DataRow

    'Prepare to Connect to SQL Server Database
    'using Connection String
    mySqlConnection.ConnectionString = _
    "user id=sa;pwd=;Database=northwind;Server=(LOCAL)"

    'Associate the Command Object with the Connection Object
    mySqlCommand.Connection = mySqlConnection
    'Associate the Command Object with intended SQL Statement
    mySqlCommand.CommandText = "Select * from Categories"
```

```
        'Associate the DataAdapter Object with the Command Object
        mySqlDataAdapter.SelectCommand = mySqlCommand
        'Have the DataAdapter Object Execute the SQL Statement and
        'store the result set in a DataSet DataTable named myCategories
        mySqlDataAdapter.Fill(myDataset, "myCategories")

        'Loop through the Dataset DataTable
        'Write out one DataColumn per DataRow
        For Each myDataRow In myDataset.Tables("myCategories").Rows
              Console.WriteLine(myDataRow("CategoryName").ToString())
        Next

        'Close the Database Connection
        mySqlConnection.Close()
        mySqlConnection = Nothing
        mySqlDataAdapter = Nothing
        mySqlCommand = Nothing

End Sub

Public Sub UseSqlDataReader()
        'Reference Data Provider Objects
        Dim mySqlConnection As New System.Data.SqlClient.SqlConnection()
        Dim mySqlDataReader As System.Data.SqlClient.SqlDataReader
        Dim mySqlCommand As New System.Data.SqlClient.SqlCommand()

        'Connect to SQL Server Database using Connection String
        mySqlConnection.ConnectionString = _
        "user id=sa;pwd=;Database=northwind;Server=(LOCAL)"
        mySqlConnection.Open()

        'Associate the Command Object with the Connection Object
        mySqlCommand.Connection = mySqlConnection
        'Associate the Command Object with intended SQL Statement
        mySqlCommand.CommandText = "Select * from Categories"

        'Have the DataReader Object Execute the SQL Statement and
        'store the result set in a DataReader Object
        mySqlDataReader = mySqlCommand.ExecuteReader()

        'Loop through the DataReader Object, Advancing to each Record
        'Write out one Column per Record
        While mySqlDataReader.Read()
```

```
            Console.WriteLine((mySqlDataReader.GetString(1)))
        End While

        'Close the DataReader
        mySqlDataReader.Close()
        'Close the Database Connection
        mySqlConnection.Close()

        mySqlConnection = Nothing
        mySqlCommand = Nothing


    End Sub

End Module
```

You will observe in the sample code in Listing 11-2 the ConnectionString of the System.Data.SqlClient.SqlConnection class has "user id," "pwd," and "Server" attributes. The values used to set these ConnectionString attributes may not be the same for every individual. They will certainly be different in a production application. The values that I used are for demonstration purposes only.

 TIP Using the Enterprise Manager tool, check to make sure that the SQL Server database is *started* before you attempt to run the DataBaseAccessExampleVB sample project.

When you execute this sample project, you will see the contents of the CategoryName column from the Northwind.Categories table written to the console. In the next section, you will take a look at how the ADO.NET technology is implemented using COBOL .NET.

ADO.NET with COBOL .NET Sample Code

You will notice that the ADO.NET assembly (System.Data.Dll) reference is already added for this COBOL .NET project. The coding for ADO.NET data providers and .NET Datasets can take place. The COBOL .NET sample code in Listing 11-3 for the project DataBaseAccessExampleCobol provides a good example of how to use several ADO.NET classes to query a SQL Server database.

Listing 11-3. COBOL .NET Sample Code Demonstrating the Use of ADO.NET

```
000010* Sample Code using ADO.NET Technology
000020 IDENTIFICATION DIVISION.
000030 PROGRAM-ID. MAIN.
000040 ENVIRONMENT DIVISION.
000050 CONFIGURATION SECTION.
000060 REPOSITORY.
000070* .NET Framework Classes
000080     CLASS SqlConnection  AS "System.Data.SqlClient.SqlConnection"
000090     CLASS SqlDataAdapter As "System.Data.SqlClient.SqlDataAdapter"
000100     CLASS SqlCommand As "System.Data.SqlClient.SqlCommand"
000110     CLASS SqlDataReader AS "System.Data.SqlClient.SqlDataReader"
000120     CLASS DataSet     As "System.Data.DataSet"
000130     CLASS DataTable   AS "System.Data.DataTable"
000140     CLASS DataRow     As "System.Data.DataRow"
000150     CLASS DataColumn AS "System.Data.DataColumn"
000160     CLASS DataRowCollection AS "System.Data.DataRowCollection"
000170     CLASS SystemType        AS "System.Type"
000180     CLASS DataColumnArray   AS "System.Data.DataColumn[]"
000190
000200     CLASS Sys-Integer     AS "System.Int32"
000210     CLASS Sys-String      AS "System.String"
000220     CLASS Sys-Objects     AS "System.Object[]"
000230     CLASS Sys-Object      AS "System.Object"
000240
000250* .NET Framework Properties
000260     PROPERTY PROP-ConnectionString AS "ConnectionString"
000270     PROPERTY PROP-Connection       AS "Connection"
000280     PROPERTY PROP-CommandText      AS "CommandText"
000290     PROPERTY PROP-SelectCommand    AS "SelectCommand"
000300     PROPERTY PROP-Columns          AS "Columns"
000310     PROPERTY PROP-Tables           AS "Tables"
000320     PROPERTY PROP-Rows             AS "Rows"
000330     PROPERTY PROP-DataType         AS "DataType"
000340     PROPERTY PROP-ColumnName       AS "ColumnName"
000350     PROPERTY PROP-Count            AS "Count"
000360     PROPERTY PROP-Item             AS "Item"
000370     PROPERTY PROP-ItemArray        AS "ItemArray"
000380     PROPERTY PROP-PrimaryKey       AS "PrimaryKey"
000390     PROPERTY PROP-Unique           AS "Unique".
000400*
000410 DATA DIVISION.
000420 WORKING-STORAGE SECTION.
```

```
000430    77 mySqlConnection   OBJECT REFERENCE SqlConnection.
000440    77 mySqlDataAdapter OBJECT REFERENCE SqlDataAdapter.
000450    77 mySqlCommand      OBJECT REFERENCE SqlCommand.
000460    77 mySqlDataReader   OBJECT REFERENCE SqlDataReader.
000470    77 myDataSet         OBJECT REFERENCE DataSet.
000480    77 myDataTable       OBJECT REFERENCE DataTable.
000490    77 myDataRow         OBJECT REFERENCE DataRow.
000500    77 myDataColumn      OBJECT REFERENCE DataColumn.
000510    77 myPrimaryKeyColumn  OBJECT REFERENCE DataColumn.
000520    77 myPrimaryKeyColumns OBJECT REFERENCE DataColumnArray.
000530    77 myDataRowCollection OBJECT REFERENCE DataRowCollection.
000540
000550
000560    77 mySys-String  OBJECT REFERENCE Sys-String.
000570    77 mySys-Integer OBJECT REFERENCE Sys-Integer.
000580    77 mySys-Objects OBJECT REFERENCE Sys-Objects.
000590    77 mySys-Object  OBJECT REFERENCE Sys-Object.
000600    77 myDisplayString PIC x(30).
000610    77 myInt          PIC S9(9) COMP-5.
000620    77 myOtherInt     PIC S9(9) COMP-5.
000630    77 NOT-END-OF-READ PIC 1 USAGE BIT.
000640    01 NULL-X         PIC X(1).
000650 PROCEDURE DIVISION.
000660
000670      Perform 0000-OptionalPreTableBuild.
000680      Perform 1000-UseSqlDataAdapter.
000690      DISPLAY " "
000700      Perform 2000-UseSqlDataReader.
000710
000720      DISPLAY "Enter X and Press Enter to Exit.".
000730      ACCEPT NULL-X.
000740      Stop Run.
000750
000760***********************************************
000770    0000-OptionalPreTableBuild.
000780*  It is possible to obtain the "schema" or table structure
000790*  directly/automatically from the SQL Server Database
000800*  This section is added for training purposes.
000810*  The information found in this section would be critical
000820*  in the case of building a disconnected .NET dataset
000830*  that may have a non-SQL Server Data Source.
000840
000850* Create a new DataTable.
000860      INVOKE DataTable "NEW" USING BY VALUE "myCategories"
```

```
000870        RETURNING myDataTable.
000880
000890* Create 1st myDataColumn.
000900     INVOKE DataColumn "NEW" RETURNING myDataColumn.
000910     SET PROP-DataType OF myDataColumn TO
000920         SystemType::"GetType"("System.Int32").
000930     SET PROP-ColumnName OF myDataColumn TO "CategoryID".
000940     SET PROP-Unique OF myDataColumn TO B"1".
000950     INVOKE PROP-Columns OF myDataTable "Add"
000960       USING BY VALUE myDataColumn.
000970
000980* Create 2nd myDataColumn.
000990     INVOKE DataColumn "NEW" RETURNING myDataColumn.
001000     SET PROP-DataType OF myDataColumn TO
001010         SystemType::"GetType"("System.String").
001020     SET PROP-ColumnName OF myDataColumn TO "CategoryName".
001030     INVOKE PROP-Columns OF myDataTable "Add"
001040       USING BY VALUE myDataColumn.
001050
001060* Create 3rd myDataColumn.
001070     INVOKE DataColumn "NEW" RETURNING myDataColumn.
001080     SET PROP-DataType OF myDataColumn TO
001090         SystemType::"GetType"("System.String").
001100     SET PROP-ColumnName OF myDataColumn TO "Description".
001110     INVOKE PROP-Columns OF myDataTable "Add"
001120       USING BY VALUE myDataColumn.
001130
001140* Create 4th myDataColumn.
001150     INVOKE DataColumn "NEW" RETURNING myDataColumn.
001160     SET PROP-DataType OF myDataColumn TO
001170         SystemType::"GetType"("System.Byte[]").
001180     SET PROP-ColumnName OF myDataColumn TO "Picture".
001190     INVOKE PROP-Columns OF myDataTable "Add"
001200       USING BY VALUE myDataColumn.
001210
001220* Assign primary key column to CategoryID column.
001230     INVOKE DataColumnArray "NEW" USING BY VALUE 1
001240         RETURNING myPrimaryKeyColumns.
001250     INVOKE PROP-Columns OF myDataTable "get_Item"
001260       USING BY VALUE "CategoryID"
001270       RETURNING myPrimaryKeyColumn.
001280     INVOKE myPrimaryKeyColumns "Set"
001290       USING BY VALUE 0 myPrimaryKeyColumn.
001300     SET PROP-PrimaryKey OF myDataTable TO myPrimaryKeyColumns.
```

```
001310
001320* Reference the DataSet.
001330     INVOKE DataSet "NEW" RETURNING myDataSet.
001340* Associate the Table with the Dataset.
001350     INVOKE PROP-Tables OF myDataSet "Add"
001360        USING BY VALUE myDataTable.
001370
001380***************************************************
001390    1000-UseSqlDataAdapter.
001400
001410*   Reference Data Provider Objects
001420       INVOKE SqlConnection "NEW"  RETURNING  mySqlConnection
001430       INVOKE SqlDataAdapter "NEW" RETURNING  mySqlDataAdapter
001440       INVOKE SqlCommand "NEW"     RETURNING  mySqlCommand
001450
001460*   Prepare to Connect to SQL Server Database
001470*   using Connection String
001480       SET PROP-ConnectionString OF mySqlConnection TO
001490       "user id=sa;pwd=;Database=northwind;Server=(LOCAL)"
001500
001510*   Associate the Command Object with the Connection Object
001520       SET PROP-Connection OF mySqlCommand TO mySqlConnection
001530*   Associate the Command Object with intended SQL Statement
001540       SET PROP-CommandText OF mySqlCommand TO "Select * from Categories"
001550*   Associate the DataAdapter Object with the Command Object
001560       SET PROP-SelectCommand OF mySqlDataAdapter TO mySqlCommand
001570
001580*   Have the DataAdapter Object Execute the SQL Statement and
001590*   store the result set in a DataSet DataTable named myCategories
001600     INVOKE mySqlDataAdapter "Fill"
001610       USING BY VALUE myDataSet, "myCategories"
001620
001630*   Loop through the Dataset DataTable
001640*   Write out one DataColumn per DataRow
001650     INVOKE PROP-Tables OF myDataSet "get_Item"
001660             USING BY VALUE "myCategories"
001670        RETURNING myDataTable
001680
001690       SET myDataRowCollection to PROP-Rows OF myDataTable
001700       SET mySys-Integer to PROP-Count of myDataRowCollection
001710
001720          SET myOtherInt TO mySys-Integer
001730          PERFORM VARYING myInt
001740              FROM 1 BY 1 UNTIL myInt > myOtherInt
```

```
001750
001760                    INVOKE PROP-Rows OF myDataTable "Find"
001770                    USING BY VALUE myInt RETURNING myDataRow
001780
001790                    SET mySys-Objects TO PROP-ItemArray OF myDataRow
001800                    INVOKE mySys-Objects "Get"
001810                      USING BY VALUE 1 RETURNING mySys-Object
001820                    SET myDisplayString to mySys-Object::"ToString" ()
001830                    DISPLAY myDisplayString
001840                 END-PERFORM.
001850
001860*  Close the Database Connection
001870      INVOKE mySqlConnection "Close".
001880
001890      SET mySqlConnection TO NULL.
001900      SET mySqlDataAdapter TO NULL.
001910      SET mySqlCommand TO NULL.
001920      SET myDataTable TO NULL.
001930
001940*************************************************
001950    2000-UseSqlDataReader.
001960
001970*  Reference Data Provider Objects
001980          INVOKE SqlConnection "NEW"  RETURNING  mySqlConnection
001990      INVOKE SqlCommand "NEW"     RETURNING  mySqlCommand
002000
002010*  Connect to SQL Server Database using Connection String
002020      SET PROP-ConnectionString OF mySqlConnection TO
002030      "user id=sa;pwd=;Database=northwind;Server=(LOCAL)"
002040      INVOKE mySqlConnection "Open"
002050
002060*  Associate the Command Object with the Connection Object
002070      SET PROP-Connection OF mySqlCommand TO mySqlConnection
002080*  Associate the Command Object with intended SQL Statement
002090      SET PROP-CommandText OF mySqlCommand TO "Select * from Categories"
002100
002110*  Have the DataReader Object Execute the SQL Statement and
002120*  store the result set in a DataReader Object
002130      SET mySqlDataReader TO mySqlCommand::"ExecuteReader" ()
002140
002150*  Loop through the DataReader Object, Advancing to each Record
002160*  Write out one Column per Record
002170          SET NOT-END-OF-READ TO mySqlDataReader::"Read" ()
002180          PERFORM UNTIL NOT-END-OF-READ = B'0'
```

```
002190                    SET myDisplayString to mySqlDataReader::"GetString" (1)
002200                    DISPLAY myDisplayString
002210                    SET NOT-END-OF-READ TO mySqlDataReader::"Read" ()
002220                END-PERFORM.
002230
002240*   Close the DataReader
002250      INVOKE mySqlDataReader "Close".
002260*   Close the Database Connection
002270      INVOKE mySqlConnection "Close".
002280
002290      SET mySqlConnection TO NULL.
002300      SET mySqlCommand TO NULL.
002310
002320 END PROGRAM MAIN.
```

NOTE   The values used to set the ConnectionString attributes ("user id," "pwd," and "Server") of the System.Data.SqlClient.SqlConnection class may not be the same for each individual. The appropriate values for your installation may differ.

As you can see in the COBOL .NET sample code in Listing 11-3, working with the ADO.NET classes is rather straightforward. Depending on your data needs, you can choose to use either the DataReader class or the DataAdapter class—whichever is more appropriate. Additionally, you may build your DataTable manually (as shown in Listing 11-3) or obtain the schema/structure directly from the SQL Server database.

Summary

This chapter's goals were as follows:

- To provide an overview of the SQL Server Enterprise Manager tool

- To discuss the use of the SQL Server Query Analyzer tool

- To explore the ADO.NET technology

I did warn you at the beginning of the chapter about the content contained in this chapter. Certainly, it is a lot to absorb. Nevertheless, can you imagine trying to become a serious Web/Windows .NET developer without these types of skill sets?

Although there are many other types of data sources for your business applications (as discussed in Chapter 10), relational database–type applications are arguably the most popular.

In this chapter, you learned about SQL Server's main client tools: Enterprise Manager and Query Analyzer. You then explored the ADO.NET technology. You were introduced to the .NET Data Provider and Dataset managed classes.

In the next chapter, you will examine the world of XML. During that discussion, I will introduce you to the "other" data-related .NET namespace: *System.XML.*

To Learn More

The following are some suggested supplemental references to further your retraining effort.

Books

ADO.NET and ADO Examples and Best Practices for VB Programmers, 2nd Edition, by William (Bill) Vaughn (Apress, 2002):

http://www.apress.com/book/bookDisplay.html?bID=79.

Advanced Transact-SQL for SQL Server 2000, by Itzik Ben-Gan and Dr. Tom Moreau (Apress, 2000):

http://www.apress.com/book/bookDisplay.html?bID=72.

Code-Centric: T-SQL Programming with Stored Procedures and Triggers, by Garth Wells (Apress, 2001):

http://www.apress.com/book/bookDisplay.html?bID=73.

Database Programming with Visual Basic .NET, by Carsten Thomsen (Apress, 2001):

http://www.apress.com/book/bookDisplay.html?bID=21.

Magazines

.NET Magazine:

http://www.fawcette.com/dotnetmag/

Visual Studio Magazine:

http://www.fawcette.com/vsm/

XML & Web Services Magazine:

http://www.fawcette.com/xmlmag/

Web Sites

.NET Architecture Center:

http://msdn.microsoft.com/architecture/

.NET Data Access Architecture Guide:

http://msdn.microsoft.com/library/en-us/dnbda/html/daag.asp

About Microsoft Data Engine (MSDE):

http://msdn.microsoft.com/library/en-us/off2000/html/acconAboutMSDE.asp

ADO.NET Primer:

http://msdn.microsoft.com/library/en-us/dnsql2k/html/sql_adonetprimer.asp

DB2 Universal Database (IBM's database product):

http://www-3.ibm.com/software/data/db2/udb/features.html

Fujitsu NetCOBOL for .NET:

http://www.netcobol.com/products/windows/netcobol.html

Microsoft Application Blocks for .NET:

http://msdn.microsoft.com/library/en-us/dnbda/html/daab-rm.asp

Microsoft Community (discussion groups, e-newsletters, and so forth):

http://communities2.microsoft.com/

Microsoft Patterns & Practices:

http://msdn.microsoft.com/practices/

Microsoft SQL Server 2000 Home Page (Microsoft's database product):

http://www.microsoft.com/sql/default.asp

MSDN:

http://msdn.microsoft.com

NetCOBOL for .NET QuickStart Tutorial for ADO.NET and XML:

http://quickstartcobol.eraserver.net/quickstartcobol/howto/

Oracle9*i* Database (Oracle's database product):

http://www.oracle.com/ip/deploy/database/oracle9i/

CHAPTER 12

XML in a Managed Environment

A Happy Trio: .NET, Data, and XML

In this chapter

- Learning to leverage the .NET Dataset's support for XML

- Exploring the System.Xml namespace

- Reviewing the .NET namespaces for overall XML support

BEFORE I BEGIN THIS chapter's discussion, I need to point out a few things about this chapter and the topic of XML. In this chapter, I will *not* mention to you that XML is an acronym for *Extensible Markup Language*. You already know that. Additionally, I will *not* take the time to provide any emphasis on how the entire .NET platform leverages the XML technology. That point was clearly stated in Chapter 2 and again in Chapter 4.

To continue, you will *not* see any details on the basic XML terminology in this chapter. This is only because you have already acquainted yourself with terms such as "documents," "elements," "attributes," and "Schema" while digesting the XML material presented in one of the prerequisite chapters (specifically, Chapter 4 in the section "XML Learning Kick Start"). On the same note, it is only right that I do *not* spend any time reintroducing the XML-related query and transformation technologies (i.e., XSL, XSLT, XPath, and XQuery) in this chapter. You already learned about these technologies in the section "XSL, XSLT, XPath, and XQuery" in Chapter 4.

NOTE   Please pardon me for assuming that you have taken advantage of the references provided at the end of Chapter 4 in the "To Learn More" section to further familiarize yourself with these topics. As you progress through *this* chapter, you will occasionally seek out more details and choose to leverage the additional groupings of informative references that are provided at the end of *this* chapter in the "To Learn More" section.

In this chapter, I see *no* need to rehash each mainframe analogy presented earlier in Chapter 4. Besides, I am sure that you recall (from that earlier chapter) the mainframe analogy that suggested that XML was the modern-day version of the legacy Electronic Data Interchange (EDI) technology. Certainly, you now understand that both XML and EDI both serve as approaches to data packaging and data description, so it would simply be redundant and wasteful to elaborate on that point in this chapter.

On the other hand, in this chapter, I *will* discuss how XML and the .NET Dataset (ADO.NET) are supported in unison. From there, I *will* review the *System.Xml* namespace and provide an overview of several managed objects that directly support reading and writing XML and XML schemas. I will conclude the chapter by stretching beyond the System.Xml namespace to introduce the "other" .NET namespaces that are available for XML support. I am sure that you will find that the XML topics that *are* included in this chapter will help move your XML expertise several .NET retraining steps forward.

XML and the .NET Dataset

As you know, the .NET Dataset object (from the System.Data namespace) is a key component of the ADO.NET technology. I introduced these managed objects in Chapter 11. You have seen how flexible this in-memory data store can be. You can easily use the .NET Dataset as a *disconnected relational* database that allows you to query the Dataset in much the same way as you would an actual database. But that is not all that the .NET Dataset can do.

Microsoft designed the .NET Dataset (or just *Dataset*) to support a *relational* view and a *hierarchical* view simultaneously. This has significantly increased the usefulness and flexibility of the Dataset. You can easily use the Dataset as a container for your relational data or XML—your *hierarchical* data. Let's now explore how you can go about writing and reading XML directly to and from a .NET Dataset.

NOTE For those of you *reformed* mainframe programmers who have had the pleasure of programming with IBM's Information Management System (IMS) on the mainframe, the word "hierarchical" may send shivers up your spine. Fear not. As you work with XML, experiencing again the parent/child structures, you will find that the .NET platform provides for a pleasurable and productive programming experience. As the mainframe IMS "data store" had its value, XML certainly has its value—and then some. Yes, the two technologies represent data in a *hierarchical model*. That is where the similarity ends. XML *extends* on from there, earning the "X" in its name.

Exploring the Dataset Class

In order to write XML to and read XML from the System.Data.Dataset class, you will first need to drill down into the Dataset class to identify the exposed methods. For that reason, I have executed the Class Viewer (WinCV.exe) tool from the Visual Studio .NET (VS .NET) command prompt and captured the "member" information for the Dataset class. The partial Class Viewer display in Listing 12-1 shows most of the methods exposed by the Dataset class.

Listing 12-1. A Partial Class Viewer Display of the System.Data.Dataset Class

```
//from module
'c:\winnt\assembly\gac\system.data\1.0.3300.0__b77a5c561934e089\system.data.dll'
public class System.Data.DataSet :
. . .
    // Fields
. . .
    // Constructors
. . .
    // Properties
. . .
    // Events
. . .
    // Methods
public void AcceptChanges();
public virtual void BeginInit();
public void Clear();
public virtual System.Data.DataSet Clone();
public System.Data.DataSet Copy();
```

```
            public virtual void Dispose();
            public virtual void EndInit();
            public virtual bool Equals(object obj);
            public System.Data.DataSet GetChanges();
            public System.Data.DataSet GetChanges(System.Data.DataRowState rowStates);
            public virtual int GetHashCode();
            public virtual object GetService(Type service);
            public Type GetType();
            public string GetXml();
            public string GetXmlSchema();
            public bool HasChanges();
            public bool HasChanges(System.Data.DataRowState rowStates);
            public void InferXmlSchema(string fileName, string[] nsArray);
            public void InferXmlSchema(System.Xml.XmlReader reader, string[] nsArray);
            public void InferXmlSchema(System.IO.TextReader reader, string[] nsArray);
            public void InferXmlSchema(System.IO.Stream stream, string[] nsArray);
            . . .
            public System.Data.XmlReadMode ReadXml(string fileName);
            public System.Data.XmlReadMode ReadXml(string fileName, XmlReadMode mode);
            public System.Data.XmlReadMode ReadXml(System.IO.TextReader reader);
            public System.Data.XmlReadMode ReadXml(System.Xml.XmlReader reader);
            public System.Data.XmlReadMode ReadXml(System.Xml.XmlReader reader, XmlReadMode)
            public System.Data.XmlReadMode ReadXml(System.IO.TextReader reader, XmlReadMode)
            public System.Data.XmlReadMode ReadXml(System.IO.Stream stream);
            public System.Data.XmlReadMode ReadXml(System.IO.Stream stream, XmlReadMode mode);
            public void ReadXmlSchema(string fileName);
            public void ReadXmlSchema(System.IO.TextReader reader);
            public void ReadXmlSchema(System.Xml.XmlReader reader);
            public void ReadXmlSchema(System.IO.Stream stream);
            public virtual void RejectChanges();
            public virtual void Reset();
            public virtual string ToString();
            public void WriteXml(string fileName);
            public void WriteXml(string fileName, System.Data.XmlWriteMode mode);
            public void WriteXml(System.IO.Stream stream);
            public void WriteXml(System.IO.Stream stream, System.Data.XmlWriteMode mode);
            public void WriteXml(System.IO.TextWriter writer);
            public void WriteXml(System.Xml.XmlWriter writer);
            public void WriteXml(System.IO.TextWriter writer, System.Data.XmlWriteMode mode);
            public void WriteXml(System.Xml.XmlWriter writer, System.Data.XmlWriteMode mode);
            public void WriteXmlSchema(string fileName);
            public void WriteXmlSchema(System.IO.Stream stream);
            public void WriteXmlSchema(System.Xml.XmlWriter writer);
            public void WriteXmlSchema(System.IO.TextWriter writer);
```

```
} // end of System.Data.DataSet
```

Looking at the Class Viewer display in Listing 12-1, you can decipher from the method names alone that the vast majority of the Dataset methods are provided for XML support. From the available methods, you will focus on the following three XML-related Dataset methods:

- *System.Data.Dataset.ReadXML*

- *System.Data.Dataset.GetXML*

- *System.Data.Dataset.WriteXML*

Using the ReadXML, GetXML, and WriteXML Methods

For basic XML/Dataset reading and writing, you will be using the ReadXML, GetXML, and WriteXML Dataset methods. You will find that they are extremely simple to use. Basically, you can use the ReadXML method to load an XML file (a file typically ending with the .xml suffix) into a Dataset. The GetXML method and the WriteXML method are similar. They both support the extraction of Dataset contents in XML format. However, the GetXML method outputs to a String variable, whereas the WriteXML method expects to output to a disk-based XML file.

TIP Both the ReadXML and WriteXML methods support an XML format called *DiffGram*. Generally speaking, the DiffGram XML format is used by the .NET Framework when it needs to serialize the contents of a Dataset. The ReadXML and WriteXML methods have overloaded constructors that allow a parameter to be passed in to indicate the Read or Write mode. The *System.Data.XmlReadMode* and *System.Data.XmlWriteMode* enumerations are used for this purpose. The value of DiffGram is listed among other enumerated Read and Write mode values.

The following sample projects (both in COBOL .NET and Visual Basic .NET [VB .NET]) demonstrate the simplicity of writing XML to and reading XML from the .NET Dataset. In the samples, you will see the necessary ADO.NET coding to connect to the Northwind database and query the Customers table. Before you continue, consider launching one of the SQL Server client tools. Take this opportunity to review the structure and contents of the Northwind database and the Customers table (see Figure 12-1).

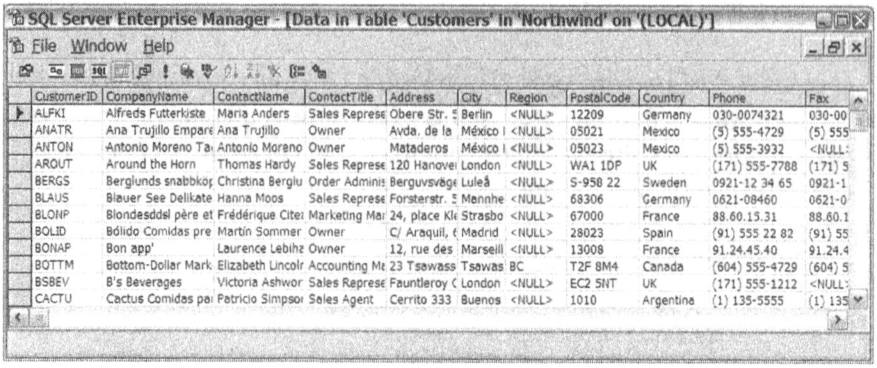

Figure 12-1. A subset of the Northwind.Customers table beginning with the ALFKI CustomerID and ending with the CACTU CustomerID

Each of the sample projects displays XML to the console window and creates an XML file. If you were to capture the XML displayed to the console[1] or actually open the saved XML file, you would see formatted XML as shown in Listing 12-2. (Notice that I have included only a snippet of the actual XML beginning with the ALFKI CustomerID and ending with the CACTU CustomerID.)

Listing 12-2. Formatted XML

```
<?xml version="1.0" standalone="yes"?>
<NewDataSet>
  <myCustomers>
    <CustomerID>ALFKI</CustomerID>
    <CompanyName>Alfreds Futterkiste</CompanyName>
    <ContactName>Maria Anders</ContactName>
    <ContactTitle>Sales Representative</ContactTitle>
    <Address>Obere Str. 57</Address>
    <City>Berlin</City>
    <PostalCode>12209</PostalCode>
    <Country>Germany</Country>
    <Phone>030-0074321</Phone>
    <Fax>030-0076545</Fax>
  </myCustomers>
  <myCustomers>
    <CustomerID>ANATR</CustomerID>
```

---

1. You may find it necessary to increase the value of the console window's Screen Buffer Size Height setting (select Properties ➤ Layout tab) to capture the extended output stream produced by these sample projects. I typically increase the console window's Screen Buffer Size Height setting from its low default setting (300) up to a much higher value (9999).

```
    <CompanyName>Ana Trujillo Emparedados y helados</CompanyName>
    <ContactName>Ana Trujillo</ContactName>
    <ContactTitle>Owner</ContactTitle>
    <Address>Avda. de la Constitución 2222</Address>
    <City>México D.F.</City>
    <PostalCode>05021</PostalCode>
    <Country>Mexico</Country>
    <Phone>(5) 555-4729</Phone>
    <Fax>(5) 555-3745</Fax>
  </myCustomers>
  <myCustomers>
    <CustomerID>ANTON</CustomerID>
    <CompanyName>Antonio Moreno Taquería</CompanyName>
    <ContactName>Antonio Moreno</ContactName>
    <ContactTitle>Owner</ContactTitle>
    <Address>Mataderos  2312</Address>
    <City>México D.F.</City>
    <PostalCode>05023</PostalCode>
    <Country>Mexico</Country>
    <Phone>(5) 555-3932</Phone>
  </myCustomers>
  <myCustomers>
    <CustomerID>AROUT</CustomerID>
    <CompanyName>Around the Horn</CompanyName>
    <ContactName>Thomas Hardy</ContactName>
    <ContactTitle>Sales Representative</ContactTitle>
    <Address>120 Hanover Sq.</Address>
    <City>London</City>
    <PostalCode>WA1 1DP</PostalCode>
    <Country>UK</Country>
    <Phone>(171) 555-7788</Phone>
    <Fax>(171) 555-6750</Fax>
  </myCustomers>
  <myCustomers>
    <CustomerID>BERGS</CustomerID>
    <CompanyName>Berglunds snabbköp</CompanyName>
    <ContactName>Christina Berglund</ContactName>
    <ContactTitle>Order Administrator</ContactTitle>
    <Address>Berguvsvägen  8</Address>
    <City>Luleå</City>
    <PostalCode>S-958 22</PostalCode>
    <Country>Sweden</Country>
    <Phone>0921-12 34 65</Phone>
    <Fax>0921-12 34 67</Fax>
```

```
      </myCustomers>
      <myCustomers>
        <CustomerID>BLAUS</CustomerID>
        <CompanyName>Blauer See Delikatessen</CompanyName>
        <ContactName>Hanna Moos</ContactName>
        <ContactTitle>Sales Representative</ContactTitle>
        <Address>Forsterstr. 57</Address>
        <City>Mannheim</City>
        <PostalCode>68306</PostalCode>
        <Country>Germany</Country>
        <Phone>0621-08460</Phone>
        <Fax>0621-08924</Fax>
      </myCustomers>
      <myCustomers>
        <CustomerID>BLONP</CustomerID>
        <CompanyName>Blondesddsl père et fils</CompanyName>
        <ContactName>Frédérique Citeaux</ContactName>
        <ContactTitle>Marketing Manager</ContactTitle>
        <Address>24, place Kléber</Address>
        <City>Strasbourg</City>
        <PostalCode>67000</PostalCode>
        <Country>France</Country>
        <Phone>88.60.15.31</Phone>
        <Fax>88.60.15.32</Fax>
      </myCustomers>
      <myCustomers>
        <CustomerID>BOLID</CustomerID>
        <CompanyName>Bólido Comidas preparadas</CompanyName>
        <ContactName>Martín Sommer</ContactName>
        <ContactTitle>Owner</ContactTitle>
        <Address>C/ Araquil, 67</Address>
        <City>Madrid</City>
        <PostalCode>28023</PostalCode>
        <Country>Spain</Country>
        <Phone>(91) 555 22 82</Phone>
        <Fax>(91) 555 91 99</Fax>
      </myCustomers>
      <myCustomers>
        <CustomerID>BONAP</CustomerID>
        <CompanyName>Bon app'</CompanyName>
        <ContactName>Laurence Lebihan</ContactName>
        <ContactTitle>Owner</ContactTitle>
        <Address>12, rue des Bouchers</Address>
        <City>Marseille</City>
```

```
      <PostalCode>13008</PostalCode>
      <Country>France</Country>
      <Phone>91.24.45.40</Phone>
      <Fax>91.24.45.41</Fax>
  </myCustomers>
  <myCustomers>
      <CustomerID>BOTTM</CustomerID>
      <CompanyName>Bottom-Dollar Markets</CompanyName>
      <ContactName>Elizabeth Lincoln</ContactName>
      <ContactTitle>Accounting Manager</ContactTitle>
      <Address>23 Tsawassen Blvd.</Address>
      <City>Tsawassen</City>
      <Region>BC</Region>
      <PostalCode>T2F 8M4</PostalCode>
      <Country>Canada</Country>
      <Phone>(604) 555-4729</Phone>
      <Fax>(604) 555-3745</Fax>
  </myCustomers>
  <myCustomers>
      <CustomerID>BSBEV</CustomerID>
      <CompanyName>B's Beverages</CompanyName>
      <ContactName>Victoria Ashworth</ContactName>
      <ContactTitle>Sales Representative</ContactTitle>
      <Address>Fauntleroy Circus</Address>
      <City>London</City>
      <PostalCode>EC2 5NT</PostalCode>
      <Country>UK</Country>
      <Phone>(171) 555-1212</Phone>
  </myCustomers>
  <myCustomers>
      <CustomerID>CACTU</CustomerID>
      <CompanyName>Cactus Comidas para llevar</CompanyName>
      <ContactName>Patricio Simpson</ContactName>
      <ContactTitle>Sales Agent</ContactTitle>
      <Address>Cerrito 333</Address>
      <City>Buenos Aires</City>
      <PostalCode>1010</PostalCode>
      <Country>Argentina</Country>
      <Phone>(1) 135-5555</Phone>
      <Fax>(1) 135-4892</Fax>
  </myCustomers>
  . . .
</NewDataSet>
```

In the sample code projects, I decided to first load the result set (relational, data) into a Dataset and then write out the XML to a disk file named myCustomers.xml. The newly created XML file is then read into a second *disconnected* Dataset. The contents of that second Dataset are then displayed to the console window in XML format.

TIP When you choose to manually build your DataColumn using the System.Data.DataColumn namespace, you can use the System.Data.SqlTypes namespace to help set the DataType property. Mapping the native data types within SQL Server to the data types in your program can sometimes be tricky. Using the SqlTypes objects for type mapping will help prevent loss of data precision and integrity.

COBOL .NET Sample Code

The sample code in Listing 12-3 is part of the ReadWriteXMLDatasetExample-Cobol project (a console project type). Please review the code. As usual, I have included many useful comments in the code. Feel free to experiment, change the code, and explore the flexibility of these ADO.NET Dataset methods (recall the various *overloaded* forms of the methods shown earlier in the section "Exploring the Dataset Class"). As demonstrated in this sample, working with XML can be rather simple. The WriteXML, ReadXML, and GetXML methods of the Dataset class are used.

NOTE The COBOL .NET project type requires that you manually add a reference to the ADO.NET assembly (System.Data.Dll). The steps for adding an assembly reference in VS .NET were introduced earlier (see the section "VS .NET Feature: The Object Browser" in Chapter 7).

Listing 12-3. A COBOL .NET Sample Project Demonstrating the Use of the ADO.NET Dataset

```
000010* Sample Code demonstrating ADO.NET's support for XML Technology
000020 IDENTIFICATION DIVISION.
000030 PROGRAM-ID. MAIN.
000040 ENVIRONMENT DIVISION.
000050 CONFIGURATION SECTION.
```

```
000060 REPOSITORY.
000070* .NET Framework Classes
000080      CLASS SqlConnection  AS "System.Data.SqlClient.SqlConnection"
000090      CLASS SqlDataAdapter As "System.Data.SqlClient.SqlDataAdapter"
000100      CLASS SqlCommand As "System.Data.SqlClient.SqlCommand"
000110      CLASS DataSet    As "System.Data.DataSet"
000120      CLASS DataTable  AS "System.Data.DataTable"
000130      CLASS DataRow    As "System.Data.DataRow"
000140      CLASS DataColumn AS "System.Data.DataColumn"
000150      CLASS SystemType       AS "System.Type"
000160      CLASS DataColumnArray  AS "System.Data.DataColumn[]"
000170
000180      CLASS Sys-Integer    AS "System.Int32"
000190      CLASS Sys-String     AS "System.String"
000200      CLASS Sys-Object     AS "System.Object"
000210
000220* .NET Framework Properties
000230      PROPERTY PROP-ConnectionString AS "ConnectionString"
000240      PROPERTY PROP-Connection       AS "Connection"
000250      PROPERTY PROP-CommandText      AS "CommandText"
000260      PROPERTY PROP-SelectCommand    AS "SelectCommand"
000270      PROPERTY PROP-Columns          AS "Columns"
000280      PROPERTY PROP-Tables           AS "Tables"
000290      PROPERTY PROP-DataType         AS "DataType"
000300      PROPERTY PROP-ColumnName       AS "ColumnName"
000310      PROPERTY PROP-Item             AS "Item"
000320      PROPERTY PROP-PrimaryKey       AS "PrimaryKey"
000330      PROPERTY PROP-Unique           AS "Unique"
000340      PROPERTY PROP-IgnoreSchema     AS "IgnoreSchema"
000350
000360* .NET Framework Enumerations
000370      ENUM     ENUM-XmlWriteMode     AS "System.Data.XmlWriteMode".
000380
000390 DATA DIVISION.
000400 WORKING-STORAGE SECTION.
000410    77 mySqlConnection    OBJECT REFERENCE SqlConnection.
000420    77 mySqlDataAdapter   OBJECT REFERENCE SqlDataAdapter.
000430    77 mySqlCommand       OBJECT REFERENCE SqlCommand.
000440    77 myDataSet1         OBJECT REFERENCE DataSet.
000450    77 myDataSet2         OBJECT REFERENCE DataSet.
000460    77 myDataTable        OBJECT REFERENCE DataTable.
000470    77 myDataColumn       OBJECT REFERENCE DataColumn.
000480    77 myPrimaryKeyColumn  OBJECT REFERENCE DataColumn.
000490    77 myPrimaryKeyColumns OBJECT REFERENCE DataColumnArray.
```

```
000500    77 myENUM-XmlWriteMode OBJECT REFERENCE ENUM-XmlWriteMode.
000510
000520    77 mySys-String   OBJECT REFERENCE Sys-String.
000530    77 mySys-Integer  OBJECT REFERENCE Sys-Integer.
000540    77 mySys-Object   OBJECT REFERENCE Sys-Object.
000550    77 myXmlFile      OBJECT REFERENCE Sys-String.
000560    77 myDisplayString PIC x(38550).
000570    77 myInt          PIC S9(9) COMP-5.
000580    77 myOtherInt     PIC S9(9) COMP-5.
000590    01 NULL-X         PIC X(1).
000600 PROCEDURE DIVISION.
000610
000620    Perform 0000-OptionalPreTableBuild.
000630    Perform 1000-UseSqlDataAdapter.
000640    Perform 2000-ReadWriteXML.
000650    DISPLAY " "
000660
000670    DISPLAY "Enter X and Press Enter to Exit.".
000680    ACCEPT NULL-X.
000690    Stop Run.
000700
000710***********************************************
000720    0000-OptionalPreTableBuild.
000730* It is possible to obtain the "schema" or table structure
000740* directly/automatically from the SQL Server Database
000750* This section is added for training purposes.
000760* The information found in this section would be critical
000770* in the case of building a disconnected .NET dataset
000780* that may have a non-SQL Server Data Source.
000790
000800* Create a new DataTable.
000810    INVOKE DataTable "NEW" USING BY VALUE "myCustomers"
000820        RETURNING myDataTable.
000830
000840* Create 1st myDataColumn.
000850    INVOKE DataColumn "NEW" RETURNING myDataColumn.
000860    SET PROP-DataType OF myDataColumn TO
000870        SystemType::"GetType"("System.String").
000880    SET PROP-ColumnName OF myDataColumn TO "CustomerID".
000890    SET PROP-Unique OF myDataColumn TO B"1".
000900    INVOKE PROP-Columns OF myDataTable "Add"
000910      USING BY VALUE myDataColumn.
000920
000930* Create 2nd myDataColumn.
```

```
000940      INVOKE DataColumn "NEW" RETURNING myDataColumn.
000950      SET PROP-DataType OF myDataColumn TO
000960          SystemType::"GetType"("System.String").
000970      SET PROP-ColumnName OF myDataColumn TO "CompanyName".
000980      INVOKE PROP-Columns OF myDataTable "Add"
000990        USING BY VALUE myDataColumn.
001000
001010* Create 3rd myDataColumn.
001020      INVOKE DataColumn "NEW" RETURNING myDataColumn.
001030      SET PROP-DataType OF myDataColumn TO
001040          SystemType::"GetType"("System.String").
001050      SET PROP-ColumnName OF myDataColumn TO "ContactName".
001060      INVOKE PROP-Columns OF myDataTable "Add"
001070        USING BY VALUE myDataColumn.
001080
001090* Create 4th myDataColumn.
001100      INVOKE DataColumn "NEW" RETURNING myDataColumn.
001110      SET PROP-DataType OF myDataColumn TO
001120          SystemType::"GetType"("System.String").
001130      SET PROP-ColumnName OF myDataColumn TO "ContactTitle".
001140      INVOKE PROP-Columns OF myDataTable "Add"
001150        USING BY VALUE myDataColumn.
001160
001170* Create 5th myDataColumn.
001180      INVOKE DataColumn "NEW" RETURNING myDataColumn.
001190      SET PROP-DataType OF myDataColumn TO
001200          SystemType::"GetType"("System.String").
001210      SET PROP-ColumnName OF myDataColumn TO "Address".
001220      INVOKE PROP-Columns OF myDataTable "Add"
001230        USING BY VALUE myDataColumn.
001240
001250* Create 6th myDataColumn.
001260      INVOKE DataColumn "NEW" RETURNING myDataColumn.
001270      SET PROP-DataType OF myDataColumn TO
001280          SystemType::"GetType"("System.String").
001290      SET PROP-ColumnName OF myDataColumn TO "City".
001300      INVOKE PROP-Columns OF myDataTable "Add"
001310        USING BY VALUE myDataColumn.
001320
001330* Create 7th myDataColumn.
001340      INVOKE DataColumn "NEW" RETURNING myDataColumn.
001350      SET PROP-DataType OF myDataColumn TO
001360          SystemType::"GetType"("System.String").
001370      SET PROP-ColumnName OF myDataColumn TO "Region".
```

```
001380      INVOKE PROP-Columns OF myDataTable "Add"
001390        USING BY VALUE myDataColumn.
001400
001410* Create 8th myDataColumn.
001420      INVOKE DataColumn "NEW" RETURNING myDataColumn.
001430      SET PROP-DataType OF myDataColumn TO
001440          SystemType::"GetType"("System.String").
001450      SET PROP-ColumnName OF myDataColumn TO "PostalCode".
001460      INVOKE PROP-Columns OF myDataTable "Add"
001470        USING BY VALUE myDataColumn.
001480
001490* Create 9th myDataColumn.
001500      INVOKE DataColumn "NEW" RETURNING myDataColumn.
001510      SET PROP-DataType OF myDataColumn TO
001520          SystemType::"GetType"("System.String").
001530      SET PROP-ColumnName OF myDataColumn TO "Country".
001540      INVOKE PROP-Columns OF myDataTable "Add"
001550        USING BY VALUE myDataColumn.
001560
001570* Create 10th myDataColumn.
001580      INVOKE DataColumn "NEW" RETURNING myDataColumn.
001590      SET PROP-DataType OF myDataColumn TO
001600          SystemType::"GetType"("System.String").
001610      SET PROP-ColumnName OF myDataColumn TO "Phone".
001620      INVOKE PROP-Columns OF myDataTable "Add"
001630        USING BY VALUE myDataColumn.
001640
001650* Create 11th myDataColumn.
001660      INVOKE DataColumn "NEW" RETURNING myDataColumn.
001670      SET PROP-DataType OF myDataColumn TO
001680          SystemType::"GetType"("System.String").
001690      SET PROP-ColumnName OF myDataColumn TO "Fax".
001700      INVOKE PROP-Columns OF myDataTable "Add"
001710        USING BY VALUE myDataColumn.
001720
001730* Assign primary key column to "CustomerID" column.
001740      INVOKE DataColumnArray "NEW" USING BY VALUE 1
001750          RETURNING myPrimaryKeyColumns.
001760      INVOKE PROP-Columns OF myDataTable "get_Item"
001770        USING BY VALUE "CustomerID"
001780        RETURNING myPrimaryKeyColumn.
001790      INVOKE myPrimaryKeyColumns "Set"
001800        USING BY VALUE 0 myPrimaryKeyColumn.
001810      SET PROP-PrimaryKey OF myDataTable TO myPrimaryKeyColumns.
```

```
001820
001830* Reference the DataSet.
001840     INVOKE DataSet "NEW" RETURNING myDataSet1.
001850* Associate the Table with the Dataset.
001860     INVOKE PROP-Tables OF myDataSet1 "Add"
001870        USING BY VALUE myDataTable.
001880
001890***********************************************
001900    1000-UseSqlDataAdapter.
001910
001920* Reference Data Provider Objects
001930     INVOKE SqlConnection "NEW"  RETURNING  mySqlConnection
001940     INVOKE SqlDataAdapter "NEW" RETURNING  mySqlDataAdapter
001950     INVOKE SqlCommand "NEW"     RETURNING  mySqlCommand
001960
001970* Prepare to Connect to SQL Server Database
001980* using Connection String
001990     SET PROP-ConnectionString OF mySqlConnection TO
002000     "user id=sa;pwd=;Database=northwind;Server=(LOCAL)"
002010
002020* Associate the Command Object with the Connection Object
002030     SET PROP-Connection OF mySqlCommand TO mySqlConnection
002040* Associate the Command Object with intended SQL Statement
002050     SET PROP-CommandText OF mySqlCommand TO "Select * from Customers"
002060* Associate the DataAdapter Object with the Command Object
002070     SET PROP-SelectCommand OF mySqlDataAdapter TO mySqlCommand
002080
002090* Have the DataAdapter Object Execute the SQL Statement and
002100* store the result set in a DataSet DataTable named myCustomers
002110     INVOKE mySqlDataAdapter "Fill"
002120       USING BY VALUE myDataSet1, "myCustomers"
002130
002140* Close the Database Connection
002150     INVOKE mySqlConnection "Close".
002160
002170     SET mySqlConnection TO NULL.
002180     SET mySqlDataAdapter TO NULL.
002190     SET mySqlCommand TO NULL.
002200     SET myDataTable TO NULL.
002210
002220***********************************************
002230    2000-ReadWriteXML.
002240
002250* The following XML file will be saved on your hard disk.
```

```
002260* You can locate it in the local application BIN folder
002270     SET myXmlFile TO "myCustomers.xml"
002280
002290* Demonstrate the usage of the WriteXML method
002300* Write out an XML file that originated as relational data
002310     SET myENUM-XmlWriteMode
002320        TO PROP-IgnoreSchema OF ENUM-XmlWriteMode
002330     INVOKE myDataSet1 "WriteXml" USING BY VALUE
002340      myXmlFile, myENUM-XmlWriteMode
002350
002360* Demonstrate the usage of the ReadXML method
002370* Load a 2nd Dataset from the saved XML file
002380     INVOKE DataSet "NEW" RETURNING myDataSet2
002390     INVOKE myDataSet2 "ReadXml" USING BY VALUE myXmlFile
002400
002410* Demonstrate the usage of the GetXML method
002420* Extract data from the Dataset in XML format
002430     INVOKE myDataSet2 "GetXml" RETURNING mySys-String
002440     SET myDisplayString TO mySys-String
002450     DISPLAY myDisplayString.
002460
002470 END PROGRAM MAIN.
```

Wow! You have got to admit, using COBOL (in .NET) to easily read and write XML from relational database data is great. Can you just imagine having been able to do something like this in some of the legacy mainframe COBOL applications that you have written in the past?

Of course, you've long been able to code legacy COBOL mainframe applications that extract database data and hold the data in a programmatically defined in-memory table. But when was the last time you output the in-memory table in a format similar to that of XML with such ease (you didn't even need any JCL)? And with so few lines of code? That's what I thought. Learning to leverage ADO.NET's support for XML has "programming productivity" written all over it.

Continuing your bilingual quest, you'll now take a look at the VB .NET sample code.

VB .NET Sample Code

I have included the relevant portion of the ReadWriteXMLDatasetExampleVB project in Listing 12-4. This sample (a console project type) is constructed as such to exercise each targeted Dataset method. In your own application, you may typically use one Dataset method or the other, but perhaps not all of them together.

Please take a moment and read through the following sample program logic and comments.

Listing 12-4. Sample Code from the ReadWriteXMLDatasetExampleVB Project

```vb
'This sample program demonstrates how to Read
'and Write data from/to a ADO.NET Dataset in XML
'format.
Module Module1
    Sub Main()

        Call UseSqlDataAdapter(OptionalPreTableBuild)
        Console.WriteLine(" ")
        Console.ReadLine()
    End Sub
    Public Function OptionalPreTableBuild() As DataSet
        'It is possible to obtain the "schema" or table structure
        'directly/automatically from the SQL Server Database
        'This section is added for training purposes.
        'The information found in this section would be critical
        'in the case of building a disconnected .NET dataset
        'that may have a non-SQL Server Data Source.

        ' Create new DataTable.
        Dim myDataTable As DataTable = _
        New System.Data.DataTable("myCustomers")

        ' Declare DataColumn and DataRow variables.
        Dim myDataColumn As System.Data.DataColumn
        Dim myDataRow As System.Data.DataRow

        ' Create 1st myDataColumn.
        myDataColumn = New System.Data.DataColumn()
        myDataColumn.DataType = Type.GetType("System.String")
        myDataColumn.ColumnName = "CustomerID"
        myDataColumn.Unique = True
        myDataTable.Columns.Add(myDataColumn)

        ' Create 2nd myDataColumn.
        myDataColumn = New System.Data.DataColumn()
        myDataColumn.DataType = Type.GetType("System.String")
        myDataColumn.ColumnName = "CompanyName"
        myDataTable.Columns.Add(myDataColumn)
```

```vb
' Create 3rd myDataColumn.
myDataColumn = New System.Data.DataColumn()
myDataColumn.DataType = Type.GetType("System.String")
myDataColumn.ColumnName = "ContactName"
myDataTable.Columns.Add(myDataColumn)


' Create 4th myDataColumn.
myDataColumn = New System.Data.DataColumn()
myDataColumn.DataType = Type.GetType("System.String")
myDataColumn.ColumnName = "ContactTitle"
myDataTable.Columns.Add(myDataColumn)


' Create 5th myDataColumn.
myDataColumn = New System.Data.DataColumn()
myDataColumn.DataType = Type.GetType("System.String")
myDataColumn.ColumnName = "Address"
myDataTable.Columns.Add(myDataColumn)


' Create 6th myDataColumn.
myDataColumn = New System.Data.DataColumn()
myDataColumn.DataType = Type.GetType("System.String")
myDataColumn.ColumnName = "City"
myDataTable.Columns.Add(myDataColumn)


' Create 7th myDataColumn.
myDataColumn = New System.Data.DataColumn()
myDataColumn.DataType = Type.GetType("System.String")
myDataColumn.ColumnName = "Region"
myDataTable.Columns.Add(myDataColumn)


' Create 8th myDataColumn.
myDataColumn = New System.Data.DataColumn()
myDataColumn.DataType = Type.GetType("System.String")
myDataColumn.ColumnName = "PostalCode"
myDataTable.Columns.Add(myDataColumn)


' Create 9th myDataColumn.
myDataColumn = New System.Data.DataColumn()
myDataColumn.DataType = Type.GetType("System.String")
myDataColumn.ColumnName = "Country"
myDataTable.Columns.Add(myDataColumn)


' Create 10th myDataColumn.
myDataColumn = New System.Data.DataColumn()
```

```
    myDataColumn.DataType = Type.GetType("System.String")
    myDataColumn.ColumnName = "Phone"
    myDataTable.Columns.Add(myDataColumn)

    ' Create 11th myDataColumn.
    myDataColumn = New System.Data.DataColumn()
    myDataColumn.DataType = Type.GetType("System.String")
    myDataColumn.ColumnName = "Fax"
    myDataTable.Columns.Add(myDataColumn)

    ' Assign primary key column to CustomerID column
    Dim PrimaryKeyColumns(0) As System.Data.DataColumn
    PrimaryKeyColumns(0) = myDataTable.Columns("CustomerID")
    myDataTable.PrimaryKey = PrimaryKeyColumns

    ' Reference the DataSet.
    Dim myDataSet As New System.Data.DataSet()
    ' Associate the Table with the Dataset.
    myDataSet.Tables.Add(myDataTable)
    myDataTable = Nothing
    Return myDataSet

End Function

Public Sub UseSqlDataAdapter(ByVal myDataset As DataSet)
    'Reference Data Provider Objects
    Dim mySqlConnection As New System.Data.SqlClient.SqlConnection()
    Dim mySqlDataAdapter As New System.Data.SqlClient.SqlDataAdapter()
    Dim mySqlCommand As New System.Data.SqlClient.SqlCommand()

    'Reference Dataset Objects
    Dim myDataRow As System.Data.DataRow

    'Prepare to Connect to SQL Server Database
    'using Connection String
    mySqlConnection.ConnectionString = _
    "user id=sa;pwd=;Database=northwind;Server=(LOCAL)"

    'Associate the Command Object with the Connection Object
    mySqlCommand.Connection = mySqlConnection
    'Associate the Command Object with intended SQL Statement
    mySqlCommand.CommandText = "Select * from Customers"

    'Associate the DataAdapter Object with the Command Object
```

```
            mySqlDataAdapter.SelectCommand = mySqlCommand
            'Have the DataAdapter Object Execute the SQL Statement and
            'store the result set in a DataSet DataTable named myCustomers
            mySqlDataAdapter.Fill(myDataset, "myCustomers")

            'Close the Database Connection
            mySqlConnection.Close()
            mySqlConnection = Nothing
            mySqlDataAdapter = Nothing
            mySqlCommand = Nothing

            'Pass the Disconnected Dataset to the called method
            Call ReadWriteXML(myDataset)

    End Sub

    Private Sub ReadWriteXML(ByVal ds1 As System.Data.DataSet)

            'The following XML file will be saved on your hard disk.
            'You can locate it in the local application BIN folder
            Dim myXmlFile As String = "myCustomers.xml"

            'Demonstrate the usage of the WriteXML method
            'Write out an XML file that originated as relational data
            ds1.WriteXml(myXmlFile, XmlWriteMode.IgnoreSchema)

            'Demonstrate the usage of the ReadXML method
            'Load a 2nd Dataset from the saved XML file
            Dim ds2 As New System.Data.DataSet()
            ds2.ReadXml(myXmlFile)

            'Demonstrate the usage of the GetXML method
            'Extract data from the Dataset in XML format
            Console.WriteLine(ds2.GetXml())
        End Sub
End Module
```

In the UseSqlDataAdapter method in Listing 12-4, notice how the Dataset is completely disconnected from its original data provider class (DataAdapter). You will see that the second Dataset, created in the *ReadWriteXML* method, is not associated with a data provider at all. The discussed Dataset methods are used in the ReadWriteXML method.

Not bad, huh? Now that you've gotten your feet quite wet using these three Dataset methods (WriteXML, ReadXML, and GetXML), you'll move on to examine the topic of the XML Schema. After all, there will be times when you'll want to work with the "defined structure" of your XML data.

The Dataset and the XML Schema

For a moment, let's take a closer look at the COBOL copybook. Why? Please recall reading earlier (in the section "XML Learning Kick Start" in Chapter 4) that an XML Schema is loosely analogous to the mainframe COBOL copybook. Listing 12-5 should help illustrate this point. Basically, this pseudo-code snippet is an example of what a copybook might look like if you were to create one for the SQL Server Northwind.Customers sample table. A DB2 DCLGEN "copybook" would have been slightly different (e.g., DB2 data types, database constraints listed, and so forth).

Listing 12-5. Pseudo-Code Snippet Showing What a COBOL Copybook Might Look Like for the Northwind.Customers Sample SQL Server Table

```
. . .
000060 05 myCustomer-Detail.
000070     10 CustomerID   PIC X(05).
000080     10 CompanyName  PIC X(40).
000090     10 ContactName  PIC X(30).
000100     10 ContactTitle PIC X(30).
000110     10 FullAddress  PIC X(60).
000120     10 City         PIC X(15).
000130     10 Region       PIC X(15).
000140     10 PostalCode   PIC X(10).
000150     10 Country      PIC X(15).
000160     10 Phone        PIC X(24).
000170     10 Fax          PIC X(24).
000180 05 myCustomers-TABLE REDEFINES  myCustomer-Detail.
000190     10 myCustomers OCCURS 100 TIMES.
000200        15 myCustomers-ITEM       PIC X(268).
. . .
```

Now, please compare the "copybook" example in Listing 12-5 to the XML Schema in Listing 12-6. This XML Schema corresponds to the Northwind.Customers sample SQL Server table.

NOTE I demonstrate how to create the XML Schema momentarily.

Listing 12-6. XML Schema for the Northwind.Customers Sample SQL Server Table

```xml
<?xml version="1.0"?>
<xs:schema id="NewDataSet" targetNamespace="http://tempuri.org/myCustomers.xsd"
xmlns:mstns="http://tempuri.org/myCustomers.xsd"
xmlns="http://tempuri.org/myCustomers.xsd"
xmlns:xs="http://www.w3.org/2001/XMLSchema"
xmlns:msdata="urn:schemas-microsoft-com:xml-msdata"
attributeFormDefault="qualified" elementFormDefault="qualified">
<xs:element name="NewDataSet" msdata:IsDataSet="true"
  msdata:EnforceConstraints="False">
    <xs:complexType>
      <xs:choice maxOccurs="unbounded">
        <xs:element name="myCustomers">
          <xs:complexType>
            <xs:sequence>
              <xs:element name="CustomerID" type="xs:string" minOccurs="0" />
              <xs:element name="CompanyName" type="xs:string" minOccurs="0" />
              <xs:element name="ContactName" type="xs:string" minOccurs="0" />
              <xs:element name="ContactTitle" type="xs:string" minOccurs="0" />
              <xs:element name="Address" type="xs:string" minOccurs="0" />
              <xs:element name="City" type="xs:string" minOccurs="0" />
              <xs:element name="PostalCode" type="xs:string" minOccurs="0" />
              <xs:element name="Country" type="xs:string" minOccurs="0" />
              <xs:element name="Phone" type="xs:string" minOccurs="0" />
              <xs:element name="Fax" type="xs:string" minOccurs="0" />
              <xs:element name="Region" type="xs:string" minOccurs="0" />
            </xs:sequence>
          </xs:complexType>
        </xs:element>
      </xs:choice>
    </xs:complexType>
  </xs:element>
</xs:schema>
```

Now do you see the similarity between the COBOL copybook and an XML Schema? Good. I want to show you a very easy way to create an XML Schema (typically a file ending with an .xsd suffix). One of the easiest ways to manually create an XML Schema (rather than type it out by hand) is to do it from within the VS .NET IDE.

Using one of the sample projects (ReadWriteXMLDatasetExampleVB), you can execute the Show All Files feature from within the Solution Explorer window to expose the targeted XML file: myCustomers.xml (see Figure 12-2).

CROSS-REFERENCE The steps you take to use the Show All Files feature from the Solution Explorer window were first introduced in the section "Using the VS .NET Solution Explorer" in Chapter 6.

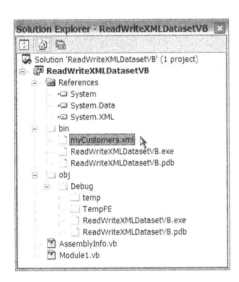

Figure 12-2. The myCustomers.xml file (in the local application bin folder) created earlier in the sample code project ReadWriteXMLDatasetExampleVB

After you select the XML file from the Solution Explorer window, you will be able to view and edit the actual XML from within the VS .NET IDE. You will also notice that there is an XML menu bar option (this only appears when you have the XML file selected). Figure 12-3 shows the option available to create the XML Schema file (using the XML menu bar and selecting XML ➤ Create Schema).

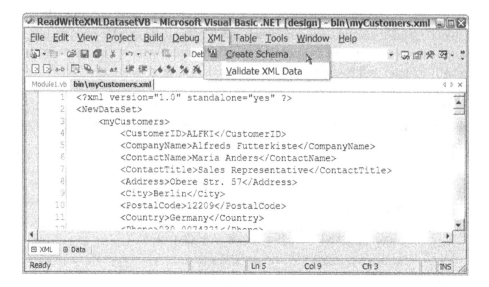

Figure 12-3. The Create Schema feature from within the VS .NET IDE

Using this Create Schema feature, you will create a file that has an .xsd suffix. This is your XML Schema file. As shown in Figure 12-4, the XML Schema file myCustomers.xsd has been created in the same folder location as the actual XML file.

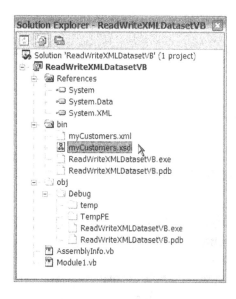

Figure 12-4. The XML Schema file located in the local application bin folder

In comparison, using this VS .NET IDE Create Schema feature is certainly preferable than having to type a schema out by hand (remember all of those copybooks you *manually* created through the years?).

Creating the XML Schema Programmatically

As great as this VS .NET Create Schema feature is, it too is considered a manual approach, albeit a modern one. You can programmatically create an XML schema using the Dataset method *WriteXmlSchema*. Two other Dataset methods provided for "accessing" the XML Schema are *ReadXmlSchema* and *GetXmlSchema*. These three Dataset methods are practically just as simple to use as the three "XML" Dataset methods used to the read/write the actual XML file. Choose the "schema creation" approach that fits your business need. It is good to be aware of your choices.

I trust that the discussion in this section provided you with a better understanding of the XML Schema. When you work with the .NET Dataset and XML, it is inevitable that you will come across the need to also work with the corresponding XML Schema. I would like to point out that other XML Schema–related topics certainly await you (e.g., Schema inference, Schema annotations, and Schema/data validation concerns). As you continue your .NET retraining, you will find the references provided in the "To Learn More" section at the end of this chapter useful.

I have discussed XML and XML Schemas, both from the perspective of the .NET Dataset. At this point, you might have the impression that you will end up using the .NET Dataset for all of your XML needs. After all, the XML support provided in the .NET Dataset is impressive.

Well, as it turns out, that is not case. There are times when you will need *more*. For example, you may have a need for more structural support (strong typing, Schema validation, and so forth) for your XML, or perhaps XML query and transformation support (XPath, XSL, and so forth). These needs will exhaust and exceed the features of the .NET Dataset (when it is used alone). Fortunately, the .NET Framework has a full offering, an entire namespace of managed objects available for your advanced XML needs. Let's now switch gears to review the .NET namespace that will serve your extended XML scenarios.

An XML Namespace: System.Xml

The System.Xml namespace objects are designed to fully support your XML needs. Your needs may range from reading and writing XML to storing XML. In fact, your application's needs may even extend to querying XML or transforming XML. There are many feature-rich System.Xml namespace objects. In this section, I provide an overview of the System.Xml namespace and the objects contained therein.

NOTE   I want to emphasize that this discussion is definitely an *overview*. A full discussion of the System.Xml namespace would likely fill an entire book. All the same, I do feel that this discussion will help shed some light on the topic and help you head in the right direction—toward continued learning.

Choosing an XML Reader or XML Writer

Basically, you could take an *either/or* approach when you choose your System.Xml class for reading. For example, *either* you choose a derived class from the *System.Xml.XmlReader* base class for fast, forward-only, read-only, non-cached type reading. *Or* you can choose the Document Object Model (DOM) class for full-featured XML document reading and manipulation. Generally speaking, the DOM class is *System.Xml.XmlDocument.* Your choice for writing is much simpler. You will want to explore the derived class *System.Xml.XmlTextWriter* for your XML output needs. Figure 12-5 shows the basic hierarchy of the *XmlReader* and *XmlTextWriter* classes.

If your reading/parsing needs point you in the direction of the XmlReader class, you would then hit another decision tree. For example, if you want the fastest reader and are willing to make a sacrifice on the feature side, then the *XmlTextReader* class might be your best bet. On the other hand, if you want to perform data/Schema validation, then the *XmlValidatingReader* class may serve your needs. The *XmlNodeReader* class is used for reading *XmlNodes* (i.e., reading portions of XML documents).

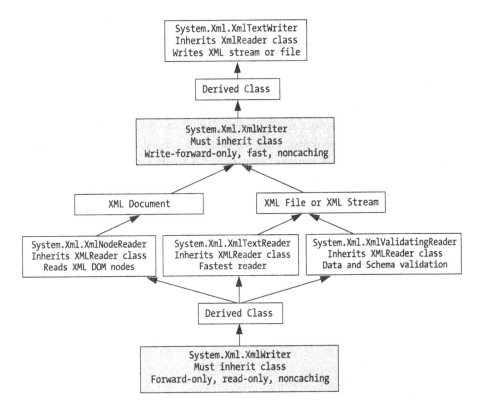

Figure 12-5. A high-level view of the System.Xml.XmlReader and System.Xml.XmlWriter family of classes

TIP Recall that I discussed the System.Data.SqlClient.SqlCommand class in Chapter 11 in the section "The System.Data.SqlClient Namespace." This particular DataProvider object exposes a method named ExecuteXmlReader. The return type of this method is System.Xml.XmlReader.

When you are ready to write XML with the XmlTextWriter class, you will generally aim to write well-formed XML documents. Fortunately, the XmlTextWriter class supports the W3C Recommendation (the Infoset Recommendation) that defines a standard of writing well-formed XML documents. Basically, the W3C Recommendation includes a definition for an XML Information Set (or Infoset). An *Infoset* is made up of any number of *information items* (such as a document, elements, attributes, and so on).

As you explore the System.Xml.XmlTextWriter class, you will encounter a collection of Write*Xxxx* methods (where *Xxxx* corresponds to the name of an Infoset information item). For example, the WriteStart*Document*, WriteStart*Element*, and WriteStart*Attribute* XmlTextWriter methods are used to write the "start" of the following information items: document, element, and attribute, respectively. If you look at the extensive list of Write*Xxxx* methods in this manner, the list may seem less exhaustive.

 CROSS-REFERENCE   You'll find the URL for the XML Information Set (Infoset) Recommendation at the end of this chapter in the "Web Sites" subsection of the "To Learn More" section.

The Document Object Model Class

One of the first things that you will come across as you dive into the Document Object Model (DOM) class (System.Xml.XmlDocument), is the realization that the class itself is derived from the *System.Xml.XmlNode* class (see Figure 12-6). The XmlDocument class simply extends the XmlNode class, providing an enhanced implementation of methods and so forth to read and manipulate the instantiated nodes. The DOM then is basically a hierarchical (parent/child) collection of nodes (or XmlNodes). You will often see a DOM presented in a tree view.

As you see in Figure 12-6, several classes are derived from the XmlNode class. Knowing this, it should be easier for you to understand the discussions, presentations, and white papers that loosely describe the XmlDocument as being "made up of" the *XmlNode*, *XmlElements*, and *XmlAttributes* classes. Either directly or indirectly, they each inherit from the XmlNode class. In your coding, you can establish logical relationships between the "nodes" creating the parent/child tree structure.

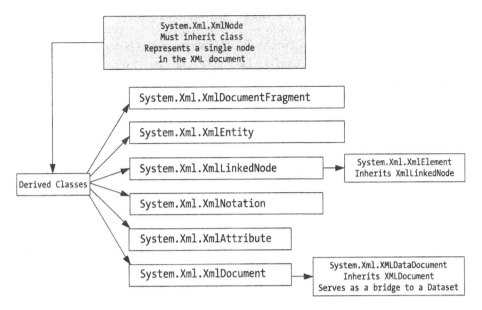

Figure 12-6. The System.Xml.XmlNode class and the classes derived from it

The DOM class, XmlDocument, has the capability to read in XML files, streams, or XmlReader objects (as illustrated in Figure 12-7). Among the many .public methods to learn about, you will want to start with the Load method. Using this method, you will be able to easily load XML data into an XmlDocument object.

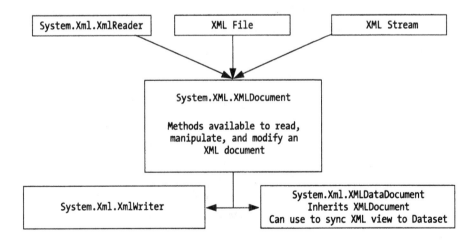

Figure 12-7. A general input and output view of the XmlDocument class

Extending the XmlDocument Class: XmlDataDocument

There is a class named *System.Xml.XmlDataDocument* that is derived from the XmlDocument class. The *XmlDataDocument* class provides yet another way to use the ADO.NET System.Data.Dataset to support your XML needs. The XmlDataDocument (or just *data document*) offers public members that enable a quick "load" of your Dataset into the data document. You can load either relational data or XML data into an XmlDataDocument object.

Once you've done this, you can manipulate the XML "view" of your data using the exposed data document methods. Optionally, you can take advantage of the synchronizing feature. That's right—you can easily *synchronize* your data document (XML view) to your Dataset (relational view). This synchronization allows a flexible handling approach when you need to update using one view or the other (in other words, using one technology/toolset or the other).

In an abbreviated fashion, that concludes this chapter's discussion of the XmlDocument class and its extended XmlDataDocument class. Obviously, many methods, properties, and so forth are exposed through each class, and all deserve further exploration. Please make a point to take on this extended exploration of the XmlDocument class (and the derived XmlDataDocument class). To finish off the chapter, you'll leave the System.Xml namespace to review several other namespaces that .NET offers for XML support.

.NET Replaces MSXML 4.0 (Almost)

Microsoft's XML parser, MSXML 4.0 (now known as *Microsoft XML Core Services* and previously described in Chapter 4 in the section "MSXML"), has historically provided much of the XML Document Object Model (DOM) support described in this section. The .NET XML managed objects largely overlap the functionality exposed in the COM-based MSXML 4.0 library.

Generally, you will want to use the managed objects offered in the various .NET XML namespaces. However, there are occasions when you should use the MSXML 4.0 product (e.g., for backward compatibility with legacy applications, to overcome the current XLST parsing performance issue, and so on). Use the .NET COM Interop feature (adding a COM reference to the Microsoft XML 4.0 MSXML4.dll, and available as free download from Microsoft's Web site) in your .NET applications to take advantage of the MSXML 4.0 library as appropriate.

For more information, please refer to the Microsoft Knowledge Base Article Q317728, which is available on the MSDN Web site.

The Other XML Namespaces

Microsoft is serious about .NET's commitment to XML. This is made obvious by the extent to which XML is used in the .NET architecture and supported through several feature-rich namespaces. In this chapter, you were introduced to the XML support available in the System.Data and System.Xml namespaces.

It may surprise you (or maybe it will not) to know that several more namespaces are dedicated to supporting XML. They each have their purpose: targeting certain XML usage scenarios. You will discover that classes from one XML namespace will often be used together with classes from a different XML namespace. For that reason, you will often "cross" namespaces, leveraging the strengths of XML objects as appropriate. The following list presents a review of these "other" XML namespaces:

System.Xml.Schema: This namespace offers classes, delegates, and enumerations used to support your XML Schema Definition (XSD) language and XML-Data Reduced (XDR) Schema needs. It strongly supports the W3C Recommendations for XML Schemas for structures and XML Schemas for data types. The classes in this namespace service the Schema Object Model (SOM). You can use the *System.Xml.Schema.XmlSchemaCollection* class through the *Schemas* property of the *System.Xml.XmlValidatingReader* class.

System.Xml.XPath: This namespace offers support for the XPath parser (query support) via several classes, interfaces, and enumerations. Two commonly used classes from this namespace are *XPathDocument* (fast, read-only cache, optimized for XSLT) and *XPathNavigator* (read-only, random access, cursor model).

System.Xml.Xsl: This namespace provides full support for the Extensible Stylesheet Transformation (XSLT) technology.[2] Although several classes and interfaces are offered in this namespace, you will likely use the *XslTransform* class most often.

---

2. Microsoft has announced (through the Microsoft Knowledge Base Article Q317691) that the COM-based Microsoft XML Core Services (MSXML 4.0) library actually offers a preferred XSLT parser. Until this is corrected through forthcoming .NET improvements, you can use the MSXML 4.0 parser/engine in your .NET applications through the COM Interop feature.

Microsoft.Data.SqlXml: This namespace represents the XML for SQL Server (SQLXML) set of managed objects. The current version of SQLXML, 3.0 SP1, is available as a free download (see the "Web Sites" subsection of the "To Learn More" section at the end of this chapter for the URL). The SQLXML offering (also known as *Web Release*) is essentially a series of "service packs" for SQL Server 2000. Its three managed classes, *SqlXmlCommand, SqlXmlParameter,* and *SqlXmlAdapter,* enable more direct XML support (XPath, XQuery, XML Templates, XML Bulk Load, and so forth) to Microsoft's SQL Server database product. Using the FOR XML clause in your SQL Server SQL queries is considered to be an "XML for SQL Server" enhancement.

System.Xml.Serialization: This namespace offers classes and delegates to assist with object serialization. Among the many managed classes offered, you will use the *XmlSerializer* class the most. Using the XmlSerializer class, you can serialize and deserialize instantiated objects to and from XML documents or streams. Object serialization is a useful technique for persisting (or saving) the state of an object so that you can later re-create an exact copy of the object. Object serialization is also useful when you want to pass the object (marshal by value) during .NET Remoting scenarios. (I further discuss .NET Remoting in Chapter 20.)

The preceding list of namespaces is provided to give you a more complete picture of the XML support available through the .NET Framework and platform. Combining this information with that of the System.Xml namespace, you are certainly off to an *informed* start. The "To Learn More" section at the end of this chapter provides additional references for your extended retraining experience.

Summary

This chapter's goals were as follows:

- To learn to leverage the .NET Dataset's support for XML

- To explore the System.Xml namespace

- To review the .NET namespaces for overall XML support

In this chapter, you saw how integrated XML is in the .NET Framework. I showed this integration by discussing and demonstrating the ADO.NET Dataset's support for XML. From there, I discussed several .NET namespaces (including System.Xml) that provide XML support. As this chapter's discussion was, in some cases, high level and in summary fashion, you will want to take advantage of the references provided in the "To Learn More" section at the end of this chapter. The material provided in this chapter should certainly assist you in getting started with and preparing for your continued learning.

The next chapter introduces the topic of user interfaces. I will discuss Windows and Web (or ASP.NET)–type applications. For this reason, (going forward) I will discontinue the regular use of the Console Application template for the sample code projects. As appropriate, most of the sample code in the future chapters will use the Windows Application, ASP.NET Web Application, or ASP.NET Web Service Project template. Undoubtedly, you will welcome this switch.

To Learn More

The following are some suggested supplemental references to further your retraining effort.

Magazines

.NET Magazine:
> http://www.fawcette.com/dotnetmag/

MSDN Magazine, "A Quick Guide to XML Schema, Part 1":
> http://msdn.microsoft.com/msdnmag/issues/02/04/xml/xml0204.asp

MSDN Magazine, "A Quick Guide to XML Schema, Part 2":
> http://msdn.microsoft.com/msdnmag/issues/02/07/XMLFiles/default.asp

MSDN Magazine, article index for the "XML Files" series of articles:
> http://msdn.microsoft.com/msdnmag/find/
> default.aspx?type=Ti&phrase=XML%20Files:

MSDN Magazine, "Run-time Serialization":
> http://msdn.microsoft.com/msdnmag/issues/02/04/net/net0204.asp

Visual Studio Magazine:
> http://www.fawcette.com/vsm/

XML & Web Services Magazine:
> http://www.fawcette.com/xmlmag/

Web Sites

Microsoft Community (discussion groups, e-newsletters, and so forth):
> http://communities2.microsoft.com/

MSDN:
> http://msdn.microsoft.com

Roadmap for XML in the .NET Framework:
> http://support.microsoft.com/default.aspx?scid=kb;[LN];Q313651

Roadmap for XML Serialization in the .NET Framework:

`http://support.microsoft.com/default.aspx?scid=kb;[LN];Q314150`

SQLXML and XML Mapping Technologies (includes a link to the free SQLXML 3.0 SP1 download):

`http://msdn.microsoft.com/sqlxml`

A Survey of Microsoft SQL Server 2000 XML Features:

`http://msdn.microsoft.com/library/en-us/dnexxml/html/xml07162001.asp`

Visual Studio .NET's XML Designer:

`http://msdn.microsoft.com/library/en-us/vsintro7/html/`
`vburfXMLSchemaDesigner.asp`

W3C Extensible Markup Language (XML):

`http://www.w3.org/XML/`

XML Core:

`http://www.msdn.microsoft.com/xml`

XML Information Set (Infoset) Recommendation:

`http://www.w3.org/TR/xml-infoset/`

XML Schema Part 0: Primer (includes links to Part 1: Structures and Part 2: Datatypes):

`http://www.w3.org/TR/xmlschema-0/`

XML Tutorial:

`http://msdn.microsoft.com/library/en-us/xmlsdk30/htm/xmtutxmltutorial.asp`

Part Four
Interfacing and
Interacting with the User

"Multiple types of screwdrivers, a few styles of hammers, and various sizes of wrenches may find their way into a well-equipped toolbox. Keep this in mind while retooling your skill set, your professional toolbox for .NET."

—*Chris Richardson*

Windows Forms, Web Forms, and No Forms

An Introduction to Windows, ASP.NET, and Web Services Development

---

In this chapter

- Discussing user interface design considerations

- Exploring Windows application and Windows Service development

- Understanding ASP.NET and XML Web services technology

THE LEGACY **COBOL** mainframe development arena has typically held that online application development is more prestigious and preferable than batch/offline programming. As a result, you have probably had the displeasure of working with a few mainframe *professionals*[1] who were known for making these types of comments:

> *"You want me to work on a batch program? You can't be serious. No, thank you. I'm now a CICS programmer! I don't do batch. I haven't 'done' batch in years and don't care to return to do any either. You'll have to get someone else, maybe one of the junior developers, to do it."*

Most will agree that this type of attitude is always unhelpful (to put it nicely), especially when the time comes to just "get the job done." Nonetheless, it does help highlight the fact that developing online applications has traditionally introduced the need for a *different* skill set, one that is typically found among more experienced developers. The resulting expectation for application *performance* and *stability* differs as well, in that it becomes more demanding.

---

1. I am using the term "professionals" rather loosely.

NOTE Granted, a delayed evening batch run can delay the CICS region from coming up the next morning. End users are never happy when that happens. Still, there is usually a buffer, a window of time during nonbusiness hours, to correct any problems experienced during batch processing. This usually shields end users from being impacted by any problems experienced during the batch process.

Online application development presents a greater potential for immediate and noticeable impact to end users. Being a successful mainframe online developer, you have learned to be sensitive to this. You have learned over time the need to design your online application's interface with the goal of providing a pleasurable and exciting user experience. On the mainframe, your experience taught you that online development brings you much closer to your end users. You will find that .NET Windows and Web development shares (and possibly exceeds) this level of intimacy with end users.

In this chapter, you will dive into the portion of .NET Windows and Web development that surrounds the user interface. I will first present to you some user interface design considerations. From there, you will tackle the .NET Windows application and Windows Service technologies. An exploration of the Active Server Pages .NET (ASP.NET) Web application and Web service toolset will follow. Throughout the chapter, where appropriate, I compare some of the .NET user interface concepts to their equivalents found in the mainframe CICS and ISPF technologies.

CAUTION I described Chapters 3 and 4 as .NET retraining prerequisite chapters. I strongly suggest that you view Chapters 5 through 12 as prerequisite chapters as well. In other words, you should read and understand the content in the chapters that precede this chapter before you take on this chapter (or any chapter following this one). The earlier chapters (Chapters 5 through 12) provide a foundational understanding of the Visual Studio .NET (VS .NET) IDE, the .NET common language runtime (CLR), the .NET Framework, and how to work with SQL Server databases and XML. Each of these "foundational" topics will be used now, as you proceed forward in this chapter (and beyond) learning to build .NET Windows and ASP.NET applications.

Developing with the User in Mind

The other day, a coworker of mine expressed extreme aggravation at the fact that one of his favorite Web sites had just begun to use pop-up boxes as a form of advertising delivery. This coworker mentioned that he would immediately discontinue visiting this particular Web site—just like that. My initial thought was that his reaction amounted to an isolated, almost knee-jerk reaction. As it turns out, I was wrong.

Later that same day, I read a news report on ZDNet.com (`http://zdnet.com.com/2100-1106-947732.html`) that discussed the extent to which this kind of pop-up advertisement proliferation has become a common frustration among Web surfers. It turns out that some people are resorting to installing software that effectively "blocks" the pop-up boxes from appearing. Others are reacting the same way that my coworker reacted, taking to a zero-tolerance approach and simply surfing to other, friendlier sites. My guess is that this "backlash" was not the Web advertiser's intended result. So what went wrong?

NOTE Pop-up ads are dying the same death of their predecessor, the scrolling banner ad. In spite of all the glittery animation, color, and attention-grabbing design, people have simply learned to ignore the majority of the banner-type ads used on Web sites.

Being User-Friendly Is Still Important

Somewhere along the way between designing a product for the end user and delivering the product, the emphasis on user-friendliness has (in some cases) been lost. As the reactions to these (excessively) popular pop-up ads have proven, user-friendliness *does* matter. Although it may be difficult for everyone to agree on exactly what being user-friendly means, I will venture to state that ultimately "friendly" in application design has something to do with the following:

- The needs of the user should be met.

- The blatant, in-your-face approach should be used conservatively.

- The application should show sensitivity to the expectations of the user.

- The user should not be inconvenienced or confused by the application.

- The application should show respect for the user's time.

- The application's information should be logically organized—not cluttered.

Sounds rather simple, right? Do you recall how some of these user-friendly design considerations were implemented when you built legacy[2] mainframe CICS applications? Certainly, you incorporated some if not all of the following considerations in your legacy CICS development:

- You placed the basic mapping support (BMS) map and Transaction-ID in the upper left and right corners of your 3270-screen layout.

- You made it obvious through your BMS map coding which fields were provided for input versus which fields were designed for output/read-only.

- You included a read-only field near the bottom of the screen for informational messages.

- You included a display near the bottom regarding any attention key assignments.

- You attempted to consistently use common attention keys (e.g., F3 for Exit, F12 for Cancel, and so forth).

Among my mainframe brothers and sisters are some who may have been following these legacy CICS screen conventions without even realizing the full impact of or reason for the conventions. Some may have not even realized that there is an actual standard promoted by IBM called Common User Access (CUA)[3] that goes into great detail in an attempt to promote the consistent creation of user-friendly interfaces. (Now you know why practically all CICS screens use an "underline" to identify input fields.) The CUA strived to promote consistency with CICS 3270 screens.

When discussing the topic of user-friendly interfaces for Windows and Web applications, "usability" seems to be the new buzzword. So, let's now explore what usability might look like when developing Windows and Web applications.

---

2. I am using the term "legacy" to acknowledge that some of the more recent/modern CICS development has moved toward actual GUIs. Because the traditional 3270 text-based designs continue to prevail, it is applicable to refer to the "legacy" CICS design for contrast/comparison.

3. The Common User Access (CUA) standard generally spoke to three user interface models: the Entry Model, the Text Subset of the Graphical Model, and the Graphical Model.

Defining Usability for Windows and Web Interfaces

Users have some common expectations when they use a Windows application. Likewise, a Web application has certain common traits that users expect to find. Basically, the more common a particular characteristic becomes and the more users start to expect it, the more appropriate it is that you consider its inclusion in your own interface design.

TIP This design decision does not speak to nor contradict the situations where creativity and uniqueness are useful and desired.

For example, users have long gotten used to having the ability to minimize, maximize, and resize their window (the "window" being used as a container for your application). Similarly, users now expect to find a vertical or horizontal scroll bar wherever one might be useful. More recently, with the popularity of e-commerce sites, the symbol of a shopping cart has even become common. This means that if you are designing an e-commerce site, you would be wise to consider the inclusion of the shopping cart symbol. Usability is an evolving, living standard.

NOTE The general Windows and Web user community constantly redefines the "standard" for Windows and Web interfaces. Rather than having a *tangible* static standard for Windows and Web interfaces, the standard is loosely defined by what is popular. Interface characteristics that are effective and convenient tend to survive and remain popular. The standard rapidly evolves as quickly and constantly as modern graphical technology itself evolves.

Usability includes basic characteristics, and yet extends beyond them. Usability speaks to the responsiveness of the application and the ease (or lack thereof) in moving from one screen to the next, or tabbing from one entry field to the next, or even navigating around the infamous pop-up windows. All of these types of actions fall under the umbrella of usability. Among the many facets of usability, the following are also included when you are developing Windows and Web interfaces:

- Using an appropriate choice of color, text font size, and text font style

- Being sensitive to any cross-browser compatibility concerns

- Using the available "screen real estate" appropriately, and finding the right ratio of "white space" to "information"

- Presenting content in an informative, purposeful, and uncluttered fashion

- Deciding whether or not to use frames

- Giving consideration to bandwidth if you are including multimedia in your Windows and Web user interface

- Deciding whether or not to include a Search field

- Identifying your target audience correctly and deciding if your interface requires any localization features

- Choosing whether or not to include a site map as a feature

- Being sensitive to accessibility concerns as mandated by the Americans with Disabilities Act

- Creating an interface that is artistically pleasant and creative yet appropriate for your business needs

- Applying security policies as appropriate

- Treating latency as a priority

The preceding list of concerns may appear to be rather exhaustive. However, it is important for you to know that it is only a partial list. That is right. When you are designing Windows and Web applications, usability is much more than just adding a button and a text box onto a form. Building professional-looking and effective Windows and Web applications is an art. In fact, there are people who have filled this "design" niche. They are commonly referred to as graphic artists (or Web designers).

NOTE The ASP.NET technology has shown a complementary approach to a development team that includes the role of the graphic artist. There is a strong move in the direction of physically separating presentation components from business logic components. This facilitates the scenario of a programmer being able to work on a component that directly serves the business logic while not disturbing the graphic artist who may concurrently be working on the presentation-oriented components.

As budgets allow, a properly staffed Windows or Web project will make sure that the skill set of a graphic artist is represented. Unfortunately, this point is often overlooked as typical software engineers, developers, and programmers embark on the creation of their first Windows or Web application, only to later discover that the internal components—the actual business logic—is impressive and superbly implemented, but the aesthetic and usability aspects of the user interface are lacking.

When the application is rolled out, it will not matter how magnificent the internal logic actually is. The end user will not care how many .NET managed objects you took advantage of in order to add the newest bells and whistles to the application. If the end user has a negative perception of your application's degree of usability, your application may be headed down the same road of doom as the scrolling banner ad and the pop-up ad.

NOTE I hope that I have made the point sufficiently clear that the role of the graphic artist and the topic of usability are critical in creating "good" Windows and Web applications. Several resources appear in the "To Learn More" section at the end of this chapter to assist your continued learning in this area. In the meantime, find out who the graphic artists are in your organization. Generally, we developers tend to underappreciate graphic artists and the work they do, often forgetting that they are helping to make our applications more usable.

It has been rumored that some developers will see a simple "Hello, World" Windows or Web application demonstrated and figure that all Windows and Web interfaces can have the same degree of usability. Therein lies the value of the discussion presented in this chapter. In the following sections, when I present to you a "Hello, World" type of Windows or Web demonstration, you will be reminded of the difference between a demonstration application and a real-world application (that exemplifies usability).

In case the "Hello, World" samples do not satisfy your appetite for "seeing code" at this time, please remember that Fujitsu and Microsoft provide additional samples. These samples came bundled with the .NET products that you installed on your hard disk. Both vendors have provided plenty of Windows- and Web-related examples. You can find the Fujitsu and Microsoft samples at the following hard drive locations: <drive>:\Program Files\Fujitsu NetCOBOL for .NET\Examples and <drive>:\Program Files\Microsoft Visual Studio .NET\FrameworkSDK\Samples, respectively. Please remember to also take advantage of the references located at the end of this chapter in the "To Learn More" section.

Let's now turn to the construction of Windows and Web interfaces. I begin by covering the .NET Windows technology. Later, I discuss the mechanics of the ASP.NET technology.

Pseudonyms and Aliases

From time to time, you will hear terms used interchangeably with the VS .NET template names of Windows Applications, Windows Services, ASP.NET Web Applications, and ASP.NET Web Services. Several of these alternative names follow:

- *Windows Applications:* Win Forms, client/server apps, desktop apps, and fat/thick client

- *Windows Services:* A new NT Service, A new Terminate and Stay Resident (TSR), long-running apps, and unattended apps

- *ASP.NET Web Applications:* Web Forms and thin client

- *ASP.NET Web Services:* XML Web services and one that I made up: "No Forms" Web app

---

Windows Development on .NET

When you are learning how to develop Windows applications, the following question is bound to come up: Is a Windows application still a viable user interface? Often, there are those who will quickly refer to the Web browser–style interface (HTML, ASP.NET, and so forth) as the *only* choice. The fact is that with .NET, both types of graphical user interfaces (GUIs) are available choices.

Depending on your business needs, there are times when a Web browser front-end will be a better choice than the Windows front-end. Yet, in other cases, a Windows application may be the appropriate user interface choice. Although you have many factors to weigh to properly choose between the two, here are just a few to get you started:

- Choose a Windows application–based interface if you need to offload the processing overhead from a centralized server to several distributed client workstations.

- Choose a Web browser–based interface if distributing a Windows application presents unwanted challenges. Even though .NET has improved the deployment of Windows applications, there is still the deployment of the .NET Framework to consider.

- Choose a Windows application–based interface if you need to leverage .NET's GDI+ graphics classes to create a graphically rich user interface.

Again, these are just a few of the possible considerations. Other considerations exist. You may have security, design, or cross-platform issues that make one choice better than another. You'll want to evaluate your business need thoroughly. The point that I want to emphasize here is that .NET does provide you with a choice between the two types of GUIs: Windows application or Web application. Having stated that point, I'll proceed with this chapter's Windows application exploration.

Leave Your Attitude at the Door, Please

If you were to take a selected veteran Web developer and ask him or her to create a Windows application, you potentially could run into the CICS versus batch type of attitude that you sometimes find among CICS veteran developers (mentioned in this chapter's introduction). Some Web developers look upon Windows development as if it is "beneath" them.

As stated earlier for those *few* CICS developers, the same applies to the *few* Web developers who may have a "negative attitude" when it comes to this topic. Having a development preference, or even a development expertise, is one thing. In some cases, a strong preference or expertise can plant the seeds for what grows into a "negative attitude." This sort of attitude is generally not helpful.

If you are not careful, a strong preference for or against a particular development tool could be blinding. In such cases, developers run the risk of letting their personal preferences cloud their judgment when they need to provide the best technical solution for a business problem.

Exploring Windows Applications

If you have ever used Microsoft Word, Microsoft Notepad, or even the Microsoft Calculator, you have used a Windows application. As you learn about .NET Windows development, you will quickly realize that it is similar to mainframe CICS development. For example, when you look at the Windows Form (also called a *Win Form*), you may compare it with a CICS BMS map. When you see the Windows Toolbox controls, such as the TextBox and Label controls, you will likely be reminded of the CICS BMS assembler macros (i.e., DFHMSD, DFHMDI, and DFHMDF).

As you explore the properties of the various Windows controls, you will be reminded of the various parameters available on the BMS macros (i.e., POS, LENGTH, ATTRB, COLOR, and INITIAL). Even when you come across the Windows Forms feature called multiple-document interface (MDI), you can loosely compare the Windows concept/feature with the practice of combining multiple CICS BMS maps to make a BMS mapset.

For those CICS mainframe developers who have been fortunate enough to have a screen painting software tool available to create mainframe CICS screens, Windows development will feel (and almost look) extremely familiar. Soon, you will be creating your own .NET Windows application. Let's now take a quick look at a simple "Hello, World" Windows application. Afterward, you will explore the technology involved in creating a Windows application.

VB .NET Does "Hello, World" in Windows

Starting with an open VS .NET IDE window, navigate to the New Project window.[4] You will notice that in Figure 13-1, I selected the Visual Basic Projects folder from the Project Types box. You will also notice that I selected Windows Application as my Templates choice. I entered **MyFirstWinFormVB** as the name of this first Windows application sample.

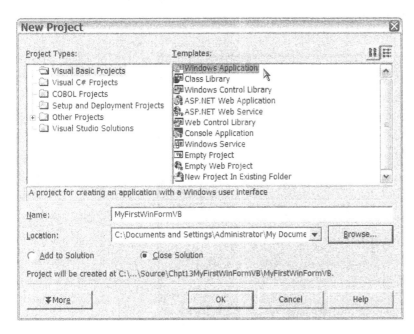

Figure 13-1. Preparing to create a new Windows application using the appropriate template

Once you have created the new project, an empty Windows Form will be displayed. For this example, you will simply add two controls onto the Windows Form: a Button control and a TextBox control. You can accomplish this by opening the Toolbox window and dragging the appropriate controls from the Toolbox window over to the Windows Form and dropping them. (Optionally, you can select

---

4. Please refer to the section "The IDE of Today and Tomorrow: VS .NET" in Chapter 5 to review the steps taken when navigating to the VS .NET New Project dialog window.

the controls and "draw" them onto the Windows Form using your left mouse button.) You can then add code as desired.

Here's a review of the steps you need to perform to add the controls to the Windows Form:

1. Open the Toolbox window by pressing the key combination Ctrl-Alt-X. (There are several other ways to open the Toolbox window.)

2. As shown in Figure 13-2, you can select the targeted control (Button, TextBox, or another control). Once you have selected a control, you can drag and drop the control onto the Windows Form, draw the selected control onto the Windows Form, or just click the Windows Form surface while the targeted control remains selected.

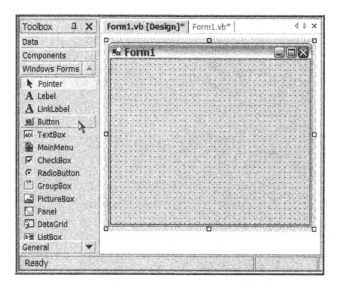

Figure 13-2. Selecting the Button control in the Toolbox

3. Choose the Code view for the Button control's Click event. To do so, you can double-click the Button control or access View Code from the Solution Explorer window. Then add the following simple line of logic: `TextBox1.Text = "Hello, World :-)"` inside of the Button control's Click event procedure. When your code entry is complete, it should look similar to the following code snippet:

```
. . .
        Private Sub Button1_Click _
        (ByVal sender As System.Object, ByVal e As System.EventArgs) _
        Handles Button1.Click
              TextBox1.Text = "Hello, World :-) "
        End Sub
. . .
```

4. Now, build and run the sample application. As you might have guessed, when you click the Button control, the text box will display the "Hello, World" message. Figure 13-3 shows the sample application running after the Button control has been clicked.

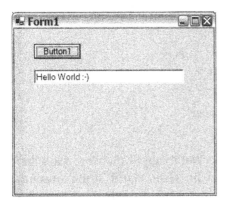

Figure 13-3. MyFirstWinFormVB executing after Button1 has been clicked

Great! Congratulations, you've created your first Windows application. It's simple, but it's a Windows application all the same. Let's turn now to the world of COBOL .NET and build another Windows application.

COBOL .NET Does "Hello, World" in Windows

Start by navigating to the VS .NET IDE New Project window. Choose COBOL Projects from the Project Types window, choose Windows Application from the Templates window, and enter **MyFirstWinFormCobol** as the name for this new project. Then click OK. At this point, you should be viewing an empty Windows Form.

After you follow the same steps that you performed in the previous section to move the controls from the Toolbox to the Windows Form, you have completed the required user interface design steps (see Figure 13-4).

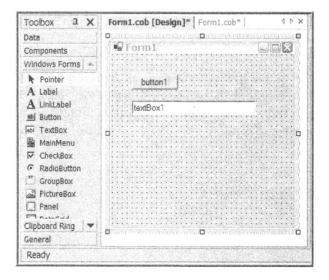

Figure 13-4. MyFirstWinFormCobol in Design view

The only other requirement for your "Hello, World" application is to add a line of code to set the Text property of the TextBox to the "Hello, World" string constant. You do this in the button1_Click method. This way, when you click the button, the TextBox content area will display the desired value. Your code in the button1_Click method should look similar to Listing 13-1.

Listing 13-1. Code Snippet from MyFirstWinFormCobol Showing the Setting of the TextBox1 Text Property

```
. . .
008630 METHOD-ID. button1_Click PRIVATE.
008640 DATA DIVISION.
008650 LINKAGE SECTION.
008660 01 sender OBJECT REFERENCE CLASS-OBJECT.
008670 01 e OBJECT REFERENCE CLASS-EVENTARGS.
008680 PROCEDURE DIVISION USING BY VALUE sender e.
008690    SET PROP-TEXT OF textBox1 TO "Hello, World".
008700 END METHOD button1_Click.
. . .
```

The only thing left to do is compile and run the sample application. Creating a Windows application is rather simple, right? Don't worry, you'll have plenty of time for building more complex, real-world applications. Although the "Hello, World" applications are extremely simple, they should help you understand how Windows applications function. In the next section, you'll dive deeper in search of a more complete understanding of the Windows application.

Introducing the System.Windows.Forms Namespace

To really understand how to build Windows applications, you need to be familiar with the *System.Windows.Forms* namespace. In order to do this, you might assume that you will start with the *Form* class. It is the Form class, after all, from which the Windows Form is instantiated. Actually, a proper exploration of the System.Windows.Forms namespace should begin with the *Control* class (as in *System.Windows.Forms.Control*). The reason for this will soon become clear.

The Form class, along with the majority of the other System.Windows.Forms namespace classes, derives from the System.Windows.Forms.Control class. The general hierarchy of the Control class is shown in Listing 13-2. You can see that the classes derived from the System.Windows.Forms.Control class are all classes that represent a "visual" type of element. See if you can locate the actual Form class.

Listing 13-2. A Partial List of the Classes Deriving Directly and Indirectly from the System.Windows.Forms.Control Base Class

```
System.Windows.Forms.Control
            System.ComponentModel.Design.ByteViewer
            System.Windows.Forms.AxHost
            System.Windows.Forms.ButtonBase
                        System.Windows.Forms.Button
                        System.Windows.Forms.CheckBox
                        System.Windows.Forms.RadioButton
            System.Windows.Forms.DataGrid
            System.Windows.Forms.DateTimePicker
            System.Windows.Forms.GroupBox
            System.Windows.Forms.Label
                        System.Windows.Forms.LinkLabel
            System.Windows.Forms.ListControl
                        System.Windows.Forms.ComboBox
                        System.Windows.Forms.ListBox
                                    System.Windows.Forms.CheckedListBox
            System.Windows.Forms.ListView
            System.Windows.Forms.MonthCalendar
```

```
System.Windows.Forms.PictureBox
System.Windows.Forms.PrintPreviewControl
System.Windows.Forms.ProgressBar
System.Windows.Forms.ScrollableControl
        System.Windows.Forms.ContainerControl
                System.Windows.Forms.Form
                System.Windows.Forms.PropertyGrid
                System.Windows.Forms.UpDownBase
                System.Windows.Forms.UserControl
        System.Windows.Forms.Design.ComponentTray
        System.Windows.Forms.Panel
                System.Windows.Forms.Design.ComponentEditorPage
                System.Windows.Forms.TabPage
System.Windows.Forms.ScrollBar
        System.Windows.Forms.HScrollBar
        System.Windows.Forms.VScrollBar
System.Windows.Forms.Splitter
System.Windows.Forms.StatusBar
System.Windows.Forms.TabControl
System.Windows.Forms.TextBoxBase
        System.Windows.Forms.RichTextBox
        System.Windows.Forms.TextBox
                System.Windows.Forms.DataGridTextBox
System.Windows.Forms.ToolBar
System.Windows.Forms.TrackBar
System.Windows.Forms.TreeView
```

Were you able to find the Form class? It's located underneath the class
that it directly inherits from, *System.Windows.Forms.ContainerControl*. The
ContainerControl class is located underneath its base class,
System.Windows.Forms.ScrollableControl. So, what does this tell you about the
Form class? For one thing, a Form is basically a special type of control; it's a container control that is also scrollable. You can deduce this from a casual observation
of the hierarchy of classes from which the Form class is eventually derived. There's
more to the Form class, though—let's now drill down further.

The Windows Forms Designer

You understand that a Windows Form is just a class from the System. Windows.Forms namespace. Perhaps you can appreciate that the Windows Form, as seen in the VS .NET IDE, is really just the visual representation (courtesy of the Windows Forms Designer) of the Form class.

This means that you could (conceivably) create an entire Windows application using just a simple text editor (outside of the VS .NET IDE) and a command-line compiler. The Form class, along with its members, is exposed and programmable, much like any other .NET Framework class. Now, why anyone would ever dream of doing this is beyond me.

The rapid application development (RAD) experience offered by drag-and-drop development should not be underestimated. Learn to fully leverage the Windows Forms Designer. By the way, if your needs are aimed in the direction of extending the Windows Forms Designer, you may wish to explore the *System.Windows.Forms.Design* namespace.

A Closer Look at the Form Class

As you create Windows applications, adding controls and business logic to the Windows Form(s), you will quickly realize that the Form class is packed with many *members* (i.e., properties, events, and methods). I suggest that you browse them, familiarize yourself with them, and experiment with them.

Taking on the daunting task of attempting to memorize the extensive list of members may be impractical. A more reasonable approach is to just familiarize yourself with the implied "groupings" of members that exist. From the VS .NET IDE browser window, I have captured a few groups of the Form class (and Control class) members. Please review the groupings of members shown in Figures 13-5 through 13-8.

Figure 13-5 shows a partial list (subset) of methods from the Form class. Notice that they each begin with the prefix "On". This group of methods is used to raise events. The targeted events may be of the Form class or the Control class.

```
OnActivated(System.EventArgs)
OnClosed(System.EventArgs)
OnClosing(System.ComponentModel.CancelEventArgs)
OnCreateControl()
OnDeactivate(System.EventArgs)
OnFontChanged(System.EventArgs)
OnHandleCreated(System.EventArgs)
OnHandleDestroyed(System.EventArgs)
OnInputLanguageChanged(System.Windows.Forms.InputLanguageChangedEventArgs)
OnInputLanguageChanging(System.Windows.Forms.InputLanguageChangingEventArgs)
OnLoad(System.EventArgs)
OnMaximizedBoundsChanged(System.EventArgs)
OnMaximumSizeChanged(System.EventArgs)
OnMdiChildActivate(System.EventArgs)
OnMenuComplete(System.EventArgs)
OnMenuStart(System.EventArgs)
OnMinimumSizeChanged(System.EventArgs)
OnPaint(System.Windows.Forms.PaintEventArgs)
OnResize(System.EventArgs)
OnStyleChanged(System.EventArgs)
OnTextChanged(System.EventArgs)
OnVisibleChanged(System.EventArgs)
```

Figure 13-5. Partial list (subset) of methods from the Form class

Figure 13-6 shows the events of the Form class. These events are raised by their respective Form methods.

```
Activated(Object, System.EventArgs)
Closed(Object, System.EventArgs)
Closing(Object, System.ComponentModel.CancelEventArgs)
Deactivate(Object, System.EventArgs)
InputLanguageChanged(Object, System.Windows.Forms.InputLanguageChangedEventArgs)
InputLanguageChanging(Object, System.Windows.Forms.InputLanguageChangingEventArgs)
Load(Object, System.EventArgs)
MaximizedBoundsChanged(Object, System.EventArgs)
MaximumSizeChanged(Object, System.EventArgs)
MdiChildActivate(Object, System.EventArgs)
MenuComplete(Object, System.EventArgs)
MenuStart(Object, System.EventArgs)
MinimumSizeChanged(Object, System.EventArgs)
```

Figure 13-6. The events of the Form class

Figure 13-7 shows a partial list of methods from the Control class. (Recall that the Form class is derived from the ContainerControl/Control lineage.) Each method shown here can be used to raise a mouse-related event.

```
OnMouseDown(System.Windows.Forms.MouseEventArgs)
OnMouseEnter(System.EventArgs)
OnMouseHover(System.EventArgs)
OnMouseLeave(System.EventArgs)
OnMouseMove(System.Windows.Forms.MouseEventArgs)
OnMouseUp(System.Windows.Forms.MouseEventArgs)
OnMouseWheel(System.Windows.Forms.MouseEventArgs)
```

Figure 13-7. Partial list of methods from the Control class

Figure 13-8 shows a partial list of events from the Control class. (Recall that the Form class is derived from the ContainerControl/Control lineage.) These are mouse-related events.

```
MouseDown(Object, System.Windows.Forms.MouseEventArgs)
MouseEnter(Object, System.EventArgs)
MouseHover(Object, System.EventArgs)
MouseLeave(Object, System.EventArgs)
MouseMove(Object, System.Windows.Forms.MouseEventArgs)
MouseUp(Object, System.Windows.Forms.MouseEventArgs)
MouseWheel(Object, System.Windows.Forms.MouseEventArgs)
```

Figure 13-8. Partial list of events from the Control class

From the preceding series of figures, you can easily see patterns that exist in the names of the Form class (and Control class) members. As you browse the list members, you will see other event and method groupings not shown here. Additionally, the Form (and Control) class offers an impressive list of properties (a group in and of itself). You will not want to forget about those.

NOTE Because all of the "visual" control classes in the System.Windows.Forms namespace are derivatives of the Control class, you will notice that a large number of the Control members (properties, methods, and events) are either inherited or overridden in the downstream derived classes. So, once you learn the most common members in one Control class derivative, you will have transferable knowledge that will carry across other classes that are also derived from the Control class.

In the "Hello, World" sample applications (MyFirstWinFormCobol and MyFirstWinFormVB) created earlier, you will recall placing a simple line of program code in the *Click* method associated with the Button control. As you code more Windows applications, you will become much more familiar with the Click method of other controls as well.

NOTE   The behavior experienced by the Form after a control is "clicked" (or any other method or event occurs) is much like the mainframe CICS application's behavior after an attention key is pressed. In your legacy mainframe CICS application you would add code at the top of your program to interrogate the CICS communication area field (Execute Interface Block Attention Identifier, or EIBAID) to detect the specific attention key that was pressed. In Windows programming, the specific event or method associated with the control or component is fired as appropriate.

So now you have a general idea of what a Windows Form is. A discussion of the Control class helped to introduce this .NET Framework class. Although this section covered the majority of the System.Windows.Forms namespace, there are a few more classes that at least deserve mention. The following section will address that need.

Revisiting the System.Windows.Forms Namespace

The Control class (discussed in the previous section) happens to be derived from the base class *System.ComponentModel.Component*. Let's now review several other classes from the System.Windows.Forms namespace that also derive from the *Component* class.

NOTE   This Component class is rather special. It serves the purpose of enabling object sharing between applications. You will learn more about the System.ComponentModel.Component class in Chapter 20.

Please take a moment to view the code snippet in Listing 13-3. I have indented several of the lines to show the implied hierarchy caused by inheritance. This represents a partial listing of System.ComponentModel.Component's derived classes.

Specifically, these are the ones that are housed in the System.Windows.Forms namespace.

Listing 13-3. A Partial Listing of System.ComponentModel.Component's Derived Classes

```
System.Windows.Forms.ColumnHeader
System.Windows.Forms.CommonDialog
            System.Windows.Forms.ColorDialog
            System.Windows.Forms.FileDialog
                        System.Windows.Forms.OpenFileDialog
                        System.Windows.Forms.SaveFileDialog
          System.Windows.Forms.FontDialog
          System.Windows.Forms.PageSetupDialog
          System.Windows.Forms.PrintDialog
System.Windows.Forms.Control
            (hierarchy presented earlier)
System.Windows.Forms.DataGridColumnStyle
            System.Windows.Forms.DataGridBoolColumn
            System.Windows.Forms.DataGridTextBoxColumn
System.Windows.Forms.DataGridTableStyle
System.Windows.Forms.ErrorProvider
System.Windows.Forms.HelpProvider
System.Windows.Forms.ImageList
System.Windows.Forms.Menu
            System.Windows.Forms.ContextMenu
            System.Windows.Forms.MainMenu
            System.Windows.Forms.MenuItem
System.Windows.Forms.NotifyIcon
System.Windows.Forms.StatusBarPanel
System.Windows.Forms.Timer
System.Windows.Forms.ToolBarButton
System.Windows.Forms.ToolTip
```

Of the classes shown in Listing 13-3, you might consider becoming familiar with the following three classes first:

- *System.Windows.Forms.CommonDialog*

- *System.Windows.Forms.Menu*

- *System.Windows.Forms.Timer*

For now, I will provide a brief, high-level summary of the CommonDialog, Menu, and Timer classes. When time allows, you will want to drill down further into each of these classes.

System.Windows.Forms.CommonDialog

If you have used "Windows" for any length of time, you have come across instances when you needed to perform tasks such as opening and saving files, manipulating the font or text color, or perhaps printing documents. In these cases, a dialog box was available for you to interact with. By using the System.Windows.Forms.CommonDialog class, you will be able to provide this same type of dialog box through your own Windows application.

System.Windows.Forms.Menu

To perform common tasks using any typical Windows application, you have certainly used the menu bar. This feature is usually located at the very top the "window." You will want to leverage the functionality of the System.Windows.Forms.Menu class to add menus to your own Windows application. Perhaps you could extend the "Hello, World" applications (MyFirstWinFormCobol and MyFirstWinFormVB) created earlier. Consider adding a menu to each sample application.

System.Windows.Forms.Timer

The System.Windows.Forms.Timer class is very useful when you want to create a "timed loop" inside your code. I suggest you spend some time experimenting with this extremely useful class. When you have a need to simulate your application "sleeping" and "waking," the Timer class may be a good choice for your application. The Timer class has property settings to allow flexible interval settings.

 TIP Remember, there are lots of existing sample applications provided by Fujitsu and Microsoft (the samples are included with the .NET products provided by each software vendor). You can find Fujitsu and Microsoft's samples at the follow hard drive locations: <drive>:\Program Files\Fujitsu NetCOBOL for .NET\Examples and <drive>:\Program Files\Microsoft Visual Studio .NET\ FrameworkSDK\Samples, respectively. Additionally, you can use the references provided in the "To Learn More" section at the end of this chapter to view other sample applications and tutorials.

Up to this point, I have covered the major portions of the System.Windows.Forms namespace. Still, I have not discussed or mentioned the handful of delegates, enumerations, and structures found in the System.Windows.Forms namespace. As your needs dictate, you will want to seek them out and review their use. The better acquainted you become with the entire System.Windows.Forms namespace, the more productive you will be as you develop Windows applications.

Let's now turn briefly to a different type of application: Windows Services. You'll want to be aware of this type of programming model, which is currently available in the Visual Basic Projects Templates group.

NOTE The fact that a .NET application runs on the Windows operating system[5] is certainly reason enough to label it as a "Windows application." Nevertheless, for simplicity, I will make the distinction between .NET Windows applications (those that have a form-type GUI) and .NET Windows Services (briefly discussed in the next section, "Exploring Windows Services"). The console application (used in the previous chapter's sample applications) is another example of a Windows application. However, this chapter's discussion excludes further mention of the console application to allow more focus on the *other* types of Windows applications.

Exploring Windows Services

The name of this particular type of application, Windows Service, is likely to cause confusion to those who are relatively new to the Windows development world. Let's start by first considering the following points:

- The Windows Service type of application was formerly called an *NT Service* (pre-.NET and pre–Windows 2000). During the pre-Windows/DOS era, these types of programs were commonly called *Terminate and Stay Resident* (TSR) programs.

---

5. Discussing the possibilities of Microsoft's .NET Framework or perhaps some other .NET creation running on non-Windows operating systems (e.g., Linux, Macintosh, and so forth) is beyond the scope of this book. Additionally, discussing the "Windows applications" that will be built using the .NET Compact Framework and Smart Device Extensions targeting the Windows CE .NET operating system (e.g., Pocket PCs, tablet PCs, and other so-called smart devices) is also beyond this book's intended scope.

- The expected design of a Windows Service does *not* include a GUI. In other words, a Windows Service does not have a Windows (Windows Form) front-end.

- A Windows Service does not make use of the System.Windows.Forms namespace as Windows applications do.

- The Windows Service type of application gets its name from the fact that the programs are typically providing a *service* and they happen to run on the *Windows* operating system.

To shed more light on what a Windows Service is, let's look at services in general first. In Chapter 11, you may recall starting the SQL Server service. Guess what? This SQL Server service is . . . well, it's an example of a *service*. As it turns out, many services run on Windows. As shown in Figure 13-9, you can use the Computer Management console (with the Services tree view node expanded) to view the installed Windows Services.

NOTE   Generally speaking, services that you create with VS .NET will be called *Windows Services*. Services that run on Windows that were not created with VS .NET are just *services* (that run on Windows). Over time, I expect that this distinction will disappear.

A Windows Service will likely remind you of some of the legacy mainframe subsystems that have existed for years. For example, on the mainframe you had the Job Entry System (JES2 or JES3) subsystem running on the system in the background. In the list of other mainframe subsystems, you might include the following:

- The security subsystem (i.e., Resource Access Control Facility [RACF], Access Control Facility [ACF2], and so forth)

- The Time Sharing Option (TSO) subsystem

- The communications device management (i.e., Virtual Telecommunications Access Method [VTAM]) subsystem

- The transaction processing (i.e., CICS) subsystem

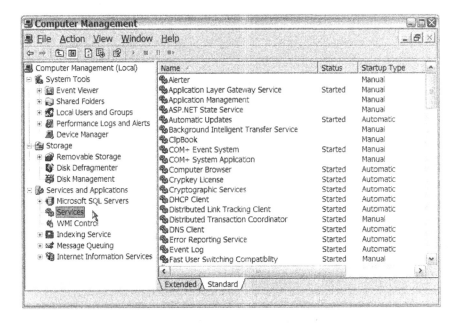

Figure 13-9. The Computer Management console with the Services tree view node expanded

Does reflecting on the legacy mainframe help put this Windows Service into perspective? Is everything clear as mud now? Do you wish that Microsoft had named the Windows Service "A Service That Runs on Windows"? Be that as it may, a Windows Service is simply a program that runs on the system in an unattended mode. Most important, with VS .NET, you can create your own Windows Service.

VS .NET Supports Windows Service

As of the writing of this book, the NetCOBOL for .NET product does not include a VS .NET project template for Windows Services. This is not a problem for you, right? You have been working toward the goal of being bilingual anyway, working with both the COBOL .NET and Visual Basic .NET (VB .NET) samples. Good for you! Technically speaking, you actually have two choices: You can choose to use the VB .NET Windows Services template, or you can choose the COBOL .NET empty template and code Windows Services without the help of a project template. You decide.

As shown in Figure 13-10, the Windows Services template is an available choice in the Visual Basic Projects Templates group.

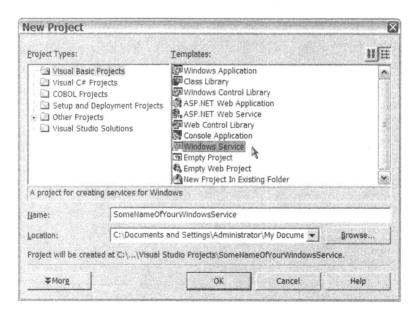

Figure 13-10. Using the VB .NET Windows Services project template to create a new Windows Service

Your continued learning about Windows Services will have you learning how to create a Windows Service and how to install your Windows Service (to have it show up in the Computer Management console). There are basically two .NET Framework classes that you will use: *System.ServiceProcess.ServiceBase* and *System.Configuration.Install.Installer.* As you can tell from the class names, you will be working with two namespaces: *System.ServiceProcess* and *System.Configuration.Install.*

Being able to easily create Windows Services with VB .NET is considered by many to be a great .NET feature. Try it out—you will likely agree that this is definitely another advantage in using .NET for Windows/Web development. Naturally, there are details that you will want to include during your research and experimentation. I refer you to the references located at the end of this chapter in the "To Learn More" section for further information on creating and installing Windows Services.

That concludes your brief (well, sort of brief) introduction to Windows Services. I trust that having this Windows Services topic immediately following the Windows applications topics (discussed in section "Windows Development on .NET") helped clear up any confusion regarding the difference between the two "Windows" technologies.

In the following section, you'll explore other types of user interfaces—specifically, those available when you develop with the ASP.NET technology.

ASP.NET Web Development

For some, the main motivation in learning to program with the .NET Framework and the .NET toolset is to create Web applications. Given the popularity and usefulness of Web-based applications, this motivation is certainly understandable.

In support of this interest, you will find in this section an introduction to the Web development technology offered through the .NET platform: Active Server Pages .NET (ASP.NET). I discuss the two portions of ASP.NET: ASP.NET Web applications and ASP.NET Web services.

CROSS-REFERENCE   In Chapter 3, I introduced the topics of HTTP, URLs, and IIS. I presented these topics as prerequisites. In this chapter, I occasionally refer to these topics and related terminology. Additionally, I introduced the topics of HTML and client-side scripting in Chapter 4. At this point, a basic understanding of both HTML and client-side scripting is assumed as you explore the ASP.NET technology in this chapter. I encourage you to revisit these earlier chapters (and the references included in the "To Learn More" sections of these respective chapters) if you need a refresher.

Understanding the ASP.NET Web Application Technology

You may have seen a .NET "Hello, World" Web application presentation before. That experience might have left you with the impression that to create a Web application, all you need to do is drag a control from the VS .NET IDE Toolbox into the ASP.NET Web Application project template—a complete Web site, just like that!

NOTE   In case you haven't seen a "Hello, World" Web application presented, don't worry. I'm going to show you one shortly.

It is true that there is a minimal amount of training needed to *begin* coding ASP.NET applications. However, I suggest that there is a big difference between *beginning* and *continuing*. In other words, continuing to become a successful ASP.NET Web developer will require that you *really* understand the ASP.NET technology. In this section, my goal is to provide you with a sound understanding of ASP.NET.

This sound understanding will serve you well as a foundation. You will be well positioned to *become* a successful ASP.NET developer. Fortunately for you, ASP.NET development has greatly surpassed its .NET predecessor, Active Server Pages (ASP), by being much more "developer-friendly." As you will discover, ASP.NET is a very feature-rich portion of .NET technology. So buckle up, this will be an exciting ride as you learn about ASP.NET.

System Level: Comparing CICS with ASP.NET

Let's take quick, side-by-side look at a few characteristics of the mainframe's CICS and the Windows operating system's IIS[6] as they relate to application development. As you know, CICS is a full-featured, system-level software package that sits on top of the mainframe operating system. With ASP.NET development, on the other hand, you have IIS. Although IIS is also a full-featured, system-level software package, it happens to sit on top of the Windows operating system.

NOTE Vendors other than Microsoft are creating Internet server software packages. Some of these "alternate" Internet servers are more common on other operating systems. For example, it is rather common to have an Apache Internet software package running on the Linux operating system. This chapter—and this book for that matter—takes a Microsoft-centric view toward Windows and Web application development. Nevertheless, just be aware that although Microsoft has good market share, there continues to be competition, which is usually a good thing.

CICS is host to a collection of system-level services (or software packages). Specifically, those services are CICS management, data management, data communication, and application programming interface. Together, these services support the CICS business applications. In other words, your application programs (presentation logic and business logic) interface with CICS through these provided services.

IIS also works with system-level software to support your business applications. Of course, the common language runtime (CLR) and the .NET Framework are there providing support for your *managed* applications. IIS relies on additional software such as the HTTP server, the Internet Server Application Programming Interface (ISAPI) software, and ASP.NET.

---

6. Feel free to revisit Chapter 3 for more information. IIS was originally introduced there.

TIP Because all HTTP requests come through the ISAPI layer (Aspnet_isapi.dll), you can code ISAPI filters to intercept, monitor, and/or modify the HTTP Web. Prior to .NET, ISAPI development (also called *ISAPI extensions*) was mainly limited to C/C++ developers. However, today the .NET Framework provides objects that can be used with any .NET-enabled language to develop routines that are analogous to ISAPI extensions. You will find these .NET Framework objects in the *System.Web* namespace as the *IHttpHandler* and *IHttpModule* interfaces. ISAPI development has long been considered advanced-level development. Please refer to the references in the "To Learn More" section at the end of this chapter for more information.

Let's examine a few more system-level comparisons. For example, you've always understood that your mainframe CICS business application required a general installation exercise. You're familiar with defining a CICS transaction, associating the transaction with your application program, and installing both the transaction and the program into the special CICS program control table (PCT) and processing program table (PPT).

Your ASP.NET Web applications also involve installation and deployment concerns. With ASP.NET, you will find yourself working with the IIS virtual directories, IIS Web site/applications folders, and in some cases, COM+ and/or the .NET Global Assembly Cache (GAC). Once your application is deployed, your ASP.NET end users will associate a URL with your Web site.

CROSS-REFERENCE I further discuss the topic of deployment (and IIS virtual directories) in Chapter 17.

During runtime, all of your CICS end users would interact with this *single* CICS transaction associated with your application. Each time this CICS transaction was initiated, your actual application program was executed. With each execution of your program, there existed the potential for a new CICS task to be created and associated with the end user. The task continued to exist on a per-user basis. In your mainframe COBOL program, you had several CICS commands to choose from that provided limited programmatic access to the transaction, task, and user.

When it is time to run your Web application, your end users will use a URL to interact (by exchanging HTTP requests and responses) with the *single* instance of your application. Each time a new user (or a user visiting again who has closed and reopened his or her browser) begins to use your application, a new session is established. A session then exists that is associated with each user. The .NET Framework provides system-level intrinsic objects that enable programmatic access to the *Application, Session,* and *User* (also to the *Server, Request,* and *Response*) intrinsic objects.

CROSS-REFERENCE   I further discuss the Application, Session, User, Server, Request, and Response .NET intrinsic objects in the section ".NET Framework Support for ASP.NET Web Applications" later in this chapter.

There are many other details on both sides of the fence (CICS and ASP.NET). I trust that I have covered enough of the basic system-level comparisons to help you feel comfortable with your new side of the fence: ASP.NET. The next section covers a few of the application-level CICS-to-ASP.NET comparisons.

Application Level: Comparing CICS with ASP.NET

I have certainly gotten the point across already that mainframe CICS application development is closely analogous to Windows and Web programming. Nevertheless, to catapult you forward into your understanding of ASP.NET, I will again refer back to those familiar legacy CICS techniques and concepts. Specifically, I will reflect on the following legacy mainframe CICS topics:

- Pseudo-conversational design

- The EIBCALEN field and the communication area length

- The EIBAID field and attention keys

- DFHCOMMAREA usage in the Linkage Section

The CICS Pseudo-Conversational Design

Probably one of the first topics you learned in mainframe CICS development was the concept of your application design moving to a *pseudo-conversational* model. This model emphasized the importance of a user interacting with your interface as if he or she were having a conversation—yet in a *disconnected* way. Thus, your

CICS transaction was removed from memory, saving resources after the completion of each program execution.

In other words, your application interface was to begin execution *each* time the user pressed an attention key (e.g., the Enter key, F1, F2, and so forth). Your application was to figure out which attention key was pressed, determine if any of the editable fields had changed, capture any data entry data, leverage the CICS DFHCOMMAREA (and possibly even CICS temporary storage [TS] queues) to retrieve and store data between executions, return a CICS screen to the end user, and actually *end* execution.

The CICS EIBCALEN Field

With the pseudo-conversational model, a CICS program would perform this execution cycle, sort of a round-trip, each time. Because each execution cycle would start with the program executing as if it was the first time executing, you added program logic to check the length of the Execute Interface Block (EIB) communications area (using the EIBCALEN field) and determine if this *was* in fact the first execution of the program.

The CICS EIBAID Field

When detecting that this was not the *first* execution (that an ongoing *pseudo-conversation* was in progress), you might have further interrogated the EIBAID field to determine which attention key had been pressed and executed any appropriate logic. In effect, this "appropriate logic" could be said to have been "tied" to the particular attention key. Meanwhile, you may have also added logic to examine each editable field's attribute byte (specifically, bit 7) to see if the Modified Data Tag (MDT) value had changed or not.

Obviously, this is a simplified high-level breakdown of the CICS application execution cycle. Nevertheless, I've gone into enough depth to be able to bring to your attention several very strong similarities. Let's turn now to ASP.NET. You'll find that the ASP.NET concepts are quite similar to those of CICS.

Looking at ASP.NET

ASP.NET is generally described as being a disconnected/stateless programming model. In fact, the protocol on which the majority of Web requests/network traffic is received (HTTP, as discussed in Chapter 3) is referred to as being a disconnected/stateless network protocol. Do you see where I'm going with this? The pseudo-conversational CICS model should remind you of the disconnected/ stateless ASP.NET model. Interesting, isn't it? But wait, there's more.

When an end user (Internet or intranet browser) sends an HTTP request to the IIS Web server, the ASP.NET server engine is responsible for carrying out a complete phased execution cycle. The Web form (or Web page) goes through these phases (conceptually similar to the CICS execution cycle). As shown in Figure 13-11, there are various page events and methods involved during this cycle.

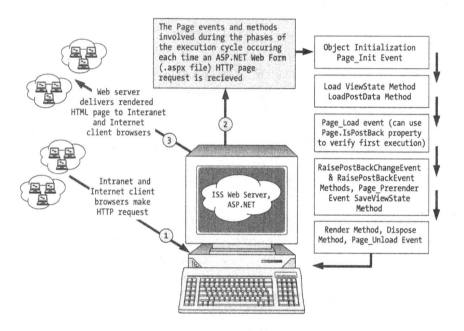

Figure 13-11. The general execution cycle of an ASP.NET HTTP request

 NOTE I will refer back to Figure 13-11 several more times in subsequent sections. Please make a note of it.

As with your mainframe CICS development, you can add logic to your ASP.NET application to influence the behavior of your application. For example, you can programmatically distinguish between the "first-time" execution and subsequent executions. Are you with me so far? Good! Let's continue.

Instead of your ASP.NET Web end user being limited to the use of CICS/ mainframe-style attention keys, you can now provide richer, more "usable" controls for your end user to interact with. Your ASP.NET application will have logic (event procedures) that associates specific routines to an interface element. You have got to admit, it really is amazing just how close ASP.NET Web development is to mainframe CICS screen development.

NOTE   You are not prohibited from using the function keys (F1, F2, key combinations, and so forth) as a means for the user to interact with the ASP.NET Web application. Visual controls have grown in popularity and remain very common. However, they are not the only choice for user interaction design.

There is one other similarity that I will just mention for now. In the CICS scenario there exists the concern of "keeping" any captured data (in memory) from previous execution cycles—possibly using the data in subsequent execution cycles. You have traditionally used the CICS DFHCOMMAREA to accomplish this on the mainframe.

As it turns out, ASP.NET offers features that directly support this same need to "save" data (between execution cycles). In ASP.NET circles, the phrases "session state" and "view state" are often used when addressing this concern. Although I briefly mention the topic of state management in this chapter, I further discuss it in Chapter 15.

CROSS-REFERENCE   I further reference the CICS DFHCOMMAREA and CICS TS queues when I discuss ASP.NET's state management in Chapter 15.

The point has been made: CICS development is similar to that of ASP.NET. This is important because you (presumably an experienced COBOL/CICS mainframe programmer) now have a jump start on learning about the ASP.NET technology. This is an opportunity for you to apply your past experience toward learning the .NET platform and the .NET toolset. You are well on your way to really understanding the ASP.NET technology. In the next section, you will create your first sample ASP.NET Web application.

Sample Code for Web Applications

The following sample applications, WebApplicationSampleCobol and WebApplicationSampleVB, demonstrate some of the basic ASP.NET concepts. You will begin with the COBOL .NET language choice for your first sample application. Following that, you will create a similar sample application using VB .NET. Please take a moment to walk through the creation of the first sample Web application, as detailed in the following steps.

TIP Although I suggest that you follow these steps to create your new ASP.NET project, you may wish to install and run the existing sample ASP.NET application that has been made available to you. In that case, you will need a small amount of preparation to get the ASP.NET sample application up and running. In Chapter 17, you will learn to create an installation/setup package. You can use the sample application in that chapter to assist you in installing the sample ASP.NET sample projects described in *this* chapter. Additionally, in case you need assistance in setting up your IIS Web server virtual directories, I cover that topic in Chapter 17 as well.

---

1. Create a new COBOL .NET ASP.NET project. In an open VS .NET IDE New Project window select COBOL Projects as your project type and ASP.NET Web Application as your template selection. Enter **WebApplicationSampleCobol** as the name of your project and **C:\Inetpub\wwwroot** as the location.[7] Once your New Project window resembles the example shown in Figure 13-12, click OK. As shown in Figure 13-13, a new folder will be created in the appropriate location.

2. Familiarize yourself with the VS .NET IDE. You will want to view the Solution Explorer window and notice the files that have been created for you (i.e., WebForm1.aspx and WebForm1.aspx.cob). Notice the Design tab and HTML tab in the WebForm1.aspx window. Additionally, notice the Toolbox that has been opened on the Web Forms tab. (You may have to manually open Solution Explorer and/or the Toolbox.)

---

7. I am assuming that you have IIS installed and running locally and that you are logged on with a user account that has administrative-level rights (over your local workstation). You may need to consult with your manager for the appropriate environment configuration used at your particular company.

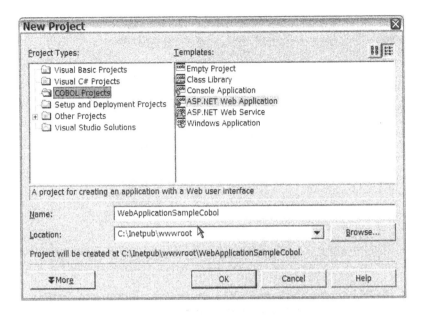

Figure 13-12. Preparing to create a new COBOL .NET ASP.NET Web application in the New Project window

Figure 13-13. A new folder is created under the C:\Inetpub\wwwroot folder location.

3. Add two Web Forms server controls to the Web Form. From the Web Forms tab of the Toolbox, drag and drop a Button server control and a TextBox server control onto the Web Form. Your Design view should look similar to the Web Form example shown in Figure 13-14.

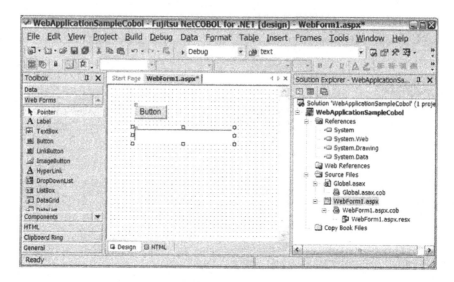

Figure 13-14. The WebApplicationSampleCobol project after Button and TextBox Web Forms server controls are added to the Web Form

4. Open the WebForm1.aspx.cob file from the Solution Explorer window by double-clicking the file name (optionally, click the View Code icon located at the top of the Solution Explorer window, or simply double-click the Web Form).

5. Add a PROPERTY statement for Text in the REPOSITORY section of the WebForm1 Class module as follows: PROPERTY PROP-TEXT AS "Text". Then build (compile) your project.

6. Add the Button1_Click method. The easiest way to do this is to first switch over to the Design view of the WebForm1.aspx file. Then double-click the Button control that you added to the Web Form. Once you have done that, add the following line of code to this "event" method: SET PROP-TEXT OF TextBox1 TO "Hello World". Your project is now ready to build and run.

TIP You can run your sample application from within the VS .NET IDE in debug mode. Optionally, you can navigate directly to your completed sample application using its URL: http://localhost/ WebApplicationSampleCobol/WebForm1.aspx.

Now, the process was not *that* bad, right? For your convenience, I have included the top portion and bottom portion of the WebForm1.aspx.cob file in Listing 13-4. Please take a moment to review the sample code.

Listing 13-4. Code Snippets from the WebApplicationSampleCobol Project's WebForm1.aspx.cob File

```
000010 IDENTIFICATION DIVISION.
000020 CLASS-ID. WebForm1 AS "WebApplicationSampleCobol.WebForm1"
000030     INHERITS CLASS-PAGE.
000040 ENVIRONMENT DIVISION.
000050 CONFIGURATION SECTION.
000060 SPECIAL-NAMES.
000070 REPOSITORY.
000080     CLASS CLASS-EVENTARGS AS "System.EventArgs"
000090     DELEGATE DELEGATE-EVENTHANDLER AS "System.EventHandler"
000100     CLASS CLASS-OBJECT AS "System.Object"
000110     CLASS CLASS-PAGE AS "System.Web.UI.Page"
000120     CLASS CLASS-BUTTON AS "System.Web.UI.WebControls.Button"
000130     CLASS CLASS-TEXTBOX AS "System.Web.UI.WebControls.TextBox"
000140     PROPERTY PROP-BUTTON1 AS "Button1"
000150     PROPERTY PROP-TEXT AS "Text"
000160
000170
000180 OBJECT.
000190 DATA DIVISION.
000200 WORKING-STORAGE SECTION.
000210 01 Button1 OBJECT REFERENCE CLASS-BUTTON PROPERTY.
000220 01 TextBox1 OBJECT REFERENCE CLASS-TEXTBOX PROPERTY.
000230 PROCEDURE DIVISION.
 . . .
<code generated by Web Forms Designer>
 . . .
001230 METHOD-ID. PAGE_LOAD AS "Page_Load" PRIVATE.
001240 DATA DIVISION.
001250 LINKAGE SECTION.
001260 01 PARAM-SENDER OBJECT REFERENCE CLASS-OBJECT.
001270 01 PARAM-E OBJECT REFERENCE CLASS-EVENTARGS.
001280 PROCEDURE DIVISION USING BY VALUE PARAM-SENDER PARAM-E.
001300 END METHOD PAGE_LOAD.
001310
001320 METHOD-ID. Button1_Click PRIVATE.
001330 DATA DIVISION.
001340 LINKAGE SECTION.
```

```
001350 01 sender OBJECT REFERENCE CLASS-OBJECT.
001360 01 e OBJECT REFERENCE CLASS-EVENTARGS.
001370 PROCEDURE DIVISION USING BY VALUE sender e.
001371     SET PROP-TEXT OF TextBox1 TO "Hello World".
001380 END METHOD Button1_Click.
001390
001400 END OBJECT.
001410 END CLASS WebForm1.
```

I copied the sample code in Listing 13-4 from the particular file referred to as
the *code-behind file*. In other words, the WebForm1.aspx.cob file contains the
"server-side" code used "behind" the WebForm1.aspx file. Listing 13-5 presents
the code contained in the WebForm1.aspx file. Notice that it only contains HTML
code at this point. Additionally, notice that the first line (which is called a *page
directive*) contains a CodeBehind= clause that makes the association between the
actual code-behind file and the HTML/UI page.

*Listing 13-5. Contents of the WebApplicationSampleCobol Project's WebForm1.aspx
File*

```
<%@ Page language="cobol" Codebehind="WebForm1.aspx.cob"
AutoEventWireup="false" Inherits="WebApplicationSampleCobol.WebForm1" %>
<!DOCTYPE HTML PUBLIC "-//W3C//DTD HTML 4.0 Transitional//EN" >
<HTML>
    <HEAD>
        <title>WebForm1</title>
        <meta name="GENERATOR" Content="Fujitsu NetCOBOL for .NET 1.0">
        <meta name="CODE_LANGUAGE" Content="cobol">
        <meta name="vs_defaultClientScript" content="JavaScript">
        <meta name="vs_targetSchema"
        content="http://schemas.microsoft.com/intellisense/ie5">
    </HEAD>
    <body MS_POSITIONING="GridLayout">
        <form id="Form1" method="post" runat="server">
        <asp:Button id="Button1"
            style="Z-INDEX: 101; LEFT: 56px; POSITION: absolute; TOP: 40px"
                runat="server" Text="Button"></asp:Button>
        <asp:TextBox id="TextBox1"
            style="Z-INDEX: 102; LEFT: 56px; POSITION: absolute; TOP: 88px"
            runat="server"></asp:TextBox>
        </form>
    </body>
</HTML>
```

Following the same steps detailed previously for the COBOL .NET sample project, I have created another sample application using VB .NET. Figure 13-15 shows an ASP.NET Web application with WebApplicationSampleVB as the project name.

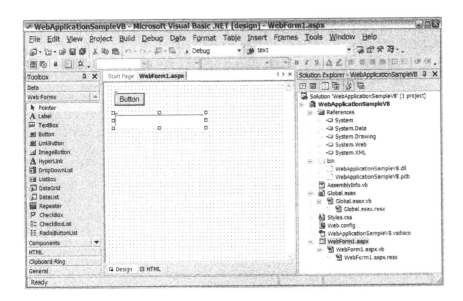

Figure 13-15. The WebApplicationSampleVB project after Button and TextBox Web Forms server controls have been added to the Web Form

The code from the WebApplicationSampleVB project's code-behind file, WebForm1.aspx.vb, is shown in Listing 13-6.

Listing 13-6. Code from the WebApplicationSampleVBl Project's WebForm1.aspx.vb File

```
Public Class WebForm1
    Inherits System.Web.UI.Page
        Protected WithEvents Button1 As System.Web.UI.WebControls.Button
        Protected WithEvents Button2 As System.Web.UI.WebControls.Button
        Protected WithEvents TextBox1 As System.Web.UI.WebControls.TextBox


#Region " Web Form Designer Generated Code "
```

483

```
'This call is required by the Web Form Designer.
<System.Diagnostics.DebuggerStepThrough()> _
Private Sub InitializeComponent()

End Sub

Private Sub Page_Init(ByVal sender As System.Object, _
ByVal e As System.EventArgs) Handles MyBase.Init
    'CODEGEN: This method call is required by the Web Form Designer
    'Do not modify it using the code editor.
    InitializeComponent()
End Sub

#End Region

Private Sub Page_Load(ByVal sender As System.Object, _
ByVal e As System.EventArgs) Handles MyBase.Load
    'Put user code to initialize the page here
End Sub

Private Sub Button1_Click(ByVal sender As System.Object, _
ByVal e As System.EventArgs) Handles Button1.Click
    TextBox1.Text = "Hello World"
End Sub

End Class
```

Looking at the code from the VB .NET code-behind file in Listing 13-6, notice the Button1_Click event method and the logic used to change the Text property of the TextBox control. Additionally, notice the Page Init and Page Load event methods. You may recall the sequence of page events shown in Figure 13-11. Recalling this sequence, you can anticipate the relative order in which the event methods are triggered.

A Word About the Code-Behind File

Inevitably, you will come across ASP.NET Web application examples showing a single-file Web Form design as opposed to a two-file Web Form design. The difference between these designs is that the single-file design will have a "script block" (resembling the following: `<script runat="server">logic</script>`) included in the HTML-based .aspx file.

The two-file Web Form design is identified by having an .aspx file and a code-behind file. The code-behind file would then contain the page and other control event-handling methods. Using VS .NET's IDE and project templates, you will typically be creating your ASP.NET projects using the two-file Web Form design. This is a good thing. Some of the advantages of the two-file code-behind design are as follows:

- Your source code, which is easily human-readable during design time, becomes more difficult for *others* to read once it is "compiled" into your assembly (DLL). This added level of privacy[8] is important to some organizations, especially when it is time to put the software distribution package together.

- During design time, you will experience better VS .NET IDE IntelliSense and debugging support.

- Events and event handlers must be manually bound.

- Separating your business logic from your presentation logic means cleaner, more maintainable code.

VS .NET: Designed with Developer Productivity in Mind

When you get a chance, consider exploring your VS .NET IDE's New Project window Project Types choices. Under the Other Projects folder, you will notice the Application Center Test Project and Enterprise Template Project choices.

You can use the Application Center Test Project to build stress/load tests for your ASP.NET applications. Optionally, you can access the Application Center Test tool by clicking the Start button and selecting Programs ➤ Microsoft Visual Studio .NET ➤ Visual Studio .NET Enterprise Features ➤ Microsoft Application Center Test.

The Enterprise Template Project is useful when you are building a large-scale application and you want to use a template that is broader than the default ASP.NET template. These two Other Projects templates are good examples of VS .NET being designed with developer productivity in mind.

---

8. Use of an "obfuscator" software tool can elevate this "level of privacy" to a "level of security."

Now that you have seen the sample "Hello, World" ASP.NET Web applications (in COBOL .NET and VB .NET), you can drill down into the .NET Framework classes. Once you learn about the .NET Framework Web namespaces, you will be well on your way to having a more complete picture of what it takes to build ASP.NET Web applications.

.NET Framework Support for ASP.NET Web Applications

The collection of .NET Framework objects for ASP.NET Web support is both extensive and exhaustive. In this section, you will learn about a subset of them. I discuss others in the later section "Understanding the ASP.NET Web Services Technology." I will defer discussing yet others until later chapters as appropriate.

The following lists of topics present the structure of my discussion of the .NET Framework support for ASP.NET (those .NET namespaces directly related to both Web application and Web services development):

Web *application* namespaces discussed in this chapter:

- *System.Web*

- *System.Web.UI*

Web *services* namespaces discussed in this chapter:

- *System.Web.Services*

- *System.Web.Services.Description*

- *System.Web.Services.Discovery*

- *System.Web.Services.Protocols*

Web *application* namespaces discussed in later chapters:

- *System.Web.UI.HtmlControls* (discussed in Chapter 14)

- *System.Web.UI.WebControls* (discussed in Chapter 14)

- *System.Web.Caching* (discussed in Chapter 15)

- *System.Web.SessionState* (discussed in Chapter 15)

- *System.Web.Mail* (discussed in Chapter 16)

- *System.Web.Security* (discussed in Chapter 18)

Web namespaces *not* discussed (please see the VS .NET Help text for more information about these namespaces):

- *System.Web.Hosting*

- *System.Web.Configuration*

- *System.Web.Services.Configuration*

- *System.Web.UI.Design*

- *System.Web.UI.Design.WebControls*

As you can see, there are quite a few namespaces for ASP.NET Web development. It's even more amazing when you compare this impressive list with the small list of .NET namespaces provided for Windows development. (Recall that there were only two: System.Windows.Forms and System.Windows.Forms.Design.) Suffice it to say, the ASP.NET development arena is feature rich.

The System.Web Namespace

Do you remember the intrinsic objects I mentioned earlier in the section "System Level: Comparing CICS with ASP.NET"? Namely, they were the Server, Application, Session, User, Request, and Response objects. Well, guess what? Among the many objects exposed in the System.Web namespace, you will find objects that have a one-to-one relationship with the so-called intrinsic objects mentioned earlier.

As you further familiarize yourself with the System.Web namespace, you will notice that the majority of its objects (classes, delegates, interfaces, and enumerations) are prefixed with "Http" (see Figure 13-16). This is understandable, given that the System.Web namespace is primarily used for the communication between the client (browser) and the server (IIS, ISAPI, and ASP.NET). Recall that the communication between the client and the server is done via HTTP.

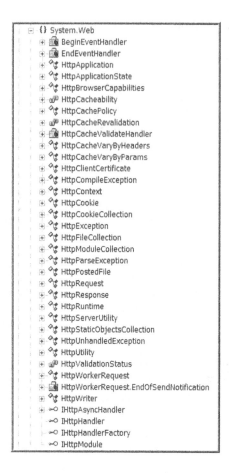

Figure 13-16. The System.Web namespace as shown in the VS .NET IDE Object Browser

Among the many interesting classes in the System.Web namespaces is the *System.Web.HttpContext* class. This class encapsulates all HTTP-request specific information (including access to the intrinsic objects). For example, you can use the *Session* property of the HttpContext class to obtain an instance of the *HttpSessionState* object. Then, using the HttpSessionState object, you can obtain the SessionID or manipulate the TimeOut value for a session. As shown in Figure 13-17, the HttpContext object includes several useful methods and properties.

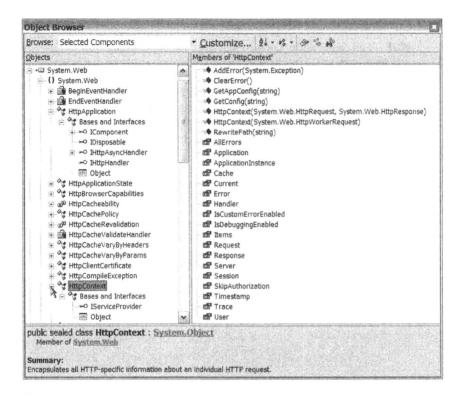

Figure 13-17. The members of the System.Web.HttpContext class as shown in the VS .NET IDE Object Browser

Another class from the System.Web namespace is the *Application* object. The Application object is exposed as *HttpApplication*. You will often see this class (and the HttpSessionState class) being used when you browse through your ASP.NET Web application's Global.asax.cob and/or Global.asax.vb file. In the "Hello, World" sample Web applications you created earlier, you may recall seeing the Global.asax.cob and/or Global.asax.vb files in the Solution Explorer window.

The Global.asax files are used as a convenient location to handle application-level events raised by ASP.NET (or by HTTP modules). As shown in Figure 13-18, the events associated with the Application intrinsic object are raised in a specific order. It would be wise to be aware of this event firing order. Each event shown in Figure 13-18 has it own significance and can be "handled" with appropriate logic (i.e., coding logic in an event method that is located inside of Global.asax.cob/ Global.asax.vb).

NOTE The *Application_OnStart* and *Application_OnEnd* event methods seen in most Global.asax.vb/Global.asax.cob modules are actually event methods triggered from the *HttpApplicationFactory* object. The HttpApplication object is created from the HttpApplicationFactory object. For more information about the HttpApplicationFactory object, please refer to the HTTP- and ISAPI-related references provided at the end of this chapter in the "To Learn More" section.

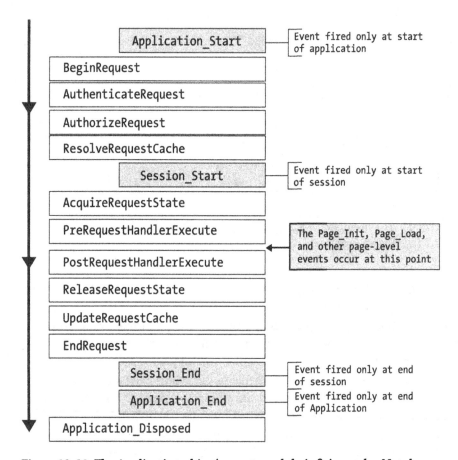

Figure 13-18. The Application object's events and their firing order. Not shown are the PreSendRequestHeaders, PreSendRequestContent, and Error events, which can fire in a nondeterministic order.

You may have noticed in Figure 13-18 the indication that the page-level events occur during the time (right after the PreRequestHandlerExecute event) that the

Application object's events are occurring. I briefly discussed the page-level events earlier in section "Looking at ASP.NET," along with Figure 13-11.

It is time to bring your exploration into the System.Web namespace to a close. You have been exposed to quite a bit with just two .NET System.Web classes: HttpContext and HttpApplication. As time allows, please revisit the System.Web namespace for continued learning. In the next section, you will dive into a different namespace that also supports Web application development: System.Web.UI.

The System.Web.UI Namespace

This particular namespace serves as the basis for the user interface controls that you will be using as you build Web pages. There is a class in this namespace called *Control* (as in *System.Web.UI.Control*). Interestingly, every control—even the page itself—derives (either directly or indirectly) from the System.Web.UI.Control class.

NOTE   For comparison, you should be reminded that in the earlier discussion on Windows development in the section "Introducing the System.Windows.Forms Namespace" that all of the user interface objects for Windows were derivatives of the System.Windows. Forms.Control class. This is, of course, more than just a naming convention. This is a good example of using inheritance and object orientation to extend a base class to more specific implementations.

This is important to realize because of the underlying benefits gained through inheritance (again, there's that object orientation that I warned you about). Once you're familiar with the base class for Web server controls (System.Web.UI.Control), then you'll basically learn everything else accumulatively. By following the inheritance lineage, you'll discover that there are more than a dozen categories of controls.

This is in contrast to the impression easily obtained from the manner in which the controls are presented in the VS .NET IDE Toolbox. I believe that a person who is new to .NET and VS .NET is at risk of being misled into thinking that there are only two types of controls: HTML controls and Web Forms controls. For example, if you were to go to the VS .NET IDE Toolbox, you would see what looks like two choices for "controls." As shown in Figure 13-19, you can select the HTML tab in the Toolbox. Optionally, as shown in Figure 13-20, you can select the Web Forms tab in the Toolbox.

Figure 13-19. The VS .NET IDE Toolbox with the HTML tab selected

Say that you want to make sense of all this and begin your research. You read somewhere that there is no such thing as HTML controls, but HTML elements do exist. You further discover that the "icons" shown on the HTML Toolbox tab represent HTML elements, not HTML controls. Then, just as you are starting to feel comfortable with your new understanding, you hear that these HTML elements can be set to "Run As a Server Control." You continue to research and discover that you can add an HTML attribute (runat="server") to these HTML elements to convert them into HTML server controls.

Assume that the next leg of your journey led you to learn about Web Forms server controls. There, you realized that the object model for Web Forms server controls is richer (more properties, methods, and so forth) than that of the HTML server controls. The choice seemed easier then. And so, your journey continues.

Figure 13-20. The VS .NET IDE Toolbox with the Web Forms tab selected

NOTE   At this point, you have half of the battle won—with controls, that is. I present a more extensive discussion of controls (e.g., Web Form controls, user controls, and so on) in the next chapter (Chapter 14). For now, simply realize that there *is* a huge difference between the "icons" shown in the HTML Toolbox tab and the Web Forms Toolbox tab. Additionally, please note that there are at least a dozen categories of Web server controls defined in the System.Web.UI namespace.

Before you go much further, take a step back for a moment—back to the System.Web.UI namespace and the System.Web.UI.Control class. After all, understanding the relative hierarchy of this base classes derivative will help in your extended learning. Consider for a moment the hierarchy of classes (ASP.NET server controls) that all inherit directly or indirectly from the System.Web.UI.Control base class, as shown in Listing 13-7.

Listing 13-7. The Hierarchy of Classes (ASP.NET Server Controls) Derived from the System.Web.UI.Control Base Class

```
System.Web.UI.Control
        System.Web.UI.BasePartialCachingControl
                System.Web.UI.PartialCachingControl
                System.Web.UI.StaticPartialCachingControl
        System.Web.UI.DataBoundLiteralControl
        System.Web.UI.HtmlControls.HtmlControl
                System.Web.UI.HtmlControls.HtmlContainerControl
                        System.Web.UI.HtmlControls.HtmlAnchor
                        System.Web.UI.HtmlControls.HtmlButton
                        System.Web.UI.HtmlControls.HtmlForm
                        System.Web.UI.HtmlControls.HtmlGenericControl
                        System.Web.UI.HtmlControls.HtmlSelect
                        System.Web.UI.HtmlControls.HtmlTable
                        System.Web.UI.HtmlControls.HtmlTableCell
                        System.Web.UI.HtmlControls.HtmlTableRow
                        System.Web.UI.HtmlControls.HtmlTextArea
                System.Web.UI.HtmlControls.HtmlImage
                System.Web.UI.HtmlControls.HtmlInputControl
                        System.Web.UI.HtmlControls.HtmlInputButton
                        System.Web.UI.HtmlControls.HtmlInputCheckBox
                        System.Web.UI.HtmlControls.HtmlInputFile
                        System.Web.UI.HtmlControls.HtmlInputHidden
                        System.Web.UI.HtmlControls.HtmlInputImage
                        System.Web.UI.HtmlControls.HtmlInputRadioButton
                        System.Web.UI.HtmlControls.HtmlInputText
        System.Web.UI.LiteralControl
        System.Web.UI.TemplateControl
                System.Web.UI.Page
                System.Web.UI.UserControl
```

```
System.Web.UI.WebControls.Literal
System.Web.UI.WebControls.PlaceHolder
System.Web.UI.WebControls.Repeater
System.Web.UI.WebControls.RepeaterItem
System.Web.UI.WebControls.WebControl
                System.Web.UI.WebControls.AdRotator
                System.Web.UI.WebControls.BaseDataList
                System.Web.UI.WebControls.Button
                System.Web.UI.WebControls.Calendar
                System.Web.UI.WebControls.CheckBox
                System.Web.UI.WebControls.DataListItem
                System.Web.UI.WebControls.HyperLink
                System.Web.UI.WebControls.Image
                System.Web.UI.WebControls.Label
              System.Web.UI.WebControls.BaseValidator
                System.Web.UI.WebControls.BaseCompareValidator
                System.Web.UI.WebControls.CustomValidator
                System.Web.UI.WebControls.RegularExpressionValidator
                System.Web.UI.WebControls.RequiredFieldValidator
                System.Web.UI.WebControls.LinkButton
                System.Web.UI.WebControls.ListControl
                        System.Web.UI.WebControls.CheckBoxList
                        System.Web.UI.WebControls.DropDownList
                        System.Web.UI.WebControls.ListBox
                        System.Web.UI.WebControls.RadioButtonList
                System.Web.UI.WebControls.Panel
                System.Web.UI.WebControls.Table
                System.Web.UI.WebControls.TableCell
                System.Web.UI.WebControls.TableRow
                System.Web.UI.WebControls.TextBox
                System.Web.UI.WebControls.ValidationSummary
        System.Web.UI.WebControls.Xml
```

While you view the hierarchy of derived server controls in Listing 13-7, observe that there are groups of classes for *System.Web.UI.HtmlControls.HtmlControl* and for *System.Web.UI.WebControls.WebControl*. Although the names may seem redundant, if you study the actual naming pattern in the hierarchy, the names will actually make sense. At the very least, they are consistent.

TIP The System.Web.UI.Page class and the System.Web.UI.Control class are two classes that you might consider focusing on as you continue your research. From there, it will be much easier to gain an understanding of the remaining server control classes in the System.Web.UI namespace. Remember that the Page class is the actual object used for your Web page. These two classes will serve as the foundation for all of your user interface–related ASP.NET Web application development.

For now, there is one other observation that I would like to point out (from the hierarchy of derived server controls). Can you spot the *System.Web.UI.Page* class? Yes, that is right. There it is—a derivative of System.Web.UI.Control. The actual Web page that you place "controls" onto during design time is itself a "control." You may recall that I referred to the Page class much earlier in this chapter. Please take a moment to revisit Figure 13-11. The figure in question illustrates the page life cycle and event firing order associated with the Page object.

NOTE You should pay particular attention to the placement/association of each class group. For example, you should notice that the System.Web.UI.Page class (and the System.Web.UI.UserControl class) derives from the System.Web.UI.TemplateControl class. This will help you understand why most of the "controls" have "common" properties, methods, and so forth.

The System.Web.UI.Page Class and Client-Side Scripts

As you may know, the use of client-side scripts (JavaScript, JScript, VBScript, and so forth) on your Web page can offer performance gains by offloading processing from the server to the client browser. Also, you can use client-side scripts to create a richer, more responsive Web Form.

Practically all of the Web pages you will see with client-side scripts will have its client-side script included in one of two ways: placed inside of a script block HTML tag or added as an attribute to an HTML element tag. In both of these cases, you will see the client-side script in the .aspx file during design time and deployment time. The script block and HTML attribute methods of client script insertion would resemble the following:

- `<script >ScriptBlockLogic</script>`

- `<A HREF="www.EclecticSoftwareSolutions.Com" onClick="alert('This will take you to my Home Page.');">`

As it turns out, you can use the System.Web.UI.Page class to separate client-side script from your HTML-based .aspx file. This is made possible through the use of any of the following public Page class methods:

- *RegisterArrayDeclaration*

- *RegisterClientScriptBlock*

- *RegisterHiddenField*

- *RegisterOnSubmitStatement*

- *RegisterStartupScript*

You can use these new System.Web.UI.Page class methods to possibly get away from needing to include any actual code in your HTML-based .aspx file. Using these methods, you can store the client-side script in your page's code-behind file. When the page is rendered, the script is combined with the HTML and sent to the client's browser for execution.

TIP   Using these Page methods for your client-side script brings another benefit. By having your client-side script located within your code-behind file, you can easily add logic to effectively build your client-side script. In other words, your client-side script can become dynamic. Your conditional server-side logic can react as needed to affect the client-side script. This is in contrast to the client-side script being physically located in the HTML-based .aspx file and becoming static.

Deciding on which Page method to use will depend on where (on the target page) you want your client-side script to be inserted. Also, depending on "when" in the page's life cycle you want the client-side script executed, one "Register"-type Page method or another will be appropriate. Keep these basic points in mind:

- Insert client-side script in the HTML form (the effect is similar to locating the script in the HTML header) if you want to explicitly call the script function for execution.

- Insert client-side script directly in the body of your HTML page when you need to include the output of the function in the resulting displayed Web page.

- Insert client-side script as an event handler if you want the appropriate event to trigger its execution.

As you recall, the topic of client-side scripting was previously acknowledged as a .NET retraining prerequisite topic (see the section "Client-Side Scripting Languages" in Chapter 4). It would certainly be appropriate to revisit the earlier client-side scripting discussion. For now, understand that using the Page methods discussed here for client-side script insertion is optional. As usual, it is good to know what your options are.

You've barely scratched the surface of the System.Web.UI namespace and the System.Web.UI.Control class topics. Nevertheless, it's time to conclude this chapter's introduction to ASP.NET Web application development. You can see that you'll definitely want to extend your learning. The references located at the end of this chapter in the "To Learn More" section should prove useful toward that goal. For now, there remains one additional portion of ASP.NET technology to briefly discuss. Let's now switch gears and focus on ASP.NET Web services.

Understanding the ASP.NET Web Service Technology

If there is one part of .NET that has received more attention (perhaps a larger share of Microsoft's marketing budget) than the others, Web services would definitely be it. The Web services technology is sometimes advertised as being *the* next generation of Web programming. Although I cannot substantiate such lofty claims, I will agree that XML Web services has much to offer and should hold a high spot on any serious Web developer's retraining agenda.

Given that there is an abundance of information publicly available already on the topic of XML Web services (or simply *Web services*), I will keep my discussion here brief. As usual, references are provided at the end of this chapter in the "To

Learn More" section for your continued learning. I begin by showing the general
architecture of a Web service application in Figure 13-21.

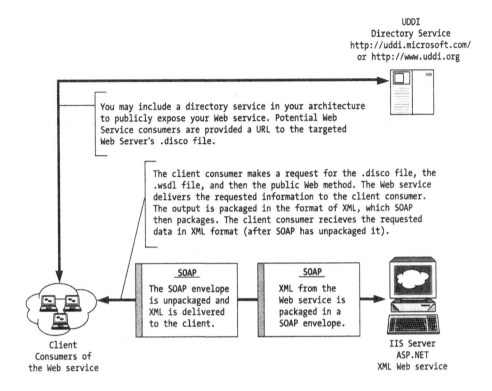

Figure 13-21. The general architecture of a Web service application

To continue my discussion of Web services, I will first revisit the mainframe
CICS started task analogy that I previously introduced in Chapter 2.

 NOTE Although the CICS LINK and XCTL commands also support the
initiation of CICS programs and the exchange of data between CICS
programs, a CICS started task runs as a separate CICS task. For this reason, the CICS started task fits as a closer analogy to the .NET XML Web
service.

A Mainframe Analogy for XML Web Services

Let's now compare Web services (synonymous with ASP.NET XML Web services) to the mainframe CICS transaction/program model referred to as a *started task*. Table 13-1 compares the basic characteristics of both.

Table 13-1. CICS Started Tasks vs. Web Services

CICS STARTED TASK	WEB SERVICE
A CICS started task is an online application that does not have a "screen type" user interface. An application programming interface (API) is used instead.	A Web service is an online application that does not have "screen type" user interface. After all, XML Web services are themselves ASP.NET Web programs (that service other programs). You use the VS .NET New Project template of ASP.NET Web service to create Web services (using COBOL .NET and/or VB .NET).
A CICS started task can be programmatically initiated (using a CICS START command) from a separately running CICS program. Additionally, you can use interval control to initiate a CICS started task based on a schedule.	A Web service can be programmatically initiated in much the same way that other Windows and Web programs are. Once a client application establishes a Web reference (usually during design time) to the Web service, a "call" is made from the client consumer to the Web service's publicly exposed method. The targeted method is required to have a <WebMethod> attribute applied. Refer to *System.Web.Services* for .NET Framework namespace support.
A CICS started task uses a temporary storage file (DFHTEMP) to facilitate the programmatic exchange of data. The CICS START/FROM and RETRIEVE/INTO commands are used to pass data to and from a CICS started task.	A Web service uses XML and Simple Object Access Protocol (SOAP) to facilitate the programmatic exchange of data. Fortunately, the mechanics of SOAP occur mostly behind the scenes. Nevertheless, be aware that SOAP is there, in the background. Refer to *System.Web.Services.Protocols* for .NET Framework support.

Table 13-1. CICS Started Tasks vs. Web Services (Continued)

CICS STARTED TASK	WEB SERVICE
A CICS started task has an implied contract in place for the structure of the data record passed using START/FROM and RETRIEVE/INTO. In other words, the layout of the data record passed has to match the layout retrieved.	A Web service has an implied contract in place that describes the service being exposed by the WebMethod. The contract is in the form of an XML document written in an XML grammar referred to as Web Services Description Language (WSDL). Refer to the two namespaces *System.Web.Services.Configuration* and *System.Web.Services.Description* for .NET Framework support.
A CICS started task is installed in the CICS program control table (PCT). The associated CICS program is then installed in the processing program table (PPT). Together, the PCT and PPT make it possible to locate a CICS started task and program when you want to initiate the online process.	A Web service can be located through the "discovery" process. The XML document referred to as the .disco file enables discovery of the Web service. Alternatively, you can use a public registry service such as the Universal Description, Discovery, and Integration (UDDI) to enable a more broad, public discovery process. A registry service would then provide a URL to the .disco file. Refer to *System.Web.Services.Discovery* for .NET Framework support.

Each of the basic characteristic comparison points in Table 13-1 shows a one-to-one match between a (mainframe) CICS started task and an (ASP.NET) XML Web service. A lot of people are amazed at how similar the two worlds are. When you have spent years being successfully trained on the mainframe platform, it sure is nice that your invested experience can be leveraged toward your continued career interests.

Noteworthy ASP.NET Web Service Observations

The first time that you use VS .NET's IDE (using the ASP.NET Web Service Project template) to create a new Web service, you will notice a few differences between the Web service project and the Web application project. For one, your default "surface," the item that looks like a Web Form, will be named with an .asmx suffix.

The .asmx suffix is characteristic of Web services (as opposed to the .aspx suffix used for Web applications).

NOTE   When you view your project files in the Solution Explorer window, you will notice that a WebService1.vsdisco file is created for you (when you use VB .NET as your language choice).

Once you open the .asmx file and navigate to the Code view, you have a nice surprise waiting for you. The ASP.NET Web service projects (both COBOL .NET and VB .NET) provide their own built-in "Hello, World" sample. All you have to do is uncomment the code (represented as a HelloWorld WebMethod), build, and run. After you uncomment the built-in WebMethod, the resulting code should resemble the code snippets in Listing 13-8.

Listing 13-8. Code Snippets of the Built-in "Hello, World" Sample Web Services

```
. . . . . .VB.NET
<WebMethod()> Public Function HelloWorld() As String
            HelloWorld = "Hello World"
End Function
```

```
. . . . . .COBOL.NET
000530 METHOD-ID. HELLOWORLD AS "HelloWorld" CUSTOM-ATTRIBUTE IS CA-WEBMETHOD.
000540 DATA DIVISION.
000550 LINKAGE SECTION.
000560 01 RET-VAL OBJECT REFERENCE CLASS-STRING.
000570 PROCEDURE DIVISION RETURNING RET-VAL.
000580     SET RET-VAL TO N"Hello World".
000590 END METHOD HELLOWORLD.
```

Not only is there a functional built-in sample, but also you will notice something else when you execute the Web service project. You will notice that a "test harness" is automatically built for you. The .asmx file dynamically builds a Web page that serves as a client consumer. You use this Web page to test your Web service. Can it get any better?

There is yet one more treat! The test page has a link available for you to view the dynamically built Web service description document (.wsdl file). While the Web service is executing, you will notice the Service Description link near the top of the test Web page. If you click the link, an XML document will be displayed (as shown in Figure 13-22).

```
  <?xml version="1.0" encoding="utf-8" ?>
- <definitions xmlns:http="http://schemas.xmlsoap.org/wsdl/http/"
    xmlns:soap="http://schemas.xmlsoap.org/wsdl/soap/"
    xmlns:s="http://www.w3.org/2001/XMLSchema"
    xmlns:s0="http://tempuri.org/"
    xmlns:soapenc="http://schemas.xmlsoap.org/soap/encoding/"
    xmlns:tm="http://microsoft.com/wsdl/mime/textMatching/"
    xmlns:mime="http://schemas.xmlsoap.org/wsdl/mime/"
    targetNamespace="http://tempuri.org/"
    xmlns="http://schemas.xmlsoap.org/wsdl/">
  + <types>
  + <message name="HelloWorldSoapIn">
  + <message name="HelloWorldSoapOut">
    <message name="HelloWorldHttpGetIn" />
  + <message name="HelloWorldHttpGetOut">
    <message name="HelloWorldHttpPostIn" />
  + <message name="HelloWorldHttpPostOut">
  + <portType name="Service1Soap">
  + <portType name="Service1HttpGet">
  + <portType name="Service1HttpPost">
  + <binding name="Service1Soap" type="s0:Service1Soap">
  + <binding name="Service1HttpGet" type="s0:Service1HttpGet">
  + <binding name="Service1HttpPost" type="s0:Service1HttpPost">
  + <service name="Service1">
  </definitions>
```

Figure 13-22. The service description XML document (.wsdl) for the sample "Hello, World" applications

There is one last difference to note between ASP.NET Web services (.asmx) and ASP.NET Web applications (.aspx). ASP.NET Web services have a special collection of .NET Framework namespaces:

- *System.Web.Services*

- *System.Web.Services.Configuration*

- *System.Web.Services.Description*

- *System.Web.Services.Discovery*

- *System.Web.Services.Protocols*

XML Web Services Continue to Evolve

The ASP.NET XML Web services arena is rather new. Many things are evolving (as I type) to help solidify its presence. Specifications, standards, and practices are being put in place as partnerships and alliances are being formed.

For example, the UDDI specification recently moved to be under the umbrella of the Organization for the Advancement of Structured Information Standards (OASIS). This happened just 2 months after Microsoft, IBM, and VeriSign submitted the WS-Security specification (a proposed standard for Web services security) to OASIS. Meanwhile, Microsoft, IBM, and BEA released the WS-Coordination and WS-Transaction specifications (proposed standards for distributed Web services and Web service–based transactions).

 NOTE The WS-Security specification for XML Web services was released in April 2002.

Microsoft, IBM, and other members of the Web Services Interoperability Organization (WS-I) are hard at work, teaming up to work on the Global XML Web Services Architecture (GXA) platform. More specifications for XML Web services are on the way. Among the specification releases expected in the future are the following:

- WS-Attachments specification

- WS-Inspection specification

- WS-Referral specification

- WS-Routing specification

The alliances formed in the WS-I, the GXA platform, and the XML Web service specifications being produced just may be what is needed to ensure the long-term success of XML Web services. Only time will tell. Certainly, this is an area that will require monitoring as it continues to evolve. Meanwhile, be aware that thousands of very useful and dependable XML Web services are being developed using VS .NET and the existing specifications and standards.

Summary

This chapter's goals were as follows:

- To discuss user interface design considerations

- To explore Windows application and Windows Service development

- To understand ASP.NET and XML Web services technology

Are you ready to create Windows and Web applications now? I trust that the topics presented in this chapter have been helpful toward that goal. You were introduced to a few user interface design considerations that apply to both Windows and Web development. Various VS .NET project templates were introduced in this chapter as well. It is likely that you now have a better picture of the types of Windows and ASP.NET applications that are possible with .NET and VS .NET. Additionally, you may have a better perspective of the .NET Framework support available for Windows and ASP.NET development.

In the next chapter you will revisit Windows and ASP.NET development. You will spend more time focusing on ways to use the various types of controls and other .NET Framework classes to add value to your Windows and ASP.NET applications.

To Learn More

The following are some suggested supplemental references to further your retraining effort.

Books

Architecting Web Services, by William Oellermann (Apress, 2001):
    http://www.apress.com/book/bookDisplay.html?bID=22.
Moving to ASP.NET: Web Development with VB .NET, by Steve Harris and Rob Macdonald (Apress, 2002):
    http://www.apress.com/book/bookDisplay.html?bID=78.
User Interface Design for Programmers, by Joel Spolsky (Apress, 2001):
    http://www.apress.com/book/bookDisplay.html?bID=10.
User Interfaces in VB .NET: Windows Forms and Custom Controls, by Matthew MacDonald (Apress, 2002):
    http://www.apress.com/book/bookDisplay.html?bID=99.

Magazines

.NET Magazine:
> http://www.fawcette.com/dotnetmag/

MSDN Magazine:
> http://msdn.microsoft.com/msdnmag/

MSDN Magazine, "Securely Implement Request Processing, Filtering, and Content
Redirection with HTTP Pipelines in ASP.NET":
> http://msdn.microsoft.com/msdnmag/issues/02/09/HTTPPipelines/default.aspx

Visual Studio Magazine:
> http://www.fawcette.com/vsm/

Windows Developer Magazine:
> http://www.wd-mag.com/

XML & Web Services Magazine:
> http://www.fawcette.com/xmlmag/

Web Sites

.NET Architecture Center:
> http://msdn.microsoft.com/architecture/

ASP.NET HTTP Modules and HTTP Handlers Overview (ISAPI type development):
> http://support.microsoft.com/default.aspx?scid=kb;en-us;Q307985

Creating Windows Applications:
> http://msdn.microsoft.com/library/en-us/vbcon/html/
> vboriCreatingStandaloneAppsVB.asp

GotDotNet (.NET samples, tutorials, and information):
> http://www.gotdotnet.com/

IBuySpy Store Application (sample application in COBOL .NET):
> http://www.ibuyspycobol.com/

IBuySpy Store Application (sample application in VB .NET and C#):
> http://www.ibuyspystore.com/

Intensity Software's NetCOBOL Samples (provided by Fujitsu Software and
Intensity Software):
> http://www.netcobolsamples.com/

Introduction to ASP.NET:
> http://msdn.microsoft.com/library/en-us/cpguide/html/
> cpconintroductiontoasp.asp

Introduction to Windows Service Applications:
> http://msdn.microsoft.com/library/en-us/vbcon/html/
> vbconintroductiontontserviceapplications.asp

Microsoft ASP.NET Home Page:

    http://www.asp.net/

Microsoft Community (discussion groups, e-newsletters, and so forth):

    http://communities2.microsoft.com/

Microsoft Patterns & Practices:

    http://msdn.microsoft.com/practices/

Microsoft TechNet How-To Web Site:

    http://www.microsoft.com/technet/treeview/default.asp?url=/technet/
    itsolutions/howto

Microsoft UDDI Business Registry Node:

    http://uddi.microsoft.com/

MSDN:

    http://msdn.microsoft.com

Specification Index for XML Web Services:

    http://msdn.microsoft.com/webservices/understanding/specs/default.asp

UDDI.org:

    http://www.uddi.org/

Windows .NET Server 2003:

    http://msdn.microsoft.com/library/default.asp?url=/nhp/
    default.asp?contentid=28001691

XML Web Services Developer Center:

    http://msdn.microsoft.com/webservices/

Adding Value to Your Interface

Learning to Exploit the .NET Framework Controls and Web Services

In this chapter

- Exploring the use of .NET's Control class to create informative Windows applications

- Discussing ways to use HTML controls and Web controls to develop interactive ASP.NET applications

- Discovering opportunities for XML Web services

HAVE YOU EVER developed an application that satisfied your end user's business requirements and at the same time was devoid of "bells and whistles"? Perhaps your end user was less than subtle when he or she criticized your application and showed dissatisfaction for the completed product. There you were, explaining the beauties of the under-the-hood .NET technology you used to build the application. Meanwhile, your end user was more concerned about why you had not used a *flashy* multicolored drop-down selection box instead of a *boring* free-form text box for data entry.

As you know, the "bells and whistles," the "icing on the cake," and the "nice-to-haves" are sometimes mistakenly regarded as being "not important" by developers and are overlooked. Obviously, the so-called extras should never take precedence over the actual business needs (including performance, reliability, and maintainability). Nevertheless, it is often these "extras" that will set your application apart from an otherwise dry, no-frills application. The challenge then is to seek out those extras that truly represent "value-added" features for your end user.

In this chapter, I discuss various ways that you can use the .NET Framework tools available to you to add value to your Windows and ASP.NET applications. This chapter's discussion will take you from the *System.Windows.Forms.Control* class (for Windows Forms) to the *System.Web.UI.Control* class (for Web Forms). In each case, you will drill down a bit beyond the respective *Form* and *Page* classes. The last portion of the chapter is devoted to XML Web services. There I present some of the most recent prospects and developments surrounding XML Web services.

NOTE Although this chapter is structured into three sections (i.e., a Windows applications section, an ASP.NET applications section, and an XML Web services section), please keep in mind that there is some overlap between the sections. For example, the first section emphasizes the importance of including design consideration for end-user communication. To illustrate the point, I have chosen to use Windows applications. Nevertheless, this need for effective end-user communication also exists in ASP.NET applications. The same could be said for the second and third sections of this chapter, as several of the points mentioned there (using ASP.NET) could loosely apply to Windows applications. I felt that the uniqueness in each platform's implementation (separate namespaces and so forth) justified the segregation into respective sections. Perhaps you will agree.

Making Your Windows Applications Informative

An application that strives to communicate with its end users is generally well regarded. In this sort of communication, your user interface design should not leave the user guessing about the "status" of a particular request/process. In our mainframe past, working on monochrome 3270-type monitors, our options for communicating status were rather limited. Sure, we mainframe CICS developers had creative ideas. However, not all 3270 terminals would support options such as flashing screen colors and reverse video.

TIP A common type of pop-up window used in Windows applications is called a *message box*. Once you incorporate the message box (actually, the *System.Windows.Forms.MessageBox* class) into your Windows application code, you simply need to call the Static (Shared in Visual Basic .NET) *Show* method, passing in the desired parameters.

In the past on the mainframe, you may have resorted to the use of crude pop-up windows on some of your ISPF/PDF-type applications to interact with the user. For your mainframe CICS applications, you generally relied on the default infamous "X" or "System" indicator at the bottom of the screen. Fearing a locked keyboard that would need to be reset, your CICS end users quickly learned that the X or System indicator communicated the status of "system busy."

> **NOTE**   Those of you mainframe programmers working on projects that involve equipping mainframe CICS applications with a Web or Windows front-end should consider yourselves lucky. Your shackles are now being removed (partially). Let those creative juices flow.

Fortunately, times have changed and tools have changed. Using the Visual Studio .NET (VS .NET) tool and the .NET Framework, you can easily add value to your Windows applications. You can use the System.Windows.Forms.Control class and its derivatives to inform and communicate with your end user. The following two classes both derive from the Control class and can be used on your Windows Form:

- *System.Windows.Forms.StatusBar*

- *System.Windows.Forms.ProgressBar*

Other Control classes add value, and even other Control classes seek to inform the end user. I explore the StatusBar and ProgressBar classes here to serve as an example for adding value in your .NET Windows application. Let's now take a look at some COBOL .NET and Visual Basic .NET (VB .NET) sample code to see how to implement these two controls.

Using Controls to Display Status

The following sample code projects are done in both VB .NET and COBOL .NET. Each uses a Windows Application project template as provided in the VS .NET IDE. You will notice in the sample code that the ADO.NET-related logic is similar to what was shown in Chapter 11. These samples leverage the available Northwind sample SQL Server database as a data source—specifically, the Categories table—and demonstrate the StatusBar and ProgressBar controls.

NOTE Other controls such as *System.Windows.Forms.ToolTip* and *System.Windows.Forms.DataGrid* are included in the sample project.

I decided to name the first project MyInformativeWinFormCobol. Once you have created the project, you can use the VS .NET IDE to initialize various properties.

You may choose to set certain properties during design time. Each control exposes a Properties window. To access this VS .NET IDE feature, after you add a control from the Toolbox to the Windows Form, select the control and press F4. Optionally, you can access the Properties windows by right-clicking the control and selecting Properties from the context window.

As shown in Figure 14-1, change the Text property of the *System.Windows.Forms.Form* class to the value **MyInformativeWinFormCobol**. The Text property will show as the form's "title" during runtime.

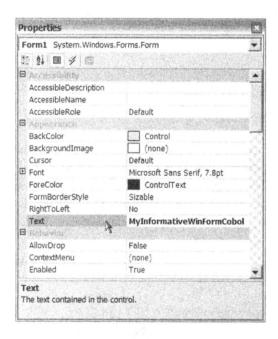

Figure 14-1. The VS.NET IDE Properties window for the System.Windows.Forms.Form control

Next, add additional controls to the Windows Form (i.e., StatusBar, ProgressBar, ToolTip, DataGrid, and Button) and modify a few properties. Using the Properties window (taking one control at a time by selecting the control and pressing F4), modify each added control as follows:

- *StatusBar:* Change the Text property to **Please Click the Button to Load the DataGrid**. During runtime, you will change this value after a selection is made.

- *ProgressBar:* Change the Visible property to **False**. You will change this value to True during runtime.

- *DataGrid:* Change the Visible property to **False**. You will change this value to True during runtime. Change the CaptionText property to **Categories Table**. Additionally, update the ToolTip property as shown in Figure 14-2.

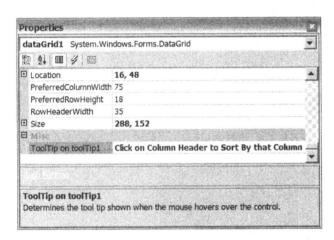

Figure 14-2. The Properties window for the System.Windows.Form.DataGrid control with the ToolTip property updated

I updated the ToolTip property for the Button control to the value **Click this Button to Load DataGrid**. This will later be apparent when you run the application and hover the mouse pointer over the Button control. Additionally, I changed the Text property of the Button control to **Click to Load DataGrid**.

NOTE The ToolTip (which you can associate with any control) itself is often referred to as being a control. Because you can find it in the Toolbox along with the other Windows controls, this is understandable. However, when you consider that it inherits directly from *System.ComponentModel.Component* instead of System.Windows.Forms.Control, it is also understandable that it should be referred to as a component or a just a class. Perhaps you can consider it to be just an exercise in semantics.

When complete, your design time view should resemble the sample application shown in Figure 14-3.

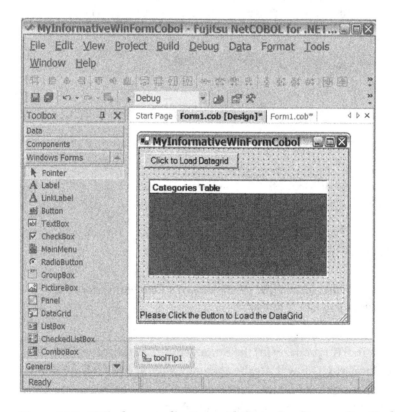

Figure 14-3. A Windows application with StatusBar, ProgressBar, ToolTip, DataGrid, and Button controls added. Several properties have been updated during design time.

Visually setting properties during design time is a common practice and perfectly acceptable as a means of initializing properties.[1] Later, if you need to, you can modify the properties in your code during runtime. Let's now turn to the code module Form1.cob (which you can access from the Solutions Explorer window) for some actual code changes.

> **TIP** Consider extending this sample application to include the *System.Windows.Forms.NotifyIcon* component. The NotifyIcon component displays an icon in the status notification area of the taskbar. Located in the Toolbox, along with the other form controls/components, you drag and drop the NotifyIcon onto the Windows Form. You would then set its properties (e.g., Icon, Visible, and Text) either during design time or runtime.

Editing the Code Module Using COBOL .NET

If you double-click the Button control (or any control on the form) while in Design view, two things will occur. First, an event handler method will be created for you. In the case of the Button control, the *button1_Click* method is created.[2] Second, you will find yourself taken from the Design view of the Form to the Source view of the Form class.

To complete the sample application MyInformativeWinFormCobol, you will need to add logic to connect to a data source and populate the DataGrid control. In the sample application, you will modify the REPOSITORY and Working-Storage COBOL .NET sections. Also, you will need to modify the button1_Click method. Listing 14-1, which I copied from the Form1.cob code file for your convenience, shows these modifications.

> **NOTE** You will notice that a portion of the sample code used here to create the ADO.NET Connection, DataAdapter, and Dataset objects was borrowed from the database access logic used in Chapter 11's sample application, DataBaseAccessExampleCOBOL.

---

1. The VS .NET IDE Windows Forms Designer actually builds code for you behind the scenes.
2. Each control has other event methods available. You can manually type others. For example, most controls expose *GotFocus* and *LostFocus* events that you can handle with appropriate methods during runtime.

Listing 14-1. Code Snippets from the Sample Application
MyInformativeWinFormCobol

```
. . .
000090 REPOSITORY.
000100     CLASS CLASS-BOOLEAN AS "System.Boolean"
000110     CLASS CLASS-CONTAINER AS "System.ComponentModel.Container"
000120     INTERFACE INTERFACE-ICONTAINER AS
000121             "System.ComponentModel.IContainer"
000130     INTERFACE INTERFACE-ISUPPORTINITIALIZE AS
000131             "System.ComponentModel.ISupportInitialize"
000140     CLASS DataColumn AS "System.Data.DataColumn"
000150     CLASS DataColumnArray AS "System.Data.DataColumn[]"
000160     CLASS DataRow AS "System.Data.DataRow"
000170     CLASS DataRowCollection AS "System.Data.DataRowCollection"
000180     CLASS DataSet AS "System.Data.DataSet"
000190     CLASS DataTable AS "System.Data.DataTable"
000200     CLASS SqlCommand AS "System.Data.SqlClient.SqlCommand"
000210     CLASS SqlConnection AS "System.Data.SqlClient.SqlConnection"
000220     CLASS SqlDataAdapter AS "System.Data.SqlClient.SqlDataAdapter"
000230     CLASS CLASS-POINT AS "System.Drawing.Point"
000240     CLASS CLASS-SIZE AS "System.Drawing.Size"
000250     CLASS CLASS-SYSTEMCOLORS AS "System.Drawing.SystemColors"
000260     CLASS CLASS-EVENTARGS AS "System.EventArgs"
000270     DELEGATE DELEGATE-EVENTHANDLER AS "System.EventHandler"
000280     CLASS CLASS-OBJECT AS "System.Object"
000290     CLASS CLASS-STA-THREAD AS "System.STAThreadAttribute"
000300     CLASS CLASS-STRING AS "System.String"
000310     CLASS SystemType AS "System.Type"
000320     CLASS CLASS-APPLICATION AS "System.Windows.Forms.Application"
000330     CLASS CLASS-BUTTON AS "System.Windows.Forms.Button"
000340     CLASS ARRAY-CONTROL AS "System.Windows.Forms.Control[]"
000350     CLASS CLASS-CONTROLCOLLECTION AS
000351           "System.Windows.Forms.Control+ControlCollection"
000360     CLASS CLASS-DATAGRID AS "System.Windows.Forms.DataGrid"
000370     CLASS CLASS-FORM AS "System.Windows.Forms.Form"
000380     CLASS CLASS-PROGRESSBAR AS "System.Windows.Forms.ProgressBar"
000390     CLASS CLASS-STATUSBAR AS "System.Windows.Forms.StatusBar"
000400     CLASS CLASS-TOOLBAR AS "System.Windows.Forms.ToolBar"
000410     CLASS CLASS-TOOLTIP AS "System.Windows.Forms.ToolTip"
000420     PROPERTY PROP-ALTERNATINGBACKCOLOR AS "AlternatingBackColor"
000430     PROPERTY PROP-AUTOSCALEBASESIZE AS "AutoScaleBaseSize"
000440     PROPERTY PROP-BUTTON1 AS "button1"
000450     PROPERTY PROP-CAPTIONTEXT AS "CaptionText"
```

```
000460      PROPERTY PROP-CLIENTSIZE AS "ClientSize"
000470      PROPERTY PROP-ColumnName AS "ColumnName"
000480      PROPERTY PROP-Columns AS "Columns"
000490      PROPERTY PROP-CommandText AS "CommandText"
000500      PROPERTY PROP-COMPONENTS AS "components"
000510      PROPERTY PROP-Connection AS "Connection"
000520      PROPERTY PROP-ConnectionString AS "ConnectionString"
000530      PROPERTY PROP-CONTROLS AS "Controls"
000540      PROPERTY PROP-CONTROLTEXT AS "ControlText"
000550      PROPERTY PROP-DATAGRID1 AS "dataGrid1"
000560      PROPERTY PROP-DATAMEMBER AS "DataMember"
000570      PROPERTY PROP-DataSource AS "DataSource"
000580      PROPERTY PROP-DataType AS "DataType"
000590      PROPERTY PROP-DROPDOWNARROWS AS "DropDownArrows"
000600      PROPERTY PROP-EMPTY AS "Empty"
000610      PROPERTY PROP-HEADERFORECOLOR AS "HeaderForeColor"
000620      PROPERTY PROP-LOCATION AS "Location"
000630      PROPERTY PROP-NAME AS "Name"
000640      PROPERTY PROP-PrimaryKey AS "PrimaryKey"
000650      PROPERTY PROP-PROGRESSBAR1 AS "progressBar1"
000660      PROPERTY PROP-SelectCommand AS "SelectCommand"
000670      PROPERTY PROP-SHOWTOOLTIPS AS "ShowToolTips"
000680      PROPERTY PROP-SIZE AS "Size"
000690      PROPERTY PROP-STATUSBAR1 AS "statusBar1"
000700      PROPERTY PROP-TABINDEX AS "TabIndex"
000710      PROPERTY PROP-Tables AS "Tables"
000720      PROPERTY PROP-TEXT AS "Text"
000730      PROPERTY PROP-TOOLBAR1 AS "toolBar1"
000740      PROPERTY PROP-TOOLTIP1 AS "toolTip1"
000750      PROPERTY PROP-Unique AS "Unique"
000760      PROPERTY PROP-VISIBLE AS "Visible"
000770      PROPERTY PROP-WINDOW AS "Window"
000780      .
. . .
000990 WORKING-STORAGE SECTION.
001000 01 mySqlConnection OBJECT REFERENCE SqlConnection.
001010 01 mySqlDataAdapter OBJECT REFERENCE SqlDataAdapter.
001020 01 mySqlCommand OBJECT REFERENCE SqlCommand.
001030 01 myDataSet OBJECT REFERENCE DataSet.
001040 01 myDataTable OBJECT REFERENCE DataTable.
001050 01 myDataRow OBJECT REFERENCE DataRow.
001060 01 myDataColumn OBJECT REFERENCE DataColumn.
001070 01 myPrimaryKeyColumn OBJECT REFERENCE DataColumn.
001080 01 myPrimaryKeyColumns OBJECT REFERENCE DataColumnArray.
```

```
001090 01 myDataRowCollection OBJECT REFERENCE DataRowCollection.
001100 01 myCLASS-STRING OBJECT REFERENCE CLASS-STRING.
001110 01 myDisplayString PIC X(30).
001120 01 myInt PIC S9(9) COMP-5.
001130 01 myOtherInt PIC S9(9) COMP-5.
001140 01 NOT-END-OF-READ PIC 1 USAGE BIT.
001150 01 statusBar1 OBJECT REFERENCE CLASS-STATUSBAR.
001160 01 progressBar1 OBJECT REFERENCE CLASS-PROGRESSBAR.
001170 01 dataGrid1 OBJECT REFERENCE CLASS-DATAGRID.
001180 01 button1 OBJECT REFERENCE CLASS-BUTTON.
001190 01 toolTip1 OBJECT REFERENCE CLASS-TOOLTIP.
001200 01 components OBJECT REFERENCE INTERFACE-ICONTAINER.
   . . .
019200 METHOD-ID. button1_Click PRIVATE.
019210 DATA DIVISION.
019220 LINKAGE SECTION.
019230 01 sender OBJECT REFERENCE CLASS-OBJECT.
019240 01 e OBJECT REFERENCE CLASS-EVENTARGS.
019250 PROCEDURE DIVISION USING BY VALUE sender e.
019260     SET PROP-VISIBLE OF progressBar1 TO B"1"
019270     INVOKE progressBar1 "Increment" USING BY VALUE 10
019280     SET PROP-TEXT OF statusBar1 TO "Updating DataGrid"
019290
019300*****************************************************************
019310* Create a new DataTable.
019320     INVOKE DataTable "NEW" USING BY VALUE "myCategories"
019330         RETURNING myDataTable.
019340
019350* Create 1st myDataColumn.
019360     INVOKE DataColumn "NEW" RETURNING myDataColumn.
019370     SET PROP-DataType OF myDataColumn TO
019380         SystemType::"GetType"("System.Int32").
019390     SET PROP-ColumnName OF myDataColumn TO "CategoryID".
019400     SET PROP-Unique OF myDataColumn TO B"1".
019410     INVOKE PROP-Columns OF myDataTable "Add"
019420       USING BY VALUE myDataColumn.
019430
019440* Create 2nd myDataColumn.
019450     INVOKE DataColumn "NEW" RETURNING myDataColumn.
019460     SET PROP-DataType OF myDataColumn TO
019470         SystemType::"GetType"("System.String").
019480     SET PROP-ColumnName OF myDataColumn TO "CategoryName".
019490     INVOKE PROP-Columns OF myDataTable "Add"
019500       USING BY VALUE myDataColumn.
```

```
019510
019520      INVOKE progressBar1 "Increment" USING BY VALUE 10
019530
019540* Create 3rd myDataColumn.
019550      INVOKE DataColumn "NEW" RETURNING myDataColumn.
019560      SET PROP-DataType OF myDataColumn TO
019570          SystemType::"GetType"("System.String").
019580      SET PROP-ColumnName OF myDataColumn TO "Description".
019590      INVOKE PROP-Columns OF myDataTable "Add"
019600        USING BY VALUE myDataColumn.
019610
019620* Create 4th myDataColumn.
019630      INVOKE DataColumn "NEW" RETURNING myDataColumn.
019640      SET PROP-DataType OF myDataColumn TO
019650          SystemType::"GetType"("System.Byte[]").
019660      SET PROP-ColumnName OF myDataColumn TO "Picture".
019670      INVOKE PROP-Columns OF myDataTable "Add"
019680        USING BY VALUE myDataColumn.
019690
019700      INVOKE progressBar1 "Increment" USING BY VALUE 10
019710
019720* Assign primary key column to CategoryID column.
019730      INVOKE DataColumnArray "NEW" USING BY VALUE 1
019740          RETURNING myPrimaryKeyColumns.
019750      INVOKE PROP-Columns OF myDataTable "get_Item"
019760        USING BY VALUE "CategoryID"
019770        RETURNING myPrimaryKeyColumn.
019780      INVOKE myPrimaryKeyColumns "Set"
019790        USING BY VALUE 0 myPrimaryKeyColumn.
019800      SET PROP-PrimaryKey OF myDataTable TO myPrimaryKeyColumns.
019810
019820* Reference the DataSet.
019830      INVOKE DataSet "NEW" RETURNING myDataSet.
019840* Associate the Table with the Dataset.
019850      INVOKE PROP-Tables OF myDataSet "Add"
019860        USING BY VALUE myDataTable.
019870
019880      INVOKE progressBar1 "Increment" USING BY VALUE 10
019890
019900*   Reference Data Provider Objects
019910      INVOKE SqlConnection "NEW"   RETURNING  mySqlConnection
019920      INVOKE SqlDataAdapter "NEW" RETURNING  mySqlDataAdapter
019930      INVOKE SqlCommand "NEW"      RETURNING  mySqlCommand
019940
```

```
019950*  Prepare to Connect to SQL Server Database
019960*  using Connection String
019970     SET PROP-ConnectionString OF mySqlConnection TO
019980     "user id=sa;pwd=;Database=northwind;Server=(LOCAL)"
019990
020000*  Associate the Command Object with the Connection Object
020010     SET PROP-Connection OF mySqlCommand TO mySqlConnection
020020*  Associate the Command Object with intended SQL Statement
020030     SET PROP-CommandText OF mySqlCommand TO "Select * from Categories"
020040*  Associate the DataAdapter Object with the Command Object
020050     SET PROP-SelectCommand OF mySqlDataAdapter TO mySqlCommand
020060
020070     INVOKE progressBar1 "Increment" USING BY VALUE 10
020080
020090*  Have the DataAdapter Object Execute the SQL Statement and
020100*  store the result set in a DataSet DataTable named myCategories
020110     INVOKE mySqlDataAdapter "Fill"
020120       USING BY VALUE myDataSet, "myCategories"
020130
020140*************************************************************
020150     SET PROP-VISIBLE OF dataGrid1 TO B"1"
020160     SET PROP-DataSource OF dataGrid1 TO myDataSet
020170     SET PROP-DATAMEMBER OF dataGrid1 TO "myCategories"
020180*************************************************************
020190*  Close the Database Connection
020200     INVOKE mySqlConnection "Close".
020210
020220     INVOKE progressBar1 "Increment" USING BY VALUE 10
020230
020240     SET mySqlConnection TO NULL.
020250     SET mySqlDataAdapter TO NULL.
020260     SET mySqlCommand TO NULL.
020270     SET myDataTable TO NULL.
020280
020300*************************************************************
020310     INVOKE progressBar1 "Increment" USING BY VALUE 40
020320     SET PROP-VISIBLE OF dataGrid1 TO B"1"
020330     SET PROP-TEXT OF statusBar1 TO "Completed Filling DataGrid"
020340
020350 END METHOD button1_Click.
       . . .
```

When you review the code in Listing 14-1, you will notice the inclusion of code to manipulate various properties on the controls. For example, code is included to "turn on" the Visible property of the DataGrid and ProgressBar controls. The StatusBar's Text property is set at the beginning and end of the button1_Click method. Notice also the use of the ProgressBar control's *Increment* method. In this case, the arbitrary value used to "increment" the ProgressBar gradually moves it from a value of 0 to 100.

> **NOTE** This sample application accesses the Northwind sample database. Check to see if your SQL Server service is active. The ADO.NET Connection object requires your service to be active to establish a connection to the data source.

The sample application in Listing 14-1 is a very basic example of adding a few controls to a Windows Form using COBOL .NET. Several of the controls used serve the purpose of communicating with the end user. The StatusBar and ProgressBar controls represent easy ways to add "informative" value to your .NET Windows applications. In the next section, you will take a quick look at the same sample application implemented with VB .NET.

Editing the Code Module Using VB .NET

In support of your bilingual programming language approach, I have created a new project in the VS .NET IDE using the VB .NET Windows Application project template. Given that this project accomplishes the same thing that the COBOL .NET version does, a comparison of the two should be rather straightforward. Nevertheless, just to keep things interesting for you, I have altered the design approach slightly with the VB .NET version of the sample application, which is named MyInformativeWinFormVB.

Rather than use the Properties window during design time, I have added code in the *Form1_Load* method (in the Form1.vb code module file) to initialize the controls. During runtime, the end result will be identical to what was achieved with the COBOL .NET version of the sample application. Please take a moment to review the sample code in Listing 14-2.

Listing 14-2. A Code Snippet from the Sample Application MyInformativeWinFormVB

```vb
Public Class Form1
    Inherits System.Windows.Forms.Form
. . .
(excluding code generated by Win Forms designer)
. . .
Private Sub Form1_Load(ByVal sender As System.Object, _
    ByVal e As System.EventArgs) Handles MyBase.Load
            'set all controls with initial values
            Me.Text = "MyInformativeWinFormVB"
            Button1.Text = "Click to Load Datagrid"

            With ToolTip1
                .SetToolTip(Button1, _
                "Click this Button to load Datagrid")
                .SetToolTip(DataGrid1, _
                "Click on Column Header to Sort By that Column")
            End With
            With DataGrid1
                .Visible = False
                .CaptionText = "Categories Table"
            End With

            ProgressBar1.Visible = False
            StatusBar1.Text = _
            "Please Click the Button to Load the DataGrid"

End Sub

Private Sub Button1_Click(ByVal sender As Object, _
    ByVal e As System.EventArgs) Handles Button1.Click
            ProgressBar1.Visible = True
            ProgressBar1.Increment(10)
            StatusBar1.Text = "Updating DataGrid"
            Call UseSqlDataAdapter(OptionalPreTableBuild)
End Sub

Public Function OptionalPreTableBuild() As DataSet
            'It is possible to obtain the "schema" or table structure
            'directly/automatically from the SQL Server Database
            'This section is added for training purposes.
            'The information found in this section would be critical
```

```
'in the case of building a disconnected .NET dataset
'that may have a non-SQL Server Data Source.

' Create new DataTable.
Dim myDataTable As DataTable = _
New System.Data.DataTable("myCategories")

' Declare DataColumn and DataRow variables.
Dim myDataColumn As System.Data.DataColumn
Dim myDataRow As System.Data.DataRow

' Create 1st myDataColumn.
myDataColumn = New System.Data.DataColumn()
myDataColumn.DataType = System.Type.GetType("System.Int32")
myDataColumn.ColumnName = "CategoryID"
myDataColumn.Unique = True
myDataTable.Columns.Add(myDataColumn)

ProgressBar1.Increment(10)

' Create 2nd myDataColumn.
myDataColumn = New System.Data.DataColumn()
myDataColumn.DataType = Type.GetType("System.String")
myDataColumn.ColumnName = "CategoryName"
myDataTable.Columns.Add(myDataColumn)

' Create 3rd myDataColumn.
myDataColumn = New System.Data.DataColumn()
myDataColumn.DataType = Type.GetType("System.String")
myDataColumn.ColumnName = "Description"
myDataTable.Columns.Add(myDataColumn)

' Create 4th myDataColumn.
myDataColumn = New System.Data.DataColumn()
myDataColumn.DataType = Type.GetType("System.Byte[]")
myDataColumn.ColumnName = "Picture"
myDataTable.Columns.Add(myDataColumn)

' Assign primary key column to CategoryID column
Dim PrimaryKeyColumns(0) As System.Data.DataColumn
PrimaryKeyColumns(0) = myDataTable.Columns("CategoryID")
myDataTable.PrimaryKey = PrimaryKeyColumns
```

```
                    ' Reference the DataSet.
                    Dim myDataSet As New System.Data.DataSet()
                    ' Associate the Table with the Dataset.
                    myDataSet.Tables.Add(myDataTable)
                    myDataTable = Nothing
                    Return myDataSet

                    ProgressBar1.Increment(10)
        End Function


        Public Sub UseSqlDataAdapter(ByVal myDataset As DataSet)
                    'Reference Data Provider Objects
                    Dim mySqlConnection As New System.Data.SqlClient.SqlConnection()
                    Dim mySqlDataAdapter As New System.Data.SqlClient.SqlDataAdapter()
                    Dim mySqlCommand As New System.Data.SqlClient.SqlCommand()

                    'Reference Dataset Objects
                    Dim myDataRow As System.Data.DataRow

                    'Prepare to Connect to SQL Server Database
                    'using Connection String
                    mySqlConnection.ConnectionString = _
                    "user id=sa;pwd=;Database=northwind;Server=(LOCAL)"

                    ProgressBar1.Increment(10)

                    'Associate the Command Object with the Connection Object
                    mySqlCommand.Connection = mySqlConnection
                    'Associate the Command Object with intended SQL Statement
                    mySqlCommand.CommandText = "Select * from Categories"

                    'Associate the DataAdapter Object with the Command Object
                    mySqlDataAdapter.SelectCommand = mySqlCommand
                    'Have the DataAdapter Object Execute the SQL Statement and
                    'store the result set in a DataSet DataTable named myCategories
                    mySqlDataAdapter.Fill(myDataset, "myCategories")

                    ProgressBar1.Increment(10)

                    '****************************************************
                    With DataGrid1
                            .Visible = "True"
                            .DataSource = myDataset
                            .DataMember = "myCategories"
```

```
            End With
            '****************************************************

            ProgressBar1.Increment(60)

            'Close the Database Connection
            mySqlConnection.Close()
            mySqlConnection = Nothing
            mySqlDataAdapter = Nothing
            mySqlCommand = Nothing

            StatusBar1.Text = "Completed Filling DataGrid"
    End Sub
End Class
```

When you examine the code in Listing 14-2, you will notice that the ToolTip control has the method *SetToolTip*. This method is used to associate the ToolTip control to other controls. In this case, the ToolTip control is associated with both the Button and DataGrid controls. As shown in Figures 14-4 and 14-5, the ToolTip control can add value to your application by communicating usage tips to your end user.

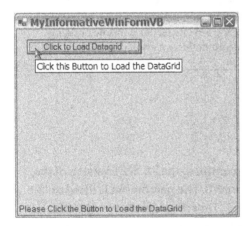

Figure 14-4. You can view the ToolTip display when you place your mouse pointer over the Button control.

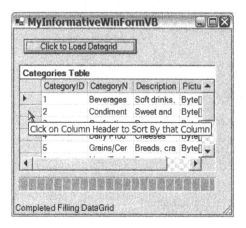

Figure 14-5. You can view the ToolTip display when you place your mouse pointer over the DataGrid control.

NOTE   The decision of whether or not to initialize your control properties during design time or runtime is a design choice. In real life, you
may come across situations where you will prefer one approach or the
other. As you have seen, the same results were achieved in the earlier
COBOL .NET project using the design-time Properties window. In both
languages, VB .NET and COBOL .NET, you have the option of initializing your controls using the design-time Properties window or using
code logic. Simply be aware that you do have a choice.

Fun with the Timer Control

Just for fun, I have added another Button control to the VB .NET version of the
sample application MyInformativeWinFormVB. The new button is listed on the
form with the Text property set to the value "TimerFun". When you click this
button, you will execute a small piece of code in the in the *Button2_Click*
event method. This code will cause the Timer control to activate. The Timer
control is a member of the *Windows.Forms* family of controls (i.e.,
System.Windows.Forms.Timer). The Timer control can remind you of the
diversity of the Windows Form controls.

TIP   Feel free to extend the COBOL .NET version of the sample application using the Timer control. As long as you know the full name of the class (in this case, System.Windows.Forms.Timer) and its members (Start, Stop, Interval, and so forth), adding it to your COBOL .NET code is rather easy. Incidentally, this Timer control logic provides an example of the code needed to associate an event with an event handler.

By the way, if you run this TimerFun logic on a Windows 2000 or Windows XP system (a system that supports layering), you will get a chance to see a demonstration of one of the coolest properties that has been added to the Windows Form class: the *Opacity* property. As shown in Listing 14-3, you can use the Windows Form Opacity property to bring a Windows Form to varying degrees of transparency. Bravo, bravo! Viva la .NET!

Listing 14-3. Code Snippet from the MyInformativeWinFormVB Project Showing the Timer Control Being Used

```
Private Shared tm As New System.Windows.Forms.Timer()
Private Shared Cycles As Int32
Private Sub Button2_Click(ByVal sender As System.Object, _
ByVal e As System.EventArgs) Handles Button2.Click
    Cycles = 0
    Call FunWithTimer()
End Sub
Public Sub TimerEventProcessor(ByVal myObject As Object, _
ByVal myEventArgs As EventArgs)
    Cycles += 1
    Me.Opacity = 0.1 * Cycles
    If Cycles > 10 Then
       tm.Stop()
    End If
End Sub
Public Sub FunWithTimer()
    AddHandler tm.Tick, AddressOf TimerEventProcessor
    tm.Interval = 500
    tm.Start()
End Sub
```

Please take a moment to reflect on the namespaces that you have used in this section for Windows Forms development. You will recall[3] that each of the Windows Forms controls inherit either directly or indirectly from System.ComponentModel.Component or System.Windows.Forms.Control. Understanding the namespace hierarchy and the base classes will give you the advantage with .NET. You will leverage this advantage as you build applications that sufficiently provide your end users with pertinent information.

In the next section, I will continue the "adding value" theme, but I will switch over to Web application development. As you will see, the ASP.NET technology arena brings with it an entirely different set of concerns, challenges, and opportunities for adding value to your applications.

Making Your ASP.NET Applications Interactive

Practically all Web-based business applications offer some form of interaction with their end users. That interaction may be in the form of hyperlinks, input fields, Submit buttons, or some type of navigation feature. Providing the right type of interaction for your Web site is important. Because interaction design affects your users' experience, you can easily see the connection that this topic has with the concern for adding value to your application's user interface.

Deciding among the many types of user interface interaction then becomes a developer's challenge. Among the many application design considerations, the following three points are arguably the most critical:

- Making the application responsive

- Providing user validation

- Managing state and cache

In the sections that follow, I discuss the first two points in the preceding list. You will explore the role that the various .NET Framework control classes can play to help you achieve your design goals. I focus on the third point in the next chapter (Chapter 15).

Making the Application Responsive

If you are developing applications for an intranet community, you have already been greeted with the reality that end users do not like to wait. When you are

---

3. This topic was originally introduced in Chapter 13.

building an application to serve the Internet community, your users' expectations will vary. For example, if a user is stuck with a slow dial-up connection, your application's lack of responsiveness is potentially hidden. However, just wait until your user switches to a lightning-fast Internet connection. At some point, the user may even get a broadband solution. When that happens, the true bottlenecks will be revealed.

CROSS-REFERENCE   In Chapter 13, I acknowledged that several categories of controls existed that are all available to the ASP.NET developer. In that chapter, I also introduced the entire hierarchy of control classes that are derived from the System.Web.UI.Control base class.

Hopefully, you would have used the .NET Framework and ASP.NET to remove any processing latency found in your application. In every design decision, your choice of user interface control could impact the performance of your application. In other words, you need to carefully consider your needs before you freely drag and drop controls from the VS .NET IDE Toolbox.

TIP   If you do consider the use of a client-side script, keep a couple of things in mind. Some users configure their Web browsers to have scripting capability disabled. Additionally, remember to refer back to the special Page methods that are available to help insert your script code into the .aspx file (see the section "The System.Web.UI.Page Class and Client-Side Scripts" in Chapter 13). Your choice to use or not to use a client-side script can result in a missed opportunity. The more proficient you become with the use of client-side scripts (e.g., JavaScript) for some of your client-side processing needs, the more choices you will have when developing for responsiveness.

Server Controls: To Use or Not to Use?

You might have the initial impression that you should use server controls at every opportunity. Actually, the exact opposite is true. You should use server controls only when you need to. If your Web Form user interface requires only simple display rendering, then strongly consider using an HTML tag. Generally speaking, try to avoid any unneeded trips (or rather, round-trips) to the Web server. The HTML tags alone will process on the client side, in the client's browser.

> **NOTE**   The namespaces System.Web.UI.HtmlControls and System.Web.UI.WebControls both provide server controls.

In cases when your user interface design includes the need to communicate with the server (e.g., you need to store or retrieve data from the database), you will want to use server controls. Additionally, if your business requirements call for the need to programmatically manipulate the attributes of your HTML tags, handle control events, or maintain view-state between postback events, server controls may be a good choice for you.[4]

> **NOTE**   In Chapter 13, I pointed out that the HTML tab in the VS .NET Toolbox displays HTML elements. Understand that if you take an HTML element and add the `runat="server"` HTML attribute to that element, you have basically created a server control (an HTML server control). In contrast, the controls displayed on the Web Forms tab in the VS .NET Toolbox are already server controls (rather, Web server controls). Either way, as far as *where* the processing takes place, a server control *is* a server control.

HTML Server Controls vs. Web Server Controls

Assume that you already know that the classes found in the System.Web.UI. WebControls namespace offer a much richer object model than those offered by the System.Web.UI.HtmlControls namespace. You can then review a few other advantages that Web server controls offer over HTML server controls. For example, with Web server controls

- The output (HTML, and possibly client script) generated by the server as part of the server process can be multibrowser compatible. Web server controls are able to render based on the capabilities of the browser.

---

4. This depends slightly on your willingness and ability to use client-side scripting. It's wise to consider learning JavaScript. This will enhance your Web development choices.

- The exposed object model (properties, methods, and so forth) against which you program is more consistent across controls. This leads to a more productive programming experience.

- You can gain access to advanced controls such as the AdRotator, Calendar, DataGrid, and Repeater. Additionally, you gain access to advanced validation classes such as the *ValidationSummary* and *BaseValidator* classes.

- There is a one-to-one mapping with the respective user interface elements. HTML server controls, on the other hand, are not consistent. In some cases they have a one-to-many mapping. In some of the cases where a one-to-one mapping does exist with HTML server controls, the name used in the Toolbox does not match the name of the resulting HTML element.[5]

To be fair, there is at least one advantage that HTML server controls offer: backward compatibility. Some will seek out the HTML controls to speed up an upgrade of their legacy Web applications (those built with classic ASP and Visual Basic 6.0). Otherwise, Web server controls are going to be your best bet—that is, when you need a *server* control.

Controls, Controls, Controls, and More Controls

Among the common categories of HTML server controls and Web server controls, you have many choices—certainly enough choices to get you off to a powerful developing start. All of them, in one way or another, seek to add value to your ASP.NET applications. Nevertheless, at some point you will come across the need to explore some of the other categories of controls.

You will find the following categories of controls briefly summarized in the sections that follow:

- Literal controls

- User controls

- Composite controls

- Custom controls

---

5. I suppose that Microsoft did this to make the HTML tab more similar to the Web Forms tab. They failed. With the HTML tab, the Label icon in the Toolbox is a <div> HTML tag. With the Web Forms tab, the Label icon in the Toolbox is an <asp:Label> HTML tag.

Literal Controls

ASP.NET uses these controls to store all the text-based data found on a Web page that does not require server processing. This would include all of the HTML elements and all other readable text. By accessing the object model of the literal control class, you can add and remove the text-based contents.

You will come across two "literal" controls—*literally*—that both inherit directly from the System.Web.UI.Control base class: *System.Web.UI.LiteralControl* and *System.Web.UI.WebControls.Literal*. ASP.NET itself creates the literal control class System.Web.UI.LiteralControl on your behalf (you can create it in your server-side code). You can find the System.Web.UI.WebControls.Literal literal control class in the Toolbox[6] (in the Web Forms tab).

By the way, you can view the *Literal* literal control as a lightweight alternative to the *Label* server control. On the other hand, you can instantiate the *LiteralControl* literal control in your server-side code and add it to the *Page.Controls* collection. Explicit use of either will depend on your needs.

User Controls

The *UserControl* class is also part of the System.Web.UI namespace. You work with user controls as you would a Page class. Notice that both the UserControl class and the Page class inherit from the *System.Web.UI.TemplateControl* class. You can add user controls to your project as text-based files that use a suffix of .ascx.

Use the UserControl class when you want to capture a Web page user interface that you want to reuse on multiple pages in the same project. You can place one or more user controls onto a Web page. It may help if you think of user controls as miniature pages. (See the upcoming sidebar titled "Looks Like a Page, Acts Like a Page, but They Called It a User Control.")

Composite Controls

When you take two or more existing server controls, inherit from their respective base classes, and assemble them together to create a new control, you have created a *composite* control. Microsoft has apparently used this approach to create some of their advanced server controls, for example, the *LinkButton* class. The LinkButton class appears to be the combination of a HyperLink control and a Button control, taking on characteristics of both controls.

---

6. If you dig deep enough you will find that the visual version of the literal control (the one located in the Toolbox) gets translated and stored along with other HTML/text into the ASP.NET-generated System.Web.UI.LiteralControl class during runtime.

Custom Controls

Similar to a composite control, a *custom* control is a control that you create yourself. Where the custom control differs is that rather than combining existing controls to create a new control, you typically just code your program logic to inherit from one targeted base control class. You then add your own logic to extend the capabilities found in the base class.

Looks Like a Page, Acts Like a Page, but They Called It a User Control

As you work with user controls (those .ascx files), you will discover that these objects look and act a lot like pages—perhaps *miniature* pages. Why then, you may ask, did Microsoft decide to call them "user controls"? As much as I may take stabs at the various naming decisions made by Microsoft, there is usually a good reason behind their decisions.

There they sat, I imagine, around a big table (in a dark, smoke-filled room) talking about how the page is itself a control. Then, after much debate, they decided that it was reasonable to describe a miniature "page" that you create and design yourself to be a user control.

If they had invited me to the naming session meeting, I could have pointed out to them that it is not the user control that is misleadingly labeled; rather, the page is. I could have suggested to the Microsoft marketing folks that they could have appended the word "control" to the word "page" to create the term "page control." Having done so, then they could have either kept the term "user control" or gone with a term like "miniature page control." What do you think: "page control" and "miniature page control"?

You know, I wonder why Microsoft has not called me yet. Nevertheless, to help clear up the user control versus page confusion, keep the following points in mind:

- Both the Page class (*System.Web.UI.Page*) and UserControl class (*System.Web.UI.UserControl*) inherit from the same base class (*System.Web.UI.TemplateControl*).

- Pages can be requested directly via an HTTP request. User controls, on the other hand, are hosted on pages (or inside of other user controls). You programmatically can make use of the properties and methods of user controls from your hosting page's server-side code.

- Even though VS .NET offers a great "Add New Item" option for adding Web user controls to projects, you can create a user control manually.

- You can convert an existing page to a user control by performing the following steps:

    1. Change the .aspx suffix extension to .ascx.

    2. Remove the <!DOCTYPE>, <HTML>, <BODY>, and <FORM> markup tags.

    3. Change the HTML @Page directive to be an HTML @Control directive.

    4. Change your code-behind logic to inherit System.Web.UI.UserControl instead of System.Web.UI.Page.

    5. Add a ClassName to the @Control directive for strong typing ability.

- The UserControl object experiences page-level events (Page Init, Page Load, and so forth) similar to those experienced by the Page object.

- With a couple of exceptions, using a user control is similar to using a Web server control (e.g., it includes the runat="server" attribute). Rather than dragging and dropping from the Toolbox, you can drag and drop from the Solution Explorer. When you use the drag-and-drop approach, an @Register directive is added to the "hosting" .aspx page file for you.

With such a varied offering of Control classes, the .NET Framework and ASP.NET have an answer to practically all of your user interface development needs. Basically, the Control classes offer opportunities for code reuse. Code reuse translates into increased developer productivity. Increased developer productivity means more time to concentrate on incorporating the right kind of value-added features to your user interface. The focus then returns to the user and the user's experience.

The following section continues that focus on the user in presenting the topic of validation. You will learn about yet another available choice for adding value to your user interface.

Providing User Validation

When you create an online application and you are designing the user interface, there is a thought process that takes place. There is that moment when you try to put yourself into the shoes of the end user. You may find yourself wondering, "If I were a user, what would I do in this scenario?"

Positioning yourself on the receiving end of that question, you make design considerations to support this anticipated end-user interaction. Experience then teaches you that the end user will not always "behave" as the user interface expects them to. So, you have learned to code defensively.

As a result, typical design considerations for online applications will include the need to validate the input received from the user. Although this is done on the end user's behalf, your user's perception of the validation logic is usually equivalent to the amount of value that has actually been added to the application. The type of interactive validation feedback delivered by your application's user interface easily influences the perceptions held by the end user.

NOTE   Most mainframe CICS developers will recall enhancing CICS BMS map processing by adding user validation logic. Some of us used the infamous symbolic cursor positioning technique (moving a –1 to the length attribute) for the field being validated, whereas others relied on manipulating the field's extended attributes using IBM's standard DFHBMSCA copybook. Given the tools available, both approaches were acceptable means of providing feedback to the end-user community.

As luck would have it, ASP.NET provides two .NET Framework classes to assist with user validation: *System.Web.UI.WebControls.BaseValidator* and *System.Web.UI.WebControls.ValidationSummary*.

.NET Supports User Validation

I'll begin by briefly reviewing the .NET Framework classes that you can use for ASP.NET user validation. The System.Web.UI.WebControls.BaseValidator class serves as a base class from which five classes are derived:[7]

- *System.Web.UI.WebControls.CompareValidator:* Compares a fixed value to the value present in a targeted input control.

- *System.Web.UI.WebControls.RangeValidator:* Compares an Input control's value to that of two fixed values using the two fixed values as a range.

- *System.Web.UI.WebControls.CustomValidator:* As the name of this class implies, you can create your own validating algorithm.

---

7.   The System.Web.UI.WebControls.CompareValidator
     and System.Web.UI.WebControls.RangeValidator classes derive
     from the System.Web.UI.WebControls.BaseCompareValidator.
     The System.Web.UI.WebControls.BaseCompareValidator class is
     derived from the System.Web.UI.WebControls.BaseValidator class.

- *System.Web.UI.WebControls.RegularExpressionValidator:* Compares the value of an Input control against a regular expression pattern. You have the flexibility to provide your own expression. Optionally, you can use the pre-packaged expressions provided by the Web Forms Designer.

- *System.Web.UI.WebControls.RequiredFieldValidator:* Simply checks to verify that a nonblank value has been entered or that a selection has been made.

Each validation control can be "tied" to an Input control on the Web page. Typically, you use the *validator* control to write an error message or display an error indicator to alert the user. You can use the System.Web.UI.WebControls.ValidationSummary class (which inherits directly from the *System.Web.UI.WebControls.WebControl* class) to display a summary of validation errors produced by one or more of the actual validation controls.

To help with your understanding of the validation controls, I have included several of the validation server controls in a sample application. Let's take a look at some code.

Code Sample to Demonstrate User Validation

Using the ASP.NET Web Application project template in VS .NET, I created a new project. In the New Project window, I entered the name **MyWebUseValidationCobol**. As shown in Figure 14-6, you can find the validation server controls under the Web Forms tab in the VS .NET IDE Toolbox. I dragged and dropped a few of them onto the Web Form from the Toolbox (rather than typing in the HTML by hand).

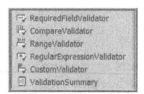

Figure 14-6. The validation server controls as seen in the VS .NET IDE Toolbox

As shown in Figure 14-7, I placed a collection of controls onto the Web Form. I used the HTML tab in the Toolbox for my labels (HTML elements). I used the Web Forms tab in the Toolbox for the server controls (e.g., the TextBox controls, a Button control, and the validation controls).

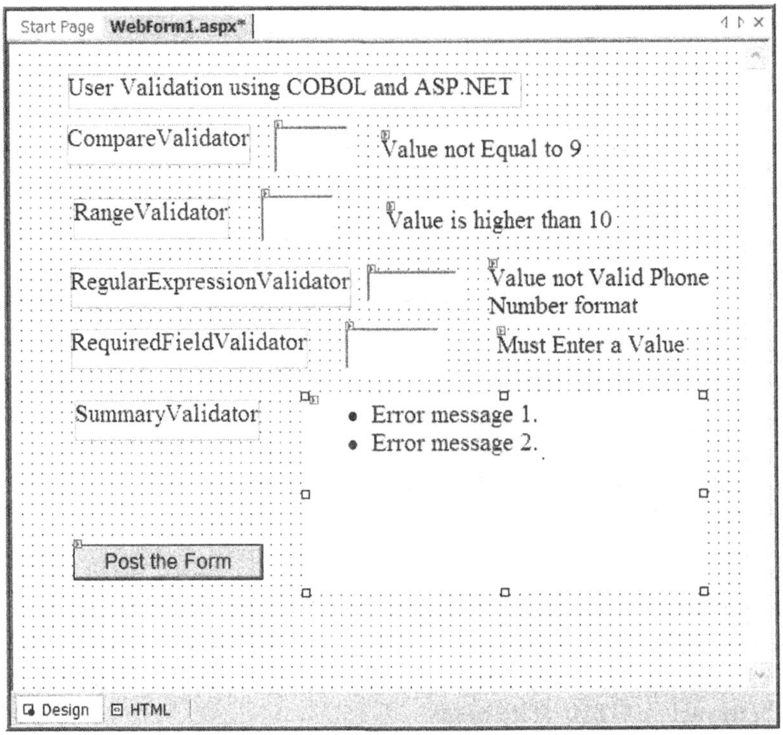

Figure 14-7. The sample application MyWebUseValidationCobol after all labels, TextBox controls, and validator controls have been added

After I placed all of the controls onto the Web Form, I proceeded to change the properties on each validator control. In the sample application, each validator control will be "associated" to the TextBox control that is immediately to the left of the validator control. I accomplished this "control association" by right-clicking each validator control and selecting Properties (see Figure 14-8) while in Design view. I then edited the *ControlToValidate* property and other properties.

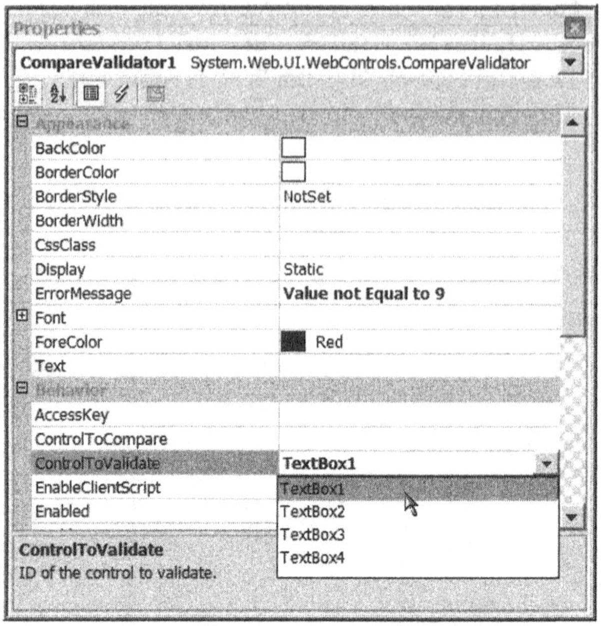

Figure 14-8. Updating the ControlToValidate property. Optionally, you can edit the HTML directly to modify each control's properties as needed.

As for the remaining properties, I will leave the color set to its default color (red) and use simple error messages. In your real-life development, you would typically create user-friendly messages. You could switch over to the HTML view and browse or edit the actual HTML statements.

I have included snippets of the generated HTML in Listings 14-4 through 14-6 for your viewing pleasure. To view this HTML in your ASP.NET Web application's WebForm1.aspx file, use the HTML tab.

The Forms Designer generated the HTML in Listing 14-4 as I was working with the TextBox server controls in Design view. Notice the use of the `runat="server"` attribute.

Listing 14-4. A Code Snippet from the MyWebUseValidationCobol Sample

```
. . .
<asp:TextBox id="TextBox1" style="Z-INDEX: 102; LEFT: 213px;
     POSITION: absolute; TOP: 64px"
     runat="server" Width="60px" Height="37px">
</asp:TextBox>
<asp:TextBox id="TextBox2" style="Z-INDEX: 103; LEFT: 202px;
     POSITION: absolute; TOP: 118px"
     runat="server" Width="59px" Height="37px">
```

```
</asp:TextBox>
<asp:TextBox id="TextBox3" style="Z-INDEX: 105; LEFT: 287px;
      POSITION: absolute; TOP: 177px"
      runat="server" Width="73px">
</asp:TextBox>
<asp:TextBox id="TextBox4" style="Z-INDEX: 106; LEFT: 269px;
      POSITION: absolute; TOP: 222px"
      runat="server" Width="76px" Height="33px">
</asp:TextBox>
. . .
```

Listing 14-5 shows the HTML snippet generated on behalf of the Label that I dragged and dropped from the HTML tab of the Toolbox. Notice the absence of the runat="server" attribute.

Listing 14-5. The HTML Generated on Behalf of the Label

```
. . .
<DIV style="DISPLAY: inline; Z-INDEX: 107; LEFT: 46px; WIDTH: 86px; POSITION:
      absolute; TOP: 63px; HEIGHT: 32px"
      ms_positioning="FlowLayout">CompareValidator
</DIV>
<DIV style="DISPLAY: inline; Z-INDEX: 112; LEFT: 51px; WIDTH: 86px; POSITION:
      absolute; TOP: 121px; HEIGHT: 32px"
      ms_positioning="FlowLayout">RangeValidator
</DIV>
<DIV style="DISPLAY: inline; Z-INDEX: 109; LEFT: 48px; WIDTH: 86px; POSITION:
      absolute; TOP: 175px; HEIGHT: 32px"
      ms_positioning="FlowLayout">RegularExpressionValidator
</DIV>
<DIV style="DISPLAY: inline; Z-INDEX: 110; LEFT: 48px; WIDTH: 86px; POSITION:
      absolute; TOP: 223px; HEIGHT: 32px"
      ms_positioning="FlowLayout">RequiredFieldValidator
</DIV>
<DIV style="DISPLAY: inline; Z-INDEX: 111; LEFT: 51px; WIDTH: 86px; POSITION:
      absolute; TOP: 279px; HEIGHT: 32px"
      ms_positioning="FlowLayout">SummaryValidator
</DIV>
. . .
```

Listing 14-6 shows a portion of the HTML generated as a result of placing each validation server control on the Web Form and using the Forms Designer to manipulate the Properties window. Notice that the runat="server" attribute is included to indicate that these controls are *server* controls.

Listing 14-6. The HTML Generated As a Result of Placing Each Validation Server Control on the Web Form

```
. . .
<asp:CompareValidator id="CompareValidator1"
      style="Z-INDEX: 113; LEFT: 299px; POSITION: absolute; TOP: 72px"
      runat="server" ErrorMessage="Value not Equal to 9"
      ControlToValidate="TextBox1" ValueToCompare="9">
</asp:CompareValidator>
<asp:RangeValidator id="RangeValidator1"
      style="Z-INDEX: 114; LEFT: 303px; POSITION: absolute; TOP: 128px"
      runat="server" ErrorMessage="Value is higher than 10"
      ControlToValidate="TextBox2" MaximumValue="10">
</asp:RangeValidator>
<asp:RegularExpressionValidator id="RegularExpressionValidator1"
      style="Z-INDEX: 116; LEFT: 385px; POSITION: absolute; TOP: 173px"
      runat="server" ErrorMessage="Value not Valid Phone Number format"
      ControlToValidate="TextBox3"
      ValidationExpression="((\(\d{3}\) ?)|(\d{3}-))?\d{3}-\d{4}">
</asp:RegularExpressionValidator>
<asp:RequiredFieldValidator id="RequiredFieldValidator1"
      style="Z-INDEX: 117; LEFT: 391px; POSITION: absolute; TOP: 226px"
      runat="server" ErrorMessage="Must Enter a Value"
      ControlToValidate="TextBox4">
</asp:RequiredFieldValidator>
<asp:ValidationSummary id="ValidationSummary1"
      style="Z-INDEX: 118; LEFT: 240px; POSITION: absolute; TOP: 280px"
      runat="server" Width="312px" Height="147px">
</asp:ValidationSummary>
. . .
```

For this sample application, the only time I actually touched the HTML code was when I performed some minor "code formatting" to create an optimal copy-and-paste page display. However, nothing is stopping anyone from going the reverse order (i.e., typing the HTML in and then viewing the result in Design view). In fact, you can drag and drop HTML elements from the Toolbox (HTML tab) directly into the HTML code. That is, if you are interested in minimizing your typing effort.

Let's now run the sample application (press F5 with the project open in the VS .NET IDE). After you enter a few test values and click the Button to post the Form, all expected results are produced. You will notice (see Figure 14-9) that each validator control is showing the appropriate error message. Additionally, the SummaryValidator control is showing a compiled summary of all of the error messages. How nice!

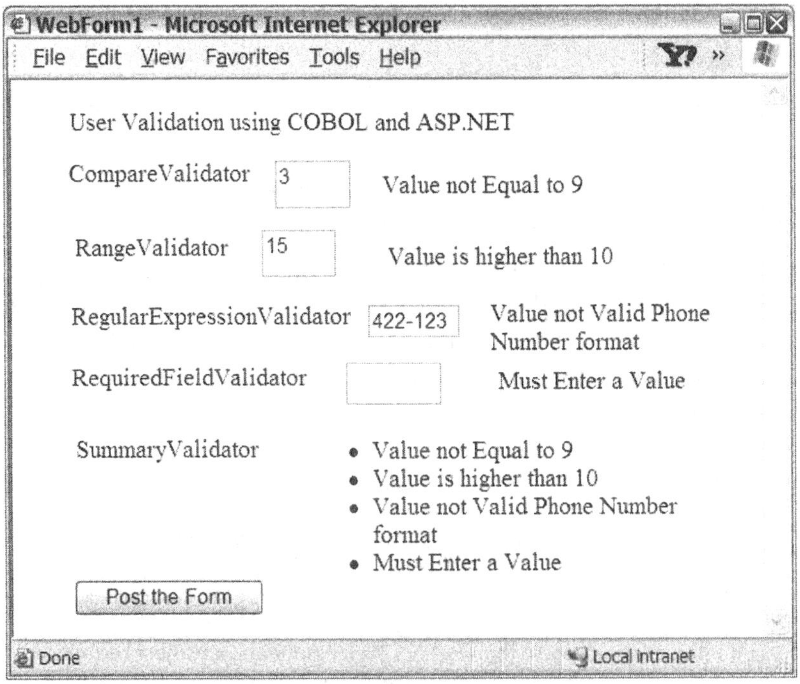

Figure 14-9. Executing the sample application ASP.NET application (MyWebUseValidationCobol) to demonstrate the use of validation controls

Using the .NET Framework and ASP.NET, it is extremely easy to add professionally styled validation to your user interface. With the right touch, this will be a welcomed change for your Web application. Just think how impressed your end users will be with the obvious effort toward adding true value to your user interface.

NOTE Obviously, in a real-life application you would add additional logic. Perhaps you would include business logic to capture and possibly store the data once it is validated. Given what you have learned about ADO.NET, adding a database connection to SQL Server should not present a big challenge for you. Other enhancements might include the addition of Web Form pages or other TextBox and Label controls. You could use the additional controls or pages to provide a "redisplay" of the validated data. Providing some type of confirmation to the user generally communicates that the data has been validated, received, and saved.

Isn't it amazing what you can do with ASP.NET? What you can now do in minutes with ASP.NET would have certainly taken much, much longer using mainframe tools to build a similar CICS application. Just think what your project managers will say when they find out that .NET fully supports a rapid application development (RAD) approach that enables you to create a complete data entry form with validation in less than an hour. Perhaps your future project timelines can be shortened a bit.

NOTE The sample application MyWebUseValidationCobol was created using the COBOL .NET ASP.NET Web Application project template. The ASP.NET Web Forms Designer basically built the HTML code (click, click, click). Given that, the resulting HTML would look virtually identical if I had chosen to use the VB .NET Web Application project template (instead of the COBOL .NET template). That being the case, I will leave it up to you to experiment with the VB .NET project template as you extend your training experience.

Throughout this section, I discussed adding value for your end user as he or she interacts with your application. I used user validation as an example scenario where interaction is common between your end user and your application. There are other scenarios. As you come across them, I am sure that the .NET Framework, ASP.NET, and VS .NET will serve your needs and then some.

In the next section you will take a high-level look at some possible opportunities for adding value made available through XML Web services. The ASP.NET XML Web service platform is no stranger to the need for value-added development. You will continue focusing on adding value, but with a different type of interface: the application interface.

Adding Value with XML Web Services

Although Web services do not actually have a graphical user interface, it is still possible to add value to their interface—that is, their *application* interface. When you think about it, its very name, "service," implies added value. You could then say that developing XML Web services that provide valuable services to Web service consumers is a reasonable requirement. The following discussion should help jump start your journey toward satisfying the requirement to develop value-added XML Web services.

It just so happens that an excellent example of Web services adding value for a group of end users is right at your fingertips: VS .NET. Recall that Chapter 5 introduced several features on the VS .NET Start Page that require an Internet connection.

Those VS .NET features include the following: What's New, Online Community, Headlines, Search Online, Downloads, XML Web Services, and Web Hosting. In each case, the VS .NET application seamlessly integrates with an online source of data (a Web service) to add value to you, the VS .NET end user. Microsoft's example provides guidance as to how XML Web services and a value-added service can be brought together. Where, then, are other examples of XML Web services adding value? What else is available to help you develop the XML Web services of tomorrow?

CROSS-REFERENCE You too can tap into VS .NET, integrating other Web service data sources. Recall that Chapter 5 introduced you to the opportunities exposed in VS .NET's object model.

To help answer these questions, you can monitor the current events surrounding XML Web services. As it turns out, Microsoft and several other vendors recently announced the availability of software development kits, toolkits, application programming interfaces (APIs), and other software[8] to serve as conduits for the creation of many value-added XML Web services. I provide the following list of recent XML Web service advances to possibly inform those involved in value-added XML Web service development:

- Microsoft Web Services Enhancements 1.0 for Microsoft .NET (WSE)

- Microsoft .NET Services and .NET Messenger Service APIs

---

8. Most of the software development kits (SDKs) and toolkits are free to download and "experiment" with.

- Microsoft MapPoint .NET XML Web service

- Microsoft Universal Description, Discovery, and Integration .NET Software Development Kit (UDDI .NET SDK)

- Microsoft Office XP Web Services Toolkit 2.0

- Microsoft SQL Server 2000 Web Services Toolkit (Microsoft .NET Enterprise Servers)

- Amazon.com Web services developer's kit

- Google Web APIs developer's kit

You can download each of the development kits in the preceding list to obtain the respective SDKs and APIs. Please refer to the "To Learn More" section located at the end of this chapter for the relevant URLs. The following sections will provide you with an overview of each XML Web service offering. In each case, try to see the connection between the service's use and the possible value being added for your end users.

NOTE Keep in mind that this is just a partial list of Web services opportunities that are available. These Web service products, those from other vendors not mentioned here, as well as the ones that you will create yourself, are all acknowledged.

Microsoft Web Services Enhancements 1.0 for Microsoft .NET

You will recall that there was a brief discussion of the Web Services Interoperability Organization (WS-I) and the Global XML Web Services Architecture (GXA) in the previous chapter. WSE is the first set of APIs to be officially released to enable XML Web service development using several of the WS Specifications (WS-Security, WS-Routing, DIME, and WS-Attachments). Essentially, WSE is a .NET class library, an extension to the existing .NET Framework (class library).

Microsoft .NET Services

Originally marketed as a set of subscription-based XML Web services called .NET My Services, this product offering has been recently streamlined by Microsoft (and the term "my" has been removed). The toolset offering, .NET Services, now includes two sets of subscription-based XML Web services: .NET Passport and .NET Alerts. This means that you can seamlessly integrate the authentication features of .NET Passport or the notification features of .NET Alerts directly into your own application.

Downloads are available for the respective SDKs and related documentation. Microsoft also has an SDK available (for download) called the .NET Messenger Service APIs. This SDK exposes instant messaging types of functionalities.

Microsoft MapPoint .NET XML Web Service

This Web service offering exposes Web methods that you can integrate into your own application. You can then enhance your user interface by providing maps, driving directions, opportunities to calculate distances, and proximity searches. Obviously, if your user interface is appropriate for this type of functionality, this would be an added value to your end users. An SDK is also available for this Web service offering.

Microsoft Universal Description, Discovery, and Integration .NET Software Development Kit

Microsoft has made available the Universal Description, Discovery, and Integration .NET Software Development Kit (UDDI .NET SDK). You can use the UDDI .NET SDK to integrate the features of the UDDI (enabling others to dynamically find your Web service) directly into your application. This would be similar to the UDDI feature that is exposed in the VS .NET IDE.

CROSS-REFERENCE　　I briefly discussed the UDDI in Chapter 13 in the section "XML Web Services Continue to Evolve."

Microsoft Office XP Web Services Toolkit 2.0

Those who have a need to develop using the Visual Basic for Applications (VBA) development model will be delighted with the Office XP Web Services Toolkit 2.0. Using this *free* toolkit, the Microsoft Office XP family of products (Word 2002, Excel 2002, and so forth) can now consume XML Web services. You can now enable your VBA application to use either the UDDI or Web Services Description Language (WSDL) approach to locate, reference, and consume XML data from XML Web services.

Imagine that: external data from the Web, programmatically integrated right into a Word document or an Excel spreadsheet. Your end users are sure to see this as a value-added feature.

Microsoft SQL Server 2000 Web Services Toolkit

Using this toolkit, you can create XML Web services directly from SQL Server stored procedures. If this fits the development architecture that you are seeking, using this *free* toolkit could be an easy opportunity to add value to your application. When you download this toolkit, you will also download the software package known as SQLXML 3.0. As you may recall, I introduced SQLXML 3.0 in Chapter 12.

A reference is provided in the "To Learn More" section to help get you started with your SQL Server–based XML Web service. After you successfully create your Web service, your client application (or the client applications of others) can then reference and consume the XML delivered from your XML Web service.

Amazon.com Web Services Developer's Kit

Say that you develop an ASP.NET Web application and plan to add a hyperlink that your users can use to surf over to Amazon.com. Perhaps this is beneficial because of a product that you are selling on Amazon.com. Your concern, though, is making it as easy as possible for your users to navigate back to your site when they have completed shopping on Amazon.com.

Well, Amazon.com has listened and created a free Web services developer's kit. Using this SDK, you can reference and consume data from the Amazon.com XML Web service. Then, you display the received *content* on your Web site. In other words, your users will remain parked on your application while you programmatically deliver Amazon.com product information to them. Over time, I expect many other vendors to follow Amazon.com's lead. This is yet another opportunity to add value to your own application by taking advantage of XML Web services.

Google Web APIs Developer's Kit

Have you ever used the fantastic Internet search engine, Google
(http://www.google.com)? Maybe not, huh? Have you ever used the
Yahoo! (http://www.yahoo.com) or Netscape (http://www.netscape.com)
search engines? Yes? Well, then you actually have used Google's search engine.
That is right. Google's search engine works so well that other companies have
contracted with Google to use its search engine behind the scenes on their
own Web sites.

Now you too can add Google's searching power to your own Web or Windows
application. To do this, you need to download the Google Web APIs. Currently, the
API is considered a beta version, restricts you to 1,000 daily searches, and is *free* of
charge. The API enables you to reference and consume the Google Web service.
Their Web service exposes a set of members to enable you to send in "search criteria" and receive XML representing the returned search results. The nice thing is
that the Search input field and the returned search results delivered to your end
users are seamlessly integrated into your own value-added Web user interface.
Nice, very nice!

Consider letting the Microsoft, Amazon.com, and Google XML Web service
examples inspire you to create your own XML Web services. You too can create
value-added APIs as these vendors have. Optionally, you can use the XML Web services offered by these software vendors[9] and others. As a Web service *consumer,*
you can seamlessly integrate the exposed advanced functionality into your application. In other words, you can use these Web service opportunities to easily add
value to your user and application interfaces.

Summary

This chapter's goals were as follows:

- To explore the use of .NET's Control class to create informative Windows
  applications

- To discuss ways to use HTML controls and Web controls to develop interactive ASP.NET applications

- To discover opportunities for XML Web services

---

9. There is generally a subscription fee associated with XML Web services offered by most
   software vendors.

In the three sections of this chapter, you have focused on adding value to your user and application interfaces for the benefit of your end users. In the first section, you explored a few Control classes that you could use to add value to your .NET Windows applications. The second section opened the floodgates to a full discussion of various types of Control classes available to ASP.NET applications. In that section, I suggested user validation as a way to add value to your application. In the last section, I presented several XML Web service opportunities made available by a few vendors, with hopes to inspire the creation of great XML Web services or the consumption of some of the better ones being published.

In the next chapter, you will explore managing state and cache. Although you will recognize that managing state and cache are certainly value-adding opportunities, the next chapter places significantly less emphasis on controls and the user interface.

To Learn More

The following are some suggested supplemental references to further your retraining effort.

Books

Architecting Web Services, by William Oellermann (Apress, 2001):
   `http://www.apress.com/book/bookDisplay.html?bID=22.`
Moving to ASP.NET: Web Development with VB .NET, by Steve Harris and Rob Macdonald (Apress, 2002):
   `http://www.apress.com/book/bookDisplay.html?bID=78.`
User Interfaces in VB .NET: Windows Forms and Custom Controls, by Matthew MacDonald (Apress, 2002):
   `http://www.apress.com/book/bookDisplay.html?bID=99.`

Magazines

.NET Magazine:
   `http://www.fawcette.com/dotnetmag/`
MSDN Magazine:
   `http://msdn.microsoft.com/msdnmag/`
Visual Studio Magazine:
   `http://www.fawcette.com/vsm/`

Windows Developer Magazine:

    http://www.wd-mag.com/

XML & Web Services Magazine:

    http://www.fawcette.com/xmlmag/

Web Sites

.NET Architecture Center:

    http://msdn.microsoft.com/architecture/

Amazon.com Web services developer's kit:

    http://associates.amazon.com/exec/panama/associates/join/developer/
    kit.html

ASP.NET Syntax:

    http://msdn.microsoft.com/library/en-us/cpgenref/html/
    gnconaspnetsyntax.asp

Building User-Centric Experiences with .NET Services:

    http://www.microsoft.com/netservices/userexperiences.asp

Creating Windows Applications:

    http://msdn.microsoft.com/library/en-us/vbcon/html/
    vboriCreatingStandaloneAppsVB.asp

Dr. GUI .NET #7: Conway's Game of Life as a Windows Forms Application:

    http://msdn.microsoft.com/library/en-us/dnguinet/html/
    drguinet7_update.asp

Google Web APIs developer's kit:

    http://www.google.com/apis/download.html

GotDotNet:

    http://www.gotdotnet.com/

Introduction to ASP.NET:

    http://msdn.microsoft.com/library/en-us/cpguide/html/
    cpconintroductiontoasp.asp

MapPoint .NET XML Web Service:

    http://msdn.microsoft.com/library/default.asp?url=/nhp/
    Default.asp?contentid=28001402

Microsoft .NET Alerts:

    http://www.microsoft.com/netservices/alerts/default.asp

Microsoft .NET Enterprise Servers (Microsoft SQL Server 2000 Web Services
    Toolkit):

    http://msdn.microsoft.com/downloads/topic.asp?URL=/MSDN-FILES/028/001/
    187/topic.xml

Microsoft .NET Messenger Service APIs:

http://msdn.microsoft.com/downloads/topic.asp?url=/msdn-files/028/001/359/topic.xml

Microsoft .NET Passport Software Development Kit:

http://msdn.microsoft.com/downloads/topic.asp?url=/msdn-files/028/000/123/topic.xml

Microsoft ASP.NET Home Page:

http://www.asp.net/

Microsoft Community (discussion groups, e-newsletters, and so forth):

http://communities2.microsoft.com/

Microsoft Office XP Web Services Toolkit 2.0:

http://www.msdn.microsoft.com/library/en-us/dnxpwst2/html/odc_offxpwstoolkit2.asp

Microsoft Patterns & Practices:

http://msdn.microsoft.com/practices/

Microsoft Universal Description, Discovery, and Integration .NET Software Development Kit (UDDI .NET SDK):

http://msdn.microsoft.com/downloads/topic.asp?url=/msdn-files/028/000/123/topic.xml

MSDN:

http://msdn.microsoft.com

NetCOBOL Samples (provided by Fujitsu Software and Intensity Software):

http://www.netcobolsamples.com/

Web Services Enhancements for Microsoft .NET:

http://msdn.microsoft.com/webservices/building/wse/default.aspx

Windows .NET Server 2003:

http://msdn.microsoft.com/library/default.asp?url=/nhp/default.asp?contentid=28001691

XML Web Services Developer Center:

http://msdn.microsoft.com/webservices/

CHAPTER 15

Managing Cache and State for ASP.NET

Preserving Content and Data Between Web Program Executions

In this chapter

- Understanding "output" cache management

- Discussing client-based state management

- Exploring server-based state management

YOU NEED NOT LOOK far to find an example of state and cache management on the Web these days. For example, I have often used a very popular travel Web site to expedite my travel arrangements. For me, one of the site's most impressive features is demonstrated each time I navigate through the site, backward and forward, pricing and then repricing my product selections. All preferences and selections I enter on one page are conveniently stashed away, saved, and then displayed as appropriate.

It is easy to see why I referred earlier to the topic of state and cache management as a way to add value to your ASP.NET application (see the section "Making Your ASP.NET Applications Interactive" in Chapter 14). Each time I return to this travel Web site, I am quickly reminded of the pleasurable experience I had when I used the site before. I appreciate how the site "remembers" me by greeting me by name and making available to me my previous itineraries.

NOTE The travel site I refer to in the preceding paragraph is Expedia.com (http://www.expedia.com). Given that this is not an endorsement of any kind, I would like my mention of the site here to be viewed as just an acknowledgement, a case study of state management. I am only referring to this particular company as an example. I am sure that many other travel Web sites also offer these types of user interface features.

Does this remind you of your own experiences as a Web user? Think about it. Are you generally happy to have your personalized display preferences saved for you? How about those multipage questionnaires? Do you appreciate having previously entered data not disappear when you navigate around a site? As you may have guessed, you can programmatically address each of these concerns (and more) with ASP.NET's state and cache management features.

In this chapter, you will sort out the many options available when you want to enhance your ASP.NET applications with state and cache management. I begin this chapter's discussion with a brief review of the legacy mainframe CICS environment and the methods generally used to "manage state." This will help establish a perspective toward the need to *preserve* data. Next, I discuss the ASP.NET approach to cache management. I end the chapter with a discussion of ASP.NET state management features, both client based and server based.

Legacy CICS "State Management"

In a previous chapter,[1] I discussed the pseudo-conversational CICS model. There, I suggested that the techniques used (e.g., DFHCOMMAREA usage in the Linkage Section) to support this model were analogous to common practices used with the disconnected, stateless HTTP/ASP.NET model. With these thoughts in mind, let's look further into the details of this mainframe CICS analogy.

When you coded your legacy mainframe CICS applications, you were faced with the choice to use either the MAPONLY or DATAONLY option in your SEND BMS Screen MAP program logic. Using these CICS options, you were basically controlling what data was to be transferred between client (your 3270 screen) and server (the mainframe HOST). The concept of needing to manage "content" separately from "user data" is an important concept to resurface.

---

1. See the section "Application Level: Comparing CICS with ASP.NET" in Chapter 13.

TIP You should find yourself being reminded of this type of content and data management when I discuss state and cache management throughout this chapter.

Another important concept that you can be reminded of from your mainframe CICS experience is queues, as in temporary storage (TS) queues and transient data (TD) queues. As you know, TS queues and TD queues were used as solutions for saving and passing data between program executions (and even between programs/tasks).

Although the CICS DFHCOMMAREA and the Linkage Section served this purpose as well, the CICS queues were preferred if you were working with a large quantity of data. Choosing either of the CICS queues over the CICS DFHCOM-MAREA meant that you would use less of your "main memory" and more hard disk space. For application performance and resource utilization, this design choice was generally welcomed.

NOTE In comparing the two general types of CICS queues, you will recall that the TS queue had a simpler, dynamic implementation and supported sequential and random access. On the other hand, if you wanted to use the CICS Automatic Transaction Initiation (ATI) feature or you wanted to process or print your queue data, the TD queue was a better choice. However, the TD queue did not support random access.

To complete your trip down mainframe CICS memory lane (as it pertains to managing the preservation of data), you should be reminded of two additional legacy CICS techniques. The Common Work Area (CWA) and the Terminal Control Table User Area (TCTUA) advanced CICS features were known to be useful as a means for storing and passing data between CICS transactions.

NOTE In the ASP.NET arena, the practice of preserving visual content and data between program executions is referred to as *state and cache management.* In the CICS mainframe arena, the practice of preserving visual content and data between program executions is referred to as, well, *preserving visual content and data between program executions.*

There is a simple point to take away from these CICS mainframe analogies. When it came to designing your CICS program for saving and passing data (managing the preservation of data) between program executions, you had choices. The quantity of data being saved and how you wanted to work with the data made one design choice or the other more or less appropriate. Pulling this general point from this mainframe analogy will be helpful as you turn now to dive into ASP.NET state and cache management.

The Key/Value Pairs in the Collections Namespace

The more you program in .NET, the more you will come across classes and methods that either consume or return a key/value pair structure. In those cases, if you take a moment to dig down a bit, you will usually find that the key/value pair is tied back to a specific class (structure or interface) from the *System.Collections* namespace.

Therefore, having a general understanding of the Collection classes, structures, and interfaces will move you several retraining steps forward. Effectively, this would work like reusable knowledge: Learn once (with the System.Collections namespace) and reuse the knowledge repeatedly throughout .NET.

By the way, a special bonus awaits you when you learn about the *System.Collections.Stack* class. The *Pop* and *Push* methods of the Stack class will remind you of the READQ and WRITEQ commands you used with the CICS TD queue. For example, once you Pop an item from the Stack class, it's no longer available. Doesn't this remind you of the "read once" behavior associated with the CICS (intrapartition) TD queue?

Preparation for Cache and State

A proper discussion of cache and state management will be best served by first revisiting the topics of application-level events and page-level events. Do you recall the discussions regarding page-level events and application-level events in Chapter 13? Feel free to revisit that earlier chapter for a brief review.

> **TIP** The ASP.NET application/session-level events and methods are commonly accessed in the Global.asax file. You will see the Global.asax file in the VS .NET IDE Solution Explorer window.

For your convenience, I have included two figures here that were both previously shown in Chapter 13. Figure 15-1 shows page-level events that occur to satisfy an HTTP page request. Figure 15-2 shows events that occur at the application/session level.

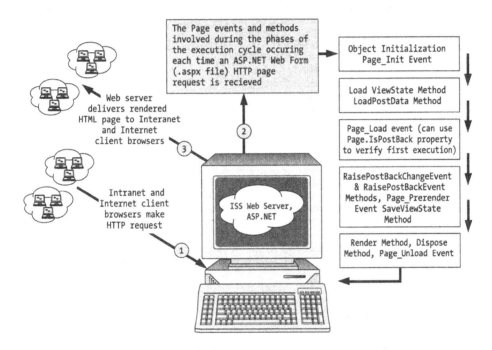

Figure 15-1. Page-level events raised in order to satisfy an HTTP page request

Please take a moment to review Figures 15-1 and 15-2. You will refer to these figures during the state and cache management discussions that follow.

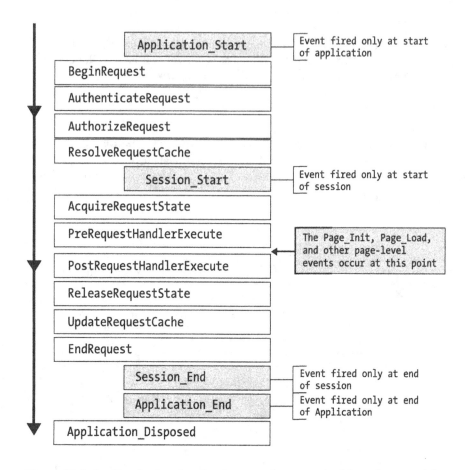

Figure 15-2. Application/session-level events that are raised in order to satisfy an HTTP page request

Save Your Cache!

At some point during your ASP.NET research and training missions, you will want to understand the concerns of working with the stateless HTTP protocol. The good news is that ASP.NET is very flexible and offers several choices. The bad news is that there are enough options available to encourage confusion. Eventually you will come across the two topics of cache management and state management, and then the confusion will begin.

On the surface, ASP.NET *cache management* appears to be similar to ASP.NET *state management*. That is, both cache and state are related to the preservation of "data" between HTTP requests. However, as you'll learn, there's a huge difference between cache management and state management. Adding to the confusion, ASP.NET has introduced a new feature referred to as *application cache,* which is really a state management feature.

In an effort to clear things up, I discuss *output cache* in the following section, which focuses on cache management. I discuss the topic of *application cache* (unofficially known as ApplicationStateOnSteroids) in the later section "Application-Level State," which focuses on state management. By the time you work through the information in this chapter, you will have a firm understanding of both cache management and state management.

Introducing Output Cache

In the earlier section "Preparation for Cache and State," I included two figures to resurface the sequence of events that occur each time an HTTP request is received by IIS and ASP.NET. You were reminded how the Application_Start and BeginRequest events began the sequenced event series. The page-level events (Page Init, Page Load, and so forth) were shown to occur a bit later. The end of the sequenced series included more application/session-level events (e.g., the EndRequest event).

As you'll see, there's an intimate connection between output cache management and the sequence of events that occurs when an HTTP request is received. Let's drill down further.

Generally speaking (in this context), the HTTP request is asking for a specific Web page. Once the request is received, the application-level events are raised, the

---

2. OK, I'm attempting to make a good point in a semihumorous fashion. Considering the seriousness surrounding a .NET retraining effort, a little harmless fun here and there can't hurt.

page-level events are raised, a few more application-level events are raised, and then the intrinsic Response object is delivered to the client's browser. The Response object contains the HTML that is rendered on the client's browser.

TIP It is never too early to think about using cache. If possible, your initial application design should include plans to take advantage of cache opportunities. A potentially huge performance gain can be realized.

When you start thinking about using the caching features of ASP.NET, you are really thinking about altering the sequence in which the application/page-level events are raised. In other words, you can cause the application-level events *PreRequestHandlerExecute* and *PostRequestHandlerExecute*, and more important, the group of page-level events, to not execute. Therefore, you could possibly avoid unneeded server-side processing.

For example, the application-level BeginRequest event is always raised. Additionally, the application-level EndRequest event is always raised. This is true regardless of your use of output cache management. On the other hand, a decision to "turn on" caching for a given page (or user control) will result in other events not being raised at all (that is, in between the raised BeginRequest and EndRequest events).

CROSS-REFERENCE I discuss the technique of enabling output cache for a page or a user control later in the section "Using Output Cache."

Generally speaking, if a page is *not* cached, the page-level events are raised in order to update the Response object with new HTML to satisfy the HTTP request. Otherwise, if a page *is* cached, there is no need to process the page-level events. The existing page (the Response object with previously rendered HTML) is retrieved from the output cache and delivered to the client that is sending the HTTP request.

Handlers, Modules, and Application-Level Events

You may have noticed (via the Global.asax file) that a pair of application-level events are associated with the "handler" execution: PreRequestHandlerExecute and PostRequestHandlerExecute. When I saw these events for the first time, I could not help but ask, "What is a *handler*?"

I discovered that an HTTP handler is a component that implements the *IHttpHandler* interface. The System.Web.HttpApplication and System.Web.UI.Page classes both implement the IHttpHandler interface and are therefore HTTP handlers. Handlers serve as "targets" for an HTTP request (much like an Internet server API or ISAPI extension).

As it turns out, a special component referred to as an *IHttpModule* works closely with the IHttpHandler. As you may have guessed, a component needs to implement the IHttpModule interface to become an HTTP module (much like an Internet server API or ISAPI filter). An example of this is an HTTP module referred to as the *OutputCache* module (*System.Web.Caching.OutputCacheModule*).

This becomes relevant when you observe that there are a pair of application-level events/methods that are obviously tied to cache: *ResolveRequestCache* and *UpdateRequestCache*. The OutputCache module is *registered* to handle these two events when (and if) they are raised.

Together, the ResolveRequestCache and UpdateRequestCache events/methods are responsible for seeing that all HTTP requests are served from the output cache when appropriate. These two events/methods are also responsible for seeing to it that the handler execution (which includes the group of page-level events/methods) is bypassed when appropriate and for checking that the output cache is updated (when appropriate) after the handler completes execution.

If you are curious, you can easily discover what the other HTTP modules are running behind the scenes ("filtering" each HTTP request before and after the handler is executed). You need only view the *Modules* property of the *HttpApplication* object. There you will find an *HttpModuleCollection* class hosting the OutputCache HTTP module, the *Session* HTTP module (*System.Web.SessionState.SessionStateModule*), and other HTTP modules.

In designing your ASP.NET application, you will want to be on the lookout for opportunities to use output cache (e.g., a page that infrequently changes). You will want to identify those cases where the HTML delivered by one Response object can satisfy the needs of multiple/subsequent HTTP requests. Under these scenarios, there is no need to execute the page-level events (and related application-level events/methods) to generate a new page. To satisfy subsequent HTTP requests, the "existing" page can be retrieved from cache.

In the following section, you will take a look at exactly how you would "turn on" output cache in your ASP.NET application. Additionally, you will examine a few of the configuration techniques used for output cache (e.g., setting cache expiration time, caching multiple versions of pages, and so forth).

Using Output Cache

You now have a basic, under-the-hood view of what output cache usage really does. With that foundational understanding, you can proceed to use output cache and still enjoy a sense of control over your ASP.NET application process, application-level events, and page-level events. The only thing that remains is a rather simple discussion of syntax and implementation.

NOTE Had I taken a more conventional approach to introducing output cache, I would have started at this point. Please keep that in mind as you seek out supplemental research material that covers the details of the ASP.NET output cache feature.

Once you identify the page (or user control) that you want to cache, you will need to do the following:

- Choose your implementation approach. Will you use the HTML-based directive or the server-side code logic (or both)?

- Determine if you want to cache multiple versions of the page (or user control).

- Determine the length of time the page (or user control) should be cached.

If you take the HTML-based directive approach for your output cache implementation, you will need to edit the .aspx file (for page caching) or the .ascx file (for user control caching). The full syntax options of the @ *OutputCache* directive are as follows:

```
<%@ OutputCache Duration="Desired#OfSeconds"
    Location="Any | Client | Downstream | Server | None"
    VaryByControl="YourControlname" VaryByCustom="browser | customstring"
    VaryByHeader="HTTPheaders" VaryByParam="YourParameterName" %>
```

You have several choices when using the @ OutputCache directive inside your .aspx or .ascx file. For example, if you want to cache a page (or user control) for 10 seconds and you do not need to distinguish between multiple versions of the page (or user control), you use the following @ OutputCache directive statement at the top of your .aspx or .ascx file:

```
<%@ OutputCache Duration="10" VaryByParam="None" %>
```

The output cache feature is flexible enough to allow you to cache multiple versions of a page (or user control). In other words, as a page (or user control) can vary by input parameter, user session, and so on, you can cache each varying version. The easiest way to accomplish this is to use the appropriate parameter option available through the @ OutputCache directive. The following example shows the approach for caching multiple versions of a page (or user control) that might vary by an input parameter. The @ OutputCache directive would cause a separate version of the page (or user control) to be cached for 10 seconds per the unique values received in MyPassedParameter (i.e., via a query string or form post).

```
<%@ OutputCache duration="10" varybyparam="MyPassedParameter" %>
```

If you prefer, you can choose to control the page (or user control) output caching from inside your server-side code-behind file(s). To manipulate the cache policy for a page, you will need to use the *SetExpires* and *SetCacheability* methods of the *Cache* class (exposed by the Response object). When you work with a user control, the *PartialCaching* metadata attribute (*System.Web.UI.PartialCachingAttribute*) is available for programmatic implementation.

ASP.NET provides extensive cache management support (both for pages and user controls). Keep in mind that it is common to see a huge performance difference in your ASP.NET applications after you properly use cache management as a way to preserve data between HTTP requests. I will now switch gears to discuss the *other* type of data preservation practice: state management.

TIP Experiment with output cache. Feel free to enhance the sample applications (StateManagementVB and StateManagementCobol) created for this chapter. Consider adding cache management support by simply adding the @ OutputCache directive to the .aspx file as discussed in this section.

State for the Stateless Protocol

Preserving content and data (rather, managing state) is appropriately considered to be a critical part of ASP.NET application design. For this reason, the .NET platform has extensive support for state management and it offers many choices to fit your needs. These choices can easily be grouped into the following two general categories:

- State management based on the client

- State management based on the server

As the categories imply, your state management design choices will be decided between preserving content/data on the client side or the server side. Once you choose between the two, you will be faced with other design choices. As shown in Figure 15-3, you can imagine having a basic decision tree for state management.

Although the choices shown in Figure 15-3 are not necessarily cut-and-dry and often offer overlapping benefits, this basic decision tree should help get you started. Otherwise, the discussions that follow provide more details that should help prepare you for making those choices.

NOTE To help demonstrate how you would implement the various state management solutions, I have created two sample ASP.NET applications: StateManagementVB and StateManagementCobol. Relevant code snippets from these sample projects are included in each related section. The user interface for the sample applications is shown later in the section "User Interface for the Sample Applications."

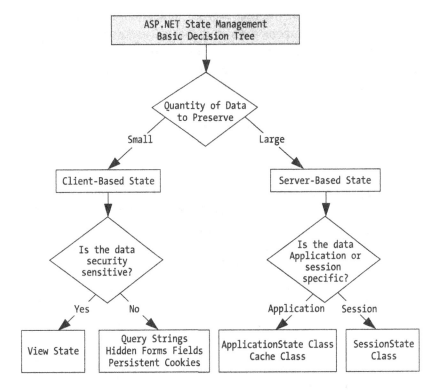

Figure 15-3. A state management decision tree for ASP.NET

Client-Based State Management

Generally speaking, you will want to look to client-based state management when you need to preserve small amounts of content/data. The following list presents the various types of client-based state management choices:

- Query strings

- Persistent cookies

- Hidden forms fields

- View state

In some cases, security concerns, user browser configurations, or just coding styles and preferences may be among the factors that will make one choice or another a better design candidate. Other factors exist that you will want to be aware of and take into consideration. In the following sections, you will drill down into each client-based state management choice for a more complete understanding.

Query Strings

The query string approach to storing and retrieving data is a very simple yet useful technique. Have you ever noticed a Web URL that included a question mark (?) as part of the URL string? If so, you have seen part of the implementation of a query string. The query string approach is an available option for programmatically passing a small amount of data from one Web page to another Web page.

TIP   To retrieve query strings, the .NET Framework support includes use of the *System.Web.HttpRequest* class. Use this class to access the intrinsic Request object and the *QueryString* property. Be aware that the values stored in the QueryString property are stored as the type *NameValueCollection* class (as in *System.Collections.Specialized.NameValueCollection*).

Say that you coded the page-to-page navigation logic using the Response object's *Redirect* method. When you code the URL parameter, you need only append a question mark symbol followed by one or more name/value pairs (e.g., `name1=value1`, `name2=value2`, and so on). The targeted page need only pull the passed values from the QueryString property of the Request object. That's it. It's that simple.

The simplicity of this client-side state management approach is certainly an important factor to consider for its use. If the data being passed is not of a sensitive nature and security is not a concern, the query string approach is certainly a viable option for client-side state management.

NOTE   When you pass data using the query string approach, you will notice that the URL and the passed query string data appears in the browser's address bar as follows: `http://www.somewebsite.com/targetedpage.aspx?name1=value1`.

Query String Code Samples

The code snippets in Listings 15-1 through 15-4 are taken from the sample projects created for this chapter.

Listing 15-1. Creating and Passing a QueryString in VB .NET

```
Response.Redirect("WebForm2.aspx?PassedQueryStringValue=" & Me.TextBox1.Text)
```

Listing 15-2. Retrieving a Passed QueryString in VB .NET

```
Me.TextBox1.Text = Request.QueryString("PassedQueryStringValue")
```

Listing 15-3. Creating and Passing a QueryString in COBOL .NET

```
001633      INITIALIZE MiscString
001634      SET MiscString1 TO PROP-TEXT OF TextBox1
001635      STRING "WebForm2.aspx?PassedQueryStringValue=" DELIMITED BY SIZE
001636           MiscString1 DELIMITED BY SPACES
001637            INTO MiscString
001638      INVOKE MyResponse "Redirect" USING BY VALUE MiscString.
```

Listing 15-4. Retrieving a Passed QueryString in COBOL .NET

```
000872      SET MyParamsObject TO PROP-PARAMS OF PROP-REQUEST OF SELF
000873      INVOKE MyParamsObject "get_Item"
000874      USING BY VALUE "PassedQueryStringValue" RETURNING MiscString1
000875      SET PROP-TEXT OF TextBox1 TO MiscString1
```

Persistent Cookies

Persistent cookies are basically small files that can be persisted (saved) to the client's local environment/hard disk. These files are then later retrieved as per the state management needs of your Web application. You would typically store small amounts of data in a cookie. Used in this way, persistent cookies are another client-based alternative for state management.

NOTE There has long been a 4096-byte maximum size limit of the cookie. Newer browsers are expected to increase the maximum size to an 8192-byte limit.

As with the query string approach, the implementation of a persistent cookies state solution is simple, requires minimal program coding to accomplish, and makes use of the Response and Request objects. Additionally, like query strings, persistent cookies should be used when security concerns do not apply and the data being persisted in the cookie is not of a sensitive nature. Nevertheless, persistent cookies (or just *cookies*) do differ from query strings in a couple of significant ways.

NOTE You should not confuse *persistent* cookies with *session* cookies. I discuss session cookies later in the section "To Be a Cookieless Session or Not to Be a Cookieless Session."

For example, the use of cookies is dependent on end users' willingness to allow cookies from your Web site. As you may know, some people are not comfortable with the idea of Web sites saving a state-holding file onto their local hard disk. You and I, as developers, may not see a problem with cookies. However, not everyone approaches the topic of cookies with open arms.

TIP The *Cookies* property of the intrinsic Response and Request objects is used to create and retrieve cookies, respectively. The objects being added and retrieved are of the types *System.Web.HttpCookieCollection* and *System.Web.HttpCookie*.

Another example of where persistent cookies differ from query strings is in the capability of persistent cookies to allow *expiration control* of the persisted file. In other words, you can use persistent cookies to maintain state beyond the life of a page, a session, or even an application.

As you can see, each state management technique has its own strengths and weaknesses. One of the cookies approach's strengths is that it has been successfully implemented in many applications. Consequently, the use of cookies continues to be a state maintenance choice worthy of serious consideration.

Persistent Cookies Code Samples

The code snippets in Listings 15-5 through 15-8 are taken from the sample applications created for this chapter. Shown in both VB .NET and COBOL .NET, the persistent cookie is created and then retrieved.

Listing 15-5. Creating a Persistent Cookie in VB .NET

```
Dim MyFirstCookie As New HttpCookie("MiscText")
MyFirstCookie.Value = Me.TextBox1.Text
MyFirstCookie.Expires = DateTime.Now.AddSeconds(15)
Response.Cookies.Add(MyFirstCookie)
```

Listing 15-6. Retrieving a Persistent Cookie in VB .NET

```
Dim myRetrievedCookie As HttpCookie
myRetrievedCookie = Me.Request.Cookies("MiscText")
Dim myCookieIsExpired As Boolean = (myRetrievedCookie Is Nothing)
If myCookieIsExpired Then
    Me.TextBox5.Text = "No Cookie"
Else
    Me.TextBox5.Text = Me.Request.Cookies("MiscText").Value
End If
```

Listing 15-7. Creating a Persistent Cookie in COBOL .NET

```
002980     INVOKE CLASS-COOKIE "NEW" USING BY VALUE "MiscText"
002981         RETURNING MyCookieObject
002990     SET PROP-VALUE OF MyCookieObject TO PROP-TEXT OF TextBox1
003000     SET NowDateTime TO PROP-NOW OF CLASS-DATETIME
003010     INVOKE NowDateTime "AddSeconds" USING BY VALUE 15
003011         RETURNING WhenToExpire
003020     SET PROP-EXPIRES OF MyCookieObject TO WhenToExpire
003030     SET MyCurrentContext TO PROP-CURRENT OF CLASS-HTTPCONTEXT
003040     SET MyResponse TO PROP-RESPONSE OF MyCurrentContext
003050     SET MyCookieCollection TO PROP-COOKIES OF MyResponse
003060     INVOKE MyCookieCollection "Add" USING BY VALUE MyCookieObject
```

Listing 15-8. Retrieving a Persistent Cookie in COBOL.NET

```
003153     SET MyCookieCollection TO PROP-COOKIES OF PROP-REQUEST OF SELF
003154     INVOKE MyCookieCollection "get_Item"
003155        USING BY VALUE "MiscText" RETURNING MyCookieObject
003156     IF MyCookieObject NOT EQUAL NULL
003158         SET PROP-TEXT OF TextBox5 TO PROP-VALUE OF MyCookieObject
003159     ELSE
003160         SET PROP-TEXT OF TextBox5 TO "No Cookie"
003170     END-IF
```

Hidden Forms Fields

Similar to cookies and query strings, hidden forms fields are used for preserving small quantities of information, when security is not an issue, to preserve page-level state. A hidden forms field is simply an HTML element turned into an HTML server control. However, during runtime, this HTML server control is invisible. As shown in Figure 15-4, the Hidden HTML element appears in the VS .NET IDE Toolbox, under the HTML tab.

Figure 15-4. The Hidden HTML element in the VS .NET IDE Toolbox

You can either type the appropriate HTML into the .aspx file or drag and drop the Hidden HTML element from the Toolbox onto your Web Form. Either way, you will want to this Hidden HTML element to an HTML server control (e.g., by adding the runat="server" HTML attribute). The following code snippet shows an example of the HTML that would be used in the .aspx file:

```
<input id="HiddenControl"
       type=hidden
       value="Your Initial Value, if desired"
runat=server>
```

To store information into the hidden forms field, you simply set the *Value* property of the HTML server control. You can accomplish this either by editing the HTML code (as shown in the preceding code snippet) or by coding logic in the server-side code-behind file.

 TIP The .NET Framework provides the *System.Web.UI.HtmlControls.HtmlInputHidden* class to expose the few class members against which you programmatically manipulate the hidden forms field. You will find that the reference terms "hidden control" and "hidden forms field" are used interchangeably.

I mentioned earlier that the hidden forms field is invisible during runtime. Well, that is not totally true. Yes, the field is invisible when you view the GUI (the Web Form). However, if you were to view the actual browser page source during runtime (by selecting View ➤ Source from your browser window), you would notice that the HTML for this hidden control is shown alongside the other HTML. More important, the content of the Value property is shown as well.

As long as the information saved in the Value property is not sensitive security-wise, this is considered acceptable. This is very important to realize. If security is an issue, the hidden forms field is not an appropriate solution for state management.

Hidden Forms Fields Code Samples

Listings 15-9 through 15-12 demonstrate the technique of populating and retrieving values with a hidden forms field.

Listing 15-9. Populating a Hidden Forms Field in VB .NET

```
Me.Hidden1.Value = Me.TextBox1.Text
```

Listing 15-10. Retrieving a Hidden Forms Field in VB.NET

```
Me.TextBox3.Text = Me.Hidden1.Value
```

Listing 15-11. Populating a Hidden Forms Field in COBOL .NET

```
SET PROP-VALUE OF Hidden1 TO PROP-TEXT OF TextBox1
```

Listing 15-12. Retrieving a Hidden Forms Field in COBOL.NET

```
SET PROP-TEXT OF TextBox3 TO PROP-VALUE OF Hidden1
```

Introducing View State

As a lead-in to the discussion of view state, let's quickly reflect back on two topics: the inheritance of System.Web.UI.Control[3] and the *page life cycle*.

The Web Form (Page class) and practically all the HTML and Web server controls inherit indirectly from the base class System.Web.UI.Control. This is important to realize because of the properties (and methods) that are inherited from the base class System.Web.UI.Control.

Among these inherited members exists a very special property: the *ViewState* property. The Page class (server control) and practically all of the other server control classes expose this inherited ViewState property. One other inherited property, *EnableViewState*, can be set on each control to True or False. Setting True per control will enable the ViewState property to preserve data for the respective control.

NOTE This is yet another example of how understanding some of the basic points of object orientation will assist you in your .NET retraining effort.

The other topic I want to reflect on was discussed in the earlier section "Preparation for Cache and State." Please notice the pair of ViewState page-level events (*LoadViewState* and *SaveViewState*) that are raised. The LoadViewState event is among the events that are raised prior to the Page Load event. On the other hand, the SaveViewState event is among the events that are raised after the Page Load event.

You can see where this is leading. Now you are ready to move on to the actual view state topic. Thanks for your patience.

---

3. This topic was previously discussed in the section "The System.Web.UI Namespace" in Chapter 13.

Using View State (the Other Hidden Forms Field)

You have basically two ways to get data into a control's ViewState property. You can use the control during runtime on the user interface by entering data into a TextBox server control during runtime. Optionally, you can programmatically set a control's ViewState property in the code-behind file.

When the SaveViewState event/method fires, the accumulated values of all available server control ViewState properties (per page) are saved to a String. This String is then used as the value of an automatically generated Hidden control (yes, another Hidden control) and sent to the browser along with the other HTML. Later, when the page is sent to the server again, the LoadViewState event/method will fire before the Page Load event takes place to restore any previously saved ViewState values.

The code in Listing 15-13 (which you can view by selecting View ➤ Source in your browser window) shows the HTML that is generated for this "other" Hidden control and sent to the browser. Because the ViewState values are hashed (and compressed), you can consider the information *somewhat* secure. Perhaps it's secure enough to be a deterrent, but not secure enough for the storage of passwords, financial information, and so forth.

Listing 15-13. The Hidden Control HMTL Generated to Support ViewState

```
<input type="hidden"
name="__VIEWSTATE"
value="a String Text that is hashed and generally indecipherable" />
```

CAUTION   The ViewState information, as shown in the browser source window, is *indecipherable*. However, a skilled hacker may be able to manipulate the Hidden control's Value property. This is something to be aware of. Yes, the ViewState approach to state management is the most secure choice among the client-side state management choices. However, you should consider the level of security that accompanies ViewState as "limited."

You will find that the .NET Framework uses the *System.Web.UI.StateBag* class as a type for storage into the ViewState property. Given the common characteristics of a key/value pair collection type, this is useful information. In other words, the *StateBag* class has properties such as *Count* and *Item*. Additionally, the StateBag class has methods such as *Add*, *Remove*, and *Clear*.

TIP For performance reasons (network traffic, object serialization, and so on), you should only have the EnableViewState property turned on (per server control, page, or user control) according to your needs. If appropriate, you can set the EnableViewState property at server, site, application, and subdirectory levels using your XML-based configuration files. (I discuss the configuration file in Chapter 18.) Optionally, you can use the *@ Page* or *@ Control* directive to control the setting of the EnableViewState property.

As time allows, it would be a good idea to drill down further to discover more facts about ViewState. For now, you must move on. At this point, you have covered each of the client-based state management solutions. Following the view state code samples section, you will turn your attention to the server-based solutions for state management.

View State Code Samples

Listings 15-14 through 15-17 demonstrate the code needed to use view state.

Listing 15-14. Populating View State in VB .NET

```
Me.ViewState("MyNewViewSTate") = Me.TextBox1.Text
```

Listing 15-15. Retrieving View State in VB.NET

```
Me.TextBox2.Text = CStr(Me.ViewState("MyNewViewSTate"))
```

Listing 15-16. Populating View State in COBOL .NET

```
003066    SET MiscString1 TO PROP-TEXT OF TextBox1
003067    SET MyViewState TO PROP-VIEWSTATE OF SELF
003068    INVOKE MyViewState "set_Item"
003069    USING BY VALUE "MyNewViewSTate" MiscString1
```

Listing 15-17. Retrieving View State in COBOL.NET

```
003171    SET MyViewState TO PROP-VIEWSTATE OF MyPage
003172    INVOKE MyViewState "get_Item"
003173    USING BY VALUE "MyNewViewSTate" RETURNING MiscObject
003174    SET PROP-TEXT OF TextBox2 TO MiscObject AS CLASS-STRING
```

Server-Based State Management

Generally speaking, the server-based state management solutions offer a higher degree of security than that offered by the client-based solutions. You should look to state-based solutions when you want to preserve relatively larger amounts of application-level or session-level state. For each level (application and session) the .NET Framework leverages each of the respective intrinsic objects.

> **NOTE**   Server-based state management is applicable to both ASP.NET applications and ASP.NET XML Web services.

Application-Level State

In the section "Preparation for Cache and State," I briefly touched on the various application-level events that are raised when an HTTP request is sent to IIS. I would like to draw your attention to two specific events/methods for this application-level state discussion: *Application_Start* and *Application_End*. You will typically see these events/methods[4] predefined in the Global.asax file.

At the moment that the Application_Start event/method is raised, two intrinsic objects are instantiated and made available: the *Application* object and the *Cache* object. These two objects continue to exist and be available until the Application_End event/method is raised. You can use either of these two objects for your needs to "globally" preserve data. In other words, potentially for the life of a given application, across multiple sessions, across multiple HTTP requests, you can preserve data.

> **NOTE**   The Cache class referred to in this section is a different .NET Framework class from the one referred to in the earlier section "Save Your Cache!" The Cache class discussed in that earlier section is exposed by the Response object and is used for output cache management. The Cache class referred to in *this* section is exposed by the *Context* and *Page* objects and is used for application-level state management.

---

4.   The raised events are *application_onStart* and *application_onEnd*. The *Application_Start* and *Application_End* methods are provided to handle the raised events.

Once you are certain that you need to preserve data at the application level (i.e., across multiple sessions), you will want to take the following points into consideration to help you choose between the two application-level state management techniques:

- The length of time you wish to "preserve" the data and the approach that you wish to take to remove the data (if you are not preserving the data indefinitely)

- The accumulated size of the preserved data

- The need to update state outside of the Start and End application-level events/methods or the need to work with a multithreaded application design

- The need for some preserved data to be associated with an external element (e.g., a file or directory) where a dependency may exist

You will now take a look at the two application-level state management techniques to see how the points in the preceding list apply to each.

NOTE   Data saved in the Application and Cache objects is granted a "global" scope. The extent of the "global" scope encompasses the entire IIS Application folder. This would typically be equivalent to the Solution folder shown in the VS .NET IDE Solution Explorer window.

Using the Application Class for State Management

In short, the following points are general guidelines to use that speak to the choice of using the Application class for application-level state management:

- Use the Application class if the accumulated size of the preserved data is small and relatively static.

- Use the Application class if you want the data to remain in memory for the entire life of the application.

- Use the Clear method of the HttpApplicationState class to explicitly remove all the contents of the collection.

- If you perform any updates to the HttpApplicationState collection outside of the Start and End application-level events/methods, use the *Lock* and *Unlock* methods to protect against concurrent update collisions.

Unfortunately, just telling you *when* to use the Application class does not really give you a solid understanding of the actual Application class. To better understand the Application class and the role it fulfills in state management, you will want to first understand some basic terminology.

For example, there is an intrinsic object identified as *application* that is actually represented by the .NET Framework *System.Web.HttpApplication* class. This particular class, *HttpApplication*, has a property called *Application*. There is a key/value pair collection type called HttpApplicationState that the Application property provides access to.

NOTE   This is a very important point that's easy to overlook. The actual Application object has a property called Application, which provides the ApplicationState collection. Wouldn't it have been nice if Microsoft had named the Application property of the Application object *ApplicationState* instead?

Confused? Don't worry. You aren't done yet. Say that you're working with the *Context* object (*System.Web.HttpContext*), and you notice that two properties are available: *Application* and *ApplicationInstance*. If you access the Application property of the Context object, you get the HttpApplicationState key/value pair collection. On the other hand, the ApplicationInstance property of the Context object provides a reference to an instance of the Application object (System.Web.HttpApplication).

Less confused? Good. Then you won't mind me mentioning that you can also access the HttpApplicationState key/value pair collection using the Application property of the Page object (the infamous System.Web.UI.Page class). In fact, you're more likely to see code that accesses the HttpApplicationState key/value pair collection using this approach.

TIP Notice that Microsoft is consistent (most of the time). Whether you are using the Application property from the Context object or the Application property from the Page object, you are getting the ApplicationState key/value pair collection. If you want to reference an instance of the Application object, you use the ApplicationInstance property of the Context object.

In other words, when you are in the code-behind file, and you just see the word "Application" being used to populate or retrieve application state data, understand that you are accessing the Application property of the Page object. Thus, you are accessing the HttpApplicationState key/value pair collection, not an instance of the Application object.

TIP You can use the Contents property of the HttpApplicationState class to obtain a reference to the HttpApplicationState object. This is useful when you want to iterate through the collection of values that may have been stored in the HttpApplicationState key/value pair collection.

Clear as mud? Great! Now, I can simply mention that the HttpApplicationState key/value pair collection is the repository for application-level state management when using the Application class.

Following the Application class code samples section, you will turn to take a look at the Cache class to review what it offers for application-level state management.

Application Class Code Samples

Listings 15-18 through 15-21 demonstrate how to use the ApplicationState class to preserve data. Notice that the Global.asax file is being used when the application-level state is captured.

Listing 15-18. Updating the Application Class in the Global.asax File in VB .NET

```
Sub Application_Start(ByVal sender As Object, ByVal e As EventArgs)
    Application("MyTimeTheAppStarted") = DateTime.Now
End Sub
. . .
Sub Application_BeginRequest(ByVal sender As Object, ByVal e As EventArgs)
    Application("MyTimeTheLastRequestWasMade") = DateTime.Now
End Sub
```

Listing 15-19. Retrieving the Application Class in VB .NET

```
Me.TextBox6.Text = Application("MyTimeTheAppStarted")
Me.TextBox7.Text = Application("MyTimeTheLastRequestWasMade")
```

Listing 15-20. Updating the Application Class in the Global.asax File in COBOL .NET

```
. . .
000290 METHOD-ID. APPLICATION_START AS "Application_Start" IS PROTECTED.
000300 DATA DIVISION.
000301 WORKING-STORAGE SECTION.
000302    01 MyHttpApplicationState   OBJECT REFERENCE CLASS-HttpApplicationState.
000303    01 NowDateTime             OBJECT REFERENCE CLASS-DATETIME.
000310 LINKAGE SECTION.
000320 01 PARAM-SENDER OBJECT REFERENCE  CLASS-OBJECT.
000330 01 PARAM-E OBJECT REFERENCE CLASS-EVENTARGS.
000340 PROCEDURE DIVISION USING BY VALUE PARAM-SENDER PARAM-E.
000341
000342    SET NowDateTime TO PROP-NOW OF CLASS-DATETIME
000343    SET MyHttpApplicationState TO PROP-APPLICATION OF SELF
000344    INVOKE MyHttpApplicationState "set_Item"
000345    USING BY VALUE "MyTimeTheAppStarted" NowDateTime
```

```
000350
000360 END METHOD APPLICATION_START.
. . .
000470 METHOD-ID. APPLICATION_BEGINREQUEST
000471          AS "Application_BeginRequest" IS PROTECTED.
000480 DATA DIVISION.
000481 WORKING-STORAGE SECTION.
000483  01 MyHttpApplicationState   OBJECT REFERENCE CLASS-HttpApplicationState.
000484  01 NowDateTime              OBJECT REFERENCE CLASS-DATETIME.
000490 LINKAGE SECTION.
000500 01 PARAM-SENDER OBJECT REFERENCE  CLASS-OBJECT.
000510 01 PARAM-E OBJECT REFERENCE CLASS-EVENTARGS.
000520 PROCEDURE DIVISION USING BY VALUE PARAM-SENDER PARAM-E.
000521
000523     SET NowDateTime TO PROP-NOW OF CLASS-DATETIME
000524     SET MyHttpApplicationState TO PROP-APPLICATION OF SELF
000525     INVOKE MyHttpApplicationState "set_Item"
000526     USING BY VALUE "MyTimeTheLastRequestWasMade" NowDateTime
000530
000540 END METHOD APPLICATION_BEGINREQUEST.
. . .
```

Listing 15-21. Retrieving the Application Class in COBOL .NET

```
003680     SET MyHttpApplicationState TO PROP-APPLICATION OF SELF
003690     INVOKE MyHttpApplicationState "get_Item"
003700     USING BY VALUE "MyTimeTheAppStarted" RETURNING MiscObject1
003710     SET PROP-TEXT OF TextBox6 TO MiscObject1::"ToString"()
003720
003730     INVOKE MyHttpApplicationState "get_Item"
003740     USING BY VALUE "MyTimeTheLastRequestWasMade" RETURNING MiscObject1
003750     SET PROP-TEXT OF TextBox7 TO MiscObject1::"ToString"()
```

Using the Cache Class for State Management

Considering that you survived my long explanation about the Application class, I will spare you the trouble this time around. However, I will offer up just two points before getting in the simple details of *why* you will want to use the Cache class.

The first point is just a reminder. The discussion in this section bears absolutely no relationship with the topic of output cache management previously discussed in the section "Save Your Cache!"

As for the other point, notice that the Cache class (*System.Web.Caching.Cache*) is exposed by the Cache property of both the Context object and the Page object. Again, Microsoft is being consistent. After all, both the Context object and Page object exposed the Application object (rather, the HttpApplicationState object).

That's it. Let's now take a look at the great features of the Cache class.

In case you did not meet the recommended criteria for using the Application class, and you still want to preserve data at the application level, the Cache class just may be the perfect solution for you. Here are the major features offered by the Cache class:

- *Easily expire data:* Avoid having to explicitly remove the preserved data from memory.

- *Easily allow for prioritization of data expiration:* It's possible to expire less-used data ahead of data being used more frequently.

- *Easily associate the preserved data with external elements (e.g., files, directories, and so on) to create dependencies:* For example, you can cause data in the cache to be removed based on whether or not its external dependent target source changes.

- *Easily implement a callback/delegate feature:* You can use the *CacheItemRemovedCallback* delegate and the *CacheItemRemovedReason* enumeration to raise/handle an event when a cached item is removed from the cache.

- *Easily avoid concurrent updating concerns:* There is no need to use a Lock/Unlock approach with the Cache class. It is completely thread-safe.

The implementation of the Cache class is rather simple, but its features are powerful. Yes, the Application class is a viable option for application-level state management. However, the opportunities made available by the Cache class might leave you wondering why the Application class would be used at all anymore.

Understand that the Application class existed before ASP.NET existed. That is, in the legacy Web (ASP) applications, this fancy Cache class did not exist as a second application-level state management option. The Application class was it.

I will dare to suggest that backward compatibility might be one of two reasons you will want to be aware of the Application class choice. You never know when you will need to maintain (or convert) a legacy Web (ASP) application. The second reason for learning about the Application class is that it is simple to use and it works.

A Quick Mainframe CICS Diversion

The callback/dependency-type features provided by the Cache class (for application-level state management) will remind you of one of the features you used in your CICS mainframe applications. When you used intrapartition CICS TD queues for data preservation, you may have had the chance to use the triggering-type feature referred to as *Automatic Transaction Initiation* (ATI). Yes, the *new* is gradually catching up with the *old*—finally.

When you need to use application-level state management in your ASP.NET application design, you will want to know what your choices are. Obviously, the two choices (the Application class and the Cache class) have overlapping features. Being aware of them should increase the chances of you implementing application-level state management properly in your application.

Following the Cache class code samples section, you will continue your server-based state management exploration and turn your attention to the topic of session-level state management.

Cache Class Code Samples

Listings 15-22 through 15-25 show the basic use of the Cache class. You will want to experiment with several other options as you continue your retraining effort.

Listing 15-22. Updating the Application Cache Class in VB .NET

```
Cache.Insert("MyApplicationCache", Me.TextBox1.Text)
```

Listing 15-23. Retrieving the Application Cache Class in VB .NET

```
Me.TextBox10.Text = CType(Cache("MyApplicationCache"), String)
```

Listing 15-24. Updating the Application Cache Class in COBOL .NET

```
003320     SET MiscString1 TO PROP-TEXT OF TextBox1
003330     SET MyApplicationCache TO PROP-CACHE OF SELF
003340     INVOKE MyApplicationCache "set_Item"
003350     USING BY VALUE "MyApplicationCache" MiscString1
```

Listing 15-25. Retrieving the Application Cache Class in COBOL .NET

```
003870    SET MyApplicationCache TO PROP-CACHE OF SELF
003880    INVOKE MyApplicationCache "get_Item"
003890            USING BY VALUE "MyApplicationCache" RETURNING MiscObject1
003900    SET PROP-TEXT OF TextBox10 TO MiscObject1::"ToString"()
```

Session-Level State

Before you dive into the specifics of ASP.NET's support for session-level management, I would like to quickly establish a common understanding of what a *session* is.

Generally speaking, when you open a browser window and send your first HTTP request to a specific Web site, you have begun a new session. As you continue your Web visit, using any available tabs, buttons, and other controls on the site, you are typically continuing your session. Closing your browser window is recognized as the end of your session.

NOTE   Some Web sites may offer login and logout features. As far as that given Web site is concerned, a login/logoff may equate to the beginning and the end of a particular session for that specific user.

A session is generally understood to be user specific, originating from a specific browser window and, in most cases, from a specific computer. When any of these variables changes, a new session is usually understood to have begun or ended. Additionally, sessions are generally understood to have an expiration period established that is enacted following a given period of inactivity.

In your ASP.NET applications, you can identify when a session starts and ends. The Session HTTP module (*System.Web.SessionState.SessionStateModule*) will raise either the *session_onStart* event or the *session_onEnd* event according to the nature of the appropriate HTTP request. These events are subsequently handled in the Global.asax file by the *session_Start* and *session_End* events/methods, respectively.

CROSS-REFERENCE   The topic of session-level events was further discussed in the previous section "Preparation for Cache and State."

With this understanding, you can define session-level state management as the preservation of data through the life of a given session. You will now take a look at the basic .NET Framework support for session state. Following that discussion, you will explore several options that you can take advantage of in ASP.NET for session-level state management.

Session State and the .NET Framework

Both the Page and Context objects expose a property called *Session*. Using the Session property, you can reference the *System.Web.SessionState.HttpSessionState* class. As you might have guessed, the HttpSessionState class provides the key/value pair type collection into which you will store your "preserved session-level data." The HttpSessionState class exposes a *SessionID* property (a 120-bit string field) that uniquely identifies each session.

Understand the subtle implication of this. When you use the word "Session" in your code-behind file, you will be referencing the Session property of the page that is providing the HttpSessionState key/value pair type collection. Optionally, you can use the Session property from the Context object for the same returned result: the HttpSessionState key/value pair type collection.

Hey, They Forgot to Create a Session Object!

I have to ask, why didn't Microsoft create a Session object? Think about it. Take into consideration that the Context object has two properties to support the "Application." The Context object exposes an Application property that provides the ApplicationState object and the ApplicationInstance property that provides the Application object.

Therefore, when I discovered that the Context object had a Session property that returns a SessionState object, I expected to find a SessionInstance property that would return a Session object. To my surprise, there is only the Session property and the SessionState object. That is it. Interesting? Giving Microsoft the benefit of the doubt, I am sure they had their reasons.

A Configuration Primer

Although Chapter 18 presents a full discussion of the XML-based configuration files, I need to cover a few basic points here that relate to session state management. At this time, I will limit the discussion to the application-level configuration file.

To begin with, the application-level XML-based configuration file (named Web.config) is located in your ASP.NET Web application folder. Typically, there is a Web.config file created, by default, for each ASP.NET application. As shown in Figure 15-5, you can access the Web.config file from the VS .NET IDE Solution Explorer window.

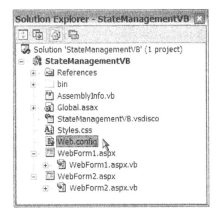

Figure 15-5. Using the VS .NET Solution Explorer window to access the Web.config file

As shown in Figure 15-6, you can also use Windows Explorer (outside of the VS .NET IDE) to navigate to your application folder to locate, browse, and edit your Web.config file.[5]

---

5. In the case of COBOL .NET, the Web.config file may not appear in the VS .NET IDE Solution Explorer window. In this case, you can use Windows Explorer outside of the VS .NET IDE to locate and edit the Web.config file.

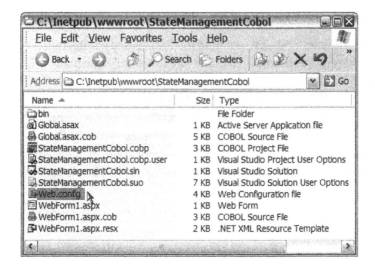

Figure 15-6. Using Windows Explorer to locate and edit the Web.config file

Whether you use Windows Explorer or the VS .NET IDE Solution Explorer window, you can double-click the Web.config file to "open" it. Once you open the Web.config file, you will see a generous number of XML statements and comments. Scroll down to near the bottom of the Web.config file and you will see the *<sessionState>* XML element. The default setting for the <sessionState> XML element should resemble the following code snippet. Note that the Web.config file created in your COBOL .NET ASP.NET application may be missing the *stateConnectionString* and *sqlConnectionString* attributes. You can manually add these two attributes if needed.

```
<sessionState
        mode="InProc"
        stateConnectionString="tcpip=127.0.0.1:42424"
        sqlConnectionString="data source=127.0.0.1;user id=sa;password="
        cookieless="false"
        timeout="20"
    />
```

The syntactical rules for the <sessionState> XML element are as follows:

```
<sessionState
        mode="Off|Inproc|StateServer|SQLServer"
        stateConnectionString="tcpip=your server: your port"
        sqlConnectionString="your sql connection string"
        cookieless="true|false"
        timeout="your desired number of minutes"
/>
```

Please take a moment to examine both of the preceding code snippets. The first one should resemble what you will see the first time you open your ASP.NET application's Web.config file.[6] The second one is a pseudo-code example that details the options that are available to you for each of the relevant <sessionState> XML attributes.

TIP   For performance reasons, you should enable session state support according to the needs of your application. To enable or disable session state support for specific pages, you have the choice of using the @ Page directive (in the .aspx file) or adding and using a *<Pages>* element in your XML-based configuration file (using the *enableSessionState* attribute). Optionally, you can use the <sessionState> XML element (mode="Off") to disable session state support for an entire application.

CROSS-REFERENCE   I further discuss the configuration file in Chapter 18.

The Web.config file is responsible for ASP.NET application-level configuration settings. As its name implies, the <sessionState> XML element deals specifically with your session state configuration choices.

---

6. The *stateConnectionString* and *sqlConnectionString* attributes may be missing when you create a Web configuration file using COBOL .NET. You can manually add these two attributes if needed.

This section was provided as a quick primer on the session state portion of the XML-based configuration file. Now that you have established a point of reference, you can move on to the remaining portions of this chapter's session-level state management discussion.

To Be a Cookieless Session or Not to Be a Cookieless Session

Given the idea of what a session is, how does ASP.NET distinguish the HTTP requests coming from one session from those coming from a different session? This is where *session cookies* (also known as *HTTP cookies*) come into the picture.

Although a session cookie is a different kind of cookie than the persisted cookie discussed earlier, it is still a cookie. In other words, the concerns of using cookies—rather, the concerns of occasionally *not* being able to use cookies—still apply.

This is where the cookieless="true|false" option comes into the picture. As shown in the earlier section "A Configuration Primer," you can edit your Web.config file to easily turn on and off the "cookieless" feature. This configuration setting has the following effect:

- cookieless="false": This is the default setting. For the life of the session, a cookie (a small file) is passed to and from the client as part of the HTTP request header. The SessionID is obtained from the HTTP cookie.

- cookieless="true": This setting will cause the SessionID to be merged with the URL (called *URL munging*). ASP.NET will then parse the URL as each HTTP request is processed to extract the SessionID.

When you use the default cookieless="false" setting, you will see something like the following in the address bar of your browser window (for the StateManagementCobol sample ASP.NET application):

```
http://localhost/StateManagementCobol/WebForm1.aspx
```

When you use the cookieless="true" setting, that same navigation appears differently in your browser's address bar. Instead, you see something that resembles the following. Notice that a 120-bit unique SessionID has been merged (munged) into the URL.

```
http://localhost/StateManagementCobol/(finpzp45o5avhf55ai4i5b45)/WebForm1.aspx
```

The use of cookies is a common practice. Nevertheless, because your client's browser may be set to not accept them, you do need to take this into consideration. Depending on your need, you can use this configuration feature to control whether or not your application even attempts to pass an HTTP (session) cookie to the client.

Fortunately, ASP.NET is intelligent enough to handle either scenario (cookieless or not) and still provide full support for session-level state management. The next decision you need to make is related to the location in which the preserved session data is maintained. As you will see, this too is controlled in the Web.config file.

In-Process vs. Out-of-Process Session State

When you use session-level state management, you have the opportunity to decide on the location where your preserved data will be stored. In other words, as you add key/value pairs into the System.Web.SessionState.HttpSessionState class, you have option of having the HttpSessionState key/value pair collection either saved in the memory (referred to as *in-process*) or saved in a database (referred to as *out-of-process*).

You would use the Web.config file to choose the "mode" for your session-level state management. The two "connection string" attributes are ignored if you are using the in-process session state mode. The following code snippet shows the three XML attributes discussed in the section:

```
. . .
mode="Off|Inproc|StateServer|SQLServer"
stateConnectionString="tcpip=your server: your port"
sqlConnectionString="your sql connection string"
. . .
```

The in-process option offers the fastest processing model. When recovery is not a concern, this option is perfect for maintaining noncritical session-level data. Additionally, if your ASP.NET application is hosted on one physical Web server and does not participate in a Web farm–type of configuration, the in-process model may be the right choice for you. It is the default configuration setting (mode="Inproc"), as seen your Web.config file.

NOTE I have provided references at the end of this chapter to assist in your continued research into the two out-of-process options. In the meantime, the in-process option can certainly get you started and headed in the right direction. Later, as your needs dictate, you can easily switch session state "modes" using the Web.config file.

The other choice, to store the HttpSessionState key/value pair collections out of process brings with it another fork in the road, another choice to make. To preserve your data using the out-of-process model (that is, out of the ASP.NET process), you need to choose between storing the session data in a state server and storing it in a SQL Server database.

The state server option (mode="StateServer") takes advantage of a Windows Service and uses the stateConnectionString XML attribute in the Web.config file. The SQL Server option (mode="SQLServer") takes advantage of an actual SQL Server database and uses the sqlConnectionString XML attribute in the Web.config file.

This brings you to the end of the session-level and server-side state management discussion. Considering the many options available for state management, it is likely that you will be able to choose the solution implementation that best fits the needs of your application. Be sure to take advantage of the references provided in the "To Learn More" section at the end of this chapter for your continued research and learning.

Following the session state code samples section, you will find a brief discussion of a few additional techniques used by ASP.NET to preserve data between each HTTP request. I loosely refer to these techniques as "other types of state management."

Session State Code Samples

Listings 15-26 through 15-29 demonstrate the use of the *Session State* class. Notice that I have chosen to use the Global.asax file when the Session State class is being updated.

Listing 15-26. Updating the Session State Class Inside the Global.asax File in VB .NET

```
Sub Session_Start(ByVal sender As Object, ByVal e As EventArgs)
    Session("MyTimeTheSessionStarted") = DateTime.Now
    Session("MyTimeTheSessionIdentity") = _
        System.Web.HttpContext.Current.Session.SessionID
End Sub
```

Listing 15-27. Retrieving the Session State Class in VB .NET

```
Me.TextBox8.Text = Session("MyTimeTheSessionStarted")
Me.TextBox9.Text = Session("MyTimeTheSessionIdentity")
```

Listing 15-28. Updating the Session State Class Inside the Global.asax File in COBOL .NET

```
000380 METHOD-ID. SESSION_START AS "Session_Start" IS PROTECTED.
000390 DATA DIVISION.
000391 WORKING-STORAGE SECTION.
000392    01 MyHttpSessionState         OBJECT REFERENCE CLASS-HttpSessionState.
000394    01 NowDateTime                OBJECT REFERENCE CLASS-DATETIME.
000395    01 MiscString1                PIC X(25).
000396    01 MyCurrentContext           OBJECT REFERENCE CLASS-HTTPCONTEXT.
000400 LINKAGE SECTION.
000410 01 PARAM-SENDER OBJECT REFERENCE  CLASS-OBJECT.
000420 01 PARAM-E OBJECT REFERENCE CLASS-EVENTARGS.
000430 PROCEDURE DIVISION USING BY VALUE PARAM-SENDER PARAM-E.
000431
000432    SET NowDateTime TO PROP-NOW OF CLASS-DATETIME
000433    SET MyHttpSessionState TO PROP-SESSION OF SELF
000434    INVOKE MyHttpSessionState "set_Item"
000435    USING BY VALUE "MyTimeTheSessionStarted" NowDateTime
000436
000437    SET MyCurrentContext TO PROP-CURRENT OF CLASS-HTTPCONTEXT
000438    SET MyHttpSessionState TO .PROP-SESSION OF MyCurrentContext
000439    SET MiscString1 TO PROP-SESSIONID OF MyHttpSessionState
000440    INVOKE MyHttpSessionState "set_Item"
000441    USING BY VALUE "MyTimeTheSessionIdentity" MiscString1
000442
000450 END METHOD SESSION_START.
```

Listing 15-29. Retrieving the Session State Class in COBOL .NET

```
003914    SET MyHttpSessionState TO PROP-SESSION OF SELF
003915    INVOKE MyHttpSessionState "get_Item"
003916    USING BY VALUE "MyTimeTheSessionStarted" RETURNING MiscObject1
003917    SET PROP-TEXT OF TextBox8 TO MiscObject1::"ToString"()
003918
003919    INVOKE MyHttpSessionState "get_Item"
003920    USING BY VALUE "MyTimeTheSessionIdentity" RETURNING MiscObject1
003921    SET PROP-TEXT OF TextBox9 TO MiscObject1::"ToString"()
```

Other Types of "State Management"

In thinking about what state and/or cache management really is, you can come to the point of looking at it as just a way to preserve data between each HTTP request. If you ignore for a moment the opportunities to persist and expire data (features made available by true state management approaches), you can entertain the idea of there being a few other "data preservation" techniques provided by ASP.NET.

Rightly so, these approaches are not acknowledged as official state or cache management choices. Nevertheless, it may be useful to be familiar with a few additional ways to preserve data between HTTP requests. With a slight stretch of definition, I suggest that these approaches do represent a *type* of *state management*. The additional approaches are as follows:

- Storing server controls in the Form variables via the Request object

- Storing all HTML and text in the LiteralControl via the Page object

- Storing data in the HashTable collection via the Context object

Form Variables via the Request Object

The *Request* object (*System.Web.HttpRequest*) exposes the *Form* property. Using this property, you can easily access a key/value collection called the *form variables*. What are form variables? Basically, form variables collectively represent all of the <Input></Input> type of controls that are on the Web Form. In other words, the server controls (e.g., TextBox, Button, Hidden, and so on) that render as HTML <Input> tags are included in this form variables key/value collection.

For example, a TextBox server control that is defined in the .aspx file with an "id" value of *Textbox1* will appear in the form variable collection with a key of *Textbox1*. The value of the TextBox's Text property will be accessible in the form variable collection. The form variables are populated automatically and stored in the Request object as it is sent from the client back to the server.

LiteralControl via the Page Object

In Chapter 14 in the section "Controls, Controls, Controls, and More Controls," I introduced and described the LiteralControl class. You understand now that ASP.NET uses the LiteralControl class to store and retrieve all "text"-based data (e.g., the rendered HTML elements) between each HTTP request. In other words, the LiteralControl class is used for the *preservation of data*—yes, another type of state management.

Using the Page object, take a look at the *Controls* property. You will see a few controls stored in the *ControlCollection* type collection. One of these controls is the LiteralControl that ASP.NET automatically creates for you. Optionally, you can create and populate your own LiteralControl control in server-side code. Of course, you would only seek to take advantage of this technique when looking for alternative approaches to data preservation.

NOTE I realize the phrase "controls stored in the ControlCollection type collection" sounds a bit redundant. However, once you get to the point of being able to digest a phrase like "the LiteralControl control, not to be confused with *the* Literal control," all the rest becomes quite easy. Again, I discussed these two controls in Chapter 14 in the section "Controls, Controls, Controls, and More Controls"—literally.

HashTable Collection via the Context Object

The Context object (*System.Web.HttpContext*) exposes an *Items* property. This particular Items property provides a key/value collection using the *IDictionary* interface. Several classes, one of which is the *HashTable*, implement the IDictionary interface. It is the HashTable class that will actually hold the key/value pairs and provide the type of data preservation resembling state management.

You will recall that the Context object encompasses an entire HTTP request and all of the objects associated with the HTTP request. Once you programmatically establish a reference to the *current context*, you have access to the HashTable key/value collection in question.

According to Microsoft's documentation, this key/value collection serves the purpose of "organizing and sharing data between an IHttpModule and an IHttpHandler." Now, "organizing and sharing data" sounds a lot like state management to me. What do you think?

CROSS-REFERENCE See the earlier sidebar titled "Handlers, Modules, and Application-Level Events" for further explanation of the IHttpModule and IHttpHandler interfaces.

User Interface for the Sample Applications

To help support the state management discussion in this chapter, I've created sample projects in both VB .NET and COBOL .NET. Throughout the chapter, I've shown code snippets taken from these sample projects. In this section, I show only the user interface.

I used the VS .NET IDE ASP.NET Application project template for each sample project. The names used for the projects are StateManagementVB and StateManagementCobol. I made the user interfaces of the StateManagementVB and StateManagementCobol sample projects identical. I added an additional Web Form (WebForm2.aspx) to each project that simply receives the redirection from the first Web Form.

As shown in Figure 15-7, I added several server controls (Buttons, Label, TextBox, and so forth) to the Web Form (WebForm1.aspx) for the sample StateManagementVB project.

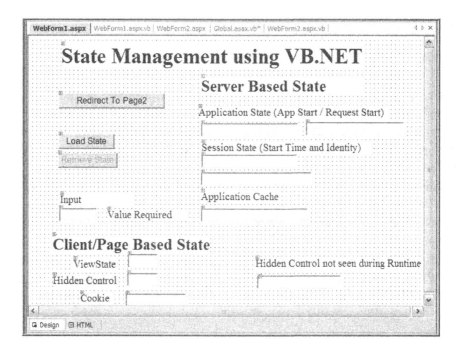

Figure 15-7. The user interface for the sample application StateManagementVB

TIP   Please give serious consideration to researching and using the ASP.NET trace feature. By turning trace support on in the XML-based Web.config file, you can generate an entire display showing the contents of your HTTP request. Once enabled, a separate page named Trace.axd can be viewed in your browser window. Additionally, you can use Trace commands in your code. The output of these commands will also appear in the Trace.axd file. Those of you who have used mainframe features such as the CICS transaction CEBR to "browse" temporary storage queues will certainly be pleased with using ASP.NET's trace feature to view the various state management containers. This feature is certainly worth your time and effort to learn about. You will not be disappointed.

Summary

This chapter's goals were as follows:

- To understand "output" cache management

- To discuss client-based state management

- To explore server-based state management

Coming from the CICS mainframe environment, I was impressed with ASP.NET's state and cache management support. My guess is that you are impressed too. Do spend some time exploring; you covered a lot of ground in this chapter, but more awaits you. As always, several references are included at the end of this chapter in the "To Learn More" section to assist you during your continued exploration.

In this chapter, I discussed output cache management. From there, I turned to state management. I divided the topic of state management into client-based and server-based subtopics. I provided a healthy amount of sample code to help illustrate the various points being discussed. As a bonus, you took a quick peek at the Web.config file during the session state discussion.

The next chapter covers reporting and information delivery.

To Learn More

The following are some suggested supplemental references to further your retraining effort.

Books

Moving to ASP.NET: Web Development with VB .NET, by Steve Harris and Rob Macdonald (Apress, 2002):
    http://www.apress.com/book/bookDisplay.html?bID=78.

Magazines

.NET Magazine:
    http://www.fawcette.com/dotnetmag/
MSDN Magazine:
    http://msdn.microsoft.com/msdnmag/
Visual Studio Magazine:
    http://www.fawcette.com/vsm/
Windows Developer Magazine:
    http://www.wd-mag.com/
XML & Web Services Magazine:
    http://www.fawcette.com/xmlmag/

Web Sites

.NET Architecture Center:
    http://msdn.microsoft.com/architecture/
ASP.NET Caching Features:
    http://msdn.microsoft.com/library/en-us/cpguide/html/
    cpconaspcachingfeatures.asp
GotDotNet:
    http://www.gotdotnet.com/
IBuySpy.com Store Application (sample application in COBOL .NET):
    http://www.ibuyspycobol.com/
IBuySpy.com Store Application (sample application in VB .NET and C#):
    http://www.ibuyspystore.com/

Introduction to ASP.NET:

http://msdn.microsoft.com/library/en-us/cpguide/html/
cpconintroductiontoasp.asp

Fujitsu NetCOBOL for .NET:

http://www.netcobol.com/products/windows/netcobol.html

Microsoft ASP.NET Home Page:

http://www.asp.net/

Microsoft ASP.NET QuickStarts Tutorial: Caching Overview:

http://www.aspng.com/quickstart/aspplus/doc/cachingoverview.aspx

Microsoft ASP.NET QuickStarts Tutorial: Managing Application State:

http://www.aspng.com/quickstart/aspplus/doc/stateoverview.aspx

Microsoft Community (discussion groups, e-newsletters, and so forth):

http://communities2.microsoft.com/

Microsoft Patterns & Practices:

http://msdn.microsoft.com/practices/

Microsoft TechNet How-To Index:

http://www.microsoft.com/technet/treeview/default.asp?url=/technet/
itsolutions/howto

Microsoft's Search the Knowledge Base Web Site:

http://support.microsoft.com/default.aspx?scid=FH;EN-US;KBHOWTO

Microsoft's State Management Recommendations:

http://msdn.microsoft.com/library/en-us/cpguide/html/
cpconchoosingserverstateoption.asp

MSDN:

http://msdn.microsoft.com

NetCOBOL Samples (provided by Fujitsu Software and Intensity Software):

http://www.netcobolsamples.com/

VBTV (Webcast built for Visual Basic developers by Visual Basic developers):

http://msdn.microsoft.com/vbtv/

Windows .NET Server 2003:

http://msdn.microsoft.com/library/default.asp?url=/nhp/
default.asp?contentid=28001691

CHAPTER 16

Reporting and Information Delivery

An Introduction to Crystal Reports for Visual Studio .NET

In this chapter

- Learning how to use Crystal Reports for VS .NET

- Exploring Crystal Reports's export feature

- Understanding report delivery options using Crystal Reports

IN THE OLD DAYS, when I was a junior-level mainframe computer operator, I spent many weekends decollating boxes of multipart printed reports and forms. *Decollating* was the process by which mainframe programmers used a machine to pull apart the multiple report copies. Using the decollating machine, I would "thread" each paper sheet copy and carbon paper sheet into alternating spindles. When the spindles would turn, the ink-filled black carbon paper would separate from each green-bar paper sheet copy. Several decollating machine jams later, I would end up with several stacks of individually printed report copies (and barrels of carbon paper).

Ink stained from head to toe, with the appearance of a soot-covered coal miner, I would load the delivery van with the printed reports. After driving across town to the corporate office, I would navigate one freight elevator, several narrow hallways, and a few flights of stairs to deliver the reports. With the printed reports in their hands, the considerate business users would often tear off the last page of the report (typically the totals page) and politely demand that I take the remaining boxes of the report (unread) to the shredding dumpster.

NOTE Allow me to point out just how prevalent the use of carbon paper was in the "old days." Today, rather than being stuck with phrases such as "electronic copies" and "digital copies," we instead have the infamous phrase "carbon copies" being used for e-mail copies (i.e., the acronym "cc" when sending multiple "copies" of electronic e-mails).

Yes, times have certainly changed[1] since the old days. High-speed printers and copiers have made carbon paper practically extinct. Electronic delivery of information is now common and expected. Users still have their demands. Except now, users demand the ability to manipulate the "digital softcopy"—to get their "totals page" and more. To the developer, *reporting* has taken on a whole new meaning.

In this chapter, I discuss the features that exist in .NET to support modern-day reporting. I explore the use of the Visual Studio .NET (VS .NET) Crystal Reports feature for report creation and display. From there, I discuss several report and information delivery options using Crystal Reports. The support provided by Crystal Reports for various file format exports as well as XML Web service publishing should make this chapter an interesting read.

Using Crystal Reports for VS .NET

Crystal Reports for VS .NET (from Crystal Decisions, Inc.) is a fully functional reporting tool integrated into the VS .NET IDE. Using this reporting tool, you can programmatically expose your data to end users in virtually any reporting format. Whether your users want reports shown on their Web browser screen with navigation bars and attractive graphs or exported as spreadsheets, Crystal Reports for VS .NET can fulfill your programmatic reporting needs.

---

1. I have always wanted to personally thank the National Cash Register Corp. (now NCR Corp.) for developing No Carbon Required (NCR) paper. The increasing use of NCR paper eventually brought a welcomed break from the messy and labor-intensive carbon paper–based "multipart" copies.

NOTE   At this time, Fujitsu Software's NetCOBOL for .NET product provides only limited support in VS .NET for Crystal Reports. Although the
Crystal Reports Viewer is available from the VS .NET Toolbox, the Crystal Reports Template and Crystal Reports Gallery are currently not
available in COBOL .NET (rather, NetCOBOL for .NET) to create a .NET
project. You may want to investigate the alternative of creating Crystal
Reports template (.rpt) files outside of your NetCOBOL project. This
way, you can add the .rpt files to your NetCOBOL project and bind the
.rpt files to your Crystal Reports Viewer control right inside NetCOBOL
project. I expect that a later version of Fujitsu's NetCOBOL for .NET
product will support the ability to create your Crystal Reports template
(.rpt) files while working inside the VS .NET IDE. For now, you will
exploit your bilingual abilities and practice using Crystal Reports with
VB .NET only.

A full-featured Crystal Reports product is available to users and developers to
use outside the VS .NET IDE. Understand that the two versions of Crystal Reports
(the version integrated into VS .NET and the stand-alone version outside of VS
.NET) are essentially the same. For your purposes here, the biggest difference
between the two versions relates to choosing which user interface you would use
to design/create the report template. I limit this chapter's focus to the use of
Crystal Reports via the VS .NET interface.

TIP   You can use existing Crystal Reports templates previously built
with the stand-alone Crystal Reports product in your VS .NET project.

Currently, the Crystal Reports product provided with .NET is a special edition
of Crystal Reports v8. It is optimized for .NET. For an extra fee, you can upgrade to
the recently released Crystal Reports v9. Both v8 and v9 offer upgrade options that
allow you to increase the number of concurrent licensed connections to higher
levels that may be more appropriate for your production needs. Consider visiting
the Crystal Decisions Web site for further licensing and upgrade details.

For now, the Crystal Reports v8 version provided with VS.NET is certainly adequate for your training, prototyping, and small-scale production deployments. To

help introduce you to this great .NET reporting feature, I discuss the following topics in the sections that follow:

- The Crystal Reports class library

- The Crystal Reports template

- The Crystal Reports Viewers

NOTE   You will often see the acronym CR used when you research the topic of Crystal Reports. Although I would love to tell you that this distinguished acronym stands for the initials of my name, Chris Richardson, I must admit that it really stands for Crystal Reports.

The Crystal Reports Class Library

Once you start adding Crystal Reports assemblies into your Windows and Web applications, you will make available an entire *additional* class library. This section presents a brief introduction to this special class library. The next section covers one of the easiest ways to incorporate Crystal Reports assemblies into your application.

For now, it will help to be somewhat familiar with the Crystal Reports class library, as provided by Crystal Decisions. As shown in the following list, the Crystal Reports class library represents a handful of namespaces:

- *CrystalDecisions.CrystalReports.Engine:* This namespace contains classes that collectively provide support to the Crystal Reports reporting engine. I further discuss this namespace in the section "The Crystal Reports Template."

- *CrystalDecisions.ReportSource:* This namespace provides the *ICachedReport* interface. This interface provides caching support between either of the Crystal Reports Viewers (Web Forms Viewer or Windows Forms Viewer) and the Crystal Reports reporting engine.

- *CrystalDecisions.Shared:* Using the collection of classes provided in this namespace, you are able to customize, configure, and control your *Viewer* and *ReportDocument* objects.

- *CrystalDecisions.Web:* Specifically, the *CrystalReportViewer* and *CrystalReportViewerBase* classes are provided in this namespace. I discuss these two classes in the section "The Crystal Reports Viewer."

- *CrystalDecisions.Web.Services:* This namespace provides one class, *ServerFileReportManager*, which you would use when you want to expose Crystal Reports as a Web service. I discuss this topic in the section "Electronic Report Delivery."

- *CrystalDecisions.Web.Services.Enterprise:* This namespace provides one class, *EnterpriseReportManager*, which you would use when you want to consume a Crystal Reports report file (.rpt) that has been exposed as a Web service. I discuss this topic in the section "Electronic Report Delivery."

- *CrystalDecisions.Windows.Forms:* The Windows Forms Viewer control is provided by this namespace. The *CrystalReportViewer* class in this namespace is virtually identical to the one that is used for a Web application. Using an ASP.NET Web application, I discuss the CrystalReportViewer class in the section "The Crystal Reports Viewers."

As the prefix of each Crystal Reports namespace indicates, this product (the group of assemblies, the class library, and so forth) is provided by Crystal Decisions. Hence, you will be prompted to register your Crystal Reports product the first time you attempt to use it. Do not worry, the Web-based registration is free and painless.

Let's now turn to look at one of the ways you can add the Crystal Reports assemblies into your application.

The Crystal Reports Template

A report built with the Crystal Report Engine is essentially a visual representation of one specific class: *ReportDocument*. This class is provided by the CrystalDecisions.CrystalReports.Engine namespace. Although you have a few ways to go about creating a Crystal Reports report (instantiating the ReportDocument class), you will use the design-time creation approach here. This technique results in a report file (.rpt) being saved in your application folder (visible in the VS .NET IDE Solution Explorer).

To begin, you will use the VS .NET IDE to create a new ASP.NET Web application. Using VB .NET as your language choice,[2] name the project CrystalReportsExampleVB. Next, follow this series of steps to incorporate a Crystal Reports template into the CrystalReportsExampleVB project:

1. Add a new item to the project in any of the following three ways: press Ctrl-Shift-A; select Project ➤ Add New Item from the Standard toolbar; or select the CrystalReportsExampleVB project in the Solution Explorer window and access the pop-up context window by right-clicking and then selecting Add ➤ Add New Item. As shown in Figure 16-1, you will select the "Crystal Report" template from the Templates area of the Add New Item dialog box.

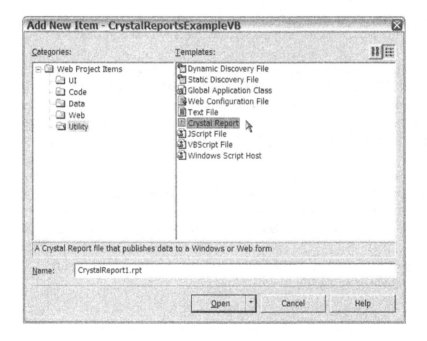

Figure 16-1. Selecting the Crystal Report template from the Add New Item dialog box

---

2. As noted earlier, COBOL .NET currently does not provide full support for the Crystal Reports feature. I use VB .NET for the following sample application demonstration. Perhaps you can consider this to be one of the reasons why being bilingual is a good idea.

2. Choose an "expert" from the Crystal Report Gallery (see Figure 16-2). Several Crystal Report experts are available. Experts are similar to what other software packages call "wizards" or "designers." For now, use the default setting of Standard. Click OK.

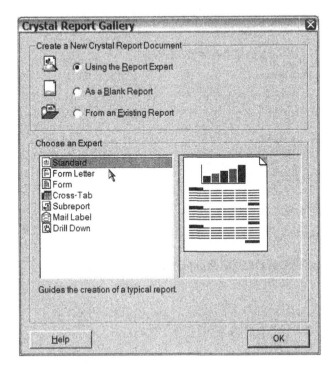

Figure 16-2. Selecting an "expert" from the Crystal Report Gallery dialog box

3. Connect the report template to a data source.[3] You will use the Pubs sample SQL Server database. Choose the Data tab and select OLE DB (ADO). Then, follow the next few dialog box prompts to establish your connection to the Pubs sample SQL Server database. As shown in the following figures (Figures 16-3 and 16-4), the prompts are rather simple. Click Finish at the last Data tab prompt.

---

3. In Chapter 11, I introduced the sample databases packaged with a typical SQL Server database installation. I used the Pubs sample SQL Server database in this demonstration. You can use other databases. In fact, you can even connect to nondatabase data sources.

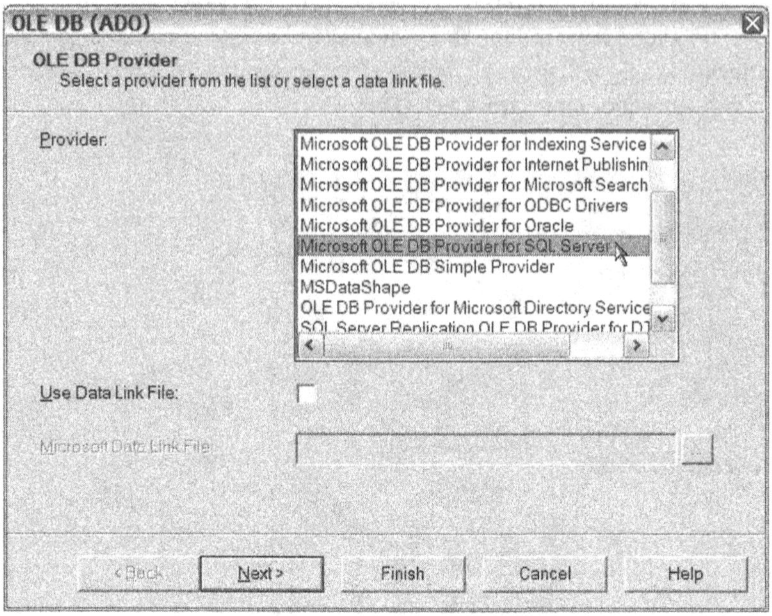

Figure 16-3. Selecting the Microsoft OLE DB Provider for SQL Server option

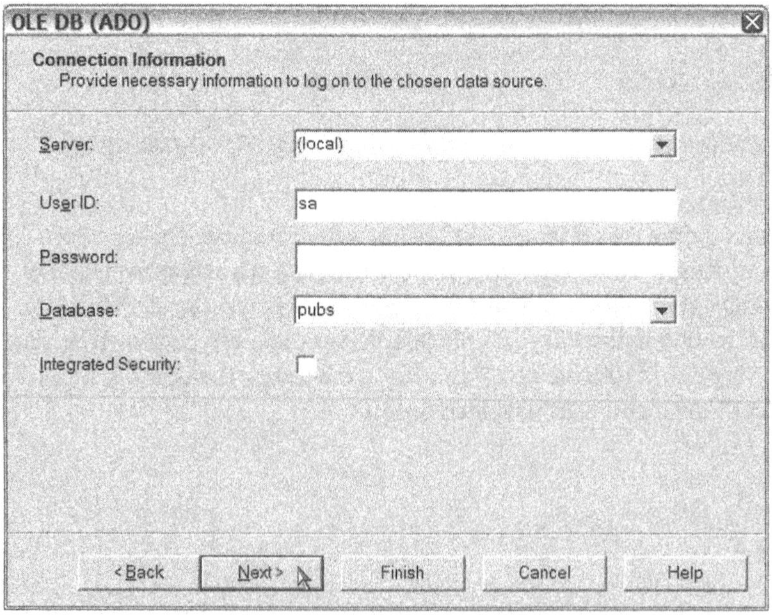

Figure 16-4. Entering the appropriate connection information to connect to the Pubs sample SQL Server database

NOTE You can use databases other than the Pubs sample SQL Server database. Additionally, you can use nondatabase sources.

4. Insert table(s) from the data source. You will use the "sales" table from the Pubs sample database (see Figure 16-5). After you insert the sales table, click Next.

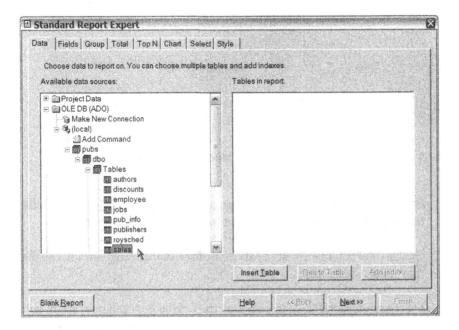

Figure 16-5. Inserting the sales table from the Pubs sample database

5. On the Fields tab, select fields and modify the column headings. Click Add All to add all the available fields and modify the column headings (see Figure 16-6). Click Next.

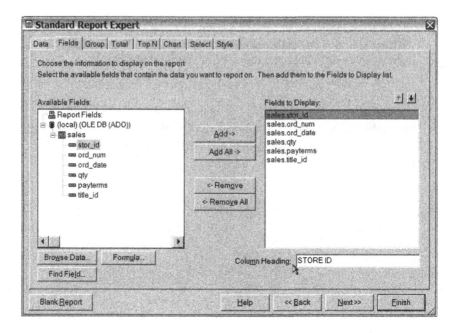

Figure 16-6. Adding all available fields and modifying the column headings

6. On the Group tab, specify any grouping. For your sample application, add the stor_id field to the Group By box (see Figure 16-7). Click Next.

7. On the Total tab, specify any fields to use for summarizing. You will use the "qty" field. Click Finish.

Once you have clicked Finish to complete the Crystal Report Expert steps, you will be returned to your open project in VS .NET. You will notice that a few things have changed:

- The ReportDocument file (.rpt) and several "CrystalDecisions" references have been added to your project (as shown in Figure 16-8).

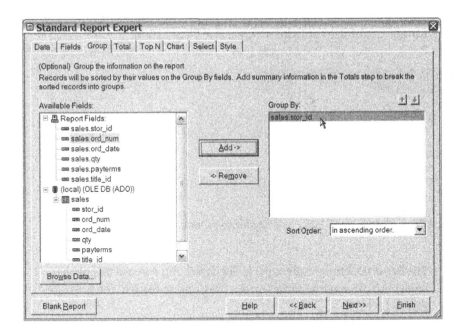

Figure 16-7. Adding the stor_id field to the Group By box

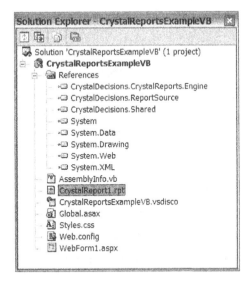

Figure 16-8. The VS .NET IDE Solution Explorer window showing the Report file and Crystal Decisions references

- The Field Explorer window will be displayed. You can use this window to further customize the fields settings (see Figure 16-9).

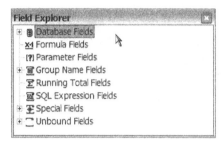

Figure 16-9. The VS .NET IDE Field Explorer window

- The ReportDocument file (.rpt) is displayed. You can use this page to adjust the placement, names, properties, and so forth of the fields (see Figure 16-10).

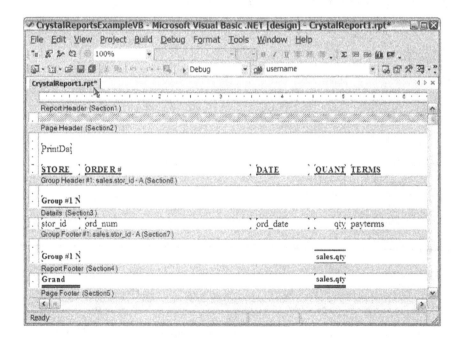

Figure 16-10. The ReportDocument file (.rpt)

NOTE   If you use Solution Explorer's Show All feature, you will be able to view the code-behind file (.vb) that is created for the ReportDocument file (.rpt).

That completes the steps of adding a Crystal Reports report template (or ReportDocument file) to your project. In the next section, you will walk through the steps needed to add a Crystal Reports Viewer to your sample project. Using the Viewer, you will be able to view the ReportDocument file during runtime, with data displayed.

TIP   This is a good time to save your CrystalReportsExampleVB sample project.

The Crystal Reports Viewers

It is easiest to describe the Crystal Reports Viewer as just another control existing in the VS .NET Toolbox that serves the specific purpose of displaying Crystal Reports's ReportDocument file. The Crystal Reports Viewer CrystalReportViewer class is first derived from the CrystalReportViewerBase class. The base class and namespace of the CrystalReportViewerBase class actually varies.

When used in a Windows application, the Crystal Reports Viewer (using the CrystalDecisions.Windows.Forms namespace) is a Windows control that inherits from the *System.Windows.Forms.Control* class as one of its base classes. On the other hand, when the Crystal Reports Viewer is used in a Web application (using the CrystalDecisions.Web namespace), it is a Web server control deriving from the *System.Web.UI.WebControls.WebControl* class.

Fortunately, both the Windows and Web versions of the Crystal Reports Viewer are basically identical. You simply need to learn one. For the discussion here, I refer to the Web version of the Crystal Reports Viewer used in a Web application.

You will add a Crystal Reports Viewer to the WebForm1.aspx file (in the CrystalReportsExampleVB project) to demonstrate its use. To accomplish this, perform the following three steps:

1. Add a CrystalReportViewer server control from the VS .NET Toolbox. As shown in Figure 16-11, the CrystalReportViewer control is available in the Web Forms tab of the VS .NET Toolbox.

Figure 16-11. The CrystalReportViewer server control in the VS .NET Toolbox

2. Once you've added the CrystalReportViewer server control to the Webform1.aspx file, you should observe the additional "Crystal" references that are added, as shown in the VS .NET Solution Explorer window in Figure 16-12.

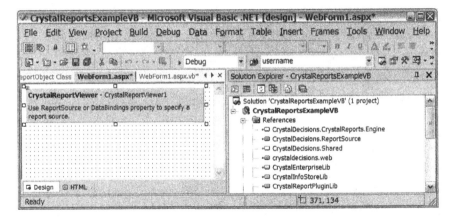

Figure 16-12. The CrystalReportViewer server control has been placed onto the Webform1.aspx file.

3. Bind the CrystalReportViewer server control to the ReportDocument file. The following code snippet shows the few lines of code used to bind the Viewer to its "source." This code will be added to the PageLoad method in WebForm1.aspx's code-behind file:

```
With CrystalReportViewer1
        .DisplayGroupTree = False
        .ReportSource = Server.MapPath("CrystalReport1.rpt")
        .DataBind()
End With
```

Once you've added the preceding few lines of code, you can execute the CrystalReportsExampleVB sample project. If all went well, the report will be shown in your browser window (see Figure 16-13).

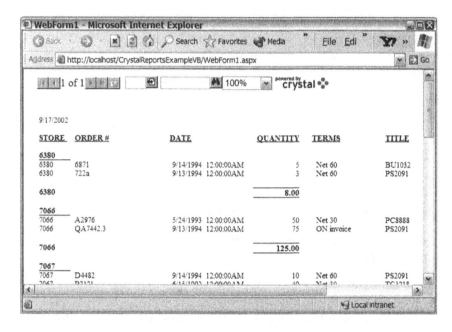

Figure 16-13. The report as shown in the browser window when executing the CrystalReportsExampleVB sample application

TIP   There are many options available to customize the Crystal Reports Viewer. The Crystal Reports class library will be a helpful source when you want to know the additional options that are available to further customize the Viewer. Additionally, please take advantage of the references provided at the end of this chapter in the "To Learn More" section.

Potential Exception Messages

During my initial development with Crystal Reports for VS .NET, I received a few exception messages. The exception messages were the result of both user (me) error and configuration concerns. Nevertheless, I was able to successfully address each exception. The following should prove helpful in the event that you have the same experience:

- *"LogOnException: Logon failed" message:* After receiving this error message, I noticed that my SQL Server Service was not "started." Once I corrected that problem, this error message did not reappear.

- *"Access to the path C:\Program Files\Microsoft Visual Studio .NET\Crystal Reports\Viewers is denied" message:* After receiving this error message, I researched the Crystal Decisions Knowledge Base Web site (see the "To Learn More" section at the end of this chapter for the URL) and located article c2010763. According to this article, "resetting" your VS .NET Toolbox (right-click the Toolbox and select Customize Toolbox ➤ Reset) "adds the ASPNET account with read and write permissions to the C:\Program Files\ Microsoft Visual Studio .NET\Crystal Reports\Viewers folder". I also experimented with my local Access Control List setup for the Viewers folder (trying a "shared" security setting) and had good results.

- *"LoadSaveReportException: Error in File . . . Access to report file denied" message:* I received this error when I attempted to "load" the report file for export (see the section "Electronic Report Delivery" later in this chapter). Researching the Crystal Decisions Knowledge Base Web site brought me to article c2010773, which suggests "to resolve this error message, set the export destination folder to a different location or grant the ASPNET user full read/write access to the destination folder".

CAUTION One way to give the ASPNET user full read/write access is to modify your Machine.config file. However, do so with extreme caution. Make sure to back up your XML-based Machine.config file before attempting any updates. Generally speaking, this approach is acceptable for stand-alone, development-mode scenarios. Your XML-based Machine.config file is located at C:\WINNT\Microsoft.NET\ Framework\<version number>\CONFIG. In this file, the setting for ASPNET's userName="machine" setting can be changed to user-Name="SYSTEM". Again, this is generally acceptable in stand-alone, development-mode scenarios. A more appropriate solution for granting "permissions" to your assembly will require an introduction to the topic of code access security. I further discuss this security topic in Chapter 18. In the meantime, feel free to take advantage of the code access security Web reference provided at the end of this chapter in the "Web Sites" subsection of the "To Learn More" section.

You have now seen how to create a Crystal Reports ReportDocument file and how to display that file using the Crystal Reports Viewer. I liken the HTML-based browser report display to a type of report delivery, perhaps electronic distribution. In the next section I expand on the topic of electronic report distribution (using Crystal Reports for VS .NET).

Electronic Report Delivery

In the previous section, you used a browser to display the Crystal Reports ReportDocument. Believe it or not, that *is* a type of report delivery. Yes, it's a stretch to define it as such. However, if you consider that an end user is able to print the displayed HTML from the browser's toolbar (by selecting File ➤ Print or pressing Ctrl-P), it's not that difficult to consider the browser display as a type of report delivery.

Certainly, this is better than loading a ton of reports into a delivery van for offsite users. Using your ASP.NET Web application, you can easily "deliver" reports across the world, just like that. This, of course, opens the floodgates for value-added enhancements. In the sections that follow, I discuss the following types of report delivery enhancements:

- Export format options

- E-mail delivery

- XML Web services

Export Format Options

Crystal Reports for VS .NET is flexible and supports various export options. To meet the various demands and expectations of the modern-day end user, you can use Crystal Reports for VS .NET to export reports in a variety of formats. Among the most popular "report" formats to export are

- Microsoft Word documents (.doc)

- Microsoft Excel spreadsheets (.xls)

- Adobe Acrobat Portable Document Format (PDF) files (.pdf)

To take advantage of Crystal Reports's exporting feature, you will need to familiarize yourself with the Crystal Reports class library (discussed earlier in section "The Crystal Reports Class Library"). Specifically, you need to use the following three namespaces:

- CrystalDecisions.CrystalReports.Engine

- CrystalDecisions.Shared

- CrystalDecisions.Web

I have modified the ASP.NET Web sample project CrystalReportsExampleVB to add exporting features. Two new Web Forms (Webform2.aspx and Webform3.aspx) and several Web server controls have been added to the project to assist with navigating back and forth between each Web Form (see Figure 16-14).

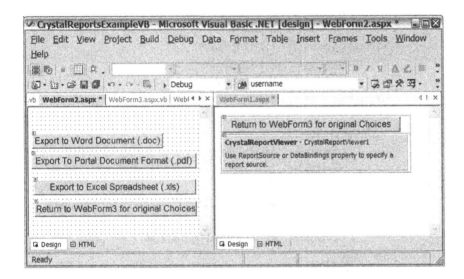

Figure 16-14. The ASP.NET Web sample project CrystalReportsExampleVB with a few enhancements added to provide navigation between each Web Form. WebForm2.aspx will be used to add "export" logic.

In the Click event/method for several Web server buttons on WebForm2.aspx, a small amount of code has been added to accomplish an "export." Please review the code snippets in Listings 16-1 through 16-3.

Listing 16-1. Code to Export a Crystal Reports ReportDocument in Microsoft Word (.doc) Format

```
Private Sub Button2_Click(ByVal sender As System.Object, _
ByVal e As System.EventArgs) Handles Button2.Click

    Dim CrReport As New _
    CrystalDecisions.CrystalReports.Engine.ReportDocument()
    CrReport.Load(Server.MapPath("CrystalReport1.rpt"))
    Dim CrExportOptions As CrystalDecisions.Shared.ExportOptions
    Dim CrDiskFileDestinationOptions As New _
    CrystalDecisions.Shared.DiskFileDestinationOptions()
    Dim CrFormatTypeOptions As New _
    CrystalDecisions.Shared.PdfRtfWordFormatOptions()

    CrDiskFileDestinationOptions.DiskFileName = _
    Server.MapPath("myfirstCR.doc")
    CrFormatTypeOptions.FirstPageNumber = 1
    CrFormatTypeOptions.LastPageNumber = 2
    CrFormatTypeOptions.UsePageRange = True
    CrExportOptions = CrReport.ExportOptions

    With CrExportOptions
            .ExportDestinationType = _
            CrystalDecisions.Shared.ExportDestinationType.DiskFile
            .ExportFormatType = _
            CrystalDecisions.Shared.ExportFormatType.WordForWindows
            .DestinationOptions = CrDiskFileDestinationOptions
            .FormatOptions = CrFormatTypeOptions
    End With
    CrReport.Export()


End Sub
```

Listing 16-2. Code to Export a Crystal Reports ReportDocument in Adobe Acrobat PDF (.pdf) Format

```
Private Sub Button3_Click(ByVal sender As System.Object, _
 ByVal e As System.EventArgs) Handles Button3.Click

    Dim CrReport As New _
    CrystalDecisions.CrystalReports.Engine.ReportDocument()
    CrReport.Load(Server.MapPath("CrystalReport1.rpt"))
    Dim CrExportOptions As CrystalDecisions.Shared.ExportOptions
```

```
Dim CrDiskFileDestinationOptions As New _
CrystalDecisions.Shared.DiskFileDestinationOptions()
Dim CrFormatTypeOptions As New _
CrystalDecisions.Shared.PdfRtfWordFormatOptions()

CrDiskFileDestinationOptions.DiskFileName = _
Server.MapPath("myfirstCR.pdf")
CrFormatTypeOptions.FirstPageNumber = 1
CrFormatTypeOptions.LastPageNumber = 2
CrFormatTypeOptions.UsePageRange = True
CrExportOptions = CrReport.ExportOptions

With CrExportOptions
        .ExportDestinationType = _
        CrystalDecisions.Shared.ExportDestinationType.DiskFile
        .ExportFormatType = _
        CrystalDecisions.Shared.ExportFormatType.PortableDocFormat
        .DestinationOptions = CrDiskFileDestinationOptions
        .FormatOptions = CrFormatTypeOptions
End With
CrReport.Export()


End Sub
```

Listing 16-3. Code to Export a Crystal Reports ReportDocument in Microsoft Excel (.xls) Format

```
Private Sub Button4_Click(ByVal sender As System.Object, _
 ByVal e As System.EventArgs) Handles Button4.Click

        Dim CrReport As New _
        CrystalDecisions.CrystalReports.Engine.ReportDocument()
        CrReport.Load(Server.MapPath("CrystalReport1.rpt"))
        Dim CrExportOptions As CrystalDecisions.Shared.ExportOptions
        Dim CrDiskFileDestinationOptions As New _
        CrystalDecisions.Shared.DiskFileDestinationOptions()
        Dim CrFormatTypeOptions As New _
        CrystalDecisions.Shared.ExcelFormatOptions()

        CrDiskFileDestinationOptions.DiskFileName = _
        Server.MapPath("myfirstCR.xls")
        CrFormatTypeOptions.ExcelTabHasColumnHeadings = True
        CrFormatTypeOptions.ExcelUseConstantColumnWidth = False
        CrExportOptions = CrReport.ExportOptions
```

```
With CrExportOptions
        .ExportDestinationType = _
        CrystalDecisions.Shared.ExportDestinationType.DiskFile
        .ExportFormatType = _
         CrystalDecisions.Shared.ExportFormatType.Excel
        .DestinationOptions = CrDiskFileDestinationOptions
        .FormatOptions = CrFormatTypeOptions
End With
CrReport.Export()

End Sub
```

In Listings 16-1 through 16-3, you will notice very subtle differences between the syntax required to export each report format. Please take a moment to review the code. Feel free to experiment with the many available options. The Crystal Reports class library will be a helpful source when you want to know the additional options available to further customize each report format. As always, references are provided at the end of this chapter in the "To Learn More" section to assist in your continued retraining efforts.

 TIP   In your actual applications, you will want to add exception handling logic. Additionally, you will typically rename your server controls,
Web Forms, report files, and so forth from their default names to more
functional and descriptive names.

Run the sample application and export each report format. As shown in Figure 16-15, each report format export will result in a file being created. In a real-world Web application, you would definitely have chosen to create an IIS virtual directory for the destination of the reports (I further discuss the creation of IIS virtual directories in Chapter 17) instead of exposing your application folder.

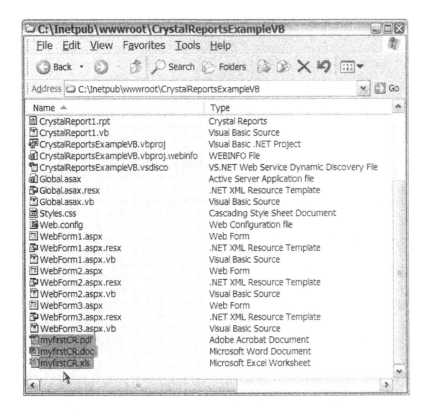

Figure 16-15. Using Windows Explorer outside of the VS .NET IDE to verify the creation of the exported report formats

As you can see in Figure 16-16, I have added a few HREF controls to WebForm3.aspx (of the CrystalReportsExampleVB sample project) to view the contents of each exported file format. In a production application, the HREF would typically contain the URL that points back to an IIS virtual directory (as noted earlier, I discuss the creation of IIS virtual directories in Chapter 17) instead of using the approach shown in this sample application.

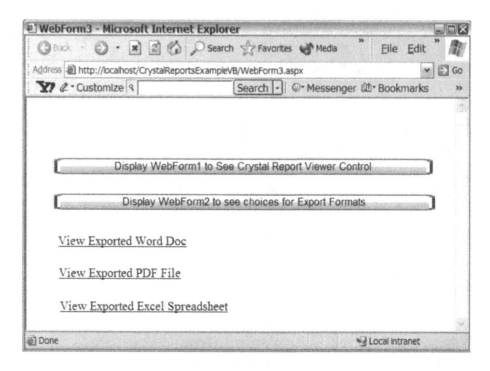

Figure 16-16. WebForm3.aspx of the CrystalReportsExampleVB sample project with a few HREF controls added

TIP   You will need to have Adobe Acrobat Reader software installed to view files exported in the Adobe Acrobat PDF (.pdf) format. The Adobe Acrobat Reader software is available as a free download from the Adobe Web site (http://www.adobe.com/).

In modern-day reporting, multiple formats are delivered right to the browser. You have got to admit, this is really great. Once the desired format is electronically delivered to the end user, he or she is free to print the report. Well, it only gets better. Suppose you want to use e-mail as a delivery vehicle. It is certainly possible. In the next section, you will explore the e-mail alternative to report distribution.

Windows Forms Controls for Printing

In the event that you are creating a .NET Windows application and wish to add "normal" printing capability to your application, you are in luck. .NET provides the following four classes that you will want to further explore:

- *PrintPreview:* System.Windows.Forms.PrintPreviewControl

- *PrintDialog:* System.Windows.Forms.PrintDialog

- *PageSetup:* System.Windows.Forms.PageSetupDialog

- *PrintDocument:* System.Drawing.Printing.PrintDocument

As you use these .NET Framework classes, you will be reminded of working with the mainframe COBOL Report Writer feature—except I believe the .NET Framework classes are more developer-friendly.

E-mail with SMTP

As you certainly know, the use of e-mail is very popular. This is a good thing. As a developer, you can take advantage of e-mail as a report delivery vehicle. The .NET platform provides a set of managed classes to support sending e-mail using the Collaboration Data Objects for Windows 2000 (CDOSYS) message component. This set of classes is provided via the System.Web.Mail namespace.

CROSS-REFERENCE The CDOSYS message component was originally discussed in Chapter 10.

Before I get into the code needed to implement an SMTP e-mail delivery solution, I need to mention a couple of points:

- You will need the SMTP service installed on your IIS Web server in order to send e-mail from your Web application using the SMTP managed classes.

- If your organization happens to use Microsoft Exchange Server for e-mail relaying, you will need to properly connect and configure your installed SMTP service to the Exchange Server. With this type of setup, you will need appropriate access permissions to the Exchange Server to complete your SMTP configuration. However, it is possible to send e-mails using SMTP without the use of Exchange Server, assuming that SMTP and your Internet connection are properly configured.

CROSS-REFERENCE SMTP was originally introduced in Chapter 3, and Exchange Server was originally introduced in Chapter 10.

NOTE The setup and configuration of the SMTP service and/or Exchange Server are beyond the scope of this text. However, I provide several references at the end of this chapter in the "To Learn More" section to point you in the right direction. Otherwise, your organization's network administration group should be able to provide further assistance.

As shown in Figure 16-17, the SMTP service will appear in your Computer Management console if it is installed as part of your IIS Web server installation.

By the way, if you have SMTP set up locally without Exchange Server, your sent e-mail will simply sit in the SMTP queue waiting for delivery. That is OK for now. At least you can verify that your programming task was completed. An SMTP installation will include the default setup of a "mailroot" folder structure as shown in Figure 16-18. As you can see in Figure 16-19, an Internet e-mail message is easily identifiable in the SMTP queue.

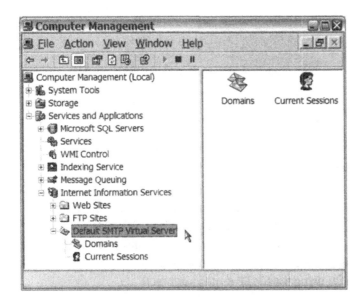

Figure 16-17. The Computer Management console showing the SMTP service installed

Figure 16-18. The mailroot folder structure for SMTP e-mail support

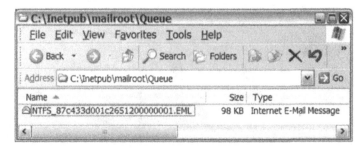

Figure 16-19. An Internet e-mail message in the SMTP queue

Now that that's out of the way, you'll take a look at how simple the actual programming is for SMTP e-mail. Further enhancing the CrystalReportsExampleVB sample project, I've added a few server controls that will facilitate the attempted send of the e-mail using SMTP. Listing 16-4 demonstrates how to send the report files (previously exported) using the SMTP e-mail approach.

Listing 16-4. Sending E-mail Attachments with System.Web.Mail Managed Classes and SMTP

```vb
Private Sub Button3_Click(ByVal sender As System.Object, _
    ByVal e As System.EventArgs) Handles Button3.Click

    Dim MyEmailMessage As New System.Web.Mail.MailMessage()
    MyEmailMessage.To = TextBox1.Text
    MyEmailMessage.From = TextBox1.Text
    MyEmailMessage.Subject = "A Satisfied Customer"
    MyEmailMessage.BodyFormat = System.Web.Mail.MailFormat.Text
    MyEmailMessage.Body = "Sending an SMTP Email is easy!"

    Dim myattachment1 As System.Web.Mail.MailAttachment = New _
    System.Web.Mail.MailAttachment(Server.MapPath("myfirstCR.doc"))
    MyEmailMessage.Attachments.Add(myattachment1)

    Dim myattachment2 As System.Web.Mail.MailAttachment = New _
    System.Web.Mail.MailAttachment(Server.MapPath("myfirstCR.pdf"))
    MyEmailMessage.Attachments.Add(myattachment2)

    Dim myattachment3 As System.Web.Mail.MailAttachment = New _
    System.Web.Mail.MailAttachment(Server.MapPath("myfirstCR.xls"))
    MyEmailMessage.Attachments.Add(myattachment3)

    System.Web.Mail.SmtpMail.Send(MyEmailMessage)

End Sub
```

NOTE If your assembly does not have the appropriate security permissions, you may experience an exception/error message when you execute the SMTP Send method. As discussed in the earlier section "Potential Exception Messages," there are solutions for this type of problem.

As you can see from Listing 16-4, the logic is rather simple. The support provided by .NET via the System.Web.Mail namespace makes sending e-mail a viable report delivery option. In the next section, you will take a look at another report delivery approach. Having options is really a great characteristic of the .NET platform that enables you to pick the solution that best fits your business needs.

What About the HTML Mailto URL?

You can also send e-mail using a simple HTML mailto URL. Using either the <a> HTML anchor element or the HyperLink Web server control, the HREF attribute value can be set to an e-mail address. This approach to sending e-mail is different from the SMTP approach. It is much simpler and you do not need an SMTP server or Exchange Server setup. You simply need to be connected to the Internet.

However, this simpler approach does not provide the rich .NET managed object module that enables value-added features such as adding attachments. The CrystalReportsExampleVB sample project has a HyperLink Web server control added to WebForm3.aspx that will send an e-mail for demonstration purposes.

XML Web Services

The Crystal Reports ReportDocument report file (.rpt) has the ability to be converted to an XML Web service. The process to do this is so easy it is amazing. The scenario would simply be that you want to expose your report as XML via the Internet. In other words, you can use this feature as yet another way to deliver your report to the end user. The end user, in this case, would use an application (e.g., a Windows or ASP.NET application) to consume the XML.

CROSS-REFERENCE   I covered the topic of XML Web services in Chapter 13 in the section "Understanding the ASP.NET Web Service Technology."

The two Crystal Reports class library namespaces you use during this process are CrystalDecisions.Web.Services and CrystalDecisions.Web.Services.Enterprise. Let's now revisit the sample application to review the simple technique involved in converting the Crystal ReportDocument report file to an XML Web service.

As shown in Figure 16-20, you need to select the Crystal ReportDocument report file in Solution Explorer. Then, you'll want to right-click and select "Publish as web service" from the drop-down context menu. That's it!

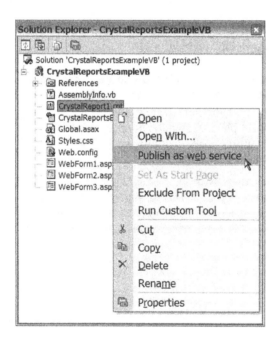

Figure 16-20. Publishing the Crystal ReportDocument report file as a Web service

Notice that when you complete these few steps, an .asmx file appears in the VS .NET Solution Explorer window (see Figure 16-21). In the case of the sample application, the new file is named CrystalReport1Service.asmx. Basically, that is your XML Web service.

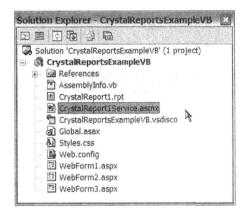

Figure 16-21. Viewing the VS .NET Solution Explorer window showing the .asmx file for the new XML Web service

Testing the XML Web Service

The easiest way to test your XML Web service is to navigate directly to the .asmx file. You can do this by typing the appropriate address (i.e., **http://localhost/ CrystalReportsExampleVB/CrystalReport1Service.asmx**) into your browser address bar. Optionally, you can modify the CrystalReport1Service.asmx file by right-clicking and selecting Set As Start Page. Then, when you start the sample project, the automatic XML Web service testing harness will display (see Figure 16-22).

You'll need to customize the CrystalReport1Service.asmx.vb code-behind file to fully enable the testing ability of the testing harness. In fact, you can customize the automatic XML Web service testing harness in virtually any other way you see fit. For example, you can modify the entry "banner page" to display your company's name. Additionally, for confidentiality reasons, you may choose to suppress some of functionality that's exposed by default.

Feel free to experiment with the sample application to continue your retraining effort. You might even create a separate .NET application (using COBOL .NET or VB .NET, Windows or ASP.NET) to serve as a consuming client application. In other words, you can create an application that makes use of the VS .NET Solution Explorer's Add Web Reference feature. This client application would then "consume" the XML returned from the XML Web service. The references provided in the "To Learn More" section should be helpful to you as you continue your journey.

Figure 16-22. The CrystalReport1Service.asmx file as seen in the automatic XML Web service testing harness

Summary

This chapter's goals were as follows:

- To learn how to use Crystal Reports for VS .NET

- To explore Crystal Reports's export feature

- To understand report delivery options using Crystal Reports

This chapter introduced you to the Crystal Reports for VS .NET product from Crystal Decisions, Inc. The seamless integration of Crystal Reports into VS .NET made it easy to demonstrate several of the Crystal Reports "reporting" features. You learned how to create and modify a report file. Additionally, you learned about the Crystal Reports Viewer control, the export features, and the XML Web services publishing feature. This chapter's discussion helped put into perspective the more "modern" view of reporting and information delivery.

In the next chapter you will explore the topic of .NET application deployment.

To Learn More

The following are some suggested supplemental references to further your retraining effort.

Books

Enterprise Reports Using VB 6.0 and VB .NET, by Carl Ganz, Jr. and Jon Kilburn
 (Apress, 2003):
 http://www.apress.com/book/bookDisplay.html?bID=133.
Programming VB .NET: A Guide for Experienced Programmers, by Gary Cornell
 (Apress, 2001):
 http://www.apress.com/book/bookDisplay.html?bID=130.

Magazines

.NET Magazine:
 http://www.fawcette.com/dotnetmag/
Exchange & Outlook Magazine, DevX Newsletter (by Jim Minatel, Editor-in-Chief):
 http://www.devx.com/free/newsletters/exo/exoed031601.asp
MSDN Magazine:
 http://msdn.microsoft.com/msdnmag/
Visual Studio Magazine:
 http://www.fawcette.com/vsm/
Windows Developer Magazine:
 http://www.wd-mag.com/
XML & Web Services Magazine:
 http://www.fawcette.com/xmlmag/

Web Sites

.NET Enterprise Servers Online Books:
 http://msdn.microsoft.com/library/default.asp?url=/servers/books/
 default.asp

About SMTP:

> http://msdn.microsoft.com/library/en-us/cdosys/html/
> _cdosys_about_smtp.asp

Adobe Acrobat Reader Free Download:

> http://www.adobe.com/products/acrobat/readstep2.html

Code Access Security Basics:

> http://msdn.microsoft.com/library/en-us/cpguide/html/
> cpconcodeaccesssecuritybasics.asp

Collaboration Data Objects Roadmap:

> http://msdn.microsoft.com/library/en-us/dncdsys/html/cdo_roadmap.asp

Crystal Reports Architecture:

> http://msdn.microsoft.com/library/en-us/crystlrf/html/
> crconcrystalreportsarchitecture.asp

Crystal Reports Class Library:

> http://msdn.microsoft.com/library/en-us/crystlrf/html/
> crlrfcrystalreportsclasslibrary.asp

Crystal Reports Developer Zone:

> http://www.crystaldecisions.com/products/dev_zone/default.asp

Crystal Reports Knowledge Base Articles:

> http://support.crystaldecisions.com/library/kbase.asp

Crystal Reports: The Visual Studio .NET Reporting Standard:

> http://www.crystaldecisions.com/products/crystalreports/net/

GotDotNet:

> http://www.gotdotnet.com/

Introduction to ASP.NET:

> http://msdn.microsoft.com/library/en-us/cpguide/html/
> cpconintroductiontoasp.asp

Microsoft ASP.NET Home Page:

> http://www.asp.net/

Microsoft Community (discussion groups, e-newsletters, and so forth):

> http://communities2.microsoft.com/

Microsoft Exchange Server:

> http://www.microsoft.com/exchange/default.asp

Microsoft's Search the Knowledge Base Web Site:

> http://support.microsoft.com/default.aspx?scid=FH;EN-US;KBHOWTO

Microsoft TechNet How-To Index:

> http://www.microsoft.com/technet/treeview/default.asp?url=/technet/
> itsolutions/howto

MSDN:

> http://msdn.microsoft.com

XML Web Services Developer Center Home:

> http://msdn.microsoft.com/webservices/

CHAPTER 17

Deploying Your .NET Application

Copying Files from Your Development Environment to Your Production Environment

In this chapter

- Reviewing deployment design considerations

- Demonstrating how to use the Microsoft Windows Installer 2.0

- Exploring the manual approach to a .NET deployment

IT IS SAFE TO ASSUME that you have installed software onto a Windows platform. After all, your Microsoft .NET Framework and Visual Studio .NET (VS .NET) toolset required a lengthy installation. The Fujitsu NetCOBOL for .NET software required that you go through an installation procedure as well. Perhaps you have installed other software packages (e.g., Microsoft Office, SQL Server, Adobe Acrobat Reader, and so on). Some of your installations were initiated by simply putting in a CD-ROM. Others required that you locate and click a Setup.exe program.

In each case, as *you* have installed software, *you* were actually completing the final steps of a deployment: a software deployment process. In this chapter, you will explore several of the steps you need to take to deploy your own .NET software that you have developed.

I start off the chapter by discussing several of the choices available to you as you plan for and design your application's deployment. From there, you will explore Microsoft Windows Installer 2.0 (Windows Installer) software as it is exposed in the VS .NET IDE. Using Windows Installer, you will learn how to easily deploy .NET Windows and Web applications. The last portion of the chapter covers the manual approach to a .NET deployment.

NOTE I use the term "deployment" to refer to copying files from a development, testing, or staging environment to a production environment that is exposed to targeted end users. Some of you may be more familiar with phrases such as "implement to production," "promote to production," or "distribute to production." No matter which terms you use to describe this process, the concept is basically the same.

Deployment Considerations

Having developed on mainframe COBOL/CICS environments, you have certainly experienced various deployment scenarios. When you developed mainframe batch COBOL programs, perhaps you only needed to have your compiled load module moved from a dev/test load library (a partitioned dataset) to a production load library. In other cases, perhaps the process was more complex.

Maybe there was an elaborate process that resulted in your COBOL source being recompiled, link-edited, archived, and then copied to a production load library. Depending on the needs of your application, you would sometimes have additional concerns of defining Virtual Storage Access Method (VSAM) files and Base Generation Data Groups (GDG) files. Your deployment may have even included copying Job Control Language (JCL) members and copybooks to appropriate production libraries.

NOTE Your applications that made use of a DB2 or IMS database may have had additional deployment concerns.

All this sounds familiar, right? Of course, it would only be fair to mention the additional production deployment concerns associated with a typical mainframe CICS application. As you know, your CICS BMS screen map and load module would have been moved. Then, you would have needed to follow up on tasks such as having your CICS transaction defined in the program control table (PCT), your application program defined in the processing program table (PPT), any I/O files defined in the file control table (FCT), and finally, any transient data (TD) queues defined in the destination control table (DCT).

> **NOTE**   Obviously, this is a watered-down summary of mainframe
> deployment concerns. I do believe there is enough detail provided to
> make this mainframe analogy useful, though.

You have a few points to focus on before you dive into the .NET arena. To begin
with, when it is time to deploy your mainframe COBOL/CICS application, you
have several steps to follow. Most organizations have processes, policies, and procedures surrounding these deployment steps. There is a correlation between the
needs of your application and the resulting steps taken to complete your production deployment. Finally, a deployment done carefully and correctly will make
the difference between your end user being negatively or positively impacted.

With .NET applications, there are deployment tasks, choices, and concerns as
well. You will need to start thinking about several deployment design decisions.
Although not presented as a complete list, the following considerations should be
enough to get you started in the right direction:

- Redistribute or not redistribute the .NET Framework

- Redistribute or not redistribute the COBOL .NET runtime

- Obfuscate or not obfuscate

- Deploy the release or debug version

- Precompile, batch compile, or just-in-time (JIT) compile

- Use or not use the Global Assembly Cache (GAC)

- Use or not use a strong name for your assembly

- Deploy or not deploy multiple versions of your configuration file

- Use an automated or a manual approach for installation

A long list, huh? Please keep in mind that this list is not even complete. Nevertheless, it does speak to the most common issues that you will want to be prepared
for. In the following sections, I drill down to briefly discuss each of the previously
listed topics.

Redistribute or Not Redistribute the .NET Framework

Will you need to be concerned about the redistribution of the .NET Framework? You will want to answer this question early on, as you plan for deployment. If the target deployment machine already has the .NET Framework installed, you simply need to distribute your application. Otherwise, you first need to concern yourself with the redistribution of the system-level software.

TIP Although you *will* need the .NET Framework on your targeted production machine, you should not install VS .NET and other development tools onto the production machine. As far as .NET is concerned, the Framework can be installed alone.

It is expected that as newer machines host the future versions of the Windows operating system, this .NET Framework requirement will become less of a concern. For the time being, however, it is a concern. It is something for you to be aware of: Your .NET application expects to run on a machine that already has the .NET Framework installed.

NOTE As long as you have a licensed version of VS .NET, you can redistribute the .NET Framework to targeted machines (per your end user license agreement). The one file (Dotnetfx.exe for v1.0) that makes up the redistributable .NET Framework is available by download from Microsoft's Web site (you can also find it on your .NET product CDs). Microsoft also provides a free download referred to as the *Setup.exe Bootstrapper sample.* The Setup.exe Bootstrapper sample provides guidance for executing the Dotnetfx.exe installation program as part of your deployment process.

The targeted machine (where your application will actually execute) must meet additional software and hardware requirements. Please refer to the Microsoft documentation (and the references provided at the end of this chapter) for more details on the redistributable package for the .NET Framework.

Redistribute or Not Redistribute the COBOL .NET Runtime

Throughout this text, I have acknowledged the possibility that you might decide to develop with Visual Basic .NET (VB .NET) or COBOL .NET. If you decide to go with the COBOL .NET choice, keep in mind that you will incur additional concerns when it is time to distribute your application.

As it turns out, there are additional files that you will need to (re)distribute. These "extra" files represent the runtime needed to support Fujitsu's NetCOBOL for .NET product (or rather, COBOL .NET—the term I have chosen as an unofficial reference).

As shown in Figure 17-1, the files are conveniently grouped in one folder.

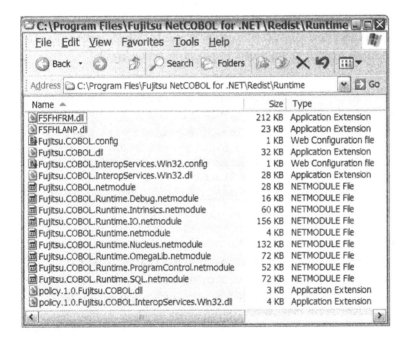

Figure 17-1. C:\Program Files\Fujitsu NetCOBOL for .NET\Redist\Runtime

According to Fujitsu's product documentation, these "additional" files must be installed into the GAC.

CROSS-REFERENCE   I further discuss the GAC in the section "Use or Not Use the Global Assembly Cache (GAC)" later in this chapter.

Obfuscate or Not Obfuscate

If you have developed an application that includes the type of sensitive source code that you would not want your customers (or competitors) seeing, you may want to look into the topic of *obfuscation*. The threat of intellectual property theft is real. It is possible to take compiled code through a process called *decompilation*. At the end of this process, your original source can be reconstructed or reverse engineered. That is, unless you use an obfuscation product.

The job of an obfuscation product is to safely "scramble" the internals of your distributable modules, making them nearly impossible to decompile.

NOTE   The concern of obfuscation does not apply as much to Web-based (ASP.NET) applications. Although Web-based applications contend with the wit of hackers and virus authors, the threat of decompilation generally applies to instances where the actual compiled modules are distributed to the end user.

Because internal applications are not necessarily exposed to nontrusted parties, you might be more interested in obfuscation in instances where your end user is an external user (working for a different company). If you feel that the routines, calculations, and algorithms packaged in your application are not *that* unique, you might conclude that there is nothing worth stealing. You will have to be the judge of that.

One of the most popular obfuscation products for .NET is Dotfuscator from PreEmptive Solutions.[1] It is expected that the Dotfuscator product will be integrated into a future version of VS .NET.[2] In the meantime, you can obtain the

---

1. PreEmptive Solutions announced the availability of the Dotfuscator product for Microsoft .NET applications at the VSLive! event in San Francisco on February 13, 2002.

2. According to a recent GotDotNet "featured site" article (http://www.gotdotnet.com/featured_site/preemptive/default.aspx), PreEmptive Solutions is a member of Microsoft's Visual Studio Integrator Program (VSIP).

Community Edition of Dotfuscator through a free download offer made available by PreEmptive Solutions.

> **CROSS-REFERENCE**   I have included the PreEmptive Solutions URL in the "Web Sites" subsection of the "To Learn More" section at the end of this chapter. Feel free to visit the PreEmptive Solutions Web site to read more about their obfuscation product.

The Community Edition of Dotfuscator is advertised as being "fully functional" and "free for evaluation, personal, or academic use." PreEmptive Solutions also offers a Professional Edition of Dotfuscator. If you were to purchase the Professional Edition, you could take advantage of the advertised feature "one year of support and upgrades."

Naturally, there are other software vendors creating obfuscation products for .NET applications.[3] For the time being, PreEmptive Solutions is apparently leading the pack.

Deploy the Release or Debug Version

In your mainframe experience, you have likely come across the occasion to troubleshoot a production problem. In some of those cases, you may have had the assistance of formatted COBOL memory dumps, interactive debugging, or perhaps File-AID–type information. All of this depended heavily on how you compiled your mainframe COBOL problem. Typically, your program would have been compiled using the most optimal compiler directives.

As you know, what is most optimal for normal production processing is not always most optimal for troubleshooting. The same quandary exists with your .NET applications. When you build your .NET applications, you can choose either the Release option or the Debug option to configure your projects/solution.

When you view an open project in the VS .NET IDE, the Solutions Configurations drop-down box is visible on the Standard toolbar. You can either make your choice there or navigate deeper to the Configuration Manager dialog box. As shown in Figure 17-2, the Configuration Manager is exposed as a choice on the Standard toolbar. The Configuration Manager window makes available a more flexible configuration for your solutions (see Figure 17-3).

---

3.   These same vendors are creating obfuscation products for other platforms as well (e.g., Java).

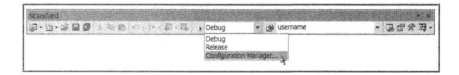

Figure 17-2. The VS .NET Standard toolbar exposing the Solutions Configurations drop-down box

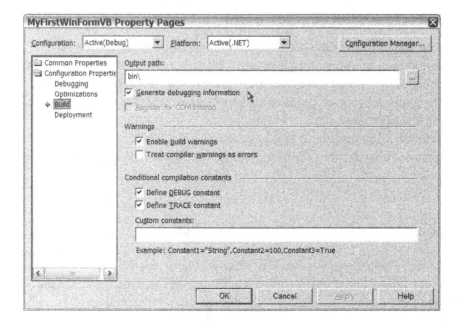

Figure 17-3. The Configuration Manager dialog box

Now comes the fun part. Which choice should you make: Release or Debug?

If you choose Debug, you will create the debug symbols file. This is the .pdb file that is located in your <application>\bin folder. The mapping (MSIL to source code) enabled by this file is invaluable during any reasonable debugging effort. However, if you distribute this .pdb file with your application, you will make it that much easier for a would-be intellectual thief to decompile and reverse engineer your .NET application.

On the other hand, if you choose Release, your production application will be built in its most optimal form. However, in the event that you need to troubleshoot a production problem, you will need to rebuild the solution to reap the benefits of interactive debugging.

Consider the alternative approach of combining the generation of debugging symbols with the Release setting. As shown in Figure 17-4, this is as simple as selecting a check box (that is unchecked by default) on the project property pages.

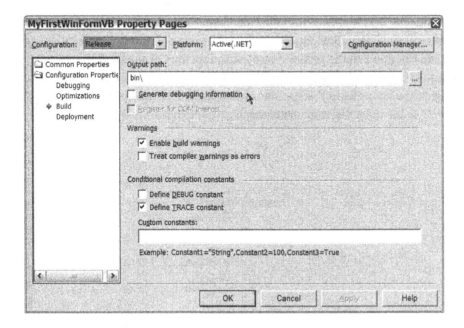

Figure 17-4. The project property pages Build options showing the check box used to selectively generate debugging information

To make this approach complete, you might even consider using a symbol server to help manage the debugging symbol (.pdb) files that you will be generating rather than include them when you deploy your application. Microsoft makes available a public symbol server that you can direct your VS .NET IDE configuration setting to. Optionally, you can create your own symbol server on your intranet or local server.

TIP Please refer to your .NET Platform SDK documentation for more information on symbol servers. I have included a Web reference at the end of this chapter to help your research efforts.

Precompile, Batch Compile, or Just-in-Time (JIT) Compile

The discussion of various compilation options is not necessarily a deployment consideration, per se. However, it does help bring to the surface an issue that you might consider addressing in your post-deployment process.

You will recall that I introduced the topic of Microsoft intermediate language (MSIL) in Chapter 8 in the section "Understanding the Common Language Runtime." In that earlier section, you learned that your .NET source code goes through a few "compilation" steps before actually executing. As shown in Figure 17-5, the objective is to create machine code that actually executes.

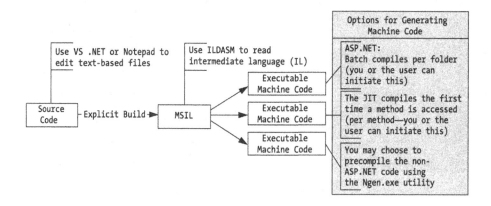

Figure 17-5. The basic options to generate machine code

As part of your post-deployment process, you might choose to initiate the batch compilation and just-in-time (JIT) compilation in your ASP.NET applications (by being the first to "hit" specific pages and methods). Then, your users will experience the lighting-fast execution of the machine code each time. For your non-ASP.NET applications, you have the option of using the Ngen.exe utility to precompile targeted methods to avoid your users initiating the JIT compilation.

Use or Not Use the Global Assembly Cache (GAC)

In the pre-.NET development arena, the most common way to "locate" an assembly (.dll) during runtime was to use the registry. In Chapter 3 in the section "System Registry," I compared the Windows registry with common mainframe practices used to "locate" executables. As part of that earlier discussion, I used the mainframe JCL STEPLIB/JOBLIB and System Master Catalog as analogies.

There was a common thread in that earlier discussion as I contrasted the mainframe and .NET environments. Regardless of the platform, there is a need for multiple applications to be able to locate shared components being targeted for execution.

With .NET, the Global Assembly Cache (GAC) serves this purpose. The GAC provides a location to store managed assemblies destined to be shared across application boundaries. .NET provides a utility, Gacutil.exe, that you can use to manage the GAC (adding or removing assemblies). You can use the .NET Framework Configuration tool Mscorcfg.msc to manage the GAC. Additionally, you can use the Microsoft Windows Installer product to add assemblies to and remove assemblies from the GAC.

 TIP Using the GAC will introduce complexities into your deployment process. Therefore, I offer this rule of thumb: Consider using the GAC only if you have an assembly (.dll) that will be shared by multiple applications on the same physical machine. Otherwise, leave your assemblies in the <application>\bin folder as private assemblies.

The next time you have a project open in your VS .NET IDE, execute the project. Then, while the project is executing, view the Debug tab of the VS .NET IDE Output window. The display in that window will show you exactly which portions of your project are coming from the GAC. To demonstrate this, I will use the sample project MyFirstWinFormVB (from Chapter 13). As shown in Figure 17-6, during an application's execution, the VS .NET IDE Output window indicates the location from which each assembly is loaded and executed.

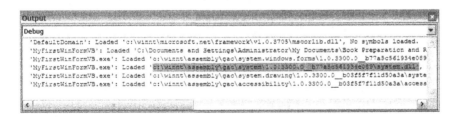

Figure 17-6. The VS .NET IDE Output window. Notice that the shared assembly System.dll was loaded and executed from the GAC.

In the event that your application's needs justify the use of the GAC, you'll need to create a strong name for your assembly. In the next section, you'll turn to further explore the topic of strong names.

CROSS-REFERENCE   Please refer to the "To Learn More" section at the end of this chapter for more information on the GAC and the Gaculil.exe utility.

Use or Not Use a Strong Name for Your Assembly

If you want to use the versioning feature that .NET offers, you will need to generate a *strong name* for your assembly. A strong name also ensures the uniqueness of your assembly name. A strong name is required in the case of your assembly being used as a shared assembly (in the GAC). The creation of a strong name for your assembly is commonly referred to as "signing your assembly."

NOTE   A few strong name facts: .NET provides a utility, Sn.exe, to assist you in creating an assembly strong name. You can create a strong name for your private and shared assemblies. If your assembly is intended to be an Enterprise Services (COM+) component, you must create a strong name for your assembly. (This topic is further discussed in Chapter 19.)

Although versioning and name uniqueness may sound like great benefits, you should seek to use these features only if you really need them. In other words, there is a cost incurred in using these benefits. One particular cost is incurred when you sign your assembly: Your deployment process becomes a bit more complex.

To reap the benefits of versioning, your applications will point to specific "versions" of the strong-named assembly. Later, when you need to deploy a new version of the strong-named assembly, you must take extra steps to force existing applications to reference the new version of the strong-named assembly.

There is no doubt that versioning is a great feature enabled by signing an assembly. Just understand what this introduces into your deployment process.

CROSS-REFERENCE   Please refer to the "To Learn More" section at the end of this chapter for resources you can look to for more information on strong names and the Sn.exe utility.

Deploy or Not Deploy Multiple Versions of Your Configuration File

I remember using mainframe JCL OVERRIDE statements during my legacy COBOL development and testing. The JCL OVERRIDE statements provided an easy way to use nonproduction resources. For example, I would use a JCL OVERRIDE statement to the test database during my testing phase. The problem came when I would occasionally leave the OVERRIDE statements in and deploy my application to production while still pointing to test resources. This type of deployment concern continues to exist, even with .NET.

The .NET environment offers an XML-based configuration file (or just *config file*). I briefly introduced this file in Chapter 15. You can use the config file to store most of your resource directive statements. For example, your database connection string information will typically be placed in the config file. Both ASP.NET and Windows applications can take advantage of the config file approach by using the Web.config file or the ApplicationName.exe.config[4] file, respectively.

CROSS-REFERENCE   Chapter 18 presents a full discussion of the XML-based config file.

The settings (e.g., database connection string) placed in your config file during your development and testing are likely to be changed when it's time to prepare for your production deployment. This means that you need to either create multiple versions of the config file or remember to edit the file as appropriate. My guess is that you don't want to end up deploying your application to

---

4. Microsoft's documentation mentions a naming convention of *ApplicationName.exe.config* for the Windows application configuration file. The config file that matches that naming convention is automatically created for you. You actually create the App.config file. When you "build" your solution/project, the App.config file is copied to the \bin folder with the name of *ApplicationName.exe.config*. You then continue to edit the App.config that remains in the application folder. This automatic copying scenario repeats with subsequent builds.

production while still referring to test-based resources. As I recall, that's frowned upon.

One approach is to create multiple versions of your config file. In other words, create a config file for each environment with self-documenting names (coming from the mainframe, this will look and feel rather familiar). As shown in Figure 17-7, you can then use the Override file feature in the Deployment section of the VS .NET IDE project property pages.

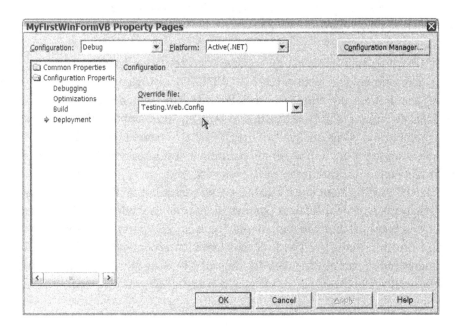

Figure 17-7. Override file feature in the Deployment section of the VS .NET IDE project property pages

Can you believe it? They are even calling them "override files." Just like in the old days. Wow, talk about coming full circle—this is almost scary. At any rate, you can use this *new* VS .NET feature to point to the appropriate config file as you prepare for each phase of your deployment process.

Use an Automated or a Manual Approach for Installation

On the mainframe, you may have used tools that served to automate a production deployment. Some of these tools simply copied modules. Others may have integrated the source management check-in and sign-off processes together with the copying and archiving of modules. You will be pleased to know that the Windows/ .NET platform also offers you the choice of automating your software installation.

Generally, the choice that you make to automate or not to automate will depend mostly on the complexity and needs of your application. In the simplest of cases, you can stick with the manual installation approach. On the other hand, automation will likely be a better choice in the following scenarios:

- For most ASP.NET installations

- For all .NET Windows application installations where an end user is involved in the deployment process

- For all .NET Windows application installations where Internet/browser-based distribution is an option

- For all .NET Windows Service installations

- For all cases where the GAC is used[5]

- For all cases where any scripting is needed

- For all cases where application resources are used (e.g., Event Log, Message Queuing, or Performance Counter)

- For most cases where Enterprise Services (COM+) components are used

CROSS-REFERENCE   I further discuss Enterprise Services (COM+) components in Chapter 19.

---

5.   This would include (but is not limited to) all cases where you need to redistribute Fujitsu's NetCOBOL for .NET runtime. In other words, if you develop your applications using COBOL .NET, an automated deployment is suggested.

The preceding list includes most of the common development/deployment scenarios where automating your deployment process will be most attractive. Once you decide to head down the path of automation, you will come to a fork in the road. You will need to decide between the following:

- Using the Microsoft Windows Installer software that is already integrated into VS .NET

- Purchasing a sophisticated automation software package from the choices available on the market

NOTE   Microsoft has joined other software vendors in the quest to provide software deployment and management products. Microsoft offers a product called Application Center that helps fill the need. In addition, the company Wise Solutions has created a product called Wise for Visual Studio .NET that integrates nicely into VS .NET. These products and others are often considered during any serious software evaluation line-ups.

As with any software purchase, you and your organization will need to conduct a proper product evaluation. In the meantime, I suggest you take advantage of the tools already included in your VS .NET toolset. You may discover that you already have enough software to meet your immediate needs.

CROSS-REFERENCE   Microsoft has published a free downloadable guide titled "Team Development with Visual Studio .NET and Visual Source-Safe." You should refer to this document as a starting point for procedural guidance. It will especially be useful if you have a development team using VS .NET and Visual SourceSafe (VSS). I provide the URL for this document in the "Web Sites" subsection of the "To Learn More" section at the end of this chapter.

Let's now explore how you can use the Microsoft Windows Installer software tool to help automate your .NET software deployment. In the section "The Manual

Approach: XCOPY or Copy" later in this chapter, you'll explore the alternative to deployment automation: doing it the manual way, without Windows Installer.

Automate with Microsoft Windows Installer 2.0

Microsoft Windows Installer 2.0 software is integrated into VS .NET. Using this software, you can create deployment packages. Your packages will include a Windows Installer (.msi) file, a Setup.exe file, and possibly other needed files.

> **NOTE** You can use Windows Installer for both ASP.NET (Web applications and Web services) and .NET Windows applications. Both COBOL .NET and VB .NET support this "automated" approach to deployment.

To learn how to use Windows Installer, you'll create a few deployment packages using the sample applications from Chapter 13. First, you'll create a deployment package for your MyFirstWinFormCobol COBOL .NET sample Windows application. Next, you'll create a deployment package for your WebApplicationSampleCobol COBOL .NET sample ASP.NET application.

> **NOTE** You will also use the MyFirstWinFormVB VB .NET sample Windows application and WebApplicationSampleVB VB .NET sample ASP.NET application. It will be helpful to note any differences you experience between the two language implementations while you attempt to build deployment packages.

When you create deployment packages using Windows Installer, the basic approach is to open your application solution where you have one or more projects. Then, add a deployment project to your application solution. Finally, you "add" the files that make up your application project to the deployment project.

In the following sections you'll learn how to create deployment packages using Windows Installer and VS .NET.

Creating a Deployment Package for a Windows Application

Start by opening the MyFirstWinFormCobol.sln sample application in your VS .NET IDE. Next, follow these steps:

1. Add a deployment project to your application solution. From the Standard toolbar, select File ➤ Add Project ➤ New Project (see Figure 17-8).

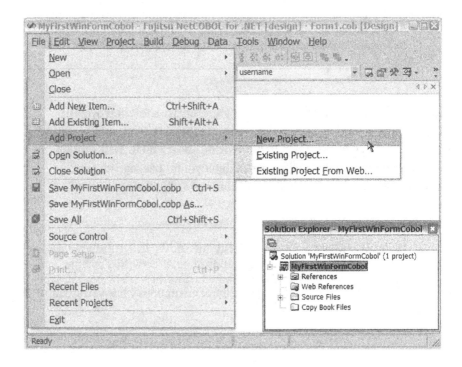

Figure 17-8. Preparing to add a deployment project to your existing solution

2. In the Add New Project window, open the Setup and Deployment Projects Project Types folder. Choose the Setup Project template. For this demonstration, change the default name of the new project from Setup# to **MyFirstWinFormCobolSetup**. When you've finished, click OK (see Figure 17-9). Optionally, you can use the Setup Wizard template.[6]

---

6. Fujitsu's NetCOBOL for .NET product currently does not support the VS .NET Setup Wizard template feature. For the time being, you will not be able to use this feature in your COBOL .NET projects. Feel free to explore this feature with your VB .NET applications.

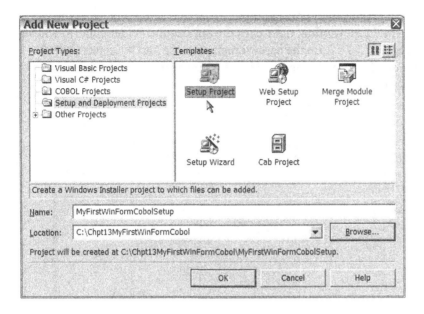

Figure 17-9. Choosing the Setup Project template

3. Notice the File System Editor in the VS .NET IDE. Also, notice that the Solution Explorer window shows the addition of the new setup project (see Figure 17-10).

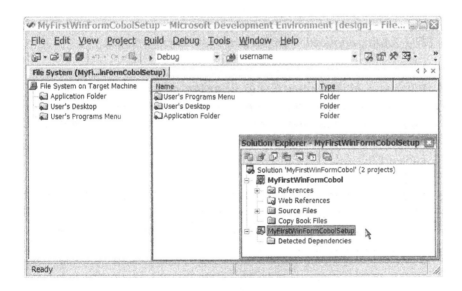

Figure 17-10. The VS .NET IDE showing the File System Editor and the updated Solution Explorer display

4. Add the application project output to the new setup project. In the File System Editor window, right-click the Application Folder node. As shown in Figure 17-11, from the context menu choose Add ➤ Project Output. Optionally, select Action ➤ Add ➤ Project Output from the Standard toolbar.

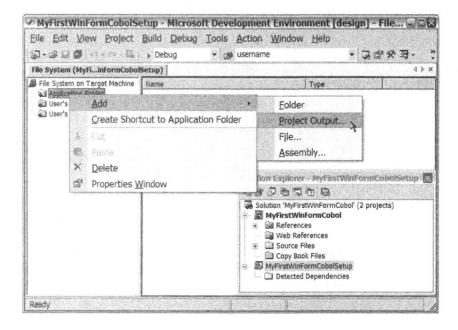

Figure 17-11. Adding application project output to the setup project

5. In the Add Project Output Group dialog box, choose the application project from the Project drop-down list. Leave the default of Active in the Configuration drop-down box, or select Debug or Release as appropriate. As shown in Figure 17-12, the sample demonstration only shows one choice. Click OK.

6. Build your setup project. From the Standard toolbar, select Build ➤ Build MyFirstWinFormCobolSetup. As shown in Figure 17-13, your VS .NET IDE Output window will provide information indicating the success (or failure) of your build.

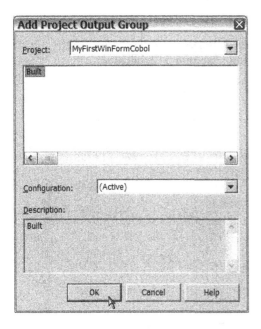

Figure 17-12. The Add Project Output Group dialog box

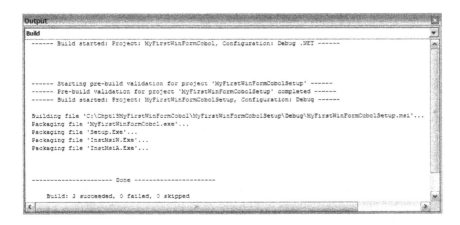

Figure 17-13. The VS .NET IDE Output window. Notice the messages showing that the Setup.exe and MyFirstWinFormCobolSetup.msi files were created.

7. Test the setup project. From your open VS .NET IDE, select the new setup project. From the Standard toolbar, select Project ➤ Install (see Figure 17-14).

NOTE The Install option will only appear under the Project menu
when the setup project in Solution Explorer is highlighted.

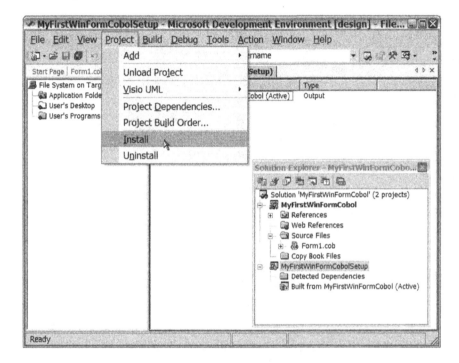

Figure 17-14. Testing the setup project

TIP Usually, you will not want to leave your application installed,
especially if you were just testing the setup project. This will give
you a good opportunity to also test your ability to "uninstall" your
application. To accomplish this in VS .NET, first make sure the setup
project is highlighted in Solution Explorer. Then, select Project ➤
Uninstall. Optionally, you use the Windows Add or Remove Programs
feature, which you access from the Control Panel, to install or uninstall
your .NET Windows application.

8. Notice the files are created for you within your setup project folder (see Figure 17-15). You will want to distribute this entire folder. You can use the Setup.exe file to initiate the installation.

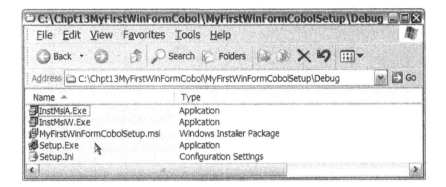

Figure 17-15. The setup project folder and contents to be distributed

 NOTE   Keep in mind that if the machine you are targeting for installation does not already have the Microsoft .NET Framework or Fujitsu
NetCOBOL for .NET product installed, a redistribution of software
modules may be needed. Either way, you can accomplish this through
your Microsoft Windows Installer package.

Add a Shortcut to Your Windows Application

If you want, you can add a shortcut to your installation setup package from either your user's desktop or the Programs menu. To do this, simply select the output created in your File System Editor's Application Folder. Then follow these steps:

1. Access the context menu. Right-click the Application Folder output node (see Figure 17-16). Optionally, you can select Action ➤ Add ➤ Project Output from the Standard toolbar to initiate the process rather than right-clicking and selecting from the context menu.

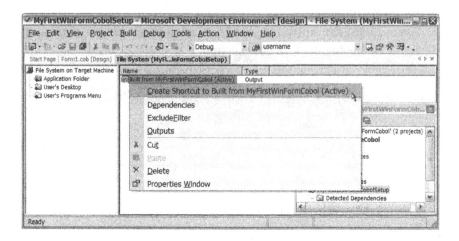

Figure 17-16. Creating a shortcut to your user's desktop or Programs menu

2. Select Create Shortcut to Built from MyFirstWinFormCobol. Choose an appropriate name for your shortcut.

3. Drag the renamed shortcut from your File System Editor's Application Folder to either the File System Editor's User's Desktop folder or the User's Programs Menu folder.

4. Rebuild your Setup project. From the Standard toolbar, select Build ➤ Build MyFirstWinFormCobolSetup.

The steps detailed in this section and the previous section are sufficient to install a .NET Windows application. In both demonstrations, a project written in COBOL .NET was used. Although the steps to install a VB .NET Windows application are basically the same, I have a few noteworthy differences to share in the following section. Given your bilingual approach, this information should be of value.

Noted Differences for Your VB .NET Windows Application

Using the MyFirstWinFormVB sample application, I began by following the same "deployment setup" steps performed in the earlier COBOL .NET sample. In the VS .NET environment, I opened the MyFirstWinFormVB VB .NET project and added a new project using the Setup Project template. From that point, I noticed the following few differences:

- The Add Project Output Group window provides choices that appear to offer a more granular level of setup customization. As shown in Figure 17-17, I used the Primary output choice to complete this step of the setup process. The COBOL .NET project did not offer this level of flexibility—the Add Project Output Group window showed only the Built choice.

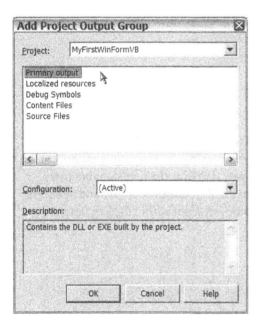

Figure 17-17. The Add Project Output Group window for a VB .NET Windows application

- The Dependencies window provides a meaningful display. It shows the additional files/assemblies that Windows Installer has detected and flagged as a dependency for your deployment. In the VB .NET project, you can easily access the Dependencies window. While you have the Setup project selected, simply select Action ➤ Dependencies from the Standard toolbar (see Figure 17-18). Unfortunately, this Dependencies window is sort of hidden in the COBOL .NET project.

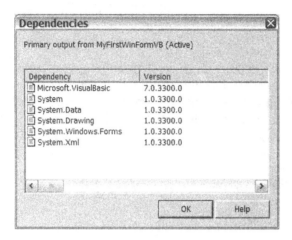

Figure 17-18. The Dependencies window for a VB .NET Windows application

- To "locate" the Dependencies window in COBOL .NET, you need to go through a few extra steps. Start by accessing the Properties window of the Application Folder output file. Then, skip over the first Dependencies property that you see. Navigate to the KeyOutput property and open the node. Select the Dependencies property from within the KeyOutput property (see Figure 17-19).

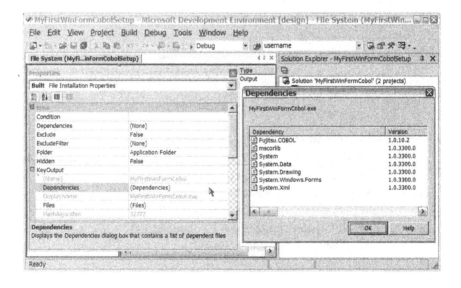

Figure 17-19. The Dependencies window for a COBOL .NET Windows application

These are simply observations. Depending on your need for these features, the differences may or may not impact your eventual deployment. Using the sample applications, I was able to successfully create a Windows Installer setup project in both VB .NET and COBOL .NET.

Two additional treats were provided by the VB .NET implementation in the Output window and in the Add New Project window. You'll now take a closer look at these last two noted observations.

The following helpful message in the Output window reminded me that the .NET Framework needs to be redistributed. The message also included instructions regarding the steps to take. This proved to be extremely helpful.

. . .

```
WARNING: This setup does not contain the .NET Framework which must be installed
on the target machine by running dotnetfx.exe before this setup will install. You
can find dotnetfx.exe on the Visual Studio .NET 'Windows Components Update'
media. Dotnetfx.exe can be redistributed with your setup.
```

. . .

As you know, the preceding helpful message is not shown in the Output window when you use COBOL .NET. No big deal, right? I just think that maybe Fujitsu might use this as an example to enhance their NetCOBOL for .NET product. Perhaps they could display not only the .NET Framework message, but also a helpful message regarding the need to redistribute the required NetCOBOL runtime files.

To finish off this series of "VB .NET versus COBOL .NET" deployment-related observations, let's briefly visit the topic of the Setup Wizard template.

You may recall that one of the first steps you took for deployment project setup was choosing a template from the VS .NET Add New Project window. I wanted to try out a few of the template choices, so the Setup Wizard template choice caught my attention. As shown in Figure 17-20, the Setup Wizard option is one choice out of five.

When I tested out the Setup Wizard template using VB .NET, my impression was that it is simple and basic but useful. I can see that this is a productivity feature, a real time-saver. With that in mind, I then wanted to try the Setup Wizard template with the COBOL .NET sample application. As shown in Figure 17-21, apparently the Fujitsu NetCOBOL for .NET product does not support this VS .NET feature.

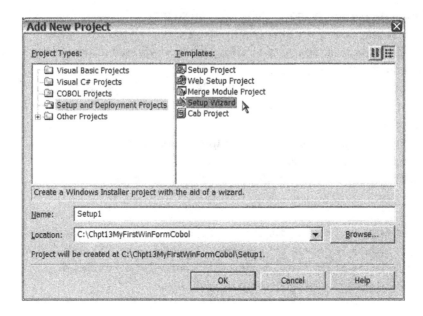

Figure 17-20. The VS .NET Add New Project window with the Setup Wizard template choice highlighted

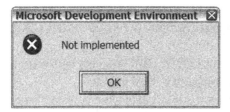

Figure 17-21. The message I received when attempting to use the Setup Wizard template in a COBOL .NET project (Windows and/or ASP.NET)

NOTE I recently contacted Fujitsu's tech support regarding their level of support for a few of the VS .NET setup features. Basically, I decided to provide feedback on my experience of using their product. Because they've always expressed appreciation for such feedback, I'm convinced that the few "areas for improvement" that I've mentioned to them have made it onto a "wish list." Beyond that, Fujitsu's tech support has indicated that future releases of Fujitsu's NetCOBOL for .NET product will likely improve on their already exceptional VS .NET setup/deployment implementation. On that note, I'd like to acknowledge Fujitsu for providing adequate support in VS .NET to use the most essential features of Microsoft's Windows Installer. At the same time, I do feel that pointing out the few "areas for improvement" to them (which I've done) will prove to be helpful. I encourage you to contact Fujitsu's tech support and let them know how important or unimportant any of these Windows Installer features (e.g., the Add Project Output Group window and the VS .NET Setup Wizard template) are to you.

So far, you've looked only at .NET Windows applications. Now you'll turn to ASP.NET. Although it's similar to Windows applications, the deployment process for ASP.NET applications introduces additional learning opportunities.

In the next section, I demonstrate the process of setting up a deployment project targeting a Web server. As you'll see, there are a few differences between setup projects that target a Web server versus those that support Windows-type applications (stand-alone servers or individual workstations).

Creating a Deployment Package for an ASP.NET Application

Begin by opening the WebApplicationSampleCobol.sln COBOL .NET sample application (this was the sample application you created in Chapter 13). Now, in the VS .NET IDE environment, you'll perform the same beginning steps you did in the earlier section "Creating a Deployment Package for a Windows Application." In other words, you'll go to the Standard toolbar and select File ➤ Add Project ➤ New Project.

From this point forward for ASP.NET, the process changes slightly. Perform the following steps:

1. As shown in Figure 17-22, you'll choose the Web Setup Project template (instead of the Setup Project template that you used for the Windows application). Click OK on the Add New Project window.

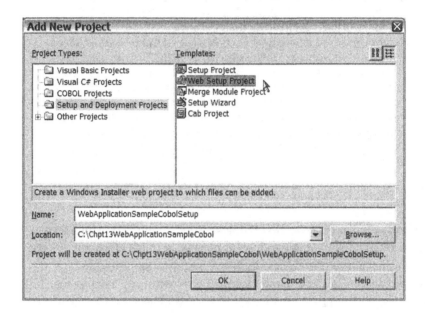

Figure 17-22. Choosing Web Setup Project from the Add New Project window. The new project will be named WebApplicationSampleCobolSetup.

2. You'll be taken to the File System Editor in the VS .NET IDE. This view is similar to the one you saw before for the Windows application. However, this time you'll want to right-click the bin subfolder[7] underneath the Web Application Folder node (see Figure 17-23).

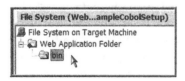

Figure 17-23. The bin subfolder underneath the Web Application Folder node in the File System Editor

---

7. The requirement to "right-click the bin subfolder" only applies to COBOL .NET projects. When you use VB .NET, you right-click the Web Application Folder.

3. Choose Add ➤ Project Output. Optionally, from the Standard toolbar you can choose Action ➤ Add ➤ Project Output. Follow the prompts to complete this step.

4. Add the content files. In the VS .NET IDE File System Editor, right-click the Web Application Folder node. Then choose Add ➤ File. Optionally, from the Standard toolbar you can choose Action ➤ Add ➤ File (see Figure 17-24).

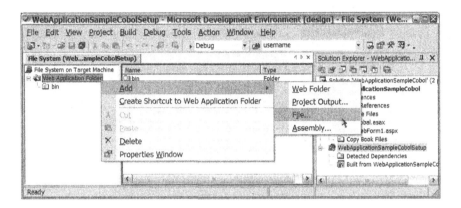

Figure 17-24. Adding the content files

5. Navigate to your application folder. In the Add Files window, select all of the content files. You can use the Ctrl or Shift key to select multiple files (see Figure 17-25). Click Open.

6. Review your VS .NET File System Editor window and your VS .NET Solution Explorer window. As shown in Figure 17-26, the appropriate files have been added to the to the application folder belonging to the Web Setup project.

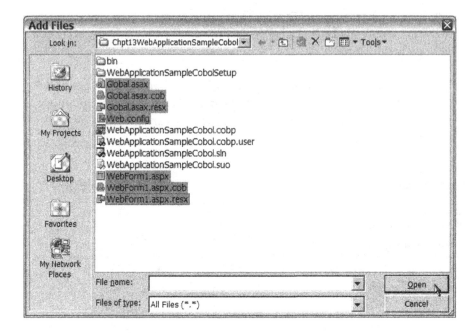

Figure 17-25. The Add Files window with all content files selected

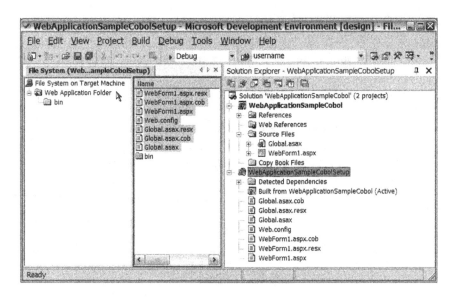

Figure 17-26. The content files have been added to the Web setup project.

7. Begin IIS properties configuration. In the VS .NET IDE File System Editor, right-click the Web Application Folder to access the Properties window.

8. Continue IIS properties configuration. As shown in Figure 17-27, for demonstration purposes, you'll edit the VirtualDirectory property in the Properties window. Notice that the default value is set to the name of the Web setup project (WebApplicationSampleCobolSetup). You'll change the value to **MyVirtualHome**.

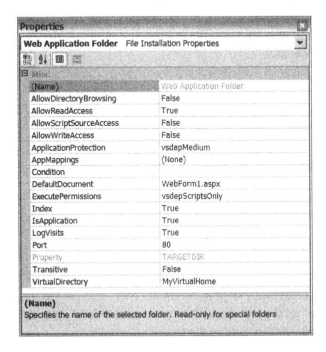

Figure 17-27. Using the VS .NET IDE File System Editor to change the VirtualDirectory property and the DefaultDocument property in the Properties window

9. Complete IIS properties configuration. As shown in Figure 17-27, you'll edit the DefaultDocument property in the Properties window. Notice that the default value is set to default.aspx. Change this to **WebForm1.aspx**. After you make this change, close the Properties window. As your needs dictate, you can use this Properties windows to configure additional IIS properties.

10. Build the WebApplicationSampleCobolSetup project.

11. Test the installation. In the VS .NET IDE Solution Explorer window, select the WebApplicationSampleCobolSetup project. From the Standard toolbar choose Project ➤ Install.

12. Test your ASP.NET Web application. Open your Web browser (e.g., Internet Explorer, Netscape). Type the URL value **http://localhost/ MyVirtualHome** into the address bar.

That completes the steps needed to create your Web setup project. You can execute this Windows Installer package (initiated by the Setup.exe file) on your local machine or the appropriate targeted machine (assuming that the minimum software and hardware requirements are met). The entire setup project folder needs to be available for installation.

 TIP It may be that your "targeted" machine is on the other end of a "hosting" arrangement contract. You may want to check out the few free hosting alternatives offered for ASP.NET applications and XML Web services. Refer to your VS .NET Start Page for more information.

Automated? Yeah, Right!

You might ask what exactly is "automated" with this deployment approach. After all, you are required to take a great many steps to create the Web setup project. In spite of the steps needed to set up the process, it truly is automated. Really, it is. By using this *automated* approach, you are getting the following benefits:

- The IIS configuration (virtual directory creation and default document setting) is being accomplished without your needing to use the IIS MMC.

- You can use the normal Windows Add or Remove Programs feature. This is extremely helpful when you want to uninstall your application. By simply "removing" your application with one click via the Windows Add or Remove Programs feature, your IIS virtual directory and the physical files will be removed.

- You can reuse your Web setup project repeatedly. In other words, create once, but install multiple times, even on multiple machines if appropriate.

- You avoid introducing errors during the installation process. If you get it right the first time, it should be right every time.

All of these benefits are invaluable, even with this simple application. The more complicated your application becomes, the more valuable these (and other) benefits become.

NOTE If your application is required to support unmanaged components (e.g., legacy COM DLLs) using the .NET COM Interop feature, your deployment will involve extra steps.

Any Noted Differences for Your VB .NET ASP.NET Application?

Don't worry, there are only a couple of noteworthy differences between the COBOL .NET and VB .NET implementations of the Web setup project. The following list quickly reviews those differences. Remember, these are simply observations I'm sharing with you for the purpose of expediting your retraining experience.

- When I added the application project into the Web setup project, I had better results right-clicking the Web Application Folder node than the bin subfolder. Clicking the bin folder only applies to COBOL .NET.

- When you add the content files in the Add Files window, a few extra files are located in the application folder (see Figure 17-28).

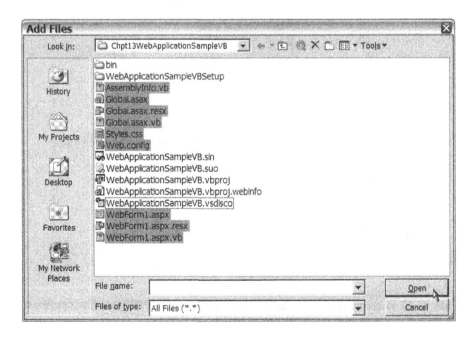

Figure 17-28. Adding the content files in the Add Files window for a VB .NET ASP.NET application. By the way, if this was an ASP.NET XML Web service, I would have also added the .vsdisco file.

I've covered most of the basic Microsoft Windows Installer features found in VS .NET. Speaking to the power and flexibility that this software harnesses, there remain many other features awaiting your discovery. In the next section, I point out a few of these remaining features.

Learning More About the Windows Installer in VS .NET

As you continue your retraining journey, you will find that there is yet more to learn about Windows Installer. For example, Windows Installer provides a set of editors to support further customization of the setup projects in the VS .NET IDE. This set of editors is available to both Windows applications (Setup Project template) and ASP.NET applications (Web Setup Project template).

You have already learned about the File System Editor. As shown in Figure 17-29, there are five other VS .NET Windows Installer editors. Using these other Windows Installer editors, your setup projects and Web setup project can evolve from the basic and crude type (e.g., those you created in this chapter using my sample code examples) to the polished and professional type (e.g., those similar to the one Microsoft created for the installation of the .NET Framework and .NET tools).

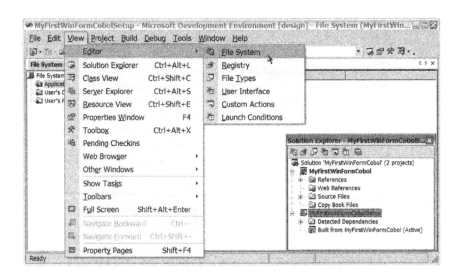

Figure 17-29. With the setup project selected, from your VS .NET Standard toolbar you can access the Editor menu by selecting View ➤ Editor.

Optionally, you can access the selection of Windows Installer editors from the VS .NET Solution Explorer window. As shown in Figure 17-30, there is a row of icons for the editors. The first icon represents the File System Editor.

Figure 17-30. The row of icons on the Solution Explorer window used for navigating to the Windows Installer editors

As you continue to explore and learn, plan to revisit the VS .NET environment to make use of these Windows Installer editors. The references provided in the "Web Sites" subsection of the "To Learn More" section at the end of this chapter will be helpful.

TIP Be sure to explore the Merge Module Project template found in the VS .NET Add New Project window. The Merge Module Project template is designed for component installation. Merge modules can help you organize portions of a larger setup project. Additionally, third-party software vendors will occasionally include merge modules specifically designed for their products. For example, you will find that the inclusion of a merge module in your deployment setup project is essential if your targeted application includes any Crystal Reports functionality. Crystal Decisions provides an excellent white paper detailing this requirement: http://support.crystaldecisions.com/communityCS/ TechnicalPapers/crnet_deployment.pdf.

Are you ready now to learn about the manual approach for .NET deployment? I know, you're probably asking "Why?" That's a good question. Let's continue.

The Manual Approach: XCOPY or Copy

Generally speaking, you should use the manual approach only for nonproduction deployments. In other words, if you want to move your files from one development machine over to another development or testing machine, the manual approach is appropriate.

However, as soon as you start preparing for production (and even when you are preparing for staging) you will want to begin to create your Windows Installer[8] setup projects. After all, even your setup projects need to be tested.

TIP   The more complex your application, the more certain that the manual approach is not appropriate. Use of the GAC or IIS can also be used as deciding factors. See the section "Automated or Manual Installation" earlier in this chapter for other factors to weigh when you want to choose between a manual and an automated deployment.

As part of your retraining effort, you *should* know how to manually install your .NET application. In this section, I cover two choices for manual deployment:

- The XCOPY approach

- The Copy Project approach

XCOPY-Based Deployment

In several .NET conferences that I had the pleasure of attending, I observed that most attendees generally got excited when the topic of XCOPY-based deployment was mentioned. I find it highly ironic, now that the dust has started to settle, that XCOPY-based deployment is discouraged and frowned upon. Oh, well.

Even stranger, each time I saw XCOPY-based deployment demonstrated, the presenter was either dragging and dropping or copying and pasting files and folders. Why is that strange? There is an XCOPY DOS-era command available (see Figure 17-31). However, not even once did I see the conference presenters open the Command window to actually execute the XCOPY DOS command. I suppose "XCOPY" sounds cooler than "dragging and dropping" or "copying and pasting." Oh, well.

NOTE   You can use the XCOPY DOS command to "copy" files and folders.

---

8. Optionally, you might consider using a competing third-party product.

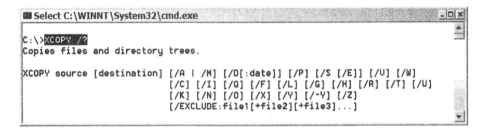

Figure 17-31. At a command prompt, you can enter **XCOPY /?** *to see a listing of all of the options/switches available for use with the XCOPY DOS command.*

Suffice it to say, if you can drag and drop or copy and paste your application files, you can proudly say that you are using the XCOPY-based deployment approach. Just keep in mind that there is an XCOPY DOS command that you can use as well. The bottom line is, there is value in both types of "deployment" approaches. The following points speak to this value:

- *The drag and drop or copy and paste approach:* Compared to the "registering DLLs" type of deployment normally associated with Wintel legacy COM objects, the drag and drop or copy and paste approach can be considered a productivity feature. Consider limiting this approach to the deployment of "small" applications.

- *Using the XCOPY command:* The power of the XCOPY command is best seen when you are attempting to deploy a Web project that has a large number of screens (.aspx files). You can use command-line switches with the XCOPY command to easily filter out any specific files that you may not need to deploy (.resx or .vb files). Additionally, you can execute the XCOPY command from within a DOS batch file (.bat).[9]

In the next section you will take a look at one other way to manually deploy your .NET application.

The Copy Project Feature

A VS .NET special Copy Project feature is available[10] when you are working with ASP.NET applications. With your application project selected, you can access

---

9. DOS batch files on Windows are very similar to the mainframe CLIST and REXX scripts that you may have created.

10. According to Microsoft's documentation, "FrontPage Server Extensions must be installed on the target server to use the Copy Project command."

this feature from the Standard toolbar by selecting Project ➤ Copy Project (see Figure 17-32).

NOTE At this time, it appears that the VS .NET Copy Project feature is not available for COBOL .NET projects. Consider trying the VS .NET Copy Project feature using VB .NET.

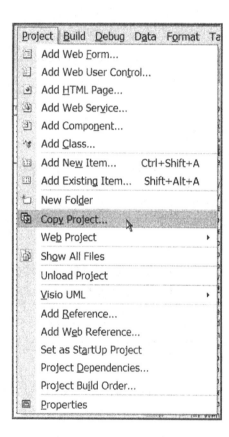

Figure 17-32. Accessing the VS .NET Copy Project feature

Once you launch the VS .NET Copy Project feature, you need to perform the following tasks:

1. Select the destination project folder. This will equate to the IIS virtual directory.

2. Select the Web access method. For demonstration purposes, I chose FrontPage, which is the default.

3. Select the scope of your "copy." For demonstration purposes, I chose to copy the minimum files needed. This is the default setting.

As shown in Figure 17-33, the default settings are typically suitable.

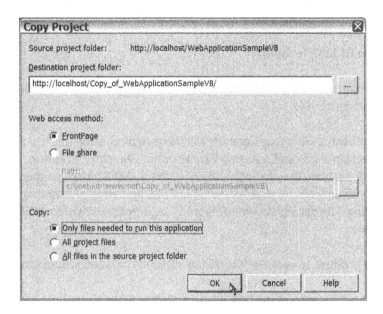

Figure 17-33. The Copy Project window with default settings

If you are using the Copy Project deployment approach or the XCOPY deployment approach, you will be sacrificing several benefits. For example, when it comes to your ASP.NET application, you will need to perform your basic IIS configuration manually. The following section gives you a few pointers for a basic IIS configuration task.

NOTE   During my testing, the VS .NET Copy Project feature successfully created an IIS virtual directory. Not bad! Nevertheless, it is likely that you will want to further configure the virtual directory that the Copy Project feature creates for you.

A Basic IIS Configuration Task

When you manually deploy an ASP.NET application, at a minimum, you will need to create an IIS virtual directory. The steps you need to perform to accomplish this task are as follows:

1. From the Windows Control Panel, select Administrative Tools. Optionally, click the Start button and select Programs ➤ Administrative Tools ➤ Internet Information Services.

2. Launch the IIS MMC snap-in.

3. In the left pane of the IIS MMC snap-in, open the tree view to expose the Default Web Site node.

4. Launch the Virtual Directory Creation Wizard by right-clicking the Default Web Site node and selecting New ➤ Virtual Directory, as shown in Figure 17-34. Note that the look and feel of the IIS MMC snap-in varies slightly depending on the version of the Windows operating system that you are using. The display shown in Figure 17-34 is typical of Windows XP Professional.

5. Follow the prompts to complete the virtual directory creation. Click Next.

6. Enter the desired name of the new virtual directory at the Virtual Directory Alias prompt. In Figure 17-35 I entered **MyTestVirtualDirectory** for demonstration purposes. Click Next.

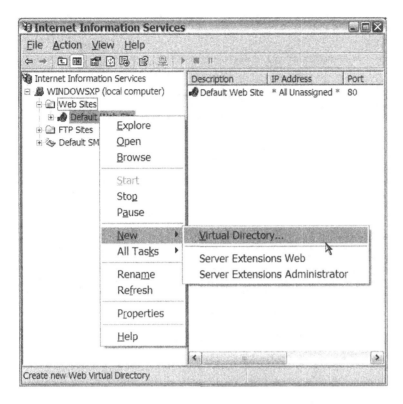

Figure 17-34. Launching the Virtual Directory Creation Wizard

7. At the Web Site Content Directory prompt, enter the physical location
   where your files will be stored. For demonstration purposes, I entered
   C:\Inetpub\wwwroot\WebApplicationSampleCobol (see Figure 17-36).
   You can use the Browse button to help locate the correct folder location.
   Click Next.

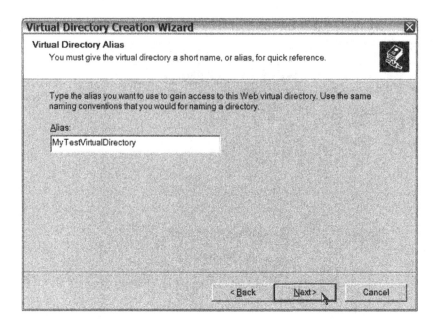

Figure 17-35. Enter the desired name for your virtual directory at the Virtual Directory Alias prompt.

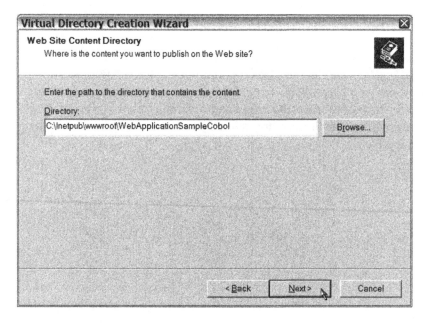

Figure 17-36. Enter the physical location where your files will be stored at the Web Site Content Directory prompt.

8. At the Access Permissions prompt, leave the defaults as set. As shown in Figure 17-37, the defaults should be sufficient for this demonstration. Click Next and then click Finish.

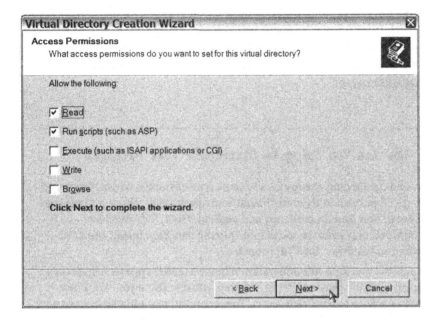

Figure 17-37. The Access Permissions prompt

9. As shown in Figure 17-38, your new IIS virtual directory has been created for you. You can further customize the virtual directory through the specific virtual directory's properties window (to access this window, right-click the specific virtual directory).

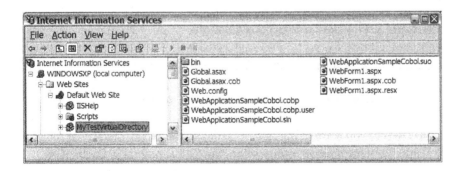

Figure 17-38. The new MyTestVirtualDirectory virtual directory

10. Test the virtual directory. In your Web browser, enter the following in the address bar to browse a specific document in the virtual directory: **http://localhost/MyTestVirtualDirectory/webform1.aspx**.

That's it. That's all you need to do to create a basic IIS virtual directory. Keep in mind, however, there's much more for you to learn before you can consider yourself an IIS administrator. As your retraining needs dictate, consider visiting the Web sites listed in the "Web Sites" subsection of the "To Learn More" section at the end of this chapter.

How Are You Going to Distribute Your Package?

You may end up needing to copy files to some type of storage device, download files using FTP, publish from within Visual SourceSafe (VSS), or use a shared network folder to drag and drop or copy and paste to. For a .NET Windows application, you may even decide to look into the new Zero Install and Zero Administration Windows (ZAW) approach.

The Zero Install and Zero Administration Windows (ZAW) approach involves a two-step distribution process. In the first step, you distribute your Windows application package to your Web server. The second step is initiated by your end users navigating to your Web site with their browser, clicking a hyperlink, and downloading the Windows application to their desktop.

Summary

This chapter's goals were as follows:

- To review deployment design considerations

- To demonstrate how to use the Microsoft Windows Installer 2.0

- To explore the manual approach to a .NET deployment

In this chapter you learned about several deployment considerations. Several new concepts were introduced: obfuscation, the Global Assembly Cache (GAC), and strong naming, to name a few. These new concepts supported the manual versus automated deployment discussion.

From there, you walked through several demonstrations that provided you with a solid understanding of how to use the Windows Installer in VS .NET. Toward the end of the chapter, you briefly explored both the XCOPY and Copy Project deployment approaches. As part of that section, you saw a demonstration of a basic IIS configuration task: the creation of a virtual directory.

In the next chapter you will explore the topics of .NET configuration and security.

To Learn More

The following are some suggested supplemental references to further your retraining effort.

Magazines

.NET Magazine:
> http://www.fawcette.com/dotnetmag/

Exchange & Outlook Magazine, DevX Newsletter (by Jim Minatel, Editor-in-Chief):
> http://www.devx.com/free/newsletters/exo/exoed031601.asp

MSDN Magazine:
> http://msdn.microsoft.com/msdnmag/

Visual Studio Magazine:
> http://www.fawcette.com/vsm/

Windows Developer Magazine:
> http://www.wd-mag.com/

XML & Web Services Magazine:
> http://www.fawcette.com/xmlmag/

Web Sites

.NET Architecture Center:
> http://msdn.microsoft.com/architecture/

.NET Enterprise Servers Online Books:
> http://msdn.microsoft.com/library/default.asp?url=/servers/books/
> default.asp

.NET Framework Redistributable Package Technical Reference:
> http://msdn.microsoft.com/library/en-us/dnnetdep/html/dotnetfxref.asp

Creating Windows Applications:
> http://msdn.microsoft.com/library/en-us/vbcon/html/
> vboriCreatingStandaloneAppsVB.asp

Deploying .NET Applications: Lifecycle Guide:
> http://msdn.microsoft.com/library/en-us/dnbda/html/DALGRoadmap.asp

Dotfuscator (obfuscator software by PreEmptive Solutions):

`http://www.preemptive.com/dotfuscator/index.html`

EggHeadCafe.com Tips and Tricks (.NET tips and articles):

`http://www.eggheadcafe.com/tipstricks.asp`

Fujitsu NetCOBOL for .NET:

`http://www.netcobol.com/products/windows/netcobol.html`

GotDotNet:

`http://www.gotdotnet.com/`

Introduction to ASP.NET:

`http://msdn.microsoft.com/library/en-us/cpguide/html/`
`cpconintroductiontoasp.asp`

IISFAQ (online guide for installing and configuring IIS):

`http://iisfaq.com/`

Microsoft Application Center 2000:

`http://www.microsoft.com/catalog/display.asp?subid=22&site=10616`

Microsoft ASP.NET Home Page:

`http://www.asp.net/`

Microsoft Community (discussion groups, e-newsletters, and so forth):

`http://communities2.microsoft.com/`

Microsoft Patterns & Practices:

`http://msdn.microsoft.com/practices/`

Microsoft's Search the Knowledge Base Web Site:

`http://support.microsoft.com/default.aspx?scid=FH;EN-US;KBHOWTO`

Microsoft TechNet How-To Index:

`http://www.microsoft.com/technet/treeview/default.asp?url=/technet/`
`itsolutions/howto`

MSDN:

`http://msdn.microsoft.com`

Placing a .NET Assembly in the GAC Using MMC and Sn.exe:

`http://www.wimdows.net/articles/article.aspx?aid=12`

Symbol Servers and Symbol Stores:

`http://msdn.microsoft.com/library/en-us/debug/base/`
`symbol_servers_and_symbol_stores.asp`

Team Development with Visual Studio .NET and Visual SourceSafe:

`http://msdn.microsoft.com/library/en-us/dnbda/html/tdlg_rm.asp`

Windows .NET Server 2003:

`http://msdn.microsoft.com/library/default.asp?url=/nhp/`
`default.asp?contentid=28001691`

Wise for Visual Studio .NET:

`http://www.wise.com/visualstudio.asp?bhcp=1`

XML Web Services Developer Center Home:

`http://msdn.microsoft.com/webservices/`

Part Five
Advanced .NET Technologies

"Learning to develop .NET applications can be good for your career. I have always found career *security to be much more secure than* job *security."*

—Chris Richardson

Configuration for .NET Applications

Controlling the Behavior of Your Application Using Various Customization Features

In this chapter

- Discussing the use of Web page and user control directives

- Demonstrating the use of custom attributes and reflection

- Explaining the role of XML-based files configuration files

- Understanding the .NET Framework configuration namespaces

- Exploring the configuration needed for code access security

THE TERM "CONFIGURATION" represents an area of concern that surrounds every software development effort, on the mainframe and off the mainframe. Generally speaking, configuration touches on those "extra" tasks that are needed for controlling and influencing the behavior of your application. Typically, this type of behavior control and influence is addressed outside of your basic code development.

I have split the broad topic of configuration into five focused subtopics in this chapter. The first of those five subtopics is the use of Web page and user control directives. The second is custom attributes and reflection. XML-based files' configuration files is the third subtopic. The fourth subtopic is what is known as the .NET Framework configuration namespaces. The fifth and final subtopic is the configuration concerns of code access security. I introduce the .NET Framework Configuration tool as part of that code access security discussion.

NOTE   The discussions in this chapter, which cover various aspects of
.NET application configuration, are more appropriate for someone
who has achieved a considerable level of comfort with the material in
most of the chapters that preceded this chapter.

Configuration with Directives

In earlier chapters, you saw and used directives. First, in Chapter 13 in the section
"Sample Code for Web Applications," you saw the Page directive when I briefly discussed the manner in which the Web page was configured to use a code-behind
file. The following code snippet, which is taken from Chapter 13, should look
familiar:

```
<%@ Page language="cobol" Codebehind="WebForm1.aspx.cob"
AutoEventWireup="false" Inherits="WebApplicationSampleCobol.WebForm1" %>
```

Then, as you progressed through the book you arrived at Chapter 15. In that
chapter in the section "Using Output Cache," I introduced the OutputCache
directive. I discussed the syntax that you use with this directive when you want to
configure the output cache setup for your Web application. The following code
snippet, which is taken from Chapter 15, is provided for your convenience:

```
<%@ OutputCache Duration="10" VaryByParam="None" %>
```

The Family of .NET Directives

The directives, whether used on the Web page (.aspx) or on the user control (.ascx),
will influence, control, and *direct* the behavior of your application. In other words,
you use directives to configure your application. The two .NET directives you were
introduced to earlier are part of a slightly larger group of .NET directives. The complete set of .NET directives follows (notice that the common syntax of each
directive requires the at symbol [@] be appended):

@ Page

@ OutputCache

@ Control

@ Reference

@ Register

@ Import

@ Implements

@ Assembly

You can use the directives in the preceding list to configure your ASP.NET applications. Listing 18-1 shows the basic syntax for each directive to give you a better idea as to the use and capability of each.

Listing 18-1. The Basic Syntax of Each .NET Directive

```
<%@ Page attribute="value" [attribute="value". . .] %>
<%@ OutputCache Duration="#ofseconds" Location="Any | Client | Downstream |
    Server | None" VaryByControl="controlname" VaryByCustom="browser |
    customstring" VaryByHeader="headers" VaryByParam="parametername" %>
<%@ Control attribute="value" [attribute="value". . .] %>
<%@ Reference page | control="pathtofile" %>
<%@ Register tagprefix="tagprefix" Namespace="namespace" Assembly="assembly" %>
<%@ Register tagprefix="tagprefix" Tagname="tagname" Src="pathname" %>
<%@ Import namespace="value" %>
<%@ Implements interface="ValidInterfaceName" %>
<%@ Assembly Name="assemblyname" %>
<%@ Assembly Src="pathname" %>
```

You will want to familiarize yourself with each directive. I suggest starting with (or rather returning to) the Page directive. When configuring your ASP.NET applications with directives, you will use this directive more than any other. From there, it will depend on the needs of your application. For example, when you create ASP.NET user controls, you will use the Control and Register directives to complete your ASP.NET user control configuration.

TIP   The following four attributes, which are available for you to use with the Page directive, will be of particular interest to you: *Buffer, ClientTarget, EnableViewState,* and *Trace.*

Beyond that, I refer you to the existing documentation available on Microsoft's MSDN Library Web site and your local Microsoft Visual Studio .NET documentation tool.

TIP Please use the link ms-help://MS.VSCC/MS.MSDNVS/cpgenref/
html/cpconpagedirectives.htm within your Microsoft Visual Studio
.NET documentation tool. There you will find an excellent write-up that
details the use of each directive.

Configuration with Custom Attributes

In Chapter 10 in the section "A Meta View of Data: Metadata," I discussed the use of
metadata as *data*. At that time, I briefly mentioned the role that attributes played
by being able to extend assembly metadata. I then scratched the surface of
attributes by quickly mentioning that there were two groups of attributes: those
that are intrinsically available to you and those that are referred to as *custom
attributes*.

In this chapter I drill down much further into the topic of attributes. I focus
both on the use of attributes for configuration and on the actual creation of
custom attributes.

You were introduced to XML Web services in Chapter 13. In that chapter
I briefly mentioned the <WebMethod> attribute as a configuration requirement if
you want to change the behavior of a publicly exposed method. The new
WebMethod-styled method would then take on the behavior of an XML Web
service member. The exact syntax from that earlier chapter is as follows:

```
. . . . . .VB.NET
<WebMethod()> Public Function HelloWorld() As String
          HelloWorld = "Hello World"
End Function
```

```
. . . . . .COBOL.NET
000530 METHOD-ID. HELLOWORLD AS "HelloWorld" CUSTOM-ATTRIBUTE IS CA-WEBMETHOD.
000540 DATA DIVISION.
000550 LINKAGE SECTION.
000560 01 RET-VAL OBJECT REFERENCE CLASS-STRING.
000570 PROCEDURE DIVISION RETURNING RET-VAL.
000580     SET RET-VAL TO N"Hello World".
000590 END METHOD HELLOWORLD.
```

The .NET Framework makes available a base class called *System.Attribute*.
From there, you will find many built-in attributes (or custom attributes)
that derive from System.Attribute. The WebMethod attribute

(*System.Web.Services.WebMethodAttribute*) is one example—an example that you have used.

TIP You are free to create your own attributes. Simply by using the *System.AttributeUsageAttribute* attribute and then inheriting the System.Attribute class into your own classes, you can create new custom attributes. As I noted in Chapter 10, this is a creative way to add documentation into your application. Documentation added this way is available as "data" even after compilation.

You can use a process referred to as *reflection* (using several classes from the System.Reflection namespace) to query the *assembly metadata*. You will recall that I demonstrated the use of reflection in Chapter 10 in the section "A Meta View of Data: Metadata." As mentioned in that earlier discussion, you can read the metadata, including any metadata associated with custom attributes. Optionally, you can use the ILDASM.exe command-line tool to read the assembly metadata (and intermediate language).

CROSS-REFERENCE In the section "Using Reflection to Retrieve the Custom Attributes" later in this chapter, I extend the reflection demonstration presented in Chapter 10 in the section "A Meta View of Data: Metadata." Although you have seen reflection demonstrated before, I now add custom attributes and several other elements to make the demonstration that much more useful.

Generally speaking, you use custom attributes to configure your .NET application. Specifically, you can use custom attributes to influence the runtime behavior of the assembly, to influence the compilation of the assembly, or to extend the assembly metadata. A partial listing of the other available predefined custom attributes appears in the next section.

The Family of Predefined Custom Attributes

When you take a closer look at the System.Attribute base class, you will notice that 190 classes derive directly from the System.Attribute base class. Certainly a generous offering available for your configuration needs. Although I would rather not show all 190 of them here, Listing 18-2 shows a few of them.

Listing 18-2. A Partial Listing of Attribute Classes That Derive Directly from the System.Attribute Class

```
System.AttributeUsageAttribute
System.CLSCompliantAttribute

. . .

System.EnterpriseServices.ApplicationAccessControlAttribute
System.EnterpriseServices.ApplicationActivationAttribute
System.EnterpriseServices.ApplicationIDAttribute
System.EnterpriseServices.ApplicationNameAttribute
System.EnterpriseServices.ApplicationQueuingAttribute
System.EnterpriseServices.AutoCompleteAttribute

. . .

System.EnterpriseServices.ComponentAccessControlAttribute
System.EnterpriseServices.COMTIIntrinsicsAttribute
System.EnterpriseServices.ConstructionEnabledAttribute
System.EnterpriseServices.DescriptionAttribute
System.EnterpriseServices.EventClassAttribute
System.EnterpriseServices.EventTrackingEnabledAttribute
System.EnterpriseServices.ExceptionClassAttribute
System.EnterpriseServices.IISIntrinsicsAttribute
System.EnterpriseServices.InterfaceQueuingAttribute
System.EnterpriseServices.JustInTimeActivationAttribute
System.EnterpriseServices.LoadBalancingSupportedAttribute
System.EnterpriseServices.MustRunInClientContextAttribute
System.EnterpriseServices.ObjectPoolingAttribute
System.EnterpriseServices.PrivateComponentAttribute
System.EnterpriseServices.SecureMethodAttribute
System.EnterpriseServices.SecurityRoleAttribute
System.EnterpriseServices.SynchronizationAttribute
System.EnterpriseServices.TransactionAttribute

. . .

System.Reflection.AssemblyAlgorithmIdAttribute
System.Reflection.AssemblyCompanyAttribute
System.Reflection.AssemblyConfigurationAttribute
System.Reflection.AssemblyCopyrightAttribute
```

```
System.Reflection.AssemblyCultureAttribute
System.Reflection.AssemblyDefaultAliasAttribute
System.Reflection.AssemblyDelaySignAttribute
System.Reflection.AssemblyDescriptionAttribute
System.Reflection.AssemblyFileVersionAttribute
System.Reflection.AssemblyFlagsAttribute
System.Reflection.AssemblyInformationalVersionAttribute
System.Reflection.AssemblyKeyFileAttribute
System.Reflection.AssemblyKeyNameAttribute
System.Reflection.AssemblyProductAttribute
System.Reflection.AssemblyTitleAttribute
System.Reflection.AssemblyTrademarkAttribute
System.Reflection.AssemblyVersionAttribute
System.Reflection.DefaultMemberAttribute
. . .
System.Security.Permissions.SecurityAttribute
System.Security.SuppressUnmanagedCodeSecurityAttribute
System.Security.UnverifiableCodeAttribute
. . .
System.Web.Services.WebMethodAttribute
System.Web.Services.WebServiceAttribute
System.Web.Services.WebServiceBindingAttribute
. . .
```

Please take a moment to review Listing 18-2. You will notice that I have pulled out a few groupings of attribute classes (from the full list of 190). Of these, I would like to highlight the following few groups:

- *Enterprise Services:* Formerly known as COM+, this topic is discussed in Chapter 19.

- *Security:* This topic is discussed in the section "Configuring for Code Access Security" later in this chapter.

- *Reflection:* This topic is discussed in the next section.

In the next section, you will take a quick look at an example of using custom attributes to extend the assembly metadata. In that context, you will see a broader range of opportunities available when you use custom attributes for configuration.

TIP Three predefined custom attributes are specific to Visual Basic .NET (VB .NET): *COMClassAttribute, VBFixedStringAttribute*, and *VBFixedArray*. Depending on your needs, you may want to keep these attributes in mind. Personally, I have used the VBFixedStringAttribute custom attribute to force the creation of a fixed-length string in a structure. Coming from a mainframe COBOL background, I found that the use of the VBFixedStringAttribute custom attribute actually looked and felt more like the fixed-length strings (e.g., PIC X) that we mainframe programmers have traditionally created.

Extending Assembly Metadata with Custom Attributes

I have created two sample applications for this discussion: AttributesExampleVB.sln and AttributesExampleCobol.sln. Each sample application is a .NET Windows application that does absolutely nothing—even less than a "Hello, World" application. For demonstration purposes, this will be sufficient.

Start by opening the VB .NET sample application, AttributesExampleVB.sln, in Visual Studio .NET (VS .NET). When you navigate to the VS .NET Solution Explorer window, you will notice the existence of a file named AssemblyInfo.vb (see Figure 18-1).

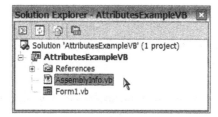

Figure 18-1. The VS .NET Solution Explorer window showing the AssemblyInfo.vb file

The AssemblyInfo.vb file is automatically created for you when you use VB .NET. I found this to be true for Console, Windows, and ASP.NET project types. Microsoft refers to the AssemblyInfo.vb file as the *assembly manifest* (the file is occasionally referred to as the *assembly information file*). After you open the AssemblyInfo.vb file, you will notice a handful of attribute statements prefaced with "Assembly" (see Figure 18-2).

Figure 18-2. The contents of the AssemblyInfo.vb (assembly manifest) file

You can modify each of these attributes as part of your assembly metadata configuration. Optionally, you can add other attributes. Please refer back to the previous section to review the "reflection" subset of attribute classes. For demonstration purposes, I modified a few of the attribute values. The following code snippet reflects the few changes that I made:

```
. . .
<Assembly: AssemblyTitle("AttributesExample")>
<Assembly: AssemblyDescription("This is the Attributes Example Using VB")>
<Assembly: AssemblyCompany("www.eClecticSoftwareSolutions.com")>
<Assembly: AssemblyProduct _
("COBOL and Visual Basic on .NET: A Guide for the Reformed Mainframe Programmer")>
. . .
```

For now, save and build the VB .NET project. Next, open the COBOL .NET sample project, AttributesExampleCobol.sln. Once you navigate over to the VS .NET Solution Explorer window, you will notice the absence of the assembly manifest file. Fear not!

The good guys over at Fujitsu worked out a different solution for us. Take a look at the project's Property Pages window. (While you are in the Solution Explorer window, right-click the AttributesExampleCobol project file and select Properties from the context menu.) As shown in Figure 18-3, under the Common Properties ➤ General tab, the assembly level attributes are exposed.

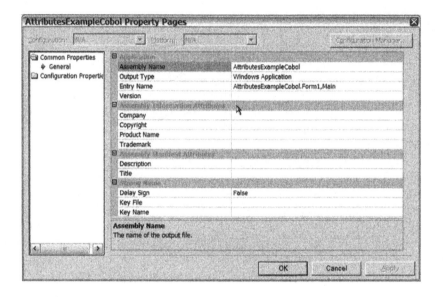

Figure 18-3. The COBOL .NET project Property Pages window showing the assembly-level attributes

After you enter the data for a few attributes, save and build the project. Being curious, after I saved and built the project, I navigated to the local application folder outside of VS .NET. I needed to take a look at the COBOL .NET raw project file (AttributesExampleCobol.cobp) just to see. Figure 18-4 shows my attribute updates.

```
AttributesExampleCobol.cobp - Notepad

File  Edit  Format  View  Help

"General"
{
"ProjectIdGuid" = "{37726A03-A900-4904-88A8-6A8D128DA779}"
"EntryName" = "AttributesExampleCobol.Form1.Main"
"OutputType" = "WinExe"
"AssemblyName" = "AttributesExampleCobol"
"RootNamespace" = "AttributesExampleCobol"
"Version" = ""
"Company" = "www.eclecticSoftwareSolutions.com"
"Copyright" = ""
"ProductName" = "COBOL and Visual Basic on .NET: A Guide for the Reformed Mainframe Programmer"
"Trademark" = ""
"Description" = "This is the Attributes Example Using COBOL"
"Title" = "AttributesExample"
"Delaysign" = "False"
"KeyFile" = ""
"KeyName" = ""
}
"Configurations"
{
```

Figure 18-4. The COBOL .NET raw project file showing the updated attributes

NOTE   You might ask why I cared if the attribute updates were stored in
the COBOL .NET raw project file. I had two reasons. First, with VB .NET,
you can edit the assembly manifest file (AssemblyInfo.vb) outside of VS
.NET—perhaps in Notepad—as it is just a text file. I wanted to see if the
same was true for COBOL .NET—that is, if you could perform the
needed edits outside of VS .NET. Second, because other assembly-level
attributes are available other than those shown in the Property Pages
window, I wanted to see how you might go about adding additional
attributes. Granted, I did not try this myself. Nevertheless, if I were to
try, my first attempt would be to add them to the project file (.cobp)
using the same syntax structure shown for the other "default"
attributes.

To make this configuration task complete, I wanted to verify that the actual
assembly metadata had in fact been extended. You will first use ILDASM to read
the MSIL and metadata. In the section "Using Reflection to Retrieve the Custom
Attributes" later in this chapter, you will see a brief demonstration showing an
alternative to using ILDASM.

As you may recall, I introduced the ILDASM tool in Chapter 6. I executed this
tool on each sample .exe file (the .exe file is located in each respective application's
\bin folder). The Manifest tab on each ILDASM display showed that in each
project, using VB .NET and COBOL .NET, the assembly metadata had been
extended. Listings 18-3 and 18-4 reflect the relevant portion of the ILDASM tool
output. Mission accomplished!

Listing 18-3. Snippet from the ILDASM Output Showing the Extended Metadata for the AttributesExampleCobol Sample Application

```
. . .
.assembly AttributesExampleCobol
{
  . . .
[mscorlib]System.Reflection.AssemblyDescriptionAttribute::.ctor(string) =
( 01 00 2A 54 68 69 73 20 69 73 20 74 68 65 20 41     // ..*This is the A
74 74 72 69 62 75 74 65 73 20 45 78 61 6D 70 6C       // ttributes Exampl
65 20 55 73 69 6E 67 20 43 4F 42 4F 4C 00 00 )        // e Using COBOL..
  .custom instance void
[mscorlib]System.Reflection.AssemblyTitleAttribute::.ctor(string) =
( 01 00 11 41 74 74 72 69 62 75 74 65 73 45 78 61     // ...AttributesExa
6D 70 6C 65 00 00 )                                   // mple..
  .custom instance void
[mscorlib]System.Reflection.AssemblyProductAttribute::.ctor(string) =
( 01 00 4D 43 4F 42 4F 4C 20 61 6E 64 20 56 69 73     // ..COBOL and Vis
75 61 6C 20 42 61 73 69 63 20 6F 6E 20 2E 4E 45       // ual Basic on .NE
54 3A 20 41 20 47 75 69 64 65 20 66 6F 72 20 74       // T: A Guide for t
68 65 20 52 65 66 6F 72 6D 65 64 20 4D 61 69 6E       // he Reformed Main
66 72 61 6D 65 20 50 72 6F 67 72 61 6D 6D 65 72       // frame Programmer
00 00 )
  .custom instance void
[mscorlib]System.Reflection.AssemblyCompanyAttribute::.ctor(string) =
( 01 00 21 77 77 77 2E 65 43 6C 65 63 74 69 63 53     // ..!www.eClecticS
6F 66 74 77 61 72 65 53 6F 6C 75 74 69 6F 6E 73       // oftwareSolutions
. . .
```

Listing 18-4. Snippet from the ILDASM Output Showing the Extended Metadata for the AttributesExampleVB Sample Application

```
. . .
.assembly AttributesExampleVB
{
  . . .
[mscorlib]System.Reflection.AssemblyProductAttribute::.ctor(string) =
( 01 00 4D 43 4F 42 4F 4C 20 61 6E 64 20 56 69 73     // ..COBOL and Vis
75 61 6C 20 42 61 73 69 63 20 6F 6E 20 2E 4E 45       // ual Basic on .NE
54 3A 20 41 20 47 75 69 64 65 20 66 6F 72 20 74       // T: A Guide for t
68 65 20 52 65 66 6F 72 6D 65 64 20 4D 61 69 6E       // he Reformed Main
66 72 61 6D 65 20 50 72 6F 67 72 61 6D 6D 65 72       // frame Programmer
00 00 )
```

```
  .custom instance void
[mscorlib]System.Reflection.AssemblyTitleAttribute::.ctor(string) =
( 01 00 11 41 74 74 72 69 62 75 74 65 73 45 78 61   // ...AttributesExa
6D 70 6C 65 00 00 )                                 // mple..
  .custom instance void
. . .
[mscorlib]System.Reflection.AssemblyCompanyAttribute::.ctor(string) =
( 01 00 21 77 77 77 2E 65 43 6C 65 63 74 69 63 53   // ..!www.eClecticS
6F 66 74 77 61 72 65 53 6F 6C 75 74 69 6F 6E 73     // oftwareSolutions
2E 63 6F 6D 00 00 )                                 // .com..
  .custom instance void
[mscorlib]System.Reflection.AssemblyDescriptionAttribute::.ctor(string) =
( 01 00 27 54 68 69 73 20 69 73 20 74 68 65 20 41   // ..'This is the A
74 74 72 69 62 75 74 65 73 20 45 78 61 6D 70 6C     // ttributes Exampl
65 20 55 73 69 6E 67 20 56 42 00 00 )               // e Using VB..
```

All right, perhaps it is not the "prettiest" display. I have just two comments. First of all, when you consider all the mainframe hexadecimal-based memory dumps that we all have combed through (fixing Abends and so forth), this ILDASM manifest display is not *that* bad. Second of all, for those who want a "nice" display, there is always the option of coding a utility application that performs reflection.

In the next section you will see a demonstration showing the use of reflection to read the assembly metadata to retrieve custom attributes—and more.

Using Reflection to Retrieve the Custom Attributes

The System.Reflection .NET Framework namespace houses about 40 classes, about 12 enumerations, and a few interfaces, structures, and delegates. Not that impressive, huh? Compared to some of the much larger .NET Framework namespaces that you have been introduced to, it is rather small. So much for passing judgment based on size. As you will see in the following demonstration, you should not underestimate the power harnessed within the System.Reflection .NET Framework namespace.

NOTE   For this reflection demonstration I have chosen to use VB .NET. As an exercise, you might consider rewriting the code using COBOL .NET. I am sure that it will be an interesting and educational experience. Bear in mind that I performed the reflection demonstration in Chapter 10 in both VB .NET and COBOL .NET.

For this demonstration, I have created a new VB .NET console project called ReflectionDemovb.sln. In the assembly manifest file (AssemblyInfo.vb), you will notice that the *AssemblyTitle* and *AssemblyDescription* attributes have been slightly modified. The following code snippet reflects the changes made to AssemblyInfo.vb:

```
. . .
<Assembly: AssemblyTitle("Reflection Demo")>
<Assembly: AssemblyDescription("This is the Reflection Demo Using VB.NET")>
<Assembly: AssemblyCompany("www.eClecticSoftwareSolutions.com")>
<Assembly: AssemblyProduct _
("COBOL and Visual Basic on .NET: A Guide for the Reformed Mainframe
Programmer")>
. . .
```

Next, I wanted to make this reflection demonstration really interesting. Therefore, I added the following class modules to the ReflectionDemovb.sln sample application:

- A *CustomAttribute.vb* class that uses the *AttributeUsage* attribute and inherits the System.Attribute class. In other words, you will create your very own custom attribute. The new custom attribute will be named *MyDocumentationAttribute*.

- A *DocumentedClass.vb* class to use the MyDocumentationAttribute custom attribute.

- An *ExampleElements.vb* class to add a variety of elements/types to the assembly. This will make the metadata that much more interesting to query. Just for fun, I included an example of the VB .NET–specific *VBFixedStringAttribute* custom attribute being used.

- A *ReflectionDrillDown.vb* class to show the real power of the System.Reflection namespace and its reflection classes.

- A *ReflectionDriver.vb* class to add some structure to the entire sample project. As you will see, it is this class that actually picks up the targeted assembly to query. For demonstration purposes, you will use the *ReflectionDemoVB* assembly as the "executing assembly."

As you will see, I have added lots of comments in the code to describe specific portions, options, and so forth. For your convenience, I provide code samples taken from the class modules. Listing 18-5 contains the CustomAttribute.vb class module.

Listing 18-5. The CustomAttribute.vb Class Module from the ReflectionDemoVB.sln Sample Application

```vb
Public Class MYCustomAttribute
    'Create your own custom attributes
    '(1) Use the AttributeUsage Tag
    '(2) Decide on AttributeTarget scope, etc.
    '(3) Use "Attribute" suffix
    '(4) Inherit System.Attribute
    <AttributeUsage(AttributeTargets.All, AllowMultiple:=True)> _
    Public Class MyDocumentationAttribute
        Inherits System.Attribute
        Public RequestNumber As String
        Public RequestNotes As String
        Public Sub New(ByVal varDrNumber As String, ByVal varDrNotes As String)
            MyBase.New()
            RequestNumber = varDrNumber
            RequestNotes = varDrNotes
        End Sub
        Public Overrides Function ToString() As String
            Return _
            ("Request Documentation: " + RequestNumber + " " + RequestNotes)
        End Function
    End Class
End Class
```

Listing 18-6 contains the DocumentedClass.vb class module.

Listing 18-6. The DocumentedClass.vb Class Module from the ReflectionDemoVB.sln Sample Application

```vb
Public Class DocumentedClass1
    'use our Custom Attribute
    Inherits ReflectionDemo.MYCustomAttribute

    'When using our Custom Attribute below,
    'the "Attribute" suffix is optional
    <MyDocumentationAttribute("Request_123", _
    "Added Class to Support new Business Rule")> _
    Public Class myDocumentedClass
        <MyDocumentationAttribute("Request_456", _
        "Changed Name or Variable")> _
        Public myInt As System.Int32
```

```
            <MyDocumentationAttribute("Request_789", _
            "Changed Access attribute to Private")> _
            Private myString As System.String

            <MyDocumentationAttribute("Request_ABC", _
            "Modfied Sub Routines Scope")> _
            Public Function myDocumentedFunction() As String
                    'Do Nothing
            End Function
        End Class
End Class
```

Listing 18-7 contains the ExampleElements.vb class module.

Listing 18-7. The ExampleElements.vb Class Module from the
ReflectionDemoVB.sln Sample Application

```
'This Class was created simply to provide a variety of TYPES
'for the Reflection Demo
Public Class ReflectionClassA
    Private myArrayList As New ArrayList()
    Friend myFriendVar As String
    Public Shared mySharedVar As Boolean
    Protected myProtectedVar As Long
    Protected Friend myProtectedFRVar As Long

    Structure AStructure
        Public myStrucInteger As Integer
        Dim myStrucPubString As String
        <VBFixedString(10)> Private myStrucPriString As String
    End Structure

    Public Sub New(ByVal afield As ArrayList)
        MyBase.new()
        myArrayList = afield
    End Sub

      Public Sub New(ByVal afield As ArrayList, _
      ByVal bfield As ArrayList)
          MyBase.new()
          myArrayList = bfield
      End Sub

    Dim myArray As String() = {"A", "B", "C"}
```

```vb
        Public Property Name() As String()
            Get
                    Return myArray
            End Get
            Set(ByVal Value() As String)
                    If Value(0) <> "" Then
                            myArray(0) = Value(0)
                    End If
            End Set
        End Property


        Public Enum ScaleOfDifficulty
            VeryEasy = 1
            Easy = 2
            SlightChallenge = 3
            Challenging = 4
            Difficult = 5
            VeryDifficult = 6
        End Enum


        Public Class NestedClassA
            Private myShort As Int16
            Private myInt As Int32
            Private myLong As Int64
            Public myPublicShort As Int16
            Public myPublicInt As Int32
            Public myPublicLong As Int64
            Dim myArrayInSideOfClass As String() _
                = {"A", "B", "C", "D", "E", "F"}

            Public Sub myFirstSub()
                    Static myStaticVar As Integer
                    For myInt = 0 To 1
                            'Do nothing
                    Next
            End Sub
        End Class
End Class
```

Listing 18-8 contains the ReflectionDrillDown.vb class module.

Listing 18-8. The ReflectionDrillDown.vb Class Module from the
ReflectionDemoVB.sln Sample Application

```vb
Option Strict On
Public Class ReflectionDrillDownClass


'Use Reflection to Drill down into each Assembly TYPE
Public Shared Sub DrillDownIntoType(ByVal objType As Type)


'Use the FindMembers Reflection method to extract all Members Types
'Optionally, you can Filter by member type, BindingFlag, or Delegate.
'Use of the Reflection Delegate requires that you Modify the Delegate
'Parameter below as per your intent to Filter your FindMembers results
Dim arrayMemberInfo() As System.Reflection.MemberInfo
arrayMemberInfo = objType.FindMembers(System.Reflection.MemberTypes.All, _
                            System.Reflection.BindingFlags.Public Or _
                            System.Reflection.BindingFlags.Static _
                            Or System.Reflection.BindingFlags.NonPublic _
                            Or System.Reflection.BindingFlags.Instance, _
                            New System.Reflection.MemberFilter _
                            (AddressOf DelegateToSearchCriteria), _
                              " ")


Dim index As Integer
For index = 0 To arrayMemberInfo.Length - 1
'Treat each Member Type according to desired information
        Select Case arrayMemberInfo(index).MemberType.ToString()
            Case "Field"
'Use FieldInfo Reflection Method to Drill down into Field type Members
                Dim FieldInfo As System.Reflection.FieldInfo
                FieldInfo = CType(arrayMemberInfo(index),
                            System.Reflection.FieldInfo)


                Dim FieldInfoStr As String
                If FieldInfo.IsPublic() Then
                    FieldInfoStr = "Public"
                End If
                If FieldInfo.IsPrivate() Then
                    FieldInfoStr = "Private"
                End If
                If FieldInfo.IsStatic() Then
                    FieldInfoStr = "Static"
                End If
```

```vb
'Optionally use Reflection and conditional logic to filter as you wish
   If arrayMemberInfo(index).DeclaringType.Namespace.ToString() <> _
         "System" Then
            Console.WriteLine("MemberType - " + ControlChars.Tab + _
               arrayMemberInfo(index).MemberType.ToString() + _
               ControlChars.Tab + _
               FieldInfoStr + _
               ControlChars.Tab + _
              "Name -" + ControlChars.Tab + _
               arrayMemberInfo(index).ToString() + ControlChars.Cr)

   'Logic to support Custom Attributes - At Field Level
   GetCustomAttibutes(arrayMemberInfo(index).GetCustomAttributes(True))
   End If

Case "Method"

'Optionally use Reflection and conditional logic to filter as you wish
   If arrayMemberInfo(index).DeclaringType.Namespace.ToString() <> _
         "System" Then
            Console.WriteLine("MemberType - " + ControlChars.Tab + _
             arrayMemberInfo(index).MemberType.ToString() + _
             ControlChars.Tab + _
             "Name -" + ControlChars.Tab + _
             arrayMemberInfo(index).ToString() + ControlChars.Cr)
        'Logic to support Custom Attributes - At Member level
   GetCustomAttibutes(arrayMemberInfo(index).GetCustomAttributes(True))
   End If

  Case "Constructor"
        Console.WriteLine("Constructor - " + ControlChars.Tab + _
         arrayMemberInfo(index).MemberType.ToString() + _
         ControlChars.Tab + _
         arrayMemberInfo(index).ToString() + ControlChars.Cr)

    End Select

   Next index
End Sub


'Optionally, customize this Reflection Delegate as you wish
Public Shared Function DelegateToSearchCriteria _
   (ByVal objMemberInfo As System.Reflection.MemberInfo, _
     ByVal objSearch As Object) As Boolean
```

```
'Optionally, modify the logic below (to filter) as per your modifications
'applied at the time of executing the FindMembers methods above.
    If objMemberInfo.DeclaringType.Namespace.ToString() <> _
        objSearch.ToString() Then
            Return True
    Else
            Return False
    End If
End Function


Public Shared Sub GetCustomAttibutes(ByVal myobj() As Object)
    'Logic to support Custom Attributes
    Dim SysAttrTypeFld As System.Attribute
    Dim idxFld As Integer
    For idxFld = 0 To UBound(myobj)
        SysAttrTypeFld = CType(myobj(idxFld), System.Attribute)
        'Single out one of the VB specific Attributes
        Select Case SysAttrTypeFld.ToString()
            Case "Microsoft.VisualBasic.VBFixedStringAttribute"
                Dim obj As Microsoft.VisualBasic.VBFixedStringAttribute
                obj = CType(SysAttrTypeFld, _
                Microsoft.VisualBasic.VBFixedStringAttribute)
                    Console.WriteLine("Attribute:->" + _
                    SysAttrTypeFld.ToString() + " " + obj.Length.ToString())
            Case Else
                Console.WriteLine("Attribute:->" + SysAttrTypeFld.ToString())
        End Select
    Next
    End Sub
End Class
```

Listing 18-9 contains the ReflectionDriver.vb class module.

Listing 18-9. The ReflectionDriver.vb Class Module from the ReflectionDemoVB.sln Sample Application

```
Option Strict On
Public Class ReflectionDriverClass
    Public Sub ReflectionDemo()

        Dim MethodIndex As System.Int32
        Dim ArrayIndex As System.Int32


        'For Demo purposes, Currently Executing Assembly
```

```vbnet
'Optionally Pick up an existing referenced Assembly
'or perhaps do a late bind, and pick up unreferenced assemblies.
'Comment/Un-comment below as appropriate


'Dim UnReferencedAssemblyForLateBind As System.Object
'Dim ReferencedAssembly = New ReflectionDemo.ReflectionDriverClass()
Dim AssemblyClass As System.Reflection.Assembly
 AssemblyClass = AssemblyClass.GetExecutingAssembly()
'AssemblyClass = AssemblyClass.GetAssembly(UnReferencedAssembly.GetType)
 'AssemblyClass = AssemblyClass.GetAssembly(ReferencedAssembly.GetType)


'Use Reflection to display Assembly Attributes
'(stored in AssemblyInfo.vb file)
GetAssemblyAttributes(AssemblyClass)


'Use Reflection to report Referenced Assemblies
Dim AssemblyArray As System.Reflection.AssemblyName()
AssemblyArray = AssemblyClass.GetReferencedAssemblies()
For ArrayIndex = 0 To UBound(AssemblyArray)
    Console.WriteLine("Referenced Assemblies: " + _
     AssemblyArray(ArrayIndex).Name)
Next

'Use Reflection to list Types within Assembly
Dim MyTypes() As System.Type
MyTypes = AssemblyClass.GetTypes()


For ArrayIndex = 0 To UBound(MyTypes)
    Console.WriteLine("*************************************")
    Console.WriteLine("Type: " + MyTypes(ArrayIndex).FullName)
    If MyTypes(ArrayIndex).IsEnum Then
        Dim EnumStr() As String
        'Use Reflection to get Details of Enums
        EnumStr = System.Enum.GetNames(MyTypes(ArrayIndex))
        Console.WriteLine("   This Enumeration Contains: ")
        Dim xString As String

        For Each xString In EnumStr

            Dim sb As New System.Text.StringBuilder()
            sb.Append("    ")
            sb.Append(xString)
            sb.Append("--->")
            sb.Append(System.Enum.Format(MyTypes(ArrayIndex), _
```

```
                        System.Enum.Parse(MyTypes(ArrayIndex), xString), "d"))
                        Console.WriteLine(sb.ToString())

                Next
            Else

                'Use Reflection to display TYPE level Custom Attributes
                Dim CustAttr() As Object
                CustAttr = MyTypes(ArrayIndex).GetCustomAttributes(True)
                Dim SysAttrType As System.Attribute
                Dim idx As Integer
                For idx = 0 To UBound(CustAttr)
                    SysAttrType = CType(CustAttr(idx), System.Attribute)
                    Console.WriteLine("Attribute:->" + SysAttrType.ToString())
                Next

                'Use Reflection to get Details other TYPES
                Dim mydemo As New ReflectionDrillDownClass()
                mydemo.DrillDownIntoType(MyTypes(ArrayIndex))

            End If
            Console.WriteLine()
        Next
        Console.WriteLine(String.Empty)
    End Sub

    Public Sub GetAssemblyAttributes(ByVal AssemblyObj As _
      System.Reflection.Assembly)

        Dim CustAttr1() As Object
        CustAttr1 = AssemblyObj.GetCustomAttributes(True)
        Dim SysAttrType1 As System.Attribute
        Dim idx1 As Integer
        For idx1 = 0 To UBound(CustAttr1)
            SysAttrType1 = CType(CustAttr1(idx1), System.Attribute)

            'There are other Attributes available. These were selected
            'for Demo purposes (stored in AssemblyInfo.vb file)
            Select Case SysAttrType1.ToString()
                Case "System.Reflection.AssemblyCompanyAttribute"
                    Dim obj As System.Reflection.AssemblyCompanyAttribute
                    obj = CType(SysAttrType1, _
                    System.Reflection.AssemblyCompanyAttribute)
                    Console.WriteLine("Company: " + obj.Company)
```

```
              Case "System.Reflection.AssemblyTitleAttribute"
                  Dim obj As System.Reflection.AssemblyTitleAttribute
                  obj = CType(SysAttrType1, _
                  System.Reflection.AssemblyTitleAttribute)
                  Console.WriteLine("Assembly Title: " + obj.Title)
              Case "System.Reflection.AssemblyDescriptionAttribute"
                  Dim obj As System.Reflection.AssemblyDescriptionAttribute
                  obj = CType(SysAttrType1, _
                  System.Reflection.AssemblyDescriptionAttribute)
              Console.WriteLine("Assembly Description: " + obj.Description)
              Case "System.Reflection.AssemblyProductAttribute"
                  Dim obj As System.Reflection.AssemblyProductAttribute
                  obj = CType(SysAttrType1, _
                  System.Reflection.AssemblyProductAttribute)
                  Console.WriteLine("Assembly Product: " + obj.Product)
          End Select
      Next
      Console.WriteLine("*************************************")


    End Sub
End Class
```

Please take a moment to review each of the class modules in the preceding listings. As you will notice, meaningful comments have been added to each. When the ReflectionDemoVB sample console application is executed, a series of lines will be written to the console. I have included a portion of the reflection console output in Listing 18-10.

Listing 18-10. A Portion of the Reflection Output As It Is Written to the Console Window for the ReflectionDemoVB Sample Application

```
Assembly Title: Reflection Demo
Assembly Product: COBOL and Visual Basic on .NET: A Guide for the Reformed Mainframe
Programmer
Assembly Description: This is the Reflection Demo Using VB.NET
Company: www.eClecticSoftwareSolutions.com
*************************************
Referenced Assemblies: mscorlib
Referenced Assemblies: Microsoft.VisualBasic
Referenced Assemblies: System
Referenced Assemblies: System.Data
Referenced Assemblies: System.Xml
*************************************
Type: ReflectionDemo.MYCustomAttribute
Constructor -   Constructor     Void .ctor()
```

```
************************************
Type: ReflectionDemo.MYCustomAttribute+MyDocumentationAttribute
Attribute:->System.AttributeUsageAttribute
MemberType -    Method  Name -  System.String ToString()
Constructor -   Constructor     Void .ctor(System.String, System.String)
MemberType -    Field   Public  Name -  System.String RequestNumber
MemberType -    Field   Public  Name -  System.String RequestNotes
************************************

. . .
************************************
Type: ReflectionDemo.ReflectionClassA+AStructure
MemberType -    Field   Public  Name -  Int32 myStrucInteger
MemberType -    Field   Public  Name -  System.String myStrucPubString
MemberType -    Field   Private Name -  System.String myStrucPriString
Attribute:->Microsoft.VisualBasic.VBFixedStringAttribute 10
************************************
Type: ReflectionDemo.ReflectionClassA+ScaleOfDifficulty
   This Enumeration Contains:
   VeryEasy--->1
   Easy--->2
   SlightChallenge--->3
   Challenging--->4
   Difficult--->5
   VeryDifficult--->6
************************************

. . .
```

As shown in Listing 18-10, you can use the reflection classes while programmatically formatting/structuring the resulting output. As compared with the display that the ILDASM tool creates for you, you may wish to create an "easier to read" type of display. On the other hand, the graphical tree view of the assembly metadata provided by the ILDASM tool has its strengths as well (see Figure 18-5).

Using the ILDASM tool, you can drill down into the DocumentedClass1 and myDocumentedClass type nodes (see Figure 18-5) to see the "documentation" that was added with your custom attribute (*MYCustomAttribute.MyDocumentationAttribute*). As I discussed in the previous section, the assembly-level attributes are stored within the Manifest node.

Perhaps the reflection demonstration presented in Chapter 10 stirred your interest. I hope the reflection demonstration in this chapter provided you with a much broader picture of the capabilities and power of reflection. Combine the reflection process with custom attributes and metadata to enhance your configuration processes.

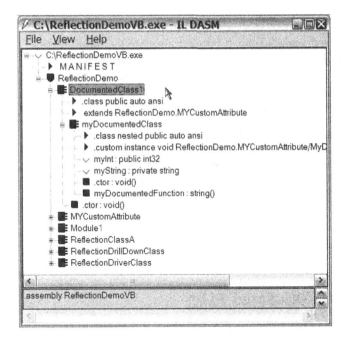

Figure 18-5. The graphical tree view display provided by the ILDASM tool using the ReflectionDemoVB assembly

Now you have seen the two choices available when you want to read metadata from an assembly. I believe that I have driven the point home that by using the process of reflection, the use of custom attributes for configuration becomes that much more attractive.

TIP   Consider enhancing the ReflectionDemoVB sample application to write the output to a text file, an XML file, or a database table.

Feel free to dig down further into the topic of custom attributes and reflection according to your needs. You will find that the topic of custom attributes extends beyond configuration and reflection. Likewise, you will find that the topic of reflection extends beyond configuration and custom attributes. This chapter's discussion exploited the intersection of these topics, as they tend to complement each other. I have included references at the end of this chapter in the "To Learn More" section that will help your continued exploration.

In the next section, you will turn your attention to the use of XML-based configuration files for your .NET application configuration needs.

CAUTION   The following section discusses the set of XML-based configuration (config) files associated with the .NET Framework. Please be
aware that if you damage either your Web.config or your App.config file,
the recovery will not be that bad. In the worst-case scenario, one application could be temporarily disabled and the associated user group will
be screaming at you. However, the same is *not* true for the
Machine.config or security-related config files. Inadvertently damaging
your Machine.config or security-related config files could be disastrous
for you. You could cripple your entire machine and all applications
running on it. This usually gets people into *big* trouble. That being
the case, you will always want to make dependable backups of the
Machine.config and security-related config files before opening them
for editing or browsing purposes.

Configuration with XML-Based Files

Let's talk about using external lookup files for configuration. As you know, some of
the preferred mainframe-based "name-value" configuration solutions typically
involved the use of smartly named partitioned datasets (PDSs). Varying slightly from
one mainframe shop to the next, the PDS files might have been referred to as
parameter libraries or *control libraries* (or maybe even *copy libraries*). When
appropriate, even JCL was leveraged to provide the right level of customization
and configuration.

Thinking about the mainframe CICS/online environment? In that case, the
topic of configuration and external "files" might take on a different meaning. For
example, it is well understood that "configuring" a CICS application involved possible updates to the program control table (PCT), processing program table (PPT),
and file control table (FCT). Where things really got interesting was when you were
given access to the CICS online configuration tools (rather than having to resort to
manual batch techniques).

A privileged few were able to use the mainframe CICS online facility called
Resource Definition Online (RDO). To use RDO, an authorized user would execute
the CEDA CICS transaction. The results of any CEDA modifications would be
stored in the CICS System Definition (CSD) file. Then this CSD file would be used
to apply updates to the PCT, PPT, and FCT. The point being, even CICS made use of
external files in typical configuration scenarios.

Hard Coding

While you were developing on the mainframe, did you ever get into trouble for hard-coding parameter or control type information into your actual code module? Perhaps you received a gentle reprimand on the condition that you promised to never hard-code again, to instead use external lookup files. Once was enough, right? Unfortunately, it is not until some programmers get burned that they truly learn the lesson. The school of hard knocks can be an effective teacher, especially if you get fired in the process.

In this section, I introduce the collection of external files used in .NET application configuration scenarios. Collectively, I refer to them as the *XML-based configuration files*. They are recognized as ending with the suffix of .config. The default config files for .NET are as follows:

- *Web.config:* This file is located in your ASP.NET application virtual directory. If you use subfolders in your Web application, you can use an additional Web.config file in each folder.

- *App.config:*[1] Commonly referred to as the *application configuration file,* App.config is located in your application directory/folder. You will typically need to manually add the App.config file into your .NET Windows application folder.

- *Machine.config:* The location of this file depends on your runtime installation path and the version of the .NET runtime. On a Windows XP platform, using version 1 of the .NET runtime, the location will typically be C:\WINNT\Microsoft.NET\Framework\v1.0.3705\CONFIG.

---

1. Microsoft's documentation mentions a naming convention of *ApplicationName.exe.config* for the Windows application configuration file. The config file that matches that naming convention is automatically created for you. You actually create the App.config file. When you "build" your solution/project, the App.config file is copied to the \bin folder with the name of ApplicationName.exe.config. You then continue to edit the App.config file that remains in the application folder. This automatic copying scenario repeats with subsequent builds.

NOTE   There are other config files: Security.config, Enterprisesec.config, Web_hightrust.config, Web_lowtrust.config, and Web_notrust.config. I defer discussion of these other config files until the section "Configuring for Code Access Security" later in this chapter.

The first config file in the preceding list, Web.config, should look familiar to you. In Chapter 15 in the section "A Configuration Primer," I discussed using this file as part of your ASP.NET session-state configuration. I discussed Web.config again later in Chapter 15 in the section "To Be a Cookieless Session or Not to Be a Cookieless Session." In the latter section, I explored the need to use this configuration file for session state configuration.

If that were not enough, I referred to the Web.config file a third and fourth time in Chapter 15 in the section "In-Process vs. Out-of-Process Session State" and in a Tip about the ASP.NET trace feature (located at the end of the chapter), respectively. More recently, in Chapter 17 I discussed a "deployment" concern of the config files.

In short, you've heard of the config files before, especially the Web.config file. Are you ready to drill down much deeper? That's great! Let's proceed.

CROSS-REFERENCE   I discuss the Security.config and Enterprisesec.config files in the section "Configuring for Code Access Security" later in this chapter.

The XML Schema for the Configuration File

On a couple of occasions, you may have noticed my use of the descriptive phrase "XML-based configuration files." Please make a note of this. The point that I want to get across is that you really should have XML on your mind (well-formed, case-sensitive XML at that) before you even think about modifying any of the config files. Taking the Web.config, App.config, or Machine.config as an example, you will notice the following required XML line at the very top of each file:

```
<?xml version="1.0" encoding="utf-8" ?>
```

Following this line, you will see the root element Configuration followed by other XML child elements. The very last line in each config file is the closing XML tag for the root Configuration element. Therefore, the following two lines of XML should be considered the minimum for any config file:

```
<configuration>
</configuration>
```

The question then becomes "What do you put in between these two XML tags?" Good question. The quick and easy answer is "You put XML child elements using well-formed XML in between the root Configuration element XML tags." Now for the realistic answer: "Depending on your configuration needs and depending on which configuration file you are using, you would select from the list of available child elements."

As for the "well-formed XML" part, I did a search in Microsoft's Visual Studio .NET documentation tool (ms-help://MS.VSCC/MS.MSDNVS/cpguide/html/cpconformatofconfigurationfiles.htm) and found the matter was documented quite nicely (see Figure 18-6).

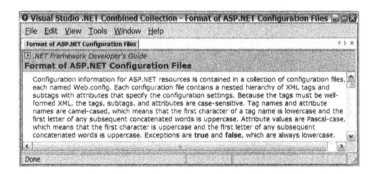

Figure 18-6. Example topic found in Microsoft's Visual Studio .NET documentation tool

Almost all of your .NET application configuration concerns will involve choosing either or both of the following two child elements (to use in between the root Configuration element XML tags):

- ASP.NET: *<system.web></system.web>*

- Application settings: *<appSettings></appSettings>*

Pertaining mostly to the Machine.config file are seven[2] other basic child elements, of which you can use one or more (in between the root Configuration element XML tags):

- Startup: *<startup></startup>*

- Runtime: *<runtime></runtime>*

- Remoting: *<system.runtime.remoting></system.runtime.remoting>*[3]

- Network: *<system.net></system.net>*

- Cryptography: *<cryptographySettings></cryptographySettings>*[4]

- Configuration sections: *<configSections></configSections>*

- Tracing and debugging: *<system.diagnostics></system.diagnostics>*

For now you'll focus mainly on the first two child elements listed previously: <system.web></system.web> and <appSettings></appSettings>. In the next section you'll take a closer look at the <system.web></system.web> child element.

Understanding `<system.web></system.web>`

You can use the <system.web></system.web> child element in either the Web.config or Machine.config file. However, you will do almost all of your editing for this child element in the Web.config file. The settings performed in the Web.config will override, per application, the settings (if any) found in the Machine.config file. The <system.web></system.web> child element only applies to ASP.NET Web applications (i.e., it is used in either the Web.config or Machine.config file).

Listing 18-11 shows the grouping of XML child elements (children of the <system.web></system.web> element) available for the element <system.web></system.web>. Several dozen child elements are available for the <system.web></system.web> element. I have intentionally omitted a few child elements from the listing. An example of one that I omitted from the listing is the

---

2. You could have more or fewer "other" basic child elements. This is controlled in your Machine.config file in the *<configSections></configSections>* XML element.

3. Chapter 20 covers the <system.runtime.remoting></system.runtime.remoting> XML child element.

4. This element is a child element of *<mscorlib></mscorlib>*.

child element, which happens to control the default client script location (aspnet_client) for several of Microsoft's Web Forms controls. As your needs dictate, consider carefully browsing your Machine.config file to discover the complete list of child elements.

*Listing 18-11. Child Elements Available for *

```
<system.web>
    <authentication></authentication>
    <authorization></authorization>
    <browserCaps></browserCaps>
    <clientTarget></clientTarget>
    <compilation></compilation>
    <customErrors></customErrors>
    <globalization></globalization>
    <httpHandlers></httpHandlers>
    <httpModules></httpModules>
    <httpRuntime></httpRuntime>
    <identity></identity>
    <iisFilter></iisFilter>
    <machineKey></machineKey>
    <pages></pages>
    <processModel></processModel>
    <securityPolicy></securityPolicy>
<serviceDescriptionFormatExtensionTypes></serviceDescriptionFormatExtensionTypes>
    <sessionState></sessionState>
    <trace></trace>
    <trust></trust>
    <webServices></webServices>
</system.web>
```

You will notice that the *<sessionState></sessionState>* child element appears in Listing 18-11 (fourth from the bottom). Less than a third of the available child elements are included in the Web.config by default. As your needs dictate, you can easily add those that remain.

In reference to Listing 18-11, you will also notice the *<trace></trace>* child element (third from the bottom). I have a few points to mention about that particular child element:

- Become familiar with the <trace></trace> child element. Once you enable a Trace.axd file, you can view it from your Web browser. This file contains lots of useful information for when you need to optimize or debug your application.

- Avoid confusing the <trace></trace> child element that is a child element of <system.web> with the other <trace></trace> child element that is a child element of <system.diagnostics>. Unfortunately, they have the same name but totally different uses.

- You can also control tracing with the @ Page directive at the ASP.NET page level.

The next step for any child element is to find out what attributes (or other child elements) are available for use. For example, you saw the attribute listing for the <sessionState></sessionState> child element earlier in Chapter 15 in the section "A Configuration Primer." As shown here, you basically have five attributes (one required and four optional) to choose from for the <sessionState></sessionState> child element (mode is a required attribute):

```
<sessionState mode="Off|Inproc|StateServer|SQLServer"
              cookieless="true|false"
              timeout="number of minutes"
              stateConnectionString="tcpip=server:port"
              sqlConnectionString="sql connection string" />
```

The attributes available for the <trace></trace> child element are as follows:

```
<system.web>
  <trace enabled="false|true"
         pageOutput="false|true"
         requestLimit="number of trace requests"
         traceMode="SortByTime|SortByCategory"
         localOnly="false|true"/>
</system.web>
```

You had already seen the Web.config file and <sessionState></sessionState> child element in earlier chapters. Nevertheless, I do believe that by presenting it here in the context of the configuration discussion, you will gain a more complete understanding. You can now continue to use the <sessionState></sessionState> child element and other <system.web></system.web> child elements for your ASP.NET configuration needs.

NOTE If you update a Web.config file while an application is executing, the CLR will recognize this change and trigger the application to recompile/reload. This "feature" is generally looked at as being a good thing. However, be aware that an application recompile/reload may introduce state management concerns.

On that note, let's shift focus toward one of the child elements of the root Configuration element: the <appSettings></appSettings> child element.

Understanding

This is one of my favorite configuration child elements. As its name implies, you should use the child element for application-level settings. In other words, in most of the instances where you might be so inclined to include hard-coded "settings" in your code modules, you would use this child element instead.

The preferred use of the child element applies to each of the occasions when I hard-coded[5] configuration information in previous sample code demonstrations, as shown in Table 18-1.

Table 18-1. Code Samples in Previous Chapters with Hard-Coded Configuration Information

CHAPTER	DESCRIPTION
Chapter 10	The names of the output .txt files were hard-coded.
Chapter 11	The database connection string was hard-coded.
Chapter 12	The names of the output .xml files were hard-coded.
Chapter 13	The HREF value (Web site URL) was hard-coded.
Chapter 14	The database connection string was hard-coded.
Chapter 15	No hard-coding, but state management was used.
Chapter 16	The exported Crystal Reports file names were hard-coded.
Chapter 17	No hard-coding, but an IIS virtual directory was created.

---

5. Yes, I did, but let that be our little secret. Go ahead, call me a hypocrite.

Yes, in each of the previous cases where the configuration settings were hard-coded, an alternative approach (i.e., using <appSettings></appSettings>) might have worked better.[6] Now, why do I mention Chapters 15 and 17?

In Chapter 15, as you know, I discussed state and cache management. You will often find state and cache management used in conjunction with configuration settings. For example, after you retrieve a specific setting from the <appSettings></appSettings> child element, you can store the value using state and cache management. You may find it appropriate, then, to store your database connection string using an application state technique.

In Chapter 17, you learned how to manually create an IIS virtual directory. Now it is fair to reemphasize one of the typical uses of virtual directories. In most cases, when you need to output files (as you did in Chapter 16 with the Crystal Reports file export logic), you would use a virtual directory as a target location, in which case you could retrieve the virtual directory name (or physical directory name) from the <appSettings></appSettings> child element. This enables you to properly configure your application.

You can use[7] the <appSettings></appSettings> child element in the Web.config file (for ASP.NET applications), the App.config file (for .NET Windows applications), and the Machine.config file (for machine-level impact). The <appSettings></appSettings> child element has a rather simple schematic, as shown in Listing 18-12. I have included the <configuration> and <system.web> elements to provide clarifying context. The <system.web> element would not apply for Windows (non-Web) applications.

Listing 18-12. The XML Schema for <appSettings></appSettings>

```
<?xml version="1.0" encoding="utf-8" ?>
<configuration>
    <appSettings>
        <add key="key" value="value"/>
        <remove key="predefined setting key"/>
        <clear/>
    </appSettings>
      <system.web>

      . . .

      </system.web>
</configuration>
```

---

6. Previous to .NET, the use of the Windows registry was more commonplace as an alternative to hard coding configuration settings. Though it is still possible to use the Windows registry, the use of XML-based configuration files is quickly becoming the preferred approach.

7. According to Microsoft's documentation, the <appSettings> child element can be used in "Web.config files that are not at the application directory level". I did not find this restriction to be true. My use of the <appSettings> child element has worked well, even with the Web.config file being located in its default application directory level location.

NOTE You can easily define other <appSettings>-type elements using other names. For example, if you want to have an element called *databaseSettings* to use in your config files, you can. To do this, you need to first edit the Machine.config file by adding an appropriate <section> entry in the <configSections> element. Optionally, you could modify the element entry that already exists for <appSettings> in the Machine.config file to have a name more to your liking. I find that the predefined <appSettings> element with its given name is flexible enough to meet my needs. Your needs may be different. Just remember to back up your Machine.config file prior to editing it. Also, consider adding lots of comments for documentation purposes.

To further demonstrate the use of the <appSettings></appSettings> child element in a typical application configuration scenario, you will use two sample applications. The following section continues on that note.

Using

The sample code I use to demonstrate the use of the child element is taken mostly from the code originally used in Chapter 14's sample applications. In other words, the original sample applications MyInformativeWinFormCobol and MyInformativeWinFormVB have been modified for this chapter to become My*Enhanced*InformativeWinFormCobol and My*Enhanced*InformativeWinFormVB.

For each sample application, the goal is to add the desired database connection string configuration into an external XML-based configuration file. Subsequently, the original hard-coded configuration coding will be replaced.

For the "modified" VB .NET sample application, an application configuration file (App.config) was added to the project folder (right-click the project file in the Solution Explorer window and select Add ➤ Add New Item), as shown in Figure 18-7.

The following code snippet reflects the code used for the VB .NET sample application, using the App.config file:

```
<?xml version="1.0" encoding="utf-8" ?>
<configuration>
    <appSettings>
        <add key="MyVBConnectionString"
        value="user id=sa;pwd=;Database=northwind;Server=(LOCAL)" />
    </appSettings>
</configuration>
```

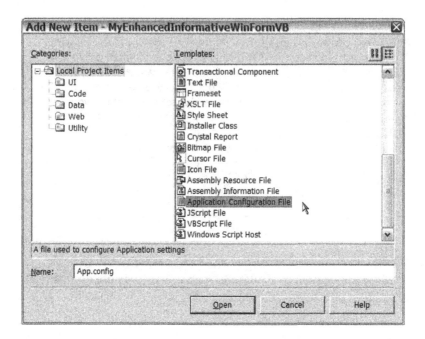

Figure 18-7. The VS .NET Add New Item window to add an application configuration file to a VB .NET Windows application

For the "modified" COBOL .NET sample application, I reluctantly chose to use the Machine.config file (see Figure 18-8). It appears that Fujitsu's NetCOBOL for .NET product does not support the VS .NET application configuration file Add New Item feature.[8]

---

8. The Fujitsu tech support team promptly responded regarding my inquiry into this matter. According to that communication, they too feel that "application-specific" configuration changes belong in an application configuration file, not in the Machine.config file. In fact, after I mentioned to them that the VS .NET Application Configuration File Add New Item feature was not available, they suggested an alternative approach to creating the App.config XML file: Use the VS .NET Dynamic Properties feature. I followed their suggestion and it worked perfectly. I tried it out by first selecting the Windows Form in Design view and viewing the properties of the Form by pressing F4. Then, I selected Dynamic Properties and selected one or more of the dynamic properties. After I clicked OK, the App.config file was created and appeared in the VS .NET Solution Explorer window. I could have edited the App.config XML file directly to add additional configuration settings. With this alternative approach suggested by the Fujitsu tech support team, I hardly had the heart to further harass them about improving their Help text to more clearly instruct developers with regard to the use of configuration files. At any rate, for sake of the demonstration here, I chose to leave the Machine.config update in for the sample application. This way, you will see how *not* to do application-specific configuration (while still using one of the XML configuration files).

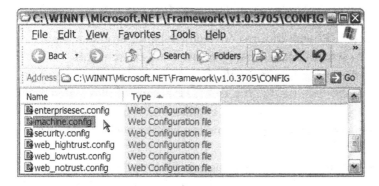

Figure 18-8. Preparing to edit the Machine.config file after making the suggested backup

The following code snippet reflects the code used for the COBOL .NET sample application, using the Machine.config file (additional child elements are shown to provide context):

```xml
<?xml version="1.0" encoding="utf-8" ?>
<configuration>
    <configSections>
    . . .
    </configSections>
    . . .
    <appSettings>
        <add key="MyCOBOLConnectionString"
        value="user id=sa;pwd=;Database=northwind;Server=(LOCAL)" />
    </appSettings>
    . . .
    <system.diagnostics>
    . . .
    </system.diagnostics>
        . . .
</configuration>
```

Now all that is left to do is implement the appropriate logic to retrieve the configuration settings from the respective config file. To accomplish that, you will need to enhance each sample application with additional code. The discussion in the section "Configuration with Configuration Namespaces" introduces the needed support provided by the .NET Framework configuration namespaces.

The Assembly Resource File: Another XML Configuration File

You may have noticed a file with the .resx extension lingering around in your application folder. As it turns out, you have another set of external XML configuration-type files other than the config files. Allow me to introduce you to the XML-based *assembly resource file*. The .resx file is automatically created by VS .NET for Windows applications and ASP.NET applications. You use the .resx file to configure applications as per globalization and localization requirements (e.g., culture, currency, and so forth).

Commonly referred to as a *resource* file, the .resx file is easily confused with the CLR *binary resource* file, which has the *.resource* extension. The .resx file is an XML-based file that has a predefined XML Schema.

The command-line tool Resource File Generator (Resgen.exe) is available to convert .resx resource files from their text/readable XML format to the binary .resources format. The binary .resources file can then be embedded/compiled into an executable/assembly. A second tool, the Windows Forms Resource Editor (Winres.exe), is available for those who want to edit a .resx or .resource file outside of the VS .NET environment.

The *System.Resources* namespace is provided to support the programmatic use of the resource files. The *ResourceManager* class (from the System.Resources namespace) enables reading and writing of resources associated with the assembly. Additionally, the *System.Globalization* namespace is available to assist you with your globalization (and localization) configuration needs.

Configuration with Configuration Namespaces

The .NET Framework offers a set of namespaces referred to as *the configuration namespaces* (seriously). Literally, the grouping is called "the configuration namespaces." This distinguished namespace grouping includes the following:

- *System.Configuration*

- *System.Configuration.Assemblies*

- *System.Configuration.Install*

From this grouping, you will focus on the System.Configuration namespace. As for the other two configuration namespaces, I provide a brief (very brief) introduction in two later sections. First, you will dig into the System.Configuration namespace.

Using the System.Configuration Namespace

About seven classes (and one interface) are contained in this namespace. I will only mention and demonstrate one of them: *ConfigurationSettings* or, rather, the *System.Configuration.ConfigurationSettings* class. The ConfigurationSettings class has one property (*AppSettings*) and one method (*GetConfig*).

You can use the GetConfig method to retrieve values from the <appSettings></appSettings> child element. However, a more typical use of the GetConfig method is to retrieve values from "any" user-defined configuration settings area. For example, if you were to create your own version of the <appSettings></appSettings> child element using a different name, you would use the GetConfig method to retrieve your configuration settings.

As I have not found the need for other user-defined configuration settings, I have yet to find a need to use the GetConfig method. The AppSettings property of the ConfigurationSettings class has worked well for me. The AppSettings property is my choice to read the configuration settings previously stored in the <appSettings></appSettings> child element in the respective config files.

Let's now return to the sample code (MyEnhancedInformativeWinFormCobol and MyEnhancedInformativeWinFormVB) to review the implementation and use of the AppSettings property of the System.Configuration.ConfigurationSettings class. As you can see from the following code snippets, the database connection string information is being retrieved from the respective config files.

Here's the original hard-coded VB .NET code (using the "hard-coded" approach) from the MyInformativeWinFormVB sample project:

```
. . .
mySqlConnection.ConnectionString = _
"user id=sa;pwd=;Database=northwind;Server=(LOCAL)"
. . .
```

Next is the updated VB .NET sample code (using a preferred configuration technique) from the MyEnhancedInformativeWinFormVB sample project:

```
. . .
Dim myConn As String = _
System.Configuration.ConfigurationSettings.AppSettings("MyVBConnectionString")
mySqlConnection.ConnectionString = myConn
. . .
```

The following is the original hard-coded COBOL .NET code (using the "hard-coded" approach) from the MyInformativeWinFormCobol sample project:

```
. . .
019970      SET PROP-ConnectionString OF mySqlConnection TO
019980          "user id=sa;pwd=;Database=northwind;Server=(LOCAL)"
. . .
```

Here's the updated COBOL .NET sample code (using a preferred configuration technique) from the MyEnhancedInformativeWinFormCobol sample project:

```
. . .
000413      CLASS CLASS-NAMEVALUECOLLECTION AS
000414          "System.Collections.Specialized.NameValueCollection"
000416      CLASS CLASS-CONFIGURATIONSETTINGS AS
000417          "System.Configuration.ConfigurationSettings"
000418      PROPERTY PROP-APPSETTINGS AS "AppSettings"
. . .
019211 WORKING-STORAGE SECTION.
019212 01 MyNewConnectionString  PIC X(100).
019213 01 MyNewAppSettings  OBJECT REFERENCE CLASS-NAMEVALUECOLLECTION.
. . .
019983      SET MyNewAppSettings TO PROP-APPSETTINGS
019984          OF CLASS-CONFIGURATIONSETTINGS
019985      INVOKE MyNewAppSettings "get_Item"
019986          USING BY VALUE "MyCOBOLConnectionString"
019987          RETURNING MyNewConnectionString
019988      SET PROP-ConnectionString OF mySqlConnection
019989          TO MyNewConnectionString
. . .
```

As shown in the preceding VB .NET and COBOL .NET demonstration code, it really is easy to break the old hard-coding habit. Using the XML-based configuration files (App.config, Machine.config, and Web.config for ASP.NET applications), your application configuration options now include a more modern, maintainable technique.

As previously mentioned, the following two sections provide a brief introduction to the "other" configuration namespaces.

Understanding System.Configuration.Assemblies

Generally speaking, this namespace contains classes used for protecting the integrity of your assembly and for assisting in your version configuration needs. Simply, the namespace contains one structure and two enumerations:

- *AssemblyHash* structure

- *AssemblyHashAlgorithm* enumeration

- *AssemblyVersionCompatibility* enumeration

The AssemblyHash structure is basically a "hash" value of the contents found in your assembly manifest (recall the discussion in the section "Extending Assembly Metadata with Custom Attributes" regarding the assembly manifest). The AssemblyHash structure has an *Algorithm* property that uses the Assembly-HashAlgorithm enumeration.

The term "hash algorithm" looks familiar, right? Earlier, when you were using the ILDASM tool, you may have noticed the ".hash algorithm" value listed in the assembly manifest (see Figure 18-9).

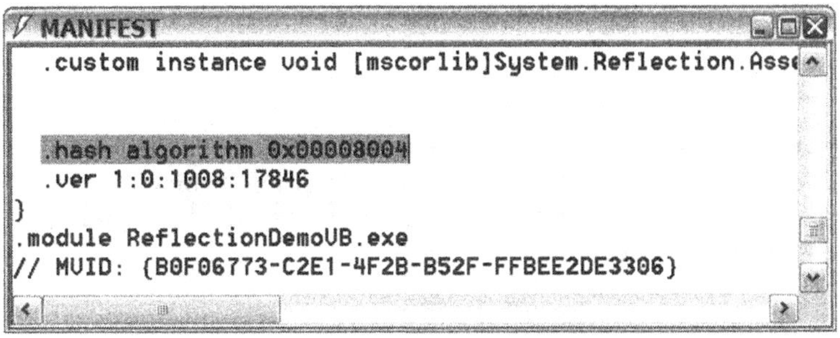

Figure 18-9. The ILDASM tool provides the ability to view the .hash algorithm value while viewing the assembly manifest

You also use the AssemblyHashAlgorithm enumeration to get or set the chosen hash algorithm, which is then used for generating strong names (using the Sn.exe utility).

You can use the AssemblyVersionCompatibility enumeration for versioning configuration. With this class, you can restrict the side-by-side capabilities of your assembly to not be able to execute with other assemblies based on same domain, same machine, or same process specifications.

Understanding System.Configuration.Install

Going down the path in pursuit of this particular configuration namespace, you will open up an entire new world. In short, this namespace provides classes, delegates, and enumerations that enable the building of *custom installers*.

Other than being relevant to software vendors, the *System.Configuration.Install* namespace is also of interest to a special group of developers. This special group of developers includes those who specialize in an area of software development known as *Windows Management Instrumentation* (WMI). The System.Configuration.Install namespace provides support for WMI development.

WMI development (using the .NET managed namespaces *System.Management* and *System.Management.Instrumentation*) involves the creation of system-type software (as opposed to business-type software). You can think of WMI applications as being similar to the set of Windows tools (e.g., the various MMC snap-ins). WMI applications provide interfaces to access management information for the Windows operating system, hardware devices, and applications.

As I mentioned, pursuit of the System.Configuration.Install namespace will lead you down a long path into another development world. This world includes the topic of WMI. As your needs dictate, feel free to continue your journey down that path.

 CROSS-REFERENCE   An entire book has been written on the topic of WMI. Additionally, several Web sites provide information on WMI. Please refer to the "To Learn More" section at the end of this chapter for these related references.

For this chapter's purposes, you will remain on the path of configuration. The next stop for you on the configuration path is code access security.

Configuring for Code Access Security

While I was writing the first half of this book, I debated about the inclusion of a security-related chapter. Was this because I thought the subject too small, too insignificant to write about? Quite the contrary, the subject is massive. It is so large that I generally felt that doing anything less than an entire book on the topic would be a disservice to you, the reader.

Then, it happened. As I was preparing the sample code for Chapter 16 (for the section "Potential Exception Messages"), I ran into "Access denied" errors. You might recall the discussion in that earlier chapter. In order to complete the simple Crystal Reports demonstration, I resorted to a quick-and-dirty solution to get around the "Access denied" issues. This incident planted the seed.

NOTE I did eventually set my Machine.config file back to its more appropriate default setting. Although your approach and needs may vary, I found that locating the Crystal Reports output files to a folder that had the appropriate permissions worked well, thus allowing the Windows operating system's native configurations to provide the appropriate access. So, just for the record, your Machine.config file should have the following attribute/value setting in the *<processModel></processModel>* child element: `userName="machine"`. Using the value of SYSTEM in Chapter 16 was just a temporary workaround.

With that experience, I decided to bite the bullet . . . well, at least part of the bullet. Yes, I decided I would include a discussion about security. However, I decided to limit the security discussion to just code access security. Then, as I have done with other detail- and feature-rich topics, I provide adequate references for your continued research, learning, and extended retraining needs in the "To Learn More" section at the end of the chapter.

CROSS-REFERENCE Several resources exist that focus solely on .NET security. Be sure to refer to the provided references in the "To Learn More" section at the end of this chapter.

Therefore, for clarification, in this section you will learn about the configuration concerns surrounding code access security. The remaining portions of the broader security topic that you may want to learn about (according to your needs, of course) are as follows:

- Cryptography, encryption, and hash algorithms

- Authentication (Passport, Active Directory, and so forth)

- Role access and authorization

- Windows impersonation

- WS-Security (GXA and security for XML Web services)

- Windows access control list (ACL)

- Secure Sockets Layer (SSL) for IIS

- Channel security for .NET Remoting

- The following security-related .NET Framework namespaces:
  *System.Security.Cryptography, System.Security.Cryptography.
  X509Certificates, System.Security.Cryptography.Xml,* and
  System.Security.Principal

The preceding list of security topics is rather lengthy, right? Stop for a moment
and think about the breadth of security topics found on the mainframe. As I recall,
there is the entire topic of the System Authorization Facility (SAF). Then, either
IBM's Resource Access Control Facility (RACF) or Computer Associates' Access
Control Facility product (now known as CA-ACF2) would come into the picture.
This left you with the opportunity to master the ins and outs of user profiles and
assuring proper access to DASD, TSO, CICS, and other resources.

In other words, being able to function in the mainframe security arena was not
a piece of cake. Likewise, functioning in the Windows security arena, even with
.NET, is not a piece of cake. Truly being functional in the security arena—the full
arena—requires continued effort. Nevertheless, the code access security information I discuss in this chapter will prove to be immediately useful and serve as a
foundation for other security topics.

In the next section you will dive into the topic of code access security and its
configuration concerns.

Code Access Security Introduction

The topic of code access security is somewhat new for the Windows development
world. Previous to .NET, the amount of security applied to an application focused
mainly on the question of "who" was attempting to execute a specific program.
With .NET, the interrogation that a specific program is subjected to gets down to a
much more granular level. Yes, the question of "who" is still important. However,
you can now get much deeper with the managed CLR environment.

With code access security, questions such as "Where did the program orig-
inate?" "Who created the program?" and "What is the program trying to do?" are
being asked. The level of control available that is exposed through code access
security gets as low-level as your needs dictate.

To further discuss code access security and the configuration concerns surrounding it, I present the following subtopics:

- Evidence

- Policy hierarchy

- Permissions

- Configuration concerns

Throughout the code access security discussion, the following security-related .NET Framework namespaces will be used:

- *System.Security*

- *System.Security.Permissions*

- *System.Security.Policy*

In the following sections when I discuss each portion of code access security, you will have the opportunity to use an assembly as an example. I created a new sample application, CodeAccessSecurityExampleVB, just for this purpose. As you will notice, this sample application borrows the file I/O logic from the sample application demonstrated in Chapter 10 in the section "Accessing Text Files in .NET the New Way."

Working with the CodeAccessSecurityExampleVB Sample Application

You should take the following information into consideration when you work with the CodeAccessSecurityExampleVB sample application:

- You will use the VS .NET Locals window to view runtime values.

- You will use reflection to examine assembly metadata.

- The "enabled" attribute for the <trace></trace> child element in the Web.config XML configuration file has been set to true.

- You will use the Trace.Write class/method to capture additional runtime values.

- To retrieve runtime values written with Trace.Write class/method, I will refer to the generated "trace" file located at http://localhost/ CodeAccessSecurityExampleVB/trace.axd.

Evidence

The first part of code access security introduces pieces of information referred to as *evidence*. That is, for example, evidence about the assembly (.dll). There are seven types of evidence:

- Site

- Url

- Zone

- ApplicationDirectory

- StrongName

- Publisher

- Hash

You will notice that the first four types of evidence speak to the question of "where" the assembly was loaded or executed from. The StrongName and Publisher types of evidence both speak to the question of "who" created the assembly. The last type of evidence, Hash, is in reference to the assembly contents (recall the earlier discussion about AssemblyHash in the section "Understanding System.Configuration.Assemblies").

Let's take a quick look at the evidence provided by the CodeAccessSecurityExampleVB assembly. To accomplish this, you will use the System.Reflection.Assembly namespace as follows:

```
Private Sub Page_Load(ByVal sender As System.Object, _
ByVal e As System.EventArgs) Handles MyBase.Load
'The following logic added for Code Access Security demonstration
'Use Reflection to retrieve Current Assembly
Dim ExecutingAssembly As System.Reflection.Assembly
ExecutingAssembly = ExecutingAssembly.GetExecutingAssembly()
. . .
End Sub
```

Then, by using a debug breakpoint, pause the execution of the assembly to review the contents during runtime. As shown in Figure 18-10, the VS .NET Locals window enables you to display the assembly. Three items appear in the assemblies evidence array: Zone, Url, and Hash.

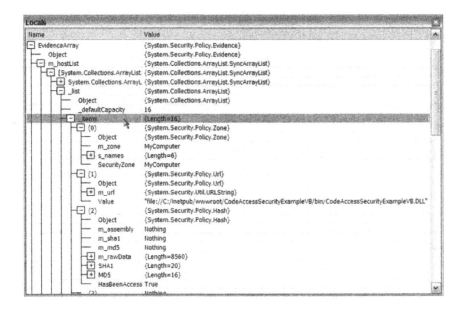

Figure 18-10. The VS .NET Locals window showing runtime information

The Url evidence value is shown (see Figure 18-10) as being file based. The encryption algorithms SHA1 and MD5 are shown as part of the Hash evidence. The Zone evidence shows as MyComputer, which is reasonable given that you are executing the code from localhost. The other possible values for Zone evidence are shown in Figure 18-11.

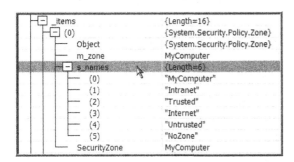

Figure 18-11. The other Zone evidence values from which the MyComputer value was assigned. The display is taken from the VS .NET Locals window during runtime.

You might ask why it is that I do not show the other four types of evidence. Consider the following explanations:

- *Site:* I am reporting on the assembly as if it is a file. Notice that the Url evidence shows the physical location of the assembly. In order to have Site evidence, you would need to modify the demonstration slightly to recognize an actual IIS Web site, in this case localhost.

- *ApplicationDirectory:* This evidence value is not available by querying the assembly. At any rate, in this case the value would be similar to the Url evidence value.

- *StrongName:* You first need to use the Sn.exe command-line tool to have StrongName evidence.

- *Publisher:* Your assembly needs to be signed with an X.509 certificate in order to have Publisher evidence. A handful of useful command-line utilities are related to the use of certificates. In fact, there is even one that you can use to create "practice" certificates. Now, that is really cool! Be sure to look into the following free tools that are bundled with the .NET Framework toolset: Makecert.exe, Cert2spc.exe, Signcode.exe, and Chktrust.exe.

Just for fun (after all, learning is fun, right?), let's explore the System.Security.Policy namespace. After you discover the existence of the *System.Security.Policy.Evidence* class, all that's left to do is add a few additional lines of code to your previous assembly reflection logic. As shown in Listing 18-13, you can access the code access security evidence information programmatically.

Listing 18-13. Using the System.Security.Policy.Evidence Class to Access Evidence Information from the Assembly

```
. . .
'Use Reflection to retrieve Current Assembly
Dim ExecutingAssembly As System.Reflection.Assembly
ExecutingAssembly = ExecutingAssembly.GetExecutingAssembly()

'Retrieve Evidence Array
Dim EvidenceArray As System.Security.Policy.Evidence _
    = ExecutingAssembly.Evidence
Dim i As IEnumerator = EvidenceArray.GetHostEnumerator
While i.MoveNext
    Dim evidence As Object = i.Current
    'Display Types of Evidence members
    Trace.Write("Evidence:   " & evidence.GetType.ToString())
```

```
      'Exclude Hash from "text" based Write, otherwise, display Evidence
      If Trim(evidence.GetType.ToString()) <> "System.Security.Policy.Hash" Then
          Trace.Write("Evidence:  " & evidence.ToString())
      End If
End While
. . .
```

Notice that the code in Listing 18-13 makes use of the Trace.Write class/
method. After you enable the trace feature,[9] you can use the browser to navigate to
the Trace.axd file. As shown in Figure 18-12, the evidence information has been
written to the trace file. It's even in XML format already. Not bad!

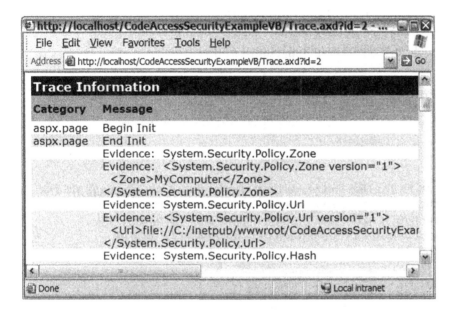

*Figure 18-12. The Trace.axd file showing the evidence information that was written
using the Trace.Write class/method*

All right, now you should be somewhat comfortable with the idea of evidence.
You'll continue drilling down further into code access security. After all, there's a
purpose for assembly modules having (or not having) evidence.

---

9. Use the Web.config XML configuration file. Set the "enabled" attribute to true for the <trace>
   child element.

Policy Hierarchy

All of the concern about evidence is for the purpose of knowing what *input* is going to be presented to any of four policy-level types. The four policy types are User, Machine, Enterprise, and AppDomain. In other words, the *System.Security.PolicyLevelType* enumeration has exactly four members (as just introduced to you). These four System.Security.PolicyLevelType enumeration members are collectively referred to as the *policy hierarchy.*

The User, Machine, and Enterprise PolicyLevelTypes are loaded from XML-based configuration files. You may recall that in the section "Configuration with XML-Based Files" there was a Note that mentioned the existence of a few other XML configuration files.

Consider Figures 18-13 and 18-14. The location and names of the specific config files are shown in each image. Additionally, the config file-to-PolicyLevelType mapping is noted with each image.

Figure 18-13. The User PolicyLevelType is loaded from a Security.config file. The exact location (path) varies depending on the user and version of the .NET Framework/CLR. In this case, the path is noted as C:\Documents and Settings\Administrator\Application Data\Microsoft\CLR Security Config\v1.0.3705.

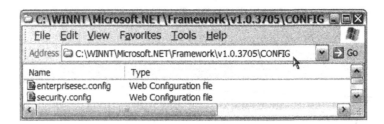

Figure 18-14. The Machine PolicyLevelType is loaded from a Security.config file. The Enterprise PolicyLevelType is loaded from the Enterprisesec.config file. The location is shown in the figure. The exact path varies depending of the version of the .NET Framework/CLR. In this case, the path is noted as C:\WINNT\Microsoft.NET\Framework\v1.0.3705\CONFIG.

You can use either the .NET Framework Configuration tool or the Code Access Security Policy tool when you want to edit the XML config files associated with the User, Machine, and Enterprise PolicyLevelTypes. Optionally, you can edit the XML in Notepad or VS .NET (this is not recommended). You can access the configuration tools as follows:

- *.NET Framework Configuration tool:* Mscorcfg.msc is a MMC snap-in. You can access it by clicking the Start button and selecting Programs ➤ Administrative Tools ➤ Microsoft .NET Framework Configuration.

- *Code Access Security Policy tool:* Access Caspol.exe, a command-line tool, by first navigating to the Visual Studio.NET Command Prompt and then entering the command **caspol** followed by the desired options.

Now you'll examine some programming code to further review these code access security objects. Please take note of the *Label* and *StoreLocation* property of each PolicyLevel. Use the following code snippet to iterate through the *PolicyHierarchy* class:

```
. . .
Dim ii As IEnumerator = System.Security.SecurityManager.PolicyHierarchy
While ii.MoveNext
Dim level As Object = ii.Current
Trace.Write("Policy Level : " & level.label)
Trace.Write("Policy StoreLocation : " & level.StoreLocation)
End While
. . .
```

After you execute the preceding code, again navigate to the Trace.axd file to retrieve the trace output. This .NET trace feature is rather nice. When you think about the effort that would have been needed on the mainframe to display and write out debugging/tracing information to a separate file, it is easy to appreciate this new VS .NET feature. As shown in the following code, the output lines were written out using the Trace.Write class/method (I modified the output slightly with regard to spacing and indentation to improve the page display):

```
Policy Level : Enterprise
   Policy StoreLocation:
   C:\WINNT\Microsoft.NET\Framework\v1.0.3705\config\enterprisesec.config
Policy Level : Machine
   Policy StoreLocation:
   C:\WINNT\Microsoft.NET\Framework\v1.0.3705\config\security.config
```

```
Policy Level : User
  Policy StoreLocation :
  C:\WINNT\Microsoft.NET\Framework\v1.0.3705\config\defaultusersecurity.config
```

Not bad, not bad at all. The security-related objects are certainly accessible. This is one of many things I find amazing about all of this. Right there on your desktop, at work[10] or at home, you're able to get to this type of information. This level of training is easily made available. Compare that with trying to squeeze a mainframe into your living room. Even if you were able to do so, can you imagine how much it would cost for RACF or ACF2 products and training? Let's continue.

I almost forgot about the fourth PolicyLevelType, AppDomain. This PolicyLevelType is handled quite differently. Tucked nicely into the System namespace is the *AppDomain* class.[11] By using the AppDomain class, you can execute its *CreateDomain* and *SetAppDomainPolicy* methods (after you instantiate a new Policy Level object with the *System.Security.Policy.PolicyLevel.CreateAppDomainLevel* method) to establish application-domain security policy.

The AppDomain policy brings exciting opportunities to restrict security policy that may have been granted by any of the higher level User, Machine, or Enterprise policy levels.

Are you ready to drill down a bit further? Good.

In the code snippet shown earlier, you took at look at the Label and StoreLocation property policy levels stored in the PolicyHierarchy class. As it turns out, each policy level contains a few other properties—in fact, they are very important properties. You can use the following property objects to examine each policy level further:

- *System.Security.Policy.PolicyLevel.NamedPermissionSets*

- *System.Security.Policy.PolicyLevel.RootCodeGroup*

In the following sections, you will take a closer look these important policy level properties.

---

10. This is assuming that your place of employment has not locked down or restricted some of these capabilities. Either way, if you consider the practical nature of acquiring your own personal computer, nothing will hold you back.

11. Of course, we will not ask why Microsoft did not put this class into one of the Security namespaces.

NOTE There is one other important policy level property:
System.Security.Policy.PolicyLevel.FullTrustAssemblies. Discussion of
this other policy level property is beyond the scope of this book.

System.Security.Policy.PolicyLevel.NamedPermissionSets

I start this section with a code snippet. I follow Listing 18-14 with a brief discussion, after you have had a chance to examine the code and its resulting output.

Listing 18-14. Reviewing the NamedPermissionSets Property

```
. . .
Dim iii As IEnumerator = System.Security.SecurityManager.PolicyHierarchy()
While iii.MoveNext()
    Dim level As System.Security.Policy.PolicyLevel = _
    CType(iii.Current, System.Security.Policy.PolicyLevel)
    Trace.Write("Policy Level: " & level.Label)
    Dim iiii As IEnumerator = level.NamedPermissionSets.GetEnumerator()
        While iiii.MoveNext()
            Dim NamedPermissionSet As System.Security.NamedPermissionSet = _
            CType(iiii.Current, System.Security.NamedPermissionSet)
            Trace.Write("  Permission set: " & NamedPermissionSet.Name)
        End While
End While
. . .
```

After you run the code in Listing 18-14, you can view the appropriate output
using the Trace.axd file (as shown in Figure 18-15).

Specific NamedPermissionSets (i.e., FullTrust, SkipVerification, Execution,
Nothing, LocalIntranet, Internet, and Everything) are *granted* by the respective
policy levels (User, Machine, Enterprise, and AppDomain) after any available
evidence is presented. Depending on any "intersections" of granted
NamedPermissionSets, a resulting permission is actually granted. In other words,
if each policy level provides a SkipVerification NamedPermissionSets after the evidence is reviewed, then the SkipVerification NamedPermissionSet is considered to
have met the intersection requirement.

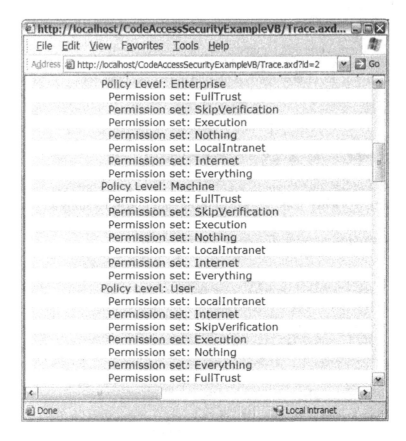

Figure 18-15. The Trace.axd file showing the available NamedPermissionSets per policy level

To drill down even further, you will use the .NET Framework Configuration tool. As previously mentioned, this tool is an MMC snap-in (using Mscorcfg.msc). You can access this tool by clicking the Start button and selecting Programs ➤ Administrative Tools ➤ Microsoft .NET Framework Configuration.

As shown in Figure 18-16, you can use the .NET Framework Configuration tool to drill down just about as far as your needs and interest can take you.

To give you a more complete idea as to what types of permissions are contained inside a NamedPermissionSet, take a look at the display shown in Figure 18-17. As you can see, an extremely granular level of control is exposed using either the .NET Framework Configuration tool or programming code. Isn't code access security intriguing?

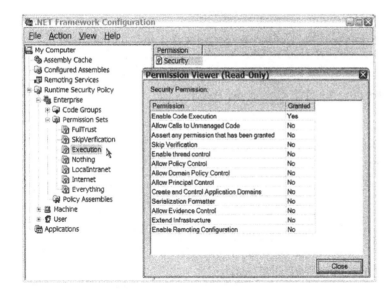

Figure 18-16. Using the .NET Framework Configuration tool to view the contents of the Execution permission set (within the Enterprise policy level). You can enable the Permission Viewer by double-clicking the Permission value in the right pane.

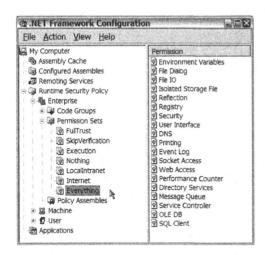

Figure 18-17. Using the .NET Framework Configuration tool to view the contents of the Everything permission set (within the Enterprise policy level)

Now, what does each policy level use when reviewing the evidence to determine which NamedPermissionSets to grant? That takes you to the other important policy level property: *RootCodeGroup*.

System.Security.Policy.PolicyLevel.RootCodeGroup

As I did in the previous section, I start this section with a code listing (see
Listing 18-15) and output display. Are you ready? Great! Here you go.

Listing 18-15. Retrieving the Code Groups per Policy Level

```
. . .
Dim iiiii As IEnumerator = System.Security.SecurityManager.PolicyHierarchy()
While iiiii.MoveNext()
    Dim level As System.Security.Policy.PolicyLevel = _
    CType(iiiii.Current, System.Security.Policy.PolicyLevel)
    Trace.Write("Policy Level: " & level.Label)
    Dim CodeGroup As System.Security.Policy.CodeGroup = level.RootCodeGroup
    Trace.Write("   Root CodeGroup MembershipCondition: " & _
    CodeGroup.MembershipCondition.ToString())
End While
. . .
```

After you execute the code in Listing 18-15, a display of output similar to the
following is retrieved:

```
Policy Level: Enterprise
    Root CodeGroup MembershipCondition: All code
 Policy Level: Machine
    Root CodeGroup MembershipCondition: All code
 Policy Level: User
    Root CodeGroup MembershipCondition: All code
```

Not terribly exciting, huh? I was tempted to modify the code to drill down into
each RootCodeGroup to review any children code groups. However, I figured you
might want to do that as part of a practice exercise. Instead, you will use the .NET
Framework Configuration tool again. Using this tool, you will be able to continue
your inquiry into the policy level code group property.

You can use the .NET Framework Configuration tool to view and/or modify
runtime security attributes. Additionally, using this tool, you can easily add
custom code groups. As shown in Figure 18-18, the Enterprise and User policy
levels do not have any default child code groups. On the other hand, as shown, the
Machine policy level has several default child code groups.

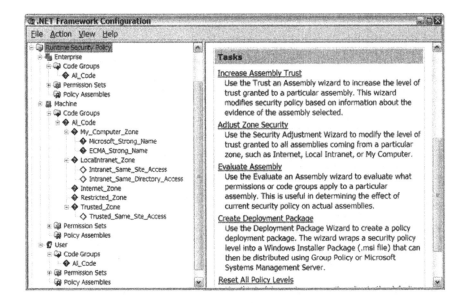

Figure 18-18. Using the .NET Framework Configuration tool to view the Enterprise policy level code group information

Now you'll explore one of the existing code groups. For demonstration purposes, you'll take a closer look at the Microsoft_Strong_Name child code group. It exists in the Machine policy level. As shown in Figure 18-19, the right pane of the .NET Framework Configuration tool window exposes an Edit Code Group Properties option. (Alternately, you can right-click a specific code group in the left pane and choose Properties.)

After you open the Properties window for a code group, you will notice three tabs: General, Membership Condition, and Permission Set. As shown in Figure 18-20, the General tab contains basic identifying information and two important property settings near the bottom of the page.

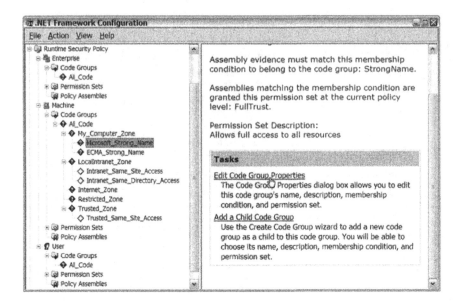

Figure 18-19. Preparing to view the properties of the Microsoft_Strong_Name child Code group in the Machine policy level

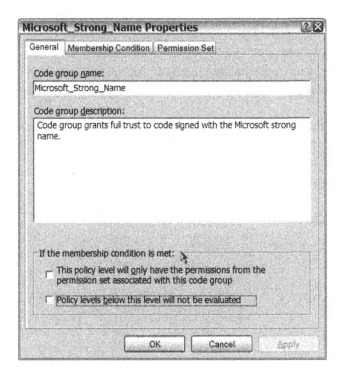

Figure 18-20. The General tab on the code group Properties window

The next tab, Membership Condition, really helps provide you with a better understanding of the code group and its relationship to evidence. Take a quick look at Figure 18-21. You will notice that the current Membership Condition setting for the Microsoft_Strong_Name child code group is Strong Name.

Figure 18-21. The current Membership Condition setting for the Microsoft_Strong_Name child code group

If you click the drop-down arrow where Strong Name is currently displayed, you see the other possible Membership Condition settings (see Figure 18-22). If I did not know better, I would swear that the list of Membership Condition choices looked like the same list of possible evidence types. In all seriousness, they are one and the same.

Figure 18-22. The list of Membership Condition choices for a code group

One more tab to go. Take a look at the Permission Set tab. As shown in Figure 18-23, the default Permission Set setting is FullTrust for this particular code group.

As you would expect, you can click the drop-down arrow to view the expected range of Permission Set choices (see Figure 18-24).

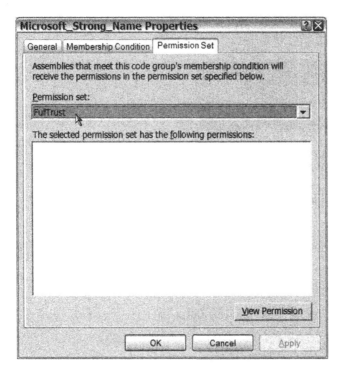

Figure 18-23. The default Permission Set setting for the Microsoft_Strong_Name child code group

---

TIP   It would be wise to click Cancel to exit the code group Properties page. This way, any changes you made inadvertently will not be saved.

Now do you have a better idea of how these pieces tie together? You have evidence, policy levels, permission sets, and code groups all working in concert with each other. Assembly evidence is presented to the policy hierarchy. The code groups that are in each policy level perform a test based on the membership conditions. Permission sets are selected from each code group that had its memberships conditions met. The group of permissions granted from all of the code groups and from all of the policy levels is then resolved and matched.

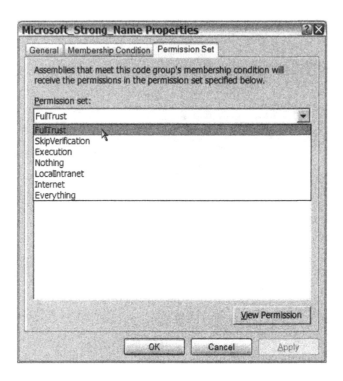

Figure 18-24. The Permission Set choices as shown in the code group Properties page

The Great Resolve (Well, Sort Of)

I could not resist the temptation to run my evidence through the available *System.Security.SecurityManager.ResolvePolicy* method to see how many and which permission sets I would end up with after going through the policy hierarchy, code groups, and so forth. Listing 18-16 shows the additional code that I added to the code access security sample application.

Listing 18-16. Executing the System.Security.SecurityManager.ResolvePolicy Method

```
. . .
Dim PermissionAgg As System.Security.PermissionSet = _
System.Security.SecurityManager.ResolvePolicy(EvidenceArray)
Trace.Write("Permission Aggregate : " & PermissionAgg.ToString)
. . .
```

After running the code in Listing 18-16, I captured the trace output. As you can see in Listing 18-17, I have two permission sets granted: *UrlIdentityPermission* and *ZoneIdentityPermission*.

Listing 18-17. The Permission Aggregate Result

```
Permission Aggregate :
<PermissionSet class="System.Security.PermissionSet"
            version="1"  Unrestricted="true">

<IPermission class="System.Security.Permissions.UrlIdentityPermission,
mscorlib, Version=1.0.3300.0, Culture=neutral, PublicKeyToken=b77a5c561934e089"
version="1"Url="file://C:/inetpub/wwwroot/CodeAccessSecurityExampleVB/bin/
CodeAccessSecurityExampleVB.DLL"/ />
<IPermission class="System.Security.Permissions.ZoneIdentityPermission,
mscorlib, Version=1.0.3300.0, Culture=neutral, PublicKeyToken=b77a5c561934e089"
version="1" Zone="MyComputer"/>

</PermissionSet>
```

As you can see, the permission sets, as determined from the evidence that was presented, were rather limited. Simply, there were just two "identity"-type permissions. Certainly, it was not much. Nevertheless, that is what the policy Resolve determined based on the associated evidence of the sample code assembly.

That concludes my high-level presentation of code access security. However, you are not done with code access security per se. In the next section you will take a brief look at the "programmatic" configuration options available to you.

Programmatic Configuration Options for Code Access Security

In the previous section you went through several code access security steps. If you had wanted to influence the outcome, you could have added/changed/removed any of the evidence information. Additionally, as previously discussed, you could manipulate the policy levels or any of the policy level properties using either the command-line tools introduced to you or the .NET Framework Configuration tool.

TIP There is a toolset available called the .NET Framework Wizards. When possible, consider looking into the features offered by this toolset. Generally, it provides a shortcut to some of the options available in the .NET Framework Configuration tool. To access this other .NET tool, simply click the Start button and select Programs ➤ Administrative Tools ➤ Microsoft .NET Framework Wizards.

As it turns out, yet another option is available to you. In this section you will focus mainly on using programming code to change the default results that you may experience with code access security.

NOTE To help stage the following demonstration, I made an adjustment to the normal ACL setting using a native configuration for the Windows operating system. The ACL setting was made to "share" the targeted folder to allow file I/O.

Listing 18-18 demonstrates a general code-based approach to configuring code access security. This type of programmatic code access security development is referred to as *imperative*. The *declarative* approach involves the use of attributes.

Listing 18-18. The Imperative Approach to Programmatically Configuring Code Access Security

```
. . .
'Demo code for Denying permissions
'****************************
Dim sPath As String = Server.MapPath("myTextFile.txt")
Dim fsPermission1 As FileIOPermission = _
New FileIOPermission(FileIOPermissionAccess.AllAccess, sPath)
fsPermission1.Deny()
. . .
```

Please review the code in Listing 18-18. You will notice that there is an explicit request for the *FileIOPermission* to be set to *Denied*. Additionally, notice the use of the Try/Catch logic for exception handling. The following trace message captured in the Trace.axd file indicating that the attempted access was denied was produced to show the success of the imperative code approach:

```
An Error Msg: Request for the permission of type
System.Security.Permissions.FileIOPermission, mscorlib, Version=1.0.3300.0,
Culture=neutral, PublicKeyToken=b77a5c561934e089 failed.
```

This underscores an important point. Using a programmatic approach (imperative or declarative), you can "take away" privileges/permissions that you may have had. In the case of the sample application, the targeted folder was given access using a normal Windows operating system native configuration. Yet, you were able to "deny" the permissions during runtime using the code access security constructs.

As your needs and interest lead you, feel free to experiment with the other programmatic methods and techniques such as demand and assert. Keep in mind that you can code similar logic for other permission sets as well.

You will find that there is much more to learn. Lots more fun waiting to be had. The references included at the end of this chapter in the "To Learn More" section should prove helpful as you continue this exploration. Although brief, this introduction should get you started in the right direction.

Configuring CAS with an XML Child Element

One option for configuring your environment to grant your assemblies permissions other than what their evidence would have resolved to is to use the *<trust>* XML element. You can use the <trust> XML child element in either the Web.config or Machine.config file. Your ASP.NET applications will feel the impact of this type of code access security configuration. As shown in the following code snippet, the syntax is rather simple:

```
. . .
  <system.web>
. . .
      <trust level="Full | High | Low | None" originUrl="url" />
. . .
  </system.web>
. . .
```

When set appropriately, the <trust> XML element will enable a "mapping" to occur to the appropriate security "trust" configuration file. Though a <trust> setting of Full will not map to a file at all, the other values are set according the *<securityPolicy>* attribute settings. In other words, these mappings are configurable via the <securityPolicy> XML child element. You will find the

<securityPolicy> element in the Machine.config file. It is recognizable as such in the following code snippet:

```
<securityPolicy>
    <trustLevel name="Full" policyFile="internal"/>
    <trustLevel name="High" policyFile="web_hightrust.config"/>
    <trustLevel name="Low" policyFile="web_lowtrust.config"/>
    <trustLevel name="None" policyFile="web_notrust.config"/>
</securityPolicy>
```

These <trust> configuration files are located in the following relative path:

```
C:\WINNT\Microsoft.NET\Framework\v1.0.3705\CONFIG.
```

As you have seen in this brief discussion, the XML configuration file approach even has applicability to the topic of configuring code access security.

Summary

This chapter's goals were as follows:

- To discuss the use of Web page and user control directives

- To demonstrate the use of custom attributes and reflection

- To explain the role of XML-based files configuration files

- To understand the .NET Framework configuration namespaces

- To explore the configuration needed for code access security

Yes, you have certainly covered a healthy amount of ground in this chapter. As you can see, the topic of configuration is broad. The chapter started by focusing on the ASP.NET page and user controls. From there you explored custom attributes, reflection, and XML-based configuration files. The later sections of this chapter's journey focused on the configuration namespaces and then code access security.

In the next chapter you will explore the topic of Enterprise Services (COM+) components.

To Learn More

The following are some suggested supplemental references to further your retraining effort.

Books

.NET Security, by Jason Bock, Pete Stromquist, Tom Fischer, and Nathan Smith (Apress, 2002):
> http://www.apress.com/book/bookDisplay.html?bID=104.

.NET System Management Services, by Alexander Golomshtok (Apress, 2003):
> http://www.apress.com/book/bookDisplay.html?bID=120.

Magazines

.NET Magazine:
> http://www.fawcette.com/dotnetmag/

MSDN Magazine:
> http://msdn.microsoft.com/msdnmag/

Visual Studio Magazine:
> http://www.fawcette.com/vsm/

Windows Developer Magazine:
> http://www.wd-mag.com/

XML & Web Services Magazine:
> http://www.fawcette.com/xmlmag/

Web Sites

.NET Architecture Center:
> http://msdn.microsoft.com/architecture/

.NET Enterprise Servers Online Books:
> http://msdn.microsoft.com/library/default.asp?url=/servers/books/
> default.asp

ASP.NET Web Application Security:
> http://msdn.microsoft.com/library/en-us/cpguide/html/
> cpconaspnetwebapplicationsecurity.asp

Configuration Files:
> http://msdn.microsoft.com/library/en-us/cpguide/html/
> cpconconfigurationfiles.asp

Creating Windows Applications:

http://msdn.microsoft.com/library/en-us/vbcon/html/
vboriCreatingStandaloneAppsVB.asp

DotNeteXtreme.com (.NET tips and articles):

http://www.dotnetextreme.com/default.asp

EggHeadCafe.com Tips and Tricks (.NET tips and articles):

http://www.eggheadcafe.com/tipstricks.asp

GotDotNet:

http://www.gotdotnet.com/

GotDotNet: Backwards Breaking Changes from Version 1.0 to 1.1:

http://www.gotdotnet.com/team/changeinfo/Backwards1.0to1.1/
default.aspx#00000106

Introduction to ASP.NET:

http://msdn.microsoft.com/library/en-us/cpguide/html/
cpconintroductiontoasp.asp

Microsoft ASP.NET Home Page:

http://www.asp.net/

Microsoft Community (discussion groups, e-newsletters, and so forth):

http://communities2.microsoft.com/

Microsoft Patterns & Practices:

http://msdn.microsoft.com/practices/

Microsoft's Search the Knowledge Base Web Site:

http://support.microsoft.com/default.aspx?scid=FH;EN-US;KBHOWTO

Microsoft TechNet How-To Index:

http://www.microsoft.com/technet/treeview/default.asp?url=/technet/
itsolutions/howto

MSDN:

http://msdn.microsoft.com

Windows .NET Server 2003:

http://msdn.microsoft.com/library/default.asp?url=/nhp/
default.asp?contentid=28001691

XML Web Services Developer Center Home:

http://msdn.microsoft.com/webservices/

CHAPTER 19

Using Enterprise
Services (COM+)

An Introduction to COM+
and Serviced Components

In this chapter

- Creating a .NET class library (.dll)

- Working with serviced components

- Reviewing the System.EnterpriseServices namespace

- Introducing the Component Services MMC snap-in

MICROSOFT HAS ANNOUNCED that their Windows XP and upcoming Windows .NET
Server products will include COM+ version 1.5. This new version of COM+ has
apparently been renamed to *Microsoft Windows Enterprise Services*. And the programming community shouts:

"Finally, Microsoft got it right!"

Given the impressive offering of *services* exposed by COM+, the new, more
encompassing name is much more appropriate. The name "Enterprise Services" is
certainly a big step for this product. If you want to have some fun, casually remind
a veteran Windows and Web developer that this product's pre-COM+ legacy name
was Microsoft Transaction Server (MTS). On the other hand, maybe you should
avoid ever mentioning this fact. The MTS and COM+ product names have always
been a sore spot with Windows and Web developers.

This chapter presents an opportunity to explore the combined use of
Enterprise Services (COM+) and .NET. The managed components that you
will integrate into COM+[1] are referred to as *serviced components*. In this

---

1. I will use the COM+ product name throughout this chapter. At some point in the future, as
   the Enterprise Services product name becomes more common, I expect that others and I will
   likely discontinue using the legacy name of COM+.

chapter, you will create serviced components and you will be further introduced
to COM+.

For perspective, before you get into programming code, you will look at the
big-picture view of Enterprise Services (COM+). From there, you will take your first
step toward creating serviced components by creating a class library (.dll) that
uses the System.EnterpriseServices namespace. After you accomplish that, you
will learn about the process of installing your serviced component into COM+.
Lastly, you will create a client to consume the class library (.dll) in its new serviced
component state.

What Is COM+?

The COM+ Microsoft product is a sophisticated runtime environment built to
provide application infrastructure support. The support found in COM+ generally
targets medium-to-large enterprise-level applications. Microsoft identified the
most complex type of service routines that developers constantly needed to
"figure out" and prepackaged a robust, almost plug-and-play reusable product.
The "plumbing" that an n-tier or 3-tier application would typically require to complete its support for middle-layer components comes with COM+ *out of the box*.

Microsoft provides the Component Services console (an MMC snap-in) to
manage COM+. Click the Start button and select Programs ➤ Administrative Tools
➤ Component Services, as shown in Figure 19-1.

Figure 19-1. Launching the Component Services console

Once you have launched the Component Services console, you will see an
MMC snap-in window. A default tree structure view is available on the left pane.
You can drill down to the preinstalled system-level COM+ applications by
double-clicking the Computers ➤ My Computer ➤ COM+ Applications nodes
(see Figure 19-2).

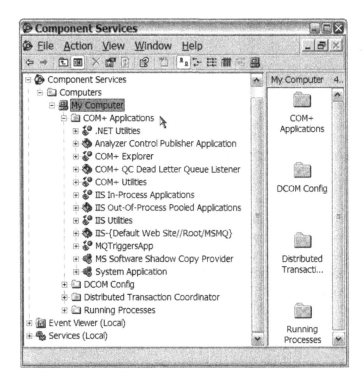

Figure 19-2. The Component Services console exposes the COM+ Applications node.

 CAUTION   Feel free to explore a bit. But do be careful. Keep in mind that these preinstalled COM+ applications support system-level services. Whatever you do, *do not delete or modify* either of these preinstalled COM+ applications.

Drill down into several of the nodes to discover the *child nodes*. You will notice that each COM+ application has a Components node (the icon that looks like a folder). As shown in Figure 19-3, the preinstalled COM+ application named System Application has five components.

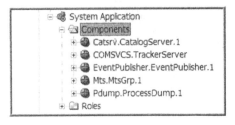

Figure 19-3. The System Application COM+ application as seen in the Component Services console

While you are exploring the System Application COM+ application, notice in the right pane (after you click the Components icon) those components displayed as round ball-like structures with a plus sign (+) on them (see Figure 19-4). In fact, one of these components may already be "spinning." These "balls" represent installed components. A spinning ball indicates that the component and the client process that is using the component are active.

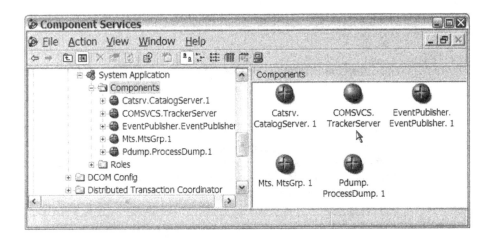

Figure 19-4. The Component Services console window shows the installed components in the right pane.

You can change the view shown in the right pane of the Component Services console window to see a varying level of detail. You can do this by selecting the View option from the toolbar (optionally, you can use the View icons, as shown in Figure 19-5).

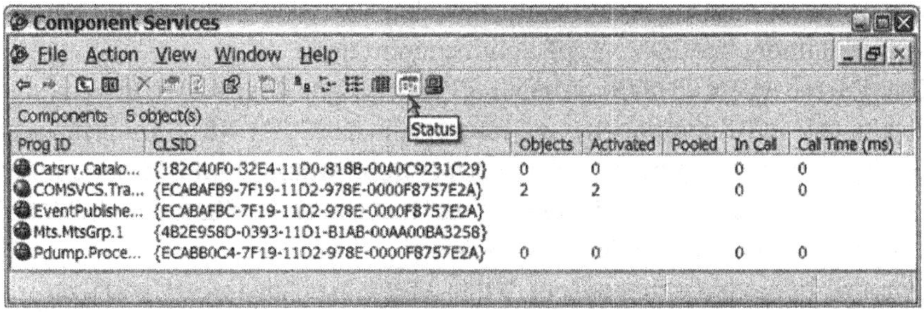

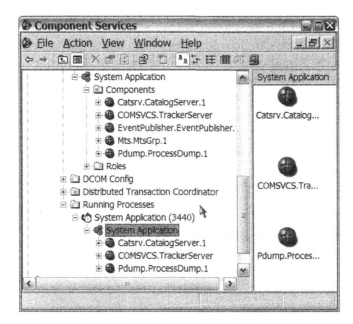

Figure 19-5. The Component Services console window with the Show/Hide Console Tree option enabled. You can use the Show/Hide Console Tree icon, located fourth from the left on the toolbar, to toggle this option. The Status view icon has been clicked to show the Status view of the components.

The last thing that I would like to point out in the Component Services console window is the Running Processes node.[2] If you look in the left pane, you will notice a folder icon labeled Running Processes. After you expand this node, you will see any COM+ applications that are actively running. As shown in Figure 19-6, at a minimum you will typically see the preinstalled System Application COM+ application.

Figure 19-6. The Running Processes node in the Component Services console window

---

2. The COM+ Running Processes folder is available on Windows XP and newer operating systems that have Enterprise Services (COM+ 1.5).

Notice the relationship between the Running Processes node and the other nodes shown under the COM+ application's parent node.

Can you see where all of this is heading? That is right. Your goal in this chapter will be to create .NET components in Visual Studio .NET (VS .NET). Then you will install those components into COM+ as COM+ applications. Your built assembly (.dll) will be represented by one of these "balls" that you will see in your own COM+ application's Components folder. How exciting!

For now, let's explore the topic of COM+ a bit more. Don't worry, you'll return to the Component Services console later.

COM+ Is Not Just for Transactions

On the mainframe when I developed COBOL/CICS programs, I recall using the term "transaction" on a daily basis. "Transaction" was ingrained into every aspect of the COBOL/CICS programming environment. Some called CICS a Transaction Processor (TP). As you know, the phrase "to create a CICS program" is synonymous with the phrase "to create a CICS transaction." During your mainframe CICS development, you depended on the simple mechanics of the transaction.

Mainframe CICS developers generally understood that CICS features such as Dynamic Transaction Backout (DTB), Emergency Restart, and the Journal/Log brought the real benefits of the CICS transaction. On the mainframe, it was generally understood that the CICS task, by default, represented a logical unit of work (LUW) and that a CICS SYNCPOINT command could limit the LUW. The point being that these CICS technologies supported the ability to do a rollback/backout if and when it was ever needed. Yes, CICS transactions were great.

Now, I ask you, is that *all* that CICS was capable of—just supporting transactions? No, of course not. As you know, CICS was capable of much more. Likewise, COM+ (Enterprise Services) provides transactional support, and COM+ is capable of much, much more.

 CROSS-REFERENCE   In Chapter 3, you were introduced to COM+. An abbreviated list of the "services" was presented at that time.

The following represents a more complete list[3] of COM+ services:

- Transactional support

- COM Transaction Integrator (COMTI)

- Compensating Resource Manager (CRM)

- Distributed Transaction Coordinator (DTC)

- Just-in-Time (JIT) Activation

- Loosely coupled events (LCE)

- Object constructor strings

- Object Pooling

- Queued Components

- Role-based security

- Shared Property Manager

- Synchronization (activity)

- Application Pooling

- Application recycling

- Applications running as NT services

- Instrumentation

- Low-Memory Activation Gates

---

3. This list was published October 2002 by the COM+ documentation team as part of the platform SDK (see http://msdn.microsoft.com/library/en-us/cossdk/htm/ services_toplevel_8uyb.asp and http://msdn.microsoft.com/library/default.asp?url=/ library/en-us/cossdk/htm/whatsnewcomplus_350z.asp).

- Partitions

- Resource Dispenser

- Services without components

- SOAP service

Granted, the transactional support of COM+ is almost all that you ever hear about. However, as you can see, transactional support is just one among many "services" offered by COM+ (hence the name "Enterprise Services").

A full discussion of each COM+ service is beyond the scope of this book. I briefly introduce two of them in section "Using Your Serviced Component." Otherwise, please use the references provided at the end of this chapter in the "To Learn More" section to assist your continued exploration into COM+ (Enterprise Services).

Database-Level Transactional Support

As you experienced on the mainframe, the transactional support provided by CICS was "separate" from the transactional support provided by DB2 DBMS technologies. Yes, it was possible to combine them to work together in one application. Yet, you understood that the CICS transactional support[4] was at the program/task level, whereas the DBMS transactional support was at the database query level.

The same contrast exists in the Windows environment when you use a DBMS such as SQL Server and a product such as COM+ (Enterprise Services). As part of your application design, choose wisely between the two levels of transactional support. If your application requires the benefits of transactional support, please be reminded that you have a choice between component level and database level.

A general approach might be to use database-level transactional support if your database updates are limited to one server, one database, and so on. As your application's level of complexity increases (e.g., multiple databases, disparate data stores, and so forth), it becomes more appropriate to look toward COM+ for transactional support.

You may even consider adding other COM+ services such as the Distributed Transaction Coordinator (DTC) and Compensating Resource Manager (CRM). The transactional support provided by COM+ greatly exceeds what is available at the database level.

---

4. When you work with transactions on the Windows platform, the ACID test applies just as it did on the mainframe/CICS platform. (As you may recall, ACID stands for *a*tomicity, *c*onsistency, *i*solation, and *d*urability.)

You now have a high-level understanding of what COM+ is. Additionally, you know how to access the Component Services console, which you can use to configure and manage COM+. Are you ready to find out how to create a .NET-managed component that you can use to access COM+ services? Good! Let's now turn to the topic of creating serviced components.

Creating a Serviced Component

In short, a serviced component is a component that inherits the class *System.EnterpriseServices.ServicedComponent*. Could it be *that* simple? That's almost the case. Let's dive quickly into demonstration mode to see just how you create a serviced component.

The sample applications you will create for this purpose involve selecting the Class Library project template. As shown in Figure 19-7, you will name the first sample application MyFirstClassLibraryCobol. You will create a Visual Basic .NET (VB .NET) versioned sample application as well. After you code and build these applications, you will end up with your very own .dll files[5] (class libraries).

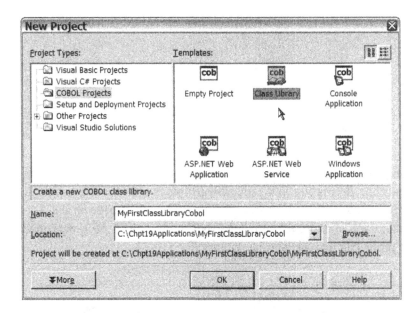

Figure 19-7. The VS .NET New Project window with the Class Library project template selected

The next thing you need to do is set a reference to the System.EnterpriseServices assembly. As you know, you do this by right-clicking the References node in

---

5. The .dll file was originally referred to as a *dynamic link library.*

the VS .NET IDE Solution Explorer window. Figure 19-8 shows the appropriate component selection that you are targeting.

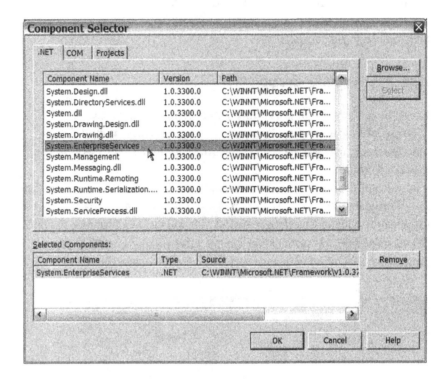

Figure 19-8. Adding a reference for System.EnterpriseServices with the VS .NET IDE Component Selector window

Following this reference-adding task, you have a few remaining steps to go: adding actual code, decorating your code with attributes, and creating a strong name key. You will notice that I have included the COBOL .NET code for the MyFirstClassLibraryCobol project and the VB .NET code for a VB .NET–versioned class library project named MyFirstClassLibraryVB.

NOTE   You must set a reference for System.EnterpriseServices in the VB .NET–versioned sample application.

Sample Class Library Code Using COBOL .NET

The code you use for the sample application MyFirstClassLibraryCobol appears in
Listing 19-1. You will notice the System.EnterpriseServices.ServicedComponent
class is inherited. Additionally, you will notice the use of a
System.EnterpriseServices attribute class.

Listing 19-1. The MyFirstClassLibraryCobol Sample Code

```
000010 IDENTIFICATION  DIVISION.
000020 CLASS-ID. MyFirstClass AS "MyFirstClassLibraryCobol.MyFirstClass"
000021         INHERITS CLASS-ServicedComponent.
000030 ENVIRONMENT DIVISION.
000040 CONFIGURATION SECTION.
000051 SPECIAL-NAMES.
000052     CUSTOM-ATTRIBUTE AutoCompleteAttribute
000053                 CLASS CLASS-AutoCompleteAttribute
000054
000060 REPOSITORY.
000070     CLASS CLASS-AutoCompleteAttribute
000071         AS "System.EnterpriseServices.AutoCompleteAttribute"
000073     CLASS CLASS-STRING AS "System.String"
000075     CLASS CLASS-ARGUMENTEXCEPTION AS "System.ArgumentException"
000076     CLASS CLASS-ServicedComponent
000077         AS "System.EnterpriseServices.ServicedComponent"
000078     CLASS CLASS-OBJECT AS "System.Object"
000079
000080 STATIC.
000090 DATA DIVISION.
000100 WORKING-STORAGE SECTION.
000110 PROCEDURE DIVISION.
000120
000130 END STATIC.
000140
000150 OBJECT.
000160 DATA DIVISION.
000170 WORKING-STORAGE SECTION.
000180 PROCEDURE DIVISION.
000190
000200 METHOD-ID. DOTRANSACTION AS "DoTransaction"
000201         CUSTOM-ATTRIBUTE IS AutoCompleteAttribute.
000202
```

```
000210 DATA DIVISION.
000220 WORKING-STORAGE SECTION.
000221   01 MyException   OBJECT REFERENCE CLASS-ARGUMENTEXCEPTION.
000222   01 MyString   PIC X(10).
000223 LINKAGE SECTION.
000224   01 InputString   OBJECT REFERENCE CLASS-STRING.
000225   01 ReturnString   OBJECT REFERENCE CLASS-STRING.
000230 PROCEDURE DIVISION USING BY VALUE InputString RETURNING ReturnString
000231     RAISING CLASS-ARGUMENTEXCEPTION.
000240*    The Input Parm is tested to be non-blank for DEMO purposes
000241     SET MyString TO InputString
000242     IF MyString NOT > SPACE
000243        INVOKE CLASS-ARGUMENTEXCEPTION "NEW"
000244        USING BY VALUE "Invalid Input Parameter"
000245        RETURNING MyException
000246        EXIT METHOD RAISING MyException
000247     END-IF
000248     SET ReturnString TO "Hello World with Enterprise Services".
000249
000250 END METHOD DOTRANSACTION.
000260
000270 END OBJECT.
000280 END CLASS MyFirstClass.
```

Please take a moment to review Listing 19-1. You will notice that one method has been included. This method, *DoTransaction*, makes use of the *AutoComplete-Attribute* class from the System.EnterpriseServices namespace. Notice that I did not use an additional attribute at the class level. I will explain this later. As you can gather, this is a very basic example of how to create a code-driven transaction.

 TIP   The *System.ArgumentException* class is included in Listing 19-1 to provide an example of .NET-style exception handling. Many other types (other than this one, which handles argument exceptions) of specific exceptions are available. The Microsoft documentation provides further details on this topic.

Now you'll quickly review the VB .NET sample code that basically accomplishes the same task.

Sample Class Library Code Using VB .NET

The sample code in Listing 19-2 was taken from the MyFirstClassLibraryVB sample application. Naturally, this class library code will inherit from the System.EnterpriseServices.ServicedComponent class. Please recall that this is one of the few definite requirements needed to convert a normal class library into a serviced component. Again, you will create a rather basic transaction using the specific function. Please take a moment to review the code in Listing 19-2.

Listing 19-2. Code from the MyFirstClassLibraryVB Sample Project

```
Imports System.EnterpriseServices
<TransactionAttribute(TransactionOption.Required)> _
 Public Class MyFirstClassLibraryVB
     Inherits System.EnterpriseServices.ServicedComponent
     Public Sub New()
         MyBase.New()
      End Sub
     <AutoComplete()> Public Function DoTransaction() _
      As String
            Return "Hello World with Enterprise Services :-)"
      End Function
End Class
```

The main difference between the code in Listing 19-2 and the COBOL .NET sample application is the use of a System.EnterpriseServices attribute at the class level. The class-level attribute is *TransactionAttribute*. In the COBOL .NET code, this attribute was omitted intentionally (but it could have been included). This attribute is used to set the *TransactionOption.Required* property. In this case, you are setting it in code. In the case of the COBOL .NET sample, you set this same property manually.

Whether you set your component transaction support using the Transaction-Attribute attribute or using the manual approach (via the Component Services MMC snap-in), you actually have five choices. For the purposes of this discussion, assume that you are using the TransactionAttribute approach. Your particular application needs will dictate which *TransactionOption* enumeration you use for the TransactionAttribute setting. I chose *TransactionOption.Required* simply for demonstration purposes.

The complete list of TransactionOption choices are as follows:

- *TransactionOption.Disabled*

- *TransactionOption.NotSupported*

- *TransactionOption.Supported*

- *TransactionOption.RequiresNew*

- *TransactionOption.Required*

Let's briefly take a look at the impact of choosing one enumeration over another. To begin with, you might wonder what the difference is between setting your TransactionAttribute with TransactionOption.Disabled and setting it with TransactionOption.NotSupported. After all, the names do imply a similar result—the *potential* to render your component as *nontransactional*. Actually, choosing NotSupported does result in having a nontransactional component. On the other hand, the choice of Disabled basically implies that you do not want your component to receive the automatic transaction management services offered by COM+.

NOTE   You might use the Disabled option if for some strange reason you want to manually control the transaction management of your component. You should be aware that if you happen to use the Regsvcs.exe tool to introduce your serviced component into COM+, the TransactionOption will default to TransactionOption.Disabled.

The remaining three TransactionOption enumeration choices will likely be of more use to you. Figuring out which one to choose is rather straightforward. Say that your component participates in a multicomponent application design. In this multicomponent design, say that you have component X that is called by a client application and initiates the logical unit of work. Then, after component X, the parent, has done some work, you may have a child component Y that gets called to do work. Perhaps a third component Z, another child, gets called to complete the logical unit of work and complete the transaction.

It's easy to imagine that you might want component X to always be created in a new transaction. This would be a chance to set your TransactionAttribute to use TransactionOption.RequiresNew. Now, let's change the scenario to have the parent component needing to participate in a transaction and needing to have the capability to create its own transaction. Assume that in this case it is not important that component X participate in a "new" transaction. This scenario is perfect for the choice TransactionOption.Required. Component X causes the creation of a new transaction if one does not exist.

The child components described in this scenario are good candidates for the TransactionOption.Supported option. This option communicates that component Y and component Z share the transaction created by component X (i.e., the parent). If component X has not created a transaction, component Y and component Z do not care. In effect, they run as nontransactional. This is what the Supported option gives you. However, if you want component Y and component Z to *really* care about the existence of a transaction, use the TransactionOption.Required setting. This allows the child components (component Y and component Z) to share an existing transaction or create their own if needed.

NOTE   Further research into the topic of COM+ transactions and object creation will have you learning about the "context." In this context, a *context* represents an organizing or grouping mechanism that COM+ uses. Each component, as it's used in COM+, gets assigned to a particular context. The transactional support implemented by your component can affect whether your component gets its own context or inherits the context of its client.

As your application designs will vary, so will your use of the TransactionOption enumeration. Having a basic understanding of these TransactionOption choices will prove to be useful. Keep in mind that you can also apply your understanding of these options to the situations where you might choose to manually set the transaction support COM+ component properties (using the Component Services MMC snap-in).

TIP   You will notice that both the VB .NET and COBOL .NET samples use the *AutoComplete* attribute (at the method/function level). Using this attribute saves you the trouble of having to explicitly call the *SetAbort* or *SetComplete* function.

The remaining task for both sample applications is to create a strong name key. Once you create the strong name key (.snk) file, you will need to add a few assembly-level attributes.

Creating a Strong Name Key (.snk)

In Chapter 17 I briefly discussed the concept of a strong name. During that discussion, I mentioned the command-line utility Sn.exe. I will now demonstrate how to use this tool to create a strong name key file for your two class libraries. The creation of a strong name key is a requirement for your serviced component.

NOTE Use of the Global Assembly Cache (GAC) is not a requirement for your serviced component. However, it is recommended that you consider putting your managed serviced component into the GAC. If your serviced component is installed as a COM+ server application, this becomes more critical. The reasoning for this speaks to the potential need for Dllhost.exe to communicate with your managed serviced component. A separate concern surrounds the use of ASP.NET and a dynamic registration installation for your serviced component. If you are not using the GAC, your assembly will be shadow-copied into the download cache. Keep these points in mind. You use the Gacutil.exe to place your managed serviced component into the GAC.

To create a strong name you will need to navigate to the Visual Studio .NET Command Prompt window (click the Start button and select Programs ➤ Microsoft Visual Studio .NET ➤ Visual Studio .NET Tools ➤ Visual Studio .NET Command Prompt) and enter **sn** followed by **-k** and *<assemblyName>*.**snk**. As shown in Figure 19-9, this is fairly straightforward.

Figure 19-9. Using the Visual Studio .NET Command Prompt window to create a strong name key (.snk) file

After you create the .snk file, physically move each .snk file to the \bin folder of each respective sample application folder. Later, in the section "Using Regsvcs.exe," you will find that placing the .snk file in your \bin folder (alongside your assembly/.dll) is a requirement for using the Regsvcs.exe command-line tool.

Adding Assembly-Level Attributes

You have seen attributes used at the assembly level before in Chapter 18. Now you will need to add an attribute setting for the strong name key file. As shown in Figure 19-10, you can update the Property Pages window to add assembly attributes for your COBOL .NET project.

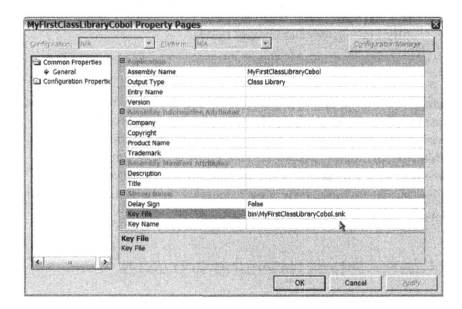

Figure 19-10. Adding the .snk file assembly-level attribute setting

For the VB .NET sample application, you add the assembly-level attributes into the AssemblyInfo.vb file. As you may recall, you access this file from the VS .NET IDE Solution Explorer window for the opened MyFirstClassLibraryVB sample project. The code snippet in Listing 19-3 shows the attributes used in the VB .NET sample application.

Listing 19-3. Assembly Attribute Code Used in the AssemblyInfo.vb File for MyFirstClassLibraryVB

```
Imports System.Reflection
Imports System.Runtime.InteropServices
Imports System.EnterpriseServices
. . .
<Assembly: ApplicationNameAttribute("MyFirstCOMPlusAppVB")>
<Assembly: AssemblyKeyFileAttribute("bin/MyFirstClassLibraryVB.snk")>
<Assembly: ApplicationActivationAttribute(ActivationOption.Library)>
<Assembly: ClassInterface(ClassInterfaceType.AutoDual)>
. . .
```

As you can observe, I used a few additional attributes for demonstration purposes. The main requirement is that I have added the attribute setting to support the inclusion of the strong name key file.

> **NOTE**   Observe the use of the assembly-level *ApplicationActivation-*
> *Attribute* attribute. The choice of "Library" as an activation type has
> important implications. I discuss this topic further in the section
> "Using the /regfile:<filename.reg> Option."

Finally, you can build each sample project. Congratulations! You have created a serviced component. Shortly, you will explore the steps you need to take to use this class library (.dll) file that you have turned into a serviced component.

While I am on the topic of the System.EnterpriseServices namespace, I will drill down just a bit. For example, there are other attributes that you could have used from the System.EnterpriseServices namespace. In the next section you will take a quick look at those.

Other *System.EnterpriseServices* Attributes

This is a good breaking point to mention the other attributes that your serviced component can make use of from the System.EnterpriseServices namespace. In most cases, the attributes represent "property settings" that you can set either in code using an attribute or manually using the appropriate MMC snap-in (I discuss the MMC snap-in used for this purpose in the section "Introducing Your Serviced Component to COM+").

I have provided Listing 19-4 for your convenience. Please refer to the available Microsoft .NET documentation for details regarding the use of each attribute.

Listing 19-4. The Available Attributes from the System.EnterpriseServices Namespace

```
System.EnterpriseServices.ApplicationAccessControlAttribute
System.EnterpriseServices.ApplicationActivationAttribute
System.EnterpriseServices.ApplicationIDAttribute
System.EnterpriseServices.ApplicationNameAttribute
System.EnterpriseServices.ApplicationQueuingAttribute
System.EnterpriseServices.AutoCompleteAttribute
. . .CompensatingResourceManager.ApplicationCrmEnabledAttribute
System.EnterpriseServices.ComponentAccessControlAttribute
```

```
System.EnterpriseServices.COMTIIntrinsicsAttribute
System.EnterpriseServices.ConstructionEnabledAttribute
System.EnterpriseServices.DescriptionAttribute
System.EnterpriseServices.EventClassAttribute
System.EnterpriseServices.EventTrackingEnabledAttribute
System.EnterpriseServices.ExceptionClassAttribute
System.EnterpriseServices.IISIntrinsicsAttribute
System.EnterpriseServices.InterfaceQueuingAttribute
System.EnterpriseServices.JustInTimeActivationAttribute
System.EnterpriseServices.LoadBalancingSupportedAttribute
System.EnterpriseServices.MustRunInClientContextAttribute
System.EnterpriseServices.ObjectPoolingAttribute
System.EnterpriseServices.PrivateComponentAttribute
System.EnterpriseServices.SecureMethodAttribute
System.EnterpriseServices.SecurityRoleAttribute
System.EnterpriseServices.SynchronizationAttribute
System.EnterpriseServices.TransactionAttribute
```

Also, please keep in mind that there are other delegates, interfaces, classes, enumerations, and structures (remember the DICES acronym?) available for your use in the System.EnterpriseServices namespace.

You are ready now to introduce your serviced component to COM+.

Introducing Your Serviced Component to COM+

You have a few choices available from which to choose when you want to introduce your serviced component to COM+. Your choice will depend on either your given set of circumstances or simply your personal preference.

Your basic choices are as follows:[6]

- Using dynamic registration

- Using manual registration with the command-line tool Regsvcs.exe

- Using manual registration with the command-line tool Regasm.exe and the Component Services console

---

6. I stumbled across the *RegistrationHelper.InsallAssembly* class method in the System.EnterpriseServices namespace. After I read its documented description, it appears to me that you can use this class method to basically create your own version of the Regsvcs.exe command-line tool. Please note that time constraints have not allowed me to try this myself. However, ultra-curious types who may be out there might consider trying it. When time allows, I am sure I will experiment with it as well.

In my own experience, I have tried all three approaches and found that each worked. Each technique offers its own advantages that you should know about as part of your retraining effort.

Registering Dynamically

You have the option to use dynamic registration as a way to get a serviced component into COM+. To use this option, you would have prepared your class library as you did with your MyFirstClassLibraryVB sample project (i.e., you would have added assembly- and class-level attributes, and inherited from the System.EnterpriseServices.ServicedComponent class).

Then, you need to add a reference to a client application to point to the .dll file output from the build of your class library. You need to add appropriate code to instantiate an object and make use of your class library/serviced component.

NOTE The use of dynamic registration requires that your client application is able to run with administrative-level security privileges.

Next, simply run the client application. The first time you pass through the code that instantiates an object from your class library/serviced component, a COM+ application will dynamically be registered.

TIP After I used the dynamic registration approach, it became obvious to me that *RegistrationHelper* executes the *System.EnterpriseServices.RegistrationHelperTx* transaction as your new COM+ application is being "added" to the COM+ catalog. This was made apparent after I created a client application to use my new COM+ application and viewed the Running Processes folder in the Component Services console display. To know that your COM+ and Windows registry updates are occurring within the safe confines of a transaction is rather comforting. Certainly, this is a thumbs up for the dynamic registration approach.[7]

---

7. According to Microsoft's documentation, Regsvcs.exe also uses the *System.EnterpriseServices.RegistrationHelperTx* transaction. It was not made apparent during my own testing. Perhaps your research will yield more conclusive results. If so, I would like to hear about it.

As shown in Figure 19-11, the Component Services console displays a new COM+ application that has been dynamically registered and installed for your MyFirstClassLibraryVB sample serviced component.

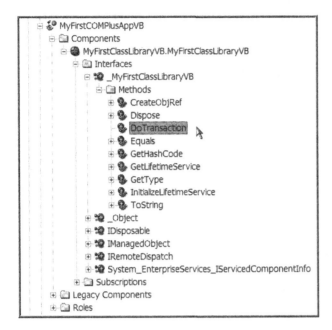

Figure 19-11. A new COM+ application for the MyFirstClassLibraryVB sample serviced component. For demonstration purposes, I have expanded a few of the nodes for the COM+ application.

You will notice that the name "MyFirstCOMPlusAppVB" was the result of using the assembly-level attribute *ApplicationNameAttribute* in the MyFirstClassLibraryVB sample serviced component. As you can see in Figure 19-11, the public methods/functions (including the DoTransaction function) are exposed. This is the result of applying the assembly-level *ClassInterfaceAttribute* attribute (using the *ClassInterfaceType.AutoDual* argument value) in the VB .NET sample application.

TIP The ClassInterfaceAttribute attribute comes from the *System.Runtime.InteropServices* namespace. You can apply this attribute at the assembly or class level.

Feel free to explore the property pages of the sample application and component. The majority of the properties shown on the property pages will relate to the attributes shown earlier in the earlier section "Other System.EnterpriseServices Attributes." That's right, you can actually modify the properties directly using the property pages. Some people prefer this approach to configuration.

The next thing you should do is delete the MyFirstCOMPlusAppVB COM+ application in preparation for the next demonstration.

CAUTION   Be careful! You do not want to delete the wrong COM+ application. To delete the sample COM+ application while you use the Component Services console, simply select the sample COM+ application and press the Delete key.

Now let's take a look at the other choices for installing/registering your serviced component into COM+.

Using Regsvcs.exe

Assume that you just completed the build of your serviced component (that contains the strong name key file and so forth). The next step, if you were using this COM+ Register option, would be to execute the Regsvcs.exe command-line tool using the .dll file that was output as you completed the build of your serviced component.

TIP   Use the Visual Studio .NET Command Prompt window to enter the Regsvcs.exe command. Additionally, be sure that your strong name key file (.snk) is located in your \bin folder along with your assembly (.dll) file. This is a requirement for executing the Regsvcs.exe command-line tool.

Using the *regsvcs /?* switch option, a display is easily generated to show the full list of command syntax options (see Figure 19-12).

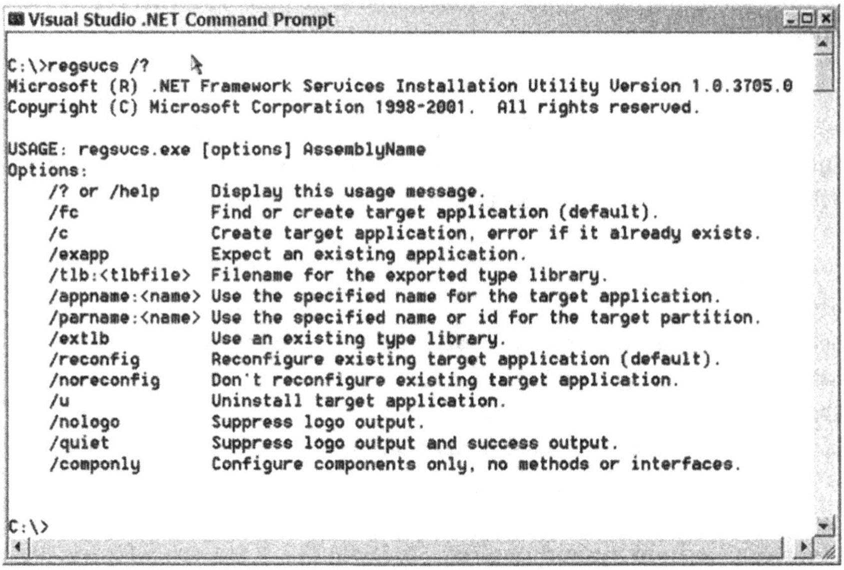

Figure 19-12. Using the regsvcs /? command syntax option to display the full list of options

Using the appropriate regsvcs command-line syntax, you accomplish the following:

1. The assembly (.dll) is loaded and registered in the Windows registry.

2. A type library (.tlb) is created for your assembly (.dll).

3. The COM+ catalog is updated to include a new COM+ application based on the type library being imported.

4. Any attributes included with serviced component are used to apply the initial configuration settings to the new COM+ application.

I chose to run the regsvcs command with minimal (default) options as shown in Listing 19-5.

Listing 19-5. Executing the Regsvcs.exe Command-Line Tool to Register the Serviced Component into COM+

```
C:\>regsvcs
 C:\Chpt19Applications\MyFirstClassLibraryVB\bin\MyFirstClassLibraryVB.dll
Microsoft (R) .NET Framework Services Installation Utility Version 1.0.3705.0
Copyright (C) Microsoft Corporation 1998-2001.  All rights reserved.

Installed Assembly:
Assembly:
 C:\Chpt19Applications\MyFirstClassLibraryVB\bin\MyFirstClassLibraryVB.dll
Application: MyFirstCOMPlusAppVB
TypeLib:
 C:\chpt19applications\myfirstclasslibraryvb\bin\MyFirstClassLibraryVB.tlb
C:\>
```

As you can see from the output display in Listing 19-5, the assembly has been installed. Additionally, a type library (.tlb) file was created and imported for me. After executing this command, I used the Component Services console tool and verified that the COM+ application had been created using the name MyFirstCOMPlusAppVB.

Out of curiosity, I looked inside my local application's \bin folder and verified that a new .tlb file was in fact there. Not bad! Of course, I could not stop there and just close my folder. I wanted to see what was inside the .tlb file. As it turns out, there is a tool included on your .NET installation disk called the OLE/COM Object Viewer.

> **NOTE** Depending on your .NET installation options, you may already be able to use the OLE/COM Object Viewer from within the VS .NET IDE (see the Tools menu).

I followed these steps to manually install the OLE/COM Object Viewer:

1. I browsed my original .NET installation disks (<CD Drive>VSENARD1\Program Files\Microsoft Visual Studio .NET\Common7\Tools on the .NET installation disks).

2. I located two files: Oleview.exe and Iviewers.dll.

3. I copied the two files (Oleview.exe and Iviewers.dll) to the location C:\Program Files\Microsoft Visual Studio .NET\Common7\Tools.

4. I navigated to the VS .NET Tools menu and chose OLE/COM Object Viewer.

After I completed these steps, I launched the OLE/COM Object Viewer tool and navigated to the location of my .tlb file. Mission accomplished! The content of my \bin\MyFirstClassLibraryVB.tlb file is shown in Listing 19-6.

Listing 19-6. The Content of the \bin\MyFirstClassLibraryVB.tlb File As Captured by the OLE/COM Object Viewer Tool

```
// Generated .IDL file (by the OLE/COM Object Viewer)
//
// typelib filename: MyFirstClassLibraryVB.tlb

[
    uuid(9BE69B56-EF21-4FA9-B664-7EC0B7BAC85E),
    version(1.0),
    custom(90883F05-3D28-11D2-8F17-00A0C9A6186D, MyFirstClassLibraryVB,
    Version=1.0.1023.16377, Culture=neutral, PublicKeyToken=c78f6c8808f9dff8)

]
    library MyFirstClassLibraryVB
{
    // TLib :      // TLib : Common Language Runtime Library :
    {BED7F4EA-1A96-11D2-8F08-00A0C9A6186D}
    importlib("mscorlib.tlb");
    // TLib :  : {4FB2D46F-EFC8-4643-BCD0-6E5BFA6A174C}
    importlib("System.EnterpriseServices.tlb");
    // TLib : OLE Automation : {00020430-0000-0000-C000-000000000046}
    importlib("stdole2.tlb");
    // TLib : Common Language Runtime Execution Engine 1.0 Library :
    {5477469E-83B1-11D2-8B49-00A0C9B7C9C4}
    importlib("mscoree.tlb");

    // Forward declare all types defined in this typelib
    interface _MyFirstClassLibraryVB;

    [
      uuid(7B2F68EF-7868-3993-8AB4-BAD7A1A654C6), version(1.0),
      custom(0F21F359-AB84-41E8-9A78-36D110E6D2F9,
      MyFirstClassLibraryVB.MyFirstClassLibraryVB)
```

```
    ]
    coclass MyFirstClassLibraryVB {
        [default] interface _MyFirstClassLibraryVB;
        interface _Object;
        interface IRemoteDispatch;
        interface IDisposable;
        interface IManagedObject;
        interface System_EnterpriseServices_IServicedComponentInfo;
    };

    [
      odl,
      uuid(9A6DAB02-62E1-3F0E-BC2E-EE3686D107D0),
      hidden,
      dual,
      nonextensible,
      oleautomation,custom(0F21F359-AB84-41E8-9A78-36D110E6D2F9,
      MyFirstClassLibraryVB.MyFirstClassLibraryVB)

    ]
    interface _MyFirstClassLibraryVB : IDispatch {
        [id(00000000), propget,
          custom(54FC8F55-38DE-4703-9C4E-250351302B1C, 1)]
        HRESULT ToString([out, retval] BSTR* pRetVal);
        [id(0x60020001)]
        HRESULT Equals(
                        [in] VARIANT obj,
                        [out, retval] VARIANT_BOOL* pRetVal);
        [id(0x60020002)]
        HRESULT GetHashCode([out, retval] long* pRetVal);
        [id(0x60020003)]
        HRESULT GetType([out, retval] _Type** pRetVal);
        [id(0x60020004)]
        HRESULT GetLifetimeService([out, retval] VARIANT* pRetVal);
        [id(0x60020005)]
        HRESULT InitializeLifetimeService([out, retval] VARIANT* pRetVal);
        [id(0x60020006)]
        HRESULT CreateObjRef(
                        [in] _Type* requestedType,
                        [out, retval] _ObjRef** pRetVal);
```

```
        [id(0x60020007)]
        HRESULT Dispose();
        [id(0x60020008)]
        HRESULT DoTransaction([out, retval] BSTR* pRetVal);
    };
};
```

Please take a moment to review the .tlb file in Listing 19-6. Viewing the content of your .tlb file will help provide you with a more complete perspective of exactly what a type library file is. As you can see, the information in this file resembles the assembly metadata that you saw when you used reflection and when you used the ILDASM.exe tool. The type library file is just another way that your assembly metadata is being captured and displayed.

Next, you'll examine your last option for registering your serviced component into COM+. Please delete the sample MyFirstCOMPlusAppVB COM+ application and delete your .tlb file from the \bin folder in preparation for the next demonstration.

Using Regasm.exe

This option also involves the use of a command-line tool: the Regasm.exe tool. Additionally, after you execute the Regasm.exe tool, you will use the Component Services console to install and configure the sample COM+ application. As you will see, this approach requires more effort. However, it is my favorite.

 TIP   Use the Visual Studio .NET Command Prompt to enter the Regasm.exe command.

As I mentioned earlier, each COM+ registration approach worked. Yes, this Regasm.exe approach involves more manual effort. It also offers its own advantages, such as more control and awareness of what is going on. For example, the Regasm.exe command has a command-line option that I really like: the ability to create and save a registry (.reg) file. The registry file could prove useful in a deployment situation.

TIP In VB .NET there is an option on the VS .NET project property pages (in the Configuration Properties ➤ Build section) that exposes a Register for COM Interop check box. Selecting this option and then building the solution will create a type library and accomplish the Windows registry task. In practice, I found this to be a viable alternative to Regasm.exe, particularly during development.

I suppose the bottom line might be that the various COM+ options are just that: options. I suggest that you try each one and decide which one best fits your needs. Incidentally, after I used this Regasm.exe approach and activated the COM+ application with my sample client application, I noticed that the resulting display shown in the Running Processes folder in the Component Services console display was more informative.

The Regasm.exe command offers a *regasm /?* option. Execute it to quickly review the syntax options available to you. Figure 19-13 shows the resulting display.

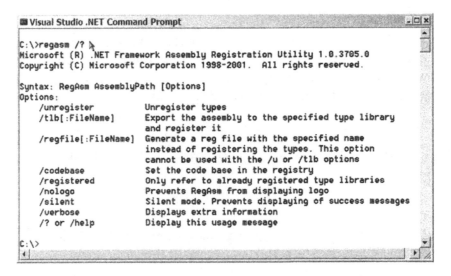

Figure 19-13. Using the regasm /? command syntax option to display the full list of options

Using the /regfile:<filename.reg> Option

Before I get into the actual installation of your COM+ applications, I'll take a quick peek at the .reg file for the VB .NET sample application. I use the */regfile* command-line switch. As shown in Figure 19-14, the generation of a registry script was successful.

Figure 19-14. Using the regasm command and the /regfile command-line switch to generate a registry script. The file will be saved at C:\MyFirstClassLibraryVB.reg.

Navigating to the saved location, I right-click the .reg file and choose Edit.

CAUTION   If you double-click a .reg file, you can potentially update your Windows registry. Be really careful with .reg files.

Viewing the .reg file with the Notepad utility (as shown in Figure 19-15) I am easily able to see exactly what will be "merged" into my Windows registry.

```
REGEDIT4

[HKEY_CLASSES_ROOT\MyFirstClassLibraryVB.MyFirstClassLibraryVB]
@="MyFirstClassLibraryVB.MyFirstClassLibraryVB"

[HKEY_CLASSES_ROOT\MyFirstClassLibraryVB.MyFirstClassLibraryVB\CLSID]
@="{E8D3132E-105D-3F7C-8A31-27028DBEAE09}"

[HKEY_CLASSES_ROOT\CLSID\{E8D3132E-105D-3F7C-8A31-27028DBEAE09}]
@="MyFirstClassLibraryVB.MyFirstClassLibraryVB"

[HKEY_CLASSES_ROOT\CLSID\{E8D3132E-105D-3F7C-8A31-27028DBEAE09}\InprocServer32]
@="C:\WINNT\System32\mscoree.dll"
"ThreadingModel"="Both"
"Class"="MyFirstClassLibraryVB.MyFirstClassLibraryVB"
"Assembly"="MyFirstClassLibraryVB, Version=1.0.1022.32968, Culture=neutral,
PublicKeyToken=c78f6c8808f9dff8"
"RuntimeVersion"="v1.0.3705"

[HKEY_CLASSES_ROOT\CLSID\{E8D3132E-105D-3F7C-8A31-27028DBEAE09}\ProgId]
@="MyFirstClassLibraryVB.MyFirstClassLibraryVB"

[HKEY_CLASSES_ROOT\CLSID\{E8D3132E-105D-3F7C-8A31-27028DBEAE09}\Implemented
Categories\{62C8FE65-4EBB-45E7-B440-6E39B2CDBF29}]
```

Figure 19-15. Viewing the C:\MyFirstClassLibraryVB.reg file with Notepad

You might say, "All right, who cares about what is in the .reg file?" The fact is, *you* should care. *Any*time that *any*thing is updating your Windows registry, you should care. Let's take a closer look at this .reg file now.

First, you will notice a few lines showing that the class identifier (CLSID) is being set using a globally unique identifier (GUID). Then, about in the middle of the .reg file display (as shown earlier in Figure 19-15), you will see the lines in Listing 19-7.

Listing 19-7. Code Snippet from the C:\MyFirstClassLibraryVB.reg File

```
. . .
[HKEY_CLASSES_ROOT\CLSID\{E8D3132E-105D-3F7C-8A31-27028DBEAE09}\InprocServer32]
@="C:\WINNT\System32\mscoree.dll"
"ThreadingModel"="Both"
"Class"="MyFirstClassLibraryVB.MyFirstClassLibraryVB"
"Assembly"="MyFirstClassLibraryVB, Version=1.0.1022.32968, Culture=neutral,
PublicKeyToken=c78f6c8808f9dff8"
"RuntimeVersion"="v1.0.3705"
. . .
```

Several things are worth noting here:

- The "version" information has been "read" from your assembly metadata. Recall the topics of assembly-level custom attributes, reflection, and metadata.

- *ThreadingModel* is set to *Both*. This means that the unmanaged COM+ client will control the apartment model. This is important to be aware of. The apartment model could possibly be either a single-threaded apartment (STA) or a multithreaded apartment (MTA).

- The InprocServer32 program is set as C:\WINNT\System32\mscoree.dll. This COM unmanaged DLL controls the COM callable wrapper (CCW) for COM Interop to occur.

Of these important points, this last one may be the most interesting. *Interoperability* is actually a .NET feature. There is language interoperability that allows one .NET language to "talk" to another .NET language. There is the runtime callable wrapper (RCW) side of COM Interoperability (COM Interop) that allows an unmanaged object to "talk" to the "managed" world. Then, there is the CCW side of COM Interop that allows a managed component to "talk" to the unmanaged world.

In other words, when you take your .NET serviced component and "register" it into the COM+ catalog, you are potentially participating using the .NET feature of COM Interop. Why is this? COM+ is a runtime environment itself. That is, it is an unmanaged runtime environment. The COM+ product existed before .NET existed. Basically, COM+ is a robust, incredibly useful *legacy* application.

There are a few things I should make clear:

- The other COM+ registration techniques (dynamic and Regsvcs.exe) also expose you to the potential of using COM Interop. On the other hand, the use of Regasm.exe and viewing the .reg file simply provided a convenient opportunity to point it out to you.

- COM Interop is not evil or bad. It is just something that you should plan and design for. Anytime you make use of any type of interoperability, you should make sure that your application design supports it.

- There is a small performance hit with COM Interop. On a case-by-case basis, you will need to weigh this small performance hit against the potential value brought by using specific COM+ services.

- When you choose the activation type for your COM+ application, be aware that the choice Library equates to being in-process. The choice Server equates to being out-of-process. It is the out-of-process model that makes use of COM Interop. Recall that you used the ActivationOption.Library argument value setting for the assembly-level ApplicationActivation-Attribute attribute in your VB .NET sample application.

The use of COM Interop is a large topic in and of itself, and it's beyond the scope of this book. I suggest that you take advantage of the references provided at the end of this chapter in the "To Learn More" section for further exploration. For now, you'll proceed to register your serviced components into COM+ using Regasm.exe and the Component Services console.

Exporting the Type Library

I executed the Regasm.exe file for both the COBOL .NET MyFirstClassLibrary-Cobol and VB .NET MyFirstClassLibraryVB sample applications. Listing 19-8 shows the command-line syntax used and resulting output display.

> **TIP** Again, use the Visual Studio .NET Command Prompt window to
> enter the regasm command.

*Listing 19-8. Using the Regasm Tool to Create a Type Library File and Perform the
Needed Windows Registry Update*

```
C:\>regasm /tlb:C:\Chpt19Applications\MyFirstClassLibraryVB\bin\MyFirstClassLibr
aryVB.tlb C:\Chpt19Applications\MyFirstClassLibraryVB\bin\MyFirstClassLibraryVB.
dll
Microsoft (R) .NET Framework Assembly Registration Utility 1.0.3705.0
Copyright (C) Microsoft Corporation 1998-2001.  All rights reserved.

Types registered successfully
Assembly exported to 'C:\Chpt19Applications\MyFirstClassLibraryVB\bin\MyFirstCla
ssLibraryVB.tlb', and the type library was registered successfully

C:\>regasm /tlb:C:\Chpt19Applications\MyFirstClassLibraryCOBOL\bin\debug\MyFirst
ClassLibraryCOBOL.tlb C:\Chpt19Applications\MyFirstClassLibraryCOBOL\bin\debug\M
yFirstClassLibraryCOBOL.dll
Microsoft (R) .NET Framework Assembly Registration Utility 1.0.3705.0
Copyright (C) Microsoft Corporation 1998-2001.  All rights reserved.

Types registered successfully
Assembly exported to 'C:\Chpt19Applications\MyFirstClassLibraryCOBOL\bin\debug\M
yFirstClassLibraryCOBOL.tlb', and the type library was registered successfully
C:\>
```

As you can see from the output display, the .tlb files were created in the
respective \bin subfolders. On this occasion, the Windows registry updates have
been performed. If you were to browse the Windows registry (using the Regedit.exe
command-line tool), you would see entries similar to what you viewed in the
.reg file.

The next step is to take the newly created type library files for each sample
application and manually register them into COM+.

Installing the COM+ Application

After you navigate to the familiar Component Services console window, you will
need to right-click the COM+ Applications node. As shown in Figure 19-16, you

will select New ➤ Application. This will begin a series of steps/prompts to add a new COM+ application.

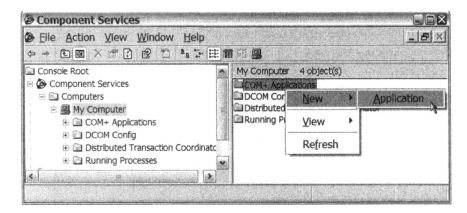

Figure 19-16. Using the Component Services console to manually add a new COM+ application

Follow this series of steps to add a COM+ application:

1. Figure 19-17 shows the first prompt for the COM+ Application Install Wizard. Click Next.

Figure 19-17. Beginning the COM+ application installation

2. Choose the "Create an empty application" option from the Install or Create a New Application window (see Figure 19-18). You will add the components in during a later step. Click Next.

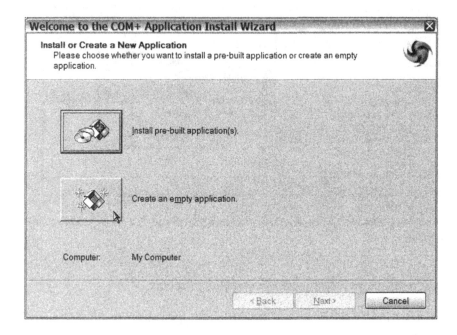

Figure 19-18. Choosing to create an empty COM+ application

3. Enter a name for the new application and choose "Library application" (see Figure 19-19) in the Create Empty Application window. Recall that the choice of Library will result in using your serviced component in an in-process model, thus avoiding any COM Interop concerns. Click Next.

4. This is the last prompt (see Figure 19-20). Congratulations! Click Finish.

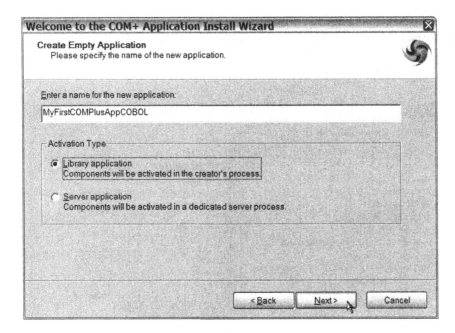

Figure 19-19. Choosing the "Library application" option

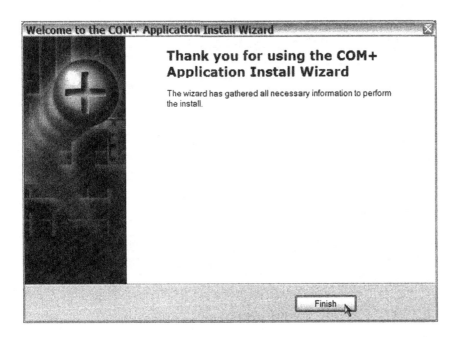

Figure 19-20. The last prompt in the COM+ Application Install Wizard. You can potentially see other prompts depending on the choices you made in earlier wizard prompts.

Now, please repeat the previous four steps for each sample application. In the end, you should have two COM+ applications. As shown in Figure 19-21, one COM+ application is named MyFirstCOMPlusAppCOBOL and the second one is named MyFirstCOMPlusAppVB.

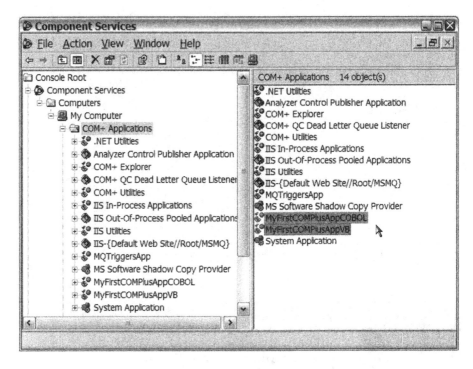

Figure 19-21. Two new COM+ applications, one for each sample application

You are almost done. The next series of steps involves adding the components into each COM+ application.

Installing the Components

Let's proceed. In these next series of steps, you will use another COM+ wizard. To launch this effort, right-click the Components folder of each sample COM+ application (see Figure 19-22).

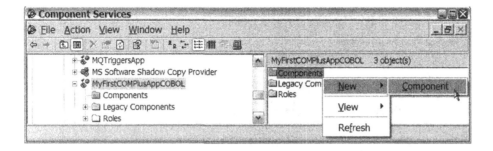

Figure 19-22. Launching the COM+ Component Install Wizard

The following series of steps takes you through the Component Install Wizard:

1. Figure 19-23 shows the first prompt for the Component Install Wizard.
   Click Next.

Figure 19-23. The Welcome screen for the Component Install Wizard

2. Select the "Install new components" option from the Import or Install a
   Component window (see Figure 19-24). Click Next.

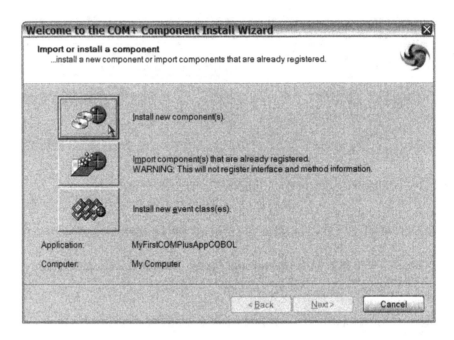

Figure 19-24. Choosing the "Install new components" option

3. In the Select Files window, navigate to the \bin folder for the appropriate sample application and select the type library (.tlb) file. After you select the .tlb file, click Open.

4. As shown in Figure 19-25, your type library and class library information is displayed. Click Next and then click Finish.

Congratulations! You have successfully added a component into the COM+ application. Now, please repeat the previous four steps for each sample application. (See Figure 19-26.)

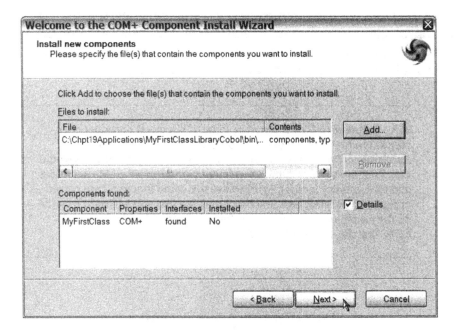

Figure 19-25. The type library and serviced component (modified class library) information is exposed in the COM+ Component Install Wizard.

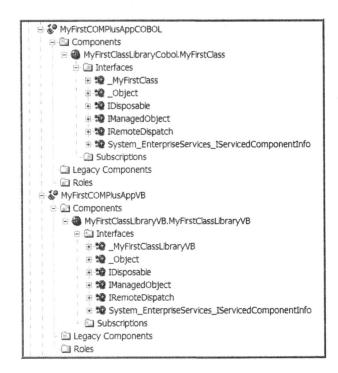

Figure 19-26. The components have been installed into the two COM+ applications.

That completes the installation of the COM+ application and serviced component. In the following section, I introduce the use of the Properties page for further COM+ configuration. Following that, you will walk through the process of building a client application that will use these two COM+ applications.

> **TIP**   I have seen it mentioned in some of Microsoft's product documentation to use the folder location C:\Program Files\ComPlus Applications for installed serviced components. In practice, this would mean deploying your application folder (containing the \bin subfolder and its contents) to this location. Give this some thought. I am considering it as a possible best practice. I imagine that you will want to settle on the folder location prior to performing any of the Windows and COM+ catalog registration steps.

Additional COM+ Application Configuration

You may have noticed that your COBOL .NET sample serviced component is missing a few attributes, both at the class level and the assembly level. For example, I added the TransactionAttribute attribute on the VB .NET sample serviced component with a value of TransactionOption.Required. However, on the COBOL .NET sample serviced component, I intentionally omitted this class-level attribute.

I did this to show that you modify the properties of an installed COM+ application using the Component Services console. Additionally, you can modify the properties of an installed serviced component. As shown in Figure 19-27, if you select and then right-click your component, you can choose Properties from the context menu.

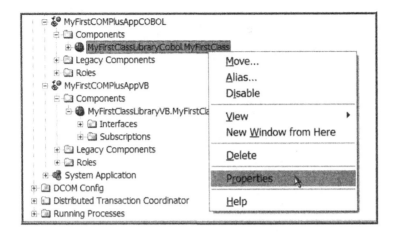

Figure 19-27. Accessing the component-level Properties page

On the Properties page, you will notice that there are several tabs available (see Figure 19-28). You can use the General tab to modify the Description value.

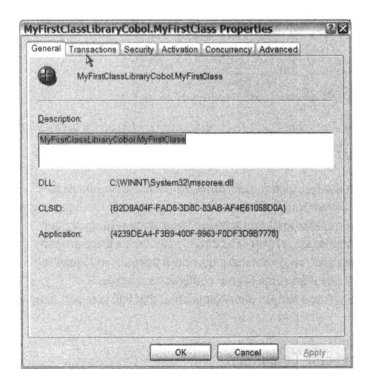

Figure 19-28. The Properties page's General tab

For this demonstration, select the Transactions tab. Under the Transaction support label, change the level of support from Not Supported to Required (see Figure 19-29). Before you leave the Properties page, click Apply. Then click OK.

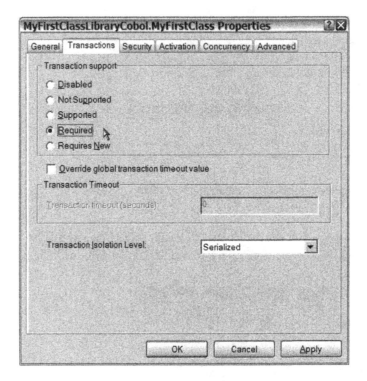

Figure 19-29. Using the Properties page's Transactions tab to change the transaction support level

As you can see on the Transactions tab, other properties are available to further customize your transaction. Give careful consideration to the Transaction Timeout and Transaction Isolation Level settings. The default settings are generally acceptable. Be that as it may, you can certainly customize these property settings to fit your particular needs. You have now been introduced to the Properties page and how to use it for some of your configuration needs.

Now you'll take a look at a simple client application that will use each sample serviced component.

Using Your Serviced Component

For demonstration purposes, I have created a simple .NET Windows application. To explore the advantages of .NET's language interoperability feature, you will create the client using VB .NET. However, you will use both the COBOL .NET and VB .NET sample serviced components.

Name the client application ServicedComponentClientVB.sln. As shown in Figure 19-30, you will add three references using the VS .NET Add Reference feature via the Solution Explorer window.

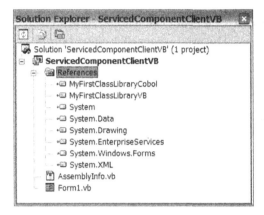

Figure 19-30. The Solution Explorer window shows the addition of references.

As you can see in Figure 19-30, the two references for your sample application .dlls and the one reference for the System.EnterpriseServices assembly have been added. The next step is to add a small amount of code. Additionally, you need to add two buttons and a TextBox to the Windows Form. Use the code in Listing 19-9 to make the client application complete. The code uses both the COBOL .NET and VB .NET sample serviced components. Language interoperability is great!

Listing 19-9. The Client Application

```
Private Sub Button1_Click(ByVal sender As System.Object, _
    ByVal e As System.EventArgs) Handles Button1.Click
    Try
        Dim mycobolclass As New MyFirstClassLibraryCobol.MyFirstClass()
        Dim mystring As String = _
            mycobolclass.DoTransaction("Remove This String To Test Exception")
        TextBox1.Text = mystring
    Catch myexception As ArgumentException
        Trace.Write(myexception.Message)
    Catch myexception As Exception
        Trace.Write(myexception.Message)
    End Try
End Sub
```

```
Private Sub Button2_Click(ByVal sender As System.Object, _
    ByVal e As System.EventArgs) Handles Button2.Click
        Dim myvbclass As New MyFirstClassLibraryVB.MyFirstClassLibraryVB()
        Dim mystring As String = myvbclass.DoTransaction
        TextBox1.Text = mystring
End Sub
```

As shown in Figure 19-31, the simple GUI for your client application is created to make clear which COM+ application will be used as you click either button.

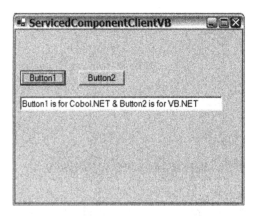

Figure 19-31. The client application is ready for use.

Before you click either of the buttons, open the Component Services console window and navigate to the Running Processes node. Then, as you proceed to click each client application (ServicedComponentClientVB) button, observe the activity reflected within the Running Processes folder/node. Figure 19-32 shows ServicedComponentClientVB as an active process with two COM+ applications.

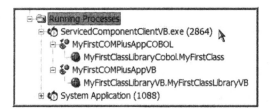

Figure 19-32. Viewing the Running Processes folder/node in the Component Services console window

If you take a peek at the right pane in the Running Processes folder/node, you can drill down into each displayed item. Various views are available. As you can see in Figure 19-33, each COM+ application is exposing its unique ID.

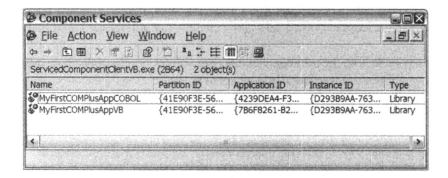

Figure 19-33. Drilling down with the Running Processes folder/node in the Component Services console window

Explore with the Component Services console tool. Using a set of sample applications such as the ones created in this chapter, you can safely explore. I'm sure that you get the sense of the feature-richness tucked away inside the COM+ product.

TIP   Consider modifying the sample applications to really take advantage of the transaction support. For example, you can expand on the exception logic that you have been shown in the sample applications to experiment with aborted transactions.

The following sections introduce other COM+ features that are available to you. As mentioned earlier, COM+ offers many services. Picking from COM+'s impressive feature list, I briefly cover the features Object Pooling and Queued Components.

COM+ Object Pooling

Object Pooling is a feature that allows COM+ to preinstantiate a pool of objects for your COM+ application. Then, as a client application makes a call to use an instance of your serviced component, COM+ will first check to see if an object is available in the pool. If so, an object is provided from the pool. If not, a new object is instantiated (up to the specified maximum pool size limit).

You may want to consider the COM+ Object Pooling feature if

- The cost incurred by executing your object's constructor is expensive relative to the length of time it takes for a client to use and release your object.

- You need to limit the number of concurrent objects. For example, there may be restrictions to resource connections or licenses.

- There is no thread affinity and no client state being used.

Assuming that your application meets each of the preceding requirements, Object Pooling may be right for you. When you use it properly, this COM+ feature can bring performance and scalability improvements.

To enable Object Pooling, navigate to the Activation tab. For demonstration purposes, in Figure 19-34 I have checked the "Enable object pooling" check box. Additionally, I have changed the Minimum Pool Size from 0 to 5.

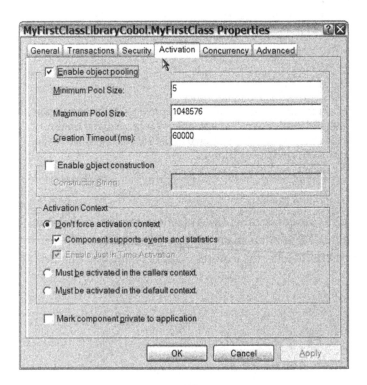

Figure 19-34. Using the Properties page Activation tab to enable the Object Pooling feature

In addition to using the Properties page (as shown in Figure 19-34) to enable the Object Pooling feature, you can use attributes in your code. Recall the list of attributes shown in the section "Other System.EnterpriseServices Attributes."

Use the sample applications provided in this chapter to freely explore the Object Pooling feature. I suggest that you enable Object Pooling on the sample COM+ application. Then, using a sample client application, notice the results. By the way, you will notice that the pooled objects all share the same CLSID. References are provided at the end of this chapter in the "To Learn More" section to assist you as you explore this and other COM+ features.

COM+ Queued Components

The COM+ Queued Components feature will certainly remind you of a product you may have worked with on the mainframe: IBM's MQSeries. That's right. Working with Queued Components will introduce (or reintroduce) you to the world of application messaging and guaranteed delivery. The COM+ Queued Components feature works closely with Microsoft's messaging product, which is called Microsoft Message Queuing (MSMQ).

NOTE MSMQ's full feature set stretches far beyond the support of Queued Components. The discussion in this section simply scratches the surface of MSMQ's full potential.

You might consider using Queued Components if

- Guaranteed delivery is critical. That is, when a client application makes a call to your serviced component, is it critical that the call is completed, even if it's done asynchronously.

- There is a need to provide support to your client application, even if the serviced component (the server application) is temporarily offline.

- The requirement to install your component on both the client and server machines does not pose any deployment concerns.

- The need to have COM+ and MSMQ installed on both the client and server machines does not pose any deployment concerns.

These are just a few points to consider. I am sure there are more. In the meantime, as you browse the Properties page of your COM+ application, understand that when you come across the Queuing tab (see Figure 19-35), you will see one of the starting points for using the Queued Components feature.

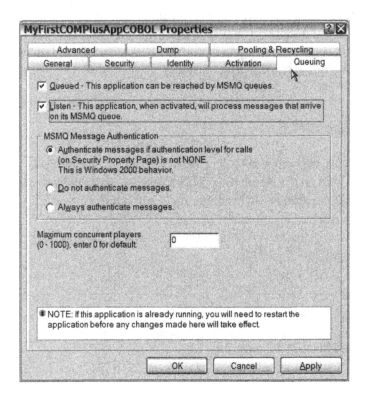

Figure 19-35. The COM+ application Properties page's Queuing tab enables the COM+ Queued Components feature.

As shown in Figure 19-35, I have modified the properties of the COBOL .NET sample COM+ application to become a queued component. In doing so, I needed to change the activation type property from Server to Library. After I did this, COM+ automatically created private queues for my new queued component in MSMQ.

To verify this for yourself, simply navigate to the Computer Management console (click the Start button and select Programs ➤ Administrative Tools ➤ Computer Management or simply right-click your My Computer icon and choose Manage). Check to make sure that you have the MSMQ product installed and that the Message Queuing Windows Service is started. Then, using the Computer Management console, you will see the MSMQ snap-in listed as Message Queuing along with your new private queues (see Figure 19-36). Not bad!

Figure 19-36. The MSMQ snap-in as seen in the Computer Management console. Notice the private queues that COM+ has created for your sample queued component.

Add in the needed code and design considerations, and you are well on your way to using the Queued Components feature of COM+. Unfortunately, I need to stop here and miss out on the fun. Please be my guest and continue on to complete this learning journey.

Summary

This chapter's goals were as follows:

- To create a .NET class library (.dll)

- To work with serviced components

- To review the System.EnterpriseServices namespace

- To introduce the Component Services MMC snap-in

In this chapter you learned how to create a class library and then how to convert that class library to a serviced component. You saw several of the System.EnterpriseServices attributes. You then created a strong name key and demonstrated alternative techniques to register your serviced component into COM+. You used the Component Services MMC snap-in to view and configure each sample COM+ application. You received brief introductions to a few COM+ features (namely, transactional support, the Object Pooling feature, and the Queued Components feature).

In the next chapter you will explore distributed and concurrent processing.

To Learn More

The following are some suggested supplemental references to further your retraining effort.

Books

COM and .NET Interoperability, by Andrew Troelsen (Apress, 2002):
http://www.apress.com/book/bookDisplay.html?bID=81.
Distributed .NET Programming in VB .NET, by Tom Barnaby (Apress, 2002):
http://www.apress.com/book/bookDisplay.html?bID=144.

Magazines

.NET Magazine:
http://www.fawcette.com/dotnetmag/
DevX and Code Magazine:
http://www.devx.com/codemag/
MSDN Magazine:
http://msdn.microsoft.com/msdnmag/
MSDN Magazine: "COM+ Integration: How .NET Enterprise Services Can Help You Build Distributed Applications":
http://msdn.microsoft.com/library/default.asp?url=/msdnmag/issues/01/10/complus/toc.asp
Visual Studio Magazine:
http://www.fawcette.com/vsm/
Windows Developer Magazine:
http://www.wd-mag.com/
XML & Web Services Magazine:
http://www.fawcette.com/xmlmag/

Web Sites

.NET Architecture Center:

http://msdn.microsoft.com/architecture/

.NET Enterprise Servers Online Books:

http://msdn.microsoft.com/library/default.asp?url=/servers/books/
default.asp

Advanced COM Interop:

http://msdn.microsoft.com/library/en-us/cpguide/html/
cpconadvancedcominterop.asp

COM+ (Component Services) Version 1.5:

http://msdn.microsoft.com/library/en-us/cossdk/htm/complusportal_9o9x.asp

COM Threading and Application Architecture in COM+ Applications:

http://msdn.microsoft.com/library/en-us/dncomser/html/comthread.asp

Enterprise Services FAQ (GotDotNet):

http://www.gotdotnet.com/team/xmlentsvcs/esfaq.aspx

The Future of COM+: Microsoft's .NET Revealed:

http://www.devx.com/upload/free/features/xml/2000/04fal00/sj0004/
sj0004.asp

GotDotNet:

http://www.gotdotnet.com/

GotDotNet: Backwards Breaking Changes from Version 1.0 to 1.1:

http://www.gotdotnet.com/team/changeinfo/Backwards1.0to1.1/
default.aspx#00000106

Microsoft ASP.NET Home Page:

http://www.asp.net/

Microsoft Community (discussion groups, e-newsletters, and so forth):

http://communities2.microsoft.com/

Microsoft Patterns & Practices:

http://msdn.microsoft.com/practices/

Microsoft's Search the Knowledge Base Web Site:

http://support.microsoft.com/default.aspx?scid=FH;EN-US;KBHOWTO

Microsoft TechNet How-To Index:

http://www.microsoft.com/technet/treeview/default.asp?url=/technet/
itsolutions/howto

MSDN:

http://msdn.microsoft.com

Understanding Enterprise Services (COM+) in .NET:

http://msdn.microsoft.com/library/en-us/dndotnet/html/entserv.asp

Windows .NET Server 2003:

http://msdn.microsoft.com/library/default.asp?url=/nhp/
default.asp?contentid=28001691

Windows Server 2003 and Enterprise Services:

http://msdn.microsoft.com/library/en-us/dnentsrv/html/
windotnetsvr_dotnetentpsvs.asp

Developing for the Enterprise

An Introduction to Distributed, Asynchronous, and Concurrent Application Models

---

In this chapter

- Revisiting Microsoft Message Queuing (MSMQ)

- Explaining asynchronous processing

- Introducing .NET Remoting

- Covering multithreading

IN PLANNING THE TOPIC lineup for this chapter, I stopped and thought. The realization that this would be the last chapter in the book weighed heavily on my mind. For a moment, I reflected on the subject matter covered in the previous 19 chapters.[1] I thought about the humble retraining prerequisites chapters and the subsequent foundational .NET and Visual Studio .NET (VS .NET) chapters. This reminded me of the chapters that followed, in which you were finally able to dive into .NET Windows and Web development and supporting technologies such as ADO.NET and XML. Wow—you have come a long way.

Continuing to review some of the earlier chapters, I found several stated goals that this book was to accomplish:

- To provide mainframe-oriented guidance to tackling .NET

- To serve as a bridge from the mainframe world to the new .NET universe

---

1. Honestly, I chuckled as I was reminded of the bits and pieces of shameless attempted humor sprinkled here and there—from the *reformation* conjugations to the loose use of acronyms (e.g., TEN, CLR, DICES, and CR).

- To serve as a complete guide to continued learning as you transition from being a mainframe programmer to being (what I like to call) an enterprise developer

I can comfortably say that this book is well positioned to meet each of its stated goals. Well, almost.

The fact is, there's more—a lot more—to learn, particularly along the lines of becoming an enterprise developer. So, don't loosen your seat belt just yet. You might even consider tightening it a bit. Taking into account[2] the material planned for this chapter, you *are* well on track toward completely fulfilling the stated goals of this book, and then some.

The topics that I have accumulated for this chapter have several things in common. For example, each topic is somewhat related to the distributed, asynchronous, or concurrent processing model. Each topic introduces a processing model more commonly found in large-scale, multiuser, enterprise-wide applications. Additionally, each topic is easily complex enough to justify the space of an entire book (or, at least several chapters) for full, detailed coverage.[3]

In this chapter, you will begin by revisiting Microsoft Message Queuing (MSMQ). You will recall that I briefly introduced MSMQ during the earlier COM+ discussion in Chapter 19. This time, you will get chance to see several MSMQ features demonstrated. From there, you will move on to the topic of *asynchronous processing*. You will receive a high-level introduction to the topic of .NET Remoting. At the end of the chapter, you will get a healthy glimpse into the topic of multithreading.

NOTE   You will use the Windows MSMQ product in the first two sections of this chapter. The MSMQ product is free and bundled with the Windows XP and Windows 2000 operating systems. You should verify that you have installed this product locally. To do so, navigate to the Computer Management Console by clicking the Start button and selecting Programs ➤ Administrative Tools ➤ Computer Management (or simply right-click your My Computer icon and choose Manage). If the MSMQ product is installed and if the Message Queuing Windows service is started, you will see the MSMQ snap-in listed as Message Queuing in the Computer Management console.

---

2. Be sure to check out the appendixes that follow this chapter. I am sure that the supplementary information that I have included there will be worth your while.

3. This same point could be made for the majority of topics covered in the previous chapters, hence the abundance of references in the "To Learn More" sections.

Distributed, Asynchronous, and Concurrent Application Models

The business applications that you build will vary greatly. The scale of the applications will also vary. You will build small, single-user applications; medium-sized applications; and large, enterprise-wide applications. When your development needs expand to the enterprise-wide level, you will eventually need to incorporate a few advanced .NET technologies into your arsenal. Your application designs will grow eventually to distributed, asynchronous, or concurrent application models.

That is right. Distributed, asynchronous, and concurrent application models are looked at as being "complex and advanced" topics. These application models are generally thought of as being for large-scale, multiuser, enterprise-wide Windows and Web applications. Now, what does this mean to you?

Coming from the mainframe environment, you are likely saying to yourself: "OK, Chris, what is the big deal? Application development on the mainframe is almost always about large-scale, multiuser, enterprise-wide applications."

Furthermore, you may be wondering about the simple demonstration applications that you have seen so far. Though you did get your feet wet with tons of great .NET technology, the applications were small and simple. My concern is that this may have left you wondering about the samples you've seen so far. Yes, you have built very simple "Hello, World" applications in most of the previous chapters.

You may be wondering why it was that the .NET console, Windows, and Web sample applications that you built did not appear to address the "enterprise-wide" type of business requirements. Looking at a simple "Hello, World" sample application, it takes a giant leap of faith and imagination to visualize that same application scaling upward to handle hundreds (even thousands) of users. For the most part, this speaks to the strength of the .NET and Windows/Web platform development: You can accomplish so much with such little effort.

Yes, you experienced a high degree of simplicity in the use of many of the .NET topics covered in earlier chapters. This fact can easily mislead you into thinking that only small, single-user applications have been built using those .NET technologies (e.g., ASP.NET, ADO.NET, and so forth). This is definitely not the case. More often than not, you can use the material covered in the previous chapters to build small-, medium-, and large-scale applications.

NOTE The success of the World Wide Web can serve as a reminder of what is possible when "growing" your applications. Everything that you have learned about .NET can easily apply to all types of Windows and Web applications.

Be that as it may, you will eventually come across the need to scale your Windows and Web applications to better address special distributed, asynchronous, or concurrent demands. You are then taking your potentially high-end application to *its* own next level, relatively speaking. This means that your design approach will need to incorporate techniques to answer new questions. You need to give some thought to satisfying the business requirements through a meaningful application design. In some cases, this will mean using a distributed, asynchronous, or concurrent application model.

Planning for Distributed, Asynchronous, or Concurrent Mainframe Applications

Think for a moment about some of the mainframe applications that you built in the past. When you built large-scale, multiuser, enterprise-wide mainframe COBOL/CICS applications, what were the requirements that your application needed to address? Were there special design considerations introduced to satisfy those types of requirements? Given your background, certainly you have come across the following mainframe scenario–based questions before:

- Will you need to remotely execute your CICS transaction using Distributed Program Link (DPL), further distributing an already distributed application model?

- Does your CICS program design require you to use the CICS START and RETRIEVE commands for simultaneous transaction processing, which introduces concurrent and asynchronous processing characteristics to your application?

- With your batch COBOL program, what input class (controlling the system initiator choice) should you use in your JCL? Are there any dispatching priority settings needed for the system initiator? The concurrent nature of batch program processing is often taken for granted.

The topics covered in this chapter will remind you of similar distributed, asynchronous, and concurrent mainframe technologies. For example, you can easily compare MSMQ and asynchronous processing on the Windows platform with IBM's MQSeries product and other supporting technologies that you may have used on the mainframe. You can also easily compare the .NET Remoting feature with the mainframe CICS DPL feature. Finally, the topic of .NET multithreading may remind you of CICS's inherent multitasking and multithreading capabilities and CICS's START/RETRIEVE feature.

Granted, these are rather loose comparisons. But you certainly get the point. Having said that, I will now switch gears and dive into the first one of these "complex and advanced" topics:[4] Microsoft Message Queuing.

Revisiting Microsoft Message Queuing (MSMQ)

The MSMQ product is Microsoft's Windows platform solution to compete against IBM's MQSeries product and similar products. Any exposure that you have had to the MQSeries product will act as transferable knowledge now for this chapter's MSMQ discussion.

> **NOTE** IBM has recently announced that they are renaming and rebranding the MQSeries product. They have merged the MQSeries product with the WebSphere product family to become WebSphere MQ (http://www-3.ibm.com/software/ts/mqseries/mq_renaming.html).

Given that, I won't spend time reminding you that these "messaging" types of products have more to do with the storage of *data* into queues than they do with the storage of *messages*.[5] I can only hope that you'll forgive me for not mentioning how a messaging product such as MSMQ helps to provide a connectionless type of guaranteed delivery between disparate systems and components. Instead, I'll spend time exploring ways that a .NET application can use MSMQ and demonstrating how MSMQ can be used as part of a distributed processing model.

---

4. Obviously, becoming informed, applying the right amount of research, and practicing can turn an otherwise "complex and advanced" topic into just another skill set under your belt, another feather in your cap, and another paragraph on your resume.

5. Of course, this would depend on your definition of the word "messages." If you strictly define the word to only apply to e-mail messages, then you might be better served looking into a product like Exchange Server. However, if you loosely define the messages to include any serializable object, then a product like MSMQ just might make a good fit into your architecture.

In this section, you'll learn that you can easily access the MSMQ product from within VS .NET using the Server Explorer window feature. Therefore, as long as you have VS .NET open, you don't necessarily need to be reminded that you can also access MSMQ via the snap-in in the Computer Management console (click the Start button and select Programs ➤ Administrative Tools ➤ Computer Management or simply right-click your My Computer icon and choose Manage).

NOTE As you recall, Chapter 19 explored the topic of MSMQ as part of the introduction to the Queued Components COM+ feature. At that time, I mentioned the requirement of having MSMQ installed.[6] Additionally, there is the requirement that the Message Queuing service be started. These requirements are equally applicable for this chapter's discussion.

Now, let's look at some code.

Setting Up for the Sample Applications

To begin, you will create two sample applications: MyMSMQExampleCOBOL and MyMSMQExampleVB (COBOL .NET and VB .NET, respectively). Both samples use the Windows Application project template. The SQL Server– and ADO.NET-related code used in each sample project was "borrowed" from Chapter 18's demonstration applications (the applications named MyEnhancedInformativeWinFormCobol and MyEnhancedInformativeWinFormVB).

To keep things interesting, I have created an "interoperability" opportunity. You will use the COBOL .NET sample application to implement logic that will load the MSMQ queue. Then, the VB .NET sample application will access the same MSMQ queue to retrieve the loaded message. This architecture will show that an MSMQ queue can be shared between different applications—even applications written in different languages. Having multiple applications interact in this fashion is one way to achieve interoperability.

---

6. The MSMQ product is a free bundled feature on the Windows XP and Windows 2000 operating systems.

Specifically, the sample applications will be designed to accomplish the following:

- The MyMSMQExampleCOBOL sample application will expose functionality to connect to the Northwind SQL Server sample database.

- The MyMSMQExampleCOBOL sample application will create and load an ADO.NET Dataset.

- The MyMSMQExampleCOBOL sample application will load the ADO.NET Dataset into an MSMQ private queue named ".myMSMQexample".

- The MyMSMQExampleVB sample application will retrieve the ADO.NET Dataset from MSMQ.

- The MyMSMQExampleVB sample application will display the retrieved ADO.NET Dataset using a DataGrid control.

MSMQ is a tool that you can use to easily enable your applications to interact. The application process model demonstrated in this section is best described as being both distributed and interoperative (see Figure 20-1).

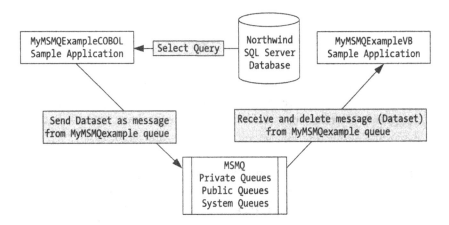

Figure 20-1. Application flow for the MyMSMQExampleCOBOL and MyMSMQExampleVB sample applications

To get things set up for the demonstration, I need to actually create an MSMQ queue. As previously mentioned, on this occasion I will demonstrate the approach of accessing MSMQ from within the VS .NET IDE. Keep in mind that you always have the choice to access MSMQ from the Computer Management console. Now you'll quickly walk through the steps of accessing MSMQ from within the VS .NET IDE:

1. Open the VS .NET IDE Server Explorer window. From your VS .NET IDE Standard toolbar, select View ➤ Server Explorer. Optionally, press Ctrl-Alt-S (see Figure 20-2).

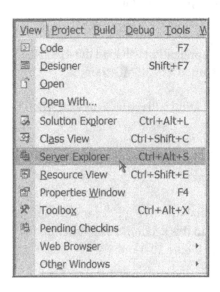

Figure 20-2. Accessing the VS .NET IDE Server Explorer window

2. Expand the Message Queues node. Observe the existence of the Private Queues, Public Queues, and System Queues nodes (see Figure 20-3). Also, notice that you can access other "server"-type products from the Server Explorer window (i.e., SQL Server, Event Logs, and so forth).

3. Create a new MSMQ private queue by right-clicking the Private Queues node and selecting Create Queue (see Figure 20-4). If your computer is connected to a local area network (LAN), you might explore the use of the Public Queues node. The System Queues node is used by the system.

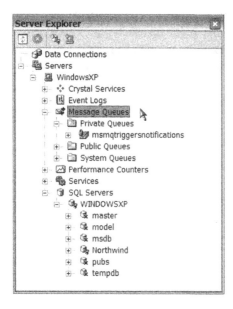

Figure 20-3. The VS .NET IDE Server Explorer window showing the Message Queues node and nodes for several other server products

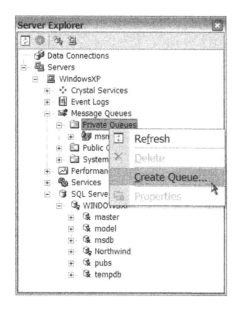

Figure 20-4. Preparing to create a new MSMQ private queue

4. Name the private queue. For this demonstration, I chose the name "myMSMQexample". Notice the "Make queue transactional" check box. Leave this box unchecked. You can experiment with this option later when you extend the sample applications. Click OK after you have entered the name (see Figure 20-5).

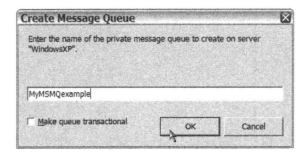

Figure 20-5. Entering the name for the new private queue

That's it! As shown in Figure 20-6, the newly created MSMQ private queue is ready for use.

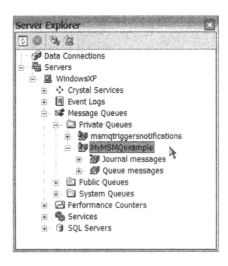

Figure 20-6. The new myMSMQexample private queue is ready for use.

Completing the Sample Applications

Now that you've created your new MSMQ queue, it's time to complete the sample applications. First, you'll add a few basic controls to the Windows Form of both MyMSMQExampleCOBOL and MyMSMQExampleVB. Next, you'll add your own myMSMQexample MSMQ private queue to each project.

To do this, first prepare your VS .NET windows such that you have both the Server Explorer window and the sample application MyMSMQExampleVB open. Then, while you are viewing the Form1.vb Windows Form in Design view, drag and drop the myMSMQexample MSMQ queue from the Server Explorer window to the Design view of the Form1.vb Windows Form (see Figure 20-7).

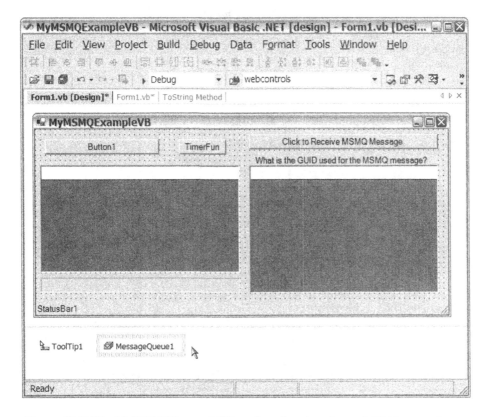

Figure 20-7. The MyMSMQExampleVB project showing the myMSMQexample MSMQ private queue in the VS .NET components tray with the default name of MessageQueue1

TIP   Dragging and dropping the MSMQ queue onto your design surface will look and feel like the familiar task of dragging and dropping
controls from the VS .NET Toolbox. Other server-type products shown
in the Server Explorer window also support the drag-and-drop
approach.

Repeat this dragging and dropping procedure for the
MyMSMQExampleCOBOL project (see Figure 20-8).

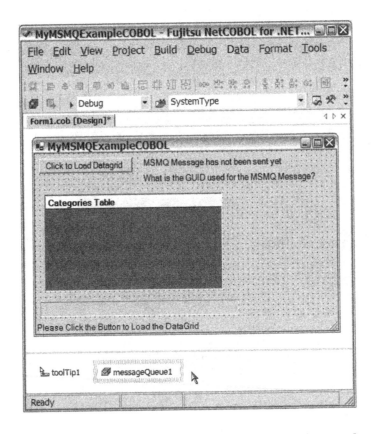

*Figure 20-8. The MyMSMQExampleCOBOL project showing the myMSMQexample
MSMQ queue in the VS .NET components tray with the default name of
MessageQueue1*

Changing the Path Value

Viewing your open project in the VS .NET IDE (Design view), take a moment to view the property pages (right-click the MessageQueue1 icon located in the component tray and select Properties or select the MessageQueue1 icon and press F4) for MessageQueue1, which sits in the component tray. Among the properties exposed, you will notice a Path property. Basically, this associates this instance of the *System.Messaging.MessageQueue* class to your private queue myMSMQexample.

When you use the Server Explorer MSMQ drag-and-drop feature, you will want to be aware that leaving the Path value at its default setting will limit your message queues to only being functional on the original computer used during initial development. Why? Notice that the default Path value appends the name of your development machine to the remaining portion of the Path. In most real-life development scenarios, you will want to change the Path value to be more *generic*. That is, if you plan to deploy your application to other machines, you will want the Path value to be more generic. You accomplish this by editing the Path value *machineName*/Private$/QueueName by replacing *machineName* with a period (.). The end result is ./Private$/QueueName. Optionally, consider creating your MSMQ queues dynamically in code during runtime (i.e., `Dim MessageQueue1 As New System.Messaging.MessageQueue(".\Private$\MyMSMQExample")`.

You will come across application design considerations where the dynamic approach may be more appropriate (sometimes it is more efficient). In other cases, you may find that the Server Explorer drag-and-drop feature (a RAD feature) will meet your needs. Be aware of your choices and choose wisely. (The sample applications use this generic path approach to enable proper MSMQ functionality on multiple machines.)

All that is left now is to add a few lines of code. The code snippet in Listing 20-1 shows the pertinent portions of code that were added to the MyMSMQExampleCOBOL sample application.

Listing 20-1. Code Snippets from the MyMSMQExampleCOBOL Sample Application

```
000010 IDENTIFICATION DIVISION.
000020 CLASS-ID. Form1 AS "MyMSMQExampleCOBOL.Form1"
000030     INHERITS CLASS-FORM.
000040 ENVIRONMENT DIVISION.
000050 CONFIGURATION SECTION.
000060 SPECIAL-NAMES.
000070     CUSTOM-ATTRIBUTE STA-THREAD CLASS CLASS-STA-THREAD
000080     .
000090 REPOSITORY.
. . .
000300     CLASS CLASS-GUID AS "System.Guid"
000310     CLASS CLASS-MESSAGEQUEUE AS "System.Messaging.MessageQueue"
. . .
000920 STATIC.
000930 DATA DIVISION.
000940 WORKING-STORAGE SECTION.
000950 PROCEDURE DIVISION.
000960
000970 METHOD-ID. MAIN AS "Main" CUSTOM-ATTRIBUTE IS STA-THREAD.
000980 DATA DIVISION.
000990 WORKING-STORAGE SECTION.
001000 01 TEMP-1 OBJECT REFERENCE Form1.
001010 PROCEDURE DIVISION.
001020     INVOKE Form1 "NEW" RETURNING TEMP-1.
001030     INVOKE CLASS-APPLICATION "Run" USING BY VALUE TEMP-1.
001040 END METHOD MAIN.
001050
001060 END STATIC.
001070
001080 OBJECT
001090     .
001100 DATA DIVISION.
001110 WORKING-STORAGE SECTION.
001120 01 myGUID OBJECT REFERENCE CLASS-GUID.
. . .
001370 PROCEDURE DIVISION.
001380
001390 METHOD-ID. NEW.
001400 PROCEDURE DIVISION.
001410     INVOKE SELF "InitializeComponent".
001420 END METHOD NEW.
```

```
. . .
025940 METHOD-ID. button1_Click PRIVATE.
025950 DATA DIVISION.
025960 WORKING-STORAGE SECTION.
025970 01 MyNewConnectionString  PIC X(100).
025980 01 MyNewAppSettings  OBJECT REFERENCE CLASS-NAMEVALUECOLLECTION.
025990 01 MyGUIDString PIC X(50).
026000
026010 LINKAGE SECTION.
026020 01 sender OBJECT REFERENCE CLASS-OBJECT.
026030 01 e OBJECT REFERENCE CLASS-EVENTARGS.
026040 PROCEDURE DIVISION USING BY VALUE sender e.
. . .
026980     INVOKE mySqlDataAdapter "Fill"
026990       USING BY VALUE myDataSet, "myCategories"
027000
. . .
027100
027110     SET mySqlConnection TO NULL.
027120     SET mySqlDataAdapter TO NULL.
027130     SET mySqlCommand TO NULL.
027140     SET myDataTable TO NULL.
027150
. . .
027210     SET myGUID TO CLASS-GUID::"NewGuid"()
027220     SET MyGUIDString TO myGUID::"ToString"()
027230     INVOKE messageQueue1 "Send"
027240     USING BY VALUE myDataSet, MyGUIDString
027250     SET PROP-TEXT OF label1 TO "MSMQ Message has been Sent!"
027251     SET PROP-TEXT OF label2 TO MyGUIDString
027260
027270 END METHOD button1_Click.
027280
027290 END OBJECT.
027300 END CLASS Form1.
```

Please take a moment to read through the code in Listing 20-1. To save space, I left out the portions of the application (the ADO.NET-related code) that you've seen before. You'll notice that the bulk of your concerns are between lines 027210 and 027251 of the code. Lines 000300 and 000310 are rather important as well. I'm sure you get the point.

Listing 20-1 shows that the System.Messaging.MessageQueue class is referenced to expose the private queue that you dragged and dropped onto the form from the Server Explorer window. Then, on line 027230, the *Send* method is invoked to "send" a message to your MSMQ private queue, myMSMQexample.

You may have noticed the addition of the GUID class in the sample code (in line 027210). I included this mainly for fun. No, actually, this is my way of providing a rock-solid and proven demonstration showing that the same MSMQ message that you "send" to the myMSMQexample queue is exactly the same message that you later "receive" from the same myMSMQexample queue.[7] After all, a globally unique identifier (GUID) is virtually guaranteed to be unique. In real life, you might use a more meaningful ID for the message label.

The only other thing to mention for the MyMSMQExampleCOBOL sample is related to the choice to "send" an ADO.NET Dataset. You might wonder if you can send other things—other classes, other objects, and so forth. There are basically two restrictions:

- The "message" item is limited to a 4MB size.

- The "message" item has to be serializable.

That is it. The size has to be reasonable and you need to be able to serialize the object that gets stored as an MSMQ message.

Just in case you were wondering how I knew that the ADO.NET Dataset met the serializable requirement, take a look at Figure 20-9. As you can see from the portion of the VS .NET Help text, the System.Data.Dataset class is decorated with the <serializable> attribute. Additionally, notice that the *ISerializable* interface is implemented. Keep these points in mind if and when you get around to creating your own custom classes as MSMQ message candidates.

TIP The *System.Data.DataTable* class is also marked as being serializable. From what I have noticed, all of the basic data types are also marked as serializable (System.String, System.Int32, System.Array, and so forth).

---

7. In other words, this is not a "smoke-and-mirrors" demonstration. The same can be said for each demonstration sample application found throughout this entire book. Unfortunately, the same is not always true with some of the sample applications floating about in the public domain and in some conferences. Programmer, beware!

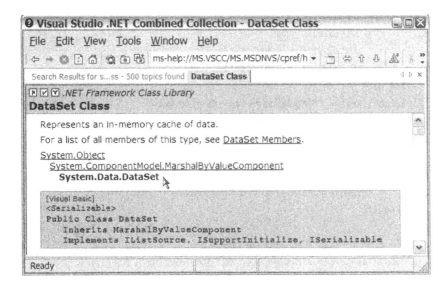

Figure 20-9. A portion of the VS .NET Help text for the System.Data.Dataset class. Many other .NET Framework classes are serializable, and you can also create your own serializable classes.

The last portion of setup for your sample applications deals with the MyMSMQExampleVB sample application. Recall that you will use the VB .NET project to "receive" the message from your private MSMQ queue. The code snippet in Listing 20-2 shows the relevant code used in the MyMSMQExampleVB sample application. This listing represents the code used in the *Button3_Click* event/method.

Listing 20-2. Code Snippet Taken from the MyMSMQExampleVB Sample Application

```
Private Sub Button3_Click(ByVal sender As System.Object, ByVal e As
    System.EventArgs) Handles Button3.Click
    Dim myNewDataset As System.Data.DataSet
    Dim myMessage As System.Messaging.Message
    Try
        MessageQueue1.Peek(New TimeSpan(0))

        myMessage = MessageQueue1.Receive
        myMessage.Formatter = New _
        System.Messaging.XmlMessageFormatter(New Type() {GetType(DataSet)})
        myNewDataset = CType(myMessage.Body, DataSet)

        '***************************************************
```

```
        With DataGrid2
                .Visible = "True"
                .DataSource = myNewDataset
                .DataMember = "myCategories"
        End With
        Button3.Text = "MSMQ Message removed from Queue"
        Label1.Text = myMessage.Label
    Catch myexception As System.Messaging.MessageQueueException
        If myexception.MessageQueueErrorCode = _
            System.Messaging.MessageQueueErrorCode.IOTimeout Then
            MsgBox("Please Load the MSMQ Message first")
        End If
    End Try
    'Example code to Load MSMQ Private Queue
    'Dim myGuid As String = System.Guid.NewGuid.ToString
    'MessageQueue1.Send(myDataset, myGuid)
End Sub
```

NOTE   Though it's not shown here, the VS .NET Solution Explorer window indicates that a *reference* has been added to the *System.Messaging* assembly.

Take a moment to review Listing 20-2. You will see that an object is created for the *System.Messaging.Message* class to expose properties and methods. Otherwise, observe that the *Peek* and *Receive* methods are used on the *messageQueue1* object. Many other useful classes are available for use in the *System.Messaging* namespace. Definitely consider familiarizing yourself with this feature- and class-rich namespace.

To get the whole demonstration up and running, simply run both sample projects (MyMSMQExampleVB and MyMSMQExampleCOBOL). If you want, you can start with the COBOL .NET-versioned project to send the MSMQ message. As shown in Figure 20-10, the GUI for MyMSMQExampleCOBOL indicates that an MSMQ message has been sent. Notice the GUID displayed on the form.

View the MSMQ private queue in the VS .NET Server Explorer window before executing the MyMSMQExampleVB sample application. As shown in Figure 20-11, the sent message shows in the myMSMQexample private MSMQ queue. Notice that the GUID (as the message label) is displayed alongside the message.

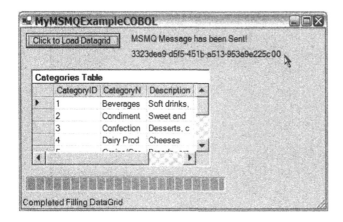

Figure 20-10. After executing the MyMSMQExampleCOBOL sample application

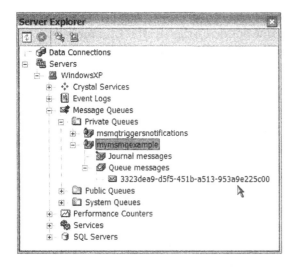

Figure 20-11. The myMSMQexample private MSMQ queue with one message

Next, run the MyMSMQExampleVB sample application. If you click the button at the top-right corner of the form, you will receive the one MSMQ message from your myMSMQexample private MSMQ queue (see Figure 20-12). Notice the GUID displayed on the form.

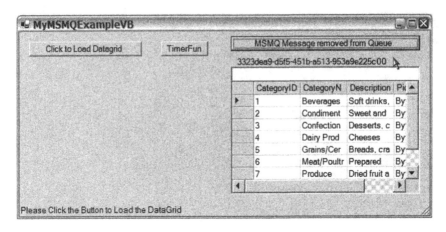

Figure 20-12. After executing the MyMSMQExampleVB sample application

Before you send another message with the MyMSMQExampleCOBOL sample application, proceed to click the same button on the MyMSMQExampleVB sample application again. As shown in Figure 20-13, a message box will appear.

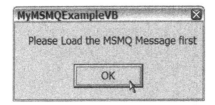

Figure 20-13. The message box logic is coded as part of the exception-handling response.

Any previous experience that you have had with the IBM MQSeries product (perhaps on the mainframe) will have acquainted you with the expected behavior of a message being deleted from the queue after it was received. As you know, this is normally a desired feature: guaranteed, one-time delivery. Naturally, you can change your code slightly to implement logic that will receive but not delete an MSMQ message.

You may notice that when you look at the VS .NET Server Explorer window, the MSMQ message still appears even after it has been deleted (or it does not appear after it has been sent). If you refresh the display (as shown in Figure 20-14), the most current content status will correctly display.

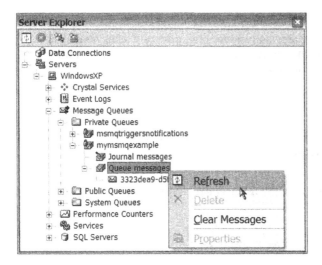

Figure 20-14. Refreshing the MSMQ Queue display from the VS .NET Server Explorer window

You can extend both sample applications to use other MSMQ features. For example, you can explore the option of making your queue transactional. So far, I have described only a couple of the most basic MSMQ features to give you a general idea and possibly point you in the right direction. In the next section, you will explore the MSMQ tool a bit further.

NOTE   The previous examples' approach demonstrated the use of MSMQ in a synchronous processing model. MSMQ supports both the synchronous and asynchronous processing models.

Asynchronous Processing

As you know, in your average mainframe batch application, the asynchronous processing model is almost nonexistent. It is not until you incorporate tools such as MQSeries that your existing mainframe batch application models are extended beyond their common linear, sequential processing design. Other than that, your previous mainframe CICS experience using the CICS START/RECEIVE commands certainly qualifies as exposure to asynchronous processing.

TIP By identifying any mainframe similarities and using analogies where possible, I am attempting to increase the chance of your transferable knowledge surfacing.

Generally speaking, the following three scenarios are common when you talk about asynchronous processing:

- A nonblocking call being made from a client-type application to a server-type application

- A nonblocking call processing at some nondeterminate time and disconnected from the ongoing operational capability of the client-type application

- A nonblocking call (in some cases) providing a response to the original client-type application

When you develop with .NET, asynchronous processing includes the implementation and use of the *System.IAsyncResult* interface. You will grow to know this interface as basically representing the status of an asynchronous request (i.e., a nonblocking call). A few base classes and properties are associated with the IAsyncResult interface. You will often see one or more of these IAsyncResult members whenever an application is designed to use the asynchronous processing model.

Specifically, *AsyncResult* and *WebClientAsyncResult* are the two classes that natively implement the IAsyncResult interface. The four public properties exposed by the IAsyncResult interface are simply *AsyncState, AsyncWaitHandle, CompletedSynchronously,* and *IsCompleted.* Other than that, there is one delegate, *AsyncCallback.* You use this delegate when you want to "call back" a client's method after the asynchronously processed request (nonblocking call) completes.

NOTE If you take a closer quick look at the AsyncResult class, you will notice that it comes from the *System.Runtime.Remoting.Messaging* namespace. This alone provides an indication of the close interrelationships among such .NET technologies as Remoting, messaging, and asynchronous processing.

Let's move now to a practical example to demonstrate the use of asynchronous processing in a .NET application.

Using MSMQ for Asynchronous Processing

The topic of asynchronous processing can easily be explained and demonstrated without the use of MSMQ. At the same time, it is good to know that the MSMQ tool provides wonderful support for asynchronous processing. Given that, I will leverage your knowledge about MSMQ to help demonstrate the use of asynchronous processing in a .NET application. Later, I will introduce you to a several other areas where the .NET Framework supports asynchronous processing.

This MSMQ/asynchronous processing demonstration will use the Windows Application VS .NET project template. You will exercise both your COBOL .NET and VB .NET skills.[8] As shown in Figure 20-15, you will implement a simple yet extendable asynchronous processing scenario.

Before you get into the code-centric portion of the demonstration, you will need to perform several setup tasks. Please note the following prerequisite tasks:

1. Create a folder at C:\MSMQ-ASYNC-DEMO (optional).

2. Create two .NET Windows sample projects. Name these new .NET Windows projects MyMSMQAsyncAndTriggerCOBOL and MyMSMQAsyncAndTriggerVB.

3. Copy both application executables (.exe) and place them inside the C:\MSMQ-ASYNC-DEMO folder for organizational purposes (optional).

4. Launch the Computer Management console tool by clicking the Start button and selecting Programs ➤ Administrative Tools ➤ Computer Management. Optionally, you can simply right-click your My Computer icon and choose Manage.

5. Use the Services MMC snap-in to verify that both the Message Queuing service and Message Queuing Triggers service show a status of "started." You can access the Services MMC snap-in via the Computer Management console.

---

8. Isn't being bilingual fun?

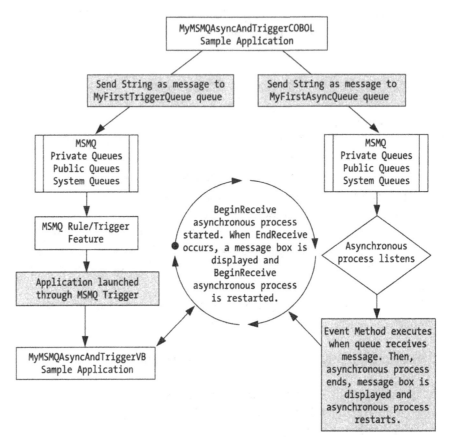

Figure 20-15. The application flow of the MSMQ/asynchronous processing demonstration

6. Create two MSMQ private queues. You can use the same procedure you learned earlier in the chapter to create the two queues. Optionally, use the Computer Management console to access the MSMQ snap-in. I chose to name the two new MSMQ Queues MyFirstTriggerQueue and MyFirstAsyncQueue. The queues were left as *not* transactional.[9]

7. Create an MSMQ rule and trigger.[10] You will walk through this task later in the section "Creating an MSMQ Trigger."

---

9. Although you won't make use of this feature during this demonstration, you certainly should make a mental note of the availability of this transactional feature. If your application design recognizes a logical unit of work surrounding the sending and receiving of MSMQ messages to/from one or more queues, the MSMQ transactional feature can offer great value.

10. The use of an MSMQ rule and trigger is not necessarily needed to implement an asynchronous processing model. I just wanted to show you another MSMQ feature that you can leverage.

With the exception of the MSMQ trigger, you should feel relatively comfortable accomplishing each prerequisite task in the preceding list. If not, please consider reviewing earlier portions of this chapter, earlier chapters, and the supplementary help sources (MSDN, VS .NET Help, and so forth). Let's turn now to the sample applications.

TIP When you use the VS .NET IDE's Server Explorer drag-and-drop feature, consider changing the default MSMQ Queue Path value (*machineName*/Private$/*QueueName*) to a generic setting by replacing *machineName* with a period (.). The intended end result would be ./Private$/*QueueName*. Use the Design view property pages to view and edit the MSMQ queue path. I previously mentioned this in the section "Revisiting Microsoft Message Queuing (MSMQ)." I used the generic setting to enable the sample application's capability to function properly on multiple machines.

The Sample Applications

As you can see in Figures 20-16 and 20-17, the two new MSMQ queues are being used in both sample projects. You will notice that each sample project presents a Windows Form along with a minimal use of Button and Label controls.

When you develop a .NET application that will use MSMQ's asynchronous processing support, you will use the System.IAsyncResult interface through either of the following System.Messaging.MessageQueue class method combinations:

- *MessageQueue.BeginReceive* and *MessageQueue.EndReceive*

- *MessageQueue.BeginPeek* and *MessageQueue.EndPeek*

In the first MSMQ demonstration (in the MyMSMQExampleVB sample application), you saw the use of the MessageQueue.Receive and MessageQueue.Peek methods. Notice the absence of the word "Begin" in the method names that you used earlier.

In the earlier MyMSMQExampleVB example, you were not initiating an asynchronous processing model. Particularly, the MessageQueue.Receive method easily demonstrates an example of a potentially "blocking" call. If you had coded to allow the sample code to execute the MessageQueue.Receive method when the targeted MSMQ queue was empty, the application would have just "waited" until a message was placed in the queue.

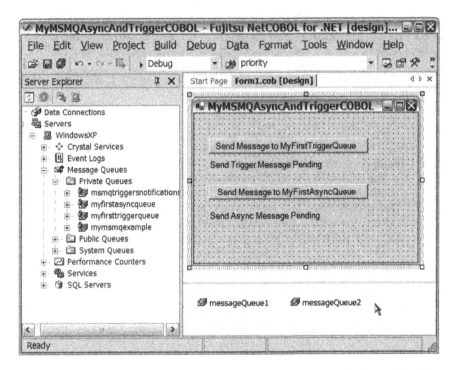

Figure 20-16. The GUI/Design view of the MyMSMQAsyncAndTriggerCOBOL sample project

TIP Consider experimenting with the previous MyMSMQExampleVB sample code by temporarily commenting out the line that uses MessageQueue1.Peek. This Peek method was actually serving the purpose of getting around the possibility that the queue may have been empty. When the queue was empty, the Peek method simply raised an exception. Observe the use of the Try/Catch logic. The exception was *handled* by displaying a message box.

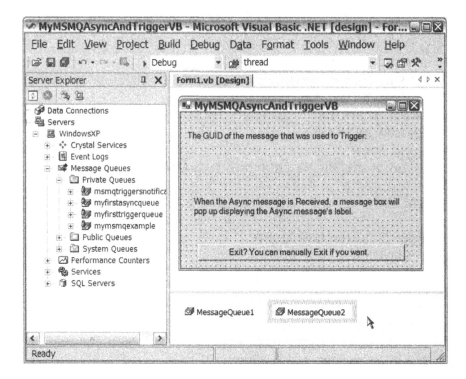

Figure 20-17. The GUI/Design view of the MyMSMQAsyncAndTriggerVB sample project

Yes, on the surface this might appear to mimic an asynchronous processing model. However, the problem is that the "waiting" application (the client) would not have been allowed to continue processing. Processing would have just "waited" at the point the MessageQueue.Receive method was executed. This type of "client blocked while waiting" scenario is in contradiction to the basic asynchronous processing model.

Now you'll take a quick peek at the code that was used in each sample project. You'll start with the COBOL .NET portion of the demonstration (see Listing 20-3). Notice that I've included only the most relevant portion of the MyMSMQAsyncAndTriggerCOBOL sample project. In this case, that is the event/method logic for the two Windows Button controls.

Listing 20-3. Code Snippet from the MyMSMQAsyncAndTriggerCOBOL Sample Project

```
000010 IDENTIFICATION DIVISION.
000020 CLASS-ID. Form1 AS "MyMSMQAsyncAndTriggerCOBOL.Form1"
000030     INHERITS CLASS-FORM.
000040 ENVIRONMENT DIVISION.
000050 CONFIGURATION SECTION.
000060 SPECIAL-NAMES.
000070     CUSTOM-ATTRIBUTE STA-THREAD CLASS CLASS-STA-THREAD
000080     .
000090 REPOSITORY.
. . .
017680 METHOD-ID. button1_Click PRIVATE.
017690 DATA DIVISION.
017700 WORKING-STORAGE SECTION.
017710 01 MyGUIDString PIC X(50).
017720 01 MyMsgString  PIC X(25).
017730 LINKAGE SECTION.
017740 01 sender OBJECT REFERENCE CLASS-OBJECT.
017750 01 e OBJECT REFERENCE CLASS-EVENTARGS.
017760 PROCEDURE DIVISION USING BY VALUE sender e.
017770
017780              MOVE "TRIGGER" TO MyMsgString
017790     SET myGUID TO CLASS-GUID::"NewGuid"()
017800     SET MyGUIDString TO myGUID::"ToString"()
017810     INVOKE messageQueue1 "Send"
017820     USING BY VALUE MyMsgString, MyGUIDString
017830     SET PROP-TEXT OF label1 TO MyGUIDString
017840
017850 END METHOD button1_Click.
017860
017870 METHOD-ID. button2_Click PRIVATE.
017880 DATA DIVISION.
017890 WORKING-STORAGE SECTION.
017900 01 MyGUIDString PIC X(50).
017910 01 MyMsgString  PIC X(25).
017920 LINKAGE SECTION.
017930 01 sender OBJECT REFERENCE CLASS-OBJECT.
017940 01 e OBJECT REFERENCE CLASS-EVENTARGS.
017950 PROCEDURE DIVISION USING BY VALUE sender e.
017960
017970              MOVE "ASYNC" TO MyMsgString
017980     SET myGUID TO CLASS-GUID::"NewGuid"()
```

```
017990      SET MyGUIDString TO myGUID::"ToString"()
018000      INVOKE messageQueue2 "Send"
018010      USING BY VALUE MyMsgString, MyGUIDString
018020      SET PROP-TEXT OF label2 TO MyGUIDString
018030
018040 END METHOD button2_Click.
018050
018060 END OBJECT.
018070 END CLASS Form1.
```

Please take a moment to review Listing 20-3. For this demonstration, I chose to send String objects to the respective MSMQ private queues. Recall that the String class is serializable (as is the ADO.NET Dataset used in the previous MSMQ demonstration).

Next, take a look at the code used in the VB.NET sample project MyMSMQAsyncAndTriggerVB (see Listing 20-4). You will need to expand the code region noted as "Windows Form Designer generated code". Notice that the demonstration code is placed after the *InitializeComponent()* call.

Listing 20-4. Code Snippet from MyMSMQAsyncAndTriggerVB

```
Public Class Form1
 Inherits System.Windows.Forms.Form
#Region " Windows Form Designer generated code "
    Public Sub New()
        MyBase.New()
        'This call is required by the Windows Form Designer.
        InitializeComponent()
          'Add any initialization after the InitializeComponent() call
          Call MyMSMQReceive()
    End Sub

    Private Sub MyMSMQReceive()
        Dim myStringMsg As String
        Dim myMessage As System.Messaging.Message
        Try
            MessageQueue1.Peek(New TimeSpan(0))
            myMessage = MessageQueue1.Receive
            myMessage.Formatter = New _
          System.Messaging.XmlMessageFormatter(New Type() {GetType(String)})
            MyStringMsg = CType(myMessage.Body, String)
            '****************************************************
            Label2.Text = myMessage.Label
        Catch myexception As System.Messaging.MessageQueueException
```

```
                    If myexception.MessageQueueErrorCode = _
                       System.Messaging.MessageQueueErrorCode.IOTimeout Then
                          Label2.Text = "The MSMQ needs to be loaded first"
                    End If
                End Try


                ' Add an event handler
                AddHandler MessageQueue2.ReceiveCompleted, _
                AddressOf MyMSMQBeginReceive
                ' Begin the asynchronous receive
                MessageQueue2.BeginReceive()
            End Sub


            Public Shared Sub MyMSMQBeginReceive(ByVal source As Object, _
            ByVal asyncResult As System.Messaging.ReceiveCompletedEventArgs)
                'Connect to the MSMQ queue.
                Dim myqueue As System.Messaging.MessageQueue = _
                CType(source, System.Messaging.MessageQueue)


                'End the asynchronous BeginReceive
                Dim myMessage As System.Messaging.Message = _
                myqueue.EndReceive(asyncResult.AsyncResult)


                'Example code to exit application
                'Application.Exit()
                MsgBox("Message received: " & myMessage.Label)
                myqueue.BeginReceive()


                ''Example code to Load MSMQ Private Queue
                'Dim mymsg As String = "ASYNC"
                'MessageQueue1.Send(mymsg, "ASYNC")
            End Sub
    . . .
    Private Sub Button1_Click(ByVal sender As System.Object, _
        ByVal e As System.EventArgs) Handles Button1.Click
            'exit application
            Application.Exit()
        End Sub
End Class
```

In Listing 20-4, the expected logic to receive the MSMQ String type message has been included. The logic shown for the MyMSMQBeginReceive subprocedure actually implements the asynchronous processing. In other words, the two lines of coding in Listing 20-5 are almost all that you need.

Listing 20-5. Code Snippet from MyMSMQAsyncAndTriggerVB Highlighting the Code Needed to Initiate Asynchronous Processing

```
. . .
        ' Add an event handler
        AddHandler MessageQueue2.ReceiveCompleted, _
        AddressOf MyMSMQBeginReceive
        ' Begin the asynchronous receive
        MessageQueue2.BeginReceive()
. . .
```

As you can see, these two lines of code accomplish the task of adding an event handler to the MyMSMQBeginReceive subprocedure. The targeted event is the *ReceiveCompleted* method being raised from MessageQueue2. The second line of code shown simply starts the asynchronous process with the *BeginReceive* method. While this MyMSMQAsyncAndTriggerVB sample application continues to execute, the *BeginReceive* method will be there, listening/running in the background and waiting for a message to be received into the specified MSMQ private queue.

NOTE   When you execute the BeginReceive function without a parameter (as I did), you are requesting that the asynchronous process wait for an MSMQ message indefinitely. Alternatively, you can specify a timeout parameter using the *System.TimeSpan* format.

The logic shown inside the MyMSMQBeginReceive subprocedure ends the asynchronous receive by receiving the MSMQ message. Notice the BeginReceive method being used again to resume the asynchronous receive process. In a real-life application, you would typically "do something" with the received message. For demonstration purposes, a message box will be used to simply provide visual notification that the message has been received.

Before you move on to the topic of MSMQ trigger setup, this is a good time to do a bit of preliminary testing. During a development life cycle, this phase of testing could be referred to as *unit testing*.

A Preliminary Test

Let's do a quick test. Execute the MyMSMQAsyncAndTriggerCOBOL sample application. Proceed to click each of the two buttons a few times. Observe that the
GUI displays the GUID on each Label control (see Figure 20-18).

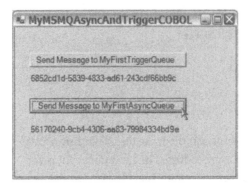

*Figure 20-18. The MyMSMQAsyncAndTriggerCOBOL sample application reflects
the GUID of each message sent to the MSMQ private queues.*

Next, use the Computer Management console to view the status of your two
MSMQ private queues. As shown in Figure 20-19, several messages have accumulated that indicate a successful preliminary test. You will notice (in Figure 20-19)
the step of manually purging the queues (right-click the Queue Messages folder
and select All Tasks ➤ Purge). Each private queue should be manually *purged* after
the preliminary test is complete.

Finally, manually execute the MyMSMQAsyncAndTriggerVB sample project.
Assuming the MSMQ private queues are empty, you should see that the Windows
Form GUI display from the Label control reflects that fact. Next, simply test the
one Button control to manually exit the application.

Do not discount the significance of testing this single Button control that
simply executes one code instruction:

```
Application.Exit()
```

I need to point out that this little Button control feature demonstrates the significant value gained from the asynchronous processing model. This Button
control actually works. What's the big deal, right? Think about it. You can use this
Button control to interact with your application *while* the BeginReceive asynchronous process is running in the background. In other words, the BeginReceive
call is *not* blocking the execution of the Button1_Click event method.

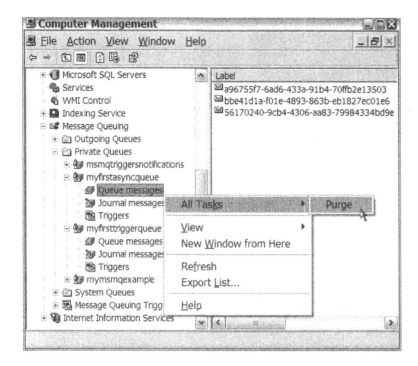

Figure 20-19. Using the Computer Management console to view the MSMQ private queues and to manually purge the accumulated messages

Establishing a nonblocking call while the client application is allowed to continue processing is one of the most significant aspects of the asynchronous processing model.

Your last unit test will be to follow this simple test script:

1. Execute the MyMSMQAsyncAndTriggerCOBOL sample application. Use the appropriate button control to place *just one* message into the MyFirstTriggerQueue MSMQ queue.

2. Manually execute the MyMSMQAsyncAndTriggerVB application. This time, the Label control should reflect that the MSMQ message was received. The GUID value being displayed provides an easy way to match one-to-one the sent message to the received message (see Figure 20-20).

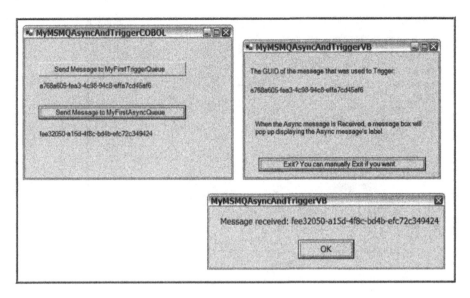

Figure 20-20. A side-by-side display of each sample application and the resulting message box during one phase of the preliminary unit testing

3. Use the appropriate Button control on the sample application MyMSMQAsyncAndTriggerCOBOL to place *just one* message into the MyFirstAsyncQueue. You should notice that the MyMSMQAsyncAndTriggerVB sample application automatically displays a message box. The message box should reflect the appropriate GUID value.

TIP During your preliminary testing, you might even place a few breakpoints in the VS .NET IDE code view window. This will give you the opportunity to step through your code and interactively debug if needed.

This completes your preliminary unit testing. Close each VS .NET IDE window. To simplify this demonstration a bit, copy both sample executables (.exe) to one common folder, C:\MSMQ-ASYNC-DEMO (see Figure 20-21). You will return to these executables in the next section.

Figure 20-21. Place the sample executables in the C:\MSMQ-ASYNC-DEMO to simplify the demonstration path displays.

In the next section you will walk through the creation of an MSMQ rule and trigger.

Creating an MSMQ Rule and Trigger

After you launch the Computer Management console and navigate to the Message Queuing node, you will notice a Message Queuing Triggers node (see Figure 20-22). You will start here. Notice that the Computer Management console window exposes the existence of the Outgoing Queues node (directly underneath the main Message Queuing node). It is good to be aware of this. If for any reason connectivity to your private or public queue is unavailable, your MSMQ messages will accumulate in the Outgoing Queues until such time that connectivity is reestablished.

NOTE   You will need administrative-level security on your local work-station to use the MSMQ trigger feature. Normally, for a development machine, this requirement is acceptable and granted.

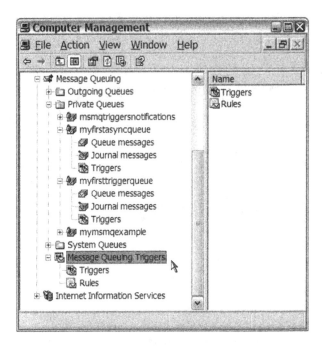

Figure 20-22. The Message Queuing Triggers node as shown in the Computer Management Console window

Follow these steps to create an MSMQ rule:

1. Right-click the Rules node and select New ➤ Rule (see Figure 20-23). A series of prompts will follow.

2. Enter a name and description in the New Rule window. You can use any name that you feel to be appropriate (see Figure 20-24). Click Next.

Figure 20-23. Preparing to create a new MSMQ rule

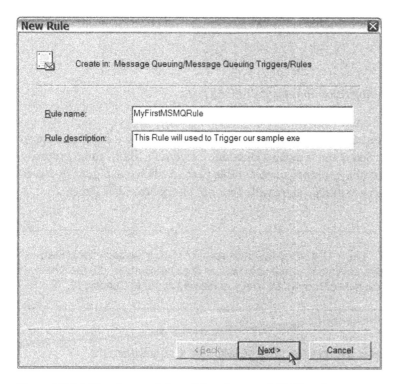

Figure 20-24. Naming and describing the new MSMQ rule

3. Add one or more conditions. Using the drop-down list, choose and add as appropriate. As shown in Figure 20-25, I have added just one condition. Click Next.

Figure 20-25. Adding conditions for your MSMQ rule

4. Next, you can choose to trigger a COM component or a stand-alone executable. Select the "Invoke standalone executable (EXE)" radio button and enter the appropriate executable path (as shown in Figure 20-26). Be sure to select the "Interact with desktop" check box. Click Finish.

NOTE The "COM component invocation" choice available for MSMQ triggers would have applied to the use of a class library (.dll) file. This was the type of project file that you learned about in Chapter 19.

That completes the creation of an MSMQ rule. Congratulations!

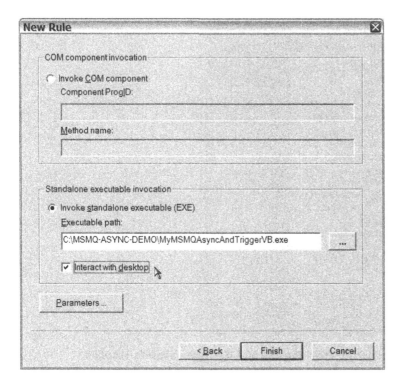

Figure 20-26. Specifying the standalone executable choice. Also, the "Interact with desktop" option is checked.

Next, you need to create an MSMQ trigger to use the MSMQ rule you just created. To initiate the short series of MSMQ trigger creation prompts, you can use the same Message Queuing Triggers node area you used to create the MSMQ rule. Optionally, you can navigate upward and use the Triggers node area located underneath the Private Queues node (see Figure 20-27).

I found that using the Triggers node underneath the Private Queues node (MyFirstTriggerQueue) worked well. If you choose this route, you are spared the need to enter the queue path name information. Personally, I prefer not having to enter the queue path name information. It's up to you. I'm choosing to use the Triggers node underneath the Private Queues node. Start the series of MSMQ trigger creation prompts by right-clicking the Triggers node. Then select New ➤ Trigger and follow the short series of prompts.

1. The first prompt asks you to enter the name of the MSMQ trigger. As shown in Figure 20-28, I have entered an appropriate name. I chose to change the message processing type from Peeking to Retrieval. This will cause the MSMQ message to be removed from the queue. I left the remaining settings at their default values. Notice that the "Queue path name" field is already filled in. Click Next.

Figure 20-27. Preparing to initiate the MSMQ trigger creation prompts

Figure 20-28. Entering the name for the new MSMQ trigger

2. The last prompt gives you the chance to attach your trigger to any existing MSMQ rules. Proceed to attach the one rule that is shown (see Figure 20-29). Click Finish. That is it!

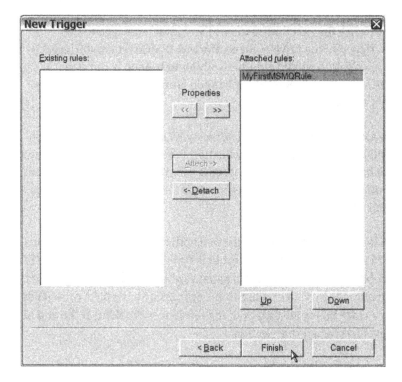

Figure 20-29. Attaching the MSMQ rule to the MSMQ trigger

TIP   During my development and testing, I needed to use the Services MMC snap-in to stop and restart the Message Queuing Triggers service a few times (the Services MMC snap-in is exposed in the Computer Management console). Of course, this came after editing the properties of my existing triggers and rules. You may or may not have the same experience. As an afterthought, I decided to adopt a practice of stopping the Message Queuing Triggers service before I edited existing triggers. Then I started the Message Queuing Triggers service after I was done. This seemed to work better. Additionally, I found it helpful to detach and reattach my rules a few times while tweaking the conditions.

You can now conduct your full *integration testing* by following these few steps:

1. Navigate to the folder location C:\MSMQ-ASYNC-DEMO and execute MyMSMQAsyncAndTriggerCOBOL.exe by double-clicking the .exe file.

2. When you click the first button to send an MSMQ message to the MyFirstTriggerQueue private queue, the MyMSMQAsyncAndTriggerVB sample application should automatically launch. Keep in mind that as the MyMSMQAsyncAndTriggerVB application launches, an asynchronous "request cycle" has begun.

3. Send an MSMQ message to the MyFirstAsyncQueue private queue. The MyMSMQAsyncAndTriggerVB application should automatically display a message box when an MSMQ message is sent to the MyFirstAsyncQueue private queue. The asynchronous process is resumed after the message box is displayed.

That concludes this chapter's demonstration with MSMQ and asynchronous processing. The MSMQ product has many other features that you can explore. The .NET Framework has many other classes to assist your use of the MSMQ product. You can further explore the use of asynchronous processing as well. As your needs dictate, please consider taking advantage of the references provided at the end of this chapter in the "To Learn More" section.

Other .NET Support for Asynchronous Processing

The .NET Framework exposes support for asynchronous processing in several areas (in addition to MSMQ). In any case, the basic model/approach will look familiar to you. You will recognize that the *BeginXXX* and *EndXXX* methods (methods beginning with the "Begin" and "End" prefixes) are available. Consider the following opportunities for introducing asynchronous processing into your application design:

- When you do file I/O, you will notice that there are *FileStream.BeginRead* and *FileStream.BeginWrite* methods available.

- When you do stream I/O, the *Stream.BeginRead* and *Stream.BeginWrite* methods work well for controlling an asynchronous cycle.

- When you do socket I/O, the *Socket.BeginReceive* method may be useful

- When you do networking/HTTP logic, look for *HttpSimpleClientProtocol.BeginInvoke*.

- When you work with ASP.NET XML Web services, *System.Web.Services.Protocols.WebClientAsyncResult* will come in handy.

- When you work with ASP.NET Web Forms, look for the following application-level method: *HttpApplication.AddOnBeginRequestAsync*.

- When you work with .NET Remoting channels (HTTP and TCP) and proxies, consider using the *RemoteAsyncDelegate.BeginInvoke* method.

You'll now turn your attention to an alternative .NET offering for distributed processing.

.NET Remoting

You have been introduced to several areas where distributed processing is supported in the .NET development arena. For example, an application that uses .NET XML Web services is supporting a distributed processing model. The book's previous discussions about MSMQ and COM+ introduced ways to use .NET- and Windows-based products with distributed processing models. With that, it would be a disservice[11] to you if I did not introduce to you the newest .NET distributed processing feature: *.NET Remoting*.

> **NOTE**   .NET Remoting is .NET's replacement for the Distributed Component Object Model (DCOM) Windows legacy feature.

The distributed processing feature .NET Remoting is primarily available for .NET client applications to be able to communicate with .NET server applications, potentially in a loosely coupled design. Such communication can occur between applications hosted on the same machine, on the same LAN, or on remotely located machines. On the other hand, XML Web services (and even MSMQ) fills the gap when disparate types of applications, runtimes, and even platforms need to communicate. You should consider .NET Remoting as one of your alternatives for distributed processing, particularly when each application involved is a "managed" application (i.e., a .NET application).

---

11. By just introducing a topic and not providing a thorough and complete discussion, I equally run the risk of doing you a disservice. Bear in mind, this book is designed to be a guide, not a complete reference. Please approach this discussion with that perspective. I can't emphasize enough that you should take advantage of the end-of-chapter references.

NOTE You can use .NET Remoting over TCP or HTTP network protocols.

You will notice that the .NET Framework provides significant support for .NET Remoting. The *System.Runtime.Remoting* namespace provides the basis from which to build these types of distributed applications. The System.Runtime.Remoting "supporting" namespaces are as follows:

- *System.Runtime.Remoting.Activation*

- *System.Runtime.Remoting.Channels*

- *System.Runtime.Remoting.Channels.Http*

- *System.Runtime.Remoting.Channels.Tcp*

- *System.Runtime.Remoting.Contexts*

- *System.Runtime.Remoting.Lifetime*

- *System.Runtime.Remoting.Messaging*

- *System.Runtime.Remoting.Metadata*

- *System.Runtime.Remoting.Metadata.W3cXsd2001*

- *System.Runtime.Remoting.MetadataServices*

- *System.Runtime.Remoting.Proxies*

- *System.Runtime.Remoting.Services*

As you can see from the impressive preceding list, there is certainly support available in the .NET Framework for Remoting. If you look at the naming convention used in the list of namespaces, you will get an idea of the topical nature taken with further learning into the area of Remoting. In other words, drilling down into the collection of Remoting namespaces will take you down the learning path of the following .NET Remoting technologies:

- *Object activation:* Client-side versus server-side, using marshal by value or marshal by reference.

- *Transport channels:* Using the *TcpChannel* or *HttpChannel* .NET Framework classes depending on the chosen protocol.

- *Contexts:* Context-bound objects (versus context-agile objects) and the proper use of the *SynchronizationAttribute* attribute. You will learn about the synchronization domain when you explore the SynchronizationAttribute attribute.[12]

- *Object lifetime:* Use of lease periods and determining whether to use *SingleCall* objects or *Singleton* call objects.

- *Messaging:* Working with the AsyncResult class for asynchronous processing. Also, using the Message object for remote calls and passing data.

- *Metadata and proxies:* Using SoapSuds.exe to extract and convert metadata to/from XML Schema. Using proxies to forward your object calls.

- *Sinks:* Creating and registering your sink to be on the receiving or sending end of your transport channels. Also creating message sinks and formatter sinks.

- *Formatters:* Using *SoapFormatter* or *BinaryFormatter* to serialize and deserialize your objects depending on the format of your message.

Please consider exploring the previously listed Remoting namespaces. You will find that, for Microsoft, this technology was not an afterthought. For you, learning about this technology should not be an afterthought either.

---

12. Interestingly enough, there are two SynchronizationAttribute classes. One lives in the System.EnterpriseServices namespace. The other lives in the System.Runtime.Remoting.Contexts namespace. The former is used for COM+ (Enterprise Services) synchronous scenarios. The latter is used both for asynchronous and synchronous needs, as long as the object is context bound.

TIP In Chapter 18, you were introduced to the Microsoft .NET Framework Configuration tool. As you explore and learn more about .NET Remoting, you will eventually come across the need to use this tool again. You will discover that developing a .NET Remoting application typically includes the need to configure communication channels. This tool exposes an option for Remoting Services. Recall that you access the Microsoft .NET Framework Configuration tool by clicking the Start button and selecting Programs ➤ Administrative Tools ➤ Microsoft .NET Framework Configuration.

I wish I could say that that was it. But there is more. Any serious attempt to learn about .NET Remoting should be accompanied by a comfortable understanding of several .NET topics not specific to .NET Remoting: application domains, synchronization domains, marshaling and serialization concerns, and object interfaces. In the simplest of terms, you will turn to .NET Remoting when you need to enable communication from one application domain to another application domain.

NOTE I briefly cover the topics application domains, marshaling and serialization concerns, and object interfaces in this book. Please use available references (including the references in the "To Learn More" section) for additional details.

Now, I need to bring this .NET Remoting discussion to an end and limit the coverage of this topic to a high-level introduction. To go much further into the details of .NET Remoting here would be going a bit beyond the scope of this book. Further learning of the topic .NET Remoting will certainly justify the use of the "To Learn More" references that I have provided. Expect to see the .NET Remoting technology implemented in your more sophisticated enterprise-level distributed applications.

TIP If there is just one point to take from this section it is this: .NET Remoting is one of several choices for building .NET distributed applications. You have been introduced to ASP.NET XML Web services, COM+, and MSMQ. These other technologies also support the distributed processing model. Each technique is available to address different business needs.

I have one additional enterprise development topic to cover: multithreading.

Introducing Multithreading

Through the years while developing on the mainframe, we all have grown comfortable with terms such as "multiprogramming," "multiprocessing," and "multitasking." With mainframe COBOL batch development, the distinction between multiprogramming, multiprocessing, and multitasking basically pointed out a level of granularity with concurrent processing. Let's review.

At a high level, multiple mainframe system initiators would concurrently process JCL Jobs. Each JCL Job had individual Job Steps that supported the concurrently processing Jobs. Each Job Step would execute your COBOL programs. Then, at a much lower level, the mainframe operating system would create one task from which resource management took place. As you know, the executing program had the option to create additional tasks (or subtasks). Coming from the mainframe, you may be more familiar with the acronym TCB, which stands for *Task Control Block*. All of these levels of "multi" processing are commonly known on the mainframe.

Now, it is time to learn about another "multi" term: *multithreading*. Generally speaking, when you use multithreading in your .NET Windows and Web applications, you are enabling your application to leverage multiple threads of execution—virtually at the same time. In some cases, you take advantage of multithreading without even being aware of it. For example, the most recent .NET sample application (in the section "Using MSMQ for Asynchronous Processing") demonstrated multithreading.

Think back for a moment. Recall the BeginReceive method that began the asynchronous process for you. At that time, I mentioned that the BeginReceive asynchronous process would be "running in the background." The fact is that the BeginReceive method created a new thread of execution. Because the new thread of execution (or simply, the *thread*) was created as a low-priority worker thread, the primary/main thread (running in the foreground) was not "blocked" by the lower priority thread that "waited" in the background.

For another moment, think further back—all the way back to Chapter 8. Recall the discussion about the garbage collector (GC). There, I mentioned that the CLR's GC ran in the background. Now, you can easily appreciate what the reference to "running in the background" really means. The GC is there, running on a lower-priority background thread.

NOTE Multithreading is a .NET feature that you should only use under three conditions. First, you absolutely must understand how to correctly implement the technique into your application design. Second, you must take your application through a rigorous testing phase. Third, you must first consider whether or not your application actually *needs* the benefits offered by multithreading.

Let's explore multithreading further.

Putting Multithreading into Perspective

You might wonder if the mainframe task is analogous to the Windows thread. The answer is yes and no. Yes, a thread is used by the operating system for scheduling and execution. No, a thread does not own memory and other resources. When it comes to the "owner" of resources, then you are really talking about the Windows process. As you will soon see, this is just one piece of the puzzle. Let's chat for a moment about processes.

CAUTION Be forewarned. The discussion that follows may appear to be rather abstract. However, if you want to efficiently, safely, and correctly use multithreading, you should give consideration to understanding each detail (and then some) contained in this section.

Defining a Process

You can easily view your active processes by launching the Windows Task Manager. Take a moment to press Ctrl-Alt-Delete to view your active processes. As shown in Figure 20-30, the Processes tab displays any active processes.

The ASP.NET application worker process

Internet Information Services (IIS) process

Dynamic link library (DLL) host process

Recent MSMQ sample applications shown as processes

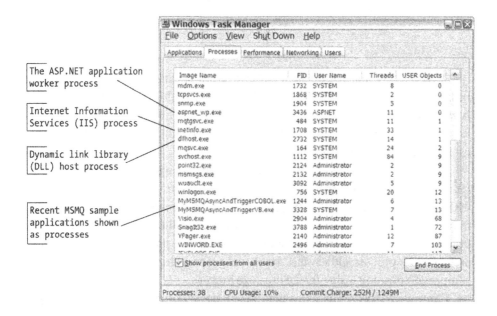

Figure 20-30. Viewing the Windows Task Manager's Processes tab. For demonstration purposes, I have executed the recent MSMQ sample applications.

In Figure 20-30, you will notice the recent MSMQ sample applications shown as processes. Additionally, you will notice that I have singled out three other processes: Aspnet_wp.exe, Inetinfo.exe, and Dllhost.exe. A complete understanding of processes will bring you to the point of knowing the purpose behind Aspnet_wp.exe, Inetinfo.exe, and Dllhost.exe.

Say that you just created an ASP.NET Web application. Then, being curious, you explored your Computer Management console MMC snap-in and noticed that you could configure your ASP.NET Web application (in the Computer Management console, select Services and Applications ➤ Internet Information Services, and then right-click your Web application and select Properties ➤ Directory Tab ➤ Application Protection). You would find that choosing the Application Protection choice of Low (IIS Process), Medium (Pooled), or High (Isolated) would cause your Web application to "run" within either the Inetinfo.exe (Low) or Aspnet_wp.exe (Medium or High) process. Hmmm, interesting.

NOTE   Using the Application Protection choice of Medium will result in sharing one instance of the Aspnet_wp.exe process. The Application Protection choice of High will result in a dedicated instance of an Aspnet_wp.exe process. Pre-.NET Web applications (ASP) used the Dllhost.exe process when either Medium or High was chosen for Application Protection.

Now, let's say that you decided to create another class library (.dll) that would be hosted in Enterprises Services (COM+). Recall that this is called a *serviced component*. Regardless of which approach you decided to take (dynamic registration, Regasm.exe, or Regsvcs.exe) to install your serviced component into the COM+ catalog, you would need to choose an activation type.

If you choose to have your COM+ application run with the activation type of Library, you'll run it in-process. If you choose to have your COM+ application run with the activation type of Server, you'll it run out-of-process. What process do you think this all applies to? That's right! Allow me to introduce to you the Dllhost.exe process. When your serviced component is running in-process, it's running inside of the client's process. Otherwise, the out-of-process choice has your serviced component running inside the Dllhost.exe process.

Can you see the implications here? If you have a simple .NET Windows application that is not using a serviced component, it will run in its own process—its own address space. On the other hand, if you have an ASP.NET Web application that happens to consume an in-process serviced component, the processes that you are actually concerned about could be either Aspnet_wp.exe or Inetinfo.exe, and possibly Dllhost.exe. Hmmm, interesting.

Now that you have a good understanding of processes, let's drop down a notch in terms of granularity. Before I discuss the infamous thread, I need to introduce two more pieces of the puzzle: the application domain and the context.

Application Domains and Contexts

In short, you can find one or more application domains in a .NET application's process. An application domain will host one or more contexts. Objects live in a context. Now, that wasn't that bad, right? Good. Let's continue.

Unless you specify otherwise, your code executes within the boundaries of the *default* application domain. A default context is created for you as well. Depending on the needs of an object and the characteristic of each particular context, an object is likely to "jump" from one context to another unless the object is a context-bound object.

TIP Consider exploring the .NET Framework's *System.AppDomain* class. You will want to learn more about default domains and the explicit creation of application domains using the *System.AppDomain.CreateDomain* method. Additionally, give strong consideration to referring back to the section "Policy Hierarchy" in Chapter 18. There you will find your first introduction to the AppDomain class. Yes, this is the same AppDomain class that you learned about in the security policy hierarchy discussion.

Application domains are made apparent each time you end a debug session while in the VS .NET IDE. You will notice that the VS .NET IDE Debug window reports on which assemblies were loaded into your application domain. You will recognize a context-bound object has either of the following characteristics: it is an object created by a class that inherits from the base class of *System.ContextBoundObject* class, or it is an object that uses the *SynchronizationAttribute* attribute from either the *System.Runtime.Remoting.Contexts* namespace or the *System.EnterpriseServices* namespace.

NOTE You might have noticed some overlap between the topics of multithreading and Remoting. That is rather perceptive of you. An understanding of application domains (and even context-bound objects) will serve you well as you further explore either multithreading or Remoting.

Now that you understand the basic idea behind processes and application domains, let's talk about the thread.

The Thread of Execution

The thread executes your managed code (your managed procedures). This thread of execution can take place within the boundaries of the default application domain. Multiple threads of execution can take place within one application domain. Additionally, one thread of execution can cross application domains. Apart from how a thread relates to an application domain, it may help to also know that a thread stores the actual stack, the current state of the CPU registers, and execution schedule information.

When you worked with MSMQ earlier in this chapter, the BeginReceive asynchronous method created a multithreading scenario for you. You should look at this as an implicit use of multithreading. Naturally, you will want to know how to explicitly work with threads to manipulate your custom multithreading processing models.

So, are *you* ready for multithreading? You think so, huh? Well, let me share a few more thoughts with you. Afterward, I promise, you will look at some multithreading code.

A Bug to Remember

Many mainframe moons ago, there was an occasion when I was rewriting a COBOL program. The rewrite was simply to move from the ANSI 74 standard to the ISO/ANSI 85 standard. After I completed the rewrite, an intermittent bug was discovered. I recall spending several days trying to track down this problem. I was eventually able to narrow the problem down to two statements that followed one after the other. One statement was an OPEN statement. The other statement was a simple READ. The strangest thing was that this portion of the logic had been "ported" over as-is from the original program, a simple OPEN statement followed by a READ statement. To make matters worse, other OPEN and READ statements that were not paired together as these two were, were working just fine.

Ultimately, I resorted to recompiling both the original ANSI 74 standard COBOL and the rewritten ISO/ANSI 85 standard program. I chose the compile option (LIST) that produced an assembly language translation listing. After doing a side-by-side comparison (from one program to the other), targeting just the two suspect lines, the cause of the problem became apparent. There, buried between nearly a dozen lines of assembly language code, I found a difference between the two programs. On the surface, both programs used the same two high-level statements. Underneath, at a lower level, the code was composed of nearly a dozen significantly different assembler language statements.

Apparently, the compiler, in its effort to produce optimized code, translated these two OPEN and READ statements in a different way than the other OPEN and READ statements. My fix was to separate these two high-level statements in an insignificant way. This was enough to trick the compiler into creating the expected correct assembler code.

You certainly recall the previous discussions about Microsoft intermediate language (MSIL) and the just-in-time (JIT) optimizations that occur with your

.NET managed code. Do you see where this is leading? That's right! Watch out. Be aware of the code that actually runs for you. Ultimately, *that* is the code that *will* matter. In the end, it's not what the high-level code looks like that matters. Rather, it's what the high-level code gets translated/optimized to that matters.

Generally, you make design decisions based on the high-level code that you "see." How the low-level version of your application runs will impact any design decisions that you have made—decisions made based on the high-level code view—for better or for worse. This becomes all the more critical when you are designing a multithreaded application.

Did you ever imagine that multithreading carried these types of low-level considerations?

Low-Level Architecture: Why?

My first exploration into multithreading left me questioning the need to *really* understand low-level architecture topics such as context-bound objects and so forth. It was not until I learned about the multithreading concerns of potential deadlocks, thread pool management, thread time slicing and starvation, unsynchronized collisions, the dangers of global variables, and corrupted shared variables that I decided to dig down further.

Yes, you can easily use multithreading without knowing or caring about context-bound objects and other low-level technical information. However, when those pesky intermittent bugs start showing up, you may regret that you ever heard the word "multithreading." After you have spent hours, days, or weeks (assuming that you have not gotten fired by that point) trying to figure out why the simple multithreading logic seems to work most of the time but not all of the time, you will want to understand what is really going on. You will appreciate what a lower-level understanding of your .NET environment really means.

Therefore, starting with a firm understanding about processes will introduce you to application domains. An understanding about context-bound objects and application domains implies that you are ready to be introduced to synchronization domains and the *SynchronizationAttribute* attribute. Understanding the value of synchronization domains means that you might have already learned about protecting the integrity of your shared variables with the *SyncLock* statement. Truly understanding when to use the SyncLock statement certainly means that you will have become equally comfortable with several *System.Threading* classes (i.e., *InterLocked*, *Monitor*, and *Mutex*).

TIP Some write-ups on the topic of multithreading seem to only mention the use of the SyncLock statement when you want to achieve synchronization. A more complete exploration will unearth at least four additional techniques: synchronization domains and the three System.Threading classes InterLocked, Monitor, and Mutex. Each synchronization technique is designed for specific scenarios. Each technique, including the SyncLock statement, has strengths and weaknesses. You should be aware of each choice and choose wisely.

With all this talk about synchronization, perhaps you may have gathered that all you really have to do is use any one of the available synchronization techniques. This is partially correct. Let's take a quick look at what I like to refer to as the ".NET Framework thread-safe" factor. As you will see, there is much to consider.

Is the .NET Framework Thread-Safe?

As you know, the .NET Framework is composed of many high-level classes and members. Fortunately, Microsoft labels each class as either being thread-safe or not thread-safe. Unfortunately, many of the .NET Framework classes are *not* thread-safe. This simply means that using any of the synchronization techniques will be that much more important when you design a multithreaded application that uses a not-thread-safe class.

Although Microsoft's NET Framework documentation states that all .NET Framework public static members (methods, properties, and fields) are thread-safe, there is still cause for concern. Notice I used the term "concern," not "alarm." When a class is not thread-safe, this simply means that you should be aware of this fact. Additionally, you should take this fact into consideration when you design your applications.

Do You Remember the Application State Management Topic?

In Chapter 15, I suggested that you "use the Lock and Unlock methods to protect against concurrent update collisions." Now it should be easier for you to appreciate the whole purpose behind that suggestion. Recall that the concern surrounded the possibility of updating the application state at any point outside the Start and End application-level events/methods. In that case, there was a possibility that two threads may have tried to update the same application state information at the same time.

The *System.Web.HttpApplicationState.Lock* method blocks other threads from accessing the application state variables. The companion method, *System.Web.HttpApplicationState.UnLock*, removes the block. In this case, the Lock and Unlock methods are implementing a form of synchronization to protect the integrity of the application variables that is made necessary by the concurrent processing of sessions on separate threads.

To give you a sense of the thread safety notifications to look for when you research the .NET Framework Help text, I have prepared a series of figures. I captured each figure in the series directly from the Microsoft Visual Studio .NET documentation tool. Let's start with Figure 20-31, which reflects an example of a completely thread-safe .NET Framework class.

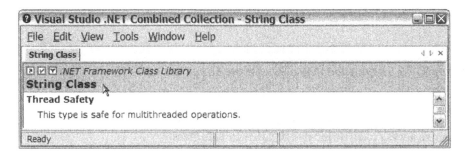

Figure 20-31. The thread safety notice for the String class

As shown in Figure 20-32, some .NET Framework classes are thread-safe for reading, but not for writing.

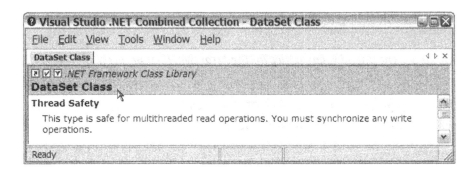

Figure 20-32. The thread safety notice for the Dataset class

Figure 20-33 displays a class that is generally not thread-safe. However, it offers a thread-safe alternative through a specified *SyncRoot* property.

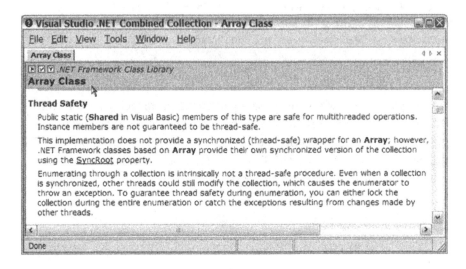

Figure 20-33. The thread safety notice for the Array class

As shown in Figure 20-34, you can use a specified thread-safe property to synchronize access to an otherwise not-thread-safe class.

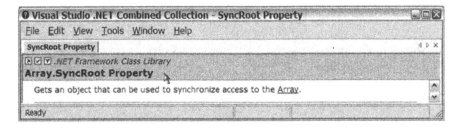

Figure 20-34. The thread safety notice for the Array.SyncRoot property

As shown in Figure 20-35, some .NET Framework classes offer limited thread safety while also offering a thread-safe wrapper class.

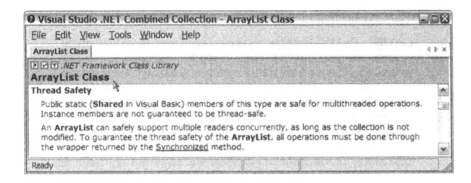

Figure 20-35. The thread safety notice for the ArrayList class

Finally, in Figure 20-36, a wrapper method is available on several .NET classes for thread-safe operations. It appears that the majority of the classes found in the System.Collections namespace offer this same wrapper method alternative.

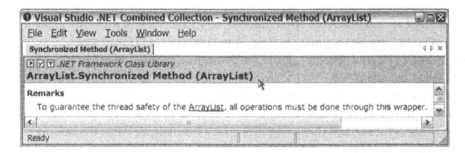

Figure 20-36. The thread safety notice for the wrapper method
ArrayList.Synchronized

This series of figures should give you a good idea of the range of thread safety support that exists across the .NET Framework. Being aware is really part of the challenge. Once you approach multithreading from this perspective, your chances for success increase dramatically.

Let's turn now to look at some actual multithreading code. That is, if you are still interested in multithreading.

CAUTION   One last warning: Incorrect use of multithreading can be hazardous to your career! In other words, be extremely careful. Give serious consideration to extensive study and research using sample applications only. Make sure you have a firm understanding of multithreading before you implement any explicit use of multithreading in your production applications. What you read in this chapter is simply an introduction to the topic of multithreading. As you can see, multithreading does involve a low-level understanding about your .NET application. This is cause for a cautious and respectful approach. Yes, explore. But be careful.

Using Multithreading

As you have gathered by now, the .NET Framework provides a namespace for the *Threading* classes. The namespace, System.Threading, offers a vast collection[13] of classes and several delegates, enumerations, and structures. To provide a general idea of how to use two common System.Threading classes (*Thread and ThreadStart*), I have created a sample .NET Windows application called MyThreadingExampleVB.

This sample application presents a Windows Form containing four Button controls, one Label control, and one TextBox control. Logic located in the Form class constructor method (*New*) executes once automatically when the sample application is loaded. At that time, the TextBox is updated with information reflecting thread statistics. Otherwise, further processing requires that you click either of the Button controls. From the top down, the buttons (when clicked) will expose the following functionality:

- Explicitly create and start a background worker thread. A loop will begin. Each iteration through the loop will update the Label control with an incremented number.

- Put the background worker thread to sleep.

---

13. Sorry, there are no interfaces in this namespace. There goes my chance to spell out one of my favorite acronyms: DICES.

- Kill the process.

- Attempt to run the loop in the main/primary thread. This will cause the sample application to "hang" and become unresponsive. This button is provided simply for demonstration purposes.

The design-time view in the VS .NET IDE of the sample application MyThreadingExampleVB is shown in Figure 20-37.

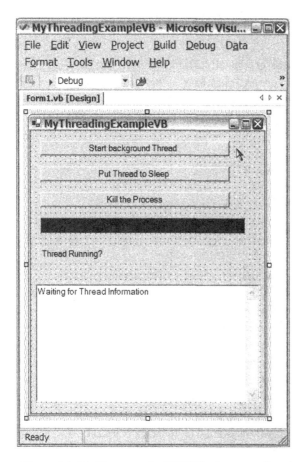

Figure 20-37. The sample .NET Windows application MyThreadingExampleVB

The code in the Form class constructor (New) method is shown in Listing 20-6.

Listing 20-6. The Form Class Constructor Method (New) of the
MyThreadingExampleVB Sample Application

```
Public Class Form1
    Inherits System.Windows.Forms.Form
#Region " Windows Form Designer generated code "
Public Sub New()
        MyBase.New()

        'This call is required by the Windows Form Designer.
        InitializeComponent()

        'Add any initialization after the InitializeComponent() call
        System.Threading.Thread.CurrentThread.Name = "MyPrimaryThread"
        Dim myappdomain As AppDomain
        myappdomain = AppDomain.CurrentDomain
        TextBox1.Text = "AppDomain: " & _
        myappdomain.ToString & vbCrLf
        TextBox1.Text = TextBox1.Text & _
        "Current Executing Thread: " & _
        myappdomain.GetCurrentThreadId.ToString & vbCrLf
        'TextBox1.Text = TextBox1.Text & "Context: " & _
        'System.Threading.Thread.CurrentContext.DefaultContext.ToString & vbCrLf

        Dim p As System.Diagnostics.Process = Process.GetCurrentProcess()
        Dim ProcessThreadArray As System.Diagnostics.ProcessThread
        TextBox1.Text = TextBox1.Text & "Name: " & _
        System.Threading.Thread.CurrentThread.Name & vbCrLf

        For Each ProcessThreadArray In p.Threads
            TextBox1.Text = TextBox1.Text & _
            "-----------------------------" & vbCrLf
            TextBox1.Text = TextBox1.Text & _
            "Thread ID: " & ProcessThreadArray.Id.ToString & vbCrLf
            TextBox1.Text = TextBox1.Text & _
          "PriorityLevel :" & ProcessThreadArray.PriorityLevel.ToString & vbCrLf
            TextBox1.Text = TextBox1.Text & _
            "ThreadState: " & ProcessThreadArray.ThreadState.ToString & vbCrLf
        Next
End Sub
. . .
```

You will notice the System.Threading namespace used in several places in Listing 20-6. Additionally, notice the following code line:

```
System.Threading.Thread.CurrentThread.Name = "MyPrimaryThread"
```

Basically, that line is assigning a name to the main/primary thread. You should also pay particular attention (in the code in Listing 20-6) to the use of the *System.Diagnostics.Process* class. This is the key to getting a collection of the available threads.

Now let's look at the remaining code used in the sample application. The code in Listing 20-7 is taken from the Click events/methods for each respective Button control.

Listing 20-7. The Remaining Code from the MyThreadingExampleVB Sample Application

```
Public Class Form1
    Inherits System.Windows.Forms.Form
#Region " Windows Form Designer generated code "
. . . (the relevant portions of code left out here already shown above)
#End Region

    Dim myThreadStart As New _
    System.Threading.ThreadStart(AddressOf ThreadingDelegateMethod)
    Dim mythread As New System.Threading.Thread(myThreadStart)
    Dim I As Int32

    Private Sub Button1_Click_1(ByVal sender As System.Object, _
    ByVal e As System.EventArgs) Handles Button1.Click
        Button1.Enabled = False
        Button4.Enabled = False
        Call ThreadingDemo()
    End Sub

    Private Sub Button2_Click(ByVal sender As System.Object, _
    ByVal e As System.EventArgs) Handles Button2.Click
        mythread.Sleep(2000)

    End Sub
```

```
Private Sub ThreadingDemo()
    mythread.Name = "MyBackGroundThread"
    mythread.Priority = Threading.ThreadPriority.BelowNormal
    mythread.Start()
End Sub

Public Sub ThreadingDelegateMethod()
    Dim myappdomain As AppDomain
    myappdomain = AppDomain.CurrentDomain

    Dim p2 As System.Diagnostics.Process = Process.GetCurrentProcess()
    Dim ProcessThreadArray2 As System.Diagnostics.ProcessThread
    TextBox1.Text = TextBox1.Text & _
    "********************************" & vbCrLf
    TextBox1.Text = TextBox1.Text & _
    "Current Executing Thread from AppDomain: " & _
    myappdomain.GetCurrentThreadId.ToString & vbCrLf
    TextBox1.Text = TextBox1.Text & "Name: " & _
     System.Threading.Thread.CurrentThread.Name & vbCrLf
    For Each ProcessThreadArray2 In p2.Threads
        TextBox1.Text = TextBox1.Text & _
        "-------------------------------" & vbCrLf
        TextBox1.Text = TextBox1.Text & "Thread ID: " & _
        ProcessThreadArray2.Id.ToString & vbCrLf
        TextBox1.Text = TextBox1.Text & "PriorityLevel :" & _
        ProcessThreadArray2.PriorityLevel.ToString & vbCrLf
        TextBox1.Text = TextBox1.Text & "ThreadState: " & _
        ProcessThreadArray2.ThreadState.ToString & vbCrLf
    Next

    Do While True
        I += 1
        Dim myMethodInvoker As New MethodInvoker(AddressOf updateLabel)
        myMethodInvoker.Invoke()
        'Call updateLabel()
    Loop
End Sub
Public Sub updateLabel()
    Label1.Text = "!! The Thread is Running !! " & i
End Sub
```

```
Private Sub Button3_Click(ByVal sender As System.Object, _
ByVal e As System.EventArgs) Handles Button3.Click
        'one way to kill a process
        'Dim p3 As System.Diagnostics.Process = _
        'Process.GetCurrentProcess()
        'p3.Kill()

        'Another way to "kill" a process
        System.Environment.Exit(0)

End Sub


Private Sub Button4_Click(ByVal sender As System.Object, _
ByVal e As System.EventArgs) Handles Button4.Click
        'This will block the primary thread
        Call ThreadingDelegateMethod()
End Sub
```

End Class

Observe that near the top of Listing 20-7 are a few lines of code that look like this:

```
Dim myThreadStart As New _
System.Threading.ThreadStart(AddressOf ThreadingDelegateMethod)
Dim mythread As New System.Threading.Thread(myThreadStart)
```

These few lines begin the creation of the worker thread. Notice the *System.Threading.ThreadStart* delegate being instantiated. Additionally, you should note the *System.Threading.Thread* class being instantiated. The remaining logic to execute (start) the new worker thread is a third line of code that uses the *Start* method. You will see that when the Button1_Click_1 event/method is executed, the worker thread is given the name MyBackGroundThread and a priority of *Threading.ThreadPriority.BelowNormal.* Then, the Start method is executed to start the new worked thread.

As per the ThreadStart delegate's instruction, ThreadingDelegateMethod is executed as the worker thread starts. The worker thread will continue to run until you kill the process (using the appropriate Button control). By the way, the BelowNormal priority was chosen to ensure that you would still be able to interact with the GUI Windows Form. After all, the main/primary thread will continue to run. You are dependent on the main/primary thread allowing you to continue interacting with the application while the worker thread runs in the background.

TIP In reference to the preceding sample code, notice the use of the *MethodInvoker* delegate to invoke the *updateLabel* subprocedure. Reportedly, this is a thread-safe approach when you use one thread to update GUI Windows Form controls that were created by a different thread (rather than just calling the updateLabel subprocedure). In this case, the main/primary thread created the controls.

Run the sample application. Before you click any of the Button controls, the sample application reflects the available information as expected (see Figure 20-38). At this point, the worker thread has not been started.

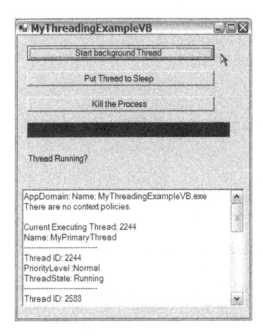

Figure 20-38. Executing the sample .NET Windows application MyThreadingExampleVB. The worker thread has not been started.

The information captured for the scrollable TextBox control is shown in Listing 20-8.

Listing 20-8. After Starting the MyThreadingExampleVB Sample Application, the Information As Written to the TextBox Control Before the Worker Thread Is Started

```
AppDomain: Name: MyThreadingExampleVB.exe
There are no context policies.


Current Executing Thread: 3780
Name: MyPrimaryThread
------------------------------
Thread ID: 3780
PriorityLevel :Normal
ThreadState: Running
------------------------------
Thread ID: 2968
PriorityLevel :Normal
ThreadState: Wait
------------------------------
Thread ID: 3844
PriorityLevel :Highest
ThreadState: Wait
------------------------------
Thread ID: 3372
PriorityLevel :Normal
ThreadState: Wait
------------------------------
Thread ID: 2840
PriorityLevel :Normal
ThreadState: Wait
------------------------------
Thread ID: 3900
PriorityLevel :Normal
ThreadState: Wait
------------------------------
Thread ID: 3148
PriorityLevel :Normal
ThreadState: Wait
```

Next, click the Button control at the top of the form to *start* the worker thread (see Figure 20-39).

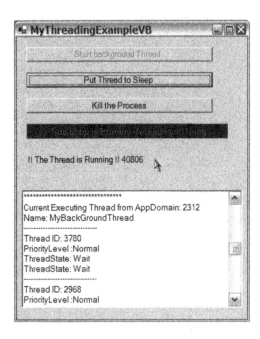

Figure 20-39. Executing the sample .NET Windows application MyThreadingExampleVB. The worker thread has been started. Notice that the Label control is being updated.

After the worker thread is started, additional information is concatenated and written to the scrollable TextBox control. The Label control reflects the incrementing value. Experiment with the button to put the worker thread to sleep. You will notice that the worker thread wakes up after the code for 2,000 milliseconds. Next, click the appropriate button to kill the process. Listing 20-9 shows the additional information captured from the TextBox control.

Listing 20-9. After Starting the Worker Thread, Additional Information Is Captured from the TextBox Control

```
********************************
Current Executing Thread from AppDomain: 2312
Name: MyBackGroundThread
-------------------------------
Thread ID: 3780
PriorityLevel :Normal
ThreadState: Wait
-------------------------------
Thread ID: 2968
PriorityLevel :Normal
ThreadState: Wait
```

```
-----------------------------
Thread ID: 3844
PriorityLevel :Highest
ThreadState: Wait
-----------------------------
Thread ID: 3372
PriorityLevel :Normal
ThreadState: Wait
-----------------------------
Thread ID: 2840
PriorityLevel :Normal
ThreadState: Wait
-----------------------------
Thread ID: 3900
PriorityLevel :Normal
ThreadState: Wait
-----------------------------
Thread ID: 3148
PriorityLevel :Normal
ThreadState: Wait
-----------------------------
Thread ID: 2312
PriorityLevel :BelowNormal
ThreadState: Running
```

As you can see from Listing 20-9, the worker thread (which has an ID of 2312) has a ThreadState of Running. The main/primary thread (which has an ID of 3780) has a ThreadState of Wait. Each time you execute this sample application, the thread ID value will change. However, the relative results will be the same.

If you want to see what will happen when the main/primary thread is allowed to run the loop, simply click the appropriate button (associated with the Button4_Click event/method). However, let me warn you: After you click this button, you will not be able to interact with the Windows Form—not even to kill the process. You will notice that the Label control does not reflect the incremented counter. To kill the process, you will need to press Ctrl-Alt-Delete. Locate and select the MyThreadingExampleVB sample application/process in the Windows Task Manager window (either on the Processes or Applications tab). On the Applications tab, click End Task. Optionally, on the Processes tab, click End Process.

As you can see, writing out information is useful, specifically for learning and demonstration purposes. During your real-life development, it is likely that you will want incorporate either of the tools discussed in the next section.

Tools to Help Monitor Your Application

During the development of your multithreaded application, rather than writing information out to a TextBox control, you may find it more useful to take advantage of one of the .NET Framework classes that are designed specifically for the purpose of writing out information to help in debugging scenarios. You have seen the System.Diagnostics.Trace class before. The *System.Diagnostics.Debug* class is another very useful .NET Framework class. I suggest that you become familiar with both as each has its advantages.

Now, there are times when you will want to use other techniques or other tools to diagnose and troubleshoot your applications. This holds true even when you are not working with multithreaded applications. Nevertheless, this is a convenient point at which to bring the topic up.

In the next sections you'll take a look at the following tools:

- The Windows Performance Monitor (Perfmon) tool

- The VS .NET IDE Threads window

- The VS .NET IDE Disassembly window

The Performance Monitor

You may recall reading about the Performance Monitor (Perfmon) in an earlier chapter. Yes, this is the same tool that I introduced to you back in Chapter 8. Recall that you can access this tool by navigating to your desktop taskbar, clicking the Start button, and selecting Programs ➤ Administrative Tools ➤ Performance. Because you have seen this tool before, I do not go into too much detail regarding its use in this section.

Start by executing the MyThreadingExampleVB sample and clicking the appropriate button control to start the worker thread. Then, while the Label control is reflecting an active background worker thread, launch the Perfmon tool.

As you have seen before, Figure 20-40 shows the Add Counters window. Select Thread from the Performance object drop-down box. Then select the Context Switches/sec counter. Notice that the "Select instances from list" selection box shows an instance available for each thread that the sample application has. Select each available instance for the sample application and click Add to add your selected counters and instances.

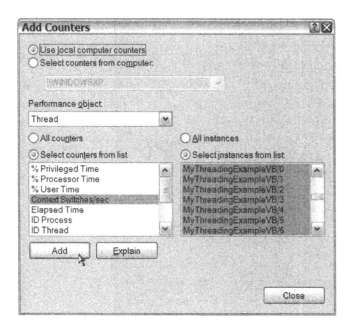

Figure 20-40. Adding performance counters

As shown in Figure 20-41, you can access the Explain Text window by clicking Explain on the Add Counters window. Click Close to close the Add Counters window.

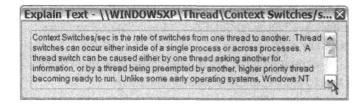

Figure 20-41. The Explain Text window

The Performance window (see Figure 40-42) shows that there is significant activity for a couple of the selected instances.

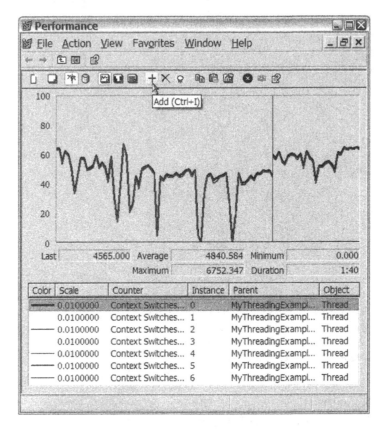

Figure 20-42. The Performance window showing activity for the sample application

Next, return to the Add Counters window. This time, select All counters for the Thread performance object (see Figure 20-43). Click Add and then click Close to close the Add Counters window.

As shown in Figure 20-44, adding all of the counters gives you much more information about the thread activity of the sample application.

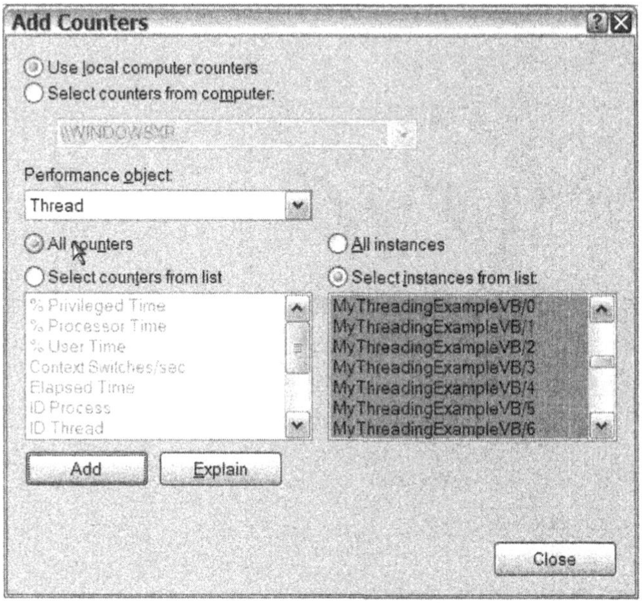

Figure 20-43. Adding all counters for the Thread performance object

After you explore this displayed information, you are able to map each instance number with a specific thread ID. You can even map the thread ID values shown here with the thread ID values written to the MyThreadingExampleVB Windows Form TextBox display. Experiment with this tool. While you look at the performance graphs, click the appropriate button on the MyThreadingExampleVB sample application to put the worker thread to sleep. Notice the change in the performance display.

Using the Perfmon tool, you can see that there are context switches occurring. In some real-life production cases, this could be a cause for concern. Otherwise, from this Perfmon tool display, you can see that while the background worker thread is active, the main/primary thread continues to be active as well. This is an important point to realize. Because you have not coded otherwise, the operating system continues to switch in and out each thread, giving each a chance to process.

For now, kill the sample application process in preparation for the next topic.

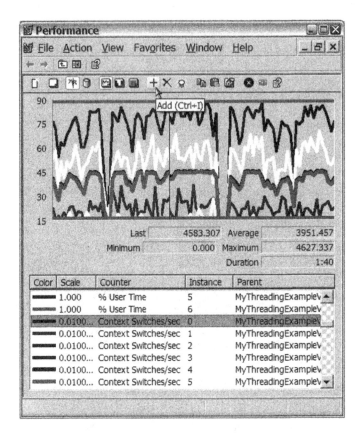

Figure 20-44. The Performance window showing more activity for the sample application

The VS .NET Threads Window

The VS .NET IDE offers several useful debug windows. One window that is particularly applicable to this multithreading discussion is the Threads window.

To prepare for the next demonstration, kill the sample application process (if you have not already done so). Then, with the MyThreadingExampleVB project open in VS .NET, place a debug breakpoint in the *ThreadingDelegateMethod* subprocedure as shown in Figure 20-45.

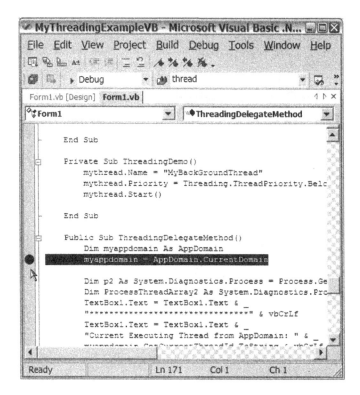

Figure 20-45. Placing a debug breakpoint

Start the MyThreadingExampleVB sample application from within VS .NET by pressing F5 (optionally, you can click the Start arrow located on the VS .NET IDE Standard toolbar). After you click the appropriate button to start the worker thread, processing will pause at your breakpoint. Once execution is paused (in break mode), navigate to the main VS .NET IDE toolbar and select Debug ➤ Windows ➤ Threads (optionally, press Ctrl-Alt-H), as shown in Figure 20-46.

As shown in Figure 20-47, the Threads window provides a very quick, code-free way to view threading information.

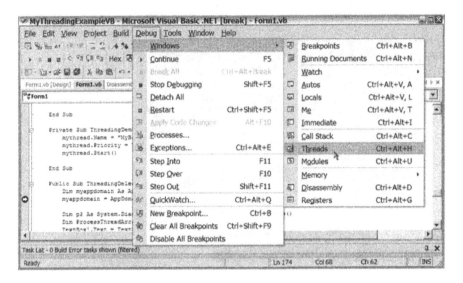

Figure 20-46. Launching the VS .NET Threads window

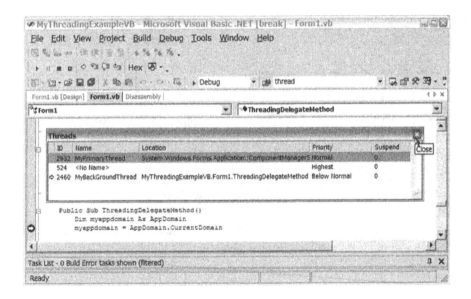

Figure 20-47. Viewing the VS .NET Threads window

Additionally, if you right-click inside of the Threads window, you will see a pop-up context window. You can use this pop-up context window for minimal thread manipulation. Use this sample application to safely explore and learn.

You can resume the processing of the sample application by pressing F5 (optionally, you can click the Continue arrow located on the VS .NET IDE Debug toolbar). By default, you can press the F11 key if you want to step through the code, line by line. There are many occasions when stepping through code interactively is useful. Those of you who have had the opportunity to use interactive debuggers on the mainframe (e.g., INTERTEST, XPEDITER, COBTEST, or even TESTCOB) will certainly feel right at home using these VS .NET debugging features.

NOTE If you leave execution paused long enough, you will need to restart the sample application. One of the "other" background threads will expire. You might consider experimenting to see if you can get around this. In the meantime, just be aware of this fact. Once you have had a chance to view the Threads window, promptly press F5 to resume execution.

Let's now take a look at another tool within the VS .NET IDE.

The VS .NET Disassembly Window

Following the same steps to place the sample application in break mode, navigate to the main VS .NET toolbar. This time, select Debug ➤ Windows ➤ Disassembly (optionally, press Ctrl-Alt-D). The VS .NET Disassembly window is shown in Figure 20-48.

While it's in break mode, the Disassembly window positions its display at the line of execution where the breakpoint was enabled. Notice that the source code is displayed along with the assembler language for the source code. Now, any mainframe programmer would have to feel right home after using this VS .NET tool. Recall that pesky mainframe COBOL bug that I mentioned to you earlier (in the section "A Bug to Remember")? Certainly, if you ever really want or need to know what lower-level code is actually running, the Disassembly window is as close as a couple of VS .NET clicks.

Can you believe it? Interactive debugging with assembler language code is available right there in your VS .NET IDE. What more could you ask for? Can it get any better? Actually, yes, it does get even better. Any programmer inclined to look at assembler language code will certainly want to view the contents of the registers as well as the actual memory content.

Using the now-familiar VS .NET navigation path, you can launch the Registers window by selecting Debug ➤ Windows ➤ Registers (optionally, press Ctrl-Alt-G), as shown in Figure 20-49.

Figure 20-48. The VS .NET Disassembly window

Figure 20-49. Viewing the VS .NET Registers window

You can launch one or more (up to four) Memory windows by selecting Debug ➤ Windows ➤ Memory ➤ Memory ? (optionally, press Ctrl-Alt-M-?). You replace ? with 1, 2, 3, or 4 depending on how many Memory windows you wish to open. See Figure 20-50.

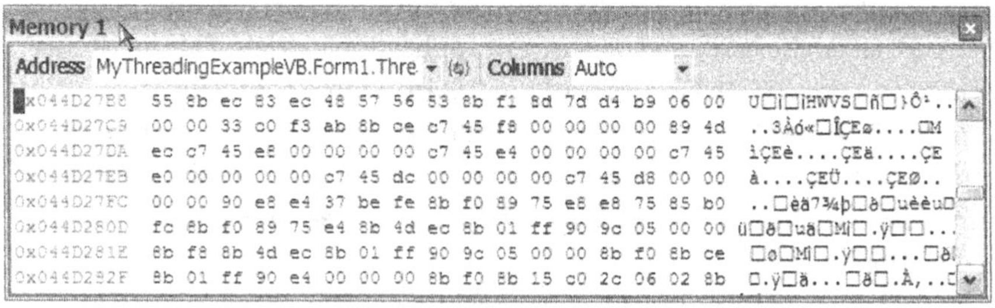

Figure 20-50. Viewing a VS .NET Memory window

You and I know that there have been times when you needed this type of low-level information. Practically every seasoned mainframe programmer has had *those* occasions of needing to view memory dumps. Granted, it's not an everyday occasion. At the same time, it's not an everyday occasion that you'll find yourself needing to build multithreaded applications, either.

One Last Shameless Plug

You *can* use this book to serve as your portal, your guide to your real-life .NET retraining journey. There remains one question though. What are your coworkers, colleagues, friends, and family—your mainframe brothers and sisters—using for *their* .NET guide? What are *they* using as their bridge into the .NET world? Sure, *you* are well on *your* way. Let's remember the others. Please consider obtaining extra copies of this book to share, to spread the word. I do think that others—those with mainframe COBOL/CICS backgrounds such as ours—will appreciate receiving a copy of this book as a gift.

Summary

This chapter's goals were as follows:

- To revisit Microsoft Message Queuing (MSMQ)

- To explain asynchronous processing

- To introduce .NET Remoting

- To cover multithreading

This chapter focused on various applications models. To that end, I covered distributed, asynchronous, and concurrent application models. This focus was presented as a needed step to position you toward a more complete .NET retraining. The tone of this chapter was directed at those aspiring to become enterprise developers. The information in this chapter, when combined with the information in each of the preceding 19 chapters, will certainly point you in the right direction.

I started the chapter's discussion by revisiting MSMQ. Using this product, I presented examples of distributed and asynchronous application models. Then, I briefly introduced the topic of .NET Remoting. I explained that .NET Remoting is another choice for creating distributed application models. Finishing the chapter, I spent a healthy amount of time covering the topic of multithreading. Using the multithreading topic, I was able to fully discuss the concerns of a concurrent processing application model. You learned about several tools that should prove helpful in your various debugging scenarios.

Explore, learn, and have fun.

To Learn More

The following are some suggested supplemental references to further your retraining effort.

Books

Advanced .NET Remoting in VB .NET, by Ingo Rammer (Apress, 2002):
    http://www.apress.com/book/bookDisplay.html?bID=108.
Distributed .NET Programming in VB .NET, by Tom Barnaby (Apress, 2002):
    http://www.apress.com/book/bookDisplay.html?bID=144.
Programming VB .NET: A Guide for Experienced Programmers, by Gary Cornell and
    Jonathan Morrison (Apress, 2001):
    http://www.apress.com/book/bookDisplay.html?bID=20.

Magazines

.NET Magazine:
    http://www.fawcette.com/dotnetmag/
MSDN Magazine:
    http://msdn.microsoft.com/msdnmag/

MSDN Magazine: "Design and Develop Seamless Distributed Applications for the
    Common Language Runtime":
    `http://msdn.microsoft.com/msdnmag/issues/02/10/NETRemoting/default.aspx`

Visual Studio Magazine:
    `http://www.fawcette.com/vsm/`

Visual Studio Magazine: "Demystify .NET App Domains and Contexts":
    `http://www.fawcette.com/vsm/2002_02/magazine/columns/blackbelt/`

Windows Developer Magazine:
    `http://www.wd-mag.com/`

XML & Web Services Magazine:
    `http://www.fawcette.com/xmlmag/`

Web Sites

.NET 247 Guide: Enterprise Remoting:
    `http://www.dotnet247.com/247reference/guide/8.aspx`

.NET Architecture Center:
    `http://msdn.microsoft.com/architecture/`

.NET Enterprise Servers Online Books:
    `http://msdn.microsoft.com/library/default.asp?url=/servers/books/`
    `default.asp`

.NET Remoting Overview:
    `http://msdn.microsoft.com/library/en-us/cpguide/html/`
    `cpconnetremotingoverview.asp`

.NET Remoting Security Solution, Part 1: Microsoft.Samples.Security.SSPI
    Assembly:
    `http://msdn.microsoft.com/library/?url=/library/en-us/dndotnet/html/`
    `remsspi.asp`

Creating Windows Applications:
    `http://msdn.microsoft.com/library/en-us/vbcon/html/`
    `vboriCreatingStandaloneAppsVB.asp`

DotNeteXtreme.com (.NET tips and articles):
    `http://www.dotnetextreme.com/default.asp`

EggHeadCafe.com Tips and Tricks (.NET tips and articles):
    `http://www.eggheadcafe.com/tipstricks.asp`

Fujitsu NetCOBOL for .NET:
    `http://www.netcobol.com/products/windows/netcobol.html`

GotDotNet:
    `http://www.gotdotnet.com/`

GotDotNet: Backwards Breaking Changes from Version 1.0 to 1.1:

http://www.gotdotnet.com/team/changeinfo/Backwards1.0to1.1/
default.aspx#00000106

IBuySpy Store Application (sample application in COBOL .NET):

http://www.ibuyspycobol.com/

IBuySpy Store Application (sample application in VB .NET and C#):

http://www.ibuyspystore.com/

Implementing a Background Process in Visual Basic .NET:

http://msdn.microsoft.com/library/en-us/dnadvnet/html/vbnet09272002.asp

Intensity Software's NetCOBOL Samples (provided by Fujitsu Software and
Intensity Software):

http://www.netcobolsamples.com/

Introduction to ASP.NET:

http://msdn.microsoft.com/library/en-us/cpguide/html/
cpconintroductiontoasp.asp

Message Queuing (MSMQ):

http://www.microsoft.com/msmq/

Message Queuing Overview and Resources:

http://www.microsoft.com/ntserver/techresources/appserv/MSMQ/
MSMQ_Overview.asp

Microsoft .NET Remoting: A Technical Overview:

http://msdn.microsoft.com/library/en-us/dndotnet/html/hawkremoting.asp

Microsoft ASP.NET Home Page:

http://www.asp.net/

Microsoft Community (discussion groups, e-newsletters, and so forth):

http://communities2.microsoft.com/

Microsoft Patterns & Practices:

http://msdn.microsoft.com/practices/

Microsoft's Search the Knowledge Base Web Site:

http://support.microsoft.com/default.aspx?scid=FH;EN-US;KBHOWTO

Microsoft TechNet How-To Index:

http://www.microsoft.com/technet/treeview/default.asp?url=/technet/
itsolutions/howto

MSDN:

http://msdn.microsoft.com

Multithreading in Visual Basic .NET:

http://msdn.microsoft.com/library/en-us/vbcn7/html/
vaconThreadingInVisualBasic.asp

NetCOBOL for .NET Training CDs:

http://www.netcobol.com/products/DotnetTrainingCD.htm

Programming the Thread Pool in the .NET Framework:

http://msdn.microsoft.com/library/en-us/dndotnet/html/progthrepool.asp

Remoting (samples):

    `http://msdn.microsoft.com/library/en-us/cpsamples/html/remoting.asp`

XML Web Services Developer Center Home:

    `http://msdn.microsoft.com/webservices/`

Using Threads:

    `http://msdn.microsoft.com/library/en-us/dv_vstechart/html/`

    `vbtchUsingThreads.asp`

Windows .NET Server 2003:

    `http://msdn.microsoft.com/library/default.asp?url=/nhp/`

    `default.asp?contentid=28001691`

Part Six
Appendixes

"How do you know when you have truly mastered a portion of .NET technology? Consider trying to explain all that you have learned to another developer. If you can successfully transfer your knowledge, you then are not only on the correct path to mastering .NET, but also clearly on your way to mastering professional growth and enrichment."

—Chris Richardson

Debugging and Testing

Essential Tips That I Needed to Share (to Clear My Conscience)

In this appendix

- Covering several VS .NET IDE tools that help you debug

- Demonstrating the Application Center Test (ACT) .NET product

---

UNDOUBTEDLY, THE MAJORITY of you will write completely bug-free code. We all do, right? Don't we all write code that compiles successfully on the first attempt and runs error-free and exception-free after it gets into production? In all seriousness, at one time or another, every developer will make use of some type of debugging tool. Additionally, we all have grown to appreciate the value of testing our code, regardless of how perfect we might think our code is.

Why then have I pushed the topics of debugging and testing all the way back to Appendix A? Frankly, these topics seemed to apply to every chapter. Therefore, I was challenged with the choice of which chapter to include coverage of debugging and testing in. However, there have been a few exceptions. Consider, for example, the following coverage:

- *Chapter 13:* I briefly mentioned the Application Center Test (ACT) product in a sidebar titled "VS .NET: Designed with Developer Productivity in Mind."

- *Chapter 18:* I demonstrated the use of both the VS .NET Locals window and the Trace.Write class/method in the section "Code Access Security Introduction." The Trace.Write class/method is a debugging tool.

- *Chapter 20:* In the section "Tools to Help Monitor Your Application," I covered in detail the Performance Monitor product, the Threads window, and the Disassembly window (the latter two being VS .NET IDE features). I briefly mentioned both the System.Diagnostics.Trace class and the System.Diagnostics.Debug class in the same section. Then, I demonstrated the technique of setting VS .NET breakpoints in the section "The VS .NET Threads Window."

You see, in a few chapters, I have touched on the topics of debugging and testing. In Chapter 20, you'll recall that you even walked through a basic unit test and integration test scenario. Yet, there's more. In this appendix, I introduce to you a few more tools. Consider the coverage of these additional tools an attempt to better prepare you for the real world where debugging and testing are assumed parts of development. Now, let's get started.

Debugging

To complement what you have already learned on the topic of debugging, you will want to know how to debug a "process" that is already running. In other words, there are occasions when you will want to know how to establish a debugging session and attach to an executable that is running outside of your VS .NET IDE. I demonstrate this type of debugging scenario in this section. Considering the exposure that you got on the mainframe to interactive debugging software (e.g., INTERTEST, XPEDITER, COBTEST, and so forth), the ability to debug in this way should feel familiar to you.

To help make this debugging discussion a bit more interesting, you'll create a Windows Service sample application to use as your targeted application for debugging. That's right. Rather than use a regular .NET Windows executable (.exe) as your targeted executing process, you'll create, install, and start a Windows Service as your executing process. Then, while the sample Windows Service is executing, you'll interactively debug the sample Windows Service application.

CROSS-REFERENCE   You will recall that Windows Services were introduced in Chapter 13. In that earlier chapter, I described a Windows Service as being an application that typically "does *not* include a GUI" and "a program that runs on the system in an unattended mode."

Before you move on to the actual debugging discussion, you first need to create your sample Windows Service application.

Creating a Windows Service to Demonstrate Debugging

You'll use Visual Basic .NET (VB .NET) as the chosen language for your sample Windows Service application. Why use VB .NET? Simply, version 1.1 of Fujitsu's NetCOBOL for .NET product doesn't offer a Visual Studio .NET (VS .NET) Windows Service project template. Yes, you could choose to use an empty COBOL .NET project template and add the appropriate assembly references and so forth. Perhaps you can save that for another day. Now, for this chapter's purposes, you'll exercise your bilingual abilities and use the VS .NET Windows Service project template for VB .NET.

NOTE If you feel that Fujitsu should add the VS .NET Windows Service project template to their NetCOBOL for .NET product, please contact them and let them know how you feel. Fujitsu's tech support has indicated to me that this feature is under consideration for a possible future release. Make sure to let them know if you are interested in the VS .NET Windows Service project template.

For demonstration purposes, you will code the Windows Services to dynamically attach to an existing MSMQ private queue. This will help create the illusion that the sample Windows Service is performing an important business process. Additionally, you will notice that I have added code to the sample Windows Service to dynamically attach to the EventLog object. Later you will use the Event Viewer to view the new EventLog entries. The Event Viewer is yet one more debugging/ monitoring tool available to you.

I could have used the drag-and-drop approach from the Server Explorer window with both the MSMQ object and the EventLog object. However, because there are times when the dynamic coding approach is more appropriate, I chose to add the needed few lines of code to dynamically create the objects.

NOTE You will attach to the private MSMQ queue MyFirstAsyncQueue that was created in Chapter 20. For simplicity, you will use the same sample application executable, MyMSMQAsyncAndTriggerCOBOL.exe, that you have in the C:\MSMQ-ASYNC-DEMO folder to send new messages to the MyFirstAsyncQueue queue.

Let's walk through the basic steps to create a Windows Service:

1. From the VS .NET IDE New Project window, choose Visual Basic Projects under the Project Types choices. Select Windows Service under the Templates choices, and name the Windows Service **MyFirstWindowsService**. Click OK. Name the class (via the Code view window), the .vb file (via the Solution Explorer window), and the Project Startup object (via the Project Properties page) **MyFirstWindowsService**.

2. Notice the two protected subprocedures *OnStart* and *OnStop*. The OnStart procedure will execute when the service is started. Naturally, the OnStop procedure will execute when the service is stopped. For this demonstration, you will not add any code into the OnStop procedure.

3. Add code to dynamically attach to an existing MSMQ private queue. Rather than drag and drop the server object from the Server Explorer window, this time accomplish the same with code. Refer to the following code snippet. Notice the two code lines immediately above the OnStart procedure. Add the familiar code to establish an asynchronous process:

```
Friend WithEvents MyMessageQueue As System.Messaging.MessageQueue
Shared MyCounter As Int32
Protected Overrides Sub OnStart(ByVal args() As String)
        'Dynamically attach to an existing MSMQ
        Me.MyMessageQueue = New System.Messaging.MessageQueue()
        Me.MyMessageQueue.Path =
        "FormatName:DIRECT=OS:.\private$\myfirstasyncqueue"
        AddHandler MyMessageQueue.ReceiveCompleted, _
        AddressOf MyMSMQBeginReceive
        ' Begin the asynchronous receive
        MyMessageQueue.BeginReceive()
    End Sub
```

4. Add the *MyMSMQBeginReceive* delegate/procedure. With the exception of the EventLog logic, most of the code in this procedure will be familiar to you.

```
Public Shared Sub MyMSMQBeginReceive(ByVal source As Object, _
        ByVal asyncResult As _
        System.Messaging.ReceiveCompletedEventArgs)
        'Connect to the MSMQ queue.
        Dim myqueue As System.Messaging.MessageQueue = _
        CType(source, System.Messaging.MessageQueue)
```

```
'End the asynchronous BeginReceive
Dim myMessage As System.Messaging.Message = _
myqueue.EndReceive(asyncResult.AsyncResult)

'use this shared variable for demonstration purposes
MyCounter += 1

Dim EventLog = New System.Diagnostics.EventLog()
With EventLog
    .BeginInit()
    .Log = "Application"
    .EndInit()
    .Source = "MyFirstWindowsService"
    .WriteEntry(MyCounter & " <-> " & myMessage.Label)
End With
myqueue.BeginReceive()
End Sub
```

5. Add an installer to the Windows Service project. In VS .NET, while you
   are viewing the design surface of the MyFirstWindowsService.vb file,
   right-click the design surface of the MyFirstWindowsService.vb file. Select
   Add Installer from the pop-up context window. As shown in your VS .NET
   Solution Explorer window, a ProjectInstaller.vb file is added to your
   Windows Service project.

6. On the design surface of the ProjectInstaller.vb file, notice the two components: ServiceProcessInstaller1 and ServiceInstaller1 (see Figure A-1).

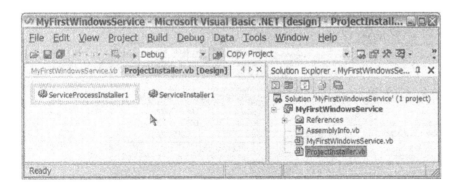

Figure A-1. The two components on the design surface of the ProjectInstaller.vb file

7. Access the property pages of the ServiceProcessInstaller1 component (select the component and press F4 or right-click the component and select Properties from the pop-up context window). Change the Account property to **LocalSystem**. This will be suitable for this demonstration's purposes.

8. Access the property pages of the ServiceInstaller1 component (select the component and press F4 or right-click the component and select Properties from the pop-up context window). Change the ServiceName property to **MyFirstWindowsService**.

9. Build the MyFirstWindowsService solution. Your Windows Service is ready to install.

Using the Visual Studio .NET Command Prompt window, enter the following command syntax to install the sample Windows Service application MyFirstWindowsService:

```
C:\>installutil C:\MyFirstWindowsService\bin\MyFirstWindowsService.exe
```

While your path information may vary, this is basically it. The Visual Studio .NET Command Prompt window display will indicate whether or not the installation was successful. You can then access the familiar Computer Management console (Services MMC snap-in) to view the newly installed MyFirstWindowsService Windows Service application. From the Services MMC snap-in, start the MyFirstWindowsService Windows Service (see Figure A-2).

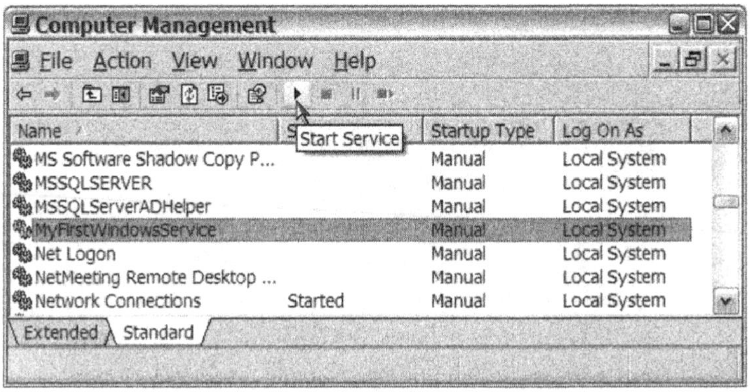

Figure A-2. Using the Services MMC snap-in to start the MyFirstWindowsService Windows Service

TIP   There is an alternative to using the Command Prompt window and installutil command to install and uninstall your Windows Service. Recall in Chapter 17 that you learned about the Microsoft Windows Installer feature. As it turns out, you can actually add a setup project to your Windows Service project. After you build your complete project, you then install your Windows Service using the Windows Installer (.msi) file and the Setup.exe file.

Later, you will want to stop the MyFirstWindowsService Windows Service from using the same Services MMC snap-in. At that time, you will want to uninstall the sample Windows Service using the following command syntax:

```
C:\>installutil /U C:\MyFirstWindowsService\bin\MyFirstWindowsService.exe
```

 TIP   You will want to stop and uninstall the Windows Service each time that you make changes to the Windows Service application source and rebuild the solution. Afterward, you repeat the install and start steps.

Access the Event Viewer using the Computer Management console (typically located underneath the System Tools tree node). Navigate to the Application node. As shown in Figure A-3, you should see a message generated from MyFirstWindowsService. If you double-click the message, you should see information indicating that the MyFirstWindowsService has started. As expected, the MyFirstWindowsService sample application has now begun an asynchronous process.

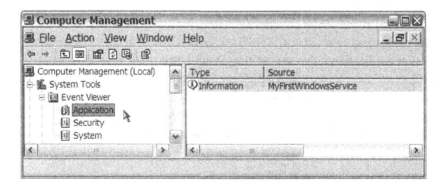

Figure A-3. Accessing the Event Viewer tool to view the application event log entries

Next, view the Windows Task Manager (press Ctrl-Alt-Delete). You will notice that the MyFirstWindowsService.exe Windows Service is listed among the other processes. As shown in Figure A-4, each process has a unique process ID (PID). In this case, the PID is 3092. The PID will likely vary each time you stop and start the Windows Service.

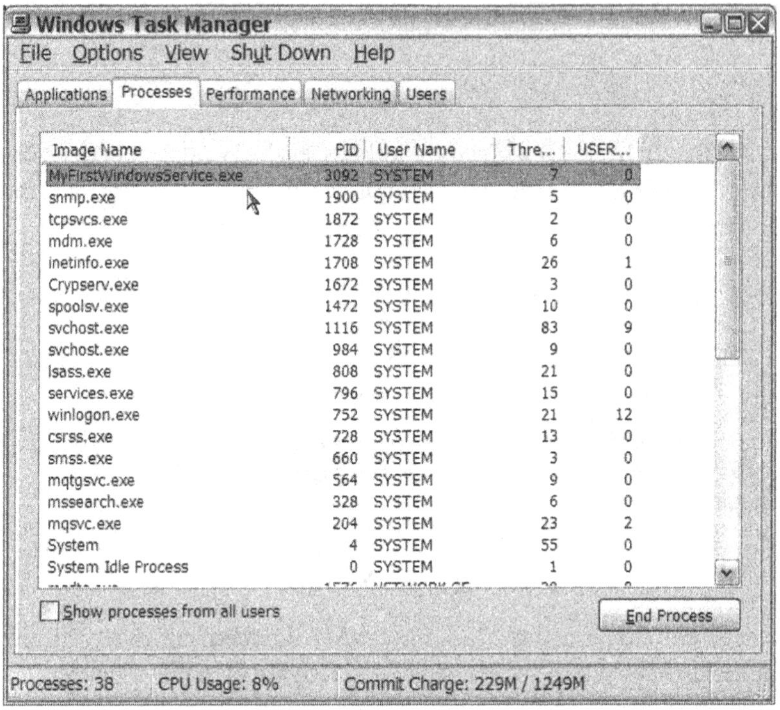

Figure A-4. Using the Windows Task Manager to view the active processes

Now execute MyMSMQAsyncAndTriggerCOBOL.exe (from the C:\MSMQ-ASYNC-DEMO folder). Use the appropriate button to send messages to the private MSMQ queue MyFirstAsyncQueue. After you have sent a few messages to the private MSMQ queue MyFirstAsyncQueue, view the Event Viewer application log to see the new Event Log entries. Choose Refresh from the Event Viewer toolbar to see the new application log entries.

Leave the MyFirstWindowsService.exe Windows Service executing. For demonstration purposes, close the VS .NET IDE window that you were using to create the MyFirstWindowsService solution. You are now ready to debug.

Debugging the Sample Windows Service

Open a new VS .NET IDE window. From this VS .NET IDE window (which does not have an opened project), select Tools ➤ Debug Processes (see Figure A-5). Optionally, press Ctrl-Alt-P while you are within the VS .NET IDE. You will now launch the VS .NET Processes window.

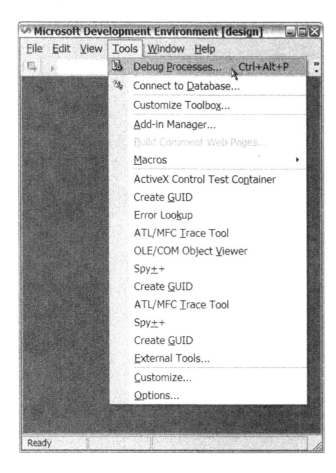

Figure A-5. Proceeding to debug an active process

From the VS .NET Processes window, locate the MyFirstWindowsService process. Then, simply follow these steps:

1. Select the MyFirstWindowsService process (with PID 3092, in this case) and click Attach. See Figure A-6.

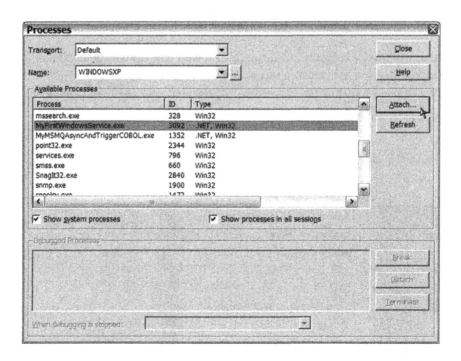

Figure A-6. Attaching to the MyFirstWindowsService process

2. An Attach to Process window will appear (see Figure A-7). Click OK. You will return to the Processes window.

Figure A-7. The Attach to Process window

3. Force a break into the process. On the Processes window, choose Break (see Figure A-8). Click Close to close the Processes window.

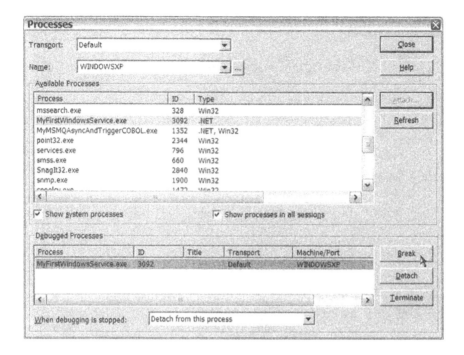

Figure A-8. Forcing a break into the attached process

4. A break should now exist in the Sub Main procedure of the MyFirstWindowsService Windows Service process (see Figure A-9).

5. Proceed with normal VS .NET IDE debugging. For example, you can place a manual debug breakpoint on code areas of interest. For demonstration purposes, I have added a breakpoint inside the MyMSMQBeginReceive subprocedure (see Figure A-10). Press F5 to allow the MyFirstWindowsService Windows Service process to move beyond the forced break and resume processing.

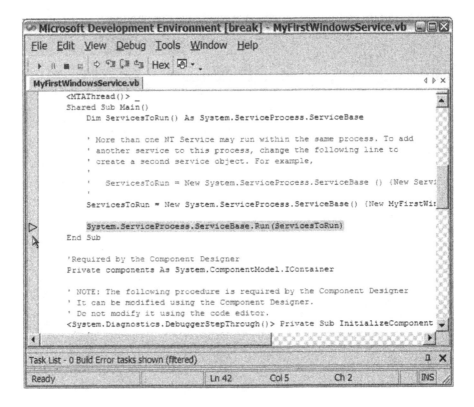

Figure A-9. Viewing the forced break in the Sub Main procedure of the MyFirstWindowsService Windows Service process

Now, return to the MyMSMQAsyncAndTriggerCOBOL.exe application (from the C:\MSMQ-ASYNC-DEMO folder). Again, use the appropriate button to send messages to the private MSMQ queue MyFirstAsyncQueue. You should see that the MyFirstWindowsService Windows Service process stops inside the MyMSMQBeginReceive subprocedure at the breakpoint.

While in break mode, hover your mouse over the *MyCounter* variable. As shown in Figure A-11, the contents of the MyCounter variable will show in a pop-up window.

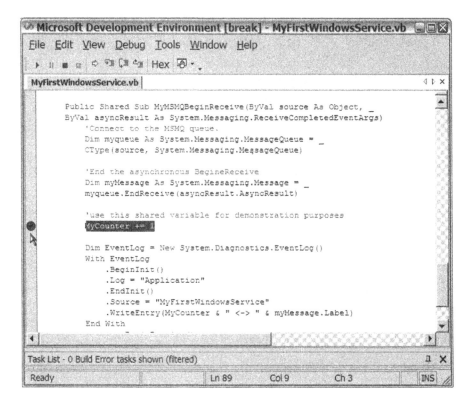

Figure A-10. Manually placing a debugging breakpoint

Press F5 to allow the process to continue normal execution. Optionally, you can step through the code, allowing executions to occur one line at a time. By default, you can press the F11 key to step through the code. Other stepping options are available on the VS .NET Debug toolbar. From this point forward, you can perform normal VS .NET debugging with the MyFirstWindowsService Windows Service process.

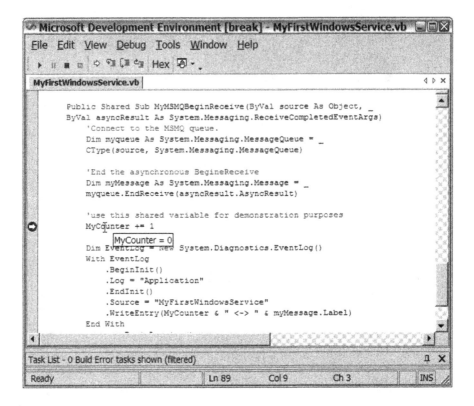

Figure A-11. The MyFirstWindowsService Windows Service process in break mode

Continue to explore by sending another message to the MSMQ queue. The MyFirstWindowsService Windows Service process will again stop at the breakpoint. While in break mode, consider exploring the VS .NET debug options. Of course, you will see the familiar Locals window. Additionally, you will want to become familiar with the other debug tools. From the VS .NET Standard toolbar, select Debug. The following list introduces some of the other debugging tools that are available from the VS .NET Debug menu:

- *Watch window and QuickWatch window:* These windows are great when you are monitoring a specific variable. Both windows allow you to add an expression that creates a conditional breakpoint. For example, you can enter break mode whenever a specific variable meets a certain condition.

- *Autos window:* When you are working with functions, the Autos window is useful for monitoring the return values from functions.

- *Exceptions window:* Consider using this tool when you are targeting a specific exception. The Exceptions window allows you to enter break mode whenever a specific exception is raised.

- *Immediate window and Command window:* From the Debug ➤ Windows menu, you can select Immediate to open a window that has a dual mode. When you are in Immediate mode, you can evaluate expressions and execute language statements. When you are in Command mode, you can enter VS .NET IDE commands (instead of always using the VS .NET IDE menu options). Use *>cmd* to switch to Command mode. Use *immed* to switch to Immediate mode.

- *Call Stack window:* Use this window when you want a quick display of the function and procedure names as they exist on the stack. This is useful when you are trying to trace the execution sequence. Also, consider using the *System.Diagnostics.StackTrace* class in code. During runtime, you can use this StackTrace class to obtain information similar to what is displayed in the Call Stack window.

- *Running Documents window:* When you are debugging ASP.NET applications, you may come across the need to debug script code (e.g., JavaScript). The Running Documents window will prove to be invaluable in such scenarios, as it allows you to attach to a document that is loaded in your process. You may have to enable script debugging on your Internet Explorer browser. (Navigate to Internet Explorer's Standard toolbar and select Tools ➤ Internet Options ➤ Advanced. Then, uncheck the "Disable script debugging" option.)

As you read the preceding list of VS .NET debug tools, I am sure you were relieved to find out that VS .NET truly does expose a full-featured debugging arsenal. As you know, the interactive debugging software that you and I used for years on the mainframe offered comparable functionality. Naturally, coming from the mainframe platform, you should expect nothing less.

TIP Using VS .NET, you can easily debug the portions of your applications that include SQL stored procedures. That is right. You can use all of the VS .NET IDE interactive debugging features (e.g., breakpoints, stepping, and so forth), even with SQL stored procedures. This feature is available through either the VS .NET Server Explorer window or the VS .NET text editor. Be sure to check the references included at the end of this appendix in the "To Learn More" section for more details.

Remember to detach from the MyFirstWindowsService Windows Service process after you have completed your debugging session. You can accomplish this from the same VS .NET Processes window you visited earlier. Please consider these additional housekeeping tasks: clearing the sample events from the event log, stopping the sample Windows Service, and uninstalling the sample Windows Service.

Let's turn now to the topic of testing.

.NET Exception Handling

Consider further exploration of the .NET Framework System.ArgumentException class (briefly mentioned in Chapter 19) along with the related .NET Try/Catch exception handling syntax. Taking into account your mainframe COBOL background, I believe you will find that .NET exception handling feels familiar to you. Please consider the following two common mainframe scenarios. You will quickly get the idea.

As you know, on the mainframe, the JCL COND statements provided a means to catch errors rising from processing. Using the appropriate COND statement parameter, you could direct the system on the appropriate action to take and how processing should proceed as errors were caught.

Similarly, in your mainframe COBOL programs, you used arithmetic statements (ADD, DIVIDE, COMPUTE, and so forth) along with the ON SIZE ERROR clause to catch errors. Recall that the ON SIZE ERROR clause provided a means for you to catch errors that may have occurred as the result of executing an arithmetic statement. You then had the chance to code defensively and direct the system to execute appropriate alternative logic.

I am sure you see how these two mainframe scenarios relate to each other and to .NET exception handling. Keep these two mainframe implementations in mind as you use .NET Try/Catch exception handling logic in your .NET development. .NET exception handling is an important coding concept to become familiar with. Additionally, you will want to become well acquainted with the .NET Framework System.ArgumentException class.

Testing

You should plan to stress test and load-test your ASP.NET applications. There are full-featured, sometimes pricey third-party products that you can purchase to assist you with this task. Then, there is Microsoft's Application Center Test (ACT) product, which comes bundled with the Enterprise edition of VS .NET. In this appendix, you will learn how to use the ACT feature. Microsoft appropriately refers to ACT as an "application life cycle development tool."

As you learned in Chapter 13, the .NET toolset includes the ACT feature. You will recall that there are two ways to access this feature. You can access ACT from within VS .NET as a project template through the Add New Project window. You can also access the ACT product by clicking the Start button and selecting Programs ➤ Microsoft Visual Studio .NET ➤ Visual Studio .NET Enterprise Features ➤ Microsoft Application Center Test.

Either approach exposes an option that allows you to record a "test script" using your Web browser. The script can then be played back to simulate actual users using the ASP.NET application. Both approaches offer the ability to simulate multiple concurrent connections. You will start by accessing ACT from within the VS .NET IDE. Later, you will walk through the alternative approach (accessing ACT from outside the VS .NET IDE).

Using ACT Inside VS .NET

For demonstration purposes, use the two sample ASP.NET applications originally created in Chapter 13. Both sample applications (WebApplicationSampleVB and WebApplicationSampleCobol) are simple "Hello, World" applications. Start by opening up WebApplicationSampleVB.sln in the VS .NET IDE. Next, perform the following steps to complete the process of setting up an ACT project in an existing solution:

1. With WebApplicationSampleVB.sln open in the VS .NET IDE, navigate to the VS .NET IDE Standard toolbar. Select File ➤ Add Project ➤ New Project. As shown in Figure A-12, the Application Center Test Projects folder is located underneath the Other Projects folder in the Add New Project window. Click OK after you select the one available template.

2. In the VS .NET IDE Solution Explorer window, locate the newly added ACT project. Right-click the ACT project in the Solution Explorer window. Select Add ➤ Add New Item from the pop-up context window.

3. As shown in Figure A-13, the Add New Item dialog box offers three default script-based templates. Select the Browser Recorded Test (.vbs) template. Click Open.

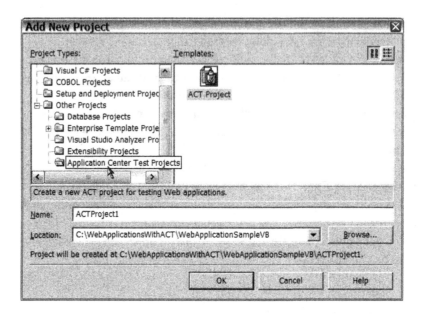

Figure A-12. The Add New Project dialog box showing the ACT Project template

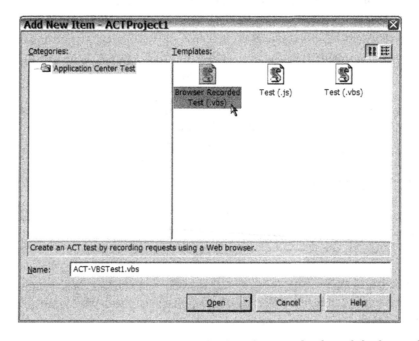

Figure A-13. The Add New Item dialog box showing the three default templates

4. A Browser Record dialog box should appear (see Figure A-14). Click Start.

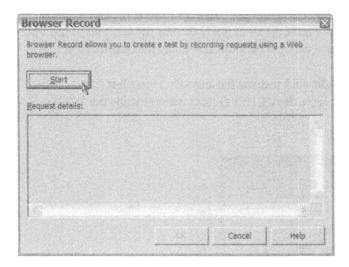

Figure A-14. Ready to start recording with the Browser Record dialog box

5. A Browser window should open. Enter the targeted Web site URL in the address bar. For demonstration purposes, I used `http://localhost/WebApplicationSampleVB/WebForm1.aspx`. This is the URL for the sample application. I then clicked the one Web Form button to generate the expected "Hello, World" text box display.

6. End the browser recording. As shown in Figure A-15, you should click the Stop button on the Browser Record dialog box to end browser recording.

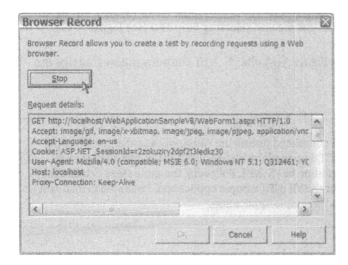

Figure A-15. Preparing to end the browser recording

7. Observe the creation of a VBScript (.vbs) file in your VS .NET Solution Explorer window. Please take a moment to view the contents of the .vbs file. You will notice that this VBScript is actually the recorded test script.

8. Start the test. Right-click the .vbs file and select Start Test (see Figure A-16). Observe the VS .NET Output window while the ACT test is running.

Figure A-16. Starting the ACT test from within VS .NET

9. After you let the ACT test run for a little while, stop the ACT test by right-clicking the .vbs file and selecting Stop Test (see Figure A-17).

10. As shown in the Figure A-18, the VS .NET Output window contains the test results.

NOTE   Once I completed testing the WebApplicationSampleVB application with ACT, I opened the WebApplicationSampleCobol sample application solution in VS .NET. Following the same steps detailed in this section for the VB .NET sample application, I was able to load-test the COBOL .NET sample application.

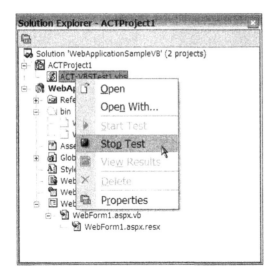

Figure A-17. Stopping the ACT test from within VS .NET

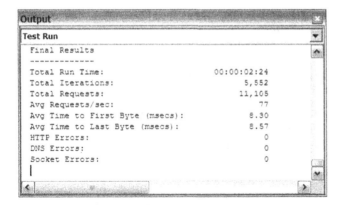

Figure A-18. The VS .NET Output window showing the ACT test results for the sample application WebApplicationSampleVB

Now, that was not that bad, right? I suggest that you refer to the references provided at the end of this chapter in the "To Learn More" section to find information that will guide you toward an accurate interpretation of the test results. Additionally, you might consider using the Performance Monitor (click the Start button and select Programs ➤ Administrative Tools ➤ Performance) while your ACT test script is running. As shown in Figure A-19, several performance counters relevant to the performance of your application may be of interest to you.

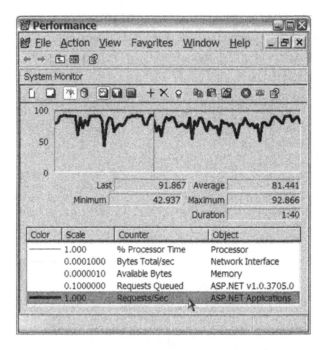

Figure A-19. The Performance Monitor

In practice, I found that using ACT in VS .NET offered one basic advantage: It promotes the storage of ACT projects inside the related .NET solution. Otherwise, using ACT from within VS .NET is somewhat limited. As your testing needs grow, you will want to leverage the more advanced features of ACT. To do this, you will need to access the stand-alone ACT product from outside VS .NET.

NOTE Be sure to close the WebApplicationSampleVB VS .NET IDE solution that contains the new ACT project. The ACT product does not allow multiple user interfaces to concurrently open the same ACT project.

Using ACT Outside VS .NET

Start by launching the ACT stand-alone product (click the Start button and select Programs ➤ Microsoft Visual Studio .NET ➤ Visual Studio .NET Enterprise Features ➤ Microsoft Application Center Test). Once ACT is launched, you should see a window similar to the one shown in Figure A-20.

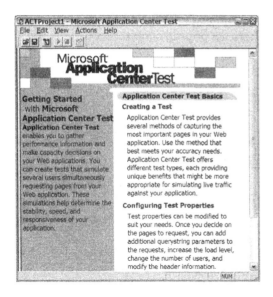

Figure A-20. The ACT stand-alone product

From the ACT menu or toolbar, you can either create a new ACT project or open an existing one. For demonstration purposes, I opened the existing ACT project created earlier for the WebApplicationSampleVB sample application (see Figure A-21).

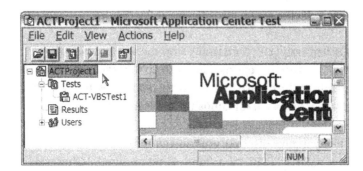

Figure A-21. Viewing an existing ACT project and existing ACT test script in the ACT stand-alone product

Take a moment to explore the ACT menu and toolbar. You will quickly discover the full support exposed to create new ACT projects and new ACT test scripts. There is support to view your ACT results. You will notice that even the test results that were created while running from within VS .NET are exposed.

Choose your existing ACT test script and run it. Right-click the ACT test script and select Start Test (see Figure A-22) from the pop-up context menu to run the existing test script.

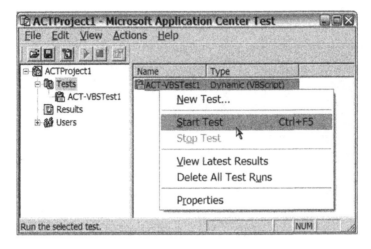

Figure A-22. Preparing to run the existing ACT test script for the WebApplicationSampleVB sample application

Once you initiate the ACT test script to run, you will notice that an ACT Test Status window opens. Using the buttons on the ACT Test Status window, you can choose to Hide/Show Details or Stop the test. There are two useful tabs: Graph and Status. As shown in Figure A-23, the Graph tab offers a similar display to that of the Performance Monitor.

After you let the ACT test script run for a while, stop the test and view the results. You will notice that the various reports that make up the results for the ACT stand-alone product are more informative than the reports shown within VS .NET. Obviously, this is one significant reason for choosing to use ACT from outside VS .NET.

As you explore further, you may discover pros and cons to the use of ACT, either within VS .NET or outside VS .NET (as a stand-alone product). Either way, I'm sure that you'll find the ACT tool to be a welcome addition to the .NET suite of tools.

NOTE ACT is the newest version of a pre-.NET load-testing tool. A previous version of this tool was known as Homer. More recently, a version was named Web Application Stress (WAS) testing tool.

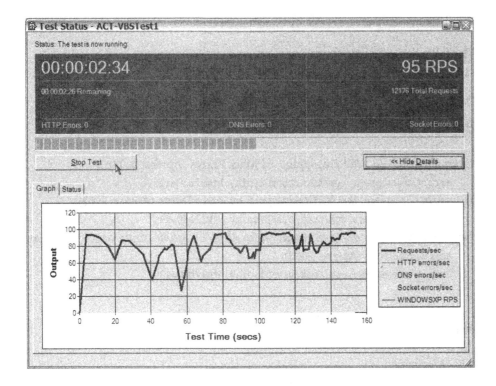

Figure A-23. Viewing the Graph tab on the ACT Test Status window

Summary

This appendix's goals were as follows:

- To cover several VS .NET IDE tools that help you debug

- To demonstrate the Application Center Test (ACT) .NET product

In this appendix, you were introduced to a collection of VS .NET debugging tools and techniques. You also learned how to debug a Windows Service. The technique of attaching a debug session to a running process (be it a Windows Service or Windows application) is certainly a desirable feather in your cap. This demonstration of this technique provided a convenient opportunity for you to discover the simplicity of using VS .NET to create a Windows Service.

The remaining portion of the appendix focused on Application Center Test (ACT) product (not to be confused with Microsoft's server product called Application Center). You learned how to use ACT both inside and outside VS .NET.

To Learn More

The following are some suggested supplemental references to further your retraining effort.

Books

Comprehensive VB .NET Debugging, by Mark Pearce (Apress, 2003):
http://www.apress.com/book/bookDisplay.html?bID=128.
Debugging Strategies for .NET Developers, by Darin Dillon (Apress, 2003):
http://www.apress.com/book/bookDisplay.html?bID=131.
Performance Tuning and Optimization for ASP.NET Applications, by Jeffrey Hasan and Kenneth Tu (Apress, 2003):
http://www.apress.com/book/bookDisplay.html?bID=135.

Magazines

.NET Magazine:
http://www.fawcette.com/dotnetmag/
MSDN Magazine:
http://msdn.microsoft.com/msdnmag/
Visual Studio Magazine:
http://www.fawcette.com/vsm/
Windows Developer Magazine:
http://www.wd-mag.com/
XML & Web Services Magazine:
http://www.fawcette.com/xmlmag/

Web Sites

.NET Architecture Center:
http://msdn.microsoft.com/architecture/
Building, Debugging, and Testing:
http://msdn.microsoft.com/library/en-us/vsintro7/html/
vxoriBuildingDebuggingandTesting.asp
Creating Windows Applications: http://msdn.microsoft.com/library/en-us/vbcon/
html/vboriCreatingStandaloneAppsVB.asp

Debugging SQL:

http://msdn.microsoft.com/library/en-us/vsdebug/html/
_core_debugging_sql.asp

GotDotNet: Backwards Breaking Changes from Version 1.0 to 1.1:

http://www.gotdotnet.com/team/changeinfo/Backwards1.0to1.1/
default.aspx#00000106

Important (Performance) Counters for Web Testing:

http://msdn.microsoft.com/library/en-us/act/htm/actml_ref_pcls.asp

Microsoft Application Center Test 1.0, Visual Studio .NET Edition (documentation):

http://msdn.microsoft.com/library/en-us/act/htm/actml_main.asp

Microsoft ASP.NET Home Page:

http://www.asp.net/

Microsoft Community (discussion groups, e-newsletters, and so forth):

http://communities2.microsoft.com/

Microsoft Patterns & Practices:

http://msdn.microsoft.com/practices/

Microsoft's Search the Knowledge Base Web Site:

http://support.microsoft.com/default.aspx?scid=FH;EN-US;KBHOWTO

Microsoft TechNet How-To Index:

http://www.microsoft.com/technet/treeview/default.asp?url=/technet/
itsolutions/howto

MSDN:

http://msdn.microsoft.com

The VS7 Debugger White Paper:

http://www.gotdotnet.com/team/csharp/learn/whitepapers/
howtosolvedebuggerproblems.doc

Windows .NET Server 2003:

http://msdn.microsoft.com/library/default.asp?url=/nhp/
default.asp?contentid=28001691

XML Web Services Developer Center Home:

http://msdn.microsoft.com/webservices/

A Sharp Primer: C# and J#

An Introduction to the Visual C# .NET and Visual J# .NET Languages

In this appendix

- Discussing the Visual C# (pronounced "C sharp") .NET language

- Covering the Visual J# (pronounced "J sharp") .NET language

DURING A RECENT CHAT with my wife, Lilia, I explained how the earlier chapters in this book advocated a *bilingual* programming approach, using both COBOL .NET and Visual Basic .NET (VB .NET) samples to demonstrate key .NET concepts. I went on to explain to my wife that I was preparing to write an appendix that would introduce two other .NET language choices.

Later, while sort of thinking out loud, I wondered if *trilingual* and *quadlingual* were grammatically correct terms that I might use to describe a development approach that includes Visual C# .NET (C#) and Visual J# .NET (J#) as language choices together with COBOL .NET and VB .NET. While still thinking out loud, I asked myself the question (repeatedly), "So, would you call it bilingual, trilingual, and quadlingual? Quadlingual, trilingual, and bilingual? Trilingual, bilingual, and quadlingual?"

My wife (perhaps realizing that I was stuck in a mental loop) responded, "Chris, you would call it developing in multiple languages."

Introducing Visual C# .NET

As you browse the Microsoft Visual Studio .NET documentation, Microsoft's MSDN Web site, or even Fujitsu's NetCOBOL for .NET sample applications, you will often come across sample applications written in Visual C# .NET. Typically, you will see this language's name abbreviated down to just C# (pronounced "C sharp"). Arguably, C# is an improved addition to the "C" family of languages.

TIP At the end of this appendix, I have included two references to Web sites that offer a free C#-to-VB .NET translation service. You may find this type of service to be helpful during the early stages of your C# learning experience.

In this section, I cover some of the basic syntax rules of C#. At the end of this appendix, you will find several references in the "To Learn More" section that you can use to further explore the C# language.

NOTE As I mentioned in Chapter 5, the C# language is one of the available language choices bundled with most of the Visual Studio .NET (VS .NET) editions.

Coming from a COBOL/mainframe background, you are likely to notice two characteristics of C# first:

- The C# language uses punctuation symbols, bracket symbols {}, and trailing semicolons (;).

- The C# language is on the opposite end of the verboseness spectrum.

Let's take closer look at these two C# characteristics.

Bracket Symbols and Semicolons

The first time you look at C# code, the use of punctuation symbols may look strange. As strange as the use of punctuation symbols first appears to be, however, their use will actually be the first thing that a COBOL developer will find to be the most familiar. Once you realize that the punctuation symbols are simply *defining the scope* for each significant code instruction/section, you will quickly be reminded of COBOL scope terminators.

I was always a fan of COBOL scope terminators. I was one of the mainframe developers who quickly adapted to the COBOL scope terminators as they were introduced in the COBOL ISO/ANSI 85 standard. I recall going through my mainframe COBOL programs happily replacing periods (.) with scope terminators.

I recall looking for conditional statements (e.g., IF, EVALUATE, PERFORM, and so on), arithmetic statements (e.g., ADD, COMPUTE, DIVIDE, and so on), input/output statements (e.g., READ, DELETE, START, and so on), and other statements (e.g., STRING, CALL, and so on). I left no stone unturned. I updated my mainframe COBOL programs with scope terminators everywhere possible. I added END-IF, END-EVALUATE, END-COMPUTE, END-READ, and END-STRING statements like you would not believe.

As you know, the removal of the periods from most COBOL code routines meant fewer coding bugs when code blocks were moved around. It meant that you could easily nest code statements and use inline techniques, cutting down on the "Go To/Branching" code styles. Yes, I quickly fell in love with COBOL scope terminators and the COBOL ISO/ANSI 85 standard at that time. The fact that one COBOL period (.) was still required to "terminate the scope" of most COBOL sections was something I learned to live with.

Now you have C# using bracket symbols. The C# open bracket symbol ({) begins scope. Of course, the C# close bracket symbol (}) ends scope. In C# code, the trailing semicolon (;) is closely analogous to the COBOL period (.).

Are you ready to look at some C# code? Great! Using C# as my language choice and the VS .NET Console Application project template, I've created a simple console application (MyFirstCSharpApplication). Listing B-1 shows a C# code snippet taken from this sample application.

Listing B-1. Code Snippet from the MyFirstCSharpApplication Sample Application

```
using System;
      /// <summary>
      /// This is my first C# Application. Coding in C# is easy.
      /// </summary>
namespace MyFirstCSharpApplication
{
      /// <remarks>The use of three slashes ("///") denotes
      /// the use of C#'s XML Documentation feature.
      /// Notice that this entire comment block appears inside of an XML
      /// element called "remarks". There are other XML elements that you
      /// can use (e.g. summary, example, etc.).
      /// You can display these XML Documentation blocks by
      /// navigating to the VS.NET Main Toolbar, clicking Tools and then clicking
      /// the "Build Comment Web Pages" menu option.
      /// After building the Comment Web Page you can save the page
      /// as part of the applications documentation.
      /// </remarks>
```

```
class Class1
{
    /// <summary>
    /// The main entry point for the application.
    /// </summary>
    [STAThread]
    static void Main(string[] args)
    {
    // Use two slash symbols ("//") for a single line comment
    /* Optionally, you can create a multi-line comment block
    * by using a single slash followed by an asterisk ("/*").
    * The end the comment block, use an asterisk followed by a slash
    */
        Console.WriteLine("Hello, .NET World.");
        Console.WriteLine("I cannot believe how simple C# is!");
        Console.WriteLine("Press Enter to Exit.");
        Console.ReadLine();
    }
}
}
```

NOTE The code used in this portion of the sample application is based on the sample applications (COBOL .NET and VB .NET) originally built in Chapter 5.

Looking at the sample application in Listing B-1, you will notice the use of the trailing semicolon (;). The C# *using* statement, as well as the *Console.Writeline* and *Console.Readline* method statements require the trailing semicolon as a statement terminator.

NOTE When the MyFirstCSharpApplication sample application is run, two lines are displayed in a console window. Pressing the Enter key will end the application and close the console window.

Additionally, you will notice that there are three pairs of bracket symbols used in the sample application. A pair of bracket symbols is recognized as one open bracket symbol ({) and one close bracket symbol (}). In the sample application, the first bracket symbol pair is used to define the scope of the MyFirstCSharpApplication namespace. The second bracket symbol pair is used for the Class1 class. The last bracket symbol pair is used to define the scope of the Main subprocedure.

TIP I have added comments in the C# code in Listing B-1 to introduce the C# XML documentation feature. Additional comments in the code sample explain the syntax used for normal inline comments.

Let's take a look at more C# code.

C#: A Terse Syntax

As previously mentioned, it's reasonable to recognize C#'s syntax as being terse. The degree to which you agree with this observation will depend on your background. If you've only coded COBOL programs on the mainframe, you might consider C# very terse. In fact, you might even look at VB .NET as less than verbose. On the other hand, if you're one of those mainframe developers who has coded using the assembler language, the slight terseness of the C# language syntax will hardly be apparent.

NOTE You can decide for yourself if C# is that terse or not. Frankly, you may not even care. Just know that there are those who spend hours debating this point.

I've added some code (specifically, the procedures DefineDataTypesSample and LogicSample) to the sample C# application to help demonstrate the essence of C# code. The additional code that I've added in MyFirstCSharpApplication is based on the (COBOL .NET and VB .NET) samples originally built for Chapter 6. I encourage you to refer back to the sample applications in Chapter 6 for line-by-line, language-to-language code comparisons.

Take a look at the code snippet in Listing B-2.

Listing B-2. Code Snippet from MyFirstCSharpApplication Showing the Procedures
DefineDataTypesSample and LogicSample

```
using System;
    . . .
namespace MyFirstCSharpApplication
{
. . .
    class Class1
    {
    . . .
        static void Main(string[] args)
        {
        . . .
//Execute Procedures
            DefineDataTypesSample();
            LogicSample();
                Console.WriteLine("Press Enter to Exit.");
            Console.ReadLine();

            . . .
        }
        static void DefineDataTypesSample()
        {
//Declare Data Items using C# Data Types
            short MyFirstNumberCsharp;
            int MySecondNumberCsharp;
            double MyThirdNumberCsharp;

    //Declare Data Items using Native .NET Data Types
            System.Int16 MyFirstNumberNative;
            System.Int32 MySecondNumberNative;
            System.Double MyThirdNumberNative;

//Place a numeric literal in Data Item
            MyFirstNumberCsharp = 32767;
            MySecondNumberCsharp = 32767;
            MyThirdNumberCsharp = 32767;

            MyFirstNumberNative = 32767;
            MySecondNumberNative = 32767;
            MyThirdNumberNative = 32767;

//Write out contents of each variable
            Console.WriteLine("MyFirstNumberCsharp= {0}",
```

```
                MyFirstNumberCsharp);
            Console.WriteLine("MySecondNumberCsharp= {0}",
                    MySecondNumberCsharp);
            Console.WriteLine("MyThirdNumberCsharp= {0}",
                    MyThirdNumberCsharp);
            Console.WriteLine("MyFirstNumberNative= {0}",
                    MyFirstNumberNative);
            Console.WriteLine("MySecondNumberNative= {0}",
                    MySecondNumberNative);
            Console.WriteLine("MyThirdNumberNative= {0}",
                    MyThirdNumberNative);
        }
        static void LogicSample()
        {
//*** Declare Data Items using .NET Data Types
            System.String MYString;
            System.Int32 MYInteger;
            System.Boolean MYBoolean = false;
            System.DateTime systemDate;


//*** Declare Data Items with C# Data Types
            int MyIndex = 0;
            int MySecondIndex;
            int MyAccum = 0;
            bool MyFlag = false;
            string MyFixedLengthString;


//*** Demonstrate creation of String Array
            string[] MonthValues =
            {"January", "February", "March",
                 "April", "May", "June",
              "July", "August", "September",
                 "October", "November", "December"};


//*** Demonstrate Intrinsic Function accessing System Date
            systemDate = System.DateTime.Now;

            Console.WriteLine("Today is {0}" ,
                    systemDate.ToShortDateString());


//*** Demonstrate Booleans, Constants, and Conditional/Computational Logic

            do
            {
```

```
                MyIndex += 1;
                if (MyIndex > 12)
                {
                        MYBoolean = true;
                        MyFlag = MYBoolean;
                }
        } while (MyFlag != true);

        if (MyFlag == true)
        {
        MYString = "The Boolean is now set to TRUE";
        MyFixedLengthString = MYString;
        Console.WriteLine(MyFixedLengthString);
        }


//*** Demonstrate usage of Conditional and Computational Logic
    for (MySecondIndex = 1; MySecondIndex <= MyIndex; MySecondIndex++)
    {
            MyAccum = MySecondIndex += 1;
    }
    MYInteger = MyAccum;


//*** Demonstrate Intrinsic Functions, Conditional/Computational Logic

        MyIndex = 1;
        MyFixedLengthString = String.Empty;
        for (int x = 0; x <= 11; x++)
        {
                switch (MonthValues[x])
                {
                        case "December":
                        case "January":
                        case "February":
                                Console.WriteLine
                                (string.Concat(MonthValues[x],
                                        " is ","Winter"));
                                break;
                        case "March":
                        case "April":
                        case "May":
                                Console.WriteLine
                                (string.Concat(MonthValues[x],
                                        " is ","Spring"));
                                break;
```

```
                    case "June":
                    case "July":
                    case "August":
                        Console.WriteLine
                        (string.Concat(MonthValues[x],
                            " is ","Summer"));
                        break;
                    case "September":
                    case "October":
                    case "November":
                        Console.WriteLine
                        (string.Concat(MonthValues[x],
                            " is ","Autumn"));
                        break;
                    default:
                        Console.WriteLine
                                ("A logic exception");
                        break;
                }
            }
        }
    }
}
```

So, what do you think? Does C# deserve its "terse" syntax reputation? Perhaps.

Please take a moment to read through the code snippet in Listing B-2. As mentioned earlier, the C# implementation mimics that of Chapter 6's sample (COBOL .NET and VB .NET) applications. Keep this in mind. If you were to do a line-by-line, language-to-language comparison (comparing this C# sample application with the sample applications coded for Chapter 6), you would observe at least the following differences:

- C# is case sensitive. All C# reserved words are lowercase.

- C# has new operators for equals (==) and not equals (!=) comparisons.

- C# uses a statement called *switch* to implement a case logic feature.

- C# has a *jump* statement specified as either *break* or *continue*.

- C# has loop logic features (e.g., *for*, *do/while*, and so on).

- C# has a unique, three-part parameter syntax for its looping *for* statement.

- C# has an *increment operator*[1] (++) that increments its operand by 1.

- C# has a *decrement operator* (--) that decrements its operand by 1.

- C# uses square brackets [] for arrays instead of parentheses ().

- C# allows intrinsic and alias named types (e.g., *int* versus *System.Int32*).

- C# introduces other access modifiers (*static void* versus *Shared Sub*).

- C# uses the word "void" to describe methods that do not return values.

You may have made other observations noting those C# syntax rules that are either familiar or new. As you further explore C#, experimenting with its powerful feature set, you will certainly accumulate more observations. Here are a few additional points that may be of interest to you:

- C# creates an application icon (app.ico) automatically by default. You will notice this file in the VS .NET Solution Explorer. The project property pages[2] expose an option to use the application icon file.

- C# will warn you if you declare a variable but fail to include code that actually uses the variable.

- C# does not use the word "NEW" for its class constructor method. Instead, the C# constructor is recognized as a method that has exactly the same name as the class itself.

- C# uses square brackets for its attribute syntax (e.g., *[STAThread]*). VB .NET uses the greater-than (>) and less-than (<) symbols.

- C# uses the colon (:) to indicate that one class is inheriting another (e.g., *myderivedclassname : mybaseclassname*) and/or that one class is implementing an interface.

- C# introduces the *ref* and *out* parameters to use when passing variable values into a called method. Using the ref parameter requires the calling

---

1. Notice that the (++) operator is used in the *for* loop statement.
2. C# and VB .NET expose this option on the project property pages. According to Fujitsu's documentation, you can use the command-line compile option `cobolc /win32icon:app.ico/ main:Main /out:yourprogramname.exe program1.cob` when you want to include an application icon file in your COBOL .NET application.

program to initialize the variable before calling the method and passing the variable value.

- C# offers a *foreach* statement as an alternative to implement looping logic.

- C# has a unique syntax for explicit type casting. You do this by first placing the desired type inside parentheses. Immediately following the close parenthesis, you then code the targeted class/method/type.

- C# program files use ".cs" as a suffix. As you know, COBOL .NET uses ".cob" and VB .NET uses ".vb".

CAUTION   The asterisk (*) in C# code has two uses. Usually, you will use it when you want to multiply two values in a typical arithmetic expression. Although it is not advisable,[3] the other use for the asterisk is to create a pointer that stores address locations. (Usually the ampersand [&] operator is used to provide the address value.) The C# coding convention directs that code blocks using address pointers should be marked *unsafe*. The use of address pointers is considered unsafe due to the GC's inability to collect pointers that exist on the heap. Be sure that when you use the asterisk, you are using it for multiplication.

Obviously, these observations deserve much more explanation. I've included them here to give you a general idea of what to expect coming from COBOL .NET or VB .NET heading into C#. Consider taking advantage of the references at the end of this appendix in the "To Learn More" section. They should point you in the right direction.

TIP   Consider using the ILDASM.exe command-line tool to view the assembly MSIL for the MyFirstCSharpApplication sample application. This will provide to you a lower-level perspective—a chance to better understand the C# implementation.

---

3. Not advisable? One of the reasons for using .NET in the first place is to take advantage of the CLR and GC features. Once you start messing around with coding techniques that get around the protection provided by the CLR, you are asking for trouble. The fact that Microsoft has labeled this feature "unsafe" should be warning enough.

To wrap up this appendix's discussion about C#, I thought it would be interesting to explore one additional side of C#. I have heard rumor that the "C# language looks like Java language syntax." Just for fun, let's take a look at how true that statement actually is.

C# Looks Like Java

I removed a Java textbook (which is based on Java 2, JDK 1.2) from my bookshelf. I purchased this book a couple of years ago and never read it. Java is a language that I have yet to code in. Now I sensed a good excuse to finally get my hands dirty. I wanted to know exactly what the Java language syntax looked like from the original source. After blowing the dust off my Java textbook, I browsed through its chapters and noticed the following:

- Java (*also*) uses the bracket symbols {} for logic block definition.

- Java (*also*) uses the semicolon (;) to terminate statements.

- Java (*also*) uses simple variable declaration syntax (e.g., *int myint;*).

That was certainly enough to capture my interest. I refilled my coffee cup and decided to read my Java textbook from cover to cover. I made the following observations during that enjoyable read:

- Java (*also*) is case sensitive. All Java reserved words are (*also*) lowercase.

- Java (*also*) has unique operators for equals (==) and not equals (!=) comparisons.

- Java (*also*) uses a statement called *swtch* to implement a case logic feature.

- Java (*also*) has a *jump* statement specified as either *break* or *continue*.

- Java (*also*) has loop logic features (e.g., *for, do/while*, and so on).

- Java (*also*) has a unique, three-part parameter syntax for its looping *for* statement.

- Java (*also*) has an *increment operator* (++) that increments its operand by 1.

- Java (*also*) has a *decrement operator* (--) that *decrements* its operand by 1.

- Java (*also*) uses two forward slashes (//) for comment lines.

- Java (*also*) uses square brackets [] for arrays instead of parentheses.

- Java (*also*) introduces other access modifiers (*static void* versus *Shared Sub*).

- Java (*also*) uses the word "void" to describe methods that do not return values.

Interesting, right? Each Java language syntax observation should remind you of the observations I made earlier during the C# discussion. Suffice it to say that there is merit to the rumors stating that C# was created using Java language syntax. Just in case you are really curious, here are two more Java observations:

- Java (*also*) does not use the word "NEW" for its class constructor method. Instead, the Java constructor is (*also*) recognized as a method that has exactly the same name as the class itself.

- Java (*also*) has a unique syntax for explicit type casting. You do this by first placing the desired type inside parentheses. Immediately following the close parenthesis, you then code the targeted class/method/type.

As you will see in the next section, the other .NET "sharp" language, J#, continues in the same direction of looking like Java. However, in the case of J#, it is not a rumor. Microsoft actually states[4] that J# "integrates the Java language syntax into the Visual Studio .NET shell."

Introducing Visual J# .NET

Similar to the C# language, the Visual J# .NET language is often abbreviated down to just J# (pronounced "J sharp"). According to Microsoft's documentation, the J# language is specifically targeted at those Java programmers and J++ programmers looking for a .NET alternative language.

---

4. After you install the J# product, take a look at the document located at *<your installed hard drive>*:\Program Files\Common Files\Microsoft Visual J# .NET Setup\ VJSharpRME1033.htm.

NOTE The newest version of VS .NET (v1.1) includes J# as a language choice. If you are using VS .NET v1.0, you can download the J# compiler separately. See http://msdn.microsoft.com/library/en-us/ dv_vjsharp/html/vjoriMicrosoftVisualJ.asp for more information and http://msdn.microsoft.com/downloads/sample.asp?url=/ MSDN-FILES/027/001/973/msdncompositedoc.xml to download the J# add-on.

As you begin your exploration into the specifics of J#, it will be impossible not to see the reoccurring disclaimers posted by Microsoft. For example, in the ReadMe document that accompanies the J# product (VJSharpRME1033.htm), Microsoft clearly states the following points:

- "Applications and services built with Visual J# will run only on the .NET Framework. Visual J# is not a tool for developing applications intended to run on a Java Virtual Machine."

- "Microsoft Visual J# .NET Redistributable Package is the redistributable package for Visual J#. The Redistributable Package will only run applications and services developed with Visual J#; Java-language applications written with other Java-language development tools will not run with the Microsoft Visual J# .NET Redistributable Package."

- "Visual J# and the Microsoft Visual J# .NET Redistributable Package have been independently developed by Microsoft, and are not endorsed or approved by Sun Microsystems, Inc."

- "Visual J# can only be installed and used on a computer that has Microsoft Visual Studio .NET installed."

Obviously, as these points illustrate, Microsoft wants to avoid creating any confusion in the Java community. Kudos and accolades to Microsoft.

J# Looks Like C#

The first time I looked at the J# language, I needed to take a very close look at J# to notice the subtle differences between it and C#. I suppose I should have expected this. Recall that C# looks like Java and J# was built using Java language syntax. How nice!

Perhaps I'm going out on a limb and stretching the use of logic and reason. Nevertheless, if someone tells me that J# is made to have Java language syntax and I can see that J# looks like C#, I then conclude that C# apparently was *also* made to have Java language syntax. It's a stretch, but that's my opinion.

Therefore, before you even look at your first line of J# code, please understand this: By being familiar with each syntax feature discussed already (for C# and for Java), you have already become familiar with the J# syntax. In other words, with the basic syntax rules discussed so far, learning *one* language actually means learning *three* languages.[5] How nice! How very nice!

As it turns out, the J# syntax has a few unique characteristics, at least when you compare it with C#. The next section briefly covers those differences.

J# Does Differ from C#

Before I even mention the few differences between J# and C#, I need to mention this one point. The few syntax differences that set J# apart from C# actually serve to make J# that much closer to Java. Let's cover a few examples.

The first example is the fact that the default extension for a J# code file is ".jsl". OK, I'll stop messing around. Now, let's take a look at some of the more interesting differences.

One of the first things you will notice in a J# program is the keyword *package*. The package keyword is analogous to the C# keyword *namespace*. Why do you suppose J# uses the term "package" instead of "namespace"? The fact that Java uses the term "package" provides you with a very good hint.

J# has a syntax feature that allows a *documentation comment* (a block of comments that can be extracted from the code). Sure, C# also has this type of syntax feature. However, the manner in which J# implements the feature is certainly different. In J#, the documentation comments are created by starting the comment block with a forward slash and two asterisks (/**). The documentation comment block concludes with an asterisk and a forward slash (*/).

NOTE In Java terms, this documentation comment feature is referred to as *Javadoc comments*. Yes, Java also uses /** and */ to implement the Javadoc comments.

---

5. Combine that with VB .NET and COBOL .NET and you have five languages presented in this book. Now, would that be quintlingual or quadlingual + 1?

To provide a shortcut for namespace names coding, J# offers the *import* statement. This is comparable to the C# *using* statement. As you might have guessed, Java also uses the import statement.

J# uses the keywords *extends* and *implements* to inherit base classes and implement interfaces, respectively. This is comparable to the use of the colon (:) in C# syntax. Of course, Java uses the keywords extends and implements when implementing similar functionality. Do you see a pattern developing here?

I'll cover just a couple more J# versus C# observations. Then you'll finally see some J# code.

J# uses the @ *Attribute* directive to attach attributes to classes, methods, and so on. You will recall that C# uses a square bracket syntax (e.g., [STAThread]) to attach an attribute at the method level.

When you read and update properties in J#, you will attach the prefixes *get_* and *set_* to the names of properties, respectively. Although this is rather different than C#, it is somewhat intuitive. If you consider that COBOL .NET, VB .NET, and C# all support the use of *Get/Set* keywords when defining properties, it's perfectly understandable why J# implements the use of get_ and set_ when reading and updating properties. Not convinced yet? All right, you caught me. Yes, Java also uses the attached get and set prefixes when accessing properties.

Finally, let's take a look at the J# language.

Finally, J# Code

Using the J# language choice and the VS .NET Console Application project template, I created a sample application (MyFirstJSharpApplication). I based my J# logic after the sample applications (COBOL .NET and VB .NET) originally built in Chapter 5 and Chapter 6. Please take moment to read the J# code logic in Listing B-3.

Listing B-3. The MyFirstJSharpApplication Sample Application

```
// The package statement is similar to the namespace statement
package MyFirstJSharpApplication;
// The import statement provides a short cut for namespace coding
// notice the asterisk (below) used as a wildcard.
import System.*;
/**
     * This is my first J# Application. Coding in J# is easy.
     * The use of the slash and two asterisks ("/**") denotes
     * the use of J#'s Javadoc like Documentation feature.
     * You will also see Javadoc comments using Tags
     * (e.g @param, @return, @see, @version, and @author).
```

```
      * You can display Javadoc comment blocks by
      * navigating to the VS.NET Main Toolbar,
      * clicking Tools and then clicking
      * the "Build Comment Web Pages" menu option.
      * After building the Comment Web Page you can save the page
      * as part of the applications documentation.
      * @author Chris Richardson
      */
public class Class1
{
      public Class1()
      {}

      /**
            * The main entry point for the application.
            * @attribute System.STAThread() */
      public static void main(String[] args)
      {
            // Use two slash symbols ("//") for a single line comment
            /* Optionally, you can create a multi line comment block
             * by using a single slash followed by an asterisk ("/*").
             * The end the comment block, use an asterisk followed by a slash
             */
            Console.WriteLine("Hello, .NET World.");
            Console.WriteLine("I cannot believe how simple J# is!");

            //Execute Procedures
            DefineDataTypesSample();
            LogicSample();

            Console.WriteLine("Press Enter to Exit.");
            Console.ReadLine();
            }
      static void DefineDataTypesSample()
      {

            //Declare Data Items using generic Object Types
            // code was added to cast the objects to J# Data Types
            short MyFirstNumberJsharp;
            int MySecondNumberJsharp;
            double MyThirdNumberJsharp;

            //Declare Data Items using Native .NET Data Types
            System.Int16 MyFirstNumberNative;
```

```
            System.Int32 MySecondNumberNative;
            System.Double MyThirdNumberNative;

            //Place a numeric literal in Data Item
            Int16 myShortvalue = (Int16) 32767;
            Int32 myIntvalue = (Int32) 32767;
            System.Double myDoublevalue = (System.Double) 32767;

            MyFirstNumberJsharp = (short) myShortvalue;
            MySecondNumberJsharp = (int) myIntvalue;
            MyThirdNumberJsharp = (double) myDoublevalue;

            MyFirstNumberNative = (System.Int16)32767;
            MySecondNumberNative = (System.Int32)32767;
            MyThirdNumberNative = (System.Double)32767;

            //Write out contents of each variable
            Console.WriteLine("MyFirstNumberJsharp= " +
                    MyFirstNumberJsharp);
            Console.WriteLine("MySecondNumberJsharp= " +
                    MySecondNumberJsharp);
            Console.WriteLine("MyThirdNumberJsharp= " +
                    MyThirdNumberJsharp);
            Console.WriteLine("MyFirstNumberNative= {0}",
                    MyFirstNumberNative);
            Console.WriteLine("MySecondNumberNative= {0}",
                    MySecondNumberNative);
            Console.WriteLine("MyThirdNumberNative= {0}",
                    MyThirdNumberNative);
    }
    static void LogicSample()
    {
            //*** Declare Data Items using .NET Data Types
            System.String MYString;
            System.Int32 MYInteger;
            boolean MYBoolean = false;
            System.DateTime systemDate;

            //*** Declare Data Items with J# Data Types
            int MyIndex = 0;
            int MySecondIndex;
            int MyAccum = 0;
            boolean MyFlag = false;
            java.lang.String  MyFixedLengthString;
```

```
        //*** Demonstrate creation of String Array
        java.lang.String[] MonthValues =
            {
                        "January", "February", "March",
                "April", "May", "June",
                "July", "August", "September",
                "October", "November", "December"};


        //*** Demonstrate Intrinsic Function accessing System Date
        //    notice that "get_" is attached to the Now method/property
        systemDate = DateTime.get_Now();

        Console.WriteLine("Today is {0}" ,
            systemDate.ToShortDateString());

//*** Demonstrate Booleans, Constants, and Conditional/Computational Logic

        do
        {
            MyIndex += 1;
            if (MyIndex > 12)
            {
                    MYBoolean = true;
                    MyFlag = MYBoolean;
            }
        } while (!(MyFlag));

        if (MyFlag)
        {
            MYString = "The Boolean is now set to TRUE";
            MyFixedLengthString = MYString;
            Console.WriteLine(MyFixedLengthString);
        }

        //*** Demonstrate usage of Conditional and Computational Logic
        for (MySecondIndex = 1; MySecondIndex <= MyIndex; MySecondIndex++)
        {
            MyAccum = MySecondIndex += 1;
        }
        MYInteger = (Int32) MyAccum;

//*** Demonstrate Intrinsic Functions, Conditional/Computational Logic
```

```
MyIndex = 1;
MyFixedLengthString = String.Empty;
for (int x = 0; x <= 11; x++)
{
    switch (x)
    {
        case 11:
        case 0:
        case 1:
            Console.WriteLine
            (java.lang.String.Concat(MonthValues[x],
                " is ","Winter"));
            break;
        case 2:
        case 3:
        case 4:
            Console.WriteLine
            (java.lang.String.Concat(MonthValues[x],
                " is ","Spring"));
            break;
        case 5:
        case 6:
        case 7:
            Console.WriteLine
            (java.lang.String.Concat(MonthValues[x],
                " is ","Summer"));
            break;
        case 8:
        case 9:
        case 10:
            Console.WriteLine
            (java.lang.String.Concat(MonthValues[x],
                " is ","Autumn"));
            break;
        default:
            Console.WriteLine
                ("A logic exception");
            break;
    }
}
}
}
```

As you can tell from looking at the J# sample application in Listing B-3, each of the Java and C# observations noted earlier are realized. I would like to mention two noteworthy differences between this J# sample and the C# sample (Listing B-2).

- In the DefineDataTypesSample method, the data types required explicit type casting. This coding characteristic is more prevalent with J#.

- The switch statement shown in the LogicSample method was changed to use ordinal values as dictated by the J# compiler.

As you explore the J# language, you will notice a scarcity of available documentation. Several references are included in the "To Learn More" section at the end of this appendix to help get you started. Between these references and my own Java textbook, I was able to work through each J# coding issue somewhat painlessly.

Summary

This appendix's goals were as follows:

- To discuss the Visual C# (pronounced "C sharp") .NET language

- To cover the Visual J# (pronounced "J sharp") .NET language

In this appendix, I covered both the C# and J# languages. During the discussion, I pointed out both the similarities and the differences between the languages. I presented sample applications to help demonstrate the syntax of each "sharp" language. Additionally, I made significant points regarding the relationship between these two languages (C# and J#) and the Java language. This appendix should serve as a good introduction, a primer, to the .NET "sharp" languages.

To Learn More

The following are some suggested supplemental references to further your retraining effort.

Books

The .NET Languages: A Quick Translation Guide, by Brian Bischof (Apress, 2001):
   http://www.apress.com/book/bookDisplay.html?bID=80.
A Programmer's Introduction to C#, Second Edition, by Eric Gunnerson (Apress, 2001):
   http://www.apress.com/book/bookDisplay.html?bID=83.
Programming C#, by Gary Cornell (Apress, 2003):
   http://www.apress.com/book/bookDisplay.html?bID=60.

Magazines

.NET Magazine:
   http://www.fawcette.com/dotnetmag/
MSDN Magazine:
   http://msdn.microsoft.com/msdnmag/
Visual Studio Magazine:
   http://www.fawcette.com/vsm/
Windows Developer Magazine:
   http://www.wd-mag.com/
XML & Web Services Magazine:
   http://www.fawcette.com/xmlmag/

Web Sites

.NET Architecture Center:
   http://msdn.microsoft.com/architecture/
C# Programmer's Reference:
   http://msdn.microsoft.com/library/en-us/csref/html/
   vcoriCProgrammersReference.asp
C# to VB .NET Translator (ASPAlliance.com version):
   http://www.aspalliance.com/aldotnet/examples/translate.aspx
C# to VB .NET Translator (KamalPatel.Net version):
   http://www.kamalpatel.net/ConvertCSharp2VB.aspx

C# Tutorials:

http://msdn.microsoft.com/library/en-us/csref/html/
vcoriCSharpTutorials.asp

GotDotNet:

http://www.gotdotnet.com/

GotDotNet: Backwards Breaking Changes from Version 1.0 to 1.1:

http://www.gotdotnet.com/team/changeinfo/Backwards1.0to1.1/
default.aspx#00000106

GotDotNet C# Community Site (various links, resources, and so on):

http://gotdotnet.com/team/csharp/

GotDotNet Visual J# .NET (various links, resources, and so on):

http://gotdotnet.com/team/vjsharp/

Introduction to C# (seminar):

http://msdn.microsoft.com/library/default.asp?url=/seminar/mmcfeed/
mmcdisplayfeed.asp?Lang=en&Product=103363&Audience=100402

J# QuickStart Tutorials:

http://samples.gotdotnet.com/quickstart/latebreaking/
default.aspx?lang=VJS

Java Developer Services (from Sun Microsystems, Inc.):

http://developer.java.sun.com/

Microsoft ASP.NET Home Page:

http://www.asp.net/

Microsoft Community (discussion groups, e-newsletters, and so forth):

http://communities2.microsoft.com/

Microsoft Patterns & Practices:

http://msdn.microsoft.com/practices/

Microsoft's Search the Knowledge Base Web Site:

http://support.microsoft.com/default.aspx?scid=FH;EN-US;KBHOWTO

Microsoft TechNet How-To Index:

http://www.microsoft.com/technet/treeview/default.asp?url=/technet/
itsolutions/howto

Microsoft Visual J# .NET download (for those using VS .NET v1.0):

http://msdn.microsoft.com/downloads/sample.asp?url=/msdn-files/027/001/
973/msdncompositedoc.xml

MSDN:

http://msdn.microsoft.com

Visual J# (add-on release information, reference, and so on):

http://msdn.microsoft.com/library/en-us/dv_vjsharp/html/
vjoriMicrosoftVisualJ.asp

Visual J# Samples:

http://msdn.microsoft.com/library/en-us/dv_vjsample/html/
vjlrfVisualJSamples.asp

Visual J# Walkthroughs:

http://msdn.microsoft.com/library/en-us/dv_vjsharp/html/
vjwlkVisualJWalkthroughs.asp

Windows .NET Server 2003:

http://msdn.microsoft.com/library/default.asp?url=/nhp/
default.asp?contentid=28001691

Religion, Landmines, and Distractions

Diversions = Opportunities to Take Your Eyes off the Ball

In this appendix

- Discussing compiler differences

- Understanding vendor and platform competition

- Covering coding style preferences

NEARLY 20 YEARS AGO, while working with a friend, a fellow mainframe programmer, I recall having a discussion about career goals and staying *focused* on the big picture. On that occasion, I was offered a piece of advice, one that I remember to this day:

> *"Remember, puppy, whatever be your goal,*
> *Keep your eye on the donut, and not the hole."*

I admit, in my younger days, I did wonder what puppies and donuts had to do with career interest. It was not until later in life that I grew to really appreciate the possible meaning and the intent behind the advice. It echoes still.

Through the years, I have interpreted and reinterpreted that piece of advice. My latest interpretation relates to a few things—possible distractions that you are likely to come across while retraining for the Windows and Web .NET arena. That, by the way, will be your focus in this appendix.

The first portion of this appendix covers a few compiler differences that some developers tend to care a lot about. From there, you will revisit the topic of vendor and platform competition. The last portion of this appendix includes some discussion about coding style preferences.

Distractions: Been There, Done That

Just coming from the mainframe over to the Windows and Web development platform, you have possibly faced adversity. It is likely that you have encountered pessimists and naysayers on both sides (mainframe and Windows/Web) of the fence.

While licking your wounds, you have tried to avoid those who seemed to have personal vendettas against anything that looked, felt, or acted like a mainframe. All along, you simply sought to broaden your skill set and build upon your respectable COBOL CICS mainframe programmer foundation. You worked hard to learn .NET and Windows and Web development. The last thing that you need is to let a distraction throw you off track.

While on the mainframe, maybe you had your share of COBOL language versus assembler language debates. But that's behind you now, right? Are these opportunities for distraction *all* behind you now? After all, you have survived the journey into the world of .NET Windows and Web development. Unfortunately, they are not. Let's take a look at a few of them now. It will serve you well to be familiar with those few distractions that are the most common.

Compiler Differences

In this book, I've advocated being *bilingual*—learning both Visual Basic .NET (VB .NET) and COBOL .NET. Other than the fact that programming is fun and using multiple languages is even more fun, being bilingual is a wise career choice. If using two .NET languages were not enough, as Appendix B showed you can even go on to include C# and J# as additional .NET language choices. The more the merrier.

TIP   Be aware that there is a faction of the Visual Basic community that is strongly defending the choice to code in VB .NET instead of in C#. At the same time, portions of the C++, J++, and Java developer communities are rallying behind C# as "the" .NET language of choice. As you broaden your skill set by picking up a second .NET language (to add to your COBOL coding skills), be aware of this heated battle going on between *some* portions of the developer community.

I believe that having flexibility in your language choice will simply open new doors for you while keeping many existing doors open. Additionally, your developing technique in each programming language typically improves as you learn other techniques common in different languages.

In the safe confines of this book, a language-neutral approach has been very easy to take. I've enjoyed the freedom of being able to focus on your retraining needs. Rather than getting into personal issues and attempting to sway you to or from one language or another, I concentrated on .NET and related development concerns. In the end, the language you happen to develop with doesn't have to be a black-and-white, either-or type of choice. At least that's how I see it.

 TIP Be sure to familiarize yourself with how some .NET languages will use either a *zero-based* index or a *one-based* index for arrays and/or collections. Some developers tend to take this particular issue very personally. Be prepared.

Unfortunately, the rest of the world is not so kind, not so liberal. In the real world, there are those who frown on developers who freely switch from one development language to the other. There are those who will even go so far as to mention disloyalty, betrayal, and treason when describing a developer who is open to trying new languages, new compilers, and so forth.

Therefore, simply be prepared to discuss why you choose to code in one specific .NET language or a combination of .NET languages. I like having those types of discussions. I have found that when you can openly discuss the pros and cons of one language or another, you have a readily available disarming tactic.

 TIP Spend some time looking into how each .NET language represents the Boolean true value. Specifically, check to see if true is represented as –1 (negative 1) or +1 (positive 1), or if the language syntax advocates using the string literal true to set a Boolean type operator. This issue is a *hot button* for some developers.

On the note of disarming tactics, try this one on for size. Let's say that you see two professional developers in heated battle over language compiler differences: *verboseness* versus *terseness*. Perhaps they are wrestling over the fact that both the COBOL and Visual Basic languages lean more toward being verbose. C#, J#, and C++, on the other hand, are generally referred to as being terse. As the two professional developers finish their wrestling competition and proceed to challenge each other in a friendly tug-of-war match, kindly interrupt them. Suggest to them that they are both wrong.

Ask them if they have coded any .NET applications using regular expressions. Tell them that they should spend some time exploring the use of the .NET Framework namespace *System.Text.RegularExpressions* (specifically, the *Regex*, *Match*, and *Group* classes). Proudly inform them that the syntax of regular expressions, hands down, exemplifies the essence of terseness—real terseness. Mention to the two dumbfounded professional developers that all .NET languages are verbose when compared with the language syntax of regular expressions.

Further, mention that all .NET languages can take advantage of the language syntax of regular expressions through the System.Text.RegularExpressions namespace. Ask these two professional developers the following question: "If all .NET languages can leverage the ultimately terse syntax of regular expressions, why not put to rest the whole verbose versus terse debate?"

Hopefully, this will be enough of an interruption to interject the thought that the terseness of a language is relative and ultimately less important than simply getting the job done. If this tactic does not work, perhaps the two professional developers can just return to their "my language is more terse than your language" debate.

Vendor and Platform Competition

It is not a secret that some companies and corporations do not get along that well with Microsoft. If you were to make a list of these companies, Sun Microsystems and IBM might be good candidates for this short list. Why Sun Microsystems and IBM?

The latest strategy in winning the developer platform war is winning the hearts and souls of developers. Sun Microsystems and IBM, along with Microsoft, are working hard to capture the attention and resulting loyalty of major portions of the developer community.

In Chapter 1, I presented to you a summary of the recent COBOL-related activities of several companies. If you look beyond COBOL, you will find other pieces of this "competition puzzle" coming together. Both Sun Microsystems and IBM are developing their own developer platforms. For the most part, their development platforms will have the opportunity to compete with Microsoft's .NET platform. That's business, right?

The problem is that you will come across individual developers who have taken it up as their own personal mission to side with one vendor or another. Effectively, some developers enlist to join the war against (or with) Microsoft. In these cases, you will come across rather heated conversations in which Microsoft's

.NET technologies are pitted against both Sun's J2EE product family and IBM's WebSphere product suite. And I do mean *heated conversations.*

 TIP IBM's announcement regarding their purchase of Rational Software Corporation will certainly heat up the "company versus company" and "developer platform versus developer platform" conversations (see http://www.ibm.com/news/us/2002/12/061.html).

More recently, the developer community has loosely referred to these heated conversations as a *holy war.* Unfortunately, some developers take this whole "business competition" thing personally. You would almost think that they actually owned one of these companies.

On the note of company ownership, consider this little experiment. The next time you come across someone who claims to "hate" Microsoft, ask that person if he or she happens to be one of the many who chooses to invest 401(k) retirement funds into Microsoft stock (either directly or through a mutual fund). More often than not, the answer you receive may surprise you.

How can you recognize those developers among us who spend way too much energy worrying about these sorts of things? If you come across someone proudly pointing out that Microsoft's C# is just a Java rip-off and that .NET's CLR is a Java Virtual Machine wanna-be, you have found your person. It's true that Microsoft's products resemble other products, other predecessors. But who cares, really?

 TIP You will notice that JavaScript is not mentioned in most of Microsoft's documentation. Microsoft's documentation clearly explains how to use JScript or VBScript as a scripting language choice. At the same time, if you happen to look at any documentation sponsored by Netscape or Sun Microsystems, JavaScript is typically the only scripting language discussed. Realize that this has a lot to do with vendor and platform competition and less to do with which scripting language might be the best language to get the job done.

Just consider this a heads-up. If you do not want to waste valuable development time debating about the ethics of business competition, simply avoid getting into these types of "Microsoft versus the world" conversations. Let Microsoft's competitors worry about competing with Microsoft. As a developer, consider simply learning and using the toolset that makes you marketable and keeps you employed.

Coding Style: Casing

Working with COBOL .NET, you have certainly come across occasions where proper casing was important. You have also discovered that VB .NET (and even C#) handles the issue of casing differently. Each compiler enforces casing syntax rules that eventually encourage formal coding styles and standards. For example, you will come across the terms "Pascal" and "Camel," as in Pascal casing and Camel casing.

Pascal casing, in which the first letter of each word is capitalized, is a coding style preferred by some. You will notice that Microsoft uses the Pascal casing convention when naming namespaces (e.g., System.Web.Services, System.Text.RegularExpressions, and so on).

Camel casing, in which the first letter of each word except the first word is capitalized, is also a popular convention. Microsoft's documentation suggests that this coding style is useful when naming variables.

The question is, should you follow Microsoft's conventions and suggestions or create your own coding style? This is where the controversy lies. Why? What you think and want personally may not be what your neighbor or your coworker thinks and wants. This is yet another opportunity for distraction—another opportunity for developers to lose focus on *the spirit of the law* while debating about *the letter of the law.*

I believe there isn't a right or wrong answer to picking a casing convention. Which way you go should depend on the agreed coding standard of your entire development team and your organization. If your team can't agree on a casing convention, you have a management issue, not a coding style issue. In the end, what's important is that your coding style is consistent with the coding style of your coworkers. This makes for more maintainable code.

Coding Style: Notation

The topic of notation as a coding style is another opportunity for disagreement. One of the most popular forms of notation is Hungarian notation. Some love it and swear by it. Others think it is a total waste of time and keystrokes.

For those who may not know, *Hungarian notation* is a coding style that suggests adding a small prefix in front of variable names to indicate the data type of the variable. For example, *strDescription* identifies a string data type. Likewise, *intCounter* identifies an integer data type. Dr. Charles Simonyi (who happens to be from Hungary), a Microsoft employee, is credited with creating this notation style, which some thought looked more like non-English words or, rather, more like *Hungarian* words.

As with any other coding style, Hungarian notation is used by some, but not everyone. If you really enjoy debating and arguing, try this little experiment. First, find someone who feels very strongly about using Hungarian notation. Next, ask this person to explain to you the premise of Hungarian notation. Then, suggest to this Hungarian notation advocate that you are going to start naming all of your .NET variables using the prefix "obj" (i.e., objDescription, objCounter, and so forth). Mention that because all .NET classes ultimately inherit from System.Object, it's clear to you that "obj" will accurately identify all of your .NET variables.

Naturally, you might not want to try this experiment with your manager or supervisor. However, it will prove to be a good conversation opener. If you can turn this debate into a productive conversation, you will be headed into the right direction. One point that you will want to explore is the need for a given team and the resulting modules that they work on to be in-sync. This will expedite the level of maintainability in your application. Having this value lost among those who would rather be *right* and have things *their way* is simply wasteful.

Coding Style: To GO TO, GoTo, goto or Not To

The coding style of using *goto* logic certainly ranks high on the list of potential landmines, sore spots, and potential arguable points. The mainframe developer community has debated about this coding style in both COBOL and assembler programs. Additionally, the Visual Basic developer community has weighed in on this contentious and controversial coding style.

As you have learned about .NET features, it is likely that you have learned that structured Try/Catch exception handling is hyped as being worlds better than the older, more traditional goto error-handling logic. Even on the mainframe, recall that the use of inline PERFORM statements was suggested as a way to help put an end to goto-style logic. All in all, the use of a goto coding style is often said to encourage the creation of spaghetti code, or code that is difficult to maintain.

Now it's time to ruffle a few feathers. Consider the following questions:

- Why did Microsoft decide to support the goto statement in the C# language?

- Why did Microsoft decide to support the goto switch-case in the C# switch statement?

- Why did Microsoft decide to include the .NET Framework class *System.CodeDom.CodeGotoStatement*?

- Why did Microsoft decide to support both structured exception handling and the legacy coding style of On Error GoTo in VB .NET?

- Why did Fujitsu decide to provide support for the GO TO statement in their NetCOBOL for .NET compiler?

Of course, I have my own answers to these questions. Maybe you have your answers as well. One explanation, perhaps one that you and I may agree on, is that there is the need to provide support that is backward compatible.

However, this argument only goes so far. Consider the following possibilities:

- VB .NET represented a housecleaning opportunity for Microsoft—a chance to "clean up" the Visual Basic language.

- C# is a new language. Because C# is a new language, what would a C# application be backward compatible with?

It appears to me that Microsoft (and Fujitsu) recognizes that not everyone agrees on whether or not goto logic is forbidden. So, to be somewhat neutral, the feature is supported. Hence, my point: You too should realize that not everyone agrees that goto logic is evil and bad. Although there may be some objective-sounding reasons against using goto logic, some will still argue in favor of using goto logic.

As you engage in these heated debates, defending your honor and your turf, remember that you and I and the guy next door all have a job to do. Of course, that is what matters. In the end, I suppose that this is just one more reason why being a developer is one of life's greatest pleasures—a treat indeed.

Summary

This appendix's goals were as follows:

- To discuss compiler differences

- To understand vendor and platform competition

- To cover coding style preferences

In this appendix, the underlying point has been that differences in opinion can often lead to unproductive debates and ultimately distract us from getting our job done. I presented a few points of controversy dealing with .NET language differences. I pointed out a few topics that often are argued as developers choose one language compiler over another. Then I spent time discussing the distractions surrounding vendor and platform competition. Additionally, I covered a few coding style topics. I pointed out how varying opinions on coding styles can get in the way and cause developers to lose sight of the most important part of their job: to create maintainable applications that meet the needs of users and customers.

To Learn More

The following are some suggested supplemental references to further your retraining effort.

Books

Regular Expressions with .NET (e-book), by Dan Appleman (Desaware, 2002):
    http://desaware.com/Ebook3L2.htm.
Visual Basic.NET or C#? Which to Choose? (e-book), by Dan Appleman (Desaware, 2002):
    http://desaware.com/Ebook2L2.htm.

Magazines

.NET Magazine:
    http://www.fawcette.com/dotnetmag/
MSDN Magazine:
    http://msdn.microsoft.com/msdnmag/
Visual Studio Magazine:
    http://www.fawcette.com/vsm/
Windows Developer Magazine:
    http://www.wd-mag.com/
XML & Web Services Magazine:
    http://www.fawcette.com/xmlmag/

Web Sites

.NET Architecture Center:
    http://msdn.microsoft.com/architecture/
.NET Framework Regular Expressions:
    http://msdn.microsoft.com/library/en-us/cpguide/html/
    cpconcomregularexpressions.asp

Compare Microsoft .NET to J2EE Technology:

http://msdn.microsoft.com/net/compare/default.asp

GotDotNet: Backwards Breaking Changes from Version 1.0 to 1.1:

http://www.gotdotnet.com/team/changeinfo/Backwards1.0to1.1/
default.aspx#00000106

Java 2 Platform, Enterprise Edition (J2EE):

http://java.sun.com/j2ee/

JavaScript Developer Central (Netscape):

http://devedge.netscape.com/central/javascript/

Microsoft Community (discussion groups, e-newsletters, and so forth):

http://communities2.microsoft.com/

Microsoft Patterns & Practices:

http://msdn.microsoft.com/practices/

Microsoft's Search the Knowledge Base Web Site:

http://support.microsoft.com/default.aspx?scid=FH;EN-US;KBHOWTO

Microsoft TechNet How-To Index:

http://www.microsoft.com/technet/treeview/default.asp?url=/technet/
itsolutions/howto

MSDN:

http://msdn.microsoft.com

"Netscape and Sun Announce JavaScript" (press release):

http://java.sun.com/pr/1995/12/pr951204-03.html

Vnunet.com: "Sun may lose war by winning Java battle" (article):

http://www.vnunet.com/News/1137515

WebSphere Developer Domain:

http://www7b.software.ibm.com/wsdd/

Windows .NET Server 2003:

http://msdn.microsoft.com/library/default.asp?url=/nhp/
default.asp?contentid=28001691

Windows Script:

http://msdn.microsoft.com/library/default.asp?url=/nhp/
Default.asp?contentid=28001169

Fujitsu's NetCOBOL for .NET

A Small Dose of Product Marketing, Courtesy of Fujitsu Software Corporation

In this appendix

- Highlighting the product features of NetCOBOL for .NET

- Presenting the documentation options for Fujitsu's .NET product

As you know, Fujitsu Software's NetCOBOL for .NET product is the first COBOL compiler available that integrates with Visual Studio .NET (VS .NET) and produces Microsoft intermediate language (MSIL). This is the compiler I used to create the COBOL-based samples throughout this book. This appendix gives you a quick description of the product's features and a few tips to direct you to the documentation provided by the software vendor, Fujitsu Software.

Product Features

NetCOBOL for .NET supports all the usual things you'd expect in a COBOL compiler today. The following sections briefly present the key .NET-related features.

MSIL Generation

The fundamental feature is that the compiler generates MSIL. This means that the output from NetCOBOL for .NET is in the same form as the output from Visual Basic .NET (VB .NET), C#, or any other true .NET language. This provides the base for other features such as inheriting from classes written in other languages and easy debugging of mixed-language applications.

.NET Data Types

Where it's appropriate, the compiler maps COBOL data types to .NET data types, and when it's not appropriate to do so, the compiler provides support for the .NET data types through OBJECT REFERENCE items. SET statements can be used to move data between COBOL and .NET-specific data types.

COBOL Syntax for .NET

NetCOBOL for .NET has taken the approach of starting with the standard object-oriented COBOL syntax and enhancing it where necessary to embrace the .NET object-oriented model. This shortens the learning curve for those already familiar with the standard object-oriented COBOL syntax.

.NET Class Inheritance

Because NetCOBOL for .NET can inherit from the classes provided with the .NET Framework, COBOL programs now have access to all the functionality available to other leading-edge languages such as C# and VB .NET. For the first time, using object orientation in COBOL has very clear, tangible benefits.

COBOL in ASP.NET Pages

When you learn how to program COBOL with .NET, NetCOBOL for .NET also provides you with the ability to apply that knowledge to programming Active Server Pages (ASP) using COBOL.

VS .NET Integration

A big boost to developers is that NetCOBOL for .NET provides the underlying support to enable COBOL application development using VS .NET. You can do things such as select COBOL templates for your projects, edit COBOL within Visual Studio as you would with other Visual Studio languages, debug with the Visual Studio debugger, and use the RAD designer features described in the next section.

Great Designers

The NetCOBOL for .NET product provides support for several types of designers. As you know, designers are intended to save you a huge amount of development time and effort. The following sections briefly introduce this impressive product offering.

Windows Forms Designer

With NetCOBOL for .NET, you can design your GUIs using the same Forms Designer that is available with VB .NET, except that you use COBOL to execute the forms and to support the events.

Web Forms Designer

You can create your ASP.NET Web pages using the Web Forms Designer, which has an interface very similar to that of the Windows Forms Designer, again with COBOL as the supporting programming language.

Web Services and Component Designer

The third designer takes care of the complexities of Web services and assembling service components, leaving you free to focus on the business functions of your COBOL applications.

Product Documentation

NetCOBOL for .NET's documentation comes in three parts: a ReadMe file, a language reference manual, and a user's guide.

ReadMe File

The ReadMe file is a simple HTML page that gives you information about the product, tips on getting started, and any limitations discovered too late to be built into the user's guide. You access it by clicking the Start button and selecting Programs ➤ Fujitsu NetCOBOL for .NET menu.

Language Reference

NetCOBOL for .NET comes with a typical COBOL language reference manual. For the most part, this manual documents the standard COBOL syntax that you are familiar with. It also contains a chapter that defines all the .NET-related syntax. This manual is provided in PDF form and is also accessed by clicking the Start button and selecting Programs ➤ Fujitsu NetCOBOL for .NET menu.

User's Guide

The user's guide for the product is provided in VS .NET Help format. It provides a lot of how-to information on using .NET features and standard information on using NetCOBOL. You access this guide from VS .NET's Help menu or Microsoft's Visual Studio .NET documentation function.

Summary

This appendix's goals were as follows:

- To highlight the product features of NetCOBOL for .NET

- To present the documentation options for Fujitsu's .NET product

In this appendix, I shared with you a sampling of the features you can find in Fujitsu's NetCOBOL for .NET product. Although the list is not intended to be exhaustive, it should give you a quick, high-level view of how you can use this product to help you build .NET applications. Several documentation options are available to help you get the most out of Fujitsu's NetCOBOL for .NET product.

To Learn More

The following are some suggested supplemental references to further your retraining effort.

Web Sites

Executive Summary for Fujitsu's NetCOBOL for .NET:
    http://www.netcobol.com/products/pdf/0602_EXSUM-NetCOBOL-NET.pdf
Fujitsu NetCOBOL for .NET:
    http://www.netcobol.com/products/windows/netcobol.html

IBuySpy Store Application (sample application in COBOL .NET):

http://www.ibuyspycobol.com/

IBuySpy Store Application (sample application in VB .NET and C#):

http://www.ibuyspystore.com/

Intensity Software's NetCOBOL Samples (provided by Fujitsu Software and
Intensity Software):

http://www.netcobolsamples.com/

Index

Special Characters

A

P

Q

Printed in the United States
By Bookmasters